S T U A R T P

MEDIA STUDIES

SECOND EDITION

LONGMAN

To Lucy Byrne

Addison Wesley Longman Limited
Edinburgh Gate, Harlow,
Essex, CM20 2JE, England
and associated companies throughout the
world.

The right of Stuart Price to be identified as the author of this Work
has been asserted by him in accordance with the Copyright,
Designs and Patents Act of 1988.

First published in Great Britain 1993
This edition 1998

ISBN 0 582 32834 9

Set in 10.25/12.5 pt Palatino
Printed in Singapore through Addison Wesley Longman China Ltd

The
publisher's
policy is to use
**paper manufactured
from sustainable forests**

Contents

Preface to the 1993 edition

Students of media studies, asked to describe the content of their subject, quite often produce a list of forms, such as television, the press, cinema and so on. It is also fairly usual to be given an outline of the kind of practical activity which goes on inside a media course. The difficulty begins when they are asked to give an account of the way they approach the subject, or required to provide a breakdown of the theories employed to investigate mass communication in general.

It would be fair to say that there has been a turning away from the practice of teaching the mass media through 'subject headings', where a bewildering variety of established topics and new developments have seemed to vie for the attention of students and their teachers. The increasingly common alternative has been to encourage students to investigate the media through the use of a variety of conceptual tools. The value of this approach has been that it has allowed teachers and students to apply theory to media texts.

The disadvantages, however, are only now making themselves plain. Some theorists have used a conceptual approach to construct a set of orthodox positions for the subject to occupy. We ought to remember that, since the media is composed of a number of quite different forms, it might be unwise to overemphasise one particular theoretical approach. The danger is that we will end up with a discipline constructed on a very narrow base, just so that a minority of critics will find the subject more 'manageable'.

For example, the fact that many individuals still rely primarily on an image-based semiology to interpret texts which have other significant components besides the visual, can only act to restrict the development of theory as well as to distort the outcome of research. It is easy to see how even the use of apparently simple terms remains problematic; different parts of the subject use different terms and concepts, which do not always 'translate' very easily from one area to another. For example, talking about genres of film is an accepted practice, but talking about genres of newspaper story would seem a little awkward.

Any outline of the subject needs to acknowledge that the theory used is drawn from a wide range of disciplines. To some extent, Media Studies remains at present a 'compilation' of theories. We need to achieve a balance between forcing the pace along, and investigating again some of the established academic traditions from which we still have much to learn. If, for example, we find that discourse analysis solves some of the problems involved in investigating ideology, or that a study of interpellation helps us to explain how media audiences are addressed and mobilised, then we should not neglect these ideas because they have emerged from studies of language and politics.

Preface to the 1998 edition

'Media Studies', which first appeared in 1993, was both a review of the subject and an intervention in the debates which surrounded it. One of the discussions current at the time (which continues in the present), concerned the general direction the subject ought to take, closely linked to the vexed question of 'level'. It seemed clear that many sources were too obscure or badly written to be of much use to students or teachers. On the other hand, most of the early books intended for an 'A' level and undergraduate audience did not appear to reach the standard required by exam boards and other professional bodies. Rather than attempt to arrest what some called 'upward academic drift', it seemed more important to recognise the advanced nature of media and communication theory, and to provide a clear guide to the field. At the same time, I thought it important to set out a number of departures from orthodox perspectives.

In recent years, what could be called the discursive turn in media and cultural studies expressed in the first edition of Media Studies (and presented in my other books as an alternative to both the structuralist orthodoxy and the postmodern 'heresy') has been considerably strengthened. However, positive developments within the subject were, for a while at least, obscured by more public events. The study of the media was attacked in some sections of the press on the grounds that it was a bogus or frivolous exercise. Although the subject itself bore little resemblance to the image of it constructed by hostile commentators, the fashion for vilifying media and cultural studies spread. An atmosphere had been created in which it became possible to make significant changes: at 'A' level, in the way the subject is structured; at undergraduate level, in the way the subject is funded. Although there is no space here to provide an overview of these events, I think we should remember that media courses, often seen as essentially leftist, have displeased many of those who would prefer to keep their own practices free from critical scrutiny.

Fortunately, the academic study of the media has continued to increase in strength and popularity and – despite an odd tendency in some theorists to celebrate their own status as consumers – has retained its critical edge. The next question must be what kind of critical perspective will be used as the subject moves away from its established traditions. The approach used in this book provides one possible route. There are other closely related developments which also seem encouraging; see for example the work of K.B. Jensen, Paul Cobley and the cultural investigations of Pertti Alasuutari.

Acknowledgements: 1st edition

The first edition of *Media Studies* was written over a period of eight months, during my time as Head of Media Education at Somerset College. I would like to thank in particular Rivers Barry and Anita Abrams, who provided friendly support and encouragement. Rivers' insight into a variety of communication issues remains highly valued. Members of the college LRC (notably Kathy Beer and Dave Ross) provided technical support, while Raoul Wedge-Thomas and Mick Garland produced a number of illustrations. Raoul created a set of excellent diagrams from my initial sketches. Examples of Mick's photography appear throughout the text; the interview he gave forms an important part of Chapter 4. I would also like to thank Saira Bradford for her hard work in making transcripts, and Sue Watling for providing notes on magazine design. Elizabeth Tarrant at Pitman was an excellent editor, while Julian Thomas showed enthusiasm throughout the process. A number of students allowed the reproduction of extracts from coursework. Above all, my thanks are due to Lucy Byrne, whose presence made the actual process of writing possible.

Acknowledgements: 2nd edition

This edition was produced in 1998. Some of the new material, particularly the work on news, has been drawn from background research produced in support of lectures given for the European Foundation and the Media Arts programme at the London College of Music and Media. Some other new material has been taken from PhD research. My colleague on the Media Arts course at the London College of Music and Media, Eryl Price-Davies, was kind enough to provide the interview on Radio broadcasting. Many thanks to Lorna Cocking and Melissa Quinn at Addison Wesley Longman for editorial support. I greatly appreciate the enthusiastic response I have received over the last few years, from students, teachers and academics.

My thanks to the following people and organisations for permission to use illustrations, transcripts and other material:

The BBC Photograph Library for the photograph of Paul McGann
BBC for the Newsnight transcript as broadcast on BBC2, 25.6.92
Birds Eye Wall's Limited for the extract from the script 'Healthy Options'
BUPA for the extract from the script 'Scanner'
Continuity Graphics and D. C. Thomson & Co Ltd for the pages from *Bucky O'Hare*
Cosmopolitan/NRS for their readership profiles
Daily Express for their front page of 26.3.92 and front pages from 2.9.97 and 3.9.97
Daily Mirror for their two pages of 25.3.92 and the pages from 18.3.97 and 4.9.97
BMP DDB Needham for the transcript and Little Boats agency for permission to use the photographs of the little girl from the Volkswagen Passat TV commercial
Ford Motor Company Limited for extract from the Ford Granada script
Friends of the Earth for campaign material on Air Pollution
The Marketing Triangle and DMB&B for the Uno Fiat campaign on behalf of Fiat Auto (UK) Ltd
Mail Newspapers/Solo Syndication and Literary Agency Ltd for the *Daily Mail* headline of 25.2.91
David Morley for the diagram of audience response from his book *The Nationwide Audience*
Radio Times for the article on *The Monocled Mutineer* and Clive Landon, who took the photographs

SOGAT '82/NGA and Labour Movement Services for leaflets produced during the Wapping dispute

The *Sun* for their front page and opinion colums from 18.3.98

GMTV for its consumer profile, March – May 1997

Daily Mail for their front page of 2.9.97

Chris Steele-Perkins and Magnum Photos Limited for the two photographs of famine victims

TVMM for the HTV social profiling guide to audience

United Nations Association for 'Pledge for the Planet'

Every effort has been made to trace and acknowledge ownership of copyright. The Publishers will be pleased to make suitable arrangements with any copyright holders whom it has not been possible to contact

SP

The position and importance of Media Studies

Media studies theory appears to have been 'compiled' from a variety of sources because the subject has its roots in film, cultural and communication studies, and in addition draws on other fields such as linguistics, sociology and psychology. There is also a considerable amount of mass communication history which requires attention. A sound knowledge of media history is necessary because we need to understand the institutions which produce and circulate media texts. This great diversity of material puts a certain amount of pressure on teachers and students, but it is exactly the variety of approach that this demands that makes up one of the subject's most positive features.

The first task must be to provide a coherent overview of mass media theory, in all its forms and with all its imperfections. If this task is not carried out, we may be left with a tightly-organised but rather small academic outpost. There may be some people in the field of media studies who believe that it is too early for this process to begin, on the grounds that the subject has not quite 'settled down'. It is worth pointing out that there are media students currently engaged in working towards a variety of qualifications in further and higher education. They need a source which at least sets out the field and some of the debates within it.

We need a thorough but not prescriptive approach which takes into account more recent developments in the subject and which allows media studies to be placed in a wider social and historical perspective. No media terminologies can be regarded as infallible keys to the subject. Although some ideas have clearly not survived the rigours of close investigation, they should still appear as important historical references in the development of the field.

Just as important is the idea that media studies should not neglect the human subject at the centre of mass communication messages. Media studies tries to demonstrate how a multiplicity of meanings can be created through the manipulation of form, content, and the foreknowledge and expectation of an audience. By starting with the concept of communication in everyday social transactions, students' own experience could be called upon, and may be used to investigate the practices which we observe in the media itself. The 'communicative background' to media studies forms an important element of Chapter 1.

THEORY AND PRACTICAL WORK

'A' level and degree courses usually contain practical modules and exercises where students have to demonstrate their understanding of ideas and issues by making their own images, programmes, tapes, magazines, and so on. The purpose of practical enquiry is not, however, to mimic mass media texts. Testing theory through practical production work may become especially useful when projects and exercises are linked to a thorough investigation of audience and industry. Practical exercises should be seen as a dynamic instrument of study which can reveal codes, structures and conventions in ways that would not be as clearly established from the analysis of published texts. The aim should be to create a media studies practice which is allowed to emerge from an integrated model of theory and practical work.

Discussion of the interplay of form and content, and the relationship between 'mainstream' and 'alternative' codes and conventions, is certainly part of a sound approach. If theory is undervalued, and treated as an adjunct to practical exercises, student work will tend to be derivative. There are clearly dangers to be avoided. In the case of film, for example, students must not use theory simply in order to help them reproduce a range of technical effects. There is little wrong with a good copy, where the copyist knows the limitations of the exercise. It is where the practitioner remains unaware of the degree of influence exerted upon his or her work that little of worth has been learned.

In order to see how meaning is created, circulated and interpreted, students must themselves be able to experiment with the creation of meaning. We should also prepare students for the movement between media forms. The adaptation of a radio script to a storyboard, the mediation of an election broadcast by a news bulletin, the filming of a comic-book narrative, and so on, all help to demonstrate how the emphasis in messages changes as different forms are used.

Whenever students are required to produce media artifacts, there are strong arguments to be made for investigating audiences and undertaking research into specific target groups. They may gain great insight into the dissemination of ideas when they are required to formulate messages and images which take into account the values, attitudes and beliefs of an audience. We should encourage our students to make experiments in media forms and to engage in group projects from the very beginning of their media and communication courses. In production work, it is important to investigate all those elements which go to make up a successful process.

Media studies bids fair to be at the centre of the further and higher education curriculum, not least because it studies an area of cultural reproduction and discourse which makes an impact on everyone who is capable of receiving its messages. I hope that students and teachers will continue to find this book a useful contribution to their work in the subject.

SP

CHAPTER 1

The background to Media Studies

COMMUNICATION – THE EXCHANGE OF MEANING BETWEEN HUMAN AGENTS

Many attempts have been made to define 'communication'. One of the most succinct is offered in Price's *The A–Z Media and Communication Handbook**, published in 1997, where communication is described as 'the **exchange of meaning** between human agents'. This definition assumes that all types of interactive process (covered by the word 'exchange') which allow any form of meaning to develop, should be considered as communication. 'Meaning' can be defined as a reference, event or action which conveys significance to human individuals. The 'exchange of meaning' between people has to take place within a certain shared **context**. This usually consists (at least in face to face communication) of four aspects:

- the physical and temporal situation they inhabit;
- the basic faculties all humans have at their disposal (spoken language, mutual awareness, etc.);
- the discursive environment which exists at the time (the general range of opinions and ideas which can be mobilised in relation to topics of conversation);
- the overall social or structural context, including the economic condition of society, the political structure, the class system, and so on.

Other definitions attempt to explain the ways in which communication is produced, or the various forms it can take. Dance and Larsen (in Watson and Hill, *A Dictionary of Communication and Media Studies*) offer this explanation:

---

* Full details of publications mentioned in the text are given in the Bibliography at the end of this book.

'The production of symbolic content by an individual, according to a code, with anticipated consumption by other(s) according to the same code.'

In this example, **symbolic content** refers to the existence of individual elements (or symbols) within the larger structures of language, mathematics or other signifying systems. Symbols (from the Ancient Greek for marks, tokens or signs) are able to describe, represent or indicate objects, ideas, concepts, and experiences – all those aspects of the real which human beings perceive and, through the process of perception and communication, re-create.

Symbolic content (in the form of utterances, words on a page, signs and so on) represents aspects of experience. In fact, some writers believe that the world cannot be understood without the use of symbols; E. Cassirer, in *The Philosophy of Symbolic Forms*, writes that 'the sign is no mere accidental cloak of the idea, but its necessary and essential organ'. This would mean that all aspects of reality, including objects, ideas and so on, must inevitably take a symbolic form. This is supported by the fact that all human cultures use names, categories, and descriptions to classify experience, providing the basis for common understanding.

If we look again at Dance and Larsen's definition, we may notice that it reveals a certain approach to communication. In the first place, it places the individual at the centre of the communication process. In some cases, however, such as the creation of broadcast material, content is produced collectively. Another point to note is the reference to **code**. A code is a system which allows a particular culture to communicate through the use of *signs*. All codes which offer the opportunity to create meaning, are called **signifying** codes. Codes may consist of written signs, graphic symbols or more informal examples of human behaviour, such as gesture or other forms of expression.

Interaction

An interaction is the **action** and **reaction** which takes place between two or more individuals, or two or more social groups. The study of communication is the study of the interactions which take place within societies. It may also include, according to some theories, those interactions which take place *between* societies. Interaction is the mobilisation of types of content.

SYMBOLIC INTERACTION

The human communicator uses a series of symbols – signs (images, words, gestures) that *stand for* things or ideas, as we have already seen. The key here to describe all the ranges of communication is **symbolic interaction**. Symbolic interaction means the *exchange* of meanings, which are encoded in language, or gesture, or in visual signs. We could add a new element and say that human communicators use a series of symbols for what they *understand to be* the environment, the real world, that they inhabit.

A QUESTION OF REALITY?

There are arguments about what the symbols we use in our interactions actually refer to: do they stand for a real, material world or a 'version' of that world?

Some thinkers have cast doubt on the ability of the human subject to get a true or complete picture of reality. According to their theories, we never get to know the real world, because we understand only the symbolic content we have built up to represent reality – the words, images and sounds which stand for some real thing or idea.

This unease about **referentiality** (the extent to which we can be sure we are referring to an actual object in the real world) can cause problems, and even contradictory definitions in the same text. Dimbleby and Burton (*see Between Ourselves*, p. 52) say at one point:

> 'There is no truth or reality out there. It is manufactured in our heads.'

Later, discussing the subject again (p. 191), they argue that:

> 'We can never deal in the original experience, the actual idea, but only in the signs which stand in place of the experience or the idea. To this extent it is a second-hand world which we live in.'

In the first quotation, there is no reality at all. It is 'manufactured in our heads'. In the second, there is presumably *something* called reality ('the original experience') because we could not otherwise gain a 'second-hand' experience of it. These arguments about reality will form an important part of our study of semiology in the next chapter. In the meantime, it might be worth noting that the question usually posed about the relationship between symbols and the real – 'Does language/symbolic content reflect or create our sense of reality?' – is in itself misleading, because it obscures what Gemma Corradi Fiumara calls 'the complex network of relations which exist between language(s) and reality in the making' (*see The Symbolic Function* p. 1). In other words, our sense of what is real depends on a dynamic process, in which symbols and the things to which they refer affect and change one another.

COMMUNICATION – ELEMENTS, FEATURES AND PROCESS

Communication is usually discussed under the following headings:

- the **elements** of communication (its component parts);
- the **features** of communication (its characteristics);
- the **process** of communication (its course of action, how it operates).

Elements

Among the authors who describe the main elements of communication are Watson and Hill (see *A Dictionary of Communication and Media Studies*). They list five basic elements which must be present for communication to take place:

- a **message**;
- an initiator (**sender**);
- a mode / vehicle (**channel**);
- a recipient (**receiver**);
- an **effect**.

Features

In *The Dynamics of Human Communication*, Myers and Myers stress six **features** of communication: it is everywhere; it is continuous; it involves the sharing of meaning; it contains predictable elements; it occurs at more than one level; and it occurs amongst both equals and 'unequals'.

It is worth expanding briefly on these points:

1 The idea that communication is *everywhere* shows us that it is impossible to avoid, and is a central feature of our whole culture.

2 Communication, some theorists argue, never stops (it is *continuous*), and has no identifiable beginning or end.

3 The idea that communication can only be found where there is some kind of *shared* meaning available leads some writers to argue that there must be interaction taking place for true communication to exist (*see* interaction, above).

4 The usefulness of having *predictable* elements is that a communication will be understood partly because there are expected (or conventional) elements in it which people anticipate in certain situations or contexts.

5 The idea of having different *levels* means that communication may happen, for example, between two individuals, between groups of individuals, and between the mass media and its audiences.

6 The idea of *equals* and *unequals* refers to people inhabiting different social and personal positions, because of age, gender, ethnicity, and so on. This idea will become very important when we examine theories of power (or domination and subordination).

Process

One definition of the *process* of communication describes it as 'the transmission of a thought, an instruction, a wish, an idea, a feelling from one person to another' (Gurevitch and Roberts, *Issues in the Study of Mass Communication and Society*, p. 12).

Watson and Hill describe the process of communication as one which begins when a **message** is thought up by a **sender**, who then *encodes* the message before transmitting it through a particular **channel** to a **receiver**, who in turn *decodes* the message with a certain **effect** as an outcome. This model of the process of communication could be applied where communication takes place between two individuals or two groups and where there is no interference by a third party.

On the face of it, nothing could be more straightforward than Fig 1.1. As an example, imagine that the **message** is a simple request or even an instruction: 'Meet me at six', which is vocalised by a young man (the **sender**) using the **channel**

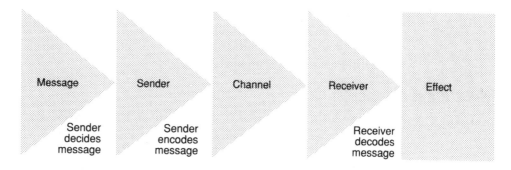

Fig 1.1 A simple diagram of the communication process

of his own voice, which results in his friend (the **receiver**) hearing, understanding and acting upon the message (the **effect**).

In fact, there are a number of factors that this diagram has ignored. One problem raised by communication theorists is how accurately the message *received* reflects the message which was originally sent. Another problem is the clarity of the message itself. In the example above, the message is rather ambiguous – *where* exactly is the meeting to take place? Also, the notion of 'interference' or 'noise', some kind of disturbance which acts to disrupt the coherence of the message (usually occurring as the **message** travels along the **channel**), has always intrigued communication theorists.

CHANGING ROLES IN THE PROCESS OF COMMUNICATION

The original diagram (Fig 1.1) could be misleading in another way, in the sense that communication does not very often end with the *effect*. The participants *change roles*, alternating as sender and receiver. A more accurate diagram, though still of a very simple process, would look like that in Fig 1.2.

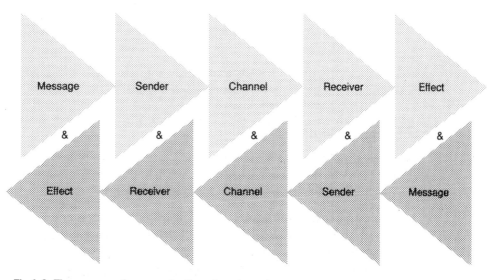

Fig 1.2 The process of communication: changing roles

The message now has a much clearer relationship to the effect. This is not to suggest that the channel need remain the same. The first time that a message is sent, it might be delivered through the channel of the human voice; the next instance might find a handwritten note being used.

THE WEAKNESS OF PROCESS?

So far, we have only studied the *obviously measurable evidence* of communication. For example, we might say that the spoken or written word, or a group of gestures, or a set of visual symbols, makes up the evidence of a communication. Where some **process theories** have shown weakness is in their neglect of what may lie *behind* this surface evidence.

INTENTION AND CONTEXT

When senders choose a message, all sorts of pressures may force them to *adapt* the message to the circumstances with which they are faced. This means that the original message will be shaped, from the moment it is first thought up, by *more factors than simply the need to communicate an idea*. There is a lot to be discovered about the first stage, the origin of the message. Perhaps the beginning of the diagram should be drawn differently, with a question mark placed between the message and the sender:

The content of any message depends very much on:

1 **The intention** of the sender
2 **The available language or symbolic forms**, which will act to structure the message
3 **The context**, as the sender understands it, within which the message is delivered
4 **The communicative possibilities or discourses** which have, in the past, presented themselves in the same sort of context.

Chapter 2 will investigate more fully this idea that messages are shaped by a number of different factors, some of them outside the control of the sender.

Categories of communication

Communication can also be separated into different types or **categories**. The ability to decribe these categories is important at this stage, though the chief purpose of this book will be to examine mass communication.

1 **Intrapersonal communication**. This category is understood as communication within the self. It includes thought processes, diary entries, notes to oneself – in fact any form of communication that helps personal reflection and organisation. Many theorists regard this as the 'bedrock' of all communication, but also as one category which is only properly understood when revealed in the context of

'interpersonal' communication. Some writers do not regard the intrapersonal as a true category at all, because to do so lends support to the idea of a 'split self', with one part of the self able to reply to the other. For a full discussion of this issue, see *Communication Studies*, by Stuart Price (1996).

2 **Interpersonal communication.** This refers to communication between people, which is usually face to face, and usually between two individuals. It does not simply consist of written and spoken communication, but also of non-verbal interaction (body language and facial expression) used as an important context or support to the verbal exchange.

3 **Group communication.** This is usually taken to mean communication within clearly identifiable groups, or between different groups of people. It is worth realising that groups are brought together, or come together, for quite a variety of reasons. Some authors distinguish between large and small groups, and explore how different rules apply to each case.

4 **Mass communication.** This category is often used to describe the type of communications initiated, or prompted, by the large institutions of the mass media. However, according to some views (*see* Dimbleby and Burton, *More than Words*, p. 8), there are other mass communicators besides the mass media, including the postal system. We may be reluctant to accept the Post Office as an example, however, because there is not a *mass audience* in receipt of a *universal message*. In other words, a postal system (whether public or private) may not share many of the criteria which go to make mass communication except the scale of the operation. In Chapter 3 on Audience there is an investigation of how far a stable, identifiable 'mass' audience can ever really exist for any mass communication.

5 **Extrapersonal communication.** This type of communication is generally described as that which takes place either *without* human involvement (communication between machines) or, more loosely, interaction *between* human beings and machines. Whether the latter is in fact really a form of intrapersonal communication (the person sitting alone at a computer terminal or a word processor) remains a matter of debate. But it is clear that any machine must at some point be programmed by a human operator before two or more machines are able to pass messages and signals along any electronic channel.

POWER, MASS COMMUNICATION AND SOCIETY

Power exists in all interactions and in all communicative relationships. How is power defined? There are two basic meanings of the term:

1 Power is the **capacity to do something,** to affect our immediate environment. Power may be used in this way by groups, by individuals, by large public or private bodies.

2 Power also means the **domination** of one individual/group/corporation **over** any other or set of others.

Both these definitions allow that power is the possession of the ability to shape action.

At the **individual** level, Weber described power as 'the probability that an actor in a social relationship will be in a position to carry out his (her) own will despite resistance.' At the **societal** level, Poulantzas described power as 'the capacity of a class to realise its specific objective interests'. (*See* McLennan on power in *The Power of Ideology*, p. 37).

Good, clean communication?

It would be naive to imagine that an **interpersonal** interaction, because it is based on one-to-one communication, is somehow 'pure', and free from the struggle for **influence** and **power** which is so clearly a feature of *mass* communication.

It also seems that the idea that 'good communication' will lead *by its very nature* to all sorts of benefits (such as 'greater understanding' between individuals and groups) can only be misleading. It is quite easy to imagine a situation where greater understanding of some points of view may lead to an extremely *negative* response (for example, it is probably better not to know what the person who shouts from a passing car has actually said).

The point, however, is that there is no interaction in which power of some sort is *not* at stake. The hierarchies of age, ethnicity, gender, even appearance and 'social acceptability' all work to structure our access to communication and power. (It is not enough, nevertheless, to assume that a white, middle-aged, middle-class male will always have access to a kind of undiluted social power in all situations; but such an individual is more likely to receive the benefits of his subject position when he is placed in a hierarchy which functions through social inequality.)

Communication between 'unequals'?

Schramm (*see* Myers and Myers, p. 9) writes:

'Communication is now seen as a transaction in which both parties are active ... The parties are not necessarily equally active ... but to both parties the transaction is in some way functional. It meets a need or provides a gratification.'

This definition may signal a significant move away from the idea that communication is a process based on a kind of 'free and equal' transaction. The transaction, in Schramm's words, is 'in some way functional'. How exactly it 'meets a need, provides a gratification,' is not explored. Schramm does not answer the question of how we *define* activity in communication. Instead, it seems the non-powerful, non-influential partner is to take a more limited role in the process.

Rhetorical sensitivity

Another theory which puts forward the idea that communication is based on the mutual *benefit* of the parties concerned, without considering the related issues of power, is called **rhetorical sensitivity**. This imagines a positive and beneficial model of interpersonal communication. It is 'a way of thinking about what should be said and then a way of deciding how to say it' (*see* Myers and Myers, p. 7, Hart).

Although rhetorical sensitivity implies a kind of mutual benefit, it is of course perfectly easy to use such a device as a way of gaining *individual* power. Much 'anti-social' communication, in the author's opinion, is *disguised* as mutual, interactive, or being sensitive to the needs of others. Choosing how to say something is all about choosing the most effective type of discourse for the aim one has in mind. It may also benefit another person, but this could be a side-effect of the real intention.

Mass communication: imitating the personal mode

Rhetorical sensitivity can be used on the interpersonal level (to influence people for good or ill) but we should be aware of how often models *taken from personal communication* can be 'translated' to mass communication uses. Some forms of 'communication' which depend on quite staggering inequalities of power can be presented as not only intimate, but based on equality and respect.

If we take the example of an election, some communicators (politicians) are anxious to make their messages conform to an 'interpersonal' model. They seem to adopt a 'domestic' and broadly 'democratic' mode of discourse to match the occasion. There are many different reasons for being sensitive, some of which can be entirely selfish.

Mass communicators use models of interpersonal communication in order to make their message effective, which means to say it is recognised by an **audience** as an **address**. Students of the media need to bear in mind that the mass media are not just one branch of human communication; they are built upon and continue to imitate human interaction. All mass media forms depend on the use of symbolic content: the formal elements of language, images, gestures, intonation and so on. However, they also display a dependence on *interactive* and *personalised* models: film may contain fantasies of interaction; politicians on the radio may address audiences as though they are able to interact personally with them; magazines may address a reader as though that reader is intimately known.

Differences between mass and interpersonal communication

In their introductory study of interpersonal and mass communication, Gurevitch and Roberts (*see Issues in the Study of Mass Communication and Society*), note that there are two major differences between the categories. They note (p. 13) that:

1 Interpersonal communication involves 'at any given moment one "transmitter" who communicates with one or a few receivers'. (This is correct, unless we insist that the definition of interpersonal communication is that which takes place between only two individuals.) They contrast this with mass communication, where one or more 'transmitters' communicate (or at least send messages) to a very large number of 'receivers'.

2 Mass communication is 'mediated' through a specific set of technologies which stand between the senders and receivers.

What are the implications of these two major differences? First, that there may be greater questions of influence and power at work when the scale of communication increases; second, that when this wider mode of communication gives rise to a set of technologies, the real (as opposed to the suggested) immediacy of interaction is lost. Some theorists, as McQuail puts it (*Communication*, p. 164), believe that it is not:

> '... the techniques [of the mass media] themselves which make any essential difference to the communication process, but rather the particular uses to which they have been put, the new kinds of social relationship which have been made possible and ... the forms of social organisation and production which have been developed.'

We could argue with the idea that the 'techniques themselves' make no essential difference; the feeling of immediacy gained from a form like television (owing to its strong visual and auditory impact) may obscure the fact that it is a **mediation**, a representation of events. Each of the mass media forms (television, press, film, radio, etc) can alter our perception of an event in a *specific* way.

A process model of the mass media

It looks as though we might have returned to the simple model of the communication process with which we began. The differences lie in the possibility that:

- **the message** may alter by virtue of the specialisms of the sender/s and the techologies of the different channels;
- **the senders** may sometimes form a group (a media industry, conglomerate, or a subsection of these), and will begin to display collective forms of behaviour;
- **the channel** chosen for the message may possibly increase in significance and power since it will consist of a more 'complex' technology (though this is not to say that personal interactions are less complex as *examples* of communication);
- **the number of possible receivers** may perhaps multiply so vastly (while being scattered in terms of physical location) that the effects may sometimes be almost impossible to gauge; in fact, the supposed receivers (the 'target audience') may never even have received the message.

The diagram in Fig 1.3 shows a model of the mass communication process.

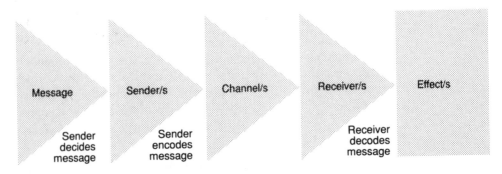

Fig 1.3 **A model of the mass communication process**

What is important to understand is that the **senders** and the **receivers** may be seen as **collectives**, but they are very different *types* of collectives. The collective which produces the messages is usually organised as a work group and as a hierarchy, with some degree of shared values and group norms. The audience which receives the mass media message is, on the other hand, much less likely to have a developed or cohesive view of itself as a collective.

Is the mass media truly communicative?

If communication is really 'a convergence process in which sender and receiver ... create and share information', then it could be argued that the relationship between the mass media and their audience is not truly 'communicative' at all. The evidence for this is easy to summarise. The mass media exercise the dominant role in the relationship. They create, or at least circulate, certain types of information, ideas, images and so on. The audience, by contrast, has only limited opportunities to make direct contact with the source of the message (through letters, 'phone-ins', 'video-box' opinions and some open-access programming), and even so does not usually initiate the communication.

While it is true that a purely structural analysis of the media is unlikely to shed light on the great variations in the way audiences consume products (the ways in which they use and enjoy texts), it is important to analyse the nature of the relationship between audience and mass media institutions. This analysis must include not just a study of the power which exists within and between people, but the power balance which exists between the mass media and those who 'consume' its output.

Some questions about society

We are beginning now to turn away from considering just how messages are sent and get from A to B to another question. What is the social context in which messages are circulated? This is one of the most difficult questions to answer, since one person's view of the society, how it operates and whether or not it is founded on a just distribution of power, may tend to clash with the views of other writers, readers, and those who study communication and the media. In order to make any progress at all, we need first to find out what we ourselves believe about the society in which we live.

One method would be to answer the following questions, and then perhaps to compare these answers with the consensus of a wider group:

- What do we mean by society?
- What kind of society do we live in?
- Why are there different classes?
- How much influence are individuals able to exercise on the state?
- What do we mean by 'equality' between men and women?
- Where can power be found in society?
- What is the role of the mass media in society?

Students of society and its communicative practices need to be aware that there are many definitions of 'communication' and 'media', partly because there are, as suggested, great differences in the way our **society** is understood. The questions posed here would be answered in different ways by every writer on the subject.

There is, however, a basic agreement about what 'society' means (among those who admit that it actually exists). Society may be defined as an organised collective at the level of the nation-state, together with the customs, practices, relationships, ideologies and culture of the people, classes and groups who make up that collective. There is no need to worry about this definition; we all have a working idea of what the term society means. What we need is an understanding of how various traditions of thought provide us with different ideas about the social environment we inhabit.

Theories of society (1)

The sociologist, David Coates (*see Traditions of Thought*, in *Society and Social Science, a reader* – 1990) describes four traditions of thought (we could call them four political approaches) which have established themselves as major ways of understanding society, including the areas of culture and economics.

David Coates calls these traditions **liberal**, **Marxist**, **social-reformist** and **conservative**. In addition, there are other perspectives and views which have made an increasing impact on how we see our society. Amongst these currents of thought are **feminist** and **ecological** approaches which, in their most radical forms, call into question the whole direction of economic and social policy. Feminism has been able to identify and criticise the way that most theories of society have neglected the family as 'one of the main sources responsible for the continued subordination of women'. (*See* Marion Price, *Still Worlds Apart?* in *Investigating Society*, Longman, 1989, p. 143). Feminism, often in alliance with psychoanalytical approaches, has made a fairly considerable impact on media theory, as we shall see in more detail later. However, its greatest impact has been on the general approach made to questions of power by all of Coates' four traditions. Each of these traditions has, to some extent, seen society as something that could be maintained, or for that matter altered, at a 'macro' level. In other words, by reinforcing or altering the major structures or social relationships through the use of legislation, reform, or even force. Feminist critiques, on the other hand (together with some libertarian or anarchist approaches), have stressed that changes which take place at the personal level might have radical implications for the conduct and structure of society as a whole.

Four traditions

LIBERALISM

This became established as a body of thought by the end of the eighteenth century. It was a clearly defined theory of economics, very much in favour of the development of capitalism. Coates desribes (p. 253) how liberalism saw society as composed of 'rational individuals in pursuit of their self-interest'.

So the people who wished to produce goods for sale and who wished to make profits and get rich were acting in a sensible way. Not only this; they were supposed to be doing the whole of society good. The extent of a society's property became a basic measure of how well individuals and the society in general were doing. The *market* would produce wealth and prosperity.

The central figure in early liberal thought was Adam Smith. He saw the pursuit of *self-interest* as beneficial for the whole society. (*See* Coates, p. 253):

> 'By pursuing his own interest he [the person in business] frequently promotes that of the society more effectively than when he really intends to promote it.'

Central direction from the state was not required. Society was made up of people driven by their own wish for success. (It seems in this theory, that those with the potential to be successful were better placed to take advantage of their energies if they belonged to the male sex.) All that was left for the state to do was to provide 'external defence and internal order'.

These notions of economic liberalism enjoyed a new lease of life when the 'radical' right wing of conservatism came to power in Britain in 1979. The economist, Milton Friedman, had a considerable influence over the policies of many western governments in the 1970s and 1980s.

MARXISM

Marx believed that individuals only truly existed in *social* relationships. In contrast to liberalism, Marxism put forward the idea that the development of society and the individual was *held back* by the concentration of private property.

Coates (p. 257) quotes Marx's view that:

> 'Men make their own history, but do not make it just as they please; they do not make it under circumstances chosen by themselves.'

Rather than support the idea that *competition* drove society forward, Marx argued that *co-operation between working people* would lead to a more positive future. It seemed to Marx that, in every period of society, production of the necessities of life had been organised in a way which divided people and caused conflict. The small number of non-producers who owned the factories, mines and shops appeared to live in comfort, supported by the labour of others. (The idea that women supported the labour of men was acknowledged by some early Marxists, but the notion that this also made them into a kind of 'sub-class' was not fully theorised, perhaps because this may have suggested in its turn that the male working class was therefore, to some degree, part of an exploitative group.)

Marx argued for a society which would be free of the division between labour and capital. Although the ruling class (referred to as the 'bourgeoisie') had developed society to a great extent, it was becoming outdated and the time of social revolution was fast approaching. Capitalism had served its purpose and now needed to go.

SOCIAL REFORMISM

Social reformism expressed a commitment to *gradual* progress and held the view that market forces alone would not produce a just society. The key to this view of society is the word 'reform'. Gradual and peaceful social change, rather than revolution, was put forward as the solution to society's ills.

Moral development, reform and education were at the centre of the whole philosophy. The nineteenth-century philosopher John Stuart Mill wished to achieve wider popular participation in representative government. Another philosopher, Jeremy Bentham, believed in attempting to obtain the 'greatest happiness of the greatest number' in society.

These philosophers believed that, as prosperity spread, conflict between the classes would decline. The economist John Maynard Keynes was an important social reformist of the 1930s, who proposed certain rescue measures for the British economy. He said that the government of the day could generate income by expanding its own labour force. Some theorists, such as Weber, believed that dictatorship would grow out of the attempt to create socialism. He made the interesting comment that (p. 277):

> 'Modern men and women possess an enhanced technical capacity to achieve ends that [are] no longer clear to them.'

CONSERVATISM

Coates reproduces a comment made by the modern conservative, Roger Scruton (p. 278): 'Conservatism becomes conscious only when forced to be so.'

Conservatives believe that there are worthwhile reasons for keeping the social system we have at present. One of these is that it is generally preferable to the alternatives. The present, with all its inequalities, is based on the accumulated wisdom of previous ages. Edmund Burke, one of the most effective philosophers of early conservatism, believed in a strong set of institutions in order to keep human passions under control. Hierarchy (the graded divisions of power in society) exists so that social order is maintained, though in some versions the ruling class have a duty to assist those less fortunate.

In the early nineteenth century some conservatives were hostile to the new capitalist class because it seemed to threaten the establishment, an aristocracy based on the ownership of land. As the capitalist class became dominant, conservatives switched their primary support to the new class. This is because traditional conservatism is an attempt to preserve something, to defend the core of an established order. It should have come as no surprise, therefore, to hear hardline 'communists' in the former Soviet Union described as conservatives.

Each of these approaches has given rise to new variations. Political positions change over time.

How may these positions be applied to the study of society and media?

Liberal, Marxist, social-reformist and **conservative** will remain labels for vaguely-remembered concepts unless we have an idea of how they are to be applied to our study. How would a 'classic' statement of each position deal with the questions we posed earlier? It would be almost impossible to find a *representative* of each position who agreed exactly with it, because people adapt their beliefs as time and circumstance demand and are anyway more creative. The answers to these questions may provide a point of comparison with the reality of politics that people describe in conversation or argument. Some of these answers make the traditions seem rather more cut and dried and perhaps more 'high-minded' than they actually are, or have been in history.

For example, because social reformism has always been a rival of the radical left, it has sometimes made its first priority the defence of the system. In practice, it has often had to manage the system as it is, putting off reforms to such a distant future that it has ended up squarely on the right of politics.

Liberal economics has found itself in close alliance with the 'Thatcherite' right of conservatism. In some ways, conservatism is no longer a defence of *all* aspects of the 'way things are'. In an economic depression conservatism has re-assessed what it thinks is most worth preserving.

Marxist thought has little influence over the making of social policy, except in so far as other traditions use it as an unpleasant contrast to their own 'moderation'. Marxism has, from the theorist's viewpoint, made significant progress in providing a clearly worked out set of cultural, media and mass communication theories.

There are also straightforward confusions at work in the description of political terms. One instance of this would be the way that the *political* meaning of liberalism is often confused with its use as an *economic* term.

Here we could remind ourselves of the questions used to draw attention to the problems of understanding and describing society, based on the four philosophies laid out by Coates. The possible answers which could be made to these questions follow after this resumé of the questions themselves:

1 What do we mean by society?
2 What kind of society do we live in?
3 Why are there different classes?
4 How much influence are individuals able to exercise on the state?
5 What do we mean by 'equality' between men and women?
6 Where can power be found in society?
7 What is the role of the mass media in society?

LIBERALISM

1 Society is a self-regulating mechanism made up of rational individuals, intent on self-improvement.
2 We live in a society where people are free and equal, but where hard work and talent can be rewarded.
3 Classes exist because different functions need to be carried out in the society, but mobility between classes is perfectly possible.

4 Individuals should be able to use the state as the guardian of society, so that the basic conditions for economic growth and individual liberty are ensured.

5 Equality between men and women is equality in marketplace opportunity.

6 Power is 'loaned' to the state through the contract made between free individuals and the state.

7 The role of the mass media is to provide accurate and reliable information, upon which rational economic decisions can be made; the media must respect the rights of the individual; the media are made up of groups of energetic entrepreneurs; the media should not be run by the state, although sensible regulation is necessary.

MARXISM

1 A society is a human organisation at a particular stage in its economic and social development.

2 Our society is a capitalist one in which the population is divided into classes; broadly speaking into working, middle and ruling classes.

3 There are different classes because some groups own the means of production, while others have only their labour to sell.

4 Individuals alone have little or no influence on the state.

5 One of the major sources of oppression is the family, as a result of its being maintained by capitalism; equality will come through revolution when economic injustices will be removed.

6 Power in society can be found in the state, which is the political instrument of the capitalist class; the working class has a kind of power, which comes into being when it acts as a conscious revolutionary collective.

7 The mass media exist to maintain the capitalist state in power.

SOCIAL-REFORMISM

1 Society is an organised collection of individuals, groups and classes.

2 We inhabit a capitalist but democratic society which needs some reform.

3 There are different classes because of inequalities of wealth and opportunity.

4 Individuals with less power and education will find it difficult to influence the state; representative democracy is therefore important.

5 Men and women should ideally be regarded as equal, but equality will only be achieved through state support for training for women, childcare, etc.

6 Power in society may reside with outdated elites and institutions.

7 The role of the mass media is to play a constructive part in a mature democracy.

CONSERVATISM

1 Society is a collection of people bound together by common traditions, outlooks and mutual responsibilities.

2 We live in a free market capitalist society.

3 A class system exists because there are differences between people's abilities and skills; a class system is part of the inherited order and worth preserving.

4 Individuals influence the state through the election of representatives.

5 Equality between men and women has to be seen within the context of the family and the natural aptitudes of each gender.
6 Power in society lies with a responsible political leadership and with the authority of established government.
7 The role of the mass media is to act as a force for social cohesion.

Theories of society (2)

It is the influence of the radical left, however, which has been most felt when it comes to carefully-argued concepts of society and its relationship to the mass media. This is why Denis McQuail in *Mass Communication Theory* (p. 62), describes a number of alternative models of society, most of which grow out of, or have a relationship to, traditional Marxist thought. These include:

- **Mass society theory**, where all the institutions which exercise power (armed forces, church, government, monarchy, the law, mass media) support and reinforce one another. The population is offered entertainment (by the mass media) as a diversion from the fact that they are in a subordinate position. People's work is routine and the whole society is centralised, with only the appearance of democracy.

- **Classic Marxist theory**, based on the idea that society is dominated by a capitalist class, which exploits the working class in order to extract surplus value from the labour that the workers carry out. The mass media are owned by the capitalist class and circulate ideas that will keep this class in power.

A number of variants of Marxist theory grew out of the original formulation, stressing either the *economic* or the *ideological* aspect of ruling class dominance. These variants are described as theories in their own right, but for our present purposes can be dealt with briefly:

1 **Political-economic theory** stresses that the information which circulates in the society is valued according to its possible *profitability*. The uneven distribution of resources prevents critical voices being heard. One development of this theory is that the media's role is to *produce* and *deliver* audiences as sources of profitability.

2 **The theories of the Frankfurt school** and Herbert Marcuse are based on the idea that the working class has been seduced from the path of liberation by a vast system which involves the mass production of goods, ideas and culture. Resistance to this overwhelming system would be found amongst 'marginal' groups in society, which do not experience the same degree of control exercised over the working class. This idea, whatever its accuracy, does allow for a positive and dynamic role to be exercised by groups which were previously marginalised in mainstream notions of radical practice. Women, ethnic groups and young people were exactly those segments of society which the European rebellions of 1968 (and the years which followed) brought into sharper focus.

3 **Theories of hegemony** come from the belief that the dominant ideas of the ruling class reproduce themselves in the *minds of the subordinate*. Ruling ideas

would become the ideas of the whole society, with a more or less voluntary acceptance of this state of affairs by the working class. In this view, the spread of certain **ideas and beliefs** has allowed capitalism to survive.

4 **Social-cultural theory** marks a departure from traditional Marxist theories. This theory tries to understand how certain groups (often the 'marginal' groups mentioned by Marcuse – *see* Frankfurt school above), make *use* of the mass culture they are offered by the media, and in turn how that mass culture draws young people, ethnic minorities and other groups, into the society.

Questions about the mass media

1 Do we believe that the mass media have a positive or a negative effect on our society, or do they have no significant influence on our lives?

2 Do the mass media make up an independent force, or are they closely linked to centres of authority, such as government?

3 Is the audience for mass media communication the 'victim' of a powerful conspiracy, or does the audience create its own meanings from the messages it receives?

4 Do the media get in the way of reality?

5 Are we ever able to know what reality is anyway, or only the words and images which describe it?

Again, the answers to these questions partly depend on the way in which we characterise (or describe) society itself and the *relations of power* which are found within it. (These relations of power are the relationship between different social forces, e.g. church and state; state and media.) Power can exist in friendships, in the workplace, in relations inside a family, and in society as a whole.

Power and authority in the mass media

In *Mass Communication Theory* (p. 32), Denis McQuail describes three alternative *models* of communication or 'modes of communication relationships'. These are:

1 **The command mode**, which considers that **there are differences in *power* and *authority* between senders and receivers,** and thinks of the receivers as being in a surbordinate or dependent position. The reason that communication takes place, according to this idea, is for purposes of *control* or *instruction*. The relationships within this mode are certainly not thought of as equal. It would be as though a sender delivered a message and allowed no feedback at all from the receiver, or at least only feedback of which the sender approved. McQuail seems to be talking here about a certain *type* of address (news programmes, leader columns in newspapers, or election broadcasts/interviews). It does not appear, however, that the command mode operates so clearly in entertainment, for example. (*See* Interpellation, later in this chapter).

McQuail believes this model of the communicative relationship is mainly a 'residual' one, by which he means that it appears as only a *remainder* of an older way of operating. To support his idea that this mode is mainly some kind of a 'leftover', McQuail says that the command mode can be 'activated' (brought into life) at times of political crisis. If it can be activated, then it must exist somewhere, ready to be used. That would suggest that it is some sort of structure. McQuail believes that it is also 'shadowed' whenever the voice of authority is given privileged access by the media.

If the command mode exists, perhaps we should imagine a **command structure** which lies *behind* the command mode. In other words, the hierarchical (top-down) organisation always exists in society and in the media. No sensible ruling class uses the command mode alone; it does not issue commands at all unless they are already part of the fabric of the law, or there is no other way of getting people to do certain things. The Gulf War would be an example of a case when the command mode was 'activated' and used by politicians, if not by the *media* as a whole (*see* Chapter 2).

2 **The service mode** is the name given by McQuail to the second mode. He describes this as 'the most normal, frequently occurring form of relationship' between senders and receivers (*see* McQuail, p. 33). Both parties are seen as united by a mutual interest 'within a market situation'. Relations are seen in a state of *balance*, but, again, they are not in a state of *equality*. This mode is supposed to apply 'most of the time' to the most frequent uses of media: for news, entertainment, ideas, etc.

3 **The associational mode** is the third of these categories. In this case, *shared beliefs* **attach a particular group or public to a specific media source**. This idea proposes that such 'attachment and attention by the receiver' (*see* McQuail, p. 33) is voluntary, and satisfying to the receiver. The needs of the groups are at least equally met. This mode cannot easily be related to the mass media and refers to forms of communication which came before the mass media, or which remain independent of it.

It appears that the three modes we have examined above have some connections with the political traditions studied before:

1 **The command mode** might find some favour with radical critics of the mass media, because it puts emphasis on the way that institutions dominate audiences. Radicals would say 'that is how things are' and perhaps use this as an argument for change. Some conservative thinkers may believe that this kind of relationship is necessary, but whether they would defend such a position in debate would depend on what they wished to achieve.

2 **The service mode**, as a description of the way things are, may receive approval from liberal or conservative thinkers because it emphasises the mutual benefits which may be obtained from a market-based relationship between media and audience.

3 **The associational mode** may attract those thinkers, possibly traditional conserv-

atives, who hanker after older, more organic forms of culture and believe that the modern media is impersonal and unauthentic.

A command structure?

McQuail believes that the mode most evident in the media is the **service** mode, but, as seen above, this can still mean that the media are organised through a **command structure**. However, we do not need to believe that the media are run as a conspiracy; nor that they are the absolute slave of the ruling class. There is an identifiable ruling class in Britain, but one which is a **coalition** of interests. It is, in other words, made up of different groups who have, under certain conditions, common interests. The **service mode** appears to have become popular with some writers because it is close to the *uses and gratifications* theory, which will form part of our study in due course.

The mass media: how powerful?

Using the miners' strike of 1984–5 as an example, Ian Connell attacked the idea that the mass media is somehow blessed with 'fabulous powers' of influence over our society and the people in it. He argued that 'the media *may* have played some part in shaping people's views of the dispute but, whether they did or not will depend upon just how the relevant programmes were watched and/or read.'

This argument is satisfactory in the sense that people bring different opinions and experiences to their 'reading' of a text. Taken on its own, however, it could be interpreted as ignoring a central charge which is often made against the media: that they are unable to offer certain kinds of representation of an event. People may well be more aware than some media pundits believe, but it is still true that our ability to exercise judgment needs to work on a *variety of sources and a variety of viewpoints*. If there are insufficient sources or representations available, then a comprehensive idea of the *possibilities* of interpretation will be lost. (Greg Philo's audience research (*see* Chapter 5) reveals how the very categories available for understanding the miners' strike seem to have been extremely limited, although people made their own sense of the event according to a host of factors, such as their own past and personal experiences.)

Although people experience massive (though admittedly uneven) exposure to media forms, audiences are not brought closer to media institutions. In fact, they show no signs of converging at all. What seems to happen is that audiences enter into a kind of dialogue with **media content**, using it and to some extent shaping it to their own ends, but remaining in the position of 'receiver'. Audiences have *enthusiasms* for media products: soap operas, films, types of music, particular magazines.

This may well mean, as some media theorists have argued, that such products are *recirculated* by audiences and given new, possibly more democratic, meanings. It does not, however, imply that the *process* of creation of meaning is democratic. We will turn shortly to the question of audience and audience use of the media, but in the meantime there is a clearly defined model of the media called 'democratic-participant'. This was described by McQuail as a situation where individuals, communities and groups 'have *rights of access* to media (rights to communicate) and rights to be served by media according to their own determination of need'. In a political environment where communities do not make public demands for a new, democratically-structured media, we might accept the notion that people are inclined to make other demands. They might, for example, wish to buy access to satellite or cable TV, rather than agitate for the power to run an independent station. It is worth asking whether the opportunities for greater media democracy actually exist.

Dominance and subordination?

Even when we inhabit society at different levels of involvement or experience, in different geographical locations or through different sub-cultures, we know something about the **values** thought important in everyday life. The mass media *are* part of our everyday life and help to express as much as to reinforce these values, but the messages they circulate are *produced* quite differently from the face-to-face, person-to-person communication in which individuals engage. The production of meaning in the media is not just organised (we all organise our thoughts and ideas, and constantly monitor their spoken effect), but organised *hierarchically*.

This means that the mass media are organised as a graded structure, with most power and influence at the top levels. Most mass media forms (TV, radio, newspapers, etc) operate through this command structure.

The idea of the *domination* of one group in society by another remains an important concept in media and communication studies. The Italian theorist Gramsci, used the concept of '*hegemony*' to describe the way that a ruling group in society exercises **the power of ideas** over subordinate groups. This does not mean to say that the ruling class just thinks up any old nonsense (though it has sometimes done so), which the poor workers accept without a murmur. Hegemony has to be reinvented, struggled over in the face of resistance, just as a parent finds that a child will sometimes follow instructions, while at other times it may resist. (Sometimes a child deliberately sets out to misunderstand the meaning of the parents'/guardian's words – a resistance to discourse – *see* Chapter 2).

This idea of powerful interests opposing much weaker and more disorganised ones has proved to be one of the most hotly debated issues in media and communication theory. There are, however, some drawbacks in describing the relationship *purely in terms of dominance and subordination*, especially in the case of a communication system like the mass media. That would be to misunderstand how the media actually works. Even in totalitarian societies, where the government controls the media, mass communicators find it difficult to speak with one voice. In Gilliam's film *Brazil* (a nightmare vision of a future which includes many uncomfortable aspects of the present) personal obsessions drown out the half-hearted propaganda of the state, and the clerks in the Records Department are at least able to avoid work by watching old movies on their computer screens.

Historically, certain individuals and groups had *social* power to communicate and *physical* power to enforce rules. Through that power, those groups were able to gain material wealth at the expense of others. This material wealth became, in itself, a symbol of the social power they held. At certain times in history, however, the simple power of argument, based on an upsurge in collective consciousness, has helped to redress the imbalance of power in society. It was the access to print enjoyed by radical and anti-monarchist groups during the English Civil War of 1642–5 (*see* Chapter 7), that helped to 'turn the world upside down'. The war was won (and then in ideological terms lost again) as much through communicative power as through the creation of the New Model Army.

Divisions at the top?

In order to think more creatively about the relationships between the powerful and the weak, we ought to look at the idea that the exercise of **domination** is never straightforward. The difference between persuading people to do things and using the threat of force is examined in the next chapter. For the moment, we will assume that the message is being received voluntarily by the audience.

In the first place, the dominant forces are not always on the same side. It depends on the issue. For instance, we could look at the widely differing views of the right-wing press in Britain when the issue of the Royal family is raised. Some newspapers on the political right (and therefore presumably close to some faction of the ruling class) take a traditionalist and largely pro-royal line (tending towards respect for the institution and its members). Others, still on the right but of a more populist type, may use stories about the Royal family to boost and maintain circulation. Secondly, the subordinate forces have to find something interesting, relevant, or useful in the message received from the dominant forces, if they are not going to ignore it completely. This means that they are not always completely overawed by the message, even though the dominant forces are apparently in a more powerful position. Linked to this there is the idea of resistance through the creation of 'sub-cultural' meanings, where the subordinate groups make new and perhaps 'deviant' readings from the mass media text.

Figures 1.4 and 1.5 may help to demonstrate the possible relationships between the different forces.

Amazing powers of resistance?

It has already been made clear that some theorists think we should be careful not to credit the mass media with too much power and influence. We have seen, with the aid of theory and some diagrams, that there are various ways of understanding the relationship between dominant and subordinate forces. There is another current in media studies which seems to credit the *subordinate* groups with a different kind of power. How meaningful is this 'power of the underdog'? Are there two *kind* of power at work in the tussle between rulers and ruled?

In his book *Understanding Popular Culture*, John Fiske celebrates what he sees as popular resistance to the dominant forces in our culture. He notes:

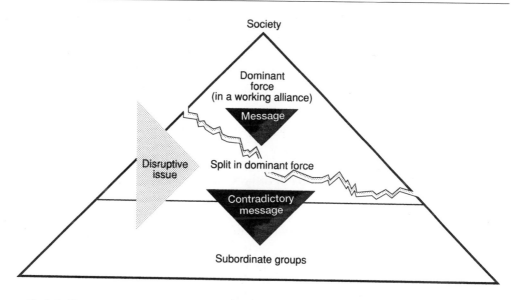

Fig 1.4 Disagreement among dominant forces: contradictory message

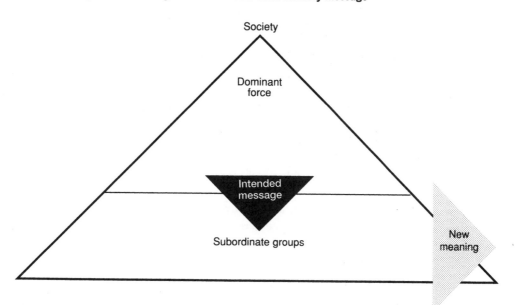

Fig 1.5 Subordinate groups create new meanings from the intended message

'... white patriarchal capitalism has failed to homogenise the thinking and culture of its subjects, despite nearly two centuries of economic dominance ...'

By 'failed to homogenise' he means that the dominant forces in our society (white patriarchal capitalism) have failed to make everyone's outlook and culture the same. However, is it possible for any force in society to make everyone's thinking and culture the same? Is this, in fact, really what 'white patriarchal capitalism' has tried to do?

'White patriarchal capitalism' as a description of the dominant powers is rather confusing. It is not necessarily an *equal* partnership divided into exact thirds – white, partriarchal and capitalist. Which bits of the white patriarchal capitalist *alliance* are dominant in any situation at any one time is difficult to work out, but certain factors will definitely come into play:

- There is the question of how many of the subordinated women, ethnic minorities and anti-capitalists *oppose* the dominant system, or enter the system with the intention of *changing* it (if it *can* be changed bit by bit before it changes the people who get inside it).
- There is the problem of how far the subordinate groups identify with some of their oppressor's views, or how far they may dislike other dominated groups more than their rulers.
- There is also the problem of what is happening in the society at the time. (For example, if the racist sections of the ruling alliance are going to interfere with profit, then it may be that they are controlled and kept quiet. If investment in the training of a flexible workforce is seen as being a more important issue than short-term profit, then the profit motive may be underplayed.)

All one culture?

It would appear that 'white patriarchal capitalism' has *not* always tried to make all culture the same. The fact that this force is an alliance means that some parts of the whole may prefer a very wide, diversified culture. There *have* been social and political tendencies which have tried to restrict the free expression of ideas, but the urge to capture new markets has sometimes led to a capitalist onslaught on such forces.

According to Tony Bennett in *The Media: Contexts of Study*, the growth of newspaper sales and increased advertising revenue in the 1840s had a number of liberalising effects on the press. It 'financed the development of independent news gathering resources', 'rendered newspapers less dependent upon official intelligence', and furthermore encouraged some publishers not to accept secret service bribes, because they wished to maximise sales in an expanding market. Overall, Tony Bennett (p. 45) argues that:

> '... many commercial newspapers were ... supporting middle-class campaigns for reform and were often consciously promoting a system of values that challenged the leadership role of the aristocracy.'

In conclusion, Fiske's original description of capitalism gives no sense of the complexity of the past two hundred years, the phases of development and the range of popular resistance to dominant ideas. There is no sense of the internal fights and compromises which are a feature of all ruling alliances – and of all other groups for that matter.

Torn jeans – cultural resistance?

We should perhaps treat with caution those theories which seem to avoid the problem of *relations of power* by crediting the 'subordinated' with such an ability to resist their rulers that they fly from the grasp of domination like a piece of wet soap.

One of the most memorable examples of an idea of *cultural* resistance (where the person or group concerned does not resist *economically* or *politically*, e.g. by throwing spanners into machinery, or going on strike, or refusing to fight in an army) is probably represented by John Fiske's 'torn jeans'.

The idea works like this: if a company markets jeans, one possible way people could express their own values, and make some kind of resistance to dominant values, would be to buy the jeans and then make tears in them.

So far, we see: (a) the *imposition* of the capitalist order of meaning; and (b) *resistance* to it. However, the struggle is not over yet. The company in question then decides to market jeans which already have 'factory-made tears' in them. What next? Fiske's subcultural guerillas are not defeated because, as Fiske writes, 'people will always find new ways of tearing their jeans' (*see Understanding Popular Culture*, p. 29).

We have now encountered (c) *recuperation* of the original resistance by the company (i.e. making the first resistance harmless); and (d) *renewed resistance*. Fiske believes popular discontent creates new and politically progressive meanings.

At this point we had better leave these heroes to the struggle, before their jeans become less of a cultural resource than a social embarrassment!

Are the powerful inflexible?

The problem lies in the way that Fiske describes the dominant or powerful. He quotes the theorist de Certeau, who believes that 'the powerful are cumbersome, unimaginative, and over-organised' whereas the weak 'are creative, nimble and flexible' (*Understanding Popular Culture*, p. 19). Is it true that, because of their size, big institutions are 'overorganised'? Are they so unimaginative that they cannot make their messages relevant to the subordinate?

This whole model of how dominance works may be very misleading. We should realise, especially when we look at advertising in Chapter 3, that 'subcultural' meanings are often *already circulated* in mass media texts. In other words, it is sometimes easy for the subordinate (the audience) to find 'alternative' meanings in texts exactly because these meanings are already there.

Advertisers may, for example, *recognise other values* in order to neutralise or 'deal with' the objections or criticisms of certain groups. There are plenty of examples of 'green' advertisements which do exactly this. Again, texts may have 'subordinate' meanings in order to gain attention and credibility. This may be why some music records and videos use sex or bad language despite the dangers of the product being banned. Or, as Terry Lovell writes in *Pictures of Reality* (pp. 60–1).

'. . . conflict may also obtain [may happen] between the use value in question and the interests of capitalism in general . . . the conflict may be compounded by the divergence of interest between particular capitals and capitalism as a whole. Particular capitals invested in the entertainment industry have an interest in maximising profits through maximising the popularity and therefore the sale of entertainment . . .'

Recuperation/contestation

We might say that not only goods, but *values* are circulated in our society. The mass media, in particular, are concerned with the circulation of values. These values are *transitional*, i.e. not yet generally held in the society, but equally not completely despised or neglected. This will help to explain later theories on the nature of contestation (resistance to values) and recuperation (the ability to recover 'uncomfortable' ideas for re-use in a preferred form).

We might say that recuperation and contestation represent a continuous process, rather than two separate or opposite ideas. They exist where there is a relationship between the 'dominant' and 'subordinate' currents of our culture. The 'popular resistance' theory suggested by Fiske makes contestation the activity of the underdog alone. The two aspects of the process could be summed up as follows:

- **Contestation** is the idea that one of these two groups (dominant or subordinate) resists the meanings created by the other.
- **Recuperation** is the ability of one of the groups to take back the content of the resistance and turn it to their own ends.

So far, we have seen the relations of power as involving domination and subordination. This is a simple but useful idea, if we realise that the basic features of capitalist *production* are like this – one group owning the means of production and other groups doing the actual work of production.

Economics and culture

In order to **circulate**, artifacts (manufactured products) need to be produced on a large scale. Films must have a good distribution network in order to be seen by a wide audience. In order to make sense to any consumer, the product and the signs and codes which go with it must be able to be understood. In order to be understood, mass media messages (advertising messages are a good example) must rely on a shared sign-system (see the section on ideology). Therefore, the mass communicator must use elements of subordinated values, as well as dominant values.

Cultural artifacts are not likely to reflect the interests or ideas of the dominant class simply because they have been produced within its dominant mode of production. For example, when EMI signed up the Sex Pistols, we could ask if this was to make profit from the idea of rebellion.

If we just imagine that dominant production means the public are sold the ideas/products of the dominant class, this may leave us with a number of misunderstandings:

- it may encourage the idea that mainstream ideology proceeds *directly* from the centres of power;
- it may reduce our understanding of the *process* **of mediation;**

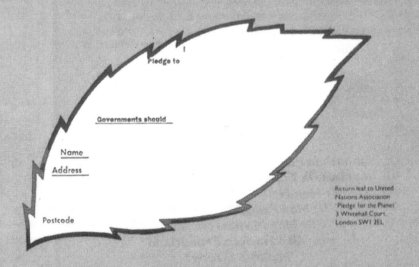

PLEDGE FOR THE PLANET

Choose your pledge from the list below, write on the leaf provided and return to us.

- **Energy:** I will use 10% less gas and/or electricity at home during the next year. **Governments** of rich nations should agree to cut carbon dioxide emissions from the burning of fossil fuels by 20% within 15 years.
- **Third World Debt:** I will write to my bank manager urging the bank to write off debts owed by the poorer countries. **Governments** of rich countries should agree to cancel debts owed them by poor nations.
- **Transport:** I will cut my car mileage by 10% during the next year. I will walk, cycle or use public transport wherever possible. **Governments** should agree to greater investment in public transport systems.
- **Recycling:** I will recycle as much waste as possible at home and/or I will help to organise recycling at work or at school. **Governments** should agree to double the amount of paper, glass, metal, and plastic that is recycled.
- **Forests:** I will not buy any products from tropical hardwood. **Governments** should commit themselves to new policies to protect the forests.
- **Overseas aid:** I will give at least 0.7% of my net income to United Nations sustainable development projects in line with the target set for governments by the United Nations. **Governments** should fulfil their commitment to the 0.7% target as soon as possible.
- **Population:** I will fully suport United Nations and other programmes designed to eradicate basic poverty and thereby to stabilise the world's population; **Governments** should increase their commitments to the UNFPA, WHO and oher relevant bodies to a minimum global sum of $5 billion per annum.
- **Common security:** I will not buy any goods from a company involved in manufacturing or selling arms or other lethal military items; **Governments** should take urgent action to strengthen the UN's conflict avoidance and conflict resolution capability and secure widespread arms control, disarmament and security agreements.
- **Trade:** I will always try to buy goods from environmentally friendly companies which promote fair trade, both nationally and internationally. **Governments** should change their trade policies so that they promote fair trade.
- **Acting locally:** I will increase the amount of time or money I give to environmental and development organisations.
- **Spreading the message:** I personally will raise 20/50/100 pledge leaves for the Tree of Life in Brazil before 1st June 1992.

Pledge to

Governments should

Name

Address

Postcode

Return leaf to United
Nations Association
'Pledge for the Planet'
3 Whitehall Court,
London SW1 2EL.

TREE OF LIFE/Pledging for the Planet, an independent initiative, is working with the One World Group of Broadcasters and organisations world-wide to raise public awareness of the issues relating to the UN Earth Summit in June 1992.

Fig 1.6 Contestation – Pledge for the Planet leaf motif
(Courtesy of United Nations Association)

- it may reinforce a mistaken view that domination and subordination are fixed positions rather than part of a process; this might encourage either a *pessimistic* view of power (e.g. Frankfurt School) or an *optimistic* view of resistance (e.g. Fiske, de Certeau) instead of a *dialectical approach* (one which looks at both sides of the question, and sees meaning created by a process of opposites acting upon each other).

It can be argued there is a wide variety of ideas circulating in any mass media text, some marked by a close relationship to hierarchies of power, but others clearly not. It is true that all goods promote themselves (when we look at sweet wrappers we may realise that they are advertising the *next* purchase as well as what is inside), but not all goods simply work to support ruling class ideology.

It is surely the case that we live in a capitalist society in which there is a wide diversification of ideas, just as there is a multiplicity of economic interests. Understanding recuperation and contestation as a process, and thus avoiding an over-emphasis of the 'dominant' over the 'subordinate' or *vice versa*, is one way of achieving a balanced methodology.

A MODEL OF POWER

As argued earlier in this chapter, there are two basic meanings of the term 'power'. It is the **capacity to do something**, to affect our immediate environment. Power may be used in this way by groups, by individuals, by large public or private bodies. Power also means the **domination** of one individual/group/corporation **over** any other or group of others. Again, we can remind ourselves that power is the possession (in both these cases) of the ability to shape action. It is no accident, however, that we have been particularly interested in examining the problem of power as **domination**.

A war of all against all?

Michel Foucault, responding to a question about power in a 1977 interview (*see Power/Knowledge*, p. 123), framed some questions of his own:

'... isn't power simply a form of warlike domination? ...
Who wages war against whom? Is it between two classes or more?
Is it a war of all against all?'

Foucault noted also (p. 142) that 'relations of power are interwoven with other kinds of relations (production, kinship, family, sexuality)'. The questions above and this statement make a useful starting-point for trying to explore power. As noted earlier, power exists in all human relationships. The mistake of some theorists has been to look at state power alone. However, we must not make the mistake of *neglecting* to consider state power.

There is a clear difference between saying, as the theorist Poulantzas once did,

We'd like to make the world a greener place.

So we've just introduced two major environmental initiatives.

You can't put a price on clear air. So we haven't.

On every Fiat with a catalytic converter the cat comes free. (Some other manufacturers would make you cough up over £500 for the privilege.)

We think it's the least we can do to reduce the levels of harmful poisons and pollutants.

As if that wasn't green enough, we've gone one greener.

If your current car was registered on or before 31st December 1989, trade it in for a new Fiat with a catalytic converter. We'll give you up to £1,200 more than it's worth. We're basing our valuations on the trade-in prices quoted in the Used Car section of What Car? magazine June 1992 issue.

Whatever the condition of your car, providing it has a valid M.O.T. certificate, we'll give you the amount shown opposite over and above the dealer's valuation when you buy the relevant new Fiat.

If, however, your car was registered on or after 1st January 1990 or you don't have a part exchange, visit your dealer anyway. He'll offer unbeatable deals on all Fiats, including our range of cleaner, greener diesels. And there are even more persuasive offers overleaf. Alternatively call 0800 717000 for further information.

So now you can protect the environment. And your bank balance.

What a breath of fresh air.

REDUCE AIR POLLUTION WALK TO A FIAT DEALER

FIAT'S GREEN PAPER

(A FIST FULL OF FIVE POUND NOTES)

TRADE IN YOUR CAR FOR A FIAT CROMA WITH CATALYTIC CONVERTER, AND WE'LL GIVE YOU AN EXTRA ALLOWANCE OF
£1,200

TRADE IN YOUR CAR FOR A FIAT TEMPRA WITH CATALYTIC CONVERTER, AND WE'LL GIVE YOU AN EXTRA ALLOWANCE OF
£1,000

TRADE IN YOUR CAR FOR A FIAT TIPO WITH CATALYTIC CONVERTER, AND WE'LL GIVE YOU AN EXTRA ALLOWANCE OF
£800

TRADE IN YOUR CAR FOR A FIAT UNO WITH CATALYTIC CONVERTER, AND WE'LL GIVE YOU AN EXTRA ALLOWANCE OF
£650

TRADE IN YOUR CAR FOR A FIAT PANDA WITH CATALYTIC CONVERTER, AND WE'LL GIVE YOU AN EXTRA ALLOWANCE OF
£500

DESIGNED FOR LIFE FIAT

*THE VALUE OF ANY VEHICLE SUBMITTED FOR TRADE-IN UNDER THIS SCHEME WILL BE DETERMINED BY THE FIAT DEALER. FIAT DEALERS RESERVE THE RIGHT TO OFFER LESS THAN THE PRICE QUOTED IN WHAT CAR? JUNE 1992. OFFER APPLIES TO NEW CARS PURCHASED AND REGISTERED BETWEEN 1.6.92 AND 31.9.92. TRADE-IN CAR MUST HAVE VALID M.O.T. CERTIFICATE. OFFER EXCLUDES THE FOLLOWING SPECIAL SERIES CARS: PANDA - PINK, SKY, MANIA; UNO CHIC; TIPO - BRIO, FORZA.

Fig 1.7 Recuperation – Fiat's Green Paper promotion
(Courtesy of Sales Promotion Agency: The Marketing Triangle, and Advertising Agency: DMB & B, for Fiat Auto (UK) Ltd)

PLANT YOURSELF BEHIND
YOU'LL LEAVE

Test driving a new Fiat could change your outlook on life.

For a start your living room or conservatory will look greener. Or even your bathroom. Why?

Because you'll be driving home with a beautiful houseplant worth up to £25 with our

green paper.[†] Or the £300 worth of BP unleaded petrol vouchers that come free with all special edition Fiats.[††] Now that really is a breath of fresh air.

Booking a test drive couldn't be easier either. Just dial 0800 717000 and we'll put your local dealer in touch with you. Like the new

TEST DRIVE A NEW FIAT
AND TAKE HOME A HOUSEPLANT.

compliments.[*] It's one of the ways we're making everyone's life a little greener this summer. Just like the new Fiat range with free catalytic converters. And up to £1,200 extra trade-in allowance on your old car in Fiat's

Fiat range, you'll find he's very friendly.

Now if you still don't find yourself beginning to turn a shade or two greener, there's more.

You could win one of 25 Fiat Unos. Simply take the leaf on this page along to any one of

*Free plant offer closes 13.07.92. Offer subject to availability. Plants may vary in size and type.
†See previous page for conditions. ††Offer applies to new special edition models purchased and registered between 01.06.92 and 31.08.92.

26

Fig 1.7 *(continued)* **Note the use of the leaf (refer to Fig 1.6)**

THE WHEEL OF A FIAT. GREENER.

the 250 Fiat showrooms before 31st August 1992 (we've got branches everywhere and they're even open today & next weekend). Check to see if your leaf matches the one on display. If you're green enough, you'll win one of 25 Fiat Unos. There's also a second chance to win by posting your leaf in the box provided.

But whatever the outcome, if you take a test drive, one thing's certain - you'll leave greener.

So go on, turn over a new leaf.

**REDUCE AIR POLLUTION
WALK TO A FIAT DEALER**

DESIGNED FOR LIFE FIAT

27

that all *social relations* are relations of *power*, and suggesting that, because power is everywhere', we are all equally at fault for the wrongs of society and the faults of the individual. Just because power is divided among very many different institutions, groups and individuals, does not mean that *central* authority in society is no longer a problem, or that the ruling class has somehow ceased to exist.

Foucault seems unable to formulate a general theory of power exactly because he made the useful observation that part of the *operation* of power takes place on a localised and individual level. He is right to be suspicious of the idea that the conflict between a 'dominant' ruling class and a 'subordinate' working class is the only real struggle in society. He is probably wrong to see power as *only* fragmented.

The idea of social conflict needs close attention because we should discover *how* the battle is fought. There has been a tendency to overestimate the power of one side or the other, as we have seen.

Power: many sources, many messages?

David Tetzlaff, of Miami University, argues that most left-wing or critical theories of power and domination have started with the assumption that power always works by *centralising* its force (*see* his article *Divide and Conquer* in *Media, Culture and Society*). He describes this as the idea that:

> 'People are controlled by getting them together, doing the same thing, thinking the same thing.'

He identifies two opposing currents of thought in this argument. He begins with Adorno and Horkheimer's theory that the culture industry moulds people into a kind of standard state of being, which can make a subordinated population ripe for fascism or some other form of authoritarian control. On the other hand, he notes that theorists like Fiske emphasise the ultimate failure of the powerful to dominate other people, because people in their various groups and sub-cultures make their own meanings from the mass-produced culture they consume. Tetzlaff believes that mass-produced culture *does* keep the capitalist system going, but that it does so by 'fragmenting' society instead of by forcing it to obey the same system of thought. In other words, mass culture keeps people in their place by dividing the population – a theory of 'divide and rule'.

Why should a system where there is, apparently, no one dominant meaning or direction in culture, be an effective means of social control? Tetzlaff argues that centralised control of meaning is difficult and even counter-productive, because it tends to produce critics. It produces critics because it has to teach the 'correct' way of seeing society. Once people have been taught the skills of understanding, they may apply their new skills in criticising the way that society is organised. Before the First World War, schools encouraged their pupils to believe in church, state and monarchy. It was an important part of how people learned their *place* in society as well as how they should *behave* in society.

By contrast, a system which produces so many *different* messages about society that an accurate picture is impossible to gain, must end by misleading large numbers of people. Tetzlaff's point is that, even when the subordinate receives mass media messages, the messages *themselves* may fail to have any connection to the real relations of power.

It is clear that most of the mass media function in the same way as other capitalist enterprises engaged in the production of other goods. It is also true that some companies have attempted to remodel their operations, using a decentralised model, which involves dismissing much of the workforce and then giving those who remain a greater say in the company's day-to-day operation. This would suggest that some companies have decentralised elements of their power in order to safeguard the core of their interests, showing the very opposite of de Certeau's 'over-organisation'.

THE USE OF MEDIA TERMS

At the beginning of this chapter, a basic model of the communication process was outlined and the weakness of process models in general was discussed. It was proposed that we attempt to understand the way that any message comes into existence by looking at the *intention* of the sender; the *available forms* in which the message could be cast; the immediate *context* in which the message is set (as the sender understands that context); and finally the *possibilities* that the sender believes to be at his or her disposal. There is a problem with the use of the term 'message' in interpersonal communication because it suggests a one-way process of limited scope. In most situations, an interaction is a complex of messages, each shaped by the one before, by the context, by the intention, etc.

The mass media message

When we turn our attention to the mass media, however, there are other factors besides the 'crafting' of the message which need to be taken into account. Personal face-to-face interaction is mediated through language and speech, and/or non-verbal communication. The mass media message (message seems appropriate here) is also mediated: first in the usual human forms, through **language** or some other **symbolic code**; then through a group of media professionals, who revise the message by selecting what they think is relevent; then by a **technology** which gives the message a *form*; once the message reaches its audience, it is again mediated through that audience's individual **subjectivities** and the **expectations** which automatically greet each genre or type of message form. The *levels of mediation* would appear as in Fig 1.8.

The place of the text

When we speak about a particular film, programme, article, advertisement and so on, it is usually referred to as a **text**. It is unfortunate that the term is used, for example, to refer both to a newspaper and also to an article which may appear inside that newspaper.

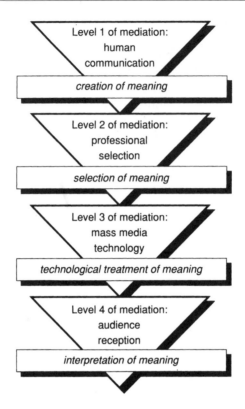

Fig 1.8 Levels of mediation

The mass media text is clearly not the same as the messages which pass during a personal interaction, in the sense that it is neither as *intimate* nor as *immediate*. That is to say, there is often a delay between its **formulation**, its **circulation** and its **reception**. It could be argued that we do see a form of 'instant' or immediate communication: television (which also at times tries to be intimate). But the difference between a news flash or election result and what used to be called television's 'seamless flow' can show us how *conventional* the usual form of the television message has become. (Note the confusion which is created when something unexpected and unprepared occurs.)

The delay which occurs between production and distribution/consumption is in fact not just a feature of mass media communication (films, programmes, advertisements, books, comics). It is also found whenever artifacts (e.g. catalogues, telephone directories) are produced by an institution or where an individual makes artifacts such as paintings or sculptures. The audience expects immediately to consume the media message at a distance from its place of origin, in 'private space'. It knows also that the mass media message is often supposed to be fixed or *closed*. Indeed, it is the 'open' text, where meaning is not spelled out for us, that we often regard as difficult or inaccessible.

Three levels of 'encoding'

To get its message across, the media text must be expressed in a code (e.g. language) which people will recognise. The text has to create its meanings through some method or system, based in the first place on the symbolic interactions that people use in everyday life. When John Fiske (*see Television Culture*, p. 4) writes that 'reality is already encoded' and gives the example of people's appearance, he has performed the useful service of reminding us that all forms of the mass media must use the basic 'human codes' upon which all meaning is based.

Fiske goes on to divide the codes of television into three. (We are, however, interested in how this might apply to all mass media and not just to television.)

Level 1 begins with an 'event' which is already encoded at the level of **reality**. This includes appearance, dress, environment, speech, expression, sound and so on.

Level 2 sees the reality being encoded by technical codes (including camera, lighting, editing, music, sound in the case of television). These technical codes transmit the conventional **representational** codes (which in television shape narrative, conflict, character, action, dialogue, setting, etc).

Level 3 is, according to Fiske, that of **ideology** where the representational codes are organised into 'coherence and social acceptability' by what Fiske sees as the structures (such as race and class) and the dominant systems of belief in our society (such as individualism, patriarchy, materialism and capitalism).

A LIST OF CONCEPTS

ADDRESS

An **address** is the deliberate direction or delivery of a message, in whatever form, from one source (an individual, a group or an institution) to any recipient, whether an individual or a collective. All mediated communication is addressed to an audience. The process begins when an addressor (for example, a broadcaster) wishes to produce an effect. The addressor's knowledge or impression of the 'target' audience helps to shape the message. *The A–Z Media and Communication Handbook* (p. 7) notes that 'the media often imitate personal forms of address in order to create a kind of "intimacy" between performer (actor, game-show host, reporter, etc.) and audience'. See also **interpellation**, below.

AGENDA-SETTING

This is the practice of selecting and emphasising certain issues and / or events from among the various topics which inform public discourse. Many definitions of **agenda-setting** argue that the media are responsible for the process. Watson and Hill, for example, believe that the media 'set the order of importance of current issues' (*see A Dictionary of Communication and Media Studies*, p. 3). O'Sullivan in *Key Concepts in Communication and Cultural Studies*, p. 8 writes that the media 'wittingly or unwittingly structure public debate and awareness'. Gill and Adams (*see ABC of Communication Studies*, p. 6) mention 'the ways in which the media decide which information and which issues are most important for the public'.

However, there are other social agencies, individuals and groups which set public agendas. Dearing and Rogers, in their book called *Agenda-Setting*, describe the process as 'an on-going competition among issue proponents to gain the attention of media professionals, the public, and policy elites'. This would suggest that the media is just one part of the contest to form points of view, and that media professionals can actually be the *target* of attempts to persuade or influence.

AUDIENCE

The aggregate of individual listeners / viewers thought to receive public forms of communication. The use of the word 'thought' is significant, because the exact composition of any audience is always difficult to calculate. **Audiences** are 'targeted' by the media but bring their own subjective understandings to individual media texts. McQuail's *Mass Communication Theory* speaks of the 'duality' of audience (p. 215), in the sense that it is 'constructed' by commercial and academic bodies, and because it refers to specific social groups, divided by class, sex, age, ethnicity and other characteristics.

Price (in *The A–Z Media and Communication Handbook*, p. 20) calls audience 'a sort of "**temporary collective**", brought into existence by the experience of listening to a concert, viewing a television programme, and so on'. Ien Ang, in *Desperately Seeking the Audience*, calls the audience a 'repertoire of practices and experiences'. This idea recognises the changeable nature of audiences, but also shows that they are, nevertheless, part of social reality.

CODE

A system which allows a specific culture to communicate through the use of *signs*. **Codes** consist of a network of signs, known as a *paradigm*, from which individual units of meaning may be chosen. The units selected are then combined as a *syntagm*, which conveys meaning within a certain cultural context. All codes are signifying codes: they refer to ideas, objects, events and entities in culture and society.

CONTEXT

The conditions which provide a structure for any act, statement, or event. **Context** can be divided into a number of categories, each a factor in shaping an event. Price's *The A–Z Media and Communication Handbook* proposes four levels of context:

- **functional context** – the purpose of an event and its subject matter, expressed through basic human faculties (the power of speech, gesture, intonation, and so on); in the case of the media, this level would also include the technology used for composing and sending out a particular message;
- **situational context** – the physical and temporal circumstances within which any event is conducted; with reference to media, this could be a radio or television studio (the point of production) and the domestic or public environment (the point of consumption);

- **discursive context** – the range of ideas and opinions which participants can draw upon when they interact;
- **social/structural context** – the state of the society itself, including its social, cultural and political condition.

DISCOURSE

In linguistics, **discourse** can mean verbal expression, or a specialised form of language, such as the 'discourse of the law'. Other meanings of discourse concentrate on the social process of creating meaning, through the use of language and other symbolic forms. Although discourse is sometimes regarded as the expression of a particular viewpoint or ideology, it is a mistake to think that it is possible to construct discourses which exactly represent a system of belief.

'Discourse' is now used in media and cultural studies to refer to the structured **representation** of events. Gunther Kress (1985) argued that 'a discourse provides a set of possible statements about a given area … and gives structure to the manner in which a particular topic, object, process is to be talked about'. Price, in *Communication Studies*, calls discourses 'social narratives,' stories which 'offer broadly plausible explanations for events in the social world'.

GENRE

A specific type of film, radio, or television production. In cinema, from which the term emerged, examples of genres could be science fiction, police dramas, martial arts movies, Westerns, action films, musicals, love stories and so on. Stephen Neale, in his book *Genre*, addressed the problem of attempting to decide where one genre begins and another ends. He saw genre as a system of (p. 19) 'orientations, **expectations** and conventions' which circulate between 'industry, text and subject'. Thus, an audience participates in the creation of genre, using expectations created through previous contact with similar texts.

IDENTITY

Identity is the 'sense of self' which each individual possesses, what I would call the 'continuity of self-consciousness'; as long as a person remains aware of his/her own personality and history, and is conscious of a continuous link between his/her past and present condition, then a consistent identity has been retained. For many centuries, philosophers regarded the individual as the measure of identity.

In the nineteenth century, however, Marx attacked the idea that individual identity could be constructed in isolation, pointing to the way that the self is constructed within the context of social relations. Raymond Williams notes in *Keywords* (p.161) that 'individual' originally meant 'indivisible' (unable to be divided). This suggests 'a necessary connection' between people. Personal identity should therefore be placed in the context of the identity of a wider group or community.

IDEOLOGY

An **ideology** is a specific example of organised belief, while ideology in general is the framework of all those ideas and beliefs which offer a coherent, but incomplete, critique of 'things as they are'. An individual ideology must 'make sense' to large numbers of people, even if they do not accept all the ideas or values it offers. *The A–Z Media and Communication Handboo*k states that (p. 111) 'ideology exists wherever signs, discourses, objects and representations, are used in an attempt to explain material reality'.

INSTITUTION

The term **institution** refers to an established form of social organisation engaged in public activity. It is a system of relationships, referring not simply to large corporations, buildings, etc., but also to the relations set up between official government bodies, industries and audiences (patterns of regulation, production, distribution and consumption). The British Broadcasting Corporation, for example, exists within a set of public relationships. In *Learning the Media*, Alvarado and his co-writers suggest a list of seven 'institutional determinants' which shape the media institution: finance, production practices, technology, legislation, circulation, **audience** construction and audience use. We should perhaps think of the core of institution as finance, production, technology, and the power of circulation.

INTERPELLATION

Interpellation is a mode of **address** which attempts to put the addressee or receiver into a position where they accept their 'place' in a **discourse**. It is also the process through which individual human subjects have their social location confirmed by the 'symbolic order' (language in its various forms). The term was used by the philosopher Althusser to express the idea that individuals cannot exist outside ideology. Interpellation attempts to reinforce a relationship based on inequality of power.

INTERTEXTUALITY

Intertextuality is a description of the way that texts, sometimes but not necessarily of the same type, reproduce recognisable elements or styles. Used mostly of television, it refers to the idea that a text is read in the light of others of a broadly similar nature. Intertextuality is sometimes produced deliberately, in order to create references which an audience will recognise. A film, for example, may contain a sequence which is echoed by an advertisement. 'Intertextuality' comes originally from studies of literature.

MEDIATION

Mediation is a process of selection and shaping which creates a range of meanings from public events. Mediation is not merely a 'bridge' from source to **audience**, or from authority to public, but a process of alteration in which the media organisation brings certain perspectives to bear on an issue. An event which is mediated is handled within the context of public and institutional values.

NARRATIVE

Narrative can be: the end-product of storytelling (a 'narrative'), the process of story-construction, a mental activity that organises data into a pattern, and a way of organising spatial and temporal data into a cause-effect chain of events. The essential part of a narrative is said to be that part which provides the most important information for an audience, allowing the viewer/reader to construct meaning by moving forwards and backwards from that point.

REPRESENTATION

Representation has two related meanings: to 'show' or present (as when a person or object is 'shown' during a theatrical performance), and 'to describe or declare to be' (in the sense, for example, of 'representing' someone as an authority on a particular issue). *The A–Z Handbook of Media and Communication* distinguishes between the two senses in the following way (p. 198):

> 'In the first case, a simple act of "showing" has taken place ... in the second case, there is more of the sense of a report, where there is no direct evidence as such to judge whether or not the statement is true.'

The second meaning includes the idea of 'symbolizing' something, perhaps in a different symbolic form to that taken by the original. The point is that the media are thought to use the process of representation to make composite descriptions of social reality, supposedly in the form of 'biased' characterisations of people, events, places, and so forth.

There is also a psychological explanation for the existence of representation as a human 'faculty'. According to this idea, human beings acquire a 'fund' of images and symbols, collected together as memories; these are then used whenever reference to the real is demanded. This theory, the 'internal symbolisation' of the external world, does not explain how the human subject is able to create meaning in situations which lie outside immediate experience.

According to Richard Dyer (in Andrew Hart's *Understanding the Media*, p. 83) representations can take a variety of forms: a *selective representation* of the real, determined to some extent by the form in which the representation is made; a *representative example* of the usual ways the mass media tends to show a certain thing, person, group or idea; the process of speaking as a *representative* of someone or something or some position; and finally, the meanings which various media create or *represent* for audiences. Representation is the *method* used by the mass media to create meanings.

SEMIOLOGY

The term **semiology** comes from the Greek 'semeion' for **sign**. Signs are usually explained as physical objects with associated mental concepts. Semiology is thus the study of signs and meaning in language, art, the mass media, sound, and in any field of human endeavour which can be reproduced for, or represented to, an individual or audience. The two major traditions of semiological work are: the structuralist model (emerging from the work of Ferdinand de Saussure), which emphasises the relationship between the sign and its place in the overall structure of language (structure producing meaning); and the pragmatist approach (associated with C.S. Peirce) which understands 'semiosis' (Peirce's term) as a continuous process of meaning-creation which allows human beings to make interpretations and to carry out actions.

THE FORMATION OF THE SUBJECT

When the communication theorists, Myers and Myers, state in *The Dynamics of Human Communication* that people 'are not born fearing God', they are obviously trying to emphasise the role of all the *social* influences which go to make up the human subject, and oppose the idea that all attitudes, values and beliefs appear 'ready made' in the infant. If we accept that human beings are not born fearing God, we might still ask if some people are born with a *predisposition* to fear God. In other words, there may be a tendency for people to believe / accept certain things, even if the precise nature of the belief will not emerge or will not take a certain form for a considerable length of time.

The debate over 'nature' *versus* 'nurture' is misleading in the sense that the person we are when *born* and the person we *become* are difficult to separate. The influences on us are not simply 'internal' and 'external' (though many philosophers have made this distinction), because we are formed by a process of interaction between these two forces. The external is only felt through our internal apprehension of it. The internal can only act upon the ground of the external. We are creatures of place, of time, of our society and of our psychology. The 'vehicle' which takes us through our experiences is our own body and physiology. As individuals, we are *socialised* – 'brought up', if you like – by many more people than just parents, guardians, families. We are influenced by peer groups, by institutions, by hierarchies, by the mass media. All of these factors influence us to different extents and at different times of our lives, with widely differing outcomes for each person.

How are people formed?

Human biologists will base much of their understanding of the subject on the extent of physical capabilities. *Psychoanalysts* will typically examine the 'structures of desire' that form the basis, in their opinion, of human actions and the desire to act. The *linguists* would tend to look at the structures of language and the available contexts of expression. The *social theorists* would study the economic and social formation of the individual. It may be that, although we need to examine these areas of study separately, it will be difficult to hold them apart.

If we are to gain a full understanding of the formation of the communicative subject, we could begin with the *physical* limitations which govern the range of our perceptions. The other areas mentioned above will follow this initial discussion.

PHYSIOLOGICAL FACTORS

Our ability to communicate will clearly depend in the first instance on the range of what we are physically able to perceive. It is an inescapable fact that there are quite dramatic limitations to what we can see, hear, smell, taste and feel. We are able to use technology to increase our range (for example, slow motion camerawork and time-lapse photography both reveal things we would normally be unable to see), but this should not obscure the fact that there are animals which can see for much greater distances than ourselves, or can hear sounds beyond our range. Human beings can only perceive one-seventieth of the total light spectrum. Thus the human infant is born into a specific set of possibilities which will help to determine the general extent of its perceptual and communicative abilities.

PSYCHOLOGICAL GROWTH

Sandy Flitterman-Lewis, in her essay on Psychoanalytical theory (*see Channels of Discourse*, Methuen, 1987, p. 172) says that such theory describes the way in which:

'... the small human being comes to develop a specific personality and sexual identity within the larger network of social relations called culture.'

Freud described the human need to repress our tendencies towards gratification (which he called the 'pleasure principle') in order to be able to get on with our day-to-day existence (the 'reality principle'). By comparison to the adult, the infant has no such mechanism for repressing its desires and needs. The infant is 'entirely under the sway of libidinal gratifications' (*see Channels of Discourse*, p. 173).

Anyone who has looked after a baby will know how the infant appears to be a mass of wants and desires. It is not possible to make a rational impact on a baby that is waiting to be fed, in the sense that it would be pointless to construct elaborate diversions when it is hungry. The baby is intent upon satisfying one of its most basic needs.

Basic instincts?

Freud believed that the intense pleasure the infant derives from suckling at the breast marked the emergence of sexuality. The whole question of sexuality and pleasure is central to the study of certain mass media forms, such as film and television. It appears that, for Freudians, a crucial stage in the formation of the subject (the person) is the idea that the *biological instinct* becomes separated from the *sexual drive*, thus allowing desire to make its first appearance. From this standpoint, the desire felt by the adult in later life would be for the *totality* of sensations once experienced as an infant. The major limitation of traditional Freudianism, however, has been its tendency to characterise the female as 'lacking' certain male attributes, and as a result possessing an 'inferior' sexuality. Freud's theories are, in the opinion of some writers, very much moulded by the social outlook of his time.

Still, the growth of desire in human beings is obviously important, particularly when considering what implications it might have for their behaviour. So far, we have a developing subject which becomes capable of desire. As soon as we accept that individuals are able to desire things beyond themselves, then we must be dealing with wider issues than just the individual. We must look at *the individual's attempts to remould his/her immediate environment*. In terms of mass media and communication studies we could also ask exactly how desire works to position us as the subject of a discourse or the target of a campaign.

Lacan: a different approach

Jacques Lacan's work on the human subject was based partly upon anthropology and, importantly from our point of view, upon linguistics (the study of language). A central belief for Lacan was that the unconscious, although hidden, is structured like language. According to Lacan, it is the interplay between 'I' and 'Thou' which *defines* the human subject. The fact that 'I' and 'You' occupy positions opposite each other helps to create the human subject, as a result of the tension between the two poles. If we know our opposite (the 'other'), then according to this theory we know the 'self'. In his early writing, the Other is the other person, about whom one entertains illusions; in his later formulation, the Other is language itself. But it is not primarily the linguistic aspect of Lacan's theory which is of immediate concern. It is rather his view of human development, one which has the virtue of emphasising, in a way that Freud did not, the exclusion of the female subject from the symbolic order of language. This, together with his description of the 'mirror phase' (discussed below), has caused Lacan to be used extensively by some feminist film theorists.

Lacan believed that the first expression or articulation of 'I' takes place when the young child moves towards recognising itself as a distinct individual. He called this the 'mirror phase'. The 'mirror' theory is described by Madan Sarup (*see Introductory Guide to Post-Structuralism and Postmodernism*, p. 10):

'At first, the child who is together with an adult in front of a mirror confuses his [*sic*] own reflection with that of his adult companion. In the second phase the child acquires the notion of the image and understands that the reflection is not a real being. Finally, in the third stage, he realizes not only that the reflection is an image, but that the image is his own and is different from the image of the Other.'

The human child's first recognition of itself in a mirror was regarded by Lacan as crucial to the formation of the ego. Lacan believed that this recognition predated the acquisition of language. Clearly, the *experimental* basis for such a theory would be difficult to establish, since this process is supposed to take place between the ages of six and eight months. The 'mirror phase' is sometimes described as a *metaphor* for human development in its very early stages.

However it is described, the 'mirror phase' remains a very sketchy and cataclysmic view of infant development, betraying an unfortunate tendency to represent a decisive and dramatic 'moment' which is at odds with more reasoned empirical studies of human development. In addition to the doubts which Lacan's 'mirror' theory has raised, there would appear to be a need for a revised view of attachment, one which puts less emphasis on the mother–child relationship so important to theorists like Freud and Lacan. Later attachments, it is now thought, can influence the effects of an early attachment, however strong that early attachment was and however important the mother has been in providing the initial support needed by the child.

Piaget and the study of human development

Despite some recent updating of his theories (particularly the unconvincing view that the human senses develop in separate stages), the psychologist Piaget produced a view of human development which stands in contrast to the broad and rather vague delineations made by Lacan. Piaget believed that youngsters automatically construct a view of reality – a way of *representing* the world and acting upon that representation. A young baby's view of the world is tied to sensing and doing, and its knowledge of the world (*see* Steinberg, Belsky and Meyer, *Infancy, Childhood and Adolescence: Development in Context*) is;

> '... structured by simple actions that can be performed on objects – shaking, mouthing, smelling, sucking, biting and so forth.'

As children mature, they become capable of using increasingly complex and abstract schemes. Children constantly absorb information and actively try to make sense of it. Two processes play an important part in this:

1 **Assimilation**, the process by which people incorporate new information into their current ways of thinking and acting.
2 **Accommodation**, where people fundamentally alter their ways of thinking or acting to adapt to new information that doesn't 'fit' an existing scheme.

The stages in Piaget's theory were as follows:

- **The sensorimotor**, which took place from birth to age two (infancy) and whose major characteristic was that thought was confined to 'action schemes'.
- **The preoperational**, which took place from about the age of two to the age of six. This stage saw the use of representational thought which was not logical but was intuitive.'
- **The concrete operational**, which lasted from about the age of six to twelve, and which involved the use of systematic and logical thought, but only with regard to concrete objects.
- **The formal operational**, a feature of adolescence and adulthood.

Some theorists argue that infants are unable to distinguish themselves from other people until after the age of eighteen months, just as Lacan argued. The developmental psychologists, Steinberg, Belsky and Meyer, (*see Infancy, Childhood and Adolescence: Development in Context*, p. 210) note that this inability to distinguish the self from another is called **symbiosis**, a sort of fusion with the mother which is thought to be essential for survival.

There is, in fact, a psychological test which may reinforce the simple observation made by Lacan about the initial inability of the child to distinguish itself as a separate being (though it does nothing to support the headier conclusions he made about sexuality and the Other). This is the 'rouge' test, in which some mark or spot is made on an infant's nose. When the infant is shown a mirror, it will perhaps look at its nose, but will not actually reach for it until it is older than twelve months. The *gradual* process of discovering a separate sense of self is described by the psychologist Mahler (*see* p. 211) as *individuation and separation*. Erikson (*see also* p. 211) looked at conflict during the infant's move towards independence and called the stage *autonomy versus shame and doubt*.

The formation and maintenance of the subject through language

One of the useful comments Lacan made was that we are all immersed in language and only have access to others through it. This is in marked contrast to Saussure, whose theories behave as though we can stand outside language and make judgments about it. If we asked how these judgments could be made, we would have to say through the system being investigated – in other words, through language.

Language arises, in all societies, from a response to the environment which human begins inhabit and experience. As Denis McQuail notes in *Communication* (p. 58):

> '... for people to co-operate, or simply to cope with environmental facts, agreed ways of denoting human experience must be arrived at.'

This is clearly an important motivation for the genesis of language as a coherent symbolic code. One way of approaching the relationship between the external world and the language which describes it, is to describe the world we experience 'at first hand' as the *empirical* world (the world of experiences), and the domain of language and signs which describes and interprets that world as the *symbolic*.

Once language was established, human beings were able to release their ideas and concepts from the constraints of their immediate present. Language carries not only the useful experiences and knowledge which can be learned from the near or distant past (written texts), but also brings us the 'dead weight' of old practices and ideologies which our culture has accumulated for generations. To acquire language is to acquire a specific culture, but at the same time language provides us with the tools to criticise and, at a symbolic level, to suggest the reformation of that culture.

CHOMSKY AND LANGUAGE

Infants in all societies appear to progress through the same stages at the same time. The process of *language development* seems to begin before words themselves put in an appearance, with very young children communicating with adults through games which involve repetition and turn-taking. No matter what language their parents speak, all babies begin to make the same sounds at the same time (*see* Steinberg, Belsky and Meyer, *Infancy, Childhood and Adolescence: Development in Context*, p. 173). By two or three months, infants begin 'cooing'; that is to say they repeat the same vowel sound, with variations in pitch. According to these authors, at the age of five months babies add consonants to the vowels and string the sounds together, such as the sound-forms 'ba-ba-ba-ba' and 'do-do-do-do'. Such sound sequences are called *babbling* and:

'... the sequence of sounds that infants make when they babble appears to be universal ... for infants everywhere, sounds made with the lips ('p' or 'b') precede sounds made with the tip of the tongue ('d' or 'n').'

Research into the biology of language has also seemed to demonstrate that week-old French infants can tell the difference between spoken French and Russian, but take a little longer to distinguish English. Such research seems to support the theory put forward by Noam Chomsky that human beings are born with an innate capacity to understand the rules of grammar that underlie natural language. Dr Jacques Mehler of the Centre Nationale de la Recherche Scientifique in Paris has argued that the ability to acquire language has a genetic basis. He has stated that the structure of the cerebral cortex is such as to make people acquire natural language in a rapid and efficient form. The structure of the brain, in his view, must closely mirror the underlying structure of language.

Chomsky had arrived at much the same conclusion through his work on the structure of language. He revolutionised linguistics at the end of the 1950s by arguing that linguistic knowledge took the form of a rule system, and that this rule system was acquired because human beings were equipped with an innate faculty for the acquisition of language. (It would seem that human beings are also 'physiologically' *built for speech*.) The evidence Chomsky offered for his theory of 'innateness' was that human languages displayed close similarities, and that children follow remarkably similar routes (and seem to go through the same stages) in acquiring language. It seems that no one actively teaches children language as such, but that they nonetheless manage to formulate accurate linguistic rules and principles.

CHICKENS AND EGGS: THEORIES OF LANGUAGE AND THOUGHT

Some theorists imagine language as having preceded thought. This proposition is called the hypothesis of *linguistic relativity*, and argues essentially that it is impossible to think about something if there is not the language available to describe that thing. By contrast, Piaget argued that language was the *external* manifestation of thought processes, and grew not from any social requirement, but from the need to organise experience and create structure.

Speech acts

The linguist, J. Dore, characterised the one-word utterances of very young children as **primitive speech acts** which consist of a simple expression and a primitive force. The way that the child would *intone* or give emphasis to the word would indicate to the parent what the child required. There are, according to this system, nine primitive speech acts. These are set out by Malcolm Coulthard in *An Introduction to Discourse Analysis* (p. 162):

1 **Labelling,** where the child identifies an object for its own benefit and without reference to adults.
2 **Requesting** (an answer), when the child would seek reassurance on some point.
3 **Requesting** (an action), where the child would ask someone to carry out some task.

4 **Practising**, where the child says something without the subject of the reference being present.
5 **Calling**, when the child seeks a response.
6 **Greeting**, an initiation of contact made by the child.
7 **Answering**, where a response from the child to a question is required.
8 **Repeating**, an example of which would be a child's repetition of an overheard word.
9 **Protesting**, which would often be incoherent or alternatively would involve the use of a simple negative.

From this (slightly rearranged) list, it would seem that these speech acts are geared to a variety of functions, *not simply the naming of objects*. Some are clearly **interactional**, that is to say they are designed to share meaning with others, or are used to elicit a clear response. Coulthard places *calling, greeting*, and *answering* in this category. Others are purely **instrumental**, designed to get a specific action carried out. An example of this category would be *requesting an action*.

From these examples, we can discover some of the ways in which the young child attempts to use symbolic content to exercise control over its environment. *How* children came to produce utterances was the subject of research carried out by the linguist Bates, who followed the development of communication through three stages. These are re-presented by Coulthard (*see* p. 166 of his book):

• **Stage one** is where the very young child has a systematic effect on the (usually adult) listener without having an intentional control over the effect created – this stage is called the *perlocutionary* phase.
• **Stage two** is a phase in which the child intentionally uses non-verbal signals to convey requests and to direct adult attention to 'objects and events' – this is known as the *illocutionary* stage.
• **Stage three** is that in which the child 'constructs propositions' in the same sequences that were previously expressed in a non-verbal way – this stage is described as the *locutionary* stage.

This description of the linguistic development of the child is useful because it reveals some aspects of the formation of the human subject. The subject moves from a state of 'unawareness' in the earliest phase, in the sense that the child uses what we might call built-in mechanisms to signal its needs. It has no control over the effects it creates during this stage. The little human being is totally dependent upon the attachment felt by the parent or other adult carer. Communication at this stage could be said to be an automatic process. Just as the infant has no control over its needs, it cannot fully control the communication of those needs.

The dawn of linguistic control is a first step to exerting some control over the individual's immediate environment. Some research (Coulthard, *see* p. 173 of his book) seems to suggest that babies of the age of seven months can 'initiate' parental speech by making certain types of protest, and that they are able by the age of twelve months to produce actions as a response to an utterance.

An important aspect of language, as it is acquired in any culture, is that it is bound by sets of rules. Languages depend on a logical consistency. McQuail (*see Communication*, p. 59) describes language as 'a system of differences or contrasts . . .

concerned with distinguishing one object, experience, concept from another.' Thus it is an important way of differentiating between, and making sense of, the various aspects of our environment.

Categories of language?

Saussure, a theorist who will appear quite prominently in the next few chapters, divided language into two major aspects. He called the first **langue**, a term which refers to the formal properties of language which can be studied and described by researchers and theorists. He called the second **parole**, which he decided was not open to systematic study. This is the language as it is actually spoken, i.e. the *practice* of the language. Taken together, the two elements combine to make **langage**.

Sociolinguistics

An important development has been the growth of studies of language which stress the *context* in which language takes place. Context is a vital factor in the overall structuring of meaning; it is for this reason that references to context will appear throughout this book. The idea that variations in 'speech behaviour' are linked to our position in the social structure is important.

Sociolinguistics is a study of language use and class, and the relationships which may exist between the two. Denis McQuail (in *Communication*, p. 65) talks of 'status groups' in society, which are:

'. . . normally differentiated by the degree of its access to power [and which is] also a community and in part a speech community.'

The individual subject born into a particular class or speech community will adopt many of the linguistic forms (and the values implicit in those forms) of that community. It is interesting to note that an aspect of the rebellions which individuals sometimes make against background and community involves the adoption of the **parole** of other 'more desirable' groups.

Jennifer Coates, in *Women, Men and Language*, argues that men and women not only speak differently, but that there are also clearly identifiable differences in their status as *social groups*. She argues that women could be considered to be a disadvantaged social group, and that children acquire a 'sex-differentiated' language. In conclusion, she proposes that men organise their talk *competitively*, while women organise their talk *co-operatively*. While some theorists may argue that this constitutes simply a clash of styles of speech, Coates remains convinced that the very competence that women display in one style of speech acts as a major disadvantage when it comes to mixed group interaction. Using the results of a careful sociolinguistic survey, Coates reaches the conclusion that (*see* p. 154):

'In mixed conversations, women do more of the interactive work, supporting others' topics, respecting others' turns, facilitating conversational flow through the use of questions. The end-product of all this is that men dominate conversation. This is unsatisfactory if such interactions are meant to be exchanges between equals.'

The question which faces the communication theorist at this point is whether women in general should adopt a different style (as they may be forced to do in many work situations) or whether it should be argued, as Coates puts it (p. 154), '... that some features of women's talk are desirable for everyone.'

Put writing in your heart

It comes as no surprise to learn that powerful classes and social groups have tended to restrict access to language, or have developed specialist forms of language in order to maintain the power of an elite. McQuail (*see Communication*, p. 65) quotes a remark made by an Ancient Egyptian: '... put writing in your heart that you may protect yourself from hard labour of any kind.' In the novel *1984*, George Orwell describes the invention of a restrictive form of language called 'Newspeak', the purpose of which is to shrink what we know as *langue* to such a degree that the possible construction of 'deviant' thought and speech (*parole*) is made increasingly unlikely. The use of forms of speech which attempt to limit the possibilities of choice will be explored further in the section on propaganda and persuasion. In the meantime, note that, quite apart from how certain choices may be 'closed down', there are strong arguments to be made that restricting a child's early access to language forms contributes to wider *social* disadvantages in many everyday situations.

Paralanguage

Spoken and written language are not the only ways of communicating. As we develop, we learn a range of **non-verbal** behaviours from our families and from our peers which can be used to reinforce, or to contradict, the spoken communication we can offer. These non-verbal devices are also known as **paralanguage**. There is a great deal of scope for individuality in the use of non-verbal communication, which includes facial expression, gesture, postures, movements of the body, proximity and actual physical contact. Gestures, in particular, can be codified in a variety of ways to explain their different uses in communication. These can be:

- **specific or intentional gestures**, such as waving, pointing, the use of gesture as insult, and so on;
- **accidental or unintentional 'gestures'**, such as blushing and fidgeting;
- **address and response gestures**, including formal and informal signals made during an interaction, intentional as in the first case;
- **gestures as metaphor**, encompassing such deliberate actions as kissing someone's hand, which carry a wider and more abstract meaning in certain contexts than might be suggested by the action alone. Context, in this case, would determine how a participant might interpret such an action: e.g. is the action carried out in private or in public?

SOCIAL THEORY AND THE FORMATION OF THE SUBJECT

The political writer Goran Therborn (*see Ideology of Power and the Power of Ideology*), was careful to distinguish between the **subjectivity** (or subject position) of an individual and the **personality** (or character structure) of the person. Therborn did not see the subject as totally dominated by the institutional framework or the society which surrounded it.

He noted, for example, that the subject *is not always completely subordinated* and that the meaning of the 'subject of the king' is quite different from the meaning of the 'subjects of history'. In the first case, we have a subject who is clearly dominated by the relationship of power. In the second case, the individuals concerned have an interactive relationship with history itself (interaction as action and reaction), helping to 'make' that history as much as the history made the individuals who struggled within it.

Subjection/qualification

Therborn believes that the sexuality and potentialities of human infants are shaped by a number of factors. The type of society they inhabit 'favours certain drives and capacities, and prohibits or disfavours others' (*see* p. 17 of his book). In other words, the society in which we live will affect the range of possibilities available to us. What happens according to this author is that the 'powers that be' use **three** basic methods of *talking to* or *addressing* the human subject:

1 Human subjects are told *what exists*: who we are, what the world is like, what our society is like, how men and women behave – and also by implication what does *not* exist.
2 They are told *what is good*: what is right, what is attractive, and by implication their opposites.
3 They are told *what is possible*: this suggests that certain ways of behaving, certain changes that we may want to see in society, are excluded from the ruling power's agenda.

Roles

Human subjects eventually come to adopt 'roles' in our society, again in the tension between the Freudian categories of 'pleasure principle' and 'reality principle'. Roles could be explained (*see* Therborn, pp. 20–1) as:

'the behaviour ... expected of persons occupying a particular social position.'

Role is clearly something 'forced' on individuals, and could be something that someone could adopt only in certain circumstances – it is obvious that some roles change with circumstance and that behaviour which might be appropriate for one kind of circumstance might be totally inappropriate in another. In addition, certain roles are unlikely to alter easily, despite the circumstances. Gender roles are not easy to break down, for example, because they are central to our conception of Self.

'Role' forms part of the subject positions we occupy, but the suggestion in the word that there might be an opportunity to drop one role in order to adopt another is quite correct. The overtones of *acting* in the term 'role' should not be ignored. We may find, for instance, that we are placed in a situation so unusual that our experience cannot provide us with a model for a new role or role behaviour. We might therefore 'fall back' on a role which approximates to what we think is expected of us.

Subjects, in my opinion, recognise from a very early age that there are a variety of possible roles for people to adopt, so they are able to speak in role, and to address others in role – they are capable of 'role-play', as suggested above. Role-play is a way of experimenting with different aspects of behaviour. I believe that the adult, despite his/her position in society, does not lose this capacity. We might argue that it is from this ability to 'act' a role in a given context that *registers of speech* appear.

The whole of infant 'society' is processed through certain beliefs. Quite beyond the considerations of class, there are some general values which apply to all young individuals growing up in the society. Some of these values are based on gender, while others relate to age, sexuality and class. As the subject goes through life, he/she has to interact with many different people in many different situations, and, as we have seen above, is called upon to *assume* different roles. The subject can choose to retain the most significant 'self', or a 'core self'. In *The Dynamics of Human Communication*, Myers and Myers describe 'ranges' of role *behaviour* as follows:

- **Physical range**, such as age, height, weight, hair colour;
- **Introspective range**, which includes all the private motivations and feelings which you may possess;
- **Role range**, which is the actual variety of roles played with different people in different situations.

If we move away from the interpersonal for a moment, we may see that authority in society certainly addresses or *speaks to* all of these different ranges. In addition, the mass media will address us in a similar way, in terms of how we might look, or how we might want to look (physical range), sometimes in terms of how we might feel (introspective range) and sometimes in terms of how we might have to function in relation to other people and society in general.

Interpellation

The Marxist philosopher, Althusser, imagined the operation of ideology in terms of the formation of human subjectivity. His work on the idea of interpellation is a very important part of our study. Althusser believed that an address works to put the subject into the position of what we originally called the 'receiver' and can now call the 'addressee'.

Interpellation works by 'hailing' the subject/addressee. In responding to the address being made, recognising that it is 'us' being spoken to, we tend to accept or adopt the subject-position being offered to us. This makes some authors believe that 'dominant' forces are able to construct positions for us to occupy. As we flick

Fig 1.9 Address: an emotional appeal
(Courtesy of SOGAT '82)

MURDOCH IS BAD NEWS

Rupert Murdoch made a staggering £47 million profit last year out of the Sun, News of the World, Times and Sunday Times.

He has just bought six American TV companies but he needs even more profits to pay for them.

So Murdoch has provoked a strike to sack over 5,000 British employees – employees who have worked on his papers for years and earned him huge profits.

People all over the country have stopped buying Murdoch's papers.

Please do the same.

Then he will have to start negotiating.

● Eric worked for the Sun for sixteen years before he was sacked by Rupert Murdoch.

Jeremy Nicholl

DON'T BUY

THE Sun   NEWS OF THE WORLD

THE ⚜ TIMES
THE SUNDAY TIMES

Published by SOGAT, NGA, AUEW & NUJ 63-67 Bromham Road, Bedford MK40 2AG. Tel: 0234 51521. Printed by Shadowdean Ltd. (TU)

Fig 1.9 (continued)

> ## "I want your beer account in France."
>
> I love France so much that I married here twelve years ago, but there are certain things I'll always miss. Good old British ale, for instance. That's something I'd like to get the French to discover and enjoy.
>
> Although our agency is young, most of us have had key jobs in major Franch and international agencies where we have acquired wide experience in a great variety of fields, including food and beverage.
>
> Why don't you give us a ring if you're thinking of looking for an advertising agency in France, or just changing your existing one?
>
> We would like to show you our work and convince you we are the right agency for your company or product.
>
> **We understand you better**

Fig 1.10 An example of address: advertising
(Courtesy of Antelme et Associés)

through the pages of a magazine, we might notice many different types of address, 'hailing' us in different ways, sometimes through the role ranges explained before. It seems clear, however, that the very *lack* of interaction between us as audience and the mass media as 'addresser' means that we often break off from the address, or will occupy some of the role positions we are offered for a short space of time, moving on elsewhere quite rapidly.

MAINTENANCE OF THE SUBJECT

A place in the world

Now we have dealt with the **formation** of the human subject, we could re-emphasise the **maintenance** of the human subject. People need to *continue* to gain a sense of themselves and their place in the world through a constant reassessment of both. Myers and Myers talk of the way people 'establish and maintain' relationships with others in order to do this, and point to the central importance of **communication** in human life.

Communication allows us to 'check' our place in the world and clearly not just through other people, but also against our perceptions of a changing environment. If we were to imagine a world in which we were *unable to communicate*, and unable *to receive communication*, all human and environmental interaction would be lost in a confusion of seemingly meaningless images and actions. As Myers and Myers say (p. 5), '... you would be without the symbolic systems you use to make sense out of your world and out of your own place within that world.' Communication keeps us operating as fully social beings. However, all the communication processes we experience within society tend to do more than simply maintain our 'balance' as rational subjects.

To a large degree, communication as we experience it in society reinforces a number of social norms which are very far from being beneficial. Our society does seem to have various 'collective madnesses', not all of them communicative, to which we subscribe as though they are perfectly rational. Our treatment of the environment is an example of something which may harm us all; yet many individuals persist, for instance, in relying exclusively on their car for transport, when a truly rational approach would suggest how harmful such conduct has become. The difference in the socialisation of boys and girls is an outstanding example of how we inherit, through communication and examples of behaviour, the society's view of what we ought to be. We think we know who we are, but perhaps we have only developed into the people we are *allowed to be*.

Production and exchange

Communication, as we have seen, is more than the sending and receiving of messages – it is the production and exchange of meaning through the **symbolic systems** we have at our disposal. John Fiske, in *Introduction to Communication Studies* (p. 2), writes that communication is central to the life of our culture and that without it the culture would die. This reinforces the idea that the importance of communication goes beyond the individual to the society as a whole.

Culture is maintained as much through interpersonal and group interaction as it is through the mass media, and is certainly felt both more subjectively and more warmly in our personal relationships.

Personality, social behaviour and communication

Although the subject (the individual) may well be 'formed' by a combination of the different factors mentioned above, there is some research which suggests that the *expression* of personality, and even the personality itself, may not always be entirely consistent. Michael Argyle, in *The Psychology of Interpersonal Behaviour*, suggests that individuals can behave in a variety of ways that are dependent on three factors. He describes these as:

1 The rules and conventions which operate in different situations (interviews, ceremonies, weddings, and so on).
2 The relationship of the human subject with other individuals.
3 The particular individuals encountered, since the behaviour the subject displays

will depend partly upon the personalities of others as well as upon his/her own personality.

However, changes in an individual's behaviour will not be in any sense random – they will be rational responses made in the face of a veriety of stimuli. There is a 'continuum' of behaviour, which the individual will display as a 'repertoire' of responses. This repertoire will cover all the social situations with which the individual has had to cope in the past.

Only human?

In *The Dynamics of Human Communication* (p. 5), Myers and Myers describe communication as 'the specific behaviour which sets human off from other species'. We know, however, that many animals have effective methods of communicating including vocal, chemical, optical and tactile communication.

Some aspects of the 'specific behaviour' mentioned by Myers and Myers seems to be shared with animals. So how does human communication differ from that of animals? In other words, what makes our communication so special?

Only a little further into their book (p. 11), we find Myers and Myers quoting the work of the communication theorists Miller and Sunnafrank, who wrote:

> 'Our first major assumption is that the basic function of all communication is to control the environment so as to realise certain physical, economic, or social rewards from it ...'

(By environment we mean not only our immediate physical surroundings but also the 'psychological climate' we inhabit, the people around us, and the social interchanges, as well as information needed for day-to-day existence.)

We might, however, argue that both humans and animals need to gain certain material rewards from their respective environments. Although some purposes are shared, we can begin to gain a sense of the differences at work when we understand the *limitations* to the 'rewards' which animals are able to obtain *from their environment* and *through their communication*. It seems that animals are unable to exploit the world in quite the same ways as the human species. This is because the extent of their intelligence, the 'social systems' this gives rise to and the resulting forms of communication all remain relatively simple.

When some types of grazing animal take to their hooves in order to escape from a predator, the herd communicates a simple message almost *unintentionally*; the purpose is the survival of the majority of the herd. The survival is the 'reward'. Some animals might be able to obtain more advanced rewards than others and might be capable of using more complex (and co-operative) modes of communication in order to obtain them. It is clear that animals gain certain benefits from their surroundings, but also that they do not have an 'economy' as such.

Generally animals do not seem capable of using either the same variety of *forms* of communication as humans (they do not speak, for example) or of possessing and exercising the same degree of *power* through communication. Having said this, it is worth noting again that human beings do not all gain the same opportunities to 'control' their environment; neither do they have equality of access to the 'power to communicate'. We still say that some human beings are treated 'like animals' and this gives us an indication of the status of both some humans and all animals in our society. Perhaps part of what sets humans apart is both the scale of their communication, and the *intentions* which lie behind their communications. We have also managed to create systems which appear to carry out communicative functions with increasingly less input from the human communicators themselves.

SUMMARY

■ COMMUNICATION: A DEFINITION

A concise definition of communication, taken from Price's *The A–Z Media and Communication Handbook*, is 'the **exchange of meaning** between human agents'. This 'exchange of meaning' between people has to take place within a certain shared **context**. Alternative definitions attempt to explain the ways in which communication is produced. Dance and Larsen offer this explanation: 'The production of symbolic content by an individual, according to a code, with anticipated consumption by other(s) according to the same code.'

■ Interaction

An interaction is the *action* and *reaction* which take place between two or more individuals, or two or more social groups.

Symbolic interaction is where the human communicator uses a series of symbols: signs (images, words, gestures) that *stand for* things or for ideas. Symbolic interaction means the exchange of meanings which are encoded in language, or gesture, or in visual signs.

■ ELEMENTS, FEATURES, AND PROCESS OF COMMUNICATION

The *elements* of communication are the component parts of it; the *features* of communication are its characteristics; and the *process* of communication is its course of action, how it operates.

■ Intention and context

When the sender chooses a message, all sorts of pressures may force him/her to adapt the message to the circumstances with which he/she is faced. This means that the 'original' message will be shaped, from the moment it is first thought up, by more factors than simply the need to communicate an idea. There is a lot to be discovered about the first stage, the origin of the message.

There are five elements which must be present for communication to take place. These five elements are: a **message**, an initiator (**sender**), a mode/vehicle (**channel**), a recipient (**receiver**), and an **effect**.

The content of the message depends very much on:
1 the intention of the sender
2 the **available language or code**, which will act to structure the message
3 the **context** within which the message is delivered

4 the **communicative possibilities** which have, in the past, presented themselves in a similar situation.

The five categories of communication may be described as:

1 **Intrapersonal** communication: this category is understood as communication within the self.
2 **Interpersonal** communication: this refers to communication, usually face to face, usually between two individuals.
3 **Group communication**: this is usually taken to mean communication within clearly identifiable groups, or between different groups of people.
4 **Mass communication**: this category is often used to describe the type of communications initiated (or prompted) by the large institutions of the mass media.
5 **Extrapersonal communication**: this type of communication is generally described as that which takes place either *without* human involvement (communication between machines) or, more loosely, interaction *between* human beings and machines.

■ POWER, MASS COMMUNICATION AND SOCIETY

Power is defined as the **capacity to do something**, to affect our immediate environment, and as the **domination** of one individual/group/corporation **over** any 'other' or set of others. *Both* these definitions allow that power is the possession of the ability to shape action. Interpersonal interaction is not free from the struggle for influence and power which is so clearly a feature of mass communication.

■ Mass communication: imitating the personal mode

Models taken from personal communication can often be 'translated' to the mass level. Some forms of 'communication' which depend on quite staggering inequalities of power can be presented as not only intimate, but based on equality and respect.

Mass communicators use models of interpersonal communication in order to make their message effective, which means to say it is recognised by an **audience** as an **address**. The mass media themselves are not just one branch of human communication; they are built upon and continue to imitate human interaction.

Differences between mass and interpersonal communication can be understood as follows: that **interpersonal** communication involves at any given moment one 'transmitter' who communicates with one or a few 'receivers'; that **mass** communication is 'mediated' through a specific set of technologies which stand between the senders and receivers.

■ Is the mass media truly communicative?

If communication is really 'a convergence process in which sender and receiver ... create and share information', then it could be argued that the relationship between the mass media and their audience is not truly 'communicative' at all.

The following questions are asked about society: What do we mean by society? What kind of society do we live in? Why are there different classes? How much influence are individuals able to exercise on the state? What do we mean by 'equality' between men and women? Where can power be found in society? What is the role of the mass media in society?

Four traditions of political approach to the media may be described: liberal, Marxist, social-reformist and **conservative**.

Questions about the media include: Do we believe that the mass media have a positive or negative effect on our society, or only a minor influence on our lives? Do the mass media make up an independent force, or are they closely linked to centres of authority, such as government? Is the audience for mass media communication the 'victim' of a powerful conspiracy, or does it create its own meanings from the message it receives? Do the media get in the way of reality?

Power and authority in the mass media: Denis McQuail describes three alternative models of communication or 'models of communication relationships': the **command** mode, the **service** mode and the **associational** mode.

The mass media: how powerful?: Ian Connell attacked the idea that the mass media is somehow blessed with 'fabulous powers' of influence over our society and the people in it; taken on its own this could be interpreted as ignoring a central charge which is often made against the media, that they are unable to offer certain kinds of representation of the event. It is still true that our ability to exercise judgment needs to work on a variety of sources and a variety of viewpoints.

Dominance and subordination are examined in relation to power. The ruling class is decribed as a coalition of interests. The idea is advanced that the dominant forces are not always in agreement. Is it possible for any force in society to make thinking and culture uniformly the same? Fiske's over-emphasis on the powers of resistance of the subordinate is examined.

The concept of recuperation/contestation is one which lies at the centre of questions about the relationships of power. **Contestation** is the idea that one of the two or more groups in a communication resists the meanings offered by another group. **Recuperation** is the ability of one of the groups to take back the content of the resistance and turn it to their own ends.

Power in society: The idea that people are controlled by getting them together, and by making them do and think the same thing is described as an outdated approach. The idea advanced here is that society is 'fragmented' and then kept under control through its divisions.

A model of power takes issue with Foucault's idea of a war of 'all against all' and suggests that there is a clear difference between saying, as the theorist Poulantzas once did, that all social relations are relations of power, and suggesting that, because power is 'everywhere', we are all equally at fault for the wrongs of society and the faults of the individual.

David Tetzlaff's identification of a 'fragmented' society where mass culture keeps people in their place by dividing the population is advanced as a useful model of power. Centralised control of meaning is seen as both difficult and counter-productive. The point Tetzlaff tries to make is that, even when the subordinate receives mass media messages, the messages themselves may fail to have any connection to the real relations of power.

■ THE MASS MEDIA MESSAGE

Four levels of mediation are suggested: Level 1: human communication (the creation of meaning); Level 2: professional selection (the selection of meaning); Level 3: mass media technology (the technological treatment of meaning); Level 4: audience reception (the interpretation of meaning).

Media terms: a list of the definitions of the media terms: address, agenda-setting, audience, code, context, discourse, genre, identity, ideology, institution, interpellation, intertextuality, mediation, narrative, representation, and semiology is given on p. 35–40.

■ The formation of the human subject

The idea that human beings are made human through a specific process can be investigated using a number of different perspectives: *human biologists* will base much of their understanding of the subject on the extent of its physical capabilities; *psychoanalysts* will typically examine the 'structures of desire' that form the basis, in their opinion, of human actions and the desire to act; *linguists* would tend to look at the structures of language and the available contexts of expression; *social theorists* would tend to look at the economic and social formation of the individual.

■ The central importance of interaction

Interaction is seen as central to human subjects and to human behaviour. A number of approaches to language and human development may be explored, including those of Lacan, Piaget and Chomsky.

Speech acts are seen to be at the forefront of human communication. Linguists like J. Dore characterise the one-word utterances of very young children as **primitive speech acts** which consist of a simple expression and a primitive force.

■ Language

Saussure divides language into two major aspects called l*angue*, a term which refers to the formal properties of language, and *parole*, the language as it is actually spoken: the *practice* of the language. Taken together, the two elements combine to make l*angage*.

Sociolinguistics is related to the way that language is used with regard to social factors like class and gender; it is important to stress the *context* in which communication takes place. It is important to see gesture and non-verbal behaviour in context.

■ Social theory and the formation of the subject

This deals with *subjection* and *qualification*, a theory of the formation of people in a social context, the type of society people inhabit tending to favour certain drives and capacities, and prohibiting or disfavouring others.

Roles and the way that human subjects eventually come to adopt 'roles' in our society are examined. The Freudian categories of 'pleasure principle' and 'reality principle' may account for some of the basic ways in which people structure their lives and make decisions. Roles could be explained as 'the behaviour . . . expected of persons occupying a particular social position'.

Interpellation (which will assume an important place in this book) is an address which works to put the subject into a position where the address is accepted and therefore the ideological interest of the addressor is served.

Three factors affect what human beings say and how they say it: the rules and conventions which operate in different situations (interviews, ceremonies, weddings and so on); the relationship of the human subject with other individuals; and the particular individuals encountered, since the behaviour displayed by the subject will depend partly upon the personalities of others (as well as upon his/her own personality).

A place in the world deals with the formation and maintenance of the human subject. People need to continue to gain a sense of themselves and their place in the world through a constant re-assessment of both. Communication allows us to 'check' our place in the world, not just through other people, but also against our perceptions of a changing environment.

Production and exchange: communication is more than the sending and receiving of messages – it is the production and exchange of meaning, through the symbolic systems we have at our disposal.

Personality, social behaviour and communication: although the subject may well be 'formed' by a combination of the different factors mentioned above, there is some research which suggests that the expression of personality, and even the personality itself, is not always entirely consistent. However, changes in an individual's behaviour will not be in any sense random: they will be rational responses made in the face of a variety of stimuli. There is a 'continuum' of behaviour, which the individual will display as a 'repertoire' of responses. This repertoire will cover all the social situations with which the individual has had to cope in the past.

Only human?: Myers and Myers describe communication as 'the specific behaviour which sets humans off from other species'. We know, however, that many animals have quite vocal or effective visual methods of communicating. Myers and Myers describe the basic function of all communication as the attempt to 'control the environment so as to realise certain physical, economic, or social rewards from it'. We might, however, argue that both humans and animals need to gain certain material rewards from their respective environments. Although some purposes are shared, we can begin to gain a sense of the differences at work when we understand the limitations to the 'rewards' which animals are able to obtain from their environment, and through their communication. It seems obvious that animals are unable to exploit the world in quite the same way as the human species. The survival of the animal in its environment is its 'reward'.

Ideology: the point of departure

WHAT IS IDEOLOGY?

In order to understand anything much about the subject of communication and media studies, and the place of semiotics and discourse analysis within it, we need to have a working understanding of ideology.

The term was first used in France at the end of the eighteenth century, by a writer called Destutt de Tracy. It meant a 'study of ideas'. As time passed, the use of the term changed and 'ideology' came to be applied to a certain type of belief system, of which an example in the eighteenth century might have been faith in a particular form of religion, or in radical theories of democracy. In the nineteenth century, the concept of ideology was presented as an undesirable belief, characteristic of a fanatical individual (as in 'ideologue'). Eventually, 'ideology' was used to refer to *belief systems* in general. So, ideology refers to ideas and beliefs – but more significantly, systems of belief.

The question remains, however: why make a particular study of ideology? Clearly, if ideology were simply a matter of private belief, without any public repercussions, it would not provoke so much comment or argument. Who would care what anyone (beyond the small group of people one knew) thought or said privately about anything?

In fact belief, truth, 'bias', myth and the creation of meaning in general, all excite controversy because most of us believe that ideology has some kind of impact in (and on) our society. The word 'system' (used above) is important. Not all ideas and beliefs qualify as ideology. An ideology must be seen as a coherent and recognisable set of beliefs. As Slavoj Zizek maintains in *Mapping Ideology* (1994), the concept 'ecology' is not ideological because it may be further defined as conservative, socialist, liberal–capitalist, feminist and so on, depending on how the causes of environmental degradation are imagined. Gregor McLennan, in *The Power of*

Ideology (p. 111), sets out three conditions which must be fulfilled if ideas and belief are to be regarded as 'ideological'.

1 the ideas concerned must be **shared** by a significant number of people;
2 the ideas must form some kind of coherent **system**;
3 the ideas must connect in some way to the use of **power** in society.

At this stage, we need to ask *how we recognise ideology in practice*. In order to recognise ideology, *we first need to know where it can be found*.

Belief and the expression of belief

If ideology is at least connected to belief, then we should have some idea where to start looking. Since belief exists in the human mind, we should concentrate for the moment on people, since they are both the 'creators' of ideology and its 'interpreters'. Unless we are prepared to look at people, both individually and in groups, we cannot even begin to guess what *forms* ideology takes.

This calls for a close study of what people say and do (not forgetting what they *create*) as individuals and as groups of individuals. Furthermore, if we are to gain some idea of why people sometimes do, say and create different things at different times, we need also to look at the different *contexts* in which they act, speak or reproduce culture. Media theory should examine the situations in which people find themselves, as well as the *purposes* they have in mind when they begin to express themselves. This, of course, is the whole problem with studying ideology and belief in the first place: ideology and belief are difficult to identify until the person or people concerned express themselves or carry out some action.

Talk and action *sometimes* make us think that belief is plain for all to see, but at times they can disguise or hide a person's or a group's true motivations. (We shall see, in Chapter 3, that the very act of expression tends to give *form* to belief – when you speak, you modify or alter subtly what you originally thought, according to your intention and the available words and ideas at your disposal.)

Even when we have worked out that something called ideology or belief exists, we must recognise that we have only identified its presence. We are still ignorant of its precise strength, significance, or place in the wider world of general ideologies and discourses. This, again, will form part of the concerns of this chapter.

Ideology: world view or distorted consciousness?

In *The Concept of Ideology*, Jorge Larrain begins his definition of ideology by showing that it has traditionally carried either a *negative* or a *positive* meaning. However, it might be more helpful to change these terms to **negative** and **neutral**.

The **neutral** meaning of ideology has usually been associated with the 'world view' (the 'outlook', or total perspective) of a particular social class, a definition linked with a view of ideology as being multiple – 'ideologies', or 'systems of belief' would explain this idea quite well. In this case, we might say that ideology 'typified' consciousness.

The **negative** meaning has largely been associated with the idea of *'false con-*

sciousness'. This definition grew from observations about ideology made by Karl Marx (1818–83), though it appears that Marx himself did not use the term as such (*see* Michelle Barrett's *The Politics of Truth*, p. 5). Marx did, however, use the term ideology to describe a form of belief which *distorted* the actual conditions of life in a class society. In Marxist terms, ideology is described as 'forms of consciousness' which determine the outlook of human beings. According to Marx, there is a difference between the true interests of people and the 'form in which these interests are experienced'. Thus, there is supposed to be a split between those ideas which influence people, and their 'true' interests. However, false or 'distorted' consciousness (often extended to include theories which portray the media as being partly reponsible for pulling the wool over people's eyes) could be explained as the inability of the working class to recognise its true interests because it has taken on the beliefs and values of the dominant class in society. (For Marxists and some other radicals, the working classes remain the focus of attention because they appear to hold the potential to change society for the better.)

At one time the idea of 'false consciousness', useful as a crude form of shorthand for more complicated problems, was offered as one reason why the working class did not rise against the state in Britain – or why it did not rally more solidly to the cause of the miners, print-workers, and so on.

The idea of false consciousness is less popular now, partly because it is difficult to form a useful picture of 'true consciousness'. The traditional definition of true consciousness took as its example those workers who have a radical and critical view of class society (usually those workers who accept the basic tenets of 'traditional' Marxist belief). Notions of 'correct' belief led in some countries to the idea that people's beliefs need to be policed. Once a system of belief in a country becomes inflexible or 'closed', then dictatorships, rather than workers' democracies, are likely to be the end result.

The second reason for the decline of ideas about 'false' beliefs, is the understandable reluctance of many theorists to accept that human behaviour is determined wholly by *class interests* or by *class position*. The class position we as individuals occupy certainly does have an influence on the way we see ourselves and the world, but the end result of this influence will be different even within the same class grouping. In brief, it seems clear that there are other factors which motivate people besides their class (for example, gender, region, ethnicity, age, income, religion, etc.).

Summing up the worth of the **negative** and **neutral** positions (what he calls negative and positive positions) on ideology, Jorge Larrain finds significant drawbacks in both cases. In the first case (*The Concept of Ideology*, p. 118) he shows that 'every point of view has an ideological character ... [ideology] ends up with very little meaning and loses its critical capability'. In the second case, 'ideology is confined to the conscious lies and illusions of political parties and groups', which Larrain feels ignores the fact that ideology also exists in the social structure itself.

In *The A–Z Media and Communication Handbook* (1997), I offered a definition of ideology as 'the general framework of all those ideas and beliefs which offer a coherent, but incomplete, critique of "things as they are".' This definition will be analysed step by step. Note first that ideology is described as a **general framework** of ideas. This reminds us that it is a large-scale structure, and not just a collection of isolated beliefs. More importantly, such a definition bears a similarity to the *neutral* view of ideology, in so far as it is seen as a widespread social phenomenon (what Slavoj Zizek in *Mapping Ideology* calls 'the indispensable medium in which individuals live out their relations'). Next, the proposition that the ideas and beliefs which make up this general framework offer a **coherent** point of view, shows that ideology provides a plausible explanation for events. The fact that it is described as **incomplete**, marks a departure from the *negative* position, which merely emphasised its distortion of reality. Ideology is 'incomplete' for three reasons: first, because society itself is made up of contradictions and controversies, second because it must work at an abstract level of description, and third because the struggle to establish the meaning of specific events, results in the neglect of other aspects of experience. In conclusion, the notion that ideological points of view offer a **critique** of society, supports the idea that they often *deliberately intend* to produce particular explanations of public events. *The A–Z Handbook*'s definition moves away from the idea of ideology as a deliberate falsity, but holds on to the useful notion that it is an *intentional intervention* in the creation of meaning.

The term ideology will, however, continue to produce a range of meanings. Slavoj Zizek points out that (p.7): 'Ideology can designate anything from a contemplative attitude that misrecognises its dependence on social reality, to an action-oriented set of beliefs, from the indispensable medium in which individuals live out their relations, to a social structure to false ideas which legitimate a dominant political power.' Students must be careful to work out which meaning is intended, from the context in which each reference is found.

Idols of the tribe

The **negative** view of ideology was expressed powerfully by Francis Bacon. Writing in *Novum Organon* (1630), Bacon suggested that people would never obtain a true picture of the world unless certain false ideas or 'idols' were discarded, or at least recognised as false. We have seen above how the notion of some form of 'true' belief, in exact opposition to 'false' belief, is unhelpful and confusing, but Bacon's work is useful for another reason. It begins to ask where ideology *comes from*. Is it carried inside us, or is it something found in society which is then passed on to us? Bacon's definition of four classes of 'idols', or false ideas, starts to made clear the difference between *internal* and *external* ideologies. The four idols were described as follows:

- **Idols of the tribe** – internal attributes which are founded in human nature itself, and which therefore cannot be avoided. They are common to all human subjects and cannot be altered.
- **Idols of the cave** – again, internal factors but peculiar to the individual, and which include his/her character, education, personality, etc. These idols cannot be discarded or ignored.
- **Idols of the market-place** – external influences which refer to the fact that people (specifically men, in Bacon's example) meet and discuss business at the marketplace. There, they enter into conversation or discourse, learning the lin-

guistic signs for things before they come to know them through their own experience.

- **Idols of the theatre** – external in character, referring to the dependence of human beings on systems of belief, on ways of interpreting the world, which they have inherited from previous generations.

This system splits ideology into two – first, as mentioned above, something 'irrational' that is *based in human nature*, and secondly, something rooted in society, or *based on relations between human beings*. (It is worth noting that, if human nature is irrational, then it is difficult to imagine any society, made up as it must be of 'irrational individuals', managing to be rational itself.)

Larrain (in *The Concept of Ideology*) poses a similar problem to that set by Bacon. Is ideology *subjective* or *objective*? By this, he means to ask if it is to be found in someone's psychological formation (*what goes on in their minds*) together with the influences created by the class or groups they belong to (**internal**), or whether it stems from the wider, not so easily 'seen' aspects of society (**external**). Once again, this interpretation of ideology is based on the negative model, the 'distortion'of reality. This distortion would exist either in the minds of people (internal) or in the very structure of the society (external).

This text will argue that ideology comes from both 'internal' and 'external' sources, and that the link between the two areas becomes more obvious once we begin to consider 'speech acts' and discourse. It will also argue that we should think of ideology as **a consequence of the interaction between people and their imagined environment**, rather than as some kind of distortion which 'hides' reality.

The problem of wondering exactly what reality *is*, and whether or not we have a 'true' picture of it, can be resolved for the purposes of our study by looking at the fact that there are *shared* understandings of what is 'real'. (This problem was briefly mentioned in Chapter 1.) By 'shared understandings', I mean simply that people within a certain culture are able to *refer back* from a description of something, to some common understanding of what that thing is. If someone tells a classroom of students that there is a dog in the yard outside, the whole group will understand what is meant, by referring to their own experience of the subject being described. They may have a *different* mental picture of the type of dog and the space it occupies, and the shared understanding of the situation may well be imperfect (distorted by the effects of discourse or ideology), but the fact that they are able to recognise the meaning intended (and to be able to refer to similar but distinct experiences), shows that we are all involved in the process of the '*re-presentation*' of the world.

Wittgenstein, examining sign-languages, described this process in the following way: 'A proposition (a statement, or assertion, especially when part of a formal system of language) is a picture of reality. A proposition is a model of reality *as we imagine it*.' (*Tractatus Logico-Philosophicus*, 1921, Emphasis supplied.) He also noted that: '. . . if I understand a proposition, I know the situation it represents.' This chapter will examine the idea that we are all involved in *re-presenting* the representations others have already made.

Althusser and ISAs

A famous example of those theories which describe the existence of ideology in its 'external' form, can be found in the work of the French Marxist Louis Althusser. In 1969 he described the existence of an **ideological state apparatus**, made up of those agencies and systems (state education, established party politics, the family, the media and so on) which help shape public consciousness, ensuring that 'subordinate' groups accept the established social order. In Zizek's words (*see Mapping Ideology*), 'religious belief, for example, is not merely or even primarily an inner conviction', but exists in 'the Church as an institution and its rituals'.

In the ISA model, the economy is still regarded as the major force in society, but it cannot reproduce all the conditions required for the smooth running of capitalism. Education, for example, is required both to train the workforce, and to get individuals to accept their role as workers. Besides ideological forms concerned with socialisation, the ruling class has the option of using the 'repressive state apparatuses' (the army, police and so on), which represent the threat of force.

We should realise that there are all sorts of pressures on individuals to express themselves in certain 'accepted' codes, which vary from situation to situation and (which some writers seem to forget) from one specific time to another. It is important to note that ideology does not exist in human subjects alone. Although we began by looking at people, the things that people have *made* also reproduce ideologies.

The very structures of society, its material forms, are 'carriers' of ideology. For example, the appearance of a government building or a palace may be seen to embody systems of belief. An imposing building is a material embodiment of the social power which lies behind it. We should understand that ideology can make itself felt in gestures, signs and pictures as well as in words. In fact, we could call the reproduction of ideology a **material practice**.

SEMIOLOGY

The term semiology comes from the Greek word *'semeion'*, meaning sign. Semiology is the study of **signs and meaning** in language, art, the mass media, sound, and indeed any field of human endeavour which can be reproduced for, or represented to, an individual or an audience. (A sign may be understood as being **a physical object with a meaning**.) It must be clear that the *representations* we see around us are drawn from a kind of **'fund'** of images and ideas that, as members of this society, we recognise as carrying a range of possible meanings. This will be our starting point when we cover the differences between semiology and discourse analysis.

At first sight, a systematic study of signs would appear to be perfectly tailored for the study of communication and the mass media. Semiology is not a 'new' field and has the appearance of a coherent system which has been developed and refined over time. Its history, however, has been marked by many differences between major theorists. In addition, some of its applications have been called into question. As a relatively new discipline which continues to draw on other fields of enquiry for many of its ideas, media studies has been the victim of a variety of intellectual 'fashions'. One of these has been the fashion for an image-based semiology which, in the author's opinion, has treated small units of meaning as though they are complete texts and has neglected areas such as sound and meaning.

Approaches to semiology

In his *Introduction to Communication Studies* (p. 42), John Fiske describes three main areas of study in semiology:

1 the sign: the word, the picture, the sound that represents meaning within a specific culture;
2 the systems into which signs are organised;
3 the culture within which these signs and systems operate.

The very fact that semiology concentrates on the *text*, whether that text is a written narrative, a photograph, or a piece of film, is part of the reason why in its older forms, it has come in for criticism. Just as **process** theories of communication underplayed the role of the receiver, so some approaches to semiology have been attacked for treating **signs themselves** as though they contained meaning, when it is clear that meaning is to be found in the **transactions which use signs**, in the *use* of signs by actual individuals and groups in specific **contexts**.

Two traditions: Saussure *vs.* Peirce?

The two major traditions of semiological work are the structuralist perspective, which emphasises the relationship between the sign and its place in the overall structure of language (in the belief that it is structure which produces meaning); and the pragmatist approach which conceives of 'semiosis' as a continuous process of meaning-creation which allows human beings to make interpretations and to carry out actions. The first tradition is associated with Ferdinand de Saussure, the second with C.S. Peirce.

Saussure, Peirce and the sign

Saussure was born in Geneva in 1857. At the age of twenty-one, having studied linguistics, he published a well-received piece on Indo–European languages. In 1881, he began work as a lecturer in Paris, eventually becoming a professor of Sanskrit and Indo–European languages at the University of Geneva. His published output was, however, quite small. The famous 'Course in General Linguistics' was compiled after his death (in 1913) by colleagues and students, working from lecture notes and other sources. In this work, Saussure was mostly concerned with language as a system. Explicit references to 'semiology' are limited – what was *left behind* after language had been considered was called semiology. Saussure began by dividing what he described as the *internal* and the *external* features of language.

He went on to concentrate on the internal aspects and *excluded* a study of external factors.

Saussure focused his attention closely upon the sign itself. He understood the sign as **a physical object with a meaning** (this definition was used at the beginning of this section). The sign, according to Saussure, is made up of a *signifier* and a *signified*. The *signifier* would be the actual image, the physical appearance of the word (some theorists think that a single word cannot be considered as a sign), the physical existence of sound. The *signified* was the idea – what Fiske calls the 'mental concept' (*Introduction to Communication Studies*, p. 47) – to which the *signifier* referred.

As an example, we might think of a photograph of a boat. It is not an actual boat – one could not use it to sail on a river. It represents a particular boat, but also represents the idea of 'boat' as a concept in general. Another example may be the word 'boat' written on a piece of paper. It does not represent a particular boat either, but instead the mental concept of 'boat'. Boat enough of this for now!

Charles Sanders Peirce (1839–1918) was an American logician and philosopher, who founded 'pragmatics', an approach to the study of meaning which states that human consciousness is mediated by *signs*. In Peirce's words, 'every thought must be interpreted by another ... all thought is in signs' (*see* Jensen *The Social Semiotics of Mass Communication*, 1995). Peirce believed that each interpretant of a sign (each idea or effect produced in the mind of a human subject) produced another sign. Instead of believing reality to be entirely dependent upon structures of language, Peirce thought that signs enable people to exert some influence over everyday experience.

Peirce's signs were part of a larger system of thought, which set out three levels of phenomena to be found in the world: Firstness (the actual quality of things, including the colour of objects, the feelings associated with events, even the taste of various foods); Secondness (what Paul Cobley in *The Communication Theory Reader* calls the 'brute' facts we encounter, the real conditions of existence which may frustrate plans and courses of action), and Thirdness (those general laws of cause and effect found in the natural world, which lie behind everyday manifestations of 'brute' facts).

We have seen that Saussure was not unduly concerned with the external, *real* thing to which the sign refers. (His boat might in fact have sunk without him noticing.) Although Saussure insisted that language was a social, and not simply an individual phenomenon, his division of language into *langue* and *parole*, and his subsequent concentration on the former (the structure of language), led to a rather abstract or *idealist* approach to linguistics. Peirce, more concerned with the real object, used the term 'semiosis' to describe the **process** or **'action' of signs**. Semiosis is produced by the relationship between sign, interpretant and object.

The **sign** or 'representamen' addresses 'somebody ... creates in the mind of that person an equivalent sign, or a more developed sign' (see K.B. Jensen's *The Social Semiotics of Mass Communication*, p. 21). The equivalent or more developed version of the original sign is called the **interpretant**. The thing to which the sign refers (the real thing in the world) is the **object**. Peirce believed, as we have seen, that each interpretant of a sign went on to produce another sign.

MESSING ABOUT IN BOATS

If we return to the concept 'boat', we can see that the word itself is the **sign** or representamen. This stands for a real boat or the conception of a boat, in the physical or mental environment (the **object**). The word calls up in the mind not the object itself, but a more developed sign, the **interpretant**. The three elements together make up a 'triad', a combination of the three elements. Cobley (*see The Communication Theory Reader*, p. 28) notes that 'an interpretant's most important role is in the contribution to a further triad in which it becomes the Sign, with a subsequent Object and another Interpretant'.

As his work progressed, Peirce became convinced that individual signs were composed of many complex elements, moving beyond the simpler icon, index, and symbol categories usually associated with his name (*see* below).

TYPES OF SIGN

Peirce suggested that the **sign** or representamen produced three further types of **Firstness** or 'first level' sign. These are:

- a **qualsign**, the basic quality of things as experienced by human subjects;
- a **sinsign**, a sign which is considered in relation to an existing thing or fact;
- a **legsign**, a sign which relates to a general law or principle.

In turn, the **object** produces three kinds of sign, at the level of **Secondness** (relating to the factual conditions of existence). These form the famous triad which has become synonymous with Peirce's name:

- **icon**, which bears some resemblance to the object it represents (a photograph, map, or passage of music which sounds like natural auditory phenomena;
- **index**, where there is a direct physical connection to the object (the smell of coffee, the noise of an engine running, the taste of sugar in confectionery);
- **symbol**, a sign related to its object only through convention (a symbol could be the CND sign, a road sign, or a unit of linguistic meaning such as a phrase or sentence).

Here, we may notice that some signs can be made up of more than one category: a road sign showing a bend in the road, for example, can be iconic, indexical and symbolic at the same time. Iconic, because it is a graphical representation of the actual shape of the bend; indexical, owing to its being placed in a physical position (before the bend appears); and symbolic, because it may include conventional elements (such as a red triangle placed around the outside of the sign, symbolising danger).

The realm of **Thirdness**, expressed through the **interpretant**, also generated three signs:

- a '**rheme**', a sign related to the interpretant in the sense of a concept;
- a '**dicent**', which has a factual connection with the interpretant;
- an '**argument**', whose relationship to the interpretant is based on reasoning or logical thought.

Taken together, these nine areas of sign-function are able to generate a vast range of possible combinations; one consequence of Peirce's work is to demonstrate the shortcomings of Saussure's legacy, concentrating as it does on a model of symbolic communication, always at one remove from experience.

Saussure, Barthes and signification

Saussure used a set of terms which have been used extensively by theorists to describe the process of meaning-creation. Saussure imagined the sign, as we have seen, as being composed of two parts: a signifier and a signified. The 'external' meaning created by these two components is called *signification*.

Saussure's lack of interest in both the social context of meaning-creation and the individual user of signs meant that an important area of study was neglected. Meaning is actually produced as the result of a kind of interaction between the reader and the text. In order to explore how this process worked, Roland Barthes invented a system which described the two orders of signification:

- **Signifier** was also described by Barthes as 'meaning' (for example, word).
- **Signified** was also described as 'form' (for example, object).

The first order is called **denotation**, which Fiske (*Introduction to Communication Studies*, p. 91) describes as 'the common sense, obvious meaning of the sign.' For example, a rose is a pretty-looking flower with a strong scent. Fiske uses the example of a photograph of a street which means, at this level, simply an urban road lined with buildings.

The second order is called **connotation**, which we might understand as the associations produced by the denotative order in the mind of the person or persons who interact with the sign. To take an example used by Barthes, a red rose may connote romance, and the presentation of red roses by one person to another may be a specific attempt at signifying romantic affection. However, we know already that connotation changes according to context, and that the traditional signified 'romance' may not be what the gift of roses means in a particular case. Connotation may also change over time, because the red rose may also now signify a political party.

Myth

Used by Barthes, this concept has the status, according to some commentators, of a third level of signification. It emerges at the same level as connotation, or *from* connotation. It works as a chain of related concepts or ideas about something within the culture. According to Fiske (*Introduction to Communication Studies*, p. 93), an example of myth could be,

'... the traditional myth of the British policeman [which] includes concepts of friendliness, reassurance ... non-aggressiveness'

Clearly, myths do not apply in all sections of society. However, if something is to be regarded as a myth, it must be an idea about something which is fairly widespread. This particular 'myth' of the traditional, moderate British policeman does not seem to have applied at the time Fiske was writing, nor does it seem to have a wide circulation at the moment. It does not even have a particular currency inside the police force, where concerns over issues of 'professionalism' or 'service' may dominate the agenda.

Some comments

Connotations are sometimes specific to one culture, beyond which they may fail to be understood. However, certain connotations have been circulated so widely that different cultures are familiar with them. Television and the cinema in particular have made certain signs and symbols universal, probably because they have at the same time created a kind of broad consumer culture that covers most of the world. We might like to think of music as having a universal meaning in terms of its emotional effect on listeners from different cultures. Some anthropologists believe that there are universal or cross-cultural meanings which can be found in body language.

Some criticisms

Something that we ought to be aware of is that the two orders of signification probably happen almost simultaneously in the human mind. Separating the two and holding them apart for purposes of analysis is quite an artificial practice.

In his early writing, Barthes appeared to identify connotation (the second order of signification) as something which 'corrupts' an innocent or natural system, denotation. In doing this, Barthes loaded connotation with a rather negative ideological meaning, although he later went on to change his mind, noting that denotation was not the 'natural' meaning of the sign, but was in fact a kind of 'superior myth' exactly because it 'pretends' to return to a meaning no one can dispute. A simple example will demonstrate this. The obvious meaning of a drawing of a man with a crown on his head is 'king'. This is denotation, pure and simple; it is now exactly the simple meaning of 'king' which is seen to operate as a myth. The *naming* of the person as king, because our society assumes that certain interpretations are 'natural', effectively closes down other possibilities. Connotation, in fact, might be *less* mythological, because different individuals may interpret the drawing not as 'the power of royalty' but as 'an actor dressed as king' or 'a person with delusions of power'. Connotation at least recognises that there are different possible interpretations of a sign. As Jorge Larrain (*The Concept of Ideology*, p. 166) notes:

> 'So ideology is no longer conceived as a connoted level but as the reduction of meaning to only one signification.'

The concern here is less with an idea that ideology is something 'wicked' which hides behind a 'natural-looking' mask. Ideologies may be thought of as a kind of fund from which people pick and choose their discourses – we all know that people sometimes repeat beliefs or ideas which are not even theirs, in order to win arguments. People often pick up the nearest argument to hand, particularly where their own interests are at stake.

One of the major limitations to Saussure is that he studied *words* or *phrases*, rather than the larger structures of discourse which will form part of the concerns of this book. The rather narrow field he explored may have helped to lead semiology into some blind alleys – for example, as mentioned at the start of this section, the tendency to look for highly significant meanings in 'signs' which, as units, are too small to bear the weight of importance placed on them. (The author has heard a description of someone's shoes as a 'text', from which a certain judgment can be made. This interest in detail tends to ignore the larger context – in this case the general appearance of the person's clothes.)

Wittgenstein, by contrast, made the smallest unit of signification not a single element (a pair of shoes), but a combination of elements (in this example it would be a whole set of clothes). It no longer seems sensible to argue that a single word can be taken as an entire sign.

DISCOURSE

Discourse has been variously defined, according to the *uses* writers have in mind for it, and the academic backgrounds from which they come. These are some of the definitions:

1 In linguistics, an utterance of greater size than the sentence.
2 In some literature studies, the utterance of language generally.
3 In some language and structuralist studies, the utterance of a specialised form of language, such as the language of the law. A form, mode, or language genre.
4 In some political and cultural enquiries, discourse is the spoken expression of ideologies, or one of the battlegrounds upon which struggles for power take place. Discourse is not used in order to get at the truth, it is used to achieve a form of power.

The description of discourse as the general use of language is *too wide* a definition to be of much use, and the definition of discourse as a language genre is a dead end. For example, if we wish to find out what the discourse of 'the law' is, we go to a place where we can hear it or read it – a courtroom or an article in a legal journal respectively. Then we can note its form, content and features. Next time we are asked what the discourse of the law is, we can whip out a nice list. So we end up by saying that the discourse of the law is the law's discourse.

Discourse as the expression of ideology

The meaning of discourse that will be pursued here is that defined by the last item above, since, as Goran Therborn says, 'ideology operates through discourse'. Going beyond this position, one can insist (using plurals deliberately) that **ideolo-**

gies are able to operate through discourses. However, it must be acknowledged that they are present in other aspects of life also, such as the physical appearance of things and hierarchical structures. If discourse comes from *speech*, these other forms must be called *expressions* of ideology.

Once ideologies are expressed through language or any other sign-system, they draw upon a range of meanings which are limited or circumscribed by their history of use, as well as by the limitations of the particular system.

The whole point about discourse is that it is a *socially constructed* way of speaking or of representing something, and that, most crucially, it is never completely pure. If it is constructed from the various currents of ideology, then it is the spoken but only partially formed expression of ideologies. Ideology only becomes social through use and expression. A private belief or ideology which remains unexpressed or unspoken is not social. Is there what Foucault called 'a will to power' in the self?

Langue and parole

When Saussure considered how *verbal language* should be investigated, he decided that it should be divided into two aspects, *langue* and *parole*. (We encountered this idea in Chapter 1.)

- **Langue** is the abstract system of rules underlying speech.
- **Parole** is human speech, characterised by Saussure as being infinite and generally arbitrary.

Saussure discarded parole as being an impossible object for systematic study. The priority chosen instead – langue – demonstrates how Saussure cut out major areas of study which are now considered vitally important. There are theorists (for example, Hodge and Kress) who have been through what they call Saussure's 'rubbish bin', following up all the areas he rejected.

Saussure also had contemporary critics. The Russian theorist Voloshinov objected to Saussure's approach, particularly his rejection of the speech act. Voloshinov took issue with Saussure's idea that the speech act is 'individual' and therefore not worthy of close study. According to Voloshinov, 'the utterance is a social phenomenon'. In other words, all 'individual' utterances are in fact born out of and given form by their position as social actions. Accordingly we should certainly *study* individual utterances. All speech acts will carry the traces of their status as social actions. We can study their internal structures and learn something about the *external* factors which have created them. It is also the case that it is useful to study utterances in their wider social and historical context.

Voloshinov spoke of two important influences on meaning: the 'social organization of participants' and the 'immediate conditions of interaction' (see Hodge and Kress, *Social Semiotics*, p. 19) For our purposes, a study of parole would be central to understanding discourse. One reason for Voloshinov's insistence on looking at the 'social origin' of the speech act is that he saw society as based on struggle and conflict between groups and classes, whose relations were therefore being constantly *renegotiated*. (This idea will be helpful when we come to examine the question of 'audience', particularly when we investigate whether ideology can truly be understood as consisting of **dominant**, **negotiated** and **oppositional** positions.)

The theorist Bakhtin (*see* Crowley, *The Politics of Discourse*, p. 4) supported this view of the social origin of speech:

> '... verbal discourse is a social phenomenon – social throughout its entire range and in each and every one of its factors, from the sound image to the furthest reaches of abstract meaning.'

We should be able to see now that Voloshinov's disagreement with the Saussurean system was based upon the idea that it was responsible for creating a kind of static, once-and-for-all meaning of the sign or utterance (*Social Semiotics*, p. 6): 'isolated, finished ... divorced from its verbal and actual context'.

Traffic lights: semiology

At this point, it might be worth reinforcing the following points: that meaning is not fixed; that it is social; that it should be understood in its context.

If we want a useful example of how 'actual' **context** (i.e. the immediate social context) gives us a real insight into what is actually happening in a system of signs, we could begin with Hodge and Kress's reworking of Leach's 'traffic lights'. This demonstration was originally (1974) supposed to show the semiotic relationship between the three colours used in the regulation of traffic. So it is really taken from studies of semiology rather than discourse.

Leach's idea was simple – what could be more straightforward than a study of only three elements? There would be an uncomplicated relationship between these basic signifiers: red, green, amber and their obvious *signifieds*: stop, go and get ready to stop/go.

Hodge and Kress (*Social Semiotics*, p. 38) explain that the signifiers are actually rather more precise, with **red** for example meaning 'motorists, stop'. They go on to explain that there are whole groups of individuals who read the **amber** light not as a signal to get ready to stop/go, but *as a signal to speed up and get through the lights before they turn to red*. Of course, such groups understand very well the precise meaning of the conventional/official intention of the light. The specific context here is both physical (according to Hodge and Kress, traffic in a major Australian city) and an organisation of participants (drivers, whichever way they choose to interpret the signals). The original, non-specific and apparently 'universal' semiology of the traffic light is shown to be an inadequate treatment of the subject, precisely because it ignores human subjects and the social context.

'Recently times have been hard for everyone': discourse

The following example is used to show how social context can be important in judging the precise meaning of an utterance. This example is hypothetical and designed to show points about discourse as a study.

A newspaper editor calls together the whole workforce of the newspaper:

> 'I am sorry that this meeting has been called at short notice. I know you are all extremely

busy, but you know also that it is has always been my policy to remain in close personal touch with all employees on the paper. As you probably appreciate, recently times have been hard for everyone. The management have had to look again at the finances of the operation. The news is not the best we might have hoped for, but it is certainly not as bad as it might have been, had we not been prudent and had such a forward-looking and reliable group of senior managers. We intend to widen our programme of generous settlements for those colleagues who wish to take up early retirement, and in addition have had seriously to re-examine the question of other forms of voluntary redundancy . . .'

When the editor (notice in this case that he/she is not the owner, the actual employer) begins to speak of 'voluntary redundancies', then the *social organisation* of all the people in that situation and the *immediate conditions of interaction* will affect meaning. The fact that the employees are the receivers of the message and the editor is, at least to start with, the sender; the fact that the editor's words are uninterrupted; the fact the editor probably wants to make a general address to the workforce but wants only individual and private responses to the offer, all show that the power of the editor is that of initiating change in the immediate situation. If, instead of the situation described above, there were a different meeting, where the editor offers the workers voluntary redundancy in the middle of a more severe recession, then the immediate conditions of the interaction (the context) might lead the workforce to see their response to the 'offer' (however widely it applied) as considerably less 'voluntary' than would be the case in a milder economic climate.

It may be useful to remember that the content, sequence and intonation of the employer's utterance may be *identical* in both situations, with exactly the same people present in the same building. It is the wider social environment which has changed (not the immediate social context) and which has caused the balance of power between the two sides to alter.

There seems to be agreement between Voloshinov and Foucault that the present distribution of discourse in society is unequal and hierarchical. Voloshinov (*The Politics of Discourse*, p. 4) pointed to the 'powerful influence ... exerted on forms of utterance by the hierarchical organisation of communication.'

In hierarchical organisation, certain types of utterance are 'appropriate' – step beyond the bounds, and the utterances one uses will be classified as irrelevant.

Class and language

We should be careful, however, not to assume from the example given above that the subordinate groups are therefore unable to reply on their own behalf. It is certainly true that once the 'discursive agenda' has been set by one group, or by one individual, or by wider social and economic circumstances, then the subordinated group will find it difficult to reply effectively to the dominant group. Why? For the reason that they will find it hard to set up *new* terms of reference for the discussion. The terms of reference for the discussion about the future of the workforce are set by external factors (recession) and the power of the newspaper magnates to translate this situation into the sacking of employees.

Some Marxists have insisted that the ideologies of the subordinate (their 'replies' to the powerful) are always formed in the language and logic of the dominant group in society. While this may be an overstatement, nevertheless the idea that the underdog often uses the language and the logic of the ruling class is obvious enough. However, we know also that it is possible to arrive at a number of different meanings in any situation which involves argument and debate.

Where do alternative discourses come from? How are people able to use an approach which depends on a different outlook?

It might be possible for the workforce in the example above to produce an entirely different plan in response to the external situation, which could involve *questioning the whole basis of the redundancies*. The workers might suggest that the whole workforce takes a pay cut, instead of accepting outright job losses (a challenge which still leaves intact the logic of the employee paying the price for recession). The workers may suggest that the management cut out all their own perks and take a pay-cut themselves (a challenge to the logic which makes the workers suffer). The only challenge the workforce cannot make, without attacking the logic of the way the whole of society is organised, is to the wider external situation.

Tony Crowley (*The Politics of Discourse*, p. 4) describes how Voloshinov demonstrates that classes (and we might say ages, genders, ethnicities) use more or less the same language, but give importance to different aspects of it:

'... given the conflictual nature of social relations, those classes will accentuate the signs of the language in different ways and thus the signs become multiaccentual and sites of conflicts in themselves.'

In other words, we have a language whose precise meanings are fought over, resulting in individual signs coming to mean more than one thing. When an employer tells his/her workforce to behave in a professional way, the employees might take issue with the meaning of the term 'professional'. But there are what may be called residual 'contaminants' in the language, in the term 'professional' which the workers and the boss cannot avoid. Ideology is not pure, and it follows that the discourses used to express it are not pure either. The author disagrees, however, with Voloshinov's idea that the ruling class tries to make signs 'eternal' and uniaccentual. In the author's view, the process of reproducing society as it is, 'stratified', for example, through class and gender, happens by virtue of the availability of different meanings, and that the most effective forms of authority are able to accept and use the range of alternative meanings which are already present in the use of the sign. This whole approach ties in closely with Tetzlaff's ideas about the diversity of culture, outlined in Chapter 1. If someone in authority has to rule others through the use of language, that language had better not be too restrictive.

On the skateboard?

We could think of ideology as being 'carried' by discourse. The trouble is, that discourse can often have a life of its own. The original ideology can be thought of as a figure which has jumped on a skateboard (the discourse). Sometimes the external forces of the social (an unexpected bend in the road) will mean that the board will need sudden adjustments to new circumstances. Sometimes, the discourse will not be able to bear the weight of the ideology. At other times, the board (the discourse) will be the wrong choice for the circumstances, and the whole of the expected movement will fail to materialise.

Expression and utterance

There are many ways of thinking about the question of ideology and its alteration in expression and utterance. For Voloshinov, 'multiaccentuality' is what maintains the virility and dynamism of the sign and gives it the capacity for further development. We can see the creation of new meanings out of old ones by examining the speech of youth in every generation; in one development, 'bad' means 'good', 'wicked' means 'excellent', and 'excellent' becomes an understatement.

THE CONCEPT OF PERSUASION

Some theorists distinguish 'persuasion' from cases of 'manipulation' by stating that in genuine instances of persuasion, the persuader 'acts in good faith' (*see* O'Keefe, *Persuasion: Theory and Research*, pp. 14-16). Manipulation may correspondingly be defined as 'managing a person by unfair influence.' Much of the debate about advertising (addressed in Chapter 3) turns on whether it is seen as persuasion or manipulation.

It is difficult to find a definition of persuasion which will satisfy all those interested in its meaning. Simons (1976) defines persuasion as 'human communication designed to influence others by modifying their beliefs, values or attitudes'. One way of approaching the problem of definition is to find a group of straightforward and uncontroversial examples which illustrate the concept. This method may be successful to start with, but it will not solve the problems of those examples which cause disagreement.

Persuasion implies a successful action

O'Keefe, in *Persuasion: Theory and Research* (pp. 14–16), notes that, 'when we say that one person has persuaded another, we ordinarily identify a *successful* attempt to influence.' It seems to be true that a notion of success is embedded in the concept of persuasion. As O'Keefe notes, 'it doesn't make sense to say "I persuaded him but failed." It does, however, make sense to say "I *tried* to persuade him but failed."'

The next point to make is that the persuader had some intention of achieving the particular goal. A further point to examine in paradigm cases of persuasion is the idea that there is some measure of free choice on the persuadee's part.

O'Keefe cites the example of 'a person knocked unconscious by a robber, who then takes the victim's money ... one would not say that the victim had been "persuaded" to give the money.' This contrasts with the idea of making charitable donations as the result of being persuaded by a TV advertisement.

Persuasion and force

Where the persuadee's freedom is minimised or questionable, then it becomes difficult to decide whether persuasion is genuinely involved. If someone hints at dire consequences if a charitable donation is not produced, then this is no longer a straightforward case. Is it possible that we need a definition which comes some way between persuasion and force, such as 'coercive persuasion'?

Persuasion and communication

One important way of understanding the issue is to realise that cases of persuasion are ones in which the effects are achieved through communication. As O'Keefe points out, throwing a person from a rooftop is quite different from talking the person into jumping off. Communication is not involved in the first case. What I would call 'manipulative persuasion' is involved in the second.

An interesting idea is that persuasion involves a change in the mental state of the persuadee. Before a person's behaviour changes (if it does), there is usually presumed to be some underlying change in their mental state. In the kind of case we will pursue, we could say that the electorate might change their minds about a certain political candidate. It is still possible that no change in action will result from the change in opinion; for various reasons, people may vote the same way as before. The point in elections is to persuade voters to alter their actions only where it suits the political party concerned. The type of mental state in this kind of study has been identified as *attitude*.

The definition of persuasion offered by O'Keefe (*Persuasion: Theory and Research*, p. 17) is:

'... a successful intentional effort at influencing another's mental state through communication in a circumstance in which the persuadee has some measure of freedom.'

Which leaves us with the question – what is it in human beings that needs to be influenced?

Attitudes, values and beliefs

These three attributes of the human personality have been variously described, but the following definitions, adapted from O'Keefe (*Persuasion: Theory and Research*) and Myers and Myers (*The Dynamics of Human Communication*), draw together the areas of agreement.

ATTITUDES

An attitude is best described as a person's general evaluation of an 'object', a person or people, an event, an incident, a commodity, an institution. Evaluation here means 'judgment about' or 'reaction to' something. Attitudes are supposed to be learned. As new learning occurs, so new attitudes may appear. Attitudes are supposed to be relatively enduring, and are not the same as temporary states such as moods. Attitudes are also supposed to affect the way that we behave.

VALUES

These are ideas about the relative worth of things and the nature of good and bad. Values often 'cluster together' to form systems of belief. Values tell people how far they may go, how they may behave and so on. Values tend to be applied to things, rather than being in the nature of things. The naming of things in language also confers values upon them. Values 'grow out of a complex interaction between basic needs and the specificity of a given environment' (Myers and Myers, p. 93). Things which are valued in one society may not be valued in another. An interesting situation arises when values of an individual or the varying values of a group contradict one another – the individual or group may then have to decide which values are most important to them (and there are lots of people around who are willing to help them 'choose').

BELIEFS

Beliefs generally express a perceived link between two aspects of a person's world. Beliefs operate as thoughts or statements about the relative truth or falsehood of a thing. Some beliefs are central to a person, whilst others are less important. 'Central' beliefs are those which are positioned in such a way that any movement of, or activation of these beliefs, will have an effect on other beliefs. Some beliefs are 'fundamental', such as belief in the material existence of certain objects. Some commentators believe that fundamental beliefs include things taught to us as children. Disruption of fundamental beliefs can cause the human subject extreme distress.

Rhetoric and persuasion

The ability to speak well, to present a good case to a group of one's peers, to influence an audience, has long been regarded as a useful skill – useful, but perhaps also dangerous. Good orators (skilful and practised public speakers) are often admired, but are rarely completely trusted.

It is worth noting that no society has ever been able to exist through coercion alone. Every expansionist society has needed a class of public orators as much as it has required the services of a military force. Soldiers are sent into battle with some form of loyalty – if not to their country, then to the men around them, or to the families they have left behind. Armies made up of mercenaries have been very effective, but soldiers who go into battle without belief or attachment to anything are unlikely to fight well.

The Homeric ideal

In the verse of the ancient poet Homer, the roles of fighter and orator are often merged in the character of the hero. The hero earns respect as much for his ability to pass on inspiration through speech, as for his ability to lead by example. (We have, of course, ceased to live in a society where leaders are expected to perform both functions. Neil Kinnock's remark after the Falklands War, that Margaret Thatcher certainly had guts but that it was a pity that British soldiers had 'had to spill theirs on Goose Green to prove it', is an interesting comment on the separation between the role of leader and the roles assigned to those who must perform the leader's will.)

Homeric oratory appears as a spontaneous and impassioned response to the circumstances of siege, battle, individual challenge and internal argument within the armed camps. We can see, however, that there were elements of structure in the speeches made by the heroes. Stock topics and certain formulaic phrases mark what they say.

Homeric speeches are notable for their appeal to the emotions. In *Greek Orators 1*, Edwards and Usher make clear a connection between the form of such speeches and the type of society the heroes were thought to inhabit (p. 5):

> '... autocratic leaders ... were not mentally conditioned to use reasoned argument when their primary purpose was simply to make their decisions known to their subjects and to call upon them to carry them out.'.

With the development of the limited democracy of fifth-century Athens, political conditions became more favourable to the development of a persuasive model of rhetoric and public speech. Obviously, if the citizens had to make a range of decisions which had previously been reserved to monarchs and dictators, their new leaders would wish to make their public arguments as effective as possible. They were 'obliged to persuade the people to adopt their policies' (p. 6). Not all the 'people' were citizens, however. Slaves had no political rights and even free women were by and large excluded from the public domain.

Rhetoric as a study

The study of rhetoric as a distinct subject began in Ancient Greece but, as with most public skills, it was turned to a variety of uses. The ability to sway an audience could obviously bring all kinds of benefits to the speaker; it should come as no surprise to learn that schools of rhetoric flourished. This use of the manipulative power of public discourse was criticised by philosophers like Plato, who considered that rhetoric should be allied with a scrupulous moral purpose.

PROPAGANDA

There are three areas to consider at this stage:

1 how propaganda should be defined;
2 how it differs from persuasion;
3 how it uses people's attitudes, beliefs, and values in the process of attaining its goals.

Definition of propaganda

In studies of communication, when the 'message' is used to promote a mutually beneficial outcome, then we may describe a 'convergence process', where the sender and receiver move closer together. In Chapter 1 we wondered whether or not, by this definition, the mass media were truly communicative. Information helps those who receive it to learn more and advance further in their understanding of their environment. One of the important features of propaganda is that it attempts to disguise itself as informative communication. The point here is that the receiver may consider that he or she is being provided with reliable information for the purposes of understanding a situation. In fact, they may be given information by the propagandist for quite different reasons.

In *Propaganda and Persuasion*, Jowett and O'Donnell describe propaganda as:

> '. . . the deliberate and systematic attempt to shape perceptions, manipulate cognitions, and direct behaviour to achieve a response that furthers the desired intent of the propagandist.'

By 'perceptions' we mean how people see and interpret things in their environment. 'Cognitions' may be defined as individual understandings of the social world.

Propaganda is not necessarily based on a series of lies. Propaganda can use the truth. Imagine for the moment that the propagandist uses the whole truth and delivers this to an audience. How on earth could this be considered to be manipulative or propagandist? The method by which the truth is told, the scale on which it is reported, and the exact timing of the reporting of this truth, may all contribute to the overall status of the message as propaganda.

Method, scale and timing

The method used to disseminate, for example, news of a minor victory in war may be crucial. If the news is sent out by the authorities to all major cities on a single sheet of paper, with the instruction to spread the news by word of mouth, then we see immediately that the impact of the news may be quite modest. If, on the other hand, all the resources of the mass media are used to circulate the information, we may see that the possible scale of the communication method used may have propaganda value in itself. However, under certain circumstances, huge rallies which use the power of mass psychology may achieve a more concentrated power than a report on the radio. If the report of the event is carefully *timed*, for example to coincide with other encouraging news, then its value as propaganda may be increased.

The same criteria may apply to discouraging news; it may be released using a minor method, possibly on a smaller scale, or perhaps may be delayed until it can be offset by more positive information.

Propaganda can be 'the truth', 'the whole truth' and 'nothing like the truth', separately or in any combination. Propaganda is about intervening in the way people make up their minds.

Propaganda and persuasion

Jowlett and O'Donnell (*Propaganda and Persuasion*, p. 13) distinguish propaganda and persuasion in the following way:

'Propaganda is a form of communication that is different from persuasion because it attempts to achieve a response that furthers the desired intent of the propagandist ... Persuasion is interactive and attempts to satisfy the needs of both persuader and persuadee.'

Of course, it seems obvious that propaganda might use persuasion, not out of any respect for the human subject, but because persuasion is effective as a device.

As we have seen propaganda may be used on a different scale (e.g. through the mass media), and its method may differ in some ways from the interpersonal ideal of persuasive interaction. Some theorists might say that its method, scale and intention are always different, but we need only to remember the way that the early Christians scratched the symbol of Christ (a fish) in the dust where travellers might pass by, or the way in which German anti-fascists scrawled criticisms of Hitler on walls during the Nazi era, to realise that propaganda is not entirely defined by a particular method or scale.

Propaganda is characterised by the fact that it is a deliberate attempt to influence the outcome of some event or to influence belief; the attempt is made in order to 'alter or maintain a balance of power that is advantageous to the propagandist' (*Propaganda and Persuasion*, p. 15). This does not mean that the propagandist will always be successful. The propagandist can only express his/her intention through the available discourses. The whole attempt to change belief has to be built on beliefs which the audience already holds.

It would perhaps be more accurate to say that propaganda is the conscious use of a particular discourse (one which may be decoded the wrong way) which will connect with the attitudes, values and beliefs of the audience, in order to further the intentions of the propagandist. What is interesting from our point of view is what happens when the mass media passes on propaganda which originates from another source. What role does the mass media play in shaping the message? This problem will be addressed when we look at an example of discourse from the coverage of the 1992 general election.

Propaganda in war

A MORAL DILEMMA: DUNKIRK

When the German army seemed poised to destroy the British Expeditionary Force and its French allies in 1940, it was clear that Britain faced what Churchill described at the time as 'a military disaster'. The only possible way of dealing with the defeat at Dunkirk was to represent the events in a different light.

The whole issue of propaganda during the struggle against the Axis powers is an indicator of how far nations are prepared to accept propaganda when faced with dire emergencies. The question to be asked is whether, if the British population had known the truth about the extent of the disaster, the result would have been a general collapse in morale.

It seems clear that the German forces understood the extent of the British defeat. There was, in this case, no point in attempting to fool the enemy, which is a reason advanced so often for the use of misleading information. The British authorities clearly had two other audiences in mind: the American nation, and the population of their own country.

There were no British correspondents on the beaches of Dunkirk. Yet, upon the evacuation of the soldiers, tales of heroism abounded: British officers bringing order to panicking French troops; a cricket match being played during a bombing run by Stukas; a wounded sailor digging shrapnel from his arm with a knife. In fact, there were plenty of tales of bravery to report. The foremost was probably the sacrifice made by those units detailed to defend the Dunkirk perimeter so that the bulk of the forces could escape.

The evacuation of Dunkirk itself was a remarkable story which was circulated widely and deserved the emphasis put upon it. However, the complete demoralisation of some units travelling through the Kent countryside was attested to by a police inspector on a rural station platform, who saw troops hurling their rifles from the windows of their train.

What should the British government and media have reported? Is there any proof that the circulation of selected 'myths' about Dunkirk helped morale? Would the circulation of the absolute truth, good and bad, have resulted in any damage at all to the British war effort?

REJOICE? THE FALKLANDS WAR

When the British Cabinet decided to send a task force to the Falkland Islands in 1982 (while discreet negotiations between Britain and Argentina were still in progress), the Royal Navy made the decision that no journalists would be permitted to accompany the expedition. Following advice from the Ministry of Defence, some reporters were allowed to travel south with the hastily-assembled task force. The figure was at first limited to six, then increased to ten. Eventually, twenty-eight reporters covered the conflict, all of them men.

The war which followed was remarkable in several respects. There was, for example, the touch-and-go nature of the British victory. (The loss of most of their helicopters meant that troops had to march overland before launching their attacks.) Most significant from our point of view, however, was the long delay between British operations and the extremely sketchy news of them which followed, several weeks later. In 1805, news of Nelson's death at Trafalgar had reached these shores in a shorter space of time than it took some reports from the Falklands to appear, despite the electronic communication supposedly at the disposal of modern reporters.

TECHNOLOGY OR CENSORSHIP?

The first point to note is that instant communication of news about the conflict (which was probably what the British public had expected) simply did not take place. This made the issue of censorship immediately obvious. The question of censorship by omission would probably not have been as noticeable had there been a little more television news footage available.

Technology played a role in ensuring that the public was left with late, incomplete and over-simplified news. Newspaper readers were treated to line drawings of soldiers in action, in appearance exactly like the contents of a war comic.

The military was not prepared to interrupt its satellite communications to provide a service for television news, and the other alternative, the use of the American DISCUS satellite, was not pursued because the British Government did not make a sufficiently high-level approach to the US authorities. In effect, the use of rather primitive communication methods, combined with the distance at which operations took place (footage was sent back to London by ship), meant military censorship was made much easier. Speaking shortly after the war (*see Gotcha! The Media, the Government and the Falklands* crisis, p. 59), the Permanent Under-Secretary at the Ministry of Defence, Sir Frank Cooper, said:

> '... if we had had transmission of television throughout, the problems of what could or could not be released would have been very severe indeed ... the criticism we have had is a small drop in the ocean compared to the problems we would have had in dealing with the television coverage.'

DIRECT CENSORSHIP: THE LESSONS OF VIETNAM?

Senior naval and army officers, viewing BBC news footage before it was released to the public on television, told the broadcasters (p. 60):

> '... not to use a picture of a body in a bag, not to use the phrase "horribly burned", not to show a pilot confess, jokingly, that he had been "scared fartless" on one mission.'

It seems to have been the memory of the detailed and exhaustive TV coverage of the Vietnam war which constantly troubled the military during the Falklands conflict. There was a widespread belief that the spectacle of the Vietnam war being 'fought in the living rooms of America' had somehow led to public disgust with the war and, as a result, to the Americans' eventual withdrawal from South East Asia.

In fact, surveys taken amongst viewers at the time found that these effects were not as 'anti-war' as they are now imagined to be. In 1967, a *Newsweek* survey found that TV coverage made 64 per cent of viewers feel more determined to 'back up the boys in Vietnam' (notice that the pro-war sentiment is always explained as support for 'our boys', rather than for war itself). Twenty-six per cent said it made them feel more hostile to the war. By the time of another *Newsweek* survey in 1972, viewers were, if anything, becoming indifferent to the war.

The fear of some in the armed forces that television coverage was capable of losing a war led to direct censorship. Patrick Bishop, an *Observer* reporter, wrote an article which repeated survivors' accounts of the loss of the British ship *Sir Galahad*. He handed it to a Ministry of Defence press officer for transmission:

> '... when I saw him again five days later ... he told me that it hadn't been sent. The

piece contained "inaccuracies"... The suppression of the piece was a simple act of censorship because it was felt the article might lower morale.'

(Rejoice!, Greenberg and Smith, pp. 12–13)

COLOUR RADIO? THE GULF WAR

Introducing a public meeting on television's coverage of the Gulf war, Sheena MacDonald (presenter of Channel 4's *This Week*) said, 'Who could have thought television could be so thrilling?' (*Free Press*, p. 2). The impression gained by many television viewers, however, was of a limited series of images, repeated time and again and supplemented by studio debates which were forced to be largely speculative because hard information was not available.

Two weeks into the conflict, the majority opinion among students taught by the author was that the Gulf war was boring and they had had enough of it. Should television viewers accept that they are unlikely, at certain times (such as during wars), to receive anything useful from their chosen medium? The London correspondent of CNN, Richard Blystone, made his opinion clear (*Free Press*) when he said:

'If you go to TV for your only news, then you're lazy.
If you go to TV for the truth, then you're a loony.'

CENSORSHIP FROM THE WORD GO

David Mannion, the editor responsible for all of ITN's programmes on ITV, was frank about the general practice followed in reporting the Gulf war (*Free Press*, p. 1):

'In Iraq, in Baghdad we said reports were subject to Iraqi censorship ... we thought it ritht, even when they were not censored, to let the viewers know we were working under those particular conditions. In Israel where reports were censored, we said they were censored. In Saudi Arabia, where we had to leave out certain details for operational reasons, we said just that – we had to leave out those details for operational reasons.'

One of the lessons applied from previous conflicts was the idea that (in the words of *New York Times* correspondent Malcolm Brown) 'the entire environment' could be controlled. The military authorities had decided to operate a 'pool' system of correspondents. The pool worked on the basis that the authorities would give controlled access to certain areas of the war zone to recognised groups of journalists; this is basically the system mentioned earlier, where a propagandist chooses the place and time of the reception of the message, except that here it is a case of control at source, at the point at which the message is created.

THE TYRANNY OF THE IMAGE?

Another feature of the Gulf war, besides the practice of leading journalists to their stories, was the provision by the military of their own war footage. A prime example would be the way that the Pentagaon released its 'video war' pictures of 'smart bombs' striking their targets. It seems that when they are given a privileged

Daily Mail

MONDAY, FEBRUARY 25, 1991   28p

The Caring Duchess . . . a fascinating new royal series starts on page 29

Allies pour into Kuwait as 5,500 Iraqis surrender

OUR TROOPS ARE DOING A GREAT JOB

Schwarzkopf: Delighted

From GEOFFREY LEVY in Saudi Arabia

THE Allies were on the brink of liberating Kuwait City from the murderous grip of Saddam Hussein last night.

Ground forces from ten nations were thrusting into the devastated emirate and southern Iraq to rout the dictator's army.

A delighted Allied commander General Norman Schwarzkopf said: 'So far, the

Mailman DAVID WILLIAMS reports from inside Kuwait — Pages TWO and THREE

offensive is progressing with dramatic success. The troops are doing a great job.'

The first day of the ground battle saw U.S. paratroopers dropping outside Kuwait City, later to be reinforced by units from the south and west — bringing hopes that the Iraqis would be cleared out within days.

In a separate thrust, Britain's Desert Rats of the 1st Armoured Division roared across Saudi Arabia's border with Iraq and were said to be speeding north in enemy territory.

Defence Secretary Tom King said British forces had sustained casualties but they were 'remarkably light'. One report last night said that 11 Allied soldiers had been killed in the initial operations.

The lack of Iraqi opposition produced elation but brought a word of caution from an otherwise ebullient General Schwarzkopf. 'I would not be honest with you if I didn't remind you that this is the very early stages,' he said. 'The war's not over yet.'

When asked whether he was trying to go

around the Iraqis, he replied: 'We're going to go around, over, through, on top, underneath and any other way it takes to beat them.'

He reported 5,500 prisoners taken and hundreds more Iraqis waving white flags at advancing forces.

As the biggest land offensive since World

War II began, Saddam's much-vaunted frontline defences were swept away like seaside sandcastles.

President Bush, after attending church, was making hourly visits to the White House operations room for briefings from the front.

Iraq claimed the offensive was a failure

and denied Allied reports about the PoWs.

The Allied units, which also included Arab contingents from Syria, Kuwait, Saudi, the Emirates, Bahrain, Qatar and Oman, surprised themselves by the speed

Turn to Page 3, Col 1

Demoralised Iraqi soldiers are captured as the Allied advance sweeps through Saddam's defences

INSIDE: Weather 2, Keith Waterhouse 8, Femail 18, Dempster's Diary 23, TV and Radio 26-28, Letters 33, Coffee Break 34, Money Mail 37-40, Sport 43-48

Fig 2.1 Propaganda in war?
(Courtesy of Mail Newspapers/Solo Syndication and Literary Agency Ltd)

glimpse of actual conditions, the mass media are pleased enough to want to repeat the images as often as possible on the small screen. Not until after the war was it revealed that only some 7 per cent of all the ordnance dropped by the US coalition forces had been 'smart' – the rest had been delivered by more conventional methods.

Had there been a triumph of communication technology over content? Had the role of the media become that of a mouthpiece for the State?

Propaganda and news values

It would seem that, in the examples of the Falklands war and more particularly the Gulf war, the propagandist role had been taken on by the State. The mass media were provided with the time and the place and the upshot was that they had little room to manoeuvre. If they wanted to be there, they had largely to operate under conditions beyond their control. I would argue that it is the everyday news values of the mass media which leads them, in extraordinary circumstances, into easy compliance with the authorities.

Public relations and propaganda

It was not only the state which was responsible for attempts to sway public opinion. In 1990 an American PR firm, Hill and Knowlton, distributed a collection of images of Kuwait to all major US networks. This formed part of a multi-million dollar campaign to create an identity for Kuwait and to build support for military action in the Gulf. One of the founder members of the organisation 'Citizens for a Free Kuwait', Fawzi Al-Sultan, was an executive director of the World Bank. The Chief Executive of Hill and Knowlton, Graig Fuller, had been a chief of staff to George Bush when Bush was Vice-President. The lines of communication between the American administration and the Kuwaiti 'Citizens' was the private PR firm. Hill and Knowlton did not have to fight for the attention of the American government. As Fuller explained in a television programme on Kuwait:

> 'As the Kuwaitis were talking to us, we were talking to people in the Administration to find out how we could be more supportive to the President's programme.'

ELECTIONS: PROPAGANDA IN PEACE?

In a society where there is formal democracy, effective propaganda has to use persuasion to achieve its desired results. In a dictatorship, or under conditions such as war which may allow those in authority to use compulsion, it is easier for those in power to 'sell' a particular idea because, in the long run, force can always be used. In those circumstances, the population knows that the threat of force or compulsion lies behind the simplest message.

The point of studying belief and *expressions* of belief in either situation, peace or war, is to find out how people **re-present** their beliefs. The propagandist or 'persuader' is never completely free to do exactly what he/she desires. A lot depends on the **intention** these people have, the **context** they find themselves in, and the ideas, phrases, and words they have at their disposal. It remains the case, however, that even under the most favourable conditions, an audience may still fail to respond in the desired manner.

With their eyes on the goal of power, politicians (at least those who work under the discipline of an agreed ideology during the time of the election) will attempt to tailor their message for the audiences they wish to attract. When a propagandist changes the exact form or content of what he/she believes in order to sway an audience, this bears a strong resemblance to the way that we are all forced to adapt what we wish to say, according to the circumstances in which we find ourselves. It is clear that we all communicate with some aim in mind, even if that aim is not particularly sinister.

In party election broadcasts and interviews which involve a direct address 'to camera', politicians take great pains to speak to their audiences as convincingly as possible. They are forced to use a broadly acceptable form of political discourse, in which certain **forms** of address will be more acceptable than others, and in which certain types of **content** must be used (just as other types of content may be safely ignored). Although, as I have remarked, a politician will attempt to tailor a message for an audience, the politician will also find that their intended message is shaped by factors largely beyond their control. The influence of the mass media must be one of the factors that politicians take into account.

Mediation of the message

When we begin to consider the role of the mass media, we are forced to look into the question of **mediation**, or how the media affects the original message offered by the 'sender'. What makes our study a bit more complicated is that politicians (as 'senders') try to take account of the mediation from the first moment the message is thought up. This does not just mean that politicians think carefully about what messages to send, but also that they think very carefully how messages ought to be framed in the first place. This is precisely what we mean when we talk about form and content.

Context and intention

At this point, because it suits our main purpose of examining the ideological dimension of discourse, it is worth returning to the straightforward distinction made earlier between context and intention. **Context** (the situation and the accepted ways of behaving in that situation) can affect the **intention** of an individual, just as the intention someone brings to a situation can affect the context. For example, if the context of a situation is a fairly private conversation, then a politician (to take an example relevant to this chapter) may be prepared to reveal more about an issue than if the context is a television interview seen by large numbers of people. His/her intention will be partly shaped by the situation. The form given by any speaker to their message will also be affected by the discourses which are actually available and which will be recognised by an audience.

Available discourses

How a party political message is to be structured will be constrained by the choice of discourses *available*, which really means working out, as I have said, which types of discourse will be easily understood and easily recognised. Adapting for a moment Stephen Neale's observations on audience and film, a party will have to take into account the 'foreknowledge and expectation' of its audience. There may be a problem if a party has a policy so new, or so 'extreme', that an audience is likely to react very negatively to the whole idea. The obvious response is to frame what is said in a recognised and trusted form. For example, part of the whole problem with the poll tax was the fact that it broke with established conventions about how to raise tax – it was perceived as a 'throw-back' to the Middle Ages. Ministers were then forced to make statements in its defence based on the idea that it was fair to expect all adults to make a contribution, or that the tax should be supported because the previous system had needed reform.

Of course, no party presents all its beliefs in the exact form that might be revealed to someone who happened to eavesdrop on a closed meeting; each party has to modify or re-emphasise certain aspects of its core beliefs in order to appeal to the attitudes, values and beliefs of its target audience. The party must 'speak' publicly. This means making a choice about what to say and how to say it. Just 'thinking aloud' on a subject can have disastrous consequences, as politicians have discovered in the past. (Figure 2.4 shows the way in which the expression of a particular belief is modified, and then interpreted by the media).

In the case of a television interview, where there may not be a chance to speak to an audience 'directly', a certain framework will be imposed on the politician. At another level, a certain *type* of programme will bring its own point of view into play, and within this situation a particular *interviewer* will bring yet another contextual pressure to bear.

Language, context, rules and norms: choices and pressures

The linguist Hymes describes four interrelated dimensions which will affect what may be said in any personal or public situation:

1 The **linguistic resources** available to a speaker – these would include different styles of speech. There are established styles in conversation and address, styles which are used generally in society.
2 **Supra-sentential structuring** – the various and differently structured linguistic events in the society – trials, religious ceremonies, debates, songs and so on. In a televised political interview, the interview itself and its status as a mass media event will provide a large structure or context for what is said.
3 The **rules of interpretation** by which an interaction or speech comes to have a certain communicative value.

PAGE 4   DAILY MIRROR, Wednesday, March 25, 1992

Health Secretary who never apologised

WHY WALDEGRAVE

COBBLERS CORNER

● TODAY we launch a new service — exposing Tory tabloid lies.

● Hysterical reports yesterday claimed Labour would impose mortgage queues for millions. The Sun, Star, Mail and Express claimed they were reporting remarks by Neil Kinnock.

● In fact, Mr Kinnock said Labour plans to control runaway credit would avert sky-high mortgages and there was no reason to believe there would be queues.

● He was backed yesterday by Britain's biggest building society, the Halifax.

Plenty of cash for loans say Halifax

By NEIL SIMPSON

THERE will be no queues for home loans under Labour, the head of Britain's biggest building society said yesterday.

Chairman Jon Foulds nailed Tory lies by revealing the society has no shortage of funds.

And the slump the Government created is so great, most folk can't afford to buy anyway.

The Halifax also revealed how badly the Tories handled the economy in 1991.

And they hit out at tight-fisted policies which have forced 390 families out of their homes every day.

"If the Government would agree to pay into mortgage rescue schemes, we could help more folk stay in their homes," said a spokesman.

Jobs

"But the Government have refused to put any money on the table."

Mr Foulds also hit out at mean Tory rules which give housing benefit to tenants on low incomes but nothing to desperate borrowers who lose their jobs. "We think this is wrong," he said.

"We have joined forces with the Council of Mortgage Lenders to try to persuade the Government to change the rules."

Foulds agreed ALL new economic statistics - on employment, output and trade - are bad.

And he admitted that Labour's "good housekeeping" plans to limit the amount people can borrow won't affect first-time buyers.

TROUBLED

HEALTH SECRETARY William Waldegrave lied his head off yesterday as he launched a savage radio attack on the Daily Mirror.

He told millions of listeners the Mirror's stories on the crumbling NHS were false.

He FAILED to give a single example to back up his smear.

And he FAILED to check his facts on true Mirror stories about tragic victims like little Carly Reavill.

But he did let slip the real reason why the Tories are so rattled by our reports. He admitted they were stories that "stick in the mind."

Mr Waldegrave made his outburst on Radio 2's Jimmy Young programme.

Ignore

He was challenged by Jimmy over revelations in yesterday's Mirror that he wrote to regional newspapers urging them to ignore our coverage of health issues in the crucial run-up to the election.

He admitted sending the letters. But he claimed:

"The dear old Daily Mirror are wide of the mark, which they usually are on health matters.

I wrote to every news editor some weeks ago to warn people that many of the individual heart-rending cases we see must be treated with very great care.

The great majority of them, when you analyse them, and when independent journalists analyse them, turn out to be false."

THE TRUTH

John Major yesterday uttered a word from a Tory slogan that sums him up perfectly

He tries to smear Mirror over 'stories that stick in the mind'

By JILL PALMER
Medical Correspondent

The Mirror has been a great purveyor of these

And when you have a heart-rending story that sticks in the mind.

So I was begging people. 'Do your own research' — don't take it that the individual cases which are given to you, either by the Mirror or by the Labour Party, or anybody else for that matter.

On the same programme, Labour's health spokesman Robin Cook said it was "perfectly proper" to expose the Tories' cash squeeze on the NHS.

Source

And he added that the source of cases highlighted by Labour was invariably a patient, or a patient's relatives.

He said: "They know far better than William Waldegrave what is actually happening to them."

We can also remind Mr Waldegrave how we tell the truth while he chooses to ignore it.

The FACT is that two little girls died because the NHS was too broke to save them.

Meningitis victim Carly, six, died last month in Welwyn Garden City, Herts, after being turned away from two major London hospitals which could not provide an intensive care bed.

Mr Waldegrave and John Major attempted to duck the issue.

Mr Major, who tried to rubbish our report on the tragedy, later admitted he was wrong.

Mr Waldegrave remained silent — and made no apology.

Eighteen-month-old Georgina Norris died in November after her heart op was twice cancelled by Great Ormond Street children's hospital.

She was sent home to Stevenage, Herts, and died six days later.

Great Ormond Street's world famous Peter Pan ward has been closed for 17 months because there is no cash to run it.

And yesterday it was revealed that a 15-year-old girl who has been waiting 2½ years for vital dental surgery has been told it will be another year before she can be treated.

Joanne Whelan, of Erdington, West Midlands, needs five teeth removed

The NHS in crisis

IF THE only reason for getting rid of this Government was the harm it has done to the National Health Service, it would be reason enough.

Despite their pretences, their crocodile tears and their mock concern, the Tories have devastated the NHS. From them we have had 13 years of ward closures, rising prescription, dental and eye-test charges and Ministerial indifference and incompetence.

That's why the NHS is in crisis. That's why, if the Tories get back, the NHS as we have known it is doomed.

Battled

They never liked the NHS. They fought against its birth, they have battled against its life and most of the Cabinet never uses it.

Even today, when the fear of defeat forces them to don the mask of hypocrisy, they promise only that from some time in the future patients won't wait for more than two years for an operation. Provided, that is, they can first get on to the waiting list, which could take another two years. Provided they live that long.

The Government's solution to the crisis is to suppress all news about it. Hospitals have been told not to talk to the newspapers until the election is safely over. Local newspapers have been warned to be careful about what they say.

What the Health Secretary, William Waldegrave, means by his threats is clear. Don't report scandals. Don't re-

MIRROR COMMENT

port cancelled operations. Don't report ambulance delays. Don't report avoidable pain. Don't report avoidable death, especially of children. And, if you do want to report it, don't ask us because we won't confirm it.

The Government boasts of the hospitals it has opened, but ignores wards empty because the nurses to staff them can't be afforded. It spends money on administrators and managers - bureaucrats who cure nothing - but puts trained medical staff on the dole.

The people do not believe their claims that the Tories care, because they know better. They do not believe that things are improving, because they can believe the evidence of their own eyes.

Skills

No one doubts the care and devotion of those who work for the NHS. Millions of people can testify to the skills with which they were treated — once they were treated.

But millions more know the agonies of a painful wait for treatment. They know the stress of hard-pressed doctors and nurses. They know that the NHS is in crisis.

And, for that reason alone, millions know to vote on April 9 to throw this Government out.

ATTACK: Cook

NO TIERS

LABOUR switched on their new-style election broadcast last night to highlight the pain and suffering caused by the ailing NHS.

Using actors, the moving TV film highlights the unfairness of the Tories' two-tier health service - the fact that cash buys care.

Two young girls are shown suffering from painful glue ear. One was soon relieved of the misery after her parents paid £200 for a private grommet operation.

The other child, whose parents could not afford such treatment, is seen crying in agony.

Message

She was forced to wait at least NINE months for an NHS operation.

Labour leader Neil Kinnock tells viewers: "If the Conservatives win, they will continue to privatise the NHS and make

Fig 2.2 Propaganda in peace time?
(Courtesy of Daily Mirror)

DAILY MIRROR, Wednesday, March 25, 1992   PAGE 5

over the tragic death of little Carly

IS A LIAR

ELECTION '92

Hopefully, it's 31st time lucky for Vera

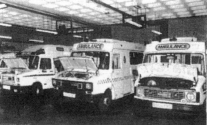

from her overcrowded mouth.

Yet her surgeon at Good Hope Hospital, Sutton Coldfield, West Midlands, is still operating on patients first seen in 1988.

Mr Waldegrave might also like to reflect on the FACTS about how the Tories have gnawed away at the NHS in their 13 years of power.

Since 1979 the NHS has lost 27,530 hospital beds for seriously-ill patients, while the private sector has 3,875 more.

The number of ancillary staff has plummeted from 172,300 to 95,700.

Yet the number of senior managers has soared from 100 to 9,740.

THE LIE-PROOF

TRIPLE heart bypass patient Vera Smith should finally undergo surgery today after her vital operation was put off a staggering 30 times.

But the 61-year-old gran – pictured left with husband Barry – is only being put out of her agony because a desperate consultant used the "old boys' network" to arrange for her to have the operation 90 miles away in London's Bart's.

The boss at the Queen Alexandra Hospital, Portsmouth, where Vera should have been treated, admitted there was nothing he could have done.

"Mrs Smith may have had to wait for months, although that was unlikely," said Richard Bishop.

"We have the beds but not enough trained intensive care staff."

Vera's husband Barry, 47, of Havant, Hants, said: "I am thoroughly disgusted.

"The last time my wife's op was cancelled she said that if she could have got herself to a window she would have thrown herself out.

"She didn't because she was in too much pain even to walk. She was inconsolable."

Finally, after an agonising TEN WEEKS of delays, Vera's consultant Michael Perry turned to the "old boys' network" – managing to find a colleague at Bart's who could carry out the op almost immediately.

Mr Smith said: "Without Mr Perry's intervention Vera would still be waiting at Portsmouth now.

"The way she has been treated is a disgrace."

999 BREAKDOWN SCANDAL

THE LIE-PROOF

BRITAIN'S ambulance service is fast becoming like the patients for whom it should cater . . . old, sick and needy.

All front-line ambulances should be replaced every three years, says the NHS Management Executive.

But dozens are still struggling on attending accidents and emergencies after NINE years.

Health authorities say they cannot afford to replace them.

In London, 60 ambulances break down each week on average and have to be "nursed" back to service in stations like the one pictured left.

Only 15 per cent of emergency calls in the city are answered within the target time of eight minutes. And complaints about the service rocketed from 460 in 1987 to 1,477 last year.

In Kent, 40 of its 160 ambulances have had three engine changes in ten years.

And it has had to borrow ambulances from as far away as Derbyshire, Devon and Wiltshire.

Ambulance crews are being cut throughout the country, and the services are relying more and more on voluntary organisations to provide specialist equipment, like heart monitors for the paramedic teams.

WITH US

By SHEREE DODD

it more like the American system."

The four-minute broadcast, set to the song Someone Really Loves You, ends with the telling message: "It's their future, don't let it end in tiers."

Shadow Health Secretary Robin Cook said the film was based on the real-life story of a girl who had to wait 11 months for a grommet op.

"We are telling a story which is relevant to the lives of us all," he said.

The broadcast, backed by a hard-hitting nationwide poster campaign, is bound to send Health Secretary Mr Waldegrave into a fury.

Mr Cook yesterday drove home his attack on the Tories with a dossier of letters from patients.

They had all been forced to pay for operations.

They could no longer bear to endure any more pain while waiting for an NHS bed.

Major in new TV cop-out

PREMIER John Major last night snubbed Neil Kinnock's challenge for a TV debate on the NHS.

The Labour leader said the clash was needed to "expose the Tory secret agenda for breaking up the health service."

Mr Major has already rejected a TV debate on their manifestoes.

THE LIE-PROOF   Barren and unable to save a single child . . . the Peter Pan ward at Great Ormond Street hospital, closed 17 months

Fig 2.3 Propaganda in peacetime?
(Courtesy of Daily Express)

1

Original or 'private' belief:

**'Privatisation will yield
good short-term profits'**

2

Expression of belief in an acceptable or 'public'
form, limited by the availability of discourses

**'Privatisation is good for the
consumer and enhances efficiency'**

3

Mediation of 'acceptable' discourse by mass media:
sometimes taking a critical perspective, sometimes a more
deferential position. Example: two newspaper headlines.

'Privatisation: selling the family silver'
(critical of policy)

or

'Privatisation: power to the people'
(celebrates policy)

Fig 2.4 Modification of a belief/mediation of a discourse

4 The **norms** which govern different types of interaction. In other words, the linguistic or spoken behaviour which is thought suited to a situation.

Speech: events and acts

Hymes went on to distinguish between **speech events** and **speech acts**. A speech event may be described as an occurrence of speech within a larger situation – it is a large *genre*, or type of speech. A speech act is usually seen as a smaller utterance within a speech event – for example, a reply to a question, a statement, a command within a longer conversation.

SPEECH EVENTS: SETTING AND PARTICIPANTS

Setting – several speech events can occur in the same situation, as for example the multiple conversations at a party (the party being the situation). All speech events must occur in time and space.

Participants – traditionally, speech has been described in terms of two participants, a speaker who transmits a message and a listener who receives it. However, while in the majority of cases the person speaking is also the addressor or the author of the 'sentiments that are being expressed and the words in which they are encoded' (Goffman, *Gender Advertisements*), there are times when stand-ins for the addressor are used (in certain situations, a spokesman or woman who might act as a mouthpiece for others). This is often the case when a television interviewer acts as the addressor on behalf of a 'public', putting questions to a politician. This leads naturally to issues concerning the roles taken by the participants in any situation where languare is used, including mediated public speech during an election.

PARTICIPANT ROLES

Hymes argues that there are at least four participant roles:

1 addressor;
2 speaker;
3 addressee;
4 hearer/audience.

Labov reports that ritual insults require at least three participant roles, one being an audience whose role it is to evaluate each contribution. (Ritual insults may be a good starting point for any enquiry into electioneering.) Once again, we must realise that the participants are able at times to change roles, just as the sender and receiver in Chapter 1 are not in a static position or relationship.

Three basic speech acts: from the classroom to politics?

The simple categories identified by Coulthard in *An Introduction to Discourse Analysis* provide an outline of the possible modes in which political speech might operate. He distinguishes between the **grammatical** categories of speech and the **situational** categories which influence that speech. Drawing on studies of what could be described as an authoritarian frame of discourse (interaction in the classroom), Coulthard outlines three basic tools which are at the disposal of the teacher. They are :

- **Statement** (This is today's lesson.)
- **Question** (What are we going to do today?)
- **Command** (Open your books at page ten.)

The grammatical 'equivalents' of these situational categories are not of central importance at present. What is important is to begin to understand the basic methods used by those attempting to influence an audience in either the short or the long term. We could start by looking at the ideas of 'statement', 'question' and 'command', since these can be applied to political speeches as well as to interaction in the classroom:

- It is important for the politician to be able to make a **statement** which can outline his/her position.
- It is important that the politician is able to **question** the position of an interviewer or the policy of a rival party.
- It is useful for the politician to **command** that certain actions be carried out.

Under the general heading of speech acts, and before moving on to speech events, it may be useful to explore what may be termed 'fashions of speech'.

FASHIONS OF SPEECH

'Fashions of speech' is an expression which bears a close relationship to the descriptive phrase used earlier, 'available discourses'. 'If I didn't enjoy this job, I'd resign', is a very frequently used expression (often by public figures). Very often it is in fact not meant to be taken literally, but is instead designed to impress on any listener the extent of the person's commitment to the job, a commitment which supposedly rises above any economic considerations.

In a similar way, there are 'fashions of speech' in political life, forming part of the 'available discourses' mentioned earlier. For example, when asked why they have (or have not) done something, politicians often reply to the effect that 'it would be grossly irresponsible of me if I raise this matter at this time ...' This remark is designed to stop or delay any further enquiry from the interviewer; it seems also to be an appeal to the supposed agreement of the audience that there is a universal 'common sense' in society and that the politician speaking is part of this consensus.

So, there appears to be a clear intention (which in a way could be adequately served by the politician simply telling the interviewer to shut up) and another implicit (or disguised) intention that can only be served by an address which simultaneously deals with the awkward line of questioning, and portrays the politician as a responsible and dependable moral figure.

Available discourses and dominant agendas

Fashions of speech should not be confused with **dominant discursive agendas** – in each area of political dialogue (such as the economy) there is a 'received wisdom' about the subject – what can be said about it and what cannot be said about it, quite apart from the 'acceptable form' of the message.

Political parties are more comfortable on ground they have traditionally been able to dominate discursively, although this does not mean that they necessarily have the best policy on that particular issue.

So far, we have established that certain terms and descriptions will make useful tools when it comes to analysing political discourse during an election. We know that what is said in a speech event is governed by the **intention** of the speakers within a given **context** (both the immediate situation and the wider social context), as well as by the **available discourses** in the language generally and the situation

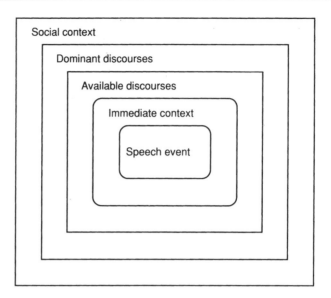

Fig 2.5 The factors governing a speech event

in particular. The discourse used will consist of a particular **form** and **content**, taken from a set of available discourses. Within these available discourses, whenever a particular topic is chosen, there will often be a **dominant discursive agenda** for that topic.

When a speech event takes place

The terms used so far – intention, context, mediation, available discourses, form and content, dominant agenda – reflect a concern with the re-presentation of ideas as a persuasive technique. This representation does not take place in the ideal environment that the politician/persuader desires, and the 'original' intention of the speaker/communicator may undergo significant changes before and during an interactive communication. The speaker must respond to the constant setting of new agendas as his/her original intention is blocked/altered/reinforced by the person with whom he/she interacts and the context in which he/she communicates.

In *An Introduction to Discourse Analysis*, Malcolm Coulthard describes the idea outlined by Hymes that there are distinct areas that need to be considered when a 'speech event' takes place:

1 **Structure**   This is the form of the event.
2 **Setting**   This refers to the fact that all speech events take place in time and space. Some of these settings, for instance a church service at Easter, may determine the range of discourses used. The setting of an event is not merely physical, but can be psychological, in the sense that the same event in different cultures can have quite different meanings, one event perhaps remaining formal while the other is informal.

3 **Participants** These are described, as we already know, as having at least four participant roles, as follows: *addressor, speaker, addressee,* and *hearer/audience.* Speech events which take place at the level of interpersonal conversation may need only an addressor and an addressee (similar to the usual communication terms 'sender' and 'receiver'). As soon as a speech event becomes more than just a conversation, then the other roles may come into use. Some situations clearly require an audience or some sort of hearer to judge the respective contributions of the main participants. As Coulthard points out, problems may arise in defining a role for some participants in an exchange, because roles tend to change according to the situation and are often not entirely clear.

4 **Purpose** This is obviously one of the major determining factors in any situation. It gives a general context to what is said, and can inform the behaviour of participants. The overall purpose of an event can clash with the purposes brought to the event by different participants.

5 **Key** This means the 'tone, manner or spirit' in which an act or event is performed. Coulthard, following the work of Hymes, explains how 'acts otherwise identical in setting, participants, message, form, etc., may differ in key.' For example, events may be serious or part of an elaborate mockery. Only the

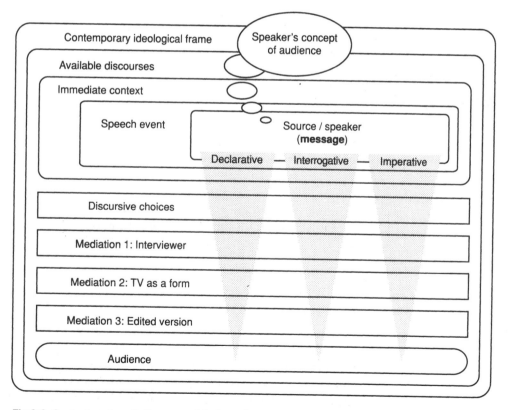

Fig 2.6 Context and mediation: a model of a politician's discourse mediated by television (*see* pp. 98–9)

difference in key would enable onlookers and participants to know what was intended.

6 **Topic**   This is the subject matter.

7 **Channels**   This has to do with the choice of the medium of transmission. For example, a message can be sent through oral, written, telegraphic, or other media.

8 **Message content**   Content is connected to the topic chosen.

9 **Message form**   The basic unit of form is the individual utterance. Hymes believed that '*how* something is said is part of *what* is said'.

This list could be extended to include the larger 'setting' which lies behind the immediate context or situation; that is the societal setting itself, or what could be called the 'supracontextual' setting, which gives form to discourse in the first place. As we will discover later, we need also to consider those 'intertextual' frames of reference (what other speech-events, speech acts and physical acts are taking place) because it is exactly the various collisions between these acts and events which set the agenda for those ideas and discourses which become dominant.

A general overview: applying Hymes' system

If we apply this overview to the subject of our analysis – television news programmes such as *Newsnight* and the *Six o'Clock News* – we can begin to lay out the areas we need eventually to draw together and analyse: the textual, contextual, intertextual and supracontextual determinants.

STRUCTURE

This would include the usual format of the news 'magazine' or programme – it may begin with a general overview of that day's news, moving on to a series of 'headlines', and might only then concentrate on individual items in detail.

SETTING

This is the studio and integrated outside broadcasts. It would not include recorded footage or tape. (The larger dimensions of setting ought perhaps to be examined also).

PARTICIPANTS

These would include the 'addressor' (the interviewer when speaking to the audience, the politician speaking to the audience), the 'speaker' (often the interviewer when speaking 'on behalf' of the audience, more obscurely the politician speaking on behalf perhaps of the nation), the 'addressee' (the politician when answering questions, the interviewer or other participants when challenged) and the 'audience' itself (usually understood as not being physically present, but sometimes appearing as a representative sample in the studio itself). Other participants may appear on footage shot before the transmission of the programme – their roles become related to the participants who remain in 'the present'.

PURPOSES OF THE EVENT

These may be to inform, entertain, amuse, educate, or even occasionally to provoke the viewer/audience. The purposes of interviewer and politician(s) may clash quite dramatically. The interests of the 'absent' audience (usually a sizeable collection of people only when television is viewed in some public place, during sporting events or elections) are usually represented by the interviewer.

KEY

This is one of the major weapons used by all sides in a programme of this type. One of the participants may, if under pressure, or because they are supremely confident of their case, or perhaps if the case is not regarded as mainstream, refuse to use the major key in the event. The key may alter dramatically; for instance, there was an alteration of key in the Conservative camp during the controversy over the Labour Party health broadcast in the 1992 election. A rather restrained and dismissive approach by John Major turned into a tone of moral outrage from Chris Patten, only to melt still later into the spirit of defensiveness represented by William Waldegrave. All these 'keys' were choices suggested to, or forced upon, the Conservative Party by events.

TOPIC

This would be best described as an agenda set out by a combination of events and available discourses. Things happen, and each party struggles to put a certain gloss on the event, in order to set the political agenda. There will be a 'professionalist' discourse maintained by the interviewers, which (although one participant in the interview may dominate the event) will consist of an attempt to put difficult questions to each politician in turn. The justification for the interviewer's method is often that he or she talks on behalf of the 'voters at home'.

CHANNEL

This is important in this case because the apparent channels adopted by the participants range across a variety of interpersonal and group models of communication, including forms like the conversation, the public speech, the discussion and so on. This, however, represents the deliberate use of certain conventions on a 'human' scale, which are then transposed to another channel, the televisual.

MESSAGE CONTENT

This would be the use of certain topics and themes in the presentations and arguments made by the participants.

MESSAGE FORM

This is one of the most interesting aspects of the way discourse is interpreted. The politician will attempt to strike a chord in the unseen audience, to present his or her arguments in a way designed to appeal to some of that audience's values, attitudes and beliefs, so far as the politician is able to judge or imagine what they are.

Appeals to certain attitudes can prepare the way for attempts to alter long- or short-term behaviour.

What follows is a transcript of a BBC 2 *Newsnight* programme, broadcast on 25 June 1992, that dealt with the subject of the 'War of Jennifer's Ear'. It represents the way in which meaning is created and mediated in a televison interview.

Jeremy Paxman introduces the programme – fragment of introduction missing

[MCU] '... capital out of the illness of a five-year-old child rippled out like some gothic earthquake today. Yesterday, Neil Kinnock claimed Labour's election broadcast was a genuine case. Today, Robin Cook said things like the girl's school, hospital and even the operation might have been changed. The parents, who were yesterday Mr and Mrs, revealed they weren't married. Labour flourished a list of ten allegedly genuine other cases, then had to apologise to at least one of the individuals who hadn't wanted to be included. The Conservatives said they'd had nothing to do with passing out details of the case, then collapsed in confusion and admitted they did. Meanwhile, Paddy Ashdown said both parties had turned the NHS into a cause of damaging, deep-seated national division.'

[Ashdown CU] 'How [applause – cut away to conference] – how much better it would be if we had spent the last twenty-four hours [CU Ashdown] not discussing the ethics of Labour's campaign, but debating how we might make the NHS once again the best health service in the world, for [applause – cut to conference] – for here is the truth of it: in all the Tory and Labour broadcasts, the speeches, the attacks, we haven't heard a single positive idea from them about the future of our precious National Health Service. They prefer to argue about themselves, when they should be [cut to conference] debating the issues.'

[CU Paxman in studio] 'Well, who came out of it best is anybody's guess. James Cox [cut to graphic of a mole on the phone] reports on the day party propaganda came [title appears on graphic; "Of Moles and Ministers"] to cry stinking fish.'

[Fade to Tory press conference, Waldegrave the subject]

[Cox VO] 'It was supposed to be the day when both Labour and Tories concentrated on the Health Service. In fact, it was not the doctors, but the spin-doctors who became a suitable case for treatment [cut to front view of press conference]. Mr Kinnock's [cut to Julie Ward] press secretary nearly burst into public tears and the youthful Mr Fixits (cut to Conservative group in discussion) on the Tory side were reduced to stumbling incoherence by a baying press corps. If there was one thing all those nice politicians were agreed on, it was that little Jennifer Bennett [*see* p. 92] and her family should never have been dragged into the mire of the campaign. It wasn't us, they each declared, it must have been the dirty unscrupulous brutes in the *other* camp. Yet, both the *Daily Express* directly, and the *Independent* by means they're still keeping mum about, did obtain and print her name.'

[Cut to Labour press conference with slogan 'It's time for Labour' in the background] 'Neil Kinnock this morning assured us, Labour's [cut to *Daily Mail* journalist] lips had been sealed [cut to Kinnock, who speaks]: 'Since we are so absolutely clear that *no one* connected with the Labour party in *any* way at all imparted any clue, let alone any specific identity, then the *only* way in which Jenny's identity could have been discovered is from some other source.'

[Cut to group of journalists and a TV camera]

[Cox VO] 'Not quite true, said the press. His personal press officer, Julie Hall, had briefed them with the Christian name, Jennifer, on Tuesday. [Cut to Julie Hall] Ms Hall defended herself in an emotional spasm.'

[Hall speaks]: 'Whichever one of you, at the briefing on that Tuesday afternoon, can tell me how, from the one word "Jennifer", you were able, when there are one in ten children in Britain who suffer from that complaint, to within hours have that story in the *Express*, I'd like to hear from you now. I think we'll find another explanation within the next 24 hours … Sorry have taken up *your* [to Kinnock] time, but I think that was the best thing to do.' [Noise]

[Cut to John Major preparing to respond to a question]
[Cox VO] 'John Major, visiting a hospital in York this morning, said Tory hands were clean.'
[Journalist's voice:] 'Was it the Conservatives?'
[Major] 'No it was not, it was most certainly not. [Laughs softly] They say they didn't leak it, that's a matter for them. No doubt it will determine in due course who did, but it certainly wasn't us.'

[Cox VO] 'But his party was involved.'
[Cut to graphic of the consultant in the case, with space for a quotation] 'Jennifer's consultant, Dr Alan Ardouin, had called Central Office before the Labour broadcast to say that [words appear] "… they had the facts wrong and I felt I should inform somebody about this."'

[Cut to Waldegrave – side on] [Cox VO] 'Today the Health Secretary William Waldegrave admitted that the Tories had received the call, and redirected it to the press.'

[Cut to Waldegrave CU – speaks] 'We advised the consultant, if he wanted to pursue this matter, a good thing to do would be to – to contact [hesitates] a newspaper that might be interested in it. Nothing wrong with that at all. Nothing wrong with that at all.' [Hubbub]

[Question in background] 'Did you give the name? Did you give the name?'
[Waldegrave] 'The name of what? Of the consultant?' [Reply] 'Yeah.'
[Waldegravel 'I–I–I–I think it – er – I think that we – er – helped the consultant to get in touch with the newspaper. There's nothing wrong with that. At all.'

[Wider shot]
[Cox VO] 'Indeed, this evening the Tory director of communications confirmed they'd not just advised the doctor, but actually called [image of documents] the *Daily Express* to tell them about his involvement [cut to Conservatives in the street]. Then there's the child's grandfather, a staunch Tory. He faxed the party complaining about the election broadcast nine days ago, but Central Office claim they took no action, and anyway he hadn't named the girl. [Cut to front page of *Independent* newspaper – headline: 'Labour plays its health service card'] Anyway, the story got out, though the *Independent*'s editor [picture on graphic replaced with picture of the editor] was careful to rule out the obvious sources.'
[Editor speaks]: 'We did not, categorically did not, get this story from a political party or a politician, or anybody directly or indirectly connected with politics.' [His picture fades]
[Cox VO] 'And tonight, in a dramatic development the doctor in the case [cut to the

doctor with a dictation machine] played tape-recordings of his conversations with the Press. The *Independent*, he said, had called him, and the newspaper already knew the girl's name *when* they called. He hadn't leaked the name of the girl, *or* her GP. [Faint sound of the tape recording: 'Yes, right, thank you very much indeed. And you wouldn't be able to tell me the name of the GP?' Doctor replies: 'I – I don't think it would be right [CU of dictation machine] for me to tell you, no.'
'All right. Well thank you very much indeed for your help.']

[Cut to doctor's face] 'The *Independent* knew the facts, I [name appears on screen: Dr Alan Ardouin, Jennifer Bennett's consultant] corrected what they thought were the facts to the *Independent*. They – they gave me the name, cos otherwise I couldn't have looked up the details of the patient.'
[Question] 'And do you know where they got their facts from?' [Reply] 'They said they had a copy of the letter from Mr Bennett to Mr Cook.'
'Can I ask you for your opinion about who did leak the child's name?'
'Well, I presume it is *somebody* who has access to Robin Cook's stationery ... because – his – his *letters* – because – the *Independent*'s Rober – er – Jonathan Foster, was quoting from – this letter – to me – asking my comm – what did I feel about it and so forth.' [Cut to mid-shot of the consultant]
'I do wish that the editor of the *Independent*, when he gave his list of people who hadn't given him the names had also included the medical profession, because I felt by implication there – that he – er – you know, hadn't excluded me as the source – but clearly I couldn't have been the source because without knowing the name first I couldn't have known what the *Independent* was talking about.'

[Cut to Cox in studio with montage of the child, Waldegrave and Robin Cook in background] 'All this might seem like a Fleet Street brawl of little relevance to the Election, but it's left both parties looking a little shabby and shop-soiled. For example, was the broadcast true, or a fictional representation merely prompted by the Bennett case? Yesterday Mr Kinnock said it was a real case of someone hurt by NHS cutbacks.'

[Cut to Kinnock and microphone] 'The particular case in this film, as I've repeatedly said [cut to a back view of Kinnock talking to the press] is a true case [back to his face] and I wish you'd show as much concern for the National Health Service as you appear to be showing for asking questions here.'

[Cut to Labour Party press conference, Robin Cook, shadow health secretary talking] 'Did you actually report ...' [Voice over] 'Today his health spokesman Robin Cook said the facts of the Jennifer Bennett case [Cut to CU of Cook] had suffered a certain reality shift.' [Cook talking] 'As I understand it the film was shot in entirely different locations from Jennifer's, and indeed as the mother has said, the school was entirely different. I think the operation that you saw on that may have been different to the one that occurred to Jennifer.'

[Cut to John Major at Conservative rally – voice over of Cox]: 'Yesterday the Prime Minister mounted his high moral horse to declare that the whole affair proved Mr. Kinnock was not fit to be his successor.'
[John Major speaks] '... none of that simple decency which the British people expect. I tell you this, their attitude tells you more about the people who lead the Labour Party than it does about the National Health Service.' [Applause – cut to John Major]. 'Such men are unfit to govern, and such men must never govern again.' [Applause]

[Voice over]: 'Yet today his colleague Mr Waldegrave [close-up of Waldegrave] admitted

Tory headquarters not only prodded *this* case into the public prints, but was assiduous-ly [wide-angle shot of Conservative press conference with slogan about NHS reforms working] encouraging more doctors to pass their horror stories to the press.' [Cut to Waldegrave, who speaks]: 'You will find that amongst these people, and amongst all this – with the stuff that Virginia has here – there are hundreds of doctors ringing in to us to say they'd like to help – and I'm afraid we are *bombarding* newspapers with their names.'

[Cut to studio – voice over]: 'Who's been damaged by the continuing slanging match? Clearly it has derailed each party's attempts to set the political agenda, and to campaign on grounds of its own choosing. Mutual accusations of sleaze and mendacity scarcely do the democatic process much good. But if there is a good side, it is that the remorseless news-management exercised by the Campaign teams has suffered a severe setback, but it all provides a somewhat sardonic refrain to the theme-tune of the original party broadcast.'

[Extracts from Labour's PEB intercut with footage of the various 'players' in this particular incident].

The Chesterfield by-election

What kind of discourses are used in the reporting of elections? Here the concern is not so much with the details of what politicians say, as with the way in which the whole spectacle of electioneering is interpreted by certain types of television pro-grammes.

The candidacy of Tony Benn in the 1984 Chesterfield by-election generated a great deal of media interest because of Benn's position as one of the standard-bearers of the Labour Party left. One of Benn's earliest criticisms of the treatment he received from the mass media was directed against Vincent Hanna, a journalist on the *Newsnight* programme. Benn regarded Hanna as 'the SDP candidate'. (SDP – Social Democratic Party.) Benn was arguing that the BBC was attempting to cir-culate the idea that the electorate in Chesterfield should vote 'tactically' to stop him from going to Westminster, In other words, that voters were being encouraged to support the candidate who posed the greatest threat to Benn and his campaign.

The journalist to whom Benn took exception, Vincent Hanna, set the tone for much of the BBC's election reporting and was widely regarded as an important figure in the whole campaign, filing reports for both *Newsnight* and *Sixty Minutes*. Hanna found that he had to defend himself publicly, making a stand on the ground of professionalism and integrity. He rejected the accusations of bias against the Labour Party candidate.

A 1984 research project, conducted by Rosalind Brunt and Martin Jordin, dis-covered that the idea of Chesterfield as a certain type of place – a decent, rather old-fashioned, largely non-political community – was presented in the *Newsnight* programme of 13 February 1984. The whole event had been 'framed' in a particu-lar ideological light; the discourse used to describe the election had made reference to moderation, common sense and privacy. Brunt and Jordin describe how the tranquillity of Chesterfield was portrayed as being shattered by the arrival of poli-tics (*International Television Studies Conference*, Sheffield, 1984, p. 13):

'... against the superficial and petty rivalries of party politics, *Newsnight*'s Chesterfield projects a particular sense of Englishness as something solid, deeply embedded and unifying ... there they all were, minding their own business, when suddenly this election came upon them and they were instantly the focus of national, indeed international media attention.'

The British electorate's disillusionment with the system, evidenced by low turn-outs at the polling booths, forms an important feature of *Newsnight*'s own jocular cynicism. Politics is portrayed, not as a natural part of life in this part of England, but as something alien and disruptive. The natural state of existence is imagined as being lived outside the realm of politics.

As the Sheffield researchers point out (p. 14), 'Its effect is to transform "the people" into the non-political subjects of someone else's political activity'. The term 'subject' is one with which we will be reasonably familiar. These are subjects, it seems, with no ability to transform their subject-position. What is most interesting from the point of view of studies of audience, is that the viewer 'at home' is also imagined as being non-political (p. 14):

'Similarly *Newsnight* renders "the Chesterfield voters", not as active participants in a political process, but as spectators of something that belongs to another world "out there".'

However, the rather simple idea that Benn was compared unfavourably with other candidates proved not to be quite true. The Liberal and Conservative candidates, despite the fact that the programme seemed interested in their campaigns, were clearly marked as minor figures, overwhelmed to some extent by their own parties. Hanna's commentaries were definitely, in their case, humorous in tone. The frame of reference adopted by the programme portrayed Benn as being 'controversial' but as almost the only serious candidate.

As a general principle, one which is followed up in a later chapter on television, it is possible for the semiology of the *imagery* used to depict an individual (in this case a candidate) to clash with the commentary. Images of Benn amongst the people of Chesterfield were in fact treated as newsworthy, without the need for a humorous commentary. Benn also had the chance to speak directly as addressor or speaker. Television in particular allows the opportunity for candidates to get a message across with a certain degree of directness. The picture of the BBC as having taken an active stand against Benn's campaign is misleading. The actual fault lay in 'framing' the whole event in a discourse which assumed that this country is not 'naturally' political, and which set the idea of moderate 'Englishness' against the concept of party politics. There was probably some truth in this idea but the point is that other discourses about the meaning of Chesterfield were much less visible. One thing we should avoid is the idea that the problem was simply some kind of media conspiracy. The *Newsnight* team works, thinks and lives in the same general social environment as anyone else in the society. They happen to occupy a specialised 'professional' position, through which they are able to communicate their view to others. They will be part of the creation of discourse, but as we know, discourse doesn't come from nowhere. Discourse has to be made out of social experience. It is impossible to 'make it up' from scratch.

THE 1992 GENERAL ELECTION AND 'THE WAR OF JENNIFER'S EAR'

The background

The mass media, under the influence of certain news values and their own party-political loyalties, picked up this 'story' and made it into a controversy with the help (deliberate or otherwise) of a number of prominent politicians, although the story had been brought to life in the first place by politicians.

There had already been a small controversy over a direct mass address used by the Conservative Party. Their curious 'double whammy' poster, attacking Labour on tax, was circulated in effect by the mass media themselves. It is no accident that, throughout the campaign, the parties appeared on television in front of backgrounds featuring election material designed to be picked up by the television cameras, and no accident that campaign posters were 'unveiled' by front-bench MPs. Political propaganda was designed for the mass media. Both events and individuals were 'packaged' for television.

One of the main techniques used successfully by the Conservatives was to make the propaganda itself an issue. If the picture of giant red boxing-gloves on the double-whammy poster was controversial, this meant that it would be seen and discussed by large numbers of people, the controversy serving to increase exposure. It is also considerably cheaper than paying for vast numbers of poster sites (though the generosity of companies which had made advance bookings to advertise their products during the election, and then allowed the Conservative Party the use of their sites, must also have helped to reduce costs).

Shaun Woodward, the Conservative's director of communications, said that they had learned lessons both from the 1987 election campaign and the Gulf War (*Sunday Times*, 15 March 1992):

'In a war you plan a campaign and then you pull in all the elements you need for it – the ships, the tanks, the planes. We're doing the equivalent of that.'

Why, however, was one of the opening shots in this 'war' a message which, for all the discussion about it, was open to different meanings? The deliberate employment of ambiguity (a word or term or action capable of signalling more than one meaning) can be useful in political campaigns, because it at least prompts discussion of the message and its significance.

Advertising expertise

Advertising is not used in elections simply to produce good 'copy'. Strategies of persuasion (dealt with in the next chapter), featuring the careful targeting of audience, do not belong exclusively to the advertiser. Political persuasion and propaganda operate in close alliance with the techniques of marketing. Advertising agencies tend to have clients from both the commercial and the political worlds, and there is sometimes a considerable overlap between agencies, the business world and political researchers, who at times appear to share personnel, methods and outlook.

The Conservative Party had office space loaned by Saatchi, where twenty or so advertising professionals worked on ideas for posters and film scripts, but significantly also where they analysed 'polls and attitudes'. The Labour Party's campaign was run by a seventeen-strong committee chaired by Neil Kinnock, but much of the day-to-day running of the campaign was carried out by a team of ten officials under the direction of Jack Cunningham. A fifty-strong 'Communications Agency', composed of volunteers from advertising companies, worked on image-making.

Polls and psychological probing

Especially during election time, the changes of opinion and attitude of panels of voters are monitored closely by political groups. Academics, strategists, advertisers, all have at their disposal a range of methods for 'taking the political temperature'. Attitude measurement techniques vary, but may be understood as a form of research and can be summarised briefly as follows (*see* O'Keefe, *Persuasion: Theory and Research*, pp. 19, 20).

DIRECT TECHNIQUES

These consist of asking the respondent for an evaluative judgment of the object under study. The methods used include **semantic differential** tests, where subjects rate the object on a seven-point scale. A possible example is shown below.

Object under study: Labour Party policy on the NHS
Good .... Bad
Positive .... Negative
Rational .... Irrational

Those asked to respond would have to mark the point on the scale which most closely corresponded to their view. The scale would already have been assigned a value at each point, which could be zero for the mid-point, through to plus three for the positive end, or minus three for the negative end. Single-item attitude measures, where there is a single question on the scale shown which the respondent must answer, is a similar method.

QUASI-DIRECT TECHNIQUES

There are also what are described by O'Keefe as 'quasi-direct' techniques. These include **paired comparison**, where the respondent has to state preferences concerning a series of objects in pairs. **Ranking procedure** involves putting a list of objects into rank order. **Thurstone attitude scales** involve assembling a pool of 'opinion statements' that indicate something about the object under study. For example, if the object of study is the Liberal Democratic Party, statements for judgment might include 'the party cares about voters', 'the party is not dynamic', 'the party is not ambitious', and so on. Eleven categories are used for sorting out the statements and, in a similar fashion to the semantic differential test, the neutral value lies at the centre of the scale. Items where respondents disagree greatly are discarded. Some items, for instance, could be interpreted by certain individuals in a negative light while others may see them as purely positive. A statement such as 'the party is not ambitious' could of course be seen from either perspective. The **Likert attitude scales** function in much the same way, except that ambiguities are discarded before the process of investigation begins.

INDIRECT TECHNIQUES

These include **physiological indices**, where the physical responses of the body are used to judge the attitude of individuals to an object. Information tests are based on the idea that a person's attitudes influence their judgment. The subject is given a multiple-choice test about factual matters, where the two possible answers are both wrong. The respondent's attitude is then worked out from the type of wrong answer they give.

VOTER-METERING

This technique, which is regarded as modern and informative, was imported from the American political scene (along with 'negative campaigning'). An audience representing a variety of gender, age, occupational and other groups from a specific constituency is shown material such as party election broadcasts. As with most investigative techniques, this method could be of use to a variety of different interest groups: politicians, pollsters, academics, media professionals and so on. Members of the audience are given a meter and asked to press a series of buttons (again, on a scale from positive to negative) in response to the points made on the broadcast. BBC 1 used this method and displayed the political loyalties of its selected audience as a series of lines superimposed on the broadcast; the lines were red, blue, yellow – and white for the uncommitted or 'floating' voter.

On certain occasions this type of investigation can be revealing. For example, on 22 March 1992, a Liberal Democrat broadcast, beginning with Simon Hughes talking about the environment, received almost universal approval. So, too, did the Ashdown message on tax, where he called for people to accept the idea of paying an extra 1p on tax in order to finance education. The only time that all lines fell (except the yellow one) was when Ashdown asked people to vote for his party. Approval of a particular message does not mean to say that votes will be cast in a certain party's favour. It seems that the Liberal Democrats were seen as occupying the high moral ground, able to deliver judgments on the state of the nation, but allowed to do so partly because they were in no danger of obtaining power.

FRAGMENTS OF DISCOURSE?

An analysis by John Cole in the same programme stressed that certain phrases (small components of speech acts) worked to gain a positive response from viewers involved in the metering experiment. Neil Kinnock, speaking about the economic condition of Britain, received approval for phrases such as 'the unemployment election' and 'the recession election', which seemed to strike a chord in those being monitored. According to the media, politicians searched for exactly this sort of effective 'sound-bite'. It is just unfortunate that terms like 'sound-bite' almost short-circuit our ability to evaluate what is actually being said.

The American version of what we might call a 'fragment of discourse' is known as a 'power phrase'; President Bush's aides made a study of positive responses to speeches made on the eve of the Gulf War, discovering that references to the idea that 'no one messes with the US' were particularly potent.

APPEALING TO THE VOTER?

One of the problems facing the measurement of audience response lies not just with the uncertainty of the methods listed above, the prejudices of the researchers, or the changeability of the audience itself. It is the difficulty of deciding what a reaction, once identified, actually means. Those voters who registered a negative reaction to the Conservatives' broadcast on Labour's tax policy (which featured a blacksmith forging a ball and chain) might have reacted negatively to the images they saw, but even so the underlying message might well have helped sway them against Labour. So what is the point of identifying the *whole* reaction as negative? It seems to have been a message that people did not like, but the fact that 'there was evidence that the attacks on Labour's tax plans were striking home with a few in the group' (*The Guardian*, Georgina Henry, 28 March 1992) suggests that, from the Conservative point of view, the broadcast had a *positive* result.

The Labour health broadcast

If we wished to emphasise visual semiology alone, the Labour health broadcast would provide a perfect case study. There was no dialogue at all during the narrative – a song acted as a commentary on the images. The narrative worked through a series of simple contrasts between the situation of two children, and can be summarised as follows.

Two young girls, one with blond hair and one with dark hair, are seen in a hospital waiting-room looking distressed. The girls look at each other. The mother of each appears concerned. Each mother strokes her daughter's head. The little girl with blond hair and her mother read a calendar which says 24 March. A computer screen tells us that this child's operation is due on 11 December. The mother seems unable to believe that there will be such a long wait.

The two little girls are seen being driven through the hospital gates by their mothers. The dark-haired girl's mother has a more expensive-looking car. They are on their way in. The blond girl looks at the other girl, but she does not return this look. The child who has to wait for her operation is then shown at school, distressed and in pain. The girl in hospital looks miserable too but then appears, smiling, on the operating table.

Back at the school, the blond girl is miserable and won't join in with the activities. The other child's operation is a success and the surgeon looks pleased. The child at school is in pain as tambourines and other instruments are being played. The child recovering in hospital receives a present from her mother – both are cheerful and happy and there are 'get well' cards in the background.

A picture of misery, the little girl at school is seen crying in a lavatory cubicle. In a kind of dumb-show, the distressed girl's mother meets her at the school gates. The girl emerges slowly, looking at the ground and, as her mother puts her hand on her shoulder, responds by holding her painful ear.

The next scene shows this girl in bed, as her mother keeps her company. The dark-haired girl also lies in bed, but is asleep with a contented smile on her face. The mother in this scene bends down and kisses the child's head. She then produces a cheque book and writes out a cheque for £200, dated 12 April 1992. The poorer mother is seen in her daughter's bedroom. Then we again see the richer parent writing the cheque. The screen is then split in two, with the dark-haired girl at the top fast asleep and the other little girl at the bottom of the screen also in bed, but turning about in discomfort.

A message appears exhorting viewers not to let the Health Service 'end in tiers'. Neil Kinnock concludes the broadcast with a short speech to camera.

NEVER WORK WITH CHILDREN AND ANIMALS?

As we will see when we consider film, any narrative may be described as a chain of events in a cause-effect relationship. The plot (the story-line) should be considered as only part of the narrative, which consists also of the devices used in telling the story. Film, and the television commercial form, are both suited to the use of narrative. In this case the narrative (story-line and the devices employed in telling it) is used to persuade an audience that there is an injustice taking place and that the NHS is under threat.

ANALYSIS: SEMIOLOGY AND IDEOLOGY

It might be useful to consider in the first place whether the simple contrast between the two girls was the most effective ploy that the Labour Party could have used. Possibly some of the power of the message was lost exactly because this contrast was given so much emphasis. The issue was personalised in a way that would perhaps not have happened had the suffering child and her family taken centre stage as victims of underfunding. Researchers found that audience response to the idea of writing out a £200 cheque for an operation was that it was a reasonable thing for a concerned parent to do. Such a response misses the point which the Labour broadcast intended to emphasise – that the poorer family had no option. The narrative device of the cheque itself, symbolising a 'two-tier' system in the NHS, distracted the audience. It produced what we might call an 'aberrant decoding', or a failure to interpret a message in the way intended by the sender, producing instead a new meaning.

OTHER DEVICES

The style of the broadcast itself (style is one of the devices used) was close to some types of dramatised documentary, but in lighting and colour it resembled commercial advertising. Did this contribute to the way that the argument over the broadcast began as an argument over the 'truth'? Had the film been uncompromisingly 'realistic', with fewer exact contrasts between the girls, the use of named individuals instead of actors, and a starker and more recognisable setting (shot perhaps in black and white), would the *genre* of the piece have made it easier to accept the message? In other words, if the form of the film had been recognised as purely documentary (although, as we shall discover, documentary is not always closest to the truth of an event), would the content have come in for less criticism? Kinnock in particular was immediately at a disadvantage when he described the events portrayed as 'true', because the public does not always take pains to distinguish between the literal truth, exact in every detail and made in a recognisable 'documentary' form, and a representation faithful to the spirit of a true case.

THE 'WAR' ITSELF

The broadcast went out on 24 March 1992. The role model for the little girl who had to wait for the operation was Jennifer Bennett, five years old at the time, whose father had approached the Labour Party about her case. The previous month, John Bennett had received a letter from the consultant treating Jennifer explaining that 'insufficient funding' had resulted in a lack of nursing cover on Sunday nights, resulting in a waiting list for overnight patients that had 'climbed enormously' (*Sunday Times*, 29 March 1992). The other child featured in the film was based on the son of the Conservative MP Michael Bates. Bates had reputedly paid £1,300 to avoid the boy having to wait for a grommet operation.

The *Six o'Clock News* on BBC 1 on 25 March described the broadcast as provoking 'the most heated exchange of the campaign so far'. The newsreader said 'Labour stand by the film, saying "It's powerful because it's true."' This remark summed up the ground Labour was forced to defend: a 'truth' about the NHS. The accompanying footage for Labour's view was film of a smiling Neil Kinnock leaning on the roof of a car to talk to the camera. When the Conservatives were represented, a serious-looking Chris Patten was seen in profile at his desk. The newsreader reported that 'the Conservatives call the broadcast despicable and sleazy and question Neil Kinnock's fitness to govern'. Paddy Ashdown was shown visiting a factory and was quoted as saying that Labour had gone 'too far'.

There are no prizes for noticing that the frame of reference adopted by the *Six o'Clock News* was not Health Service underfunding; nor was it primarily the way that Labour had represented the issue of underfunding. It was based on the idea that the heart of the news, the most important part of it, was the political row which had followed the broadcast. It is more and more the case that the mass media produce articles, news items and 'stories' during elections on how the parties present themselves. There is a lot of material also on how the media itself behaves, what it chooses to report, which journalists are involved in public rows with politicians, and so on. In one sense this is a very healthy development. In another, it is a distraction from questions of policy and fact. We now spend a great deal of time looking at the machinery which produces re-presentations of our society. The concern of the journalist seems to have been summed up by a reference to 'the smooth-running Labour campaign' which had 'run into difficulties'. Kinnock's reaction, as the questions continued during the day, makes it clear that he felt the issue of the NHS was being lost: 'The particular case in this film ... is a true case. I wish you'd show as much concern for the NHS ...' (*Six o'Clock News*). Neither of the major parties could get the media to stick to the agenda they wanted to pursue.

The earliest reactions from the Conservative Party to the broadcast were quite low key. John Major's first publicised comment was that '... it tells us more about the Labour Party than it does about the Health Service.' Soon, however, the status of the broadcast was challenged. William Waldegrave declared that it was 'a new low in political advertising'. To most people, who believe that propaganda represents a resort to lies, the Conservative contention that Labour had produced propaganda would make sense. It was the extremity of Waldegrave's remark that it was similar to *Nazi* propaganda which probably made some think that he was going 'over the top'. There was another reference to unsavoury foreign influences in Waldegrave's judgment that the Labour Party had used techniques 'we'd always hoped would never spread here from America'. On the afternoon of the 25th, Chris Patten was declaring that the Labour Party had shown they were willing to 'grub for office'. The high moral tone had been set, and the discourse used by the Conservatives had successfully avoided the issue of underfunding, because all the questions coming from the media were based on the ethics of the broadcast.

Labour attempted to seize some moral ground also, by attacking the 'personal' criticism which had been directed at Neil Kinnock. It is interesting to note that the reporter covering the controversy identified both Labour's private annoyance that they had not been better prepared, and the idea that the Conservatives had 'seized on this to try to undermine Mr Kinnock's credibility'.

ANOTHER NARRATIVE THREAD

This case provided a good story not simply because it represented a sharp political fight, but because it had a strong human interest angle. The tendency to make stories, to create structured narratives out of everyday experience, is a broadly human trait and not one that is exclusive to the mass media. The *Six o'Clock News* set out the following narrative to bring home the dramatic potential of the situation: '... as Jennifer Bennett came home from school today, the dispute about Labour's PEB reached deep into the family at the centre of the row.'

At one point in the argument, the question of waiting lists did manage to emerge, because the consultant who treated the child was questioned by television and the press over the content of his original letter to John Bennett explaining how staff shortages had been responsible for the delay in seeing Jennifer. The consultant insisted that the situation had improved considerably since the date of the letter.

CHANGING AGENDAS

Towards the end of the news programme studied here, the agenda moved towards the subject of the NHS itself. The Labour Party programme for the Health Service was actually reported in some detail. Reports about arguments over whether the proposed extra funding from a Labour government would pay for a minimum wage or for patient care showed that the issue of health spending was still an issue. The emotive broadcast and the row over its accuracy served to draw attention to the issue Labour wished to highlight, but the mass media were unable to go directly to the issue. The issue appeared as a smaller part of a news agenda focused mainly on a debate over 'truth' followed by a 'human interest' story (the Bennett family and their divided political loyalties). By 3 April, fears among some big companies that Labour might achieve victory led to several thousand high earners in the City and in advertising receiving a full twelve months' salary in advance. This payment was intended to avoid the expected increase in top-level tax should Labour have won the election.

In the absence of conclusive research, speculation about the reasons for the Conservative Party's election victory tend to become minor 'myths' in their own right. These myths then circulate and some 'solidify', coming to represent the trap to be avoided in the future, or perhaps the sure-fire method of obtaining victory under any circumstances. Circumstances change, but some of the factors which remain constant may be outlined here.

Most politicians will attempt to characterise the majority of 'right-minded' individuals as natural supporters of their own party, just as John Major talked of 'that simple decency which the British people expect' (*The Times*, 26 March 1992). It seems odd that Major should have described the British as 'not naive', since a belief in simple decency during an election would appear to be quite touching in its stupidity.

The constant factors appear to include the ability of the Conservatives to out-spend their rivals, but with a tendency to produce rather inferior party broadcasts. Their poster campaigns are circulated very successfully and seem at times to have an edge that the other parties lack. The tactic of 'scaring' voters into supporting a policy or party appears not to work in a recession, at least where the party deploy-ing the tactic is challenging a party in power. The press is certainly partisan, but the 'quality' end of the Tory market appeared anxious to seem balanced in the tone of its articles, saving most of its party political judgment for the leader pages.

MYTHS IN THE MAKING

The idea that confidence in the economy rose to such a degree as to ensure Conservative victory seems unfounded. The Labour Party's rather triumphalist pre-election rally in Sheffield may not really have put off too many voters, though there was some agreement that the event was not particularly inspiring for those outside the Labour Party's ranks. The idea that voters were scared away from Labour by the threat of higher taxation carries some credence, but it is a safer bet to say that the Liberal Democrat vote was put under pressure by John Major's state-ment that a vote for Ashdown was a vote for the Labour Party. The failure of the Liberal Democrats to hold key constituencies against the Conservatives, from whom they had been won in-by-elections, and the inability of Liberals to win in seats where Conservatives appeared weak, set the seal on the fate of the opposition parties. Persuasion cannot completely alter people's material circumstances. Most voters would appear to make their final choice based on their own material cir-cumstances, combined with their understanding of what is the most acceptable choice for the country as a whole. The simple choice offered in party propaganda was a picture of a nation either as one which required change, or one which could not afford to risk the unknown. Did one discourse result in a convincing victory? Or was the final result the simple outcome of a dysfunctional electoral system?

Re-branding the product

Stories of advertisers who 're-brand' their products in order to increase sales are quite common. This process is usually regarded as little more than a 'cosmetic' exercise, in which the product remains essentially the same. In the case of the Labour Party, however, the product had indeed changed substantially. Tony Blair made it clear to his followers that Labour had to 'modernise'. Speaking on the platform at the end of Labour's debate on the replacement of Clause Four in 1995, he promised that rumours about changes to the party's name were unfounded. In effect, the name was not changed outright but 'embellished'. The use of the title 'New Labour' had the advantage of retaining the brand (and thus recognition) but re-positioning it to attract electors who did not belong to the party's traditional base.

A change of this type, however, must also be accompanied by new ways of talking. The set of discourses which appeared in New Labour election broadcasts sounded as though they belonged to the right of the political spectrum – in this example, Anita Roddick is used to describe the virtues of business as a social force:

> 'Business is more powerful than government. It is quicker, more creative. Business is the lifeblood of the country. Only one party can represent Britain best, getting business right . . .'

The Conservatives' attempt to sully this image, based on an advertising campaign which used the slogan 'New Labour, New Danger', succeeded only in helping to reinforce the re-branding exercise.

TERMS OF DEBATE: PRESS DISCOURSES IN THE 1997 GENERAL ELECTION

The 1997 General Election resulted in a substantial victory for the Labour Party. The purpose of this study is to examine some of the **terms** upon which this victory was secured, using 'terms' in a dual sense:

i) **words** or statements used to express political concepts or ideas, and
ii) a set of **conditions** for public conduct and debate.

These two meanings are closely related. 'Terms' are those key words and phrases – tax, law and order, defence, the future, trust, leadership, unemployment, party unity, change, vision – which refer to ideas and events. They are at first sight 'neutral', in that they could be associated with any contender within the political sphere. In the 1997 election, however, certain terms were already associated with particular policies and attitudes, which could work to the advantage of one political group over another. 'Party unity', for example, once a quality supposedly foreign to the soul of Labour, soon became a concept which was almost impossible to apply to the Conservatives. Attempts by John Major to produce and inspire 'vision' did not succeed. The seizure by Labour of a vigorous and essentially authoritarian position on 'law and order', helped to make the entire idea a central element of their political creed. In the movement from 'terms' to 'concepts', and their use in public debate, we see various interest groups beginning to set out the boundaries for the political 're-alignment' which ensured 'Blairism' victory.

During election campaigns, public declarations – of belief, and of intention – are not made in a random fashion. They are part of a wider set of discourses which try to mobilise a range of values. Journalists, 'think tanks', political commentators and politicians, all attempt to set or modify the terms of debate through a series of public interventions, including speeches, advertisements, articles and broadcasts. Dearing and Rogers (see their book *Agenda-Setting*) have a name for all those who try to form agendas: they call them 'issue proponents'. Of course, we should not neglect the simpler explanations for shifts in allegiance and consciousness; changes in allegiance are rarely made on principle alone. In the run-up to the election, tales appeared in publications like *Private Eye*, describing the anxious bewilderment of certain right-wing editors, as they waited for their proprietors to tell them which party to support.

Defection to 'New Labour'

At the beginning of the 1997 election campaign, the role of the press was high-lighted by *The Sun*'s defection to the Labour Party or, more accurately, to Tony Blair as a concept. On Tuesday 18 March it carried the mighty headline 'The Sun Backs Blair', with the sub-heading 'Give change a chance'. The front page displayed, alongside the masthead, the indication that this was 'An historic announcement from Britain's No 1 newspaper'.

Although many political commentators greeted this change with great interest, it is the **terms** under which the change was made, that are most important. First, the entire front page is centred upon Blair, not the Labour Party: 'The Sun Backs Blair'. The content of the short article on the front cover reveals the The *Sun*'s perspective:

> 'This is the election for the millennium. In six weeks' time, Britain will vote for a government to take it into the 21st century. The people need a leader with vision, purpose and courage who can inspire them and fire their imaginations. *The Sun believes that man is Tony Blair. He is the best man for the job, for our ten million readers and for the country.* It is a momentous decision which we have not taken lightly because we still have reservations about some of New Labour's policies. But for all the Tories' achievements of the past 18 years, they no longer deserve our support. They are tired, divided and rudderless. They need a rest and so does the country. Blair is the breath of fresh air this great country needs. On pages 6 and 7 we explain why we are putting our trust in him.'

The use of certain hopeful but vacuous phrases echoes the rise of the 'new' politics itself: 'This is the election for the millennium'. Besides its status as a non-event, the millennium has attracted most attention as a numerical inconvenience which threatens the functions of computer-controlled technologies. Although it has been rather difficult to represent the number two and a row of noughts as a symbol of momentous change, the very poverty of the 'millennium' as an idea has allowed various groups to invest it with significance.

It is worth noting that there is no egalitarianism in the *Sun*'s outlook. Instead, the paper offers populism. People require not mutual co-operation, but 'a leader with vision'. The paper's allegiance is not offered on the basis of principle, nor as a reaction

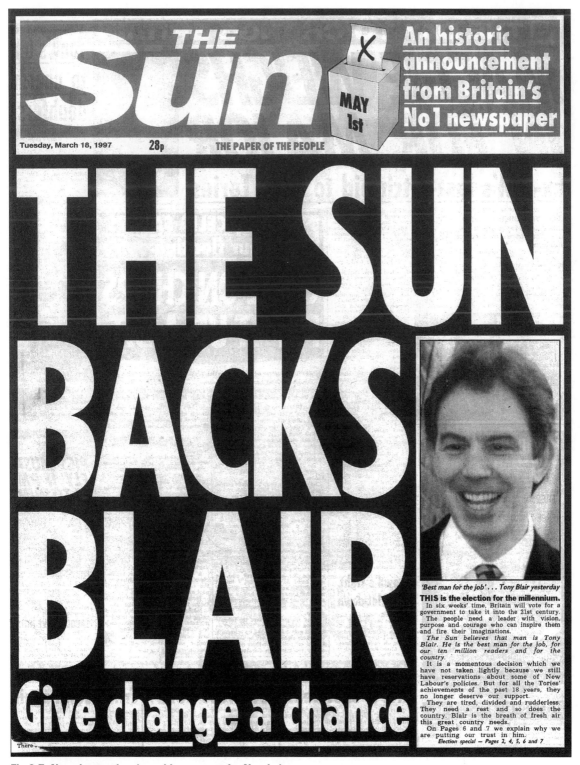

Fig 2.7 News International provides support for New Labour
(Courtesy of the Sun)

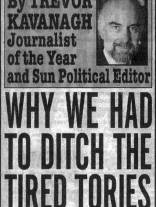

By TREVOR KAVANAGH Journalist of the Year and Sun Political Editor

WHY WE HAD TO DITCH THE TIRED TORIES

PARTY leaders – and the editors of every other national newspaper – have been waiting for months to learn who The Sun will back in the General Election.

Today we give the answer: New Labour. And in today's historic leader, we explain in detail our arguments for Tony Blair.

But this is more than simply an optimistic switch to a party which has undeniably changed, to the acute discomfort of many of its old supporters. The fact is that the Tories themselves know they are in desperate need of a rest.

We may or may not be quickly at odds with Tony Blair's regime.

But we can be absolutely certain that in the unlikely event of a Tory victory, we would witness either listless drift or a bloodbath.

How would Chancellor Ken Clarke make peace with the Right-wing majority who will give him credit for the economy, but blame him for Europe?

How would John Major, who loathes the Cabinet "bastards", feel about Michael Portillo or John Redwood as his successor?

Bickering

Because let there be no doubt, among at least a third of the Cabinet, the race is already under way to take John Major's job.

In these circumstances, how would the exhausted Tory party itself feel about being lumbered with more years of government?

Hundreds of Conservative MPs desperately want to keep their seats for personal reasons.

But in private, an astonishing number tell me they are ready for a period in Opposition, as long as they themselves are re-elected.

They cannot face the prospect of another term of bickering and backbiting.

One prominent pro-European told me, when the Tories still had a fighting chance: "I cannot bear the thought of victory. We've got to sort this

out." He spoke for a substantial rump of MPs who have worked for the election of Michael Heseltine as party leader, but would be just as happy with Mr Clarke.

But this is not a pro-Euro conspiracy. The mood is just as clear-cut on the Tory right.

At a recent dinner party attended by one present Cabinet minister and two former ministers, I suggested everything was suddenly going their way.

The economy was turning out to be solid gold, with even the EU praising us.

Germany's soaring unemployment was proving our case against a single currency and the Social Chapter. Industrialists were queuing to invest.

"You could still turn this around if you pulled your fingers out," I said.

Silence

There was a long silence. Another guest said: "You may infer that some people don't actually want to win."

Fair enough.

But is it also fair to expect The Sun, which supported the Tories in the trials and battles of the 1980s, to fight for a party which doesn't want to win?

The Conservatives need a rest from government. They should have it.

JITTERS HIT SHARES

JITTERS over the election outcome helped send shares plunging yesterday. City analysts reckoned uneasiness would continue till polling day, particularly over Labour's policy on company taxation.

But they expect a bright recovery after the poll. NatWest strategist David McBain said: "The nervousness will be short-lived. The UK is in better shape now than it has been in the past 30 years."

The FTSE index ended 51.0 down at 4373.3. The pound lost almost two cents at 1.58 U.S. dollars and four pfennings against the Deutschmark to DM2.68.

THE SUN SPEAKS ITS MIND ON THE Labour say they're so let's give them

POLITICAL COMMENTARY

THE Labour Party say they have changed. They say they are fit to govern.

So today The Sun says: Let's give them the chance to prove it.

In the past five years, John Major and the Tories have achieved the impossible: They have made themselves unelectable.

In less than three years under Tony Blair, the Labour party have done the impossible, too. They have convinced us they **ARE** electable.

That is why we are putting our trust in Blair. Such a major decision has not come easily.

Changing a government is not like changing a car – just because some parts are worn or the colour's out of fashion, it is not necessarily good sense to trade it in.

We must face

the facts

There has to be a more substantial reason than simply "It's time for a change." Remember, that's what Tory MPs thought about Maggie Thatcher and look how wrong they were.

But we must face facts. The clapped-out Tories don't deserve to win.

They have all the ingredients in place for victory: Low inflation, low interest rates, falling unemployment, huge foreign investment, public borrowing on the decline and applause for Britain from the most unlikely quarters – the European Commission and Germany.

But despite all that they are 25 points behind in the latest poll.

In 1992 they won in the middle of a recession. How can it be that in 1997 they appear set to lose during a recovery?

SIMPLE. THE COUNTRY IS SICK AND TIRED OF THEM.

After 18 years, they have become sloppy, divided and tired out. Their incompetence shines through and getting

44 DAYS TO GO

things wrong is the one thing they consistently get right. The Tories lack direction and purpose. They have been tarnished with sleaze, riddled with scandal, beset by foolishness and weakened by division.

Too many Ministers are going through the motions of government and have been for two years or more. Too many eyes are on who leads the party after Major.

Even at the Cabinet table the contenders make speeches about the leadership election when they should be talking about the General Election.

He dreams of

warm beer

Major is a decent man who does his best. But the rock-bottom state of his party, with its paralysis over Europe, shows that his best has not been good enough.

He is not a leader. He is a follower. He dreams of warm beer, cricket on the village green and old ladies cycling to church on Sundays.

He is not the man to take Britain into the 21st century. Nor can we see anyone else in his party who inspires us.

The Tories have all the right policies but all the wrong faces.

In Tony Blair, Labour has the face that fits – and many of the Tories' policies. If it works, Clony Blair has hijacked it.

But Blair's leadership qualities, his vision, his determination and his political strength are all his own work. He speaks with sincerity about the family and the importance of personal morality. He looks good and he sounds good – although substance must count

Our future . . . Tony Blair visits children at Crampton School in London yesterday

more than image. Blair showed great courage, even at the risk of his own downfall, when he took on his party when it needed reform and battered it into submission.

The result is a disciplined, co-ordinated party which knows where it is going.

Blair knows where he is going, too. Barring the greatest political upset in history, he is going into 10 Downing Street.

Labour promise to

keep taxes down

He now says of his party: "What you see is what you get." So what do we see?

We see a party which calls itself New Labour but hasn't produced many New Ideas to match.

It offers hope to those who are disillusioned with the health service, with education, with the lack of jobs for young people. But it does so while promising to do exactly what the Tories have done by keeping down taxes, borrowing and spending.

On the big issues, Labour's approach is simple: Trust us. Although they still haven't given us precise details of why

Fig 2.7 News International provides support for New Labour
(Courtesy of the Sun)

MOMENTOUS CHOICE FACING OUR COUNTRY

fit to govern Britain
the chance to prove it

FRANKLIN

TIME FOR A SPRING CLEAN

Tony Blair . . "respects The Sun"

TONY BLAIR'S MESSAGE TO Sun

TONY BLAIR said last night: "I'm absolutely delighted to learn of The Sun's support.

"The reason why The Sun is backing Labour is New Labour. I know that and respect it. Many former Conservative voters have come over to Labour for that reason.

"I want to say this to those people and to Sun readers: New Labour is real, it is here to stay. We run for office as New Labour. We will govern as New Labour. That is my bond of trust with you.

"Those things of the 80's that are working we keep, those things that aren't, we change. But it is the future we are looking to, not the past."

POLL

JOHN Major set the election ball rolling by seeking a courtesy audience with the Queen at Buckingham Palace, but her dissolution of Parliament could have been obtained by phone.

HOLE

Prescott on battle bus

LABOUR bruiser John Prescott is to tour Britain in his own election battle bus — to convince traditional Labour voters to stick with Tony Blair

The Deputy Leader's move mirrors the U.S. Presidential trail where party deputies mount their own campaigns.

But it also shows Mr Prescott is a vital figure in the party's bid for votes. One senior Labour figure said yesterday: "John will play a crucial role. He's very much in touch with our core support."

ARE YOU 18 ON BIG DAY

If you were born on May 1 1979 and will be voting for the first time, let us know where your X will go. Ring us on

0171 782 4021

We'll call you straight back.

---

we should. They make grand promises about no tax increases and no extra spending.

Well let's see them do it. If they come up with the goods, we will be the first to praise them.

But if they break the promises they have made to try to win the electon — like the Tories did over tax in 1992 — then our attack on them will be ferocious.

The Sun has not fallen in love with Blair and New Labour. We are NOT switching horses just because that's the mood of much of the country.

Our eyes have not been blinded to the inconsistencies in some of Labour's words on education, health, defence, pensions and the economy. We are giving them the chance to prove that our doubts are groundless.

But we still have great reservations about both the Tories and Labour and Europe, although we are heartened by Blair's promise that he will have no truck with a federal superstate and his recognition that there are formidable obstacles to

Britain joining a single currency. Blair says he will never let us be isolated in Europe.

If that means getting in there with his jacket off and fighting for free trade, less red tape, no restrictions on how we hire and fire and what we pay our workers then we're with him all the way.

If it means giving one-way concessions for the sake of showing we are good fellow Europeans, then we're against it.

We know Labour will sign the social chapter, the biggest Trojan horse imaginable which could have major and harmful effects on British industry and commerce from the shopfloor to the boardroom.

Will Tony Blair be tough enough?

Blair says he will veto anything which would impose on Britain the social costs that Germany and France wish they had never signed up to. But how do we know he will be strong enough? Around the nego-

tiating tables of Europe, the pressures to join in and conform are enormous.

Thatcher never wanted to join the ERM but under pressure from Major she did.

Will Blair be tougher than Maggie?

Germany's Chancellor Kohl is desperate to secure his place in the history books by founding a single European currency that will lead to a fully-integrated political and monetary union.

He sees it all going sour as Germany's economy falters, the French get awkward and the Latin countries try to cook the books. Kohl will do anything to flatter, cajole, bribe or even bully Blair into becoming a passive ally.

Will Blair, the newcomer to government, be able to resist? The answer is that we do not know and will not know until it is possibly too late.

But there is every reason to be as suspicious of the Tories as we are of Labour.

Labour say they have changed. They say they are fit to govern.

SO LET'S GIVE THEM THE CHANCE TO PROVE IT.

The Sun reserves the right to exercise its obligation to its 10 million readers to analyse most critically every step Labour take in government.

When we think they are right, we will praise them. But when we think they are wrong, we will shout so loud we will deafen them.

The Tories are in need of a rest

The Tories have had a good run. Mrs Thatcher worked miracles in transforming ordinary people's lives — but her successors (and assassins) must also shoulder the blame for their failings.

They are tired and need a rest. They need time to sort themselves out and decide if they are really radical Conservatives or just bureaucratic managers.

The Sun is putting its trust in Tony Blair.

It is up to him to make sure that our trust — and that of the voters — is not betrayed by others.

'Tories are tarnished by sleaze and weakened by division'

Fig 2.7 News International provides support for New Labour
(Courtesy of the Sun)

against restructuring, casualisation, the growth of poverty and other features of Conservative rule. In fact, Tory policies are praised. The reasons for the *Sun*'s 'momentous decision' are expressed through the positive and negative values assigned to a number of different qualities. Vision, purpose, courage, the ability to lead, to fire imaginations, to provide 'a breath of fresh air' are recognised, within the context of the election, as positive attributes. Tiredness, political division, and the state of being 'rudderless' (lacking the ability to influence direction), are the negative attributes presented in contrast.

Time for a change?

On pages six and seven, however, a lengthy editorial seems to question the simple call for change which adorns the front page. 'Changing a government is not like changing a car – just because some parts are worn or the colour's out of fashion, it is not necessarily good sense to trade it in'. This comparison appears to cast doubt on change for its own sake. However, a metaphor has already been applied to the Conservative party: it is not only 'tired' and 'divided' but also 'rudderless'. If this is taken as a precedent, then linking it to an unfashionable or worn out car is not so outrageous. The editorial, however, makes an appeal for: '... a more substantial reason than simply "It's time for a change".' The political colour of the paper is then revealed in the terms of the warning given: 'That's what Tory MPs thought about Maggie Thatcher and look how wrong they were'. The 'substantial reason' itself appears to be the *Sun*'s conviction that 'the clapped-out Tories don't deserve to win'. Despite having 'all the ingredients for victory' including 'applause ... from the most unlikely quarters – the European Community and Germany', the real problem is that 'the country is sick and tired of them'. In effect, the 'substance' of the paper's case against the Conservative party is its 'incompetence' and public tiredness with and revulsion at 'sleaze ... scandal ... foolishness ... division'. Although the editorial appears to distrust change for its own sake, the 'evidence' it provides for its own allegiance is a perception of Tory shortcomings, together with a sense of the public mood captured in the phrase used above: 'The country is sick and tired of them'. Yet the editorial is also wary of appearing to endorse this feeling: 'We are NOT switching horses just because that's the mood of much of the country'.

Significantly, Major is criticised on the basis of rhetoric he used to describe a traditionalist vision of Britain: 'He dreams of warm beer, cricket on the village green and old ladies cycling to church on Sundays'. The feeling that this is outdated and irrelevant confirms the paper in its 'modernist' discourse: 'He is not the man to take Britain into the 21st century'. Once again, such statements make it difficult for the paper to disown the notion of change for its own sake.

Throughout the article, there is an uneasiness about appearance and reality; an attraction to the superficial image that New Labour seems to project, at the same time as the 'substance' of the new leader and his policies is anxiously sought:

'... Blair's leadership qualities, his vision, his determination and his political strength are all his own work. He speaks with sincerity about the family and the importance of personal morality. He looks good and he sounds good – although substance must count more than image.'

The whole outlook of the paper on this question is inconsistent, which may explain its constant references to image and what lies behind that image. The *Sun*'s inconsistency means it cannot be ruthlessly ideological, leading to some rather peculiar outbursts. It indulges, for example, in criticisms of Blair, using a pun about 'cloning' Conservative policy which is out of place in the larger context of praise for the party's leader; 'in Tony Blair, Labour has the face that fits – and many of the Tories' policies ... if it works, Clony Blair has hijacked it'. The first part of this sentence is entirely in line with the paper's feeling that the Conservatives 'have all the right policies but all the wrong faces'. The same point, about Labour's adoption of Tory policy, is made later in the article, but this time with a negative inflection:

> 'New Labour offers hope to those who are disillusioned with the health service, with education, with the lack of jobs for young people ... but it does so while promising to do exactly what the Tories have done by keeping down taxes, borrowing and spending.'

The promotion of hope, coupled with a commitment to Conservative spending policy, is seen as a contradiction, implying that New Labour might not be able to come up with the goods if it sticks to the restrictive fiscal policies of its opponents; but the *Sun* has, in this same editorial, praised Tory policy ('The Tories have all the right policies but all the wrong faces').

The editorial goes on to reveal more about the nature of the *Sun*'s apparent populism, recommending that Blair fight the Europeans to ensure there are 'no restrictions on how we hire and fire and what we pay our workers'. The 'we' in this case would seem to align the paper with employers, rather than workers, yet the use of 'we' earlier in this diatribe refers to the British in general. What is good for Britain becomes what is convenient for one social faction. The news value known as 'Personalisation', where the impact of various social forces is attributed to the actions of an individual, is a strong feature of the paper's perspective: 'Major is a decent man who does his best ...' though inevitably '... his best has not been good enough'.

This is in line with the *Sun*'s disapproval of incompetence and its attachment to efficiency: 'the Tories lack direction and purpose'. It should be clear that there are few 'moral' arguments made here as such, merely a kind of disclaimer later in the piece: 'The *Sun* reserves the right to exercise its obligation to its 10 million readers to analyse most critically every step Labour takes in government'. This specific condition must be seen in the context of the paper's attachment to one particular myth – that of the leader betrayed by incompetent subordinates: 'Mrs. Thatcher worked miracles in transforming ordinary people's lives – but her successors (and assassins) must also shoulder the blame for their failings'. Notice that her successors must shoulder 'the blame' for failings which are not listed here, but which presumably include all the shortcomings the *Sun* has already covered. Blair is called upon to 'make sure that our trust – and that of the voters – is not betrayed by others'. In line with the paper's belief in leadership, and suspicion of less exalted persons, nameless 'others' must be monitored to ensure against some form of treachery.

Mirror, Mirror

On the same day that the *Sun* praised Blair and bemoaned the fact that the Tories could not seem to decide whether they were 'radical Conservatives or just bureaucratic managers', the *Mirror* appeared with the headline:

'I'LL WIN FOR OUR KIDS',

followed by the information that 'TONY BLAIR OPENS HIS HEART TO THE MIRROR ON HISTORIC DAY'. At the top of the newspaper a declaration reads 'Labour leader backs the paper that's always been loyal', together with the slogan 'Blair we Go! Blair we Go!' which appears beneath the masthead. The identification of Blair as the central reason for voting Labour, is promoted as strongly by the *Mirror* as it is by the *Sun*. In addition, the photograph of children serves to emphasise the forward-looking and reasonably compassionate image that New Labour wished to promote. The problem faced by the *Mirror*, however, is to differentiate between its allegiance to Labour and the support offered by the *Sun*. This is, as much as anything, a commercial necessity, brought about by the circulation war which exists between the two papers. This explains the column which appears on p. 6, next to the editorial. This column calls upon the papers to 'watch out for the Tory turncoats'. Statements made by the *Sun* before 18 March 1997, are listed in detail, revealing the highly critical perspective taken by that newspaper, including an early treatment of the theme which so occupied its attention during its call for a Labour vote: 'So with "Time for a Change" Labour you get no change', it had declared in February. After various descriptions of Blair's quality of leadership and 'brilliant' preparation for the contest, the *Mirror* sets out a series of Conservative shortcomings; the terms of its attack are essentially political in nature. It reminds its readers of:

'... the 22 tax rises and highest-ever level of taxation ... the disintegration of the health service ... the destruction of our schools ... the doubling of crime ... the record levels of government borrowing ... the million home owners trapped by negative equity ... the elderly trapped by poverty ... the young people trapped in a cycle of hopelessness.'

In contrast, the *Sun* would have found it impossible to make such direct accusations, since its political philosophy is tied to the policies which its opponents would say have created all these problems. It has to be content, therefore, with a more superficial discussion, despite its own instinct that New Labour is itself based on a surface appeal. The *Mirror*'s politics is not, however, as radical as its list of complaints might suggest. In fact, 'unemployment' (which the Sun mentioned) does not appear in the list at all, though it does feature in the article which attacks John Major's record. The *Mirror*, in common with its rival, focuses ultimately on the question of leadership: '... Mr. Major, people do want change. They want a change from you and the rest of your incompetent, reckless gang. They want this country to be run fairly, decently and honestly. *They want it to be run by Tony Blair*'.

Fig 2.8 The *Mirror* backs Blair
(*Courtesy of the Mirror*)

ON THE DAY HE ANNOUNCES ELECTION DATE,

VOICE OF THE *Mirror*

A challenge to the country

THIS is the day for which Tony Blair has waited and the nation has yearned.

The day which will herald the end of Tory rule after 18 long, hard years.

The day on which the campaign begins to elect a Labour Prime Minister for the first time for 23 years.

However tough Tony Blair's past life has been, however demanding his future will be, nothing is as crucial for him as the next six weeks.

He has prepared brilliantly for this battle. Under his leadership, Labour has developed the policies and the unity to attract voters.

But in a two-horse race, there is always the chance of the outsider winning.

No one knows that better than Mr Blair. He has warned, warned and warned again against complacency.

Mr Major wants a long campaign — the longest since the post-war year of 1918 — because he thinks Labour will trip up.

Of course, all the evidence is that it will be the Conservatives who do that. They have stumbled from crisis to crisis. They haven't seen a hole without tumbling into it or a mouth without putting their foot in it.

But Mr Blair must prepare for the miracle that John Major is hoping for – that the Tories hang together and look vaguely presentable.

Even then they will not win unless some voters forget why the Tories must not be trusted again.

So during this campaign we must constantly look back at the record. At the 22 tax rises and highest-ever level of taxation.

At the disintegration of the health service. At the destruction of our schools. At the doubling of crime. At the record levels of government borrowing.

At the million home owners trapped by negative equity. At the elderly trapped by poverty. At the young people trapped in a cycle of hopelessness.

Yesterday, in the most cynical, pathetic plea by a Prime Minister, John Major said: "If

people are looking for change, we are the change." Well, Mr Major, people do want change. They want a change from you and the rest of your incompetent, reckless, arrogant gang.

They want this country to be run fairly, decently and honestly.

They want it to be run by Tony Blair.

This election campaign is not just about votes. It is a crusade for Britain.

Like every crusade, it needs strong, firm, authoritative leadership. The tough leadership it will get from Mr Blair.

But it also needs mass support. That means all of us — united and fighting together for what we believe.

Already some former foes have jumped on the Blair bandwagon. They may be doing so for the most cynical of reasons but we welcome any sinner who repents.

Tony Blair knows *The Mirror* is not a fairweather friend, and he will be wary of those who only want to back him when the going is easy.

This election is about Mr Blair as much as it is about anything.

After the shabby, sleazy Tory years, the voters want a leader they can trust. And they know they can trust Tony Blair.

The greatest threat to his success is apathy — that his supporters stay at home, thinking victory is assured.

But he should not be denied a single vote. No majority is too big for Labour. No defeat is too great for the Conservatives.

Tony Blair has a huge job to do in the next six weeks. But so do you.

Join the crusade. Don't just go out and vote Labour yourself but make sure all your relatives, friends and workmates do, too.

May 2 will be the greatest day most of us can remember. The day when Tony Blair walks into 10 Downing Street as Prime Minister.

What a prospect. What a challenge for us all. Let's get on with it.

AND WATCH OUT FOR THE TORY TURNCOATS

THE Mirror is the only newspaper that has always remained loyal to Labour. But the party should beware Tories coming in disguise.

Here's what the Tory turncoats REALLY think of Tony Blair and his policies.

● ON January 22 *The Sun* asked if Labour's

Sun

tax policy made sense. "The answer has to be no," they went on, accusing Shadow Chancellor Gordon Brown of pinching Tory ideas.

"If all he is offering is Conservative financial restraint, why not vote for the real thing?"

● THEY repeated their copycat line on January 25.

"Why trust imitation Tories more than the real ones?" they asked.

● A MONTH later on they hadn't changed their tune. "The hollowness of Labour's

Sun

carping is clear when you consider what THEY offer voters," *The Sun* wrote.

"Much the same policies as the Tories with no more spending."

● THEIR verdict on the Shadow Chancellor's future? "It'll end in the tears of a Brown."

● *THE Sun* actually believes that nothing will be different under New Labour.

"So with 'Time For A Change' Labour you get no change," they insisted. "Mr Blair

Sun

talks a good game. But it's actions that count, not words."

● ON the "lost" voters, they said: "Major has to win back the voters who have deserted in their millions.

"People who, mistakenly, see Tony Blair as the answer."

They add: "Tony Blair wants voters to trust Labour again.

"It is easy to be tempted. But once in a while, we see behind the mask."

WHAT

Major shouted down as he claims: You have never had it so good

By NIGEL MORRIS

JOHN MAJOR'S election campaign got off to a chaotic start yesterday when he paid a flying visit to ultra-marginal Luton.

He brought with him his soapbox — his lucky charm from the last Election — but this time his good fortune deserted him.

First, his loudspeaker wouldn't work because of a glitch in the sound system. And when it was finally turned on the Premier couldn't be heard more than a few yards away.

Mr Major first stepped on to the soapbox — a small plywood case held together with black tape — when he visited Luton during the last Election. Since then it's been stored away in Downing Street.

Mr Major chose Luton to kick off his campaign because Labour has high hopes of capturing both the town's seats from the Tories on May 1.

As police struggled to hold back a crowd of about a thousand people, the Prime Minister visited the share shop in the town's Midland Bank and then a street vendor selling baked potatoes.

He couldn't make his rallying call from the steps of Luton town hall because it is Labour-controlled.

Smear

Instead, he desperately tried to make himself heard over the chanting of protesters and the cheers of Tories in St George's Square.

But his speech was only heard by a handful of journalists and by the ring of police officers around him.

Shoppers at the back of the crowd couldn't catch a word over the barracking from supporters of the Referendum Party, UK Independence Party and Green Party.

But, for the benefit of the cameras, Mr Major made clear his desperate Election tactic of smearing Labour as a "loony Left" tag.

Tory strategists are suspected of choosing Luton for the launch because of its high student population.

They were counting on young demonstrators turning out to barrack Major — giving him the chance to brand them Labour supporters.

Turning on the handful of student hecklers demanding higher grants, he said: "One suggestion of a Labour government and the demonstrators are out on the streets again."

As their chanting grew, Mr Major declared: "I have no intention of being deterred by stunt demonstrators or by the ugly chanting of the traditional Left." And he insisted: "The last

MAJOR'S BRITAIN

time I came to Luton we had a reception just like this.

"Three weeks later we won both Luton seats AND the General Election.

"Once the demonstrators are pushed to one side and ordinary people are heard I have no doubt we will have five more years."

Mr Major boasted of "some of the best economic statistics we've seen in this country for a generation".

He went on: "We have in this country an economy no one else in Europe can remotely match."

When he referred to the low inflation rate a heckler yelled at him: "Stop wittering!"

But the Premier insisted: "All the things that made this country prosperous in the last 18 years have been opposed by the other parties."

Mr Major also made clear in his brief speech that his campaign would focus on the economy, Europe and standards in schools.

He rounded off his 40-minute visit by peering through the window of the town's Age Concern charity shop.

Drain

Then he was hustled into his chauffeur-driven Daimler and back to Westminster.

But the trip left the voters unimpressed.

Student Barbara Adjei said: "It's nice that he came out here — it shakes things up.

"But he's selling the country down the drain."

And pensioner Margaret Williams added: "I've voted Tory a few times before, but never again.

"The Health Service is in a terrible state and I just don't think they care."

Housewife Hazel Dickman said she would be backing Tony Blair on May 1 "because I feel so strongly against the Tories."

Fig 2.8 The *Mirror* backs Blair
(Courtesy of the Mirror)

SUMMARY

■ **IDEOLOGY**

Ideology, a term first used in France at the end of the eighteenth century, originally meant a study of ideas, later being used to mean a certain type of belief system and eventually referring to belief systems in general. So 'ideology' refers to ideas and beliefs – but more significantly to **systems of belief**. To be regarded as ideological:

1   the ideas concerned must be shared by a significant number of people;
2   the ideas must form some kind of coherent system;
3   the ideas must connect in some way to the use of power in society.

■ **IDEOLOGY AND THE EXPRESSION OF BELIEF**

A close study of what people *say* and *do* (not forgetting what they *create*) as individuals and as collections of individuals is important to any study of ideology because this is where ideology often becomes apparent. Ideology also appears in other material practices in society (the things that people have *made* also reproduce ideologies).

Two approaches to defining ideology may be described as the **neutral** approach to ideology, usually 'the world view of a class', a definition which leads to a view of ideology as multiple ('ideologies' or 'systems of belief' would explain this idea quite well) and the **negative** approach which has largely been associated with the idea of 'distorted consciousness'.

The debate over whether ideology comes from 'external' or 'internal' sources, from the society or from the individual, is presented. This text argues that ideology comes from both internal and external sources, and that the link between the two areas may be found in 'speech acts' and discourse. Ideology is seen here as a consequence of the interaction between people and their imagined environment, rather than as some kind of distortion which 'hides' reality.

■ **SEMIOLOGY**

Semiology is the study of **signs and meaning** in language, art, the mass media, sound and indeed any field of human endeavour which can be reproduced for, or represented to, an individual or an audience. (A sign may be understood as a physical object with a meaning.) The three main areas of study are:

1   the **sign**: the word, the picture, the sound than represents meaning within a specific culture;
2   the **systems** into which signs are organised;
3   the **culture** within which these signs and systems operate.

C.S. Peirce was more concerned than **Saussure** with both the real object and the process or the 'action' of signs. Many theorists follow C.S. Peirce's classification of 'second level' signs into three types:

• **Icon** – a sign which is identical to or similar to what it represents;
• **Index** – where there is a direct link between the sign and what it represents;
• **Symbol** – where the sign has only a symbolic or 'conventional' link with what it is supposed to represent.

Barthes, following Saussure, called the first order of signification, or meaning-creation, **denotation**, or the common sense, obvious meaning of the sign. The second order he called **connotation**, which we might understand as the associations produced by the denotative order in the mind of the person or persons who interact with the sign.

Some criticisms of Barthes turn on the fact that he appeared to identify connotation (the second order of signification) as something which 'corrupts' an innocent or natural system, denotation. Later in his career, he changed his mind, noting that denotation was not the 'natural' meaning of the sign, but in fact a kind of 'superior myth' exactly because it 'pretends' to return to a meaning no one can dispute.

This textbook stresses that ideology is not just something 'wicked' which hides behind a 'natural-looking' mask, but is a kind of fund from which people pick and choose their discourses.

■ DISCOURSE

Discourse is defined according to the uses writers have in mind for it.

The definitions may be summarised as follows: in linguistics, an utterance of greater size than the sentence. In some literature studies, the utterance of language generally. In some language and structuralist studies, the utterance of a specialised form of language or a language genre. In some political and cultural enquiries, discourse is the spoken expression of ideologies, or one of the battle-grounds upon which struggles for power take place. Discourse is used to achieve a form of power.

■ Discourse as the expression of ideology

This text offers the notion that ideologies are able to operate through discourses.

The Russian theorist **Voloshinov** took issue with Saussure's idea that the speech act is 'individual' and therefore not worthy of close study. According to Voloshinov, 'the utterance is a social phenomenon'. In other words, all 'individual' utterances are in fact born out of and given form by their status as social actions.

Relations between groups and classes are therefore constantly renegotiated.

The present distribution of discourse in society is described as unequal and hierarchical.

■ THE CONCEPT OF PERSUASION

Persuasion can be distinguished from manipulation by the idea that a persuader acts in good faith, whereas manipulation, by contrast, may be defined as managing a person by unfair influence. When we say that one person has persuaded another, we ordinarily identify a *successful* attempt to influence.

■ Persuasion and force

It is proposed that where the persuadee's freedom is minimised or questionable, then it is difficult to decide whether persuasion is genuinely involved. It is possible that we need a definition which comes some way between persuasion and force, such as 'coercive persuasion'. Cases of persuasion are ones in which the effects are achieved through communication. A definition of persuasion may be 'a successful intentional effort at influencing another's mental state through communication in a circumstance in which the persuadee has some measure of freedom'.

■ ATTITUDES, VALUES AND BELIEFS

An **attitude** is a person's general evaluation of an object. Attitudes are supposed to be learned. As new learning occurs, so new attitudes may appear. Attitudes are supposed to be relatively enduring, and are not the same as temporary states such as moods. **Values** are ideas about the relative worth of things and the nature of good and bad. Values often 'cluster together' to form systems of belief. Values inform people how far they may go, how they may behave and so on. Values tend to be *applied* to things, rather than being *in the nature of* things. **Beliefs** generally express a perceived link between two aspects of a person's world. Beliefs operate as thoughts or statements about the relative truth or falsehood of a thing. Some beliefs are central to a person, whilst others are less important.

Propaganda can be defined as 'the deliberate and systematic attempt to shape perceptions, manipulate cognitions, and direct behaviour to achieve a response that furthers the desired intent of the propagandist'. Among examples of propaganda, the text mentions the Falklands War, Vietnam, and the Gulf War. In addition, the relationship between public relations and propaganda is outlined.

■ ELECTIONS

Ideas about propaganda in peace are explored. The need of politicians to use a broadly acceptable form of political discourse, in which certain **forms** of address will be more acceptable than others, and in which certain types of **content** must be used, is advanced.

Mediation of the message in political speech is considered. The question of **mediation**, or how the media affects the original message, is important, as are the form and content of the original message. Context (the situation and the accepted ways of behaving in that situation), can affect the intention behind an individual's speech, just as the intention someone brings to a situation can affect the context.

The concept of 'available discourses', from which a party or an individual is constrained to choose, is an important innovation in the view we have of what and how something may be said.

Language, rules and norms, as well as the kind of choices and pressures already mentioned, are summarised by reference to Hymes' four interrelated dimensions which will affect what may be said in any personal or public situation: the **linguistic resources** available to a speaker, the **supra-sentential structuring** (how many differently structured linguistic events there are in the society), the **rules of interpretation** by which an interaction or speech comes to have a certain communicative value, and the **norms** which govern different types of interaction.

■ SPEECH: EVENTS AND ACTS

The text goes on to distinguish between **speech events** and **speech acts**. A speech event is an occurrence of speech within a larger situation (a large genre or type of speech). A speech act by contrast is usually seen as a smaller utterance within a speech event (a reply to question, a statement, a command within a longer conversation). Participant roles are the roles taken by people during spoken communicative interactions. There are said to be at least four participant roles: addressor, speaker, addressee and hearer/audience.

Coulthard distinguishes between the grammatical categories of speech and the situational categories which influence that speech. He outlines three basic tools of speech: the statement, the question and the command. This chapter emphasises that what is said is governed by the **intention** of the speakers within the **context** (both the immediate situation and the wider social context), as well as by the **available discourses** in the language generally and the situation in particular. Within these available discourses, whenever a particular topic is chosen, there will often be a **dominant discursive agenda** for that topic. In sum, we may speak of the **textual**, **contextual**, **intertextual** and **supracontextual** determinants.

The general election of 1992 and 'The war of Jennifer's ear' (a reaction to the Labour Party health broadcast) are used to explore ideas about language choices, discourse and semiology. Polls and psychological probing are mentioned, as are various methods of investigating audience response (including semantic differential tests and voter-metering).

STUDENT ACTIVITIES

SEMIOLOGY: ANALYSIS

Identification of icon, index, symbol

Students are taken through Peirce's classification of 'second level' signs into these three types:

- **Icon** – which means a sign which is identical to or similar to what it represents;
- **Index** – where there is a direct link between the sign and what it represents;
- **Symbol** – where the sign has only a symbolic or 'conventional' link with what it is supposed to represent.

Purpose: to prepare students to identify the types of sign.

Method: a series of simple signs/drawings (not photographs) is presented and students are asked to write down what in each case they believe the sign to be: icon, index, or symbol.

Examples may be taken from road signs, warning signs displayed in public and so on. The first batch of signs must not carry any words, but they may well be combinations of icon and symbol, for example.

A good example would be a simple drawing of a dog (icon for dog), followed by a dog inside a circle with a diagonal line through the circle (combined icon and symbol for 'no dogs allowed'), and then the presentation of the word 'woof' (index for dog). Road signs in a classroom are not indices. To be an index, a road sign must correctly indicate, for example, some physical aspect of a thoroughfare.

PUBLIC RHETORIC: ANALYSIS AND PRODUCTION

Stage 1 – analysis: Claptrap

Students are shown *Claptrap*, a video of Ann Brennan being trained as a public speaker by Dr Max Atkinson, and given extracts from his book *Our Masters' Voices*. Alternatively, any footage of public figures speaking during elections or at conferences will be adequate. Transcripts of such speeches would be useful.

Purpose: to introduce students to the following 'rules' of public speech which, in the correct circumstances and context, are likely to produce applause, approval or support:

1 'The rule of three', where politicians make three-point lists in order to prepare an audience to applaud at the end of the third point.
2 Contrast or antithesis, where contrasting pairs of statements are used in order to make a point; Atkinson cites 'Man is born free but is everywhere in chains,' and President Kennedy's inaugural address, in which he said, 'Ask not what your country can do for you, ask what you can do for your country.'
3 Alliteration for emphasis.
4 Setting up positions which the speaker ascribes to his or her opponents, positions which are then easily demolished.
5 Use of the plural 'we' to describe the supposed proximity of belief and unity of purpose shown between the speaker and the audience.

Stage 2 – planning and production: Writing a speech

Method: a list of subjects of a mildly controversial nature is agreed and recorded at the front of the classroom. Students choose a topic and, as individuals, go on to produce a short piece of writing, using the different categories of rhetorical device mentioned above. They may write a piece on a subject on which they have some knowledge or about which they feel strongly, but it is sometimes better to suggest that they write from a perspective which is at odds with their real opinion, because in that way the amorality of rhetoric is easier to demonstrate.

They must first analyse the range of their own non-verbal behaviours before going on to rehearse what types of gesture are most appropriate for their speech.

Each piece will then be circulated within, or read to, a group of students rather than to the whole class, before revisions are suggested. Each group then works as a production team in the next part of the exercise.

Stage 3 – production: Recording a speech

Method: the use of a video camera, placed in a static position in an adjoining room, is helpful, in the sense that it aids both preparation and analysis after the event. The introduction of a camera does,

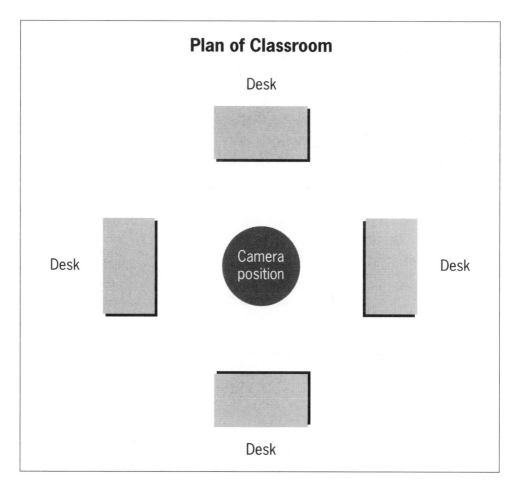

Fig 2.9 Recording group presentation in a classroom

however, alter the 'public' nature of the exercise; the advantage would be that students are able to work in small production groups of three or so, ensuring that those who are initially reluctant to speak to a large audience are still able to produce an exercise. The groups of three act as crew and as audience; the staff member may also usefully be involved with those individuals who would find it supportive.

The differences in the effectiveness of each category of rhetorical device can be demonstrated when the video recording is played back to the entire group. Alternatively, it is possible to persuade some students to make their speech before the whole class, or to set up a public speech before another class which has had no involvement in the production process.

PUBLIC DEBATE: RESEARCH AND PRODUCTION

The Interview: ideology and discourse

Students are asked to research a current issue about which there is a variety of opinion. Newspaper stories are an important source, since it may be possible to demonstrate the various ideological positions taken by different journals. Once research has been completed, students work in groups of three, acting the parts of interviewer and taking on the roles of paired adversaries in debate. (Note: it is often useful to ask students to represent the opposite point of view to their actual beliefs.)

Purpose: to move on from the tightly structured and scripted presentations made in the previous example to a situation where students are forced to respond to other points of view, and to alter their responses accordingly. They are then in a position where they have to choose between a variety of available discourses to make a case. There was a vast difference between the public speeches of Mrs Thatcher, instructive as they may be from the point of view of learning the tricks of rhetoric, and the nature of her response under pressure (the famous *Belgrano* interview, where she was interrogated by Diana Gould, a member of the public, is a case in point).

Method: the structure of a television or radio interview should be followed, and the participants prepared/rehearsed with a series of questions, at the end of which the opposing camps should be presented by the interviewer with one or two questions not anticipated by the respondents, so that the discursive choices made may be noted. The two adversaries should then be asked to sum up their positions.

The use of a television studio would be appropriate for recording these interactions, but few schools and only some colleges have such access. One alternative practice in schools is to rearrange the classroom as in Fig 2.9, so that the camera can pan across to each group; strict conditions of silence will have to be observed in the other groups while each interview is filmed, unless the other students are to play the part of a studio audience. Alternatively, students can record the interviews on audio tape.

SEMIOLOGY AND DESIGN: ANALYSIS AND PRODUCTION

Campaign materials

Students are asked to study a series of party and corporate logos, election leaflets, and political speeches in order to produce a package of election materials, consisting of a poster, badge, and campaign leaflet for an environmentalist candidate.

Purpose: to aid design work in basic and advanced production exercises, to introduce students to the idea of semiological studies having a practical application, to translate verbal rhetoric to the page, and to experiment with address and role.

Method: to assume the role of workers in a political cause who must address a set of materials to an audience. (Note: advanced work, based perhaps on the exploration of audience in Chapter 3, could produce a series of materials for a 'segmented' audience.)

ESSAY TITLES

1 'The ideologies of media institutions are revealed in the ways in which they represent people and interpret events.'

   Discuss this statement with reference to one issue that has featured in recent news reports, describing the type and range of viewpoints which are promoted.

2 'Although image-based semiology has sometimes been used as a foolproof way of interpreting media texts, it is in fact limited by a number of shortcomings.'

   What are these shortcomings, and what other methods of interpretation might help to reveal meaning in mass media texts? You may refer to any form of text which is regarded as having a significant visual element.

3 'There is an essential difference between propaganda and persuasion.'

   Discuss, with reference to any relevant examples from personal interaction and mass media communication.

4 'The discourses which politicians hope to mobilise often fail because the mass media brings its own agenda to bear on all public debates.'

   Provide evidence either to support or to attack this statement. In your response, refer to only one form of the mass media.

CHAPTER 3

'Constructing' the audience

THE MEANING OF AUDIENCE

Some writers take issue over certain uses of the term 'audience', because they are concerned that the word refers mainly to the process of hearing. Most, however, tend to stick with the term, and it is unlikely to be replaced in media and communication studies. The current use of the term in the subject refers to a great deal more than just a collection of 'hearers'.

It is also suggested by some that the usual terms used to describe how people use mass media forms, such as 'viewing' or 'watching', tend to imply that the audience is unduly passive. Some are anxious to find an alternative word for the activity they see associated with viewing television, and put forward 'reading' as a suitable term. It is worth noting first, that we should try to ensure that our understanding of the term 'activity' is not, in turn, being stretched out of all recognition. In the second place, 'reading' is already in use as a term both for the *process* of 'interaction' which takes place when a text is perused, and for the end result of that process (as in 'producing a reading of a text').

The half-life of terms

Whatever terms are used in media studies, we should accept that it is in the nature of language to change, developing as it does through use, and that certain terms take on new meanings over time. In the case of media studies, there is the usual change in the use of terms, but also a high rate of wastage, some proving that they actually explain very little, breaking down in use and then being discarded in favour of something else. The new term is then used as a sort of 'lucky charm' until it too fails to shed light on a subject which is not just expanding, but changing constantly. This implies that the tools we use may become redundant. It is also quite important that they are selected with care in the first place, bearing in mind that we cannot simply 'junk' the accumulated 'core' of the subject. We need to know what has gone before in order to make rational decisions about how to move on.

How to reach the audience?

The arguments about how research into audiences should be carried out turn on how we can observe or record response to the mass media. How exactly should people be questioned? As individuals or in groups? If in groups, how should the groups be composed? Should the researchers themselves place individuals in groups? The important work of David Morley will serve to illustrate some of these problems.

Taking a very straightforward view of the question of audience, it is clear that specific audiences do exist. There is, for example, an audience for *Eastenders*, an audience for *Channel 4 News*, and an audience for the *Independent*. The fact that these audiences are never exactly stable in terms of numbers, or that some parts of the audience do not always give their full attention to the product, or that these audiences are often separated in time and space, does not, at first, appear to matter.

Specific audiences

In *More than Meets the Eye* (p. 147), Graeme Burton defines three ways in which audiences can be specific:

1 where they are defined by the particular *product* (magazine, record, film) they consume – the *Time Out* audience, for example;
2 where there is a specific audience for a *type* of product – computer magazines, film noir, etc.;
3 where audiences belong to *pre-existing* groups (defined by age, gender, class, income, etc.)

If we deal with the last category first, we can see that the list of groups could be written out more fully. The media theorist Hartley (1982) list **seven** types of 'subjectivities' when discussing what goes to create the social position of the individual:

- self
- gender
- age group
- family
- class
- nation
- ethnicity

However, in *Television Culture*, John Fiske says that Hartley has missed out certain factors which act upon people and therefore also create subjectivities or subject positions. He adds:

- education
- religion

- political allegiance
- region
- urban versus rural background

We should note that these lists are similar to the factors which make up Therborn's view of subjectivity, but that they give no indication of which factor may be strongest at any one particular time or place, or which might act most strongly on particular individuals. It is difficult to find these answers in a list. As we shall see, we can only begin to discover answers through studying research into audience.

Different ways of defining audience

Part of the problem we are faced with is that there are different ways of thinking about (or conceptualising) audiences. We must be aware, for example, of the reasons people have for dividing audiences into separate categories. There are likely to be quite different motivations behind the investigations of, on the one hand, an advertising company (which may want to define an audience in order to sell products), and a theorist (who may wish to work out how an audience behaves for the purposes of research).

The central argument of Ien Ang's book *Desperately Seeking the Audience* is that 'television audience' (her particular concern) exists only as 'an imaginary entity, an abstraction constructed from the vantage point of the institutions, in the interest of the institutions'. This idea is worth examining, but it does not mean that the audience for a media content or form has no existence as actual individuals or collections of individuals. The way we usually think about, or understand audience, leads us into imagining that it is easily identified as some kind of 'mass'.

McQuail talks about the 'duality' of the audience. The audience may be formed either 'in response to media' (p. 215) or where 'it corresponds to an existing social group or category'. In other words (and whatever overlap there may be), we can gain a clearer picture of audience formation if we imagine that the audience has either *the media* as its source, or *society* as its source.

Methods of defining and reaching audience

The basic methods of understanding or exploring the idea of audience are listed here: some of them are based on actual investigations of audience, while others tend more to be conceptualisations or even creations of audience (ways of imagining or ways of constructing audiences). Most ways of understanding audience tend to use both research and theory. All attempts to define audience involve imagining what a particular audience might be like. (The accepted methods of finding out how an audience might *behave* will follow this list.)

First, there is the **empirical** method of counting or quantifying the number of people who use a certain product, or who are reached by what McQuail (p. 218) calls 'a given unit of media content'. The 'counting' takes place through information gained once that product has been purchased or that unit consumed. This method of investigating audience can be carried out for academic purposes, but is usually restricted to the commercial world. It has a fairly limited aim, but can be extended by producing a more detailed 'audience breakdown' which involves identifying sub-groups within the wider audience. The sub-groups might be identified according to differences in housing, income, class, region, and so on. (Why might it be useful to know which sub-groups purchase which products?) McQuail calls this concept of audience an 'aggregate of spectators, readers, listeners, viewers'.

Second, there is a view of audience as a **mass** of individuals and groups which is of a brief and inconsistent composition. This view is quite different, for example, to the Marxist view of the working class as a cohesive social mass. The 'mass' in this conception would be larger than most crowds. It could be thought of as, for example, the mass audience for cinema, radio and television. This idea of mass implies that it 'lacked self-awareness and self-identity' (McQuail, p. 31).

Third, there is the idea of an audience which is a distinct **social group** in its own right, which may be served by a particular or specialised medium, but which does not depend on that media form for its existence as a group. This might include a local audience for a local publication. McQuail calls this the 'audience as a public or social group'.

Fourth, there is the **deliberate targeting** of particular sections of the mass audience. Media industries could be seen as 'creating' sub-audiences in this way. This is both an idea about audience, and a way of segmenting specific audiences. As an idea about audience it presumes that particular social, economic, or even lifestyle groups can be persuaded that certain products and services are especially suitable for their needs. As a method, it creates boundaries between different groups in order to isolate a particular audience. However, in doing this, it sells its brand or product through an address to an audience which sometimes only comes into being at the moment of the address. (See the later outline of interpellation.) A company may decide to direct a campaign at a group which it believes has the potential to support its product. The audience they construct through this method (usually for advertising or political campaigns) is to some extent 'artificial', in that it exists as a group in relation only to a certain product. This qualification of audience often takes place before a product is sold, or when it needs to be relaunched. This is sometimes known as 'audience as market'.

Ways of studying the behaviour of audiences

There are various ways of studying the behaviour of audiences, determined by the interests of the researchers.

First, there is the **effects tradition**, which concentrates on the supposed effects that particular forms or contents of the media have on their audience. 'Forms' refer to the particular mass media outlet – television, for example. In this case, the effect of watching television *in general* would be the major consideration. Content might refer to 'violence on TV', which has long been one of the main preoccupations of groups which claim to detect a moral decline in our society.

Second, there is the research into what audiences do with the media, the uses they make of the media and the **'uses and gratifications'** they draw from it. In this case, the point is to research an identified group, so that the empirical method outlined above would come into play.

Third, there is the investigation of the ways in which **content** might be able to structure audience responses in predictable ways. This view would attempt to explain the different interpretations of mass media texts by different groups, by relating the differences to subcultural and socio-economic variables. The work of David Morley is a landmark in this kind of research.

Fourth, and deriving partly from the above, there is the study of the ways in which texts attempt to **offer positions** to an audience, from which it is invited to see experience in particular ways. The question 'How are we *positioned* by this text?' may be asked of any mass communication. We are invited to occupy a 'social space' by a text's mode of address, and are ultimately invited to occupy an ideological position – this is called interpellation.

Research methods

At this point, a brief survey of research methods is needed, if the strengths and weaknesses of different types of investigation are to be understood. A basic distinction between **quantitative** and **qualitative** methods should be appreciated. Quantitative research is concerned with the collection of facts and figures, through social surveys (finding out things from people), using questionnaires, or interviews. Ideas about broad trends in society and basic structures in social life can be gained from this approach. Quantitative data can be obtained not just from people, but from records, documents, reports and statistics. Qualitative research, on the other hand, does not often cover such a wide field, aiming instead for an in-depth view based on interviews, participant observation and the study of detailed documents of a personal / historical nature, such as autobiographies and diaries.

The type of information which may be found can also be divided into **primary data** and **secondary data**. Primary data are recorded directly by the researcher from sources. They are data which have not already been written down, recorded or processed in some way, and might include case studies, observations or surveys. Secondary data are derived from the study of recorded material, whether it is published or not, and whether or not it has already been processed by other researchers.

One of the problems faced by all researchers is that they inhabit the same general social world as their subjects, even if there are specific differences between their respective subject-positions (class differences, age differences and so on). Researchers will of course carry assumptions about what the social world is like. The methods they choose will have certain built-in biases, and the researchers will have their own political and theoretical stand-points.

Labelling, address and role

To understand how audiences which belong to so-called 'pre-existing' groups may be 'imagined' or 'pictured' by those carrying out research, we need to understand two things. First, that research into pre-existing groups may not be the sole aim of an investigation. For the marketing strategist, such research is only a starting point. He/she may be more interested in 'positioning' the audience, and will use targeting strategies relevant to the concept of 'audience as market'. Secondly, we need to realize that there is a question mark over the whole idea of the 'natural' existence of groups as they are defined by some theorists.

We would do well to remind ourselves of the subjectivities described by Fiske and Hartley before exploring how they are used as 'starting points' for different types of study. They are: self, gender, age group, family, class, nation, ethnicity, education, religion, political allegiance, region, and urban versus rural background.

A STARTING POINT: MORLEY AND THE *NATIONWIDE* AUDIENCE

David Morley's *The Nationwide Audience* is an attempt to overcome the shortcomings of theoretical approaches to audience. Morley's work was based on a study of television, and he began by dealing with the different tendencies in mass

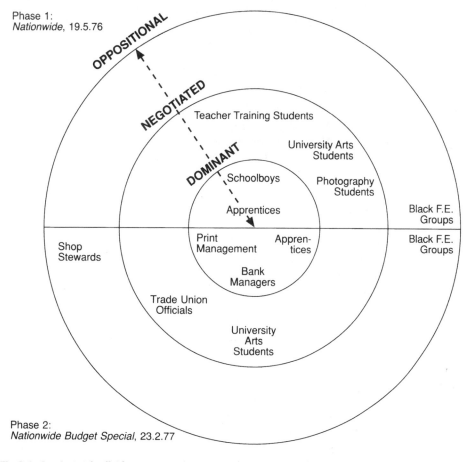

Fig 3.1 A schematic display
(Courtesy of The Nationwide Audience *by David Morley, published by The British Film Institute, 1980)*

135

communication research. He looked at the way that theorists had stressed either the central importance of the message, or the central importance of the audience and its composition. Morley saw himself at this time (1980) as part of a new approach. He did not think that the most important aspect of research was the attempt to understand the way society functions, or how audience behaviour is affected. He wished to understand how meanings are experienced by people through the process of living in society, and how these meanings are then put into a form that can be recognised and understood by other people.

Morley's project took a basic idea into account from the start, that the researcher (in the words of Robert Merton – *see* Morely's book) had to:

> '... analyse both the content of [the message] ... and the responses of the audience. The analysis of content ... gives us clues to what might be effective in it. The analysis of responses to it enables us to check those clues.'

Morley was opposed to the kind of 'effects' research which dwells exclusively on the receiver and the situation in which reception takes place. Nor was he impressed by research which concentrates on the supposed power of mass communication content to overwhelm audiences. However, his rejection of extremes did not imply any kind of 'neutral' position: the pluralist approach, which stresses how public communication forms a kind of circuit, from 'society as source' to 'society as audience' (*see* Halloran, *The Effects of Television*, p. 7), fails to take into account the complexity of the message, according to Morley.

The relationship between insitution and audience is also complex; it would appear that an audience (although essential to an institution's survival), never enjoys the privilege of initiating the 'interactions' which take place between the two. However, through its viewing habits, and to a lesser degree through the use of public campaigning and some special and limited access to parts of the mass media, it can play some part in framing the discourses of taste.

The TV message and the audience

Morley explains his view that:

> '... the TV message is treated as a complex sign, in which a preferred meaning has been inscribed, but which retains the potential ... of communicating a different meaning.'

In his book, Morley repeats the warning made by Hall, who noted that the presence of many possible alternative meanings in a message (polysemy) must not be confused with pluralism: 'connotive codes are not equal among themselves'.

Factors in different decodings

Morley investigated the idea that the various decodings arrived at by audiences might differ according to the following factors:

1 The **position people occupied** in the structures of age, sex, race and class.
2 The **involvement of people in cultural identities**, i.e. belonging to trade unions, political parties, or to specific sub-cultures based on factors like age or ethnicity.

3 The **relationship between the particular message and a group's experience of it**. In some cases an audience might be familiar with an idea or an event – in others its only contact with the content of the message may have been through the mass media.
4 The **context in which decoding takes place** and the possible differences in the detail of the decoding which may be affected by situation (college, school, work, home, etc.).

Morley's method of selecting groups for research

Class features prominently in Morley's view of the way in which groups come to exist, but he does not follow anything so simple as the notion that class position exactly determines how people behave. The categories we have used so far may be extended by Rosen's 1972 additions (*see Language and Class*) of history, traditions, job experience, residential patterns, and level of organisation to Fiske and Hartley's list of subjectivities (self, gender, age group, family, class, nation, ethnicity, education, religion, political allegiance, region, and urban versus rural background).

WHY DOES MORLEY USE GROUPS?

Morley believed that groups, rather than individuals, should be used for this type of investigation because (p. 33) 'much individually-based interview research is flawed by a focus on individuals as social atoms divorced from their social context'. What is odd here is the idea that the individual, who must carry their subjectivity, their social 'imprint' with them, is regarded as 'divorced from their social context' if they are not in the immediate presence of the group to which Morley has decided they most naturally belong!

Morley chose twenty-nine groups, of which twenty-six were eventually to form the basis of his published research. Each group was defined according to its age range, occupation, ethnicity, gender, class and political allegiance. For example, one group is described as 'a group of mainly white, male apprentice engineers; non-unionised, with a skilled working-class background, aged 20–26. Studying part-time in a Midlands polytechnic; predominantly "don't know" or Conservative in political orientation' (p. 40), while another is introduced as 'a group of West Indian women students, aged 18–19, with a working-class background, on a community-studies course full-time in a London F.E. college; predominantly "don't know" or Labour' (p. 87).

The groups were shown two *Nationwide* programmes from 1976 and 1977. Their responses were recorded on tape and interpretative judgments and speculations were then made by the author.

A useful system of interpretation?

The theorist Parkin is criticised by Morley for offering only three possible 'positions' which can be occupied by people in response to a message. Parkin's three positions are:

- 'Dominant', where the audience member or the group concerned produces a 'reading' or 'interpretation' of the message which basically agrees with the dominant viewpoint contained in it. (If, for example, it was an item in a television programme which suggested that strikes were a social evil, then the respondent would take that line.)
- 'Negotiated' where the ideological content of the message is altered to fit with the respondent's own view, and by being altered produces a new position.
- 'Oppositional', where the the dominant viewpoint is contested and a reading which opposes it is produced.

Criticisms of the *Nationwide* research

In *Television and Its Audience*, Brunt and Jordin ask several questions about the nature of Morley's research. In the first place, they note that the research does not reveal the process by which groups decode television messages. This point has led some scholars and researchers to propose the idea that there is a 'missing link' between the construction of mass media material and its reception by an audience. This link is described as the 'cognitive level'. Cognition – 'knowing', or perception – does not appear to be related directly to class, gender, ethnicity and so on. This idea is presented by Birgitta Hoijer in *Media, Culture and Society* vol. 14. (Reference to Hoijer's theory will also be made in Chapter 6.) Morley himself came to recognise that it was no good presenting demographic factors such as race or class as reasons for different decodings if no attempt was made to explain how these factors affected interpretation.

As we have already seen, the use of groups rather than individuals is not properly justified. However, going to the other extreme and setting up individual interviews will not shed light on how people use or interpret television discourses unless, as Brunt and Jordin point out, a comparative study is made between a range of individual interviews. This should find out how typical a response is for the subject-position of the individual compared with someone in a *similar* position (using many individuals with the same gender, ethnicity, age, etc.) and also how such responses contrast with individuals in *different* subject positions.

Another reservation expressed by these authors concerns Morley's practice of *giving* groups what they call (p. 237) 'a homogeneous class identity' when he also regards each group as having an *independent* existence outside the research project. Clearly, it is difficult to claim that a group exists in its own right if one of the factors (in this case class) is used to 'herd' its members into place. The 'real complexity of each group' (p. 237) is lost, because the contradictions of a subject's class-position are not explored. Class is presented as the one factor which can be relied upon to sort people into meaningful categories.

Overall, Brunt and Jordin's assessment is that the *Nationwide* research produces a negative result; there is no direct connection between social position and the way that people interpret or decode the mass communication discourses they encounter. Part of the problem, as they see it, is the attempt to place the responses of groups into the three 'bands' mentioned earlier; dominant, negotiated or oppositional.

THE WRONG VIEW OF CLASS?

It seems that some views treat class as an external structure – something which exists in society and which influences people from the outside. Clearly, people's occupations and their experience of community and history, all go to make their class position a living thing. But class is also a relationship between groups, and between institutions in our society. This means that it is quite dynamic; it changes all the time. One of the most interesting remarks made by Jordin and Brunt is that a new question should be posed in academic research of this type. That is (p. 242): 'What does this audience group do with the text it chooses to watch, and what discourses does it mobilise in the process?'

AVOIDING THE THREE 'BANDS'

It is possible to imagine that some responses to a discourse could fall exactly on the borderline of 'negotiated' and 'oppositional', and the researcher could be at a loss as to how to proceed. These artificial boundaries are not really even a useful shorthand for how people respond to messages. Brunt and Jordin prefer to say that all decodings are 'negotiated', drawing attention to how a text is used, instead of whether it fits into a category. This does not mean that they follow the current fashion for calling the audience role a 'negotiation', and then avoiding the problem of how meaning is circulated, or how power is shared within audiences and between audience and media form.

It has long been accepted in some studies of literature that there are 'preferred' meanings in a text and that other meanings (which are perhaps squeezed out or given less prominence) have a habit of reappearing. Have you ever thought that the hero you are supposed to admire is in fact less interesting than the villain? Have you wondered why the cop adventure has to start with the policemen's wife/lover being killed? How do 'alternative' ways of understanding a story push their way into a reader's mind? Some critics argue that narratives themselves always carry an 'alternative' reading, running alongside the one the author appears to suggest is 'correct'.

Jordin and Brunt argue that the 'resistance' to the dominant meaning is carried in the text itself. Presumably, this is a *potential* for resistance, since it is the incomplete meanings and contradictions carried in the text which might provide an opening for criticism through the use of the viewer's own experiences. The term 'negotiated' is used, as we have seen, to signify the way that some audience members adapt to, but also change, the meanings offered to them. 'Negotiation' could certainly be a misleading term in the context of audience response, and seems to be applied to too many situations where the parties involved are in unequal positions of power. We should realise that it refers more easily to a process in which the audience member negotiates *meaning*, rather than arguing over power itself.

RADICAL CHALLENGES TO AUTHORITY?

The idea proposed by Jordin and Brunt (p. 246) that 'radical challenges to the professional authority ... of broadcasters' are produced by audience decodings of meaning, seems rather too hopeful. Audience response is rarely a challenge to the broadcasters directly. It is more the case that their 'address' to us, their 'interpella-tion' of our subject-position, has failed.

It could be argued instead that resistance is a challenge to dominant representa-tions of what is 'normal' and 'legitimate'. What result this may have in material terms is very much open to question. Jordin and Brunt note that the very process of research involves another interpellation, this time from the researcher to the audi-ence member, in which the respondent is placed as a responsible subject who is likely therefore to answer in the official mode of discourse. It is a factor, they say, which must be taken into account.

Roles and interpellation

If, like the Marxist theorist Althusser, we imagine the dominant powers in society 'hailing' us as the subject, there is still a question over whether or not we will respond. If we do respond, do we always respond in the same way at the same time in our lives? If as infants we responded to the voice of authority (at school perhaps), then does it mean that we are 'theirs' for life, and that we will have the same reaction to any address from authority in the future? It may be thought that if this works, it does not always happen in a dramatic way. It should not be imag-ined, for example, that we are all conditioned to support this country's wars because we were taught to obey forms of authority in school. However, we may perhaps be less inclined to imagine that there is anything we can do to change our world or to challenge forms of authority.

The mass media produce a number of interpellations and a number of role-positions for us to occupy. We have come to expect a variety of role 'genres' from television news, advertising, magazines and newspapers, and so on. While this means that we are able to recognise that some part of us is being 'spoken to', we may assume the role offered for such a short space of time, and without serious consequence, that it sometimes feels as though we are engaged in a game.

It was noted earlier that direct addresses are made to us as we flick through the pages of a magazine, and that we are in the habit of engaging with an address before breaking off and moving on to another. (We should be aware that we may be addressed just as much through images as through words.) Magazines will 'speak to' different aspects of someone's personality, or different roles they are called upon to assume in real life. These roles might include friend, son/daughter, student, part-time worker, and so on. The addresses made by advertisements may ask us to do things which involve some purchase or outlay of money: to buy things, to improve things we already have, to invest in the future. Sometimes we are asked to assume certain states of mind which will encourage us to buy things. We are encouraged to sympathise, to fantasise, to be responsible, and so on.

Although it may be thought of as 'role play', the address made for commercial (rather than academic) ends forms the next part of our study of 'pre-existing' social groups. If, to pursue the example, we recognise different addresses in a magazine, we may begin to notice that the pictures and text combine to give an overall image or character to the magazine. This represents the end result of very careful market-ing and is the material evidence of 'audience profiling'.

The publishers of a magazine will certainly have carried out research into their readership. It may seem crazy to argue that the magazine is actually 'creating' its own audience through its articles, advertising, and 'house style', but this is exactly what is happening. The magazine, the commodity, is advertising itself now and in the future. Graeme Burton, in *More than Meets the Eye*, takes the example of the readership of a heavy metal magazine:

'. . . by bringing that audience into the material, the product actually defines the audience for whom the communication is intended. Heavy Metal magazines contain photographs of clothes, of fans, of performers, which define their largely male audience in the product and by providing a model for lifestyle which is assimilated into the behaviour and habits of that audience, they're shaping the material for an audience which they have already shaped through previous material.'

In the case of this kind of magazine, imagining an audience will be fairly straightforward. Most publishers will have a clear picture of the social class and the age group of the people who purchase and read a particular magazine, but for many this is not enough. The marketing expert will want to 'picture' his/her readership. This, as we shall see, involves a profile of a readership's *psychology*.

Segmentation and psychographic profiling

The ability to recognise that different groups exist, and to adjust a sales pitch or marketing technique accordingly, is only the beginning. Any audience may be further divided by the method known as segmentation. A group of black, middle-class consumers, for example, could be re-conceptualised as belonging to different *psychological* or *lifestyle* groupings. For example, groups of consumers known as Achievers, or as Strivers, or even as the Downtrodden, are all examples of categories which have been defined not just for specific campaigns, but for the general purposes of imagining what types of people inhabit the social world, how they should be spoken to and, in the case of advertising, as we shall see, to find out what products different groups of people will be prepared to buy.

Ien Ang advances the idea that we are all in danger of being forced to see audiences through the eyes of the industries, whose interest goes further than merely creating audiences so that they can sell things. She believes that industries create audiences in order to maintain their general position of power.

In order to maintain their power they must, of course, ensure that people do continue to buy what they offer! John Hartley (*Reading Television*, p. 78) said that TV institutions 'are obliged not only to speak about an audience but – crucially, for them – to talk to one as well: they need not only to represent audiences but to enter into *relations* with them'.

Obviously, if an industry is to enter into some sort of relationship with their audience, they have to picture who they will be talking to before they actually start talking. Although Hartley notes that the audience becomes an 'invisible fiction', it might be better to think of an industry as having the power to make this invisible audience 'materialise' from the shadows.

Freedom and consumption

From an audience's point of view, all sorts of goods, including cultural artefacts, help to construct what advertisers call 'lifestyle'. Debates about the degree to which audiences exercise 'freedom' in their choices, and in turn, the extent to which the sum of *any* choice made from commercial alternatives, can be described as 'freedom' *per se*, must first recognise how the capitalist system operates. Consumption has been established as the universal principle of modernity. Consumption has also become a 'right'. Production is thus geared to provide not only a bewildering range of goods, but a multiplicity of 'routes' for the expression of self-identity.

One project which has provided useful information on the way consumers assign meaning to the goods they purchase, is the Household Uses of Information Technology Project, set up by the Economic and Social Research Council. Roger Silverstone and his colleagues used the concept of a household's 'moral economy' to refer to families' 'own way of working with the social, economic and technological opportunities which frame their world' (1989, p. 1–2). Technology (manifested in things like CD-players, faxes, TV sets, etc.) is 'appropriated' by the household and undergoes a change in status, from commodity to domestic object.

Modes of consumption and theories of audience

The problems which surround any theory of media audience are compounded by the different 'modes of consumption' adopted by individual audience members. The technology available in the domestic environment, which provides 'zappers' for movement between channels, allows television programmes to be recorded, gives access to cable and satellite, and which has now introduced a rival in the form of material on the world wide web, has created 'an increasingly undisciplined and elusive set of everyday activities' (Shaun Moores, in *Satellite Television and Everyday Life*, p. 6). The realm in which these activities take place does not, according to Moores, 'lend itself to being measured'. The reason for this lies in its status as 'a dispersed domain of lived experiences and cultural meanings rather than as an object to be quantified' (Moores, p. 6). Seen from this perspective, the study of audience is not made from the perspective of 'effects', or investigated to discover 'uses and gratifications', but becomes an **ethnographic** issue, in which researchers attempt to understand the behaviour of social groups through direct contact with individuals in what Moores (p. 7) calls 'their routine daily settings'.

Other forms of investigation begin by studying the way that audience members establish their own identities in the context of interaction. In *'The Discursive Construction of Viewer Identity'* (*see* the *European Journal of Communication*, Vol. 11 (1), 1996), Paul Dickerson follows the work of Mikhail Bakhtin in arguing that 'self' could be seen as 'the consequence rather than the cause of what we say' (p. 59). This perspective is also explored in Michael Billig's *Ideology and Opinions* (1991), in which an interview on the subject of the Royal Family shows that people take positions through which they can express aspects of their identity. Rather than using interviews as a means of discovering a set of unshakeable beliefs (or ideological positions), the aim of the researcher is to explore 'live dialogic activity' (Dickerson,

p. 60) and the way in which individual identity is actively constructed during a particular social interaction.

Dickerson used an extract from the *Nine O'Clock News* to test the way his respondents framed their opinions during conversation. The tendency to regard individual statements as expressions of value within a particular discursive environment, rather than evidence of a fixed outlook, is also found in the lively work of Pertti Alasuutari. His book, *Researching Culture* (1995), reveals the difference between investigations based on a search for cultural norms (established models of behaviour and expression), and a perspective which emphasises meaning as it is found in the context of group interaction. Alasuutari argues (p. 167) that 'norm theory assumes that society or any community is held together … by a unanimity about norms that all should follow'. In contrast to this approach, his own research seemed to indicate that group norms sometimes had little real effect on group members. 'I eventually realised', writes Alasuutari, 'that when you encounter a normative statement you have to ask: what is the social meaning of each norm?' (p. 169). In other words how, and for what reasons, are norms actually used within groups? Are norms obeyed, or merely recognised as boundaries which can nevertheless be crossed? Alasuutari's central concern with meaning has implications for the way research should be conducted. In particular, caution needs to be exercised when, as is often the case, direct revelation of the researcher's hypothesis would produce meaningless responses. He insists that 'it is particularly important not to confuse two things here: the question presented in the interview and the question you have set for the study'. Alasuutari is convinced that 'a research hypothesis cannot be tested simply by asking the informants whether [the] interpretation is right'. An hypothesis cannot be presented directly, because eliciting a simple 'yes' or 'no' would negate the purpose of any investigation, which is to explore the range and meaning of respondents' answers. Alasuutari notes, however (p. 170), that 'hypotheses can … be tested by presenting questions to the informants. The trick is to word questions indirectly, to *operationalize* the hypothesis'. In sum, he describes qualitative analysis as 'reasoning and argumentation that is not based simply on statistical relations between "variables"'.

ADVERTISING: INDUSTRY AND AUDIENCE

Advertisers are particularly fond of sub-dividing social groups. It is important, from their point of view, to identify a clearly defined 'target market'. For example, certain brands of coffee are produced with different consumer profiles in mind. 'Gold Blend' might be aimed at middle-class achievers (and it's obvious that such people do exist), but also at groups which suppose that acquiring the brand will provide one element that can be *circulated* within a desirable lifestyle they wish to acquire.

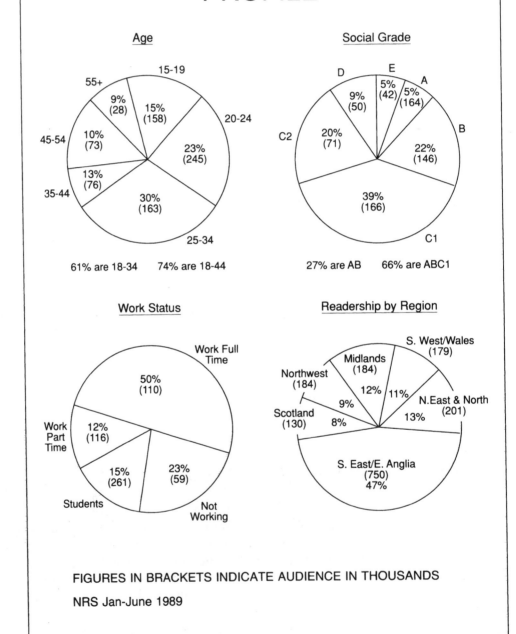

THE **COSMOPOLITAN** READER PROFILE

Age

15-19
55+
9% (28)
15% (158)
20-24
45-54
10% (73)
23% (245)
35-44
13% (76)
30% (163)
25-34

61% are 18-34   74% are 18-44

Social Grade

D
E
A
9% (50)
5% (42)
5% (164)
C2
20% (71)
B
22% (146)
39% (166)
C1

27% are AB   66% are ABC1

Work Status

Work Full Time
50% (110)
Work Part Time
12% (116)
23% (59)
15% (261)
Students
Not Working

Readership by Region

S. West/Wales (179)
Midlands (184)
Northwest (184)
12%   11%
N.East & North (201)
9%
Scotland (130)
8%   13%
S. East/E. Anglia (750) 47%

FIGURES IN BRACKETS INDICATE AUDIENCE IN THOUSANDS

NRS Jan-June 1989

Fig 3.2 A reader profile
(Courtesy of NRS for Cosmopolitan)

Table 3.1 Cosmopolitan reader profile 1991–92

	Jul–Dec 1992 %	Apr–Sept 1992 %	Jul–Dec 1991 %
Women	75.1	77.4	77.7
Men	24.9	22.6	22.3
Women			
15–19	14.9	17.7	16.1
20–24	19.6	19.9	20.0
25–34	29.2	28.0	28.4
35–44	15.9	13.4	15.2
45–54	11.8	12.2	11.7
55–64	4.8	4.2	4.1
65+	3.8	4.5	4.5
AB	26.1	27.0	25.7
C1	38.6	36.7	38.6
C2	19.0	19.9	19.7
DE	16.4	16.5	16.1

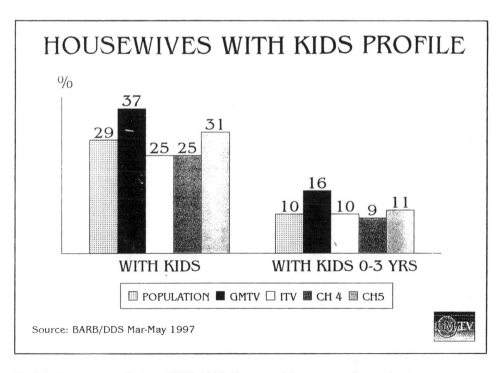

Fig 3.3 Consumer profile from GMTV, 1997. Note use of the category 'housewives'
(Courtesy of GMTV)

However, the advertising institution's approach may well change, and the groups it creates will alter according to what is perceived as fashionable in the society as a whole. Advertisers are anxious to take account of changing social fashions. The 'new man', for example, has some basis in social reality (as does his oafish cousin, the 'new lad'), but seems to appear more often in magazine advertisements because advertisers believe that it is an *effective* image. Perhaps some men quite like to be represented in this way, but advertising can only really circulate ideas and fashions (especially fashions for certain ideas) rather than starting these trends in the first place.

Lifestyle and segmentation

An interest in achieving a dynamic picture of their audience led many companies to adopt the technique known as 'lifestyle' profiling. This was not exclusively a British trend, because the internationalisation of the advertising and public relations worlds meant that the same tendencies were appearing in Western Europe and America. The idea was to combine a psychological profile of the consumer with ideas about how they conducted their life in the market-place. This idea can sound at first as though it is a bit more democratic than simply using class as a guide for marketing products. It might be the case that anyone could be labelled 'an Achiever', no matter what their background.

However, one of the early consumer profiles which used this combination of psychology and lifestyle (the McCann Erikson 'Woman Study' of 1985) revealed that class had never in fact been completely abandoned by advertisers in favour of 'psychographic' profiling. In fact, the two perspectives were simply combined. The class-position occupied by segments of the audience was central to how McCann Erikson 'imagined' or conceptualised its audience. One group, called 'the Aimless' is very clearly at the bottom of the hierarchy of social class, while the 'Traditionals' are a group at the top end of society. The different groups are represented in the McCann Erikson report by drawings of a variety of animals. The 'Downtrodden' are represented by a picture of a harassed rabbit with droopy ears, carrying heavy bags of shopping home while little rabbits run about at her feet. The drawing for 'the Aimless' shows a dog in curlers with a cigarette drooping from its lips.

MORE ANIMALS

In 1989, the French CCA (Centre de la Communication Avancée) produced the first encyclopaedia of European lifestyles, which was based on 24,000 interviews in sixteen European countries. It ran to 20,000 pages and the 'types' of people it defined included Street Cats, Herons, Doves, Elephants, Foxes, Squirrels, Owls, Sharks, Gulls and Albatrosses, Badgers and Sea-lions. But for the absence of Little Bears and other such creatures, this could be Valentine's day in the back pages of some quality newspapers.

The details of each groups are also a little puzzling. According to Mattelart, (*Advertising International*). 'Elephants [are] ... highly attracted by small specialist shops which offer personal services.' If these shops are on the small side, one might wonder how they are able to squeeze into them!

PROFILING IN EMPLOYMENT

What is particularly interesting about psychological profiling is that it is also used for social and economic purposes. Some firms hire consultants to carry out testing on their employees in order to find out whose values are closest to those of the organisation. Those employees who are in any sense lukewarm in their enthusiasm for the company's perspective may well be weeded out when redundancy or 'restructuring' takes place.

Maslow and the 'hierarchy of needs'

In *Motivation and Personality*, Abraham Maslow set out two fundamental ideas about human needs. The first was that all people have needs, but that these needs are arranged in a sort of order, with the most pressing and basic coming first on the list. Only when these needs are satisfied are people able to devote their energy to the next level of needs. The second idea was that only unsatisfied needs can motivate behaviour. Once satisfied, a need no longer acts as a motivator.

The following five 'levels' of need were placed by Maslow in a hierarchy, which is usually imagined as a pyramid structure.

1 **Physiological needs**. These concern the basic necessities which sustain life: air, water, food, elimination, sleep, and sex (there is some debate about whether sex should be included in this list).
2 **Safety needs**. This is the desire for safety from danger and deprivation.
3 **Social needs.** These are linked to the desire people have for love, acceptance into social groups, friendship and so on – they are meant to help preserve a person's social identity.
4 **Esteem needs**. This level includes the need for self-esteem, connected to feelings of competence and achievement, together with self-respect.
5 **Self-actualisation needs**. There are all about the fulfilment of one's full potential, and are linked with the expression of creativity.

QUESTIONS ON MASLOW

Why should love appear under 'social needs'? Doesn't it depend on the individual? For some, perhaps, it might constitute self-actualisation. Why are esteem needs only fulfilled when the most basic needs are already taken care of? There are many examples in history of people whose need for self-esteem has come before the fulfilment of the most basic needs – hunger strikers, for example. Aren't the social needs of some other individuals negligible by comparison with their drive for self-actualisation?

Our needs may depend not simply upon personal preferences and individual quirks, but also on the physical context in which we find ourselves. If a person is stranded on a desert island, it is certainly the case that their social esteem and self-actualisation needs will still function, but they will be forced to express these needs in a way that takes account of their environment. Short of talking to the coconuts or finding a promising footprint, their social needs in particular are unlikely to be fulfilled, and may become distorted. The 'hierarchy of needs' is perhaps not as cut and dried as it may seem.

Advertisers and the hierarchy of needs

Once again, an academic perspective has been borrowed by the corporate sector. As before, a notion of class as a static position we occupy has been grafted on to a perspective which concentrates on human growth and development. Some advertisers seem to examine social groups to discover, not their potential for development (according to the original idea, we are all supposed to have the potential to progress along Maslow's path, to reach some form of self-actualisation), but their place in the hierarchy.

Needs, hopes, dreams, fantasies are all investigated so that products, services, images may be sold more effectively. If this type of approach to advertising seems to demand a much clearer understanding of the attitudes, values and beliefs of the consumer, we might wonder if it is an approach which is similar to that of the political propagandist. Do some adverts, for example, work by anticipating not just consumer demand, but consumer protest? The BP television advert which showed wildlife in unspoilt natural surroundings anticipated public concern over the company's impact on the environment. It is a response which uses those very concerns to sell the idea that the company is pro-environment. The public's fears are admitted and re-presented from the very start. The theory of 'recuperation' (the reuse of ideas which were originally in opposition to the 'dominant' ideology) seems particularly appropriate in this case.

If the provision of information were the sole function advertising performed, then there would be little point in worrying about it. Advertising's ability to circulate messages on a global scale, together with its increasing integration with public relations, however, make it an important element in any study of power. If we were to examine the status of advertising as an informative media form, we would also have to look closely at its persuasive function.

Institution and history: the development of consumer culture

The history of advertising appears to be as old as organised commerce. Clearly, word of mouth has its limitations as a method of drawing attention to goods, once cities grow and distances between consumer and vendor increase, quite apart from the problems associated with an increase in the number of vendors. It was, however, the coming of industrialisation and the beginnings of the 'consumer culture' which led to the impetus for an explosion in the growth of advertising.

What we can be sure of is that mass society gave rise to, and was then in turn reproduced through mass culture. Mass production gave rise to mass consumption. Leiss, Klein and Jhally talk about 'the new social self' which arose when old cultures and communities were broken apart by the new concentrations of urban labour required by capitalism. This 'new self' was based on a highly individualistic outlook, matched by the tendency of the advertiser to address people as individuals.

In a situation where there is 'a truly enormous assortment of goods' confronting the individual, it might seem important for the individual to have some information about these goods. Leiss *et al.* point to 'the dramatic rise in real incomes' in the industrial West in the early stage of the consumer society (from 1900 on) which led to a higher proportion of marketing effort being directed to the satisfaction of human wants rather than basic needs (p. 53). The fact that this 'dramatic rise' was not universal, however, led advertisers to develop a primitive form of segmentation from the earliest days of the specialised agency. This segmentation tended to follow the pre-existing lines of class difference, with little need to define specialised groups like 'the Achievers'. If we take the example of car advertising in the 1920s, it made sense to regard the car as a luxury item which only the rich could afford; there would be no point in attracting different types of consumers to the product. That could only happen when there was a variety of models available at a price a substantial number of people could afford.

History: the development of the advertisement

If we need a very brief summary of the basic changes in the composition of static advertisements, before looking in more detail at the findings of research into content, we could say that the sort of 'early' advertisements which flourished in the first years of consumer society expressed meaning using, in the main, written texts to persuade the consumer to buy the product. From the 1920s, visual representation became more common. The text was then used to explain the visual elements. In the post-war period, the visual aspects of an advertising text tended to dominate and a 'reading' of an advertisement therefore became quite complex. All the internal elements of an advertisement's structure had to be related to each other, in order to create a message which made sense.

This process of development parallels the increasing use of 'psychographic' data about the characteristics of an intended audience, which we have already studied. Advertisements began to be concentrated on the supposed benefits to the consumer as a result of using the product, rather than on the product itself. This led to an increase in narrative and dramatic forms, and a steady decline in written, spoken or visually *descriptive* information. When television commercials appeared, the pre-dominance of narrative was more marked – but older methods were not discarded. (Some early television commercials employed a 'tableau' form which featured people holding up products for the public's inspection. The well-known Remington advertisements show an interesting use of this method. Dramatic narrative in this case, beyond an immediate portrayal of the product's capability, is relatively minor.)

A background to the four advertising formats

Leiss *et al.* identified four basic advertising formats, defining the way in which advertising developed in the twentieth century. Before summarising the four areas, we should first discover how Leiss and his co-workers established this overview. In order to demonstrate the steady overall decline in the number of words carried in advertising text, Leiss, Kline and Jhally made a content analysis of advertisements from 1910 to 1980 (*Social Communication in Advertising*). From an average of a 50 per cent coverage of display area in the 1910–1920 era, the coverage of words in relation to available space had dropped by 1970–80 to below

Fig 3.4 Two
examples of
American
advertisements
from 1890

Shakeresses Labeling and Wrapping the Bottles Containing the Shaker Extract of Roots, or Seigel's Syrup.

We Have Often Wondered Why

the people doubt that our medicines are made by the Shakers, but we suppose that it is because the country is filled with worthless articles made to deceive the public. So we must suffer for the faults of others. But to the afflicted this is a very important matter, because the sick and ailing are anxious to get genuine medicines, and they have faith in the Shaker articles. In view of this fact it is our duty to the public to inform them how to *learn beyond all doubt* the facts about the Shaker Extract of Roots, or Seigel's Syrup, and other Shaker remedies. Write to the *"Shaker Community,"* Mount Lebanon, N. Y., and ask if the Shaker medicines sold by A. J. White, 54 Warren street, New York City and by all dealers in medicines, are not made by the Shakers, and an answer will be returned. *The Shakers would not let their good name be used on the medicines if they were not genuine.*

TEETH!

Are easily and painlessly Filled at Home without previous experience by using Dr. Hale's Home Dental Outfit and method. It prevents toothache and early loss by stopping the cause, and secures *perfect, permanent teeth.* Every article in the outfit is warranted to be first-class. Money promptly refunded if unsatisfactory. Price, $3.00 and $5.00, with full directions, post-paid.

National Dental Supply Co.,
42 Warren St., Boston, Mass.

30 per cent. (Since then, however, it has become fashionable to produce a large amount of what advertisers call 'copy' in certain types of display advertising in magazines.) There was a corresponding increase in the visual element, between the two periods mentioned above, to over 70 per cent. (The researchers split visual representation into three areas: **product**, **person** and **setting**).

The changing relationship between written text and image is worth exploring. Even when text was the major component of an advertisement, certain types of advert used more text than others: 'alcohol and tobacco tended to use less text than … automobile ads and corporate messages' (pp. 230–1). The earlier the advertisement, the more likely it is that an illustration of the product would have made up the visual element. By the 1920s and 1930s, there were more and more advertisements where the product was no longer the only focus for illustration.

At first sight, the idea that the product should play a less important role in the images offered to the consumer may seem rather odd. Instead the product, or the effects of the product, would be emphasised through the representation of some human element. The text would then be used to draw attention to the link between the product and the human element. In other words, any 'misreading' of the advertisement was discouraged because text, image and the actual product to which they referred all reinforced one other. There was a single meaning, 'underlined', as it were, by all the elements which made up the display.

During the 1940s the use of images of people began to decline. In addition, the physical setting moved from the kind of environment in which the product might be found (a cooker in a kitchen, for example) to a wider setting, termed by Leiss *et al.* the 'social context' of use (p. 232). One of the most significant (yet hardly surprising) points made by these writers is that the technical means to reproduce images affected the kinds of information found in advertising. Just as a basic literacy would be needed to understand early advertisements, so the ability to decipher visual images must be assumed to exist in modern audiences.

The four advertising formats

The **product-information format** is a type of advertising where the product is at the centre of all other elements of the display, which point out and explain the virtues of the product. No extensive reference is made to either the user or the context of use.

The **product-image format** gives the product special qualities it might not originally appear to have – a symbolic relationship is established between the product and some abstract qualities outside the day-to-day use of the product. Leiss *et al.* use an illustration of a pack of cigarettes against the setting of a cool mountain stream.

The **personalised format** uses a direct relationship between the product and the human personality. The human element is not just part of the setting, but is central to an understanding of the product. Social interactions are made about and through the product. The product takes on human qualities. Products become 'intimate partners with use' and are at the 'centre of social interaction'.

In the **lifestyle format**, the setting is important, because it tells us how to interpret the human element and the product. This format is a combination of product-image and the personalised formats – the viewer or reader is meant to associate the product, the people and the people's use of the product with a particular kind of 'consumption style'. The product or the people using it are made to look relaxed, or sophisticated, or handsome, or rich, or a combination of these. There is an implication that the product will have some kind of positive effect in social terms, or at least that it could be used as one of the props which signify status.

Escaping from reality?

Leiss *et al.* note that 'Looking at advertisements today is a bit like walking through a carnival hall of mirrors, where the elements of our ordinary lives are magnified and exaggerated but still recognisable.' Some who write on the subject feel that advertising has become so obscure that it is in fact difficult to recognise ordinary life in it. Gillian Dyer, in *Advertising as Communication* (p. 73) notes that:

> 'It could be argued that because advertising stresses the private accumulation of goods and almost hedonistic lifestyles, it encourages people to think in terms of escape from the real world.'

It is difficult to see that we are escaping from reality by purchasing tins of beans. Dyer is probably referring to the kind of 'lifestyle' advertising which has come in for such a bad press from some quarters because of its obvious 'otherness', the distance between it and the life led by most of the population. It is certainly objectionable to watch 'conspicuous consumption' when people here and abroad are faced with such difficulties in acquiring the basics of life.

However, the problem with the theory that advertisements encourage a desire to 'escape' from our social world lies with the notion that modern advertising could somehow avoid the opposite, 'fantasy'. Any symbolic or creative exercise in representation is bound to draw on the fantasies and preoccupations of the society from which it grows. The objection should rather be that the lifestyle advertisement in particular draws its inspiration from a narrow, class-based field of elitist cultural experience. Why are the fantasies we see so often downright selfish? Why do we have limited access to the myths and fantasies of other sections of society? The answers to the last two questions lie to some extent in the view of society held by many of the top advertisers, and will be dealt with shortly.

The nature of Institution

Any consideration of advertising text and the reasons it is produced will lead to an examination of the idea of institution. Institution should not be confused with the term 'industry', which is a branch of trade or manufacture. An institution is a means of promotion or manufacture which has an agreed public character, a stable form and a set of clear-cut functions. McQuail (*see Mass Communication Theory*, p. 38) gives a breakdown of the features of the typical media institution, which may be summarised as follows:

- a concern with producing and distributing information, ideas, artifacts;

- the provision of channels for linking individuals and groups to each other;
- the public character of the reception of its messages;
- the voluntary nature of public participation in the media;
- the link between it, the market and industry;
- its relationship to state power (through regulation and the way it is used by authority).

This is not quite the place to take issue with the nature of this list, except to note that advertising as *an institution* makes an uncomfortable 'fit' here. Advertising is characterised by the way it is 'carried' through other media. By its nature, as well as by its positioning in other forms, it is less voluntary in terms of audience participation. We are listening to the radio and an advertisement intrudes. We are watching television, when suddenly an actor's voice is cut short, the film's title pops up and the 'compression' in volume (as the engineers call it) or the increase in noise (as we might describe it) signals a commercial. We walk down the street and a massive hoarding for a newspaper we hate catches our eye. Advertising is intrusive and does not quite follow the model outlined in the fourth point. It is an 'aggressive' form of mass communication.

Some of the most useful questions we could ask about Institution, when confronted with a text, are the most simple: Who produced this text? How was it produced? How widely is it going to be circulated? Who is it intended for? What is its intended effect? If we wanted to comment on it, to whom would we speak?

A glimpse of institution in the text?

'We can no more separate a media artifact from its institutional existence, than we can [separate] the classes we teach from the educational system as a whole.'

(*Learning the Media*, Alvarado, Gutch and Wollen)

The authors of *Learning the Media* stress (p. 43), that, unlike many other goods which are bought, 'the essence of a media artifact is its *dual* form as *commodity and text*'. In other words, an advertisement is not just something with a 'market value', to be sold within a certain type of economy. It also tells us things about itself, about a product, about possible ways of living in a consumer society. What it does not seem to tell us much about is the institution which produced it.

If we return to the first quotation from the work of these authors, and allow that it is impossible to separate a media artifact from its institutional existence, then might it not be possible to discover some things about the institution (advertising in general, not just one company) from an advertisement? I think it unlikely that we will come across an advert which says 'advertising may sell chocolates to you, but don't forget it also handles public campaigns which make nuclear waste appear as threatening to the environment as candy-floss.' To expect to gain such information *directly* from the ads is futile. But studying a number of advertisements *may begin* to show us how the institution as a whole is prepared to operate, what the institution is prepared to do, say and represent – and which images and discourses it seems to neglect. We would obviously be mistaken if we imagined that a single advert for expensive cigars, set in the interior of a stately home and featuring well turned out men and women sitting around enjoying themselves, was an exact expression of the values of the institution which produced it. Of course, a discourse which suggests certain values is definitely in evidence, but advertising seems to circulate other values besides the ones we might guess are present in any particular example.

We can certainly see that this institution is not above using all sorts of tricks and ploys. That tells us something. But the values the institution holds as its guiding principles cannot be located simply in textual content. The context of **production** will not be visible to the audience – the context of **consumption** will mark the place where the particular ideological 'slant' of advertising becomes clearer. While we are studying a text we may begin to notice things that we have seen in other texts. In the hypothetical cigar advertisement mentioned above, there's an open fire; a butler waits in the background; someone appears to be laughing. We might realise that these kinds of image are familiar. We may have had experience of this type of representation before. Advertising as an institution does seem to deal with certain subjects as genres, typical approaches which are seen again and again. Examples of advertisement genres or types will appear later in this chapter. We may also note that genres are restricted and that the kind of approach to products and their use is generally optimistic. Many negative aspects of social reality are excluded.

Artifacts and determinants

There are good reasons for Alvarado *et al.* to say that media artifacts 'cannot grass on their institutional determinants' (p. 45). By this, they mean that the structures and processes which created the advert can't be seen in the text itself. What we do see, however, is the evidence of an awful lot of fingerprints on the finished product. We might, through research, get some idea of the ideological determinants, or what may be called the belief systems in our culture, which shape discourses found in advertising. These belief systems are not just the property of the institutions – we recognise them because we use and reproduce them ourselves. The difference is that advertising mobilises a smaller and more restrictive number of ideas than are available in society as a whole. While ideology is not the property of the media institution alone, the rules, structures and accepted working methods within an institution mean that a certain (generally positive) approach will be made to the product and by implication to goods in general. For instance, the controversy over the Benetton campaign, examined in more detail later, lies partly in the campaign's departure from the 'upbeat' images of much advertising.

Products which advertise themselves

It seems a curious idea that things like 'dishwashers and cars' do not have (according to Alvarado *et al.*) a 'symbolic value' (p. 43). The aim of many companies, on the contrary, is to design their product in such a way that its very form and appearance will lead to its being associated with a whole host of ideas, feelings, styles. Why else design a 'family saloon' like a sports-car, when it could be the shape of a box with a big flap on the front to keep wind resistance down? Why give a car certain features and extras? The reason is to produce an effect in the onlooker. Certain attributes will act as advertisements for the product.

An interesting study of the way in which a product may come to advertise, not simply itself, but the company which produces it, the qualities associated with that company, and even attitudes and values in the society itself, can be found in Andrew Wernick's comments on the copying of the Portland vase (*Promotional Culture*). The Portland vase, currently on display in the British Museum, is a glassware pot made during the last half-century of the ancient Roman republic.

In the late eighteenth century the vase was thought of as an original and unique artifact, not merely typical of, but symbolic of the classical era. As Wernick puts it (p. 4):

> 'The details of the vase's design were less significant than what it generally connoted; as second order signifiers for classical antiquity and all that conjured up in the aesthetic sensibility of the time.'

Or, put another way, the vase stood for a version of antiquity which became popular with those elements of the upper classes which saw themselves as sensitive to, and appreciative of great art.

The eighteenth-century entrepreneur and master potter, Josiah Wedgwood, was approached by the Duke of Portland with the request that he copy the vase in all its respects, including the defects. It took Wedgwood five and a half years, using his best workers, to produce what he felt to be an acceptable and accurate copy. The significance of both the original and the copy is what concerns Wernick.

The original was a commodity, ready to be exchanged for cash in the marketplace. However, its value could be increased significantly if it also 'advertised' a range of other goods (copies). The original therefore had (and still has) an 'exhibition value'. Many items, including postcards, are sold as a result of the display of the original. As Wernick says of the copy (p. 6): 'the vase's symbolic meaning articulates with its rhetorical function precisely as an ad'. Why though, should Wedgwood undertake a difficult task which was unprofitable in the short-term?

In the first place, it was not unusual for the most labour-intensive items in Wedgwood's catalogue to be sold at a loss. The mass-produced items lower down the hierarchy of products kept up the firm's profitability. The point was (p. 7) 'to help construct a powerfully positive cultural identity for Wedgwood, his company and its hallmarked product'. The copy of the Portland vase was above all a promotional device.

The carefully organised retail operation was supported by direct advertising and took the form of published notices which drew attention to new lines, sometimes linked to a special promotional event.

PRODUCT AS ADVERTISEMENT

To return to the point that products can be symbolic (standing for themselves, a series of products, a culture, and as advertisements for the institutions and industries which stand behind them), the Portland copy projected the advertising message by 'the very appearance' of the product itself (*Promotional Culture*, p. 15). This product has a 'dual character', as an object to be sold in its own right, and as the bearer of a promotional message.

What we might call the 'sign-value' of such products (their ability to advertise) cannot be separated from the material form of the products. For instance, the form of a car may be both a promotion using symbolism and a thing to be sold. What happens in the case of the car is exactly the same process used by Wedgwood: 'promotional requirements were taken account of, before production even began' (p. 15). The image that the particular company wants to promote is given a material form in the shape of a car, vase, or whatever the product is.

The point was made in Chapter 2 that material objects may be 'carriers' of the ideological. Since semiology is the study of signs and meaning, and a sign may be understood as a physical object with a meaning, we can see how the Portland copy not only took on some of the meanings of the original, but also carried some of the ideological character of the fine art industry which produced it. This industry, in turn, was subject to the value systems of the society within which it operated. These values were therefore 'inscribed' in, or written into, or marked in the form of the object. Wernick mentions the comical result of a clash between classical 'truth' and eighteenth-century public morals, when Wedgwood was forced to avoid the introduction of naked figures into his classical reproductions, since no one 'of the present generation' would find such a representation acceptable.

One of the central arguments that Wernick makes is that the production of stylised and standardised goods (together within limited editions) became a mass medium in itself. The circulation of these promotional messages did not encourage a reply. There was no way to interact with what Wernick (p. 18) calls 'an objectified image', nor was there any way the audience could 'intervene in the construction of an ad'.

At this very early stage, before the mass media had developed, 'promotional discourse was set free from the immediacies of buying and selling to develop a life of its own'. All elements of the production and advertising process became 'more systematically involved in the definition to consumers of what the proffered goods were'. In turn, this allowed the possibility of defining in advance 'what needs and desires they might satisfy' (p. 18). If this is correct, it means that production and design make up a kind of built-in value-system, and that the advertising which follows is there to hammer home the association between the product and its supposed image. Advertising therefore does more than provide audiences with information; in attempting to shape a specific response to a product (and even to an entire company), it works as a branch of public relations. In 1978 the American Supreme Court decided that corporations had the right to advertise their opinions on social and political issues by making public advertisements. The president of the US company Hill and Knowlton declared that:

'The corporation is being politicised ... as a result ... [it] has become more conscious of using communications in all its diverse forms as a tool to accomplish its objectives ...'

(*Advertising international*, p. 179)

Advertising and economics

In the 1970s and 1980s many enterprises began to experiment with decentralisation, highlighting at the same time employee responsibility. This strategy was followed in order to give new life to companies by concentrating on their human resources. This process was chronicled and celebrated in America in the early and mid-1980s in books such as *In Search of Excellence* and *A Passion for Excellence*, whose authors referred to the experience of companies which had used the 'individual-centred' approach – one executive explained (*see* Brickman, *Solidarity*):

> '... the most commonly practised crime in industry today is a fundamental insensitivity towards personal dignity ... people need to be empowered, not managed.'

This idea has interesting consequences. If a company's success is seen to depend partly on individual managers and workers, then increased pressure to perform well will be the result. In the same way, the creation of employee 'quality circles' (where people from different levels within the company meet to discuss how things may be made more efficient) and share ownership, were directed to the basic task of keeping the workforce motivated and companies profitable. Alongside this increased interest in democracy and fairness came mass redundancies. A member of the Hay Corporation, a Saatchi-owned consultancy, revealed how white-collar workers were suddenly surplus to requirements (in Eastwest Productions, *How to Survive Lifestyle*, Channel 4, 1988):

> '... over the last five years I've observed that British companies have done quite a remarkable job of slimming down. Some of the largest corporations have lost from 5,000 to 25,000 people.'

Consultants were brought in to help these companies decide whom to remove. Psychographic profiling sometimes played a part in this process. Those who survived this process were clearly about to start working a lot harder.

Share ownership and the ads

In 1981, Nicholas Ridley proposed wider share ownership, since it would be 'the better for general political reasons'. The 'democratic' nature of government 'sell-offs' was a common feature of television advertising in the 1980s. Privatisation became the spearhead of the drive to re-commodify whole sectors of life which had previously been part of the public sector. TV commercials made an interesting turn towards emphasising the virtues of private life, private space and private consumption.

The political ground for privatisation had in fact been prepared before the official onset of 'Thatcherism'. The Labour government's 1978 Finance Act had given the green light to wider share ownership. As a consequence of effective re-structuring, and through the public celebration of sell-offs in ministerial speeches, public stunts and through the 'propaganda' of television advertising, we could argue that a section of the dominant class was able to 'recuperate' its ideological position and lead a number of new onslaughts on unionised labour, the minor and more substantial professions, and even sections of its own lower-ranking supporters.

In Britain, this greater participation in the workplace, and the new financial stake employees had in privatised companies, did not appear to apply evenly to all workers. It can be argued that the promotion of government sell-offs involved the portrayal of share-buying as a great common bond between the social classes. Television and press advertisements from this era represented different social groups as having an equal opportunity to buy shares. The types of people shown were carefully differentiated through occupational dress codes. There was no suggestion that share ownership resulted in movement between classes. Everyone seemed to know their place.

In December 1986, British Gas had around 4.5 million shareholders. By March 1987, more than one and a quarter million of these people had sold their shares and the stake of private individuals in the company had fallen from 60 per cent to 28 per cent. Individuals responded to opportunity in a way that could be described as entirely in keeping with the duality of the marketing message, which appeared to offer participation, pride in ownership and a sense of common purpose – but also appealed to a purely selfish 'common sense' based on the opportunity of making a quick profit. This second motivation was the silent partner in the whole process. It formed no part of the public discourse.

Advertisers, industries and attitudes

There is no single marketing theory which can guarantee success for an advertising campaign. Nor is there a theory so modern that it completely cuts out the use of all other methods. There is instead a 'versatile, multi-dimensional armoury' of ideas and practices which are available to the advertiser, as Leiss notes (*Advertising as Social Communication*, p. 123).

In terms of practices, an important area (though some remain doubtful of its ability to deliver useful information) is quite intensive market research. The population is already divided in a number of ways, as we have seen in our study of audience. In addition to distinctions such as class, gender and ethnicity, 'demographics, geodemographics, psychographics and life-stage' are used to provide a more precise definition of the supposed position of the consumer. One of the main reasons for the 'segmentation' we identified earlier is not just the desire to get a 'working model' of audience, but quite simply to identify where disposable income can be found, and to discover the willingness of certain groups to spend, invest or deposit money.

It was stated earlier that social class, despite all the more recent profiling methods, still seems to be the major means of definition used by many advertising researchers. A report issued in May 1990 insisted that class should be the foremost instrument of segmentation, only 'refined' by the use of other methods (Bedwell, *Media Week*). The reason for this attachment to class is clearly because it focuses on income (p. 23):

> 'The rich are also getting richer ... average personal income up from £16,800 in 1987 to £21,500 in 1989 amongst those in full-time employment ... The number of ABs claiming to have £100,000 plus stashed away has increased by almost 50 per cent to more than a third of a million.'

It is interesting to note that other definitions are used in order to keep marketing 'on track'. The point here is that segmentation begins to deal with the exact nuances of class-based behaviours. The confusion of marketing theory with ideas about the exact nature of people's attitudes, values and beliefs, is a marked trend.

The rather unpleasant effects of segmentation can be seen when it spreads beyond advertising into other areas of public space. The practice of dividing people by type is widespread in many situations where the public interacts with private industry and with the State. As we have seen, segmentation and psychological testing form part of the tools of persuasion, but they are more than this. They are rather like a form of espionage aimed at the public – and there are quite obvious political implications. It is worth noting that in America, such methods were used to identify which groups would be likely to disobey authority in times of extreme crisis.

Some agencies, notably Saatchi and Saatchi, are applying these methods in other contexts, notably through the use of lobbying groups (organisations which attempt to influence the political process). A former managing director of Saatchi, John Sharkey, spoke of the 'uncertainties [people] held about their own opinions, and also how perhaps people might be persuaded to change their views'. This particular research was carried out for the Conservative Party.

Segmentation may start with considerations of class and perhaps the straightforward 'ability to pay' but it becomes a little more sinister when the 'type' we are judged to be directly affects the kind of treatment we can expect to receive in our daily interactions with private and public bodies.

Different treatment for different 'types'

The McCann Erikson 'Woman Study', where women were divided into eight types and illustrated as different animals, reveals the way that those with the power to communicate make judgments about character and personality as it is supposed to relate to social position. The 'Hopeful Seeker' was, according to Christine Restall, Planning Director of McCann Erikson:

'. . . 16% of the population, they agree with trendy ideas without really feeling them. In a way they're a bit of a mess.'

(How to Survive Lifestyle)

The tendency of some advertisers to express the findings of research as though they express social reality may be amusing ('16% of the population' is fussily exact), but the practice of offering different services to different groups is increasing. British Airways has carried out extensive research into its customers. The results reveal an approach to the 'segmentation' of customer service:

'. . . these people [the 'hawks' who use British Airways] are efficiency-driven, they seek a certain status in life . . . also quite significant was the fact that they also desire a master/servant relationship, which we should be able to accommodate, if that's what they want.'

As indicated earlier, this is not simply the division of social and 'lifestyle' groups

(*How to Survive Lifestyle*) in order to reach a market, but the development of different styles of treatment. At the other end of the scale from the 'hawks' (who are offered a parody of deference), the implications for those who have no influence or spending power are worth noting. This description of a group designated 'the Aimless', again made by Christine Restall, illustrates the point:

> '... she really doesn't mind what happens. Life washes over her ... drifting along, quite happy watching the television, and why not?'

Or again, when we learn that certain sections of the working class 'tend by definition to be of less interest to advertisers' (voice-over, *How to Survive Lifestyle*) we know that we are witnessing a discriminatory practice. Some theorists (associated in Britain with the now defunct *Marxism Today*) placed the market and the consumer at the centre of their hopes for a democratic renewal. If, however, many of the 'freedoms' of social life are only available to those possessing significant personal wealth, then a fraction of the prosperous middle classes will continue to have a qualitatively different experience of life to a growing 'underclass'.

Divided neighbours?

The 'Acorn' method of profiling is a detailed breakdown of 'residential neighbourhood', which does not deal with psychological factors. HTV publishes an 'Acorn Household Profile' (*see* Table 3.1) which lists the following within its guide for companies wishing to use it as a medium of advertising: 'Better-off retirement areas ... less well-off council estates ... multi-racial areas ... older housing with Asians ...' and so on, together with details of the comparative percentages of each type of area, contrasting the HTV area (fewer black areas, roughly equal numbers of affluent zones) with the picture as it appears in Britain as a whole. Anglia Television produced a guide called *How Britain is Really Divided*.

The idea of an 'armoury' of theory and practices at the disposal of the advertising agencies is one which we are already familiar with, but there are limits to how the 'weapons' which fill this armoury can be used. In the first place, television commercials are constrained by the space they are allocated between programmes. They are further constrained by time. The fact that they are repeated is a further qualifying factor (roughly speaking, a viewer will tolerate the repetition of commercial material he/she enjoys).

These ads are also subject to institutional rules laid down by the Advertising Standards Authority. They also operate within the accepted 'genres' of the form. (In 1990 offence was caused by an advert which showed a child in a tub of water, being circled by a snake, and the commercial was removed despite the fact that complaints were based on distaste for the associations or connotations brought to mind by the images, rather than by any actual event within the narrative frame of the ad itself). The 'weapons' of the advertiser may also be subject to a variety of misfirings. People may not understand what is being said. They may not even see the message.

Table 3.2 HTV's segmentation by demographics/residential area
Living Standards: Acorn Household Profile

		Households			
			HTV	GB	HTV
		No.	%	%	Index
G 24	Council estates with overcrowding	407	0.0	1.4	1
G 25	Council estates with worst poverty	625	0.0	0.5	6
H 26	Multi-occupied terraces, poor Asians	0	0.0	0.3	0
H 27	Owner-occupied terraces with Asians	1 315	0.1	0.9	7
H 28	Multi-let housing with Afro-Caribbeans	2303	0.1	0.7	17
H 29	Better-off multi-ethnic areas	2 352	0.1	1.6	7
I 30	High status areas, few children	48 268	2.3	2.3	102
I 31	Multi-let big old houses and flats	28 114	1.4	1.8	75
I 32	Furnished flats, mostly single people	9 254	0.4	0.7	62
J 33	Inter-war semis, white collar workers	88 826	4.3	6.1	71
J 34	Spacious inter-war semis, big gardens	111 935	5.4	4.9	110
J 35	Villages with wealthy older commuters	76 217	3.7	2.8	131
J 36	Detached houses, exclusive suburbs	39 097	1.9	2.1	90
K 37	Private houses, well-off elderly	63 269	3.1	2.7	112
K 38	Private flats with single pensioners	19 023	0.9	2.0	45
U 39	Unclassified	683	0.0	0.0	81
Area Total		2 065 800	100.0	100.0	

Source: 1984 estimates based on 1981 Census, CACI Market Analysis Division (Courtesy of TVMM)

The Agency

Advertising agencies are usually divided into four departments. There is an immediate clash between the freedom required by the creative process on the one hand and the controlling structure of the client's brief on the other. This contradiction is institutionalised (given an actual form within the agency) by the establishment of a creative team to handle the way the campaign looks and what it says, and the use of another group which 'oversees' the whole operation from the client's point of view (the account managers).

The advertising agency is an alliance of interests, in which the 'creatives' are often seen by their superiors as having attitudes which make commercial success more difficult to attain. Tim Bell (chair of Lowe Bell Communications) was one of those engaged in mid-1990 to work on the personal image of four Cabinet ministers. In an interview in *International Journal of Advertising* (vol. 9, no. 2, p. 32) Bell characterised the 'creatives' as 'not commercial, and yet they are in a highly commercial business'. Bell thought they were in dire need of management or monitoring by 'really competent people'.

CREATIVE RISKS

It is indeed the creative team which is traditionally portrayed as hostile to the restrictions of research, and which acts on instinct. When Elliot and Michael (in the American TV series *Thirtysomething*) find themselves working as part of a creative team for the agency DAA, they hit upon the marketing concept of 'retro-snacking'. Retro-snacking is an idea they have that adults could be persuaded to revert to the sweet-eating habits they had as children. Sales of sweets would rise as a result. Eliot and Michael work on an instinct that the campaign will succeed, they have a 'gut-feeling' for the rightness of what they are doing. It is not based on research findings. For some real-life members of ad agencies, research is simply there as a 'smokescreen', designed to reassure the client and protect the account managers should a campaign flop.

TESTING ATTITUDE: FOCUS GROUPS

'Focus groups' remain a widely-used method of discovering some of the pre-occupations which exist in the minds of the consumer. Small groups of carefully selected consumers are presented with an issue, or with prototypes of campaign material. The discussions which follow are recorded. As Leiss notes (*Social Communication in Advertising*, p. 138): 'often phrases and words that participants come up with will be used in the actual copy'. Focus groups are often more in line with the approach of the creative teams, since they are orientated towards the expression of mood and feeling.

In all this, as Larry Light of BSB International explained in a television interview (*How to Survive Lifestyle*), the purpose of the advertising agency is to 'get a deeper understanding of the customer, and what really moves them'. Gillian Dyer's insistence (*Advertising as Communication*, p. 6) that 'advertisers cannot rely on rational argument to sell their goods in sufficient quantity' and that advertising 'creates desires which previously did not exist' is perhaps wide of the mark. The advertiser is keen not to scatter his/her message to the diverse winds of the market-place, and certainly will not attempt to move a population in the direction of desires which once were without existence (though the nature of human desire being so varied, it is difficult to imagine what desires there are which *could* be created from scratch.)

A CHANGING MARKET: VALUE CHANGE

Not only are advertisers anxious to understand the whole market, they are also anxious to locate 'the leading edge of value change' (*How to Survive Lifestyle*). The executive who talked of this 'leading edge' (Norman Strauss of Brand Positioning Services) links this leading edge with the 'thinkers, and the doers, and the experimenters, and the risk takers'. Perhaps Strauss is referring here to what some advertisers would call the 'self-actualised' – groups of individuals who are in advance of the rest of society.

Is this partly how the advertisers see themselves? They belong to a section of the aspirant, city-dwelling middle and upper-middle classes, whose contemporaries and acquaintances tend to be other upwardly-mobile groups who share the same cultural preoccupations (the artistic/commercial nexus) and who have broadly similar professional roles. Many of these individuals are part of a group which has been successful in education and which, until the more recent waves of redundancies in advertising, might have expected to retain a secure income.

The point about 'the leading edge' of value change, though, is that it is sometimes hostile to all that advertising stands for. Mattelart (*Advertising International*) explains that, in the late 1970s, US corporations were under extreme pressure from a variety of activist groups who saw many of their operations as immoral. An article in *Business Week* in January 1979 described how the typical corporation was forced to become 'as much a political animal as an economic machine'.

New social movements?

The movements which caused this discomfort to business are sometimes known as the 'new social movements' (*see* Colin Webster, *Here and Now*). These movements arose as an embodiment of the radical causes (including feminist, anti-racist and environmentalist strands) which followed the declining class-based movement which had flourished before the Second World War. The ideas put forward by such groups achieved quite wide currency in the public domain, largely through the mass media. Of course, many of the ideas were distorted, partly because they were circulated outside the radical context in which they had originally been set. All the same, concepts of equality and freedom had entered circulation and become part of the leading ideas of the time. Advertisers could not afford to ignore them. In fact, they helped to circulate the 'parodies' of these ideas. But why should they have wished to do this?

NEW MOVEMENTS – NEW MARKETS

The impact of the new social movements – particularly the feminist current – created new markets. Advertisers were led to consider that some of their representations of women, which previously had not caused them any disturbance, might no longer reflect what was happening in society.

This feeling that images need constant updating remains in evidence. One executive expressed the need to understand a new and more complex picture of 'the housewife' (Vic Davies, 'Mum, are you a Housewife?', *Media Week*, 1987):

> '... how well we communicate with the "housewife" will depend more on our ability to understand them [sic] as people, and less on a perception of them left over from the fifties.'

The actual change from representing women as largely home-centred and passive in the 1950s, towards images which portrayed a more active and independent, sex-orientated female of the 1960s was due to the increase in the number of women in the workforce, women who then had to be recognised as consumers in their own right. Only incidental credit is due to the 'progressive' outlook of some advertising executives. The real motor of change appears, naturally enough in a commercial enterprise, to be economic considerations. The 'counter-culture' of the late sixties and early seventies is another case in point. This new outlook seemed to hold values which were global, and vaguely communitarian. The landmark in recuperating this idea and turning it to commercial use was the 1971 Coke ad ('Hilltop'), in which a popular melody was sung by a variety of ethnic groups.

What is interesting here (and will be pursed later when considering an example of another theorist's work) is that feminism and other radical movements may not have achieved *exactly* what they set out to accomplish, but that they did achieve some measure of wider social change. This change came about partly as a result of the wide availability of advertising and other mass media 'parodies' of the original messages.

For the advertiser, the impetus to change arises from commercial considerations. He/she is usually interested in progressive social engineering. However, **mediated change** in social conditions has come about as a by-product – not change which anyone might necessarily have anticipated, but which nonetheless has had a visible impact. Radical movements themselves had to use discourses, ways of expressing their belief-systems, taken from what was available in the society – this is one of the reasons why a completely 'new' social outlook was not possible. These social movements could be said largely to have failed (although some of their aims could be accepted without too much trouble in the capitalist economy). In a way the original collective effort became changed, partly through its commercial transformation, into a more modest set of personal goals.

Advertisers, in looking to certain groups as bringing about change, are bound to move into a position which may be well in advance of other sections of the population. Mass media versions of 'forward-looking' ideas may actually create negative reactions among groups which mistake them for the originals, or dislike them so much that any resemblance to the original ideas is an irritant. The distorted representations of the aims of certain advanced groups which are circulated by the media (career feminists, lifestyle environmentalists) might act to stir up opposition to a host of 'progressive' values which may seem to characterise some sections of the well-off middle classes.

The position of the advertising agency is that of a 'privileged mediator' between the dominant groups which produce commodities, and the consumer groups which may form the market for the goods and services on offer. This intermediary, the agency, looks to its clients and its target markets for guidance in constructing the broad outlines of the advertising message. The client has the controlling interest, while the consumers are investigated, rather than consulted as equals. The money and energy devoted to discovering how people feel and where exactly their insecurities lie are not used to improve their immediate situation. They are used to make sure that commercial products are placed in the correct market-position.

When the advertisers themselves declare that 'we aren't satisfied with the results of the enterprise culture', as does Norman Strauss, they aren't abandoning consumerism into the bargain. Strauss, for example, looked about for 'a new style of value-led consumer boom' (*Washes Whiter*, BBC Productions, episode of 29 April 1990). The great trawling operations of research, together with the 'gut-feelings' of individual advertisers, are directed to the search for the next set of money-making values. Broad references to the eighties as the 'me' decade and the nineties as the 'us' decade come from the desire to find a new peg on which to hang advertising messages. The aim is to link the product to a value to which people will respond positively.

The 'soul' of the brand

Larry Light, the president of the company BSB, argues that 'people don't buy products, they buy brands'. According to Light, a brand possesses a 'deep seated emotion that is really the continuing strength of the brand'. He even goes so far as to say that a brand 'has soul'. As Light says, 'as there is more focus on branding [i.e. on giving the product or range of products a personality or image] there will be even more focus on understanding the psychology of persuasion' (*How to Survive Lifestyle*).

BENETTON: PERSUASION THROUGH CONTROVERSY?

The Benetton display advertisements which featured children in desperate poverty, including Colombian children employed as brick-makers, were part of a series of images which caused offence and controversy on an international scale. One of the reasons for the negative reactions would appear to have been the use of 'photo-journalistic' images in a context designed to sell goods. Some may claim that one of the by-products of the campaigns run by Benetton has been an increased awareness of certain social issues.

However, the de-contextualised, 'artistic' presentation of the 'real' images (of a man who had just died of Aids, of the scene of a Mafia killing) makes it difficult to see exactly in what ways an audience might make a 'social use' of the images. The advertisements which preceded Benetton's 'realist' phase were mostly set up in the studio. They worked as fairly strident semiological constructions, using 'opposition' between various images; for example, a black child was shown with two cones of hair which resemble horns, while a white child standing alongside was deliberately made to appear 'angelic'. Or again, a Catholic priest and a nun were shown kissing. Such images are accessible to a wide international market. Despite the reaction they caused, they were still broadly linked with Benetton's earlier representation of the 'family of humankind', with all its 'progressive' overtones. The departure from the original 'multi-ethnic' house style, and the move towards a kind of 'postmodern' manipulation of the image, leads us to consider how an audience interprets messages.

INVESTIGATING ADVERTISEMENTS

We can remind ourselves here of the 'basic advertising formats' described by Leiss and his co-authors. The four types, what we might call genres of address, were identified as:

- **Product information** format, in which the product is the focus of all elements of the ad.

- **Product image** format, in which the product has a symbolic relationship to some abstract domain of significance other than utility (mere practical use).
- **Personalised** format, in which the relationship between the product and the human personality defines the primary framework of the ad.
- **Lifestyle** format, in which a relationship is established between the codes of person, product, and setting by combining aspects of the product image and personalised formats.

There are also a number of ways of categorising television commercials according to what and how they are attempting to sell. These are:

- Ads for particular products – commercials which display the same or similar products or services.
- Ads which market products in similar ways, even though those products might be very different. These could be described as genres, and they often link up with the product/service definition above: e.g. car ads will often fall into the same broad genres. (Among genres in general we could identify the 'mini-adventure', the 'social realist', the 'high lifestyle', and so on.)
- Ads which don't sell anything, but which propagate a corporate image, or which are designed to persuade an audience to take a course of action which has broader political implications. An example might be share commercials made on behalf of the government. These could be produced in any one of the different genre-types.

Methods of interpreting advertisements

A number of authors have tried to describe different ways of understanding magazine or display advertisements. The reason for this interest in static adverts is quite simple. In the first place, the elements of a two-dimensional advertisement can be studied at leisure. The added complications of working out what is happening in a television or cinema commercial, where images are moving, where sound has to be taken into account, where problems of narrative arise, make interpretation more difficult. Of course, display advertisements are useful also because they can be reproduced in books.

To start with, we should examine the major approaches to the study of advertisements. Leiss *et al.* identify the two most commonly used methods, but there are also other approaches. The first of the 'major' approaches is semiological analysis.

SEMIOLOGY

Semiology concentrates upon the idea that meaning is created, both as the result of the relationship between different elements within the message or display, and as a result of a text's production and circulation in the social world.

Gillan Dyer (*Advertising as Communication*) is careful to stress that the advert has to be understood according to both the *internal* and the *external* factors which govern its meaning.

- **Internal** factors refer to the content and form of the advertising text, organised by codes and conventions which should be recognised by a 'reader' from the same culture.

- **External factors** refer to the production, circulation and consumption of the text.

Some semiologists seem to forget the external elements, spending most energy on the internal structures – the way that the different images combine, the way that words or titles qualify images. The meaning of the text then becomes a matter of their own individual explanation. Individuals can, of course, be very experienced, and may even be experts in their field – but semiology as a system of analysis has to be rather more democratic than this. If the meaning of an advert lies in the associations the text creates in the minds of its 'readership', then different groups of people will see the different elements of the text differently. (David Morley's work could be used to discover an 'overview' of the *Nationwide* text's meaning.)

If it is also important for texts to be seen in the context which produced them (the commercial strategy of which they are part), then information about advertising as an institution, its role and function in society, and if possible details of the particular company's operations, would all help in interpreting the advert. The meaning of some advertisements may only become clear through reference to other commercial texts, whether these are other ads, television programmes, films, works of art, and so on.

The three aspects of the study of a text, detailed above, may be called **textual**, **contextual** and **intertextual**. 'Textual' refers to the internal elements. 'Contextual' means how and where the text was produced, and how and where it was and will be consumed. 'Intertextual' refers to its relationship with other texts and how this relationship helps to create meaning.

CONTENT ANALYSIS

Content analysis does not really reach the depth that a semiological analysis can attain, but it can provide a more accurate 'overview' of a wider range of material, provided that it is carried out on a scale which justifies its conclusions.

The semiologist looks for descriptive categories within the material itself, but the content analyst arrives at the data already 'armed' with the categories to be used (though see Chapter 7 for Barker's critique of semiological approaches to comics). The semiologist often makes statements which grow from a general observation, but the person carrying out content analysis is able to give facts and figures about the sample (often a random sample), with the knowledge that the information will give a general picture and will reveal some precise details. There is no 'reading between the lines', or drawing conclusions which cannot be supported by evidence which is apparent to all. Evidence can also include reference to what possible images or discourses are absent; for instance, if a series of advertisements appears which deal with urban life in the larger American cities, but which contain no images relating to ethnic differences, then this in itself is a research finding and may reveal something about the ideological mould of the whole series.

Just as semiology, particularly when it is carried out on a small scale, may be unreliable because of its tendency to interpret images a little freely, then content analysis has weaknesses if it is taken as utterly scientific. For example (as

167

suggested at the beginning of the last paragraph), in order to carry out a study of any subject, categories must be constructed. It may be that the analyst wishes to investigate the 'types' of individual which appear in 'lifestyle' ads. The researcher would therefore have to come up with categories of people. The setting up and application of categories to research is called 'operationalization'. Categories, as the first order of signification (the apparently 'innocent' denotation) carry their own ideological limitations. The other drawback may be what Leiss *et al.* refer to as (p. 223) the tendency of content analysis to fail to capture meaning because:

> '... meaning cannot be captured when communication is broken down into ... categories of form and content.'

This view would argue that meaning depends on context and the 'place' of single elements in a larger structure. Stripping elements from their context and adding them up as tallies obviously does not meet the requirements of the semiologist, but general overviews of the level, status and function of words, people, objects and settings may be obtained through content analysis.

RITUAL DISPLAYS: A HUMAN BEHAVIOURAL APPROACH

Erving Goffman, in *Gender Advertisements*, presents a view of advertising which concentrates on the human figure and extracts meaning from the variety of physical poses and 'ritual displays' made between men and women, and between older and younger men. He locates this firmly in the context of the social. He claims (p. 5) that 'in our society whenever a male has dealings with a female or a subordinate male' the social situation is handled by applying what Goffman calls the 'child – parent complex'.

The relationship between children and parents is examined and certain interactive behaviour patterns noted, which are then applied by Goffman to explain why human beings of unequal power and influence appear to occupy dominant and subordinate positions in display advertising. For example, touching gestures, standing and lying positions, and so on, are all used to demonstrate Goffman's idea that the relative physical positions of human subjects reveal relationships of power.

This approach, sometimes described as 'ritual subordination', deals with one element of the semiological. What is particularly interesting here is that Goffman's examples are taken from an era of advertising whose representations look almost nothing like the gender ads we have experienced since the end of the 1970s. Subordination, as we know, exists in society, but it is completely unfashionable to show women draped over beds while clean-cut males stand in the foreground, staring into the middle distance. There are many more advertisements now which show men and women in more equal situations, and therefore more equal physical positions, as well as those which show women in plainly dominant stances, exacting revenge on unreliable men, giving them orders in the context of the workplace, etc. As a greater feeling of equality takes hold (whatever the reality of the distribution of power) then the extreme variations in posture described by Goffman are less likely to be seen.

Questions to use for an analysis of display advertisements

It is useful to prepare an analytical framework for approaching advertisements. The following is based on a combination of semiological approaches, references to types of content and ideas about the discourse and context. The 'text' itself is composed of content, mediated through a certain form.

CONTENT

This refers to what we actually see in the image, as well as what it suggests to us. Although it may be 'internal' to the text, some of the possible meanings may only be mobilised by reference to elements outside the text, such as other adverts, films, etc. In some studies, the two stages are called denotation and connotation. We might ask the following questions:

1 What is actually visible in the frame – written text, images (of people, objects, settings)?
2 What does the advert appear to be for?
3 What kind of references to our culture (lifestyle, habits, fantasies, dreams) do the images and written elements seem to make – are there identifiable icons, indexes, symbols? What kind of representations of people are shown; are famous people used to bring their status to the product, or are the famous used for the associations they bring from other mass media texts? What is the suggested meaning of all the individual elements? What are the individual connotations?
4 What is the combined effect of the elements, the connotation of the whole text; what social discourse is used by the text (how does it seem to represent the world)?
5 Are some of the references ones we have seen in advertising texts before? Is meaning created by reference to other texts (intertextuality) – are some of the references 'typical' for this type or genre of ad?

FORM

This is the way that the text is presented through technical means, as well as through the use of composition (the way that things are set out within the frame). We could ask:

1 Are the images presented in colour, or black and white – what are the general connotations of each?
2 How exactly has the colour or monochrome been used – to achieve contrast, or to create a subdued image?
3 Does the typeface or style of the written text produce any associations in the mind of the viewer; does it suggest a certain genre?
4 How is the image treated – for example, is one element in sharp focus, or is deep focus used; how is it lit; what effect on meaning might different technical choices have had?
5 What is the main focus of attention – might other subsidiary elements draw attention away?

6 Is composition used to integrate the written text? Is it used to create some sort of balance or opposition between the elements (people, objects, setting) of the image?

7 Does the image suggest a narrative?

8 Does the form suggest a discourse, expressed through all its technical and compositional features (soft focus connoting a romantic vision, 'modernism' suggested by the use of dramatic angles, certain types of lettering suggesting a scientific logic), and does this discourse clash in any way with the discourse suggested by the content?

It is not only difficult, but probably undesirable, to hold internal and external factors apart when we come to decide upon the meaning of a text. They work in a productive opposition to one another.

CONTEXT

This is concerned with where an image appears, and the overall format in which it appears (what comes before and after it – for example, an ad which is surrounded by articles and by other advertisements, in the magazine format). Questions which might be used could include:

1 Are we seeing the text in the original or proper physical context, or has the context changed? We might first have seen an ad on a poster site, but must later study it in a lecture or lesson; or a photojournalist's work may appear in a gallery after having been used in a magazine – does a change in physical context alter the meaning of the advertisement?

2 Is an image *within* a text capable of being used to create a different meaning if it is placed in some other non-commercial context?

3 Is the text given a different meaning as a result of being placed in a relationship with a text which seems to contradict it; for example an ad for alcohol which is printed near a warning about drinking and driving?

4 In what context does the image appear to have been produced? Is the production process revealed in any way; does our sense of the age of the advertisement affect our response?

This last point may be quite significant. If a text no longer has a commercial impact, perhaps because the advertising has been replaced by a new campaign (or because the product is no longer available), then it is easier to see it 'objectively', as a cultural artifact. People tend to laugh at those advertisements whose fashions and styles are within memory but which now look outdated. Ads from different cultures also tend to amuse. Advertisements which are very much older than the memories of the middle-aged may sometimes be regarded as historical documents.

THE TELEVISION COMMERCIAL

The television commercial displays some additional features, which suggests that the questions above will need to be supplemented.

CONTENT

1 What is actually visible in the frame – and what are we led to believe is going on outside it?
2 What do we hear, and what does this connote both on its own and in combination with or opposition to the image? What are the differences between speech, sound and music; why are some sound elements placed in the 'foreground' while some remain in the 'background'?
3 How is human interaction represented?

FROM

1 Are the images we see edited to produce a certain effect; are they treated electronically; are cartoon elements or computer-aided designs included?
2 Does the use of lettering sustain part of the narrative; or is it part of or identical to that used on the packaging or exterior of the product?

CONTEXT

Is the physical context one which helps to emphasise the commercial or the narrative forms (for example, are we seeing a commercial presentation, or are the adverts interrupting a film)?

Television commercials: discourse on tap

Television advertising is a form that 'absorbs and fuses a variety of symbolic practices and discourses' (Leiss, p. 145). This means that it tends to sop up many different ideas and ways of acting out ideas, bringing them together in a new form. It looks around the society and picks and chooses its influences – but of course it already carries attitudes and values around, so the new ideas will be reflected through the old ones.

The institutional position of advertising generally is that of a link 'between the major forces of cultural and commodity production' (ibid). This means that advertising acts as a kind of bridge between the habits and practices of a society, and the straightforward making and selling of goods. We could say that it uses culture to sell goods, and as the things it sells are circulated in the market-place, so the goods also sell versions of the culture.

Although the television commercial takes its discourses from a wide range of cultural reference points, there are occasions when it appears to break away from the multiple sources of representation and becomes strongly marked by one influence. When there is a discourse which is fighting to become, or which already forms, a dominant current in the society, then the commercial may reproduce the concerns of these forces in a reasonably direct way. This happens most obviously at times of a clear discursive break with the past, a departure from the accepted ways

171

of interpreting and talking about the world. A more *direct* expression of ideology may then occur. For example, the 1980 Esso advert which expressed the belief that 'you can't climb out of a recession by pointing your nose downhill' was, according to one of the team which produced it, 'very much a potted version of Thatcherism' (*Washes Whiter*, BBC Productions, 1990).

Boardroom realities?

There is a danger that the advertisers themselves might come to believe that the aspect of social reality that they inhabit can be applied to the whole of society. Certain values may be represented as being universal, when they may well be restricted to only certain sections of the social formation.

Explaining why there seemed to be so many commercials featuring boardroom rivalry and aggression, Miles Young, a director of Ogilvy and Mather, offered the idea that a whole society was being ruled by a narrow set of values (*Washes Whiter*):

'. . . the fact of the matter is, that that was the reality of the world in which we lived – we did have a city of London culture which was profoundly materialistic'.

Perhaps this means that the 'caring and sharing' adverts of the 1990s ought to be treated as a fashion. Who knows how 'progressive' the next 'leading' idea will be? We must remember, as noted earlier, that this portrayal of the 'leading' ideas will often leave wide sections of the population completely cold. In many ways, discourses about new modes of personal behaviour and new ways of expressing personal responsibility for the environment do not touch the concerns of a number of groups. One of these may include those individuals whose personal security is founded on exactly those values which are now no longer 'trendy'.

Television commercials: an analysis

The method followed here will consider both linguistic and visual meanings. The aim in each case will be to identify those currents of discourse which run through the text. The lists of questions on advertising texts set out earlier will form the background to this analysis.

CASE STUDY A **BUPA ad**

(Filmed by Eastwest Productions for *How to Survive Lifestyle* as a glimpse behind the scenes of a BUPA advertisement voice-over recording for *Scanner*).

VISUAL NARRATIVE

Young couple with small children. Woman becomes unwell. See her sitting up anxiously in hospital bed, holding husband's hand, doctor in attendance. She is put in a scanning machine. Anxiety fades as nurse smiles. Next seen in her private room with family, watching television. Doctor enters; whole group bathed in warm light.

Comment: Having discovered that men are more emotionally influenced by the sight of a woman undergoing treatment, BUPA uses women in its TV commercials. BUPA hoped to target men in particular, believing that it is usually men who pay for private health care. The aim of the advertisement was to change the image of BUPA's hospitals and present them as hi-tech and capable of undertaking major operations.

VOICE-OVER RECORDING

'To be sure of private health care they became members of BUPA. This priority was brought home to them recently when Sue fell ill. She was treated in a BUPA hospital where her problem was diagnosed with a body scanner. You see, BUPA has priorities too. No one takes a profit. Anything left over from caring for its members today is reinvested for their future, like hospitals, health screening centres and the latest medical technology. Most people choosing private health care join BUPA. BUPA – Britain feels better for it.'

VISUAL ANALYSIS

A potentially uncomfortable subject is here being represented in a visual style which, in terms of the ethnicity and middle-class appearance of the family, invites identification with their position and predicament from other white, middle-class adults in this age range. No black actors appear on screen. The earlier shots are cast in a harder light than the final shot when the woman is recovering. The intended audience might perhaps be alienated from the central character ('Sue') at the moment when she is in the scanner but the whole phase of 'treatment' is passed over fairly briefly, as if not to dwell on what is nevertheless a vital part of the advert's message.

In conclusion, the images which emerge are carefully balanced to create a brief narrative in which disruption passes quickly to resolution and the hinted-at return to normality. This is done within a 'realist' mode of representation centred on a youngish, white, middle-class family, which despite some minor alienation experienced through lighting, is to be identified with. The character of the doctor is cast as a white, middle-aged man whose mode of address and physical position in some of the shots signify authority and sympathy. The nurse who appears signifies sympathy (woman to woman) and cheerful efficiency.

VOICE-OVER ANALYSIS

First there is the opening narrative, read by an actor in an authoritative but sympathetic tone. The decision to join BUPA is presented as a past event: 'they became members'. Here we observe the couple from the outside. We are positioned as spectators of their story, privileged in our access to the narrative. But this technical device is one with which we are familiar. The first important point is that the decision to become members is an action that has already been taken, in response to an anxiety which we are all supposed to feel. If the action is in the past, it is no longer up for discussion. If it was taken in response to a 'universal' anxiety, then it is made to appear to be a sensible one.

There is a certain formality in some parts of the speech act, for instance in the words 'this priority was brought home to them'. But already there are hints of 'everyday' speech, and echoes of methods of persuasion which we may have encountered in other texts: 'be sure of' reminds us perhaps of simple advertising addresses like 'to be sure of your copy, place an order'.

Ultimately, we (unlike the characters in the advertisement) are not 'safe' – we are in the position of feeling insecurity and doubt. We are being addressed as an audience that needs private health care. The 'priority' of private care is brought home, it is not to be avoided. But the fear of being ill is not examined too closely, nor is the illness itself examined too closely. Sue is 'treated' and the nature of her illness is kept dark; it is 'diagnosed' rather than cured – no promises are in fact made in the narrative.

A direct colloquial address is made at the point where the actor explains that BUPA is not in this game for the money. A question about profits has not been asked, but is answered. Why? At 'You see . . .' the discourse, which so far has been centred on ideas of responsibility, common sense, forward planning and care for the family unit, makes a detour.

The reassurance about private health care and profits can be seen as an attempt to anticipate a criticism which could, were it not addressed, undermine the 'caring' and responsible tone of the whole message. But in talking about the issue of profits, in trying to close off that discussion, the text opens up the whole issue of 'unofficial' public discourse on health, which runs through a number of ideas and positions about saving the NHS, suffering at the end of waiting lists, going private if you had to save your kid, etc. Always, when a discourse acknowledges the existence of an alternative, some measure of risk is being run.

In order to create meaning, in order to have an impact on its selected audience, it must not 'empty' its text of all oppositional meanings. We can accept that a discourse carries a 'will to power' but it gets nowhere at all if it does not carry some of its everyday meanings – in other words, all the marks of its creation in a divided society. The trend seems to be towards acknowledging alternative points of view in order that the favoured discourse might be seen to deal with such alternatives.

The fact that the focus groups used by BUPA research are in some respects unhappy about the 'need' to go private is not the whole picture. We are offered again a common-sense explanation in a common-sense language that 'anything left over' from this caring is 'reinvested'. This is a scheme that has to be contracted into, has some degree of exclusivity, followed by the claim that 'Britain feels better for it.'

We are offered a number of ideas: BUPA has the same values as the commonsensical individual. But it invests in 'the latest medical technology', despite doubts which may arise about the funding of hi-tech methods. It is a capitalist enterprise which doesn't 'take a profit'.

CATEGORIES OF ADDRESS

There is what might be termed a 'range of discourses'. Because discourses are addressed to individuals, because we are *offered* subject-positions, they will use a number of possible approaches. They will 'speak' in different styles.

The author of this book has classified these 'styles' or modes of address:

1 the '**inclusive-personal**', characterised by appeals to a sense of community and belonging, and expressed through 'ordinary' phrasing and speech;
2 the '**inclusive-impersonal**', characterised by references again to a sense of community and belonging, but expressed through a more 'professional' language;

3 the '**exclusive-impersonal**', which works through references and expressions which completely exclude the viewer, in order perhaps to create envy of the lifestyle of the subjects who already use the product;

4 the '**exclusive-personal**', which works to show a product or lifestyle which is 'beyond' the viewer but which nevertheless addresses him/her in ordinary terms.

The advert works only through a tension between these poles of discourse, which appears as Fig. 3.5.

In the first place, the viewer might be 'excluded' from something in order to make that thing desirable. But he/she must be offered the possibility of being 'included', otherwise the product (or service) will languish on the shelves. If a different approach is used in order to motivate the viewer, positive feelings may take second place to the mobilisation of negative feelings. The audience may be addressed in formal language and held at arm's length.

In the case of the BUPA ad, the range of discourse includes 'inclusive-personal', characterised by appeals to common sense and expressed through colloquial phrasing; and the 'inclusive-impersonal' characterised by references to the expertise of the BUPA group and expressed through a more 'professional' language. There are hints of the exclusive mode, but only occasionally in the content and style of the address.

UNDERSTANDING A DISCOURSE

Part of the question we must examine is to what extent people need direct experience of an event or object or situation to be able to recognise a discourse. If we take the example of the health service, it is possible to imagine that a human subject/viewer might have seen a few programmes on the NHS, or a popular drama series like *Casualty*, without having been to hospital themselves. In this case, some of the visual references might not carry the same weight as they would with someone who had been a patient at some time.

Equally, some part of the cultural process of picking up connotations might be lost on a person whose medical experiences were confined to the privatised health care system, and who was unfamiliar with popular representations of the NHS. We can now gain a view of the differences between the range of connotations which might result from such hypothetical cases.

Our first subject might, as I have hinted, feel insulated from the 'worries' which form an important part of the advert. Nevertheless, he or she might well pick up

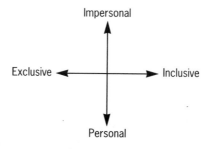

Fig 3.5 Poles of discourse

the idea that private health care 'looks' different to the widespread and largely justified view of the NHS as surviving under pressure. Depending upon the individual's own cognition, psychology and past and present position as a social subject, the sight of colour TV and private rooms may trigger a variety of responses. There is no guarantee what may happen. Direct experience is not needed for an understanding of any aspects of the ad. A completely hostile response may, for example, be based on the individual's most trusted reference-point, and this may be another representation – a programme like *Casualty*, for example.

Our second subject, the one who has had no contact with mass media representations of hospitals, may find nothing controversial in the advert. Private health care may seem the natural and universal form of medicine as it is practised.

These hypothetical cases may lead us to believe that a semiological reading needs to take account of the individual subjects who receive the message. It may also show that television, in certain circumstances, can add to the universality of our knowledge, but that the commercial text alone, because its aim is to persuade and sell, is not a reliable source of information. Considering the advanced state of visual representation which is used in television commercials, it is not a reliable source of 'truthful' images either. In addition to alternative texts, we probably need statistical information, reports from official bodies, information from hospital workers and patients, in order to give a contextual ground to the particular genre of commercial that we are dealing with.

CASE STUDY B | *Healthy Options TV commercial transcript*

The interior of a flat, marked in appearance as modern yet ordinary. Kitchen-bar in background. Central character, a young man marked as modern and ordinary also. Talks to camera.

Young man: 'While Nigel's doing a few extra circuits at the gym, I've invited Julia [Julia in background], his girlfriend, back for a spaghetti bolognese'. [The meal is displayed] It's a Healthy Options meal from Birds Eye, made to a low fat recipe, with no artificial colours or preservatives.'

[Young man brings two plates on a tray to the sofa where Julia sits. At this point, Nigel bursts in. He is short, stocky, in a casual gym top, has thinning hair.]

Nigel: 'Whoooer ... I did forty lateral raises, bench pressing with 60 kilos and a hundred and fifty sit-ups.' [Plumps himself down next to Julia]

Young man [Exchanges amused glance with audience]: 'I'm more of a squash man myself. Budge up, Nigel.' [Squeezes between the couple]

Voice-over: 'Now you don't have to be health-mad to take the Healthy Option'.

VISUAL ANALYSIS

The setting is smart enough, and yet ordinary enough, to invite comparison with the living rooms/kitchens of the intended audience. The characters are marked as young, white and inhabiting the grey area between skilled working class and the lower-middle class.

The young man at the centre of the narrative could possibly be a student (in discussion, students tend to disagree) and Julia (especially as she does not speak) has the kind of indeterminate social location which could make her role subject to the preferences of the audience. Nigel is marked as a little gauche, and his appearance is sporty, with a hint of the ridiculous in the tight cycling shorts he wears.

THE DOMINANT DISCOURSE

There are clues in the way the characters speak which point to an 'ordinary' and direct mode of communication. Inviting someone 'back for a spaghetti bolognese' is an example. Or again, 'doing a few extra circuits' is an instance of an informal language which is deemed appropriate to the intended audience and which accords also with the physical appearance of the actors.

In addition to this informality there are suggestions of a difference between the social class of the two male characters. Nigel speaks with traces of a working-class (south-east) accent. This difference is further emphasised by the slightly more 'knowing' attitude of the hero, his use of the double-entendre joke about 'squash' and the suggested social superiority of squash as a preferred sport to the arduous training which Nigel opts to do. The suggested superiority of the hero as a possible partner for Julia, as opposed to the more unsophisticated and 'unknowing' Nigel, is heavily underlined. Julia speaks not a world – she is presented as the prize which the two men fight over, though Nigel appears not to realise that he is losing.

The near-mantra (heard in so many TV ads), 'no artificial colours or preservatives' is thrown in to underline the major theme of the entire text: 'You don't have to be health-mad.'

CONCLUSION

The discourse at work is a fine example of a recuperative attempt by a major food manufacturer which intends to secure the peripheral areas of the health food market. In order to do so, it circulates meanings of 'healthiness' which are closely linked to ideas about style and a 'balanced' attitude to life. This is a muted version of the 'healthy' lifestyle whose hard-line devotees are represented as 'over the top', unreasonable, obsessive, possibly from an unsophisticated 'manual' background (in this case), and blind to the implications of the drive to fitness – they lose sight of the social drawbacks of their obsession. The humorous treatment of the subject is very effective in helping to encode this message. In sum, the discourse is inclusive-personal, with a direct address to camera by the young man with whom we are supposed to agree. There is a possible exclusion of certain social 'types' (represented by Nigel), and clearly women are given a mute role which implies they are subsidiary to the message, taking on the status of object, or a component part of the overall setting.

CASE STUDY C *Volkswagen Passat ad*

BREAKDOWN OF SHOTS

1 CU child's head at angle   SFX: Discordant noise

2 Mix from 1 – Camera pans l. to r. across city

3 Child with father's hand in street (slow motion)

4 Extreme CU man's bewhiskered face
>>> Sound: Shouting

5 CU child's reaction – surprise (slow motion)

6 CU same man as in 4, old, harangues passers-by:
>>> 'Is your life decent, is your life pure?'

7 MS/SA child jumping in air (slow motion)

8 Balding man looking in bonnet of car:
>>> 'I do not believe this!' PIANO intro

9 Child lifted by father MS/SA (slow motion)

10 Child brought up to father's head-level (slow motion)

11 LS/HA revolving shot – City from above
>>> SFX: Police siren

12 LS City streets at an angle with people crossing road

13 CU child's face (slow motion)

14 Indeterminate movement across background

15 Police officer emerges from car:
>>> 'All right guys'

16 Men back away from officer – arrest begins
>>> 'Sound: Song begins THEM THAT'S GOT

17 MS child crossing road with father
>>> SHALL HAVE

18 LA/MCU Officers slamming men down on car bonnet: sounds of struggle

19 SA/MCU Child's reaction – winces

20 Electronic news hoarding – 'Suspect in ...'   THEM THAT'S NOT

21 Mix from 20 – CU child's face as 1

22 From 21 – streets from above   SHALL LOSE

23 Child looking up CU/LA

24 Buildings seen from below, child's perspective   SO THE BIBLE

25 MS child and father cross road   SAID AND

26 CU as above
    IT STILL IS

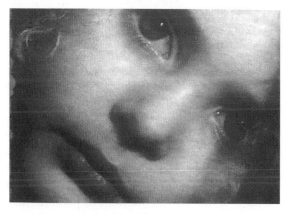

27 CU front of Volkswagen
    NEWS

28 MS father and child, child lifting leg

29 MS Passat turning
    MAMA MAY HAVE

30 CU child's face

31 HA of father opening car door for child
    PAPA

32 Child helped into car
    MAY

33 Mother seen in car's mirror   HAVE

34 Child seen from inside car clambering into back seat

35 Back door slammed, mother seen looking back   BUT GOD BLESS THE CHILD

36 CU black police officer blowing whistle

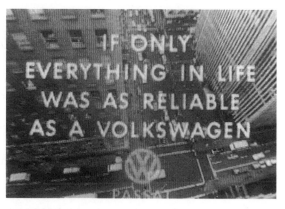

37 Father in front, mother driving, slams door
    THAT'S GOT

38 Car driving away
    HIS OWN

39 Child smiling CU
    THAT'S

40 Street seen from inside the car as it moves
    GOT HIS OWN

41 City from above HA and slogan superimposed:

'IF ONLY EVERYTHING IN LIFE WAS AS RELIABLE AS A VOLKSWAGEN'

Note: These abbreviations are:
CU: close-up; MCU: medium close up; MS: medium shot; LS: long shot; SA: straight angle; HA: high angle; LA: low angle; SFX: sound effects. *See* Chapter 5.

ANALYSIS

In a short piece on this and the general direction taken by TV commercials at the very beginning of the 1990s ('Carers and Sharers', The *Guardian*, 22 January 1990), Alex Garrett claims that this advert 'reverses the traditional male and female roles in car advertising'. He believes in addition that it 'exemplifies the shift in values which places family and environment ahead of sex appeal and power'.

It seems that Garrett sees this commercial as bearing the hallmarks of renewal; it reverses sex-roles and demonstrates a shift towards new values. One thing which tends to militate against the power of a commercial is the fact that it has to be repeated so often. In this simplest of senses then, it becomes redundant very rapidly indeed. Nevertheless, this particular example certainly made an impact for its freshness and unusual approach.

Some features immediately marked this ad out from its contemporaries. It used black and white film, discordant noise, 'odd' camera angles, a mixture of slow and standard motion, 'realistic' speech and snatches of speech, overlaid with a Billie Holliday soundtrack.

The advert appears to have a fractured and unpredictable form, a presentation of life in the city which is bewildering and alienating. However, the reason for this approach can be found in the (extremely simple) narrative. These experiences are mediated through the presence of the little girl. We do not exactly see through her eyes entirely, however, because she is herself so often in the foreground of the frame.

The method of presentation, therefore, is new only really by comparison to the frame of reference of other television commercials. In terms of film-making as a whole, this advert is in fact an exposition of a variety of well-established effects, a highly rule-bound mode associated with dream sequences, states of extreme stress, disordered perception, etc.

In terms of the narrative, we also find that the commercial offers little that is 'new'. The protective father, the child introduced to a world it doesn't understand, the mother appearing at the end and providing rescue and comfort.

Its impact lies rather in the fact that we see the other aspect of life which in most adverts remains invisible. In other words, the 'escapist' car ads show the commodity as the provider of powers of mobility, in which the owner of the car is able to cut free from the limitations of an urban life. For once, we see what it is that is being left behind, rather than endless scenic interludes with one car the only object in sight. We observe the poverty, madness and conflict which is supposed to characterise the inner-city.

Overall, the Passat commercial provides a fairly redundant message, one of escape and of the primary importance of the nuclear family. In its characterisation of those individuals we do not follow through the narrative (the old street-preacher, the man whose car has broken down, the men who are arrested) there is no attempt to make them function as 'character props' for the commodity – they are the alternative to the commodity, the reason for the commodity's existence. The car is an area of private space. In this sense, there is no attempt to rescue or recuperate these alternatives, or to speak in their language; they are simply excluded. They are there both as a freak-show (notice how their physical appearance is carefully marked off from that of the family) and as a representation of how public space has become degraded. The only solution for those who possess the means to alter their environment is the retreat from the common order of experience.

Therefore the real boldness of this advertisement lies in its outright refusal to share and its complete confidence in its ability to recuperate any small difficulties –

like, for example, the fact that the Billie Holliday song is put in a context which reverses completely the intention of its message. 'Them that's got will have, them that's not will lose', is a message which shows the reality of many lives under our social system. In its new context, it is used as a celebration of inequalities.

CONCLUSION

Through its heavily-emphasised visual orientation, this commercial works mainly through its narrative, a narrative which can of course be read as in some way 'progressive' because the mother drives the car and the father is 'caring'. (Though holding your child's hand as you cross the road is usually seen just as normal behaviour.) I would suggest that a reading of the narrative which arrives at this conclusion is only possible if one ignores the 'peripheral' elements of the story. In this case, looking beyond the text is not the first step because enough exists in the narrative frame to offer an alternative view.

The discursive elements, which include wealth, security, urban life, poverty, the nuclear family, and so on, are brought together to produce an individualist and 'exclusive' discourse which, because of the way it has cut out the possibility of a wide market, must rely on the association of the car not simply with 'lifestyle' but with the particularity of the commercial itself as a talking point, which it soon became in the letters page of the *Guardian* and in a survey of TV ads in *Media Week*. The inclusive elements of the discourse are reserved for a small audience. The larger part of the advertisement is impersonal in tone and in address. It almost loses a sense of audience through its concentration on its own form and content.

CASE STUDY D · *Granada commercial*

TRANSCRIPT

A man is driving to take up his new post in a company. We are shown how the people he is to work with spend that morning's teabreak speculating on his reputation.
Secretary: 'It's his first day today. I wonder what he's like.' [Enthusiastic, smiling up at tea lady]
Tea-lady: 'You'll like him, he's ever so nice, a real gentleman.'
[Scenes of new man in car]
Tea-lady: 'The new boss starts today, boys.'
Executive 1: 'Well, he managed it at BDT.'
Executive 2: 'It needed an insider for this job.'
Tea-lady: [Slightly mocking] 'What, like yourself?'
[More shots of the new man]
Young male: 'He's got an impressive track record.'
Young female: 'He doesn't suffer fools gladly.'
Older male: 'Well, he took BDT to number three.'
Tea-lady: 'Number two if you count South America.'
VDU female: 'I saw him, he's gorgeous.'
VDU female 2: 'He has a lovely smile.'
Tea-lady: 'He has a wife, too.'

[We see the new man turning over a home-made card: 'Good luck daddy.' He smiles at this.]

Board member: 'You, er, don't think he's too young, do you?'

Board member 2: 'Hard to say – it's a lot to take on.'

Board member 1: 'There are some very big decisions to be made.'

Board member 2: [Observing man drive into car bay – in the Granada] 'I think he's proved himself in that department, don't you?'

Board member 1: 'That's the new Granada, isn't it?'

Tea-lady: 'Course – it's the two point nine Ghia.'

Voice-over: 'The new Ford Granada. Let them know you've arrived.'

ANALYSIS: REDUNDANCY AND RENEWAL

A large number of television commercials have featured the executive as 'hero', and these have often shown the central character driving an expensive car. The advert transcribed above stands at a particular juncture. Serious ads of this sort had become less fashionable – whether the advertisers or consumers had found them increasingly ineffective or unconvincing is unclear, but a number of rather 'jokey' versions began to emerge.

This is part of a cycle. A move away from the previous car ad formula completely would have been difficult, because in the cycle of redundancy (where an idea or formula becomes stale) and renewal (where ideas not seen for a while are reintroduced) there is usually a 'bridge' between old and newer forms. The reason for this is that a complete break in the type of representation offered for a familiar product can be a risky marketing strategy. There must be some point of reference in the new material which the consumer is able to recognise. The bridge between a fresh approach and redundancy is parody, which can be considered a safer proposition than starting from scratch.

The ad contains a number of supposedly humorous touches, but it is based on an approach which is well-known in plots taken from the cinema. The audience is given a great deal of information about the central character. Nearly everyone seems to admire him. All the remarks are directed towards building up a positive image of the new boss. He is never heard to say anything. He doesn't need to – he acts, others can be impressed if they so wish.

The remarks made about him are split for the most part according to gender, except in the case of the young female executive who notes that 'he doesn't suffer fools gladly', and in the case of the all-knowing, all-seeing tea-lady. The men tend to note his performance as a manager: 'He managed it at BDT' ... 'He's got an impressive track record' ... 'He took BDT to number three' 'I think he's proved himself in that department'. The women tend to notice his attractive appearance: 'He's gorgeous' ... 'I wounder what he's like' ... 'He has a lovely smile.'

There is also an interesting division in the discourse of work and interpersonal relationships. He can be a 'perfect gentleman' to his secretary. He does not 'suffer fools gladly' – presumably those whom he perceives as incapable, inefficient and in a position of rivalry or subordination. He conforms, in fact, to a view of the ideal manager, against which others may be measured and found wanting.

TYPAGE IN ADVERTISING

The idea of typage is taken from film studies, and refers to the way that certain physical 'types' are used for certain roles. Physical appearance plays a large part in the way human interactions are governed, and this is reflected in a kind of hierarchy of attractiveness in some social situations. It is often the case in film, especially if the genre is a kind of action/romance, that the central character has to conform to a stereotyped physical appearance. In the case of the Granada ad, the individuals we see conform to the physical appearance we might expect from our experience of other texts. The women who operate the VDUs (presumably secretaries, but we are not told for sure), are young, marked as subordinate, and speculate about the new man's appearance. The speech acts they engage in are suited to the combination of their gender and their position within the company. They have a perspective shaped by their lack of access to power. One of the results of this is that they at least do not share the obsessions about managerial performance. Their discourse is subordinate, but in some senses more healthy than some of the other judgments. The less subordinated female executive is allowed to comment on the hero's managerial character.

The male executives also fit their stereotyped role-appearance; they all have certain things in common, but those differences that exist are marked by age, or by typages based on 'character'. The executive who thinks an insider would have been most suitable for the post our hero is about to occupy looks suitably wimpish and frustrated. The hero, by contrast, conforms to a certain conventional sense of what is handsome.

CLASS: A MAJOR FACTOR IN REPRESENTATION

What are we to make of the representations of different types and class-positions in this particular television commercial?

No direct address to the viewer is made in this commercial. The discourse appears to represent a broad range of classes; all employees discuss the new boss, although the tea-lady not only knows more about him but appears also to have access to business information and can make informed comments about the car he drives. She moves through all aspects of the firm's life, dispensing wisdom (this privilege seems to be allowed because she is completely removed from formal power and does not represent a threat).

The general ideological trend which lies behind this discourse can be recognised from other advertisements which attempt to show a cross-section of class. Advertisements in the 1980s for shares, for services aimed at a wide range of consumers (such as ads for banks and building societies) would be included in this genre. The message of such commercials appears to confirm the notion of classes being equal in some respect (modernist lack of deference) While still retaining watertight boundaries. All groups and classes are bound to the 'system' (in this case, the company) whatever their respective levels of engagement.

The general ideological message here is that individuals function through and behave according to their position within a hierarchy. The use of certain stereotypes attempts to confirm above all that people are in the correct position in the power hierarchy because their characters, predispositions and abilities suit them for such a role. It seems to me that there is a suggestion that the viewer also should accept the notion that things only run well when people know their place. VDU operators speak in a different mode to management, not simply because they are female, but because they are not privy to management discourses. The apparently 'modernist' or subversive touch, showing the tea-lady as sharper than the lot of them, and more astute than senior management, works only because the advertisers have selected someone at one extreme of the hierarchical scale. The negative connotation of the tea-lady's role is that she is a 'gossip'; there is no guarantee that she will not be read as such.

Discourse or interaction?

If discourse can be characterised either as 'communicative' or as 'strategic', we must recognise that advertising is not simply trying to achieve understanding between (presumably fairly equal) participants. The television commercial is intent upon getting results, and must therefore be understood as being of the 'strategic' order. If its strategies are founded on establishing understanding, then this is only because it has an instrumental goal in mind.

In other words, the TV commercial has aims which go beyond the establishment of good communication. Television advertisements as a whole operate as bearers of 'strategic' discourse; discourse is a speech act which seeks to achieve a dominant and privileged access to the circulation of ideas; it has a 'will to power'.

Progressive advertising?

We should be wary of labelling some advertising forms 'progressive', thereby supporting the notion that progress is being made, simply because there has been a move from the more overt sexism of a 'discriminatory' past to a parody of equal treatment and opportunity. In the search for renewal, for messages which make an impact with a segmented audience, the advertisers have made a strike deep into the territory of the 'oppositional' camp. They have raided the progressive ideas the left thought were theirs. The use of 'Real People' (with all their individuality and imperfection) at the beginning of the 1990s has marked another variation in marketing technique: the television commercial is set to change. The new image may 'fit' the perceived needs of the consumer, but it does so by taking the first step on a path which leads ultimately to redundancy and the comfortable laughter which greets the outdated.

Can advertising texts change the connotations of language?

In her advocacy of a 'qualitative' approach to the study of media texts, the theorist Ros Gill examines a Club 18–30 leaflet entitled 'A Woman's Right to Choose'. Although this is not a text taken from television, it illustrates very well a tendency to imagine that incorporation acts against the original progressive and radical meaning of an idea by 'stealing' its resistive discourses. This approach could be misleading, and will not assist students in understanding how discourses work.

Gill is right to say that the leaflet parodies the use of feminist language. She believes that a 'feminist researcher using content analysis' would affirm, from the positive nature of individual phrases and the occurrence of words like 'rights', 'freedom', etc., that the whole advert might be promoting feminist ideas. But this would surely depend upon context as well as the intention of the speaker. Of course, a 'right to choose' carries other possible meanings besides the one given to it by the feminist perspective.

Again, we may not be surprised that the advert is talking about choices which are confined to individual style. It is true that a slogan which is presently understood by many to be 'collectivist', concerned with rights and with collective struggle, has been transformed within the context of the text into an individualistic one. But the individualistic meaning is already present in the use of the singular 'woman', rather than the plural 'women'.

It is no argument to say as Gill does that the advert reduces choice into choice about what to consume. Any advert is bound to move the centre of its concern to the commodity it wishes to promote. A collective, inclusive and progressive address, set within the context of marketing a product, would *also* turn choice into the selection of a type of commodity. An advert is always going to do this.

The most urgent disagreement must be with Gill's conclusion, when she advances the possibility that the message may be an example of 'co-option or incorporation' of feminist images. This incorporation apparently leads to the 'emptying' of the progressive meaning of feminist images. This conclusion should be rejected.

If the text incorporates feminist language, it does so in order to strike some sort of chord with the female 'subject' of the ad. The exact response of the subject may vary considerably, from one of offence if she feels it to be a parody of her politics, to one of amusement in the case of someone who is hostile to feminist politics – there are a number of possibilities.

The most important consideration is the fact that the ad agency expects the type of language to be noticed, to strike a note of recognition in the consciousness of its target market. The context of the words and phrases is not progressive, measured by some notions of political radicalism, but the individual words and phrases carry the connotations of feminist discourses. There is no point in a parody if one cannot recognise the original in its form or content.

When advertisers use such terms, they are reproducing the original intonations in no matter how muted a form. The whole reason that Gill is studying the ad is because she recognises the use of feminist discourses. It is recognisable as an attempt to use such discourses. If Gill can see this, then others might as well – so how is the language emptied of meaning? The ad carries and even inadvertently circulates broadly feminist meanings. The whole point of 'a woman's right to choose' is surely that women in general should exercise more control over all aspects of their lives, including where they go on holiday.

The use of the word revolution, for example, may be put into contexts which limit its application as a description of traumatic social upheaval, but the meaning is not entirely lost; nor is it meant to be lost. The very effectiveness of describing some commodity as 'revolutionary' depends partially on our recognition as an audience of the social and political connotations of the word and its contrasting positioning within the theatre of consumption. The dominant meanings of the feminist phrases are what make the 18–30 advert effective. There may well be a reduction in the power of the original words through an altered context, but these dominant meanings still echo with what Gill takes to be their original feminism. In addition, the muted version achieves a circulation which may reinforce the availability of a discourse leading back to a specifically feminist practice. 'Incorporation' is actually a process in which new meanings are created – and it works both ways.

SUMMARY

■ AUDIENCE STUDIES

Audiences may be described as specific in three ways: where they are defined by the particular product (magazine, record, film) they consume; where there is a specific audience for a type of product; and where audiences belong to pre-existing groups (age, gender, class, income, etc.). Some theorists list all the different aspects of individuals' background which may help to position them, and which may affect their response to media texts; amongst these are self, gender, age group, family, class, nation, ethnicity, education, religion, political allegiance, region, and urban versus rural background.

McQuail talks about the 'duality' of the audience, which may be formed either in response to media or where it corresponds to an existing social group or category. In other words it is possible to gain a clearer picture of audience formation if we imagine that the audience has either the media as its source, or society as its source.

Methods of defining and reaching an audience may be described as empirical if they depend on counting or quantifying the number of people who use a certain product, or who are reached by a given 'unit' of media content. Another view of audience is as a mass of individuals and groups, of a brief and inconsistent composition, such as the mass audience for cinema, radio and television. Alternatively, an audience may be seen as a distinct social group in its own right, which does not depend on a media form for its existence as a group; a fourth example is where the deliberate targeting of particular sections of the mass audience 'creates' a sub-audience.

■ Approaches to the study of audience

First, there is the **effects** tradition, which concentrates on the supposed effects of particular forms or contents of the media on their audience. Second, there is the research into what audiences do with the media, the uses they make of the media, and the '**uses and gratifications**' they draw from it. Third, there is the investigation of the ways in which **content** might be able to structure audience responses in predictable ways. Fourth, and growing partly from the above, there is the study of the ways in which texts attempt to **offer positions** to an audience, from which it is invited to see experience in particular ways. The question 'How are we positioned by this text?' may be asked of any mass communication. Ideas about address are central to this book.

In research, a basic distinction is made between quantitative and qualitative methods of enquiry into audience (see the 'Student Activity' section which follows this summary). The type of information which may be found can also be divided into primary data and secondary data. One of the problems faced by all researchers is that they are part of the general social world they investigate and will have their own political and theoretical standpoints.

■ MORLEY AND THE 'NATIONWIDE' AUDIENCE

David Morley's *The Nationwide Audience* is reviewed as an attempt to overcome the shortcomings of theoretical approaches to audience. He begins by dealing with the different tendencies in mass communication research, starting with the opposing schools of thought which stressed either the central importance of the message, or the central importance of the audience and how it is composed. Morley saw himself as part of a new strategy which considered the most important aspect of research to be the attempt to understand how meanings are experienced by people through the process of living in society, and then put into a form that can be recognised and understood by other people.

Morley investigated the idea that the different decodings produced by audiences might be due to: the position people occupied in the structures of age, sex, race and class; the involvement people had in cultural identities, i.e. belonging to trade unions, political parties, or to specific sub-cultures based on factors like age or ethnicity; the relationship between the particular message and a group's experience of it; and the context in which decoding takes place.

■ Dominant, negotiated and oppositional responses

A dominant response is one where the audience member or the group concerned produces a 'reading' or 'interpretation' of the message which basically agrees with the dominant viewpoint contained in it. A negotiated response is one where the ideological content of the message is altered to fit with the respondent's own view, and by being altered produces a new position. An oppositional response is one where the dominant viewpoint is contested and a reading which opposes it is produced. Such categories of communication are over-simplified and are not used as extensively as they once were.

■ Criticisms of the 'Nationwide' research

Jordin and Brunt ask several questions about the nature of Morley's research. In the first place, they notice that the research does not reveal the way in which groups decode television messages. This realisation has led some scholars and researchers to propose the idea that there is a 'missing link' between the construction of the mass media material and its reception by an audience. This link is described as the 'cognitive level'. Cognition is 'knowing' or perception, and it does not appear to be directly related to class, gender, ethnicity and so on. Morley eventually recognised that it was no use presenting the demographic factors such as race or class as reasons for different decodings if there was no attempt to explain how these factors affected interpretation.

■ Roles and interpellation

Althusser's ideas on address (he used the term 'interpellation') are important in relation to how an audience recognises that it is being addressed.

■ Modes of consumption and theories of audience

The different 'modes of consumption' adopted by individual audience members has created 'an increasingly undisciplined and elusive set of everyday activities' (Shaun Moores). The difficulty of measuring such responses means that **ethnographic** research becomes more appropriate than 'effects' or 'uses and gratifications' approaches.

The work of researchers like Paul Dickerson concentrates on the discursive construction of viewer identity. Interviews to explore 'live dialogic activity' and the way in which individual identity is actively constructed during a particular social interaction.

Pertti Alasuutari, in *Researching Culture*, argues that the discovery of meaning should be the primary goal of audience studies, and warns against direct revelation of the research hypothesis. He notes that 'it is particularly important not to confuse two things here: the question presented in the interview and the question you have set for the study'.

■ ADVERTISING: INDUSTRY AND AUDIENCE

The fact that advertisers divide their audiences is important from the point of view of the address chosen for each sub-division of audience.

■ Lifestyle and segmentation

The need to gain precise information about the consumer led many companies to adopt the technique known as 'lifestyle' profiling, where people are designated as belonging to certain groups according to their consumption of goods and services. Psychological or psychographic profiling is also used for social and economic purposes, whereby some firms hire consultants to carry out testing on their employees in order to compare their values with those held by the organisation.

■ Maslow and the 'hierarchy of needs'

Abraham Maslow set out two fundamental ideas about human needs. The first was that people all have needs, but that these needs are arranged in a sort of order. Only when the most pressing and basic are satisfied are people able to devote their energies to the next level. Maslow described four levels of need: physiological needs, safety needs, social needs, esteem needs and the need for self-actualisation.

Advertisers have used the hierarchy of needs, but have turned a developmental model into one which merely classifies different social groups at different stages on the ladder.

■ Institution and history

The development of consumer culture is presented, together with the idea that the history of advertising appears to be as long as organised commerce. The history and development of the advertisement is analysed in its various phases, including the trend from advertising based largely on the written text to advertising based primarily on the use of imagery.

■ The nature of institution

Institution should not be confused with the term 'industry', which is a branch of trade or manufacture. An institution is a means of promotion or manufacture which has an agreed public character, a stable form and a set of clear-cut functions. McQuail gives a breakdown of the features of the typical media institution. These may be summarised as follows: a concern with producing and distributing information, ideas, and artifacts; the provision of channels for linking individuals and groups to each other; the way that the reception of its messages has a public character; the voluntary nature of public participation in the media; the existence of a link between it, the market and industry; and the fact that it has a relationship to State power.

Advertising as an *institution* makes an uncomfortable 'fit' here. It is characterised by the way it is 'carried' through other media. By its nature, it is less voluntary in terms of audience participation. It may be categorised as an 'aggressive' form of mass communication.

The question is asked whether we can see the structures and processes which create a text in the text itself, with the conclusion that there are a lot of 'fingerprints' on the finished product. We might, through research, get some idea of the ideological determinants or belief-systems in our culture which shape discourses found in advertising.

■ The Portland Vase

The original was a commodity, ready to be exchanged for cash in the market-place, but its value could be increased significantly if it also 'advertised' a range of other goods (copies). The original therefore had (and still has) an 'exhibition value'. The vase is seen as an early example of an artifact which has become an advertisement.

■ ADVERTISING AND ECONOMICS

In the 1970s and 1980s, many enterprises began to experiment with a type of decentralisation, highlighting at the same time employee responsibility. This strategy was followed in order to revitalise the base of some companies, while at the same time cutting costs.

■ Testing attitudes: focus groups

'Focus groups' remain a widely-used method of discovering certain consumer preoccupations. Small groups of carefully selected consumers are presented with an issue, or with prototypes of campaign material. The discussions which follow are recorded. Not only are advertisers anxious to understand the whole market, they are also anxious to locate 'the leading edge of value change'.

New movements in social life seem to produce new markets, in which the position of the advertising agency is that of a privileged mediator between the dominant groups which produce commodities and the consumer groups which may form the market for the goods and services on offer. Benetton could be seen as having taken to heart new ideas about society and advertising, in their attempt to achieve a high profile through the use of controversial images.

Different methods of analysing advertisements include **semiology**, which concentrates upon the idea that meaning is created as the result of the relationship between different elements within the message or display, and as a result of a text's production and circulation in the social world. **Content analysis** as a method does not really reach the depth that a semiological analysis can attain, but it can provide a more accurate 'overview' of a wider range of material, provided that it is carried out on a scale which justifies its conclusions. Irving Goffman's work on **ritual displays** presents a view of advertising which concentrates on the human figure and extracts meaning from the variety of physical poses and 'ritual displays' between men and women, and between older and younger men.

An analysis of television commercials is presented as a model of analysis which moves towards the consideration of the production of discourse. This method follows both linguistic and visual meanings. The types of address present in advertisements are identified as running along the axes shown in Fig. 3.6.

This text sees discourse as 'strategic' (as having a will to power) rather than as purely 'communicative'. In other words, the TV commercial has aims beyond the establishment of good communication. Television advertisements as a whole operate as bearers of 'strategic' discourse; discourse is a 'speech-act' which seeks to achieve a dominant and privileged access to the circulation of ideas.

A critical analysis is made of a theorist who argues that the connotative impact of feminist language can be incorporated into commercial discourses.

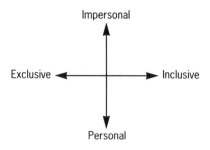

Fig 3.6 Poles of discourse

STUDENT ACTIVITIES

ADVERTISING: ANALYSIS, RESEARCH, PRODUCTION, ESSAY TITLES

Analysis: Advertisement analysis using a visual base: the semiology of the image.

Student groups are presented with a set of four two-dimensional advertising images, with written text deleted or obscured.

Purpose: to elicit response on the basis of broad connotations of meaning and to compare these with more specific address established by combination of visual and written text.

Student response: the class is divided into groups of three, with one person from each group assigned to report back the consensus of response. (If another room and supervision can be arranged, a small number of individuals may be used as a 'control' and given the image and the text together; they will need the full version of these questions in Chapter 3.)

The following questions are presented on content (using the process of denotation and connotation).

1 What images are visible in the frame (of people, objects, settings)?
2 What kind of references to our culture (lifestyle, habit, fantasies, dreams) do the images seem to make – are there identifiable icons, indexes, symbols; what kind of representations of people are shown; are famous people used to bring their status to the product, or are the famous used for the associations they bring from other mass media texts; what is the suggested meaning of all the individual elements; what are the individual connotations?
4 What is the combined effect of the elements, the connotation of the whole text; what social discourse is used by the text (how does it seem to represent the world)?
5 Are some of the references ones we have seen in advertising texts before; is meaning created by reference to other texts (intertextuality) – are some of the references 'typical' for this type or genre of advertisement?
6 What might the advert be for?

Form: this is the way that the text is presented through technical means, as well as through the use of composition (the way that things are set out within the frame). We could ask:

1 Are the images presented in colour, or black and white – what are the general connotations of each?

2 How exactly has the colour or monochrome been used – to achieve contrast, to create a subdued image?

3 How is the image treated? For example, is one element in sharp focus, or is deep focus used; how is it lit; what effect on meaning might different technical choices have?

4 What is the main focus of attention – might other subsidiary elements draw attention away?

5 Does the image suggest a narrative?

6 Does the form suggest a discourse, expressed through all its technical and compositional features (soft-focus connoting a romantic vision, 'modernism' suggested by the use of dramatic angles, certain types of lettering suggesting a scientific logic), and does this discourse clash in any way with the discourse suggested by the content?

Students should be asked, in conclusion, to comment on the possible **context,** which is concerned with where an image appears and the overall format in which it appears (what comes before and after it – for example, an ad in the magazine format which is surrounded by articles and by other advertisements). In this case, the advertisement will have been divorced from its context. Students should also be questioned about **address**. To whom is the appeal most likely to be made? When discussion has been followed through, the entire text or the text and the individuals who studied it are brought into the equation. All differences between the visual and the combined visual and written interpretations are noted and discussed.

Analysis: Commutation tests

The commutation test is a method used in media analysis to discover the exact contribution made to the production of meaning, by all the individual elements which go to make up a text. In this type of test, one part of the media text or message is removed; unlike the previous example, however, something else of a similar nature is substituted.

Students are given a series of advertisements in which the central product on display has been removed; for example, the image of a bottle of alcohol is replaced with that of a bottle of milk. Do the surrounding elements which are left seem inappropriate? Again, advertisements which use famous people to reinforce their sales are tampered with so that an unknown individual appears instead. What is the effect of this on the meaning of the image?

Purpose: to investigate how the creation of meaning is composed of individual elements. To investigate how these elements usually work in broadly similar genres. To prepare the ground for the doctoring of the image and the possibilities of new representations through techniques such as photomontage. (See Chapter 4 for information on the practice of photomontage.)

Analysis: The semiology of sound

The class is played a succession of pieces of music, from a variety of forms: classical, popular, rock, opera, folk and so on.

Purpose: to investigate cultural conventions in the use of television advertisement soundtracks.

Student response: after each piece, the following questions are answered on paper:

1 Are any particular colours suggested by the piece?

2 Is there any particular narrative which in your opinion the piece suggests?

At the end of this part of the exercise, the students are asked to go back and in each case to note down what kind of product might be advertised using the music they have heard. The results from all exercises are read aloud and this material is noted on a chart or OHP or board at the front. The presence of similarities and differences is noted and discussion about the nature of connotative meaning and audience expectation follows. (See pages 193–5 for an example from a Production Report.)

Research

A basic distinction between **quantitative** and **qualitative** methods should be appreciated. Quantitative research is concerned with the collection of facts and figures. Ideas about broad trends in society and basic structures in social life can be gained from this approach and information can be obtained, not just from people, but from records, documents, reports and statistics. Qualitative research often does not attempt to cover such a large field of investigation as the first method, but aims instead for an in-depth investigation based on interviews, participant observation and the study of detailed documents of a personal/historical nature, such as autobiographies and diaries.

The type of information which may be found can also be divided into **primary data** and **secondary data**. The first type consists of data collected by the researcher from scratch – data which are not already written down, recorded or processed in some way. Primary data might include case studies, observations or surveys. The second type consists of the study of recorded material, whether published or not, and whether or not already processed by other researchers. (*See* Figures 3.7 and 3.8.)

Conclusions from research questionnarire – attitudes on women in advertising

- Both men and women equally believe that women take a lower position in society.
- More women consume the advertising in popular magazines, some 80 per cent of women read a magazine of some kind.
- Men tend to stress the existence of negative representations of women.
- Men believe the subordinate position women take to be due mainly to tradition. Women place more importance on the influence of the media.
- More men than women felt that advertising had changed over the years.
- 80 per cent of men believed that advertising still promotes female stereotypes, compared to 100 per cent of women.
- Women are much more opposed than men to the use of sexy images.
- Both men and women state that (semi) nudity is acceptable in advertising, but a larger percentage of women were completely opposed, and no women at all felt these images were advantageous.
- Women strongly opposed the use of 'perfect women' within advertising. (93 per cent of women compared to 60 per cent of men).
- Both men and women agreed that the media reinforce stereotypes.
- * Women tend to place more blame on the media for their subordinate position. Practically all agreed that any change would surely take a long time.

Fig 3.7 An example of qualitative research, including some objective measurements
(Extract from 'A' Level Media Studies report)

Research: Content analysis of television commercials

Students are asked to make a content analysis of representation in television commercials.

Purpose: to investigate representation through a method which does not set out categories in advance (see critiques of content analysis in this chapter, and Barker's critical approach in Chapter 7), in order that broad findings about the role and function of individuals and groups may be examined.

Student response: students are asked to keep an accurate record of all roles (and those shown taking them) and actions which take place within the parameters of the survey. The same time each

I collected the following information from my respondents:

1. 42% of respondents were aged 26–35
   36% were aged 17–25
   22% were aged 36+

2. 36% had no children
   26% had 1 child
   20% had 2 children
   18% had 3 or more children

3. 38% of respondents work part-time
   32% work full-time
   30% do not work (outside the home)

4. 30% own a washer/dryer
   26% have no washer and no dryer
   24% have a washer, but no dryer
   20% have a washer and a separate dryer

Of those with no washer and no dryer:

54% use a launderette
31% go to their parents' house
15% go to a friend's house

Fig 3.8 An example of quantitative research
(Extract from 'A' Level Media Studies report)

day is chosen for a specific period, with a number of different times offered to those carrying out the study. The narrative of each commercial is noted, as is the product at the centre of each.

Information is presented in graphic form, as bar charts, pie charts or other visual representation. Information about gender, age and ethnic roles is given as a percentage of all roles investigated in the period concerned.

THE SEMIOLOGY OF SOUND: AN EXTRACT FROM A STUDENT'S PRODUCTION REPORT

A detailed textual analysis of the final product and an evaluation of its success in targeting its audience

The cassette we have produced is not by any means a work of art, but it does serve a purpose. The cassette was produced as a teaching aid for GCSE Media Studies students and its mode of address was therefore informative. It aimed to be of help to the students by widening their media knowledge as well as being entertaining. The lecture took the form of questions based on sound effects; this we felt was more interesting than setting them a formal test or a straightforward lecture on semiology. The students had never covered semiology before at all, so it was necessary for us to explain the concept to them with lecture notes. Again, the notes were used though they were not tested on these notes to help back up our demonstration.

The tape itself consisted of two sections. The first section was designed purely to show these students who had no knowledge of semiology that sound does create meaning, sometimes universally. To do this, I placed 15 pieces of sound and sound effects on to an audio cassette. We presented the pieces one by one with a question and asked the students to respond on paper. The idea was to show how sounds have meaning, and how those meanings can be altered by additional sounds or music.

The first piece on the tape was of several people laughing in a maniacal way. This was primarily used because laughter, whatever its form, can be identified without difficulty. The other reason it was used was to see if the audience could identify it as maniacal laughter. Indeed 17 out of 18 identified the sound as mad laughter or maniacs laughing or some such similar idea. This showed us straight away that the tones used in laughing can represent different emotions or mental conditions; in other words they can produce different connotations.

The second piece combined the first with a piece of 'chilling' music. Combining the two together was interesting. As we had predicted, the presence of the music altered the audience's perception of the laughter. The thought had crossed our minds that because the laughter was maniacal in the first piece, this would make the audience identify it as evil. To counter this, in the third piece the laughter was combined with what we defined as light, mildly comical music. The results showed that this music had altered the perceptions from really maniacal laughter to comically maniacal laughter from harmless people. This first example gave us a good insight into the use of music in producing meaning.

No. 4 was a single bell tolling; 17 out of 18 recognised this sound. However, in No. 5, when the sound of a howling wind was introduced, the ideas of evil and death came into play.

A critical analysis of the research, planning and production processes

To undertake a project on semiology there was a good deal of research to be done. First we had to look at theories of semiology and secondly at the use of sound on TV and radio (as our production was concerned with *sound* and meaning.)

To research the theories behind semiology we looked at books on communication. This helped us really understand the subject before undertaking any work on it. We found that many theorists made no mention of the idea of sound and meaning in semiology, so we had to relate their ideas to sound. Saussure was looked at very closely because his concept of signifier and signified was extremely relevant to our argument. The idea of a signifier (a sound, e.g. single bell tolling) having a signified meaning (e.g. death, funeral) was pertinent to the demonstrations we were making – that sounds carry a meaning of their own, quite independent from the image.

Connotation and denotation were also looked at in great detail. Our production wanted to stress that a sound has a fixed first order of significance (denotation) but its connotation (second order of significance) could be altered by context and by any other sounds or music combined with it. For example, the sound of a violin playing may be just a piece of music if I said it was part of an orchestra, but the same piece could have a romantic meaning if I said it was being played under a balcony.

Barthes' two levels of signification were closely examined by the group and related to our examples on the cassette.

We also studied linguistics, as we wanted to show how para-linguistics plays a part in sound and meaning. Crystal's study of linguistics was examined, which showed us how tone, rhythm and pace can alter the meaning of the same set of words. We also looked at intonation and how one sentence could have a different meaning by an emphasis on one word.

When it came to our research on existing sound on television and on radio we studied the use of sound on TV to anchor meaning, and the use on radio to create it. To do this we chose to carry out content analysis and semiological analysis on the material we watched. It was difficult to know which method was best for our research. Content analysis would help us study a particular aspect of the TV and radio text, whereas semiological analysis would allow us to see the messages it conveyed. Both methods seemed to be valid to our research. Using just one of the methods we felt would limit our research. Using just content analysis, which shows how many times sound has been used to create meaning, would be useful but would not show how meaning is created. Semiology would show us how but not necessarily how often. Another problem with choosing was that content analysis was quantitative.

(Courtesy of Alistair Durden)

Research projects

Research from a 'problematic' (the problem or question a student poses in order to investigate some aspect of the mass media) is useful in that it focuses the attention of a student on a specific area. The danger is that some of them may set themselves tasks which require resources beyond what may be available. For example, a project which intends to 'Investigate the ways in which women are portrayed within television commercials' is only the first part of a task, and clearly depends on the use of secondary data. If a student then decides to compare these findings with 'the roles that women actually take in society', then the help of a massive research team and the provision of a funded project to last the rest of the century would be the least he or she would need. If, however, the second part of the project was to be a comparison with the way that women wish to be represented, then a real opportunity for progressive research presents itself. The women could be selected from either the same social group, or from a variety of groups across the spectrum of social class. The numbers could be set at a reasonable level; a sample of some twenty-five for the purposes of quantitative analysis, supported by an in-depth qualitative interview of a sample of those originally questioned.

Production: Designing material in response to a creative brief

Students are put into groups and given the creative brief 'Premia Lager'. (See the reproduced hand-out Fig. 3.9 on page 196.)

Purpose: to reveal some simple aspects of audience targeting, to develop collaborative group-work, to introduce some element of design into the study of two-dimensional advertising, and to encourage the practice of keeping log-books which describe the planning and production process.

- **Stage 1**: groups produce a set of ideas and drafts for the required designs. All meetings to discuss the ideas proposed are recorded individually in log-books.
- **Stage 2**: groups agree on a production schedule for the designs. While the designs are being produced, a record of each individual's contribution to the planning and production process is kept in the logs.
- **Stage 3**: all designs are displayed and a short written piece is produced to support each person's contribution.

Production from analysis and research: advertisement storyboard

Students are asked produce a short advertisement in visual form with accompanying textual analysis.

Purpose: to manipulate representation in the narrative form.

Student response: using previous content analysis of television commercials, a picture of current practices in the production of advertisements should have been produced. If a photo-storyboard is to be used, students will need to be guided through the use of simple point and shoot cameras. Note: provided the drawings/photographs are recognisable and match the technical information, then no student is penalised for their image-based work. The final production should include the following:

1 a written script for the television commercial;

Creative brief:
Premia Gold Lager

Background:
This brand is being launched in the face of stiff competition and the proliferation of the lager market. It is being positioned as a high gravity lager eih premium image. It is to be given an expensive price and, consequently, the image must be top quality.

Advertising objective:
To position the brand as a good value for money brand, whilst being a quality product.

Target audience:
1 Heavy lager drinkers. (18–35) C1, C2, D
2 Current drinkers of strong lagers.

Desired response:
For consumers to continue consuming Premia Gold Lager.

Position:
Price plus quality = value.

Justification:
Premia Gold Lager is brewed by experts in the oldest UK brewery.

Creative guidelines:
1 The execution should be able to be used, in slightly differing ways, for up to three years.
2 The advertisements must feature the logo.

The requirement:
1 Logo
2 Poster concept board
3 Drip mat

Approval:
Director _____
Manager _____
Client _____

Fig 3.9

2 a storyboard including all relevant technical details – shot length, angle, distance, SFX (see Chapter 5 on film);
3 a close semiological analysis of two or three enlarged frames of the storyboard.
4 a detailed textual analysis of the finished product.

Stage 1: it is essential for the meaning of current practices to be discussed. Does an increased representation of women in certain roles, for example, mean that advertisers are completely 'progressive'? Or is it a matter of changing fashions in advertising? A useful starting-point for this discussion would be the showing of the *Washes Whiter* series, for its portrayal of the history of television commercials. This should be contrasted with a batch of current advertisements which concentrate on the human subject. Broad differences between the types of roles taken by different subject should be noted in discussion. Besides this, the use of gender-based voice-overs should be examined.

Stage 2: the technical mode of representation should be examined in detail, including (in specific advertisements), the length of shots, the use of ellipses in narrative, and the angle and distances used to represent different events or moods. An average length of shot should be established by dividing the length of the advertisement by the number of shots. Occasions when the shot is significantly longer or shorter should be noted, and the possible reason for this should be drawn out. Is it to represent significant action if longer, or to increase the pace of the narrative if shorter? The basic forms of notation on storyboards should be taught: angle, distance, sound effects (SFX), length of shot. (*See* Fig. 3.10 for example storyboard.)

Stage 3: analysis of the type of narratives on offer should be made, together with some investigation of the way that certain products might focus on specific settings and storylines. The concept of intertextual meanings in advertising should be established, where certain genres of advertisement begin to emerge; echoes of one advertisement and its narratives or styles will reappear in another.

Stage 4: the connotive or implicit meanings of each advertisement should be investigated, as they were in the first exercise on analysis. The concept of address and discourse should be introduced. Students will need some idea of the four advertising formats.

Stage 5: students should have reached some conclusions about: the range of available representations; the range of available narratives; and the forms of address and types of discourse which are mobilised in advertising. On the basis of this, they should produce either a commercial narrative which attempts to reproduce the types of address and range of representation seen in mainstream television advertisements, or a narrative which attempts to challenge the types of address and range of advertisements.

A delicate balance is required here between awareness of what the industry produces and awareness of its possible shortcomings. It is no use producing a parody which reinforces these shortcomings. Equally, it would be pointless if students were simply to produce a narrative which stripped out all 'retrogressive' stereotypes and replaced them with a set of impeccably correct ones. One of the solutions is the manipulation of narrative to play on the expectations of an audience; to offer a set of images, for example, which are juxtaposed with the actual functions of the characters. (See Chapter 5 for narrative, genre and expectation.)

The purpose of textual analysis: students must be able to carry out an exhaustive textual analysis of their own work, with cross-references from the images, narratives and technical details of their own work, to the following:

Storyboard

Length of shot: _____

Type of shot: _____

SFX/Speech: _____

_____

_____

Length of shot: _____

Type of shot: _____

SFX/Speech: _____

_____

_____

Length of shot: _____

Type of shot: _____

SFX/Speech: _____

_____

_____

Length of shot: _____

Type of shot: _____

SFX/Speech: _____

_____

_____

Length of shot: _____

Type of shot: _____

SFX/Speech: _____

_____

_____

Fig 3.10

1 Theorists on advertising: Leiss, Dyer, Williamson and so on. Here the basic enquiry turns on the role and function of advertising, moral questions connected with advertising, and the formats advertising uses (see 'the four advertising formats' in this chapter). Reference to the usefulness of semiology (see Chapter 2 for an introduction to semiology, and Chapters 6 and 7 for critiques of semiology as an approach).

2 The historical development of advertising images and narratives, with reference to the types of society in which they appeared.

3 Intertextuality: the recognisable cross-fertilisation between advertisements and other television and/or film narratives, with examples from studies made on an individual basis or in class.

4 The relative success of the advertisement the student has produced in creating the intended meaning. Attention should be paid to questions of narrative (how well-structured is the story?), to technical production of the story (does the sound-track work with or against the visual element? – see Chapter 6 on film), to the use of representation within the story.

See below for an example of a student response to a television commercial assignment: extract from script (the accompanying storyboard has not been shown.)

EXAMPLE OF A STUDENT RESPONSE TO A TELEVISION COMMERCIAL ASSIGNMENT: EXTRACT FROM SCRIPT

Gale's Jeans

The first shot is of a busy office. The camera pans around quickly to show people standing and walking around, or sitting at desks – the whole place is very untidy. The next shot is of a young executive dressed in a smart striped shirt with a tie and pin; it is hard to see him behind all the rubbish on his desk! The camera moves in so we just see his head and shoulders and desk top. He looks like he's really bored, and he's not doing anything. He puts his head in his hands and stares out of the window on his left. The camera follows his gaze to a large building across the street.

The building is fairly grand, a flight of steps leads up to the main entrance, above the door is a sign which reads 'Devue Fashion House'. A sleek black sports car smoothly pulls into a designated car-park space next to the steps. There is a CU shot of a fashionably dressed woman (she has black hair and clear blue eyes) as she steps out of the car. She carries a pink portfolio. The camera shot follows her as she walks past a sign where the car is parked saying 'Katherine Devue – Company Director'. The camera shot goes back to the woman walking up the steps but shot from the office with the man's profile in view.

He watches until she disappears from view, then turns away from the window looking thoughtful. He opens (CU) a drawer on his desk, scrabbles among a load of papers and brings out some designs. With his left hand he sweeps the table clear (CU) and puts the designs on the table. He glances at the sketches, which are very good fashion designs (CU); he glances at the building again (MS from behind him) and grabbing the pictures (LS) he walks determinedly away from his desk.

The next shot (LS) is of him walking across the road and up the steps of 'Devue Fashion House'. When he's inside he sees a quiet, open plan office; at one of the front desks is Katherine Devue, who has her head down and doesn't notice him. He starts to walk over to her (all LS) but is stopped by her secretary. They talk, then she goes and whispers something to Katherine who looks up, obviously sees what he's wearing (CU shot of her blue eyes looking up and down) shakes her head (LS). The secretary goes back to the man and starts to say, 'Sorry, but I'm afraid . . .', but he has rushed off. The secretary shrugs.

The man comes back again and crosses the road running (slow motion); he is wearing a pair of blue 'Gale's Jeans' and a flowing trendy white shirt. (Advert concludes with man being hired by Devue Fashion House.)

Script evaluation

The advert is a straightforward narrative based on the story of a man breaking away from his previous image to fulfil his ambition to become a fashion designer. Because the latter is far more creative he has to leave behind his 'executive' style and wear something which will reflect his creativity and individuality to his fastidious employer-to-be. By buying the product he in fact buys himself an image which helps him achieve his personal goal. He is the perfect example of what the slogan says, by buying the jeans he stands up and is noticed.

This advert has to be visually powerful because there is no speech, and so it uses visual codes and semiology to get its message across. These codes are in the actions/clothes and status of the characters; they are also part of the soundtrack and setting of the text. Each look the company director gives the persistent man says something different – they are not individually 'explained', although the audience is expected to understand the meaning for each one. If this advert had been shown in the 1950s, the meanings would have been lost on the audience, which is trained into understanding different visual codes over a period of time. Even earlier than the 1950s, narrators were used to explain the benefits of the product; today, however, we are used to advertising methods of codes, and constant explanation is not necessary. Advertisers depend, it could be said, on audience foreknowledge and expectation.

Leiss believes that 'The job of the advertiser is to know the world of segmented audiences intimately, so that the stimuli created can evoke associations with whatever is "stored" in their memories and imaginations.' This is very true of this particular text, it plays highly on imagination and on the 'freedom fantasy' of a bored office worker. It has to use images which appeal to the age group which the advert is centred upon. Sports cars, beautiful and intelligent women, piles of work and busy work-places are all things which in one way or another are a part of everyday life or fantasy. What this ad tries to do is to show the ideal and the problem – how is the problem solved? By buying the product of course. Most adverts today use this format to create a problem and then show how to solve it. Washing powder ads are a good example of this: 'Fat is impossible to budge in your clothes. What can you do to get rid of those greasy stains? New "Cleano" has been designed specifically to remove all traces of unsightly stains.' This is the general type of thing . . .
It could be said that the advert relies too heavily on audience foreknowledge about such products as jeans.

On the storyboard, shot 22 is a good example of the role reversal that occurs at the end of the ad, even without the use of speech. The man is standing in a dominant position in front of the woman; this also helps to show off the product – the 'Gale's' label on the back pocket of his jeans. Because his face can't be seen there is an element of mystery involved; the woman is the only one who can see his face – all we can see is the way in which she reacts to him – which of course is positively. The fact that the woman is sitting and the man is towering above her reveals how power changes in the relationship.

The explicit message is obvious – the meaning is anchored by the slogan 'Gale's Jeans – stand up and be noticed', but in accordance with the problems that have been pointed out, the implicit meaning of the ad may not be quite what is intended. What the message is supposed to say is that by wearing the product you will improve your image, people will think that you have individuality and style, while at the same time they help you to escape from constriction and boredom.

If this advert was going to appeal to as broad an audience as was intended, it would have to have some adjustments; price, range and availability, or a change in the situation, but using the same type of themes. The mixture of fantasy and reality, however, is probably all right, and would have the necessary appeal to much of the intended audience.

ESSAY TITLES

1 Some modern advertisers have used Maslow's 'Hierarchy of Needs' as a model for labelling or 'segmenting' their prospective audiences.

Comment on the practice of 'segmentation' in general, and the way in which the 'hierarchy of needs' has been modified to fit a commercial purpose. Refer to those examples of television commercials you have studied which appear to use 'segmentation' to represent the human subject.

2 What are the uses and/or shortcomings of a semiological approach when it comes to interpreting two-dimensional advertisements? Are there ways in which a semiological approach could be reinforced by other methods of enquiry?

Give a detailed response to these questions.

3 'It could be argued that because advertising stresses the private accumulation of goods and almost hedonistic lifestyles, it encourages people to think in terms of escape from the real world . . .' (Gillian Dyer, *Advertising as Communication*).

Does advertising encourage people to attempt to escape from reality? Discuss this question with reference to theories of audience effects.

4 Advertising is an 'aggressive' form of mass communication. Discuss.

CHAPTER 4

Photography, semiology and the image

An image is usually taken to mean a pictorial representation of something in the real world: a person, scene or object. It can be produced in a variety of ways using different media. It might be a drawing or a photograph, or again it may be three-dimensional (e.g. a sculpture). Holograms, which were first exhibited in Britain in 1976, are examples of images which appear to have three dimensions.

But we also carry images of things around in our minds. We tend to 'update' these images from time to time, although there may be some that we protect from change, retaining them as 'ideal' pictures of some part of reality.

The 'authority' of the photograph

Many authors have discussed both the nature of the photographic image, and its social impact. In *On Photography*, Susan Sontag argues (p. 153) that:

'the images that have virtually unlimited authority in a modern society are mainly photographic images.'

According to Sontag (pp. 153–4), a painting is 'never more than the stating of an interpretation', while a photograph:

'is never less than the registering of an emanation (light waves reflected by objects) – a material vestige of its subject in a way that no painting can be.'

THE PHOTOGRAPH: EARLY DEVELOPMENTS

The invention of photography should really have occurred sooner than it did, at least in the sense that the two 'halves' of the technology needed to produce photographs had existed in reasonable abundance for some time. The mechanical half of this technology was the camera obscura, a large and cumbersome instrument which had been used over many centuries by artists to trace the outline of objects. It was used in an attempt to produce a closer representation of the real; it aimed to be more than the mere 'interpretation' described by Sontag. Over time, the camera obscura was reduced in size, so that an artist was able to carry it under one arm. The essential elements of the modern camera, including the iris diaphragm and an adjustable lens tube, were already present in this early aid to drawing, some one hundred and fifty years before the invention of photography.

The chemical half of the solution to photographic representation lay in the use of silver nitrate crystals, which had the ability to react to light. In 1727 it was discovered that silver salts turn dark when exposed to light, and in the late 1790s it was discovered that chemical treatment can produce a lasting change.

The world's first photograph

The first permanent photograph was produced in 1826, by a French inventor named Niepce. Its grainy vision of a disappeared world, taken with an exposure time of eight hours from his window in Gras, is quite compelling. Although some critics have 'seen' more in the picture than most have been able to identify, it has come to stand as the moment in history which gave birth to every succeeding photographic achievement.

The historian of photography associated with the rediscovery of Niepce's early work was Helmut Gernsheim, whose *History of Photography* (published in 1955 and 1969) helped shape, for better or worse, the way that developments in the science are understood. Gernsheim's method was based on his enthusiasms as a collector. He was an individual whose own discoveries and favoured examples have given a certain bias to the study of the subject. The notion of great 'landmarks' in photography is useful only if we also bear in mind that such an approach tends to produce a distorted view of progress, which rarely proceeds in a straightforward way.

Meaning and context

Our reading of Niepce's photograph (which he called a 'heliograph', or sun-picture), greatly depends (as with all photographs) on the context in which we see it. If we were to find it reproduced in a study of photography, with a caption which indicated its status, it would obviously assume its central place in the history of photographic representation. Should it be removed to a new context, however, its meaning might not be inflected in quite the same way. Used within the general frame of advertising, for example, its indistinct outlines and indeterminate distances might easily be taken for a deliberate effect. What was once the 'best' that could be achieved may now be reproduced to order, though of course few imitations could reproduce the emotional force of this early photograph, once its status is recognised and accepted by the observer.

Developments in photography

More advanced technologies than Niepce's were soon to appear, though each had a variety of advantages and disadvantages. A number of inventions and discoveries, all occurring within a few years of each other during the 1830s and the years which followed, gave rise to a confusion of claims and counter-claims. The distinction of being recognised as the true originator of the new 'art' was fought over for a considerable time. From the early 1840s the daguerreotype photograph, named after its inventor Louis Daguerre, became the most popular method for recording the human image. Its use as a medium for producing portraits depended upon its ability to reproduce fine detail. The limitation of the system was that it could produce only one image from each exposure.

A rival system was invented by William Henry Fox-Talbot (though the system appears to have been discovered independently in Germany by two photographers called Franz von Kobell and Karl August). This used paper negatives and had the advantage that prints could be made. Fox-Talbot had been making his 'photogenic drawings' since 1835. In 1839, hearing of Daguerre's announcement of the invention of a photographic process, he hurried to reveal the details of his own work, since he was at first convinced that the two systems must be identical. In 1844, Fox-Talbot began publishing in sections a volume entitled *The Pencil of Nature*, which required the production of thousands of high quality prints, although the number of copies of the edition published was quite small. He had to set up a primitive system of mass-production in order to deal with the many prints required for this venture into publishing.

Early photography required considerable financial resources, as well as the leisure to practice what for many remained a hobby. The role of women in this process was central. Constance Fox-Talbot worked as her husband's chief assistant. A Welsh contemporary of Fox-Talbot, John Dilwyn Llewelyn, was also assisted by his wife. These women undertook the often hazardous technical work of preparing plates and fixing images. These procedures included the use of unpleasant and dangerous chemicals; yet it is the men, as the chief practitioners of the 'artistic' side of the enterprise, who are remembered in historical overviews of photography.

While some photographers of the period (such as the portraitists Hill and Adamson in Scotland) are rightly celebrated for their inventive compositions and imaginative approach, in general there was also a great deal of material which took its inspiration from the most fussy of representational art; carefully depicted scenes of rural tranquillity abound, but one curious practice would appear to be the direct imitation of 'still-life' work, including photographs of dead game such as rabbits.

The highly celebrated Victorian photographer, Roger Fenton (still best known for his sanitised pictures of the Crimean War), founded a career on what appears to be, certainly by comparison to Fox-Talbot, Hill and Adamson, some of the most lifeless and depressing work in the early history of photography. His pictures of the English landscape appear as empty as his Crimean work, while his portraits of Queen Victoria's family are almost as ghastly and pointless as some of the 'genre' photographs he composed. It is as though the 1850s had begun to produce in some circles a weighty sense of respectability, which curtailed the enthusiasm and freshness of outlook which photography had produced quite naturally in the previous decade.

How close to reality?

Fox-Talbot introduced *The Pencil of Nature* with an interesting assertion about the 'natural' status of photographic images:

> '... this little work is the first attempt to publish a series of pictures wholly executed by the new art of photogenic drawing, without any aid whatever from the artist's pencil.'

Photography had from the first impressed both practitioners and critics by its apparent closeness to reality. As we shall see in the chapter on film, a twentieth-century theorist called Kracauer produced five arguments in favour of the idea that film was naturally a 'realist' form, based on the proposition that photography, in its turn, inclined naturally towards the straightforward recording of reality. The idea that photography was particularly close to the real seems also to have been taken up by the French semiologist, Roland Barthes. To understand how these arguments can be made, we need to look at the way that photographs work to produce meaning.

Literal reality?

In answer to the question 'What is the content of the photographic message? What does the photograph transmit?', Barthes (*see* Webster, *The New Photography*, pp. 172–3) stated: 'by definition, the scene itself, the literal reality.' Barthes went on to emphasise, however, that the image/photograph is not the reality itself, but, 'at least ... its perfect analogon'. So, in the first place, the photograph is supposed to transmit literal reality. In the second, it is an analogon; it is exactly similar to the reality it transmits.

Photographs have most usually been described as 'icons', because of their apparent ability to reproduce some elements of reality. There is little doubt that icons do have a close resemblance to the objects they represent. Since the photograph appears, at first sight, to be extremely close to the thing it represents, the many claims made for its ability to transmit 'the literal reality' seem convincing.

However, we have only to ask what *differences* there are between reality and its photographic representation, to discover that photographs in no way transmit 'the literal reality'. For a start, the photograph is usually flat, working in only two dimensions, whereas reality is three-dimensional. The flat image will be confined by a frame, limiting the extent of the image and forcing every photographer to consider how to compose the shot within the frame. Also, there will be no sound to accompany the image, as would be the case in the real world.

Barthes did in fact recognise that there was a change in the general 'quality' which is transmitted as we pass from reality to image. He wrote (*see The New Photography*, p. 173):

> '... from the object to the image there is of course a reduction – in proportion, perspective, colour – but at no time is this reduction a *transformation* (in the mathematical sense of the term).'

There are serious shortcomings to this argument; if, as Barthes says, there is always a reduction from the object to the image, it is the nature of this reduction which is important. The absence in the photograph of a number of elements found in the real world shows clearly how reality is not simply reduced or altered, but actually transformed by photography. Reality and its photographic image are in fact much farther apart than Barthes leads us to believe.

The photograph: a message without a code?

If it is true that the photograph resembles reality in a limited way only, then it must follow that there is also something wrong with Barthes' idea that there is no need to set up 'a relay' between the reality and the image. By a relay, Barthes meant a code. In other words, he saw no need to construct a *link* between object and image, for the reason that he believed object and image to be so close. Barthes therefore accords 'a special status to the photographic image' (*The New Photography*, p. 173) by which he means, as we have seen, that 'it is a message without a code'. This means, presumably, that the photograph signifies the actual scene, object, or person in the real world, without needing to be explained through the codes of a specific culture.

It is difficult to imagine how a message can be interpreted if it is has no code; presumably it is simply understood as we would understand any real object in the world. Barthes' view has influenced many academic studies of photography and the image. For example, Frank Webster (*The New Photography*), argues that an icon can:

'stand on its own to constitute a sign whereas most signifying systems require the reader/viewer/hearer to introduce a cultural stock of knowledge to decipher the codes of a subject.'   (p. 172)

The idea of a photograph being able to 'stand on its own' as a sign seems reasonable. But the implication that it does not need a 'cultural stock of knowledge' to be deciphered or decoded is more difficult to accept. All signs need to be processed through the human experience of culture. Nothing in this world can create meaning unless it can make some sort of connection to the experience of people. The human subject will always need to bring his or her experience (and also inevitably culture) to bear on a sign. In *Learning the Media*, Alvarado, Gutch and Wollen make some interesting remarks about the way images are decoded and understood by their audience. They note (p. 102) that images:

'also have to be understood in terms of the relationships they construct with their spectators and in terms of the contexts of their production, exhibition and circulation.'

Images carry extra-textual meanings. There can be a variety of significations of a single image in, for example, a newspaper, on television, or in a film at the cinema.

When Barthes insists that the photograph is a 'message without a code', he seems to be led more by his ability to create memorable statements than the urge to provide clarity of explanation. Does he neglect simple evidence? The frame of a photograph is a code, as is the internal arrangement of the subject-matter, the context (as Alvarado *et al.* note above) in which the picture is produced and seen, the selection of angle, distance, lighting effects, and so on. All these codes combine to allow the image to be interpreted according to our cultural experience. The important point about a photograph is not that it has no code, but rather that it is open to a variety of different interpretations.

Therefore, when Webster insists, just as Barthes did before him, that the photograph has (p. 173) 'a capacity to signify without recourse to the interpretations of a cultural system', and that 'icons have a cultural independence lacking in other signs', he appears first to have been misled by an over-simplified view of photographs as close to the real and in the second place, to have put too much stress on icons as 'free agents'.

When Webster goes on to admit that photographs are not free from cultural systems, this does not seem to lie easily with his idea that icons have a 'cultural independence' which other signs lack. What exactly is this 'cultural independence'? How far does it extend? Does he mean that icons carry meanings which can be understood across different cultures? (A drawing can be iconic, but some drawings carry meanings which do not translate easily from one culture to another.) Is Webster arguing that icons do not depend on cultural references at all? How then could a sign stand outside a culture, and yet remain a sign?

SEMIOLOGY AND THE PHOTOGRAPH

One of the central tenets of semiology is that certain types of sign have an *arbitrary* link to the idea or thing to which they refer. This means, for example, that a sign composed of letters, like 'dog', for example, only stands for a specific sort of creature by some kind of chance. There is nothing in the sign 'dog', according to this theory, to indicate that it means a particular type of animal. How then is a sign understood by the people who see it? Saussure believed that the sign could only be understood within a system of conventions. Therefore 'dog' would carry a specific meaning because there are other words which do *not* refer to the animal. This system of conventions – meanings created through use and over time – would suggest that the sign itself has a conventional use.

If we accept the idea that certain types of sign carry meanings established through convention, can we also describe such meanings as *arbitrary*? In other words does confusion arise if we take it on trust that signs created through words are at the same time *always* conventional and arbitrary?

We could use two examples to investigate the problem. In the first place, the word 'cat' would seem to have no obvious link with the animal it signifies. However, there are words in all languages which have grown out of the sounds made by (and then associated with) animals, forces and objects. For our second example, the word 'miaow' has a clear onomatopoeic link to the sound that a cat makes, and therefore to the animal itself. (Both 'cat' and 'miaow' as signs suggest a mental concept of the animal.)

Although Saussure rejected such examples of onomatopoeia as unimportant, some words would nevertheless appear to have perfectly 'natural' roots in our experience of the objective world. From this, we might wonder if words might begin life in a 'natural' way, where there is a connection between naming and some intrinsic value such as a resemblance in sound.

The other reason for doubting Saussure's emphasis on the arbitrary nature of the sign, is that the systems in which they operate are themselves very far from being arbitrary. It would make more sense to argue that most signs have a conventional link with the things they represent, because conventions are established over time. It is the continued use of the terms 'arbitrary' and 'conventional' together, and even sometimes as interchangeable concepts, which may act as a barrier to understanding the sign.

The icon and photography

Peirce's icon is, as we have seen, a sign which resembles closely the 'object in the world'. An icon is not an arbitrary form of sign. It *resembles* the object it stands for. Understanding the nature of the iconic sign is central to any study of photography, but it is important to remember the other two categories of sign in this system, the index and the symbol. The index has a physical link to the object that it represents, while the symbol (as we have seen above) is usually explained as having only a 'conventional' or 'arbitrary' connection to the object in the world. As I have said, it is this use of the terms 'conventional' and 'arbitrary' to describe the sign, and more particularly the symbol, which I would identify as having caused problems for the study of semiology in general.

It should be clear at least that signs can be composed of more than one category. As John Fiske demonstrated in his *Introduction to Communication Studies* (p. 52), some road signs are made up of all three categories of sign. For example, the road sign which illustrates the approach of a crossroads/junction (a cross inside a red triangle) is indexical because it is linked to the crossroads by virtue of its position on the road leading up to it. It is also iconic, since the cross bears a resemblance to the crossroads, and symbolic because it is set inside a triangle.

From icons to symbols

As we have seen, there appear to be a number of things wrong with the theory of photographic meaning, where an icon, resembling the real, is independent of, or has a degree of independence from, the cultural system in which it operates. In the first place, we know that whenever we see an actual object, that object has a range of associations linked to it. This is before any image of it is made. For example, a tree may suggest more than just a tree. It may symbolise Nature, or a particular environmental problem; if it is an oak tree, it may symbolise England. Therefore, a photograph will not simply suggest the object to us, it will also carry some of the meanings of the original object.

Growing out of this first point, it is impossible for any individual or group to read an image without reference to the cultural codes they have acquired. There is no escaping the 'cultural system'. Webster notes (*The New Photography*, p. 173) that a photograph of a terrorist in a newspaper signifies the terrorist. Quite rightly, he argues that the image of the terrorist is both iconic and symbolic but arguably the image also signifies 'terrorism' as much as it refers to the occupation of the individual in the photograph. It may well be the case that photographs are now often automatically symbolic, and that their symbolic meanings arise partly because we already give meaning to the things in the real world that they represent, and partly because to photograph something is to make choices about meaning. These choices are partly influenced by representations we have already seen. In other words, we are used to seeing certain kinds or types of photograph, to which we attach certain meanings.

The role of the audience

An audience is aware of the form and context of a photograph, quite apart from its content. In fact, an audience is immediately conscious, when a photograph is presented to them, that the image must be significant in some way.

When a particular photograph achieves wide circulation, its weight as a symbol is increased. There are in fact 'genres' of photographs – we expect certain situations, such as famine, to produce certain types of image. The resonances of these images depend on their previous associations. An audience will have a prior knowledge of a class of images and will expect future representations to be linked to those which have already been circulated. (*See* Fig. 4.1.)

When Webster says that icons are present 'in a real sense' beyond the 'vagaries of an audience's reading practices' (p. 173) he recognises the role of the audience, but does not seem to give much weight to the importance of decoding, which is more than a set of 'vagaries'. Is there supposed to be a 'real' meaning which an

Fig 4.1 *(Photographed in Uganda by Chris Steele-Perkins)*

audience is unable to reach? How could this real meaning exist outside the 'vagaries' of human perception? Are theorists above ordinary perception? All these questions point to the flawed logic and idealism of some semiological approaches.

Return to the real?

As we have seen, Barthes seemed to be saying that the photograph transmits reality, and that it does so because it is iconic (i.e. it looks like the thing it shows us). But then we have to deal with the next stage of his argument, which is that the photograph can be very misleading, exactly *because* it is so close to the real. Photographs are here imagined to be powerful manipulators of human perception, precisely because they seem to give us a direct access to the real world. According to this view, the photographic image is able to mislead us because it is a special, 'direct' form of the iconic. It might appear to have a straightforward denotative message, but it is exactly its obvious meanings and its seeming closeness to reality which make it, according to Barthes, open to a symbolic interpretation.

In fact, Barthes goes much further than this, to claim that the photograph is so purely denotative that there is 'no space for the development of a second-order message' (*The New Photography*, p. 185). In other words, Barthes seems to be saying here that there are no connotations. Does this mean that there are no 'secondary meanings' present in the photograph?

At this stage, Barthes appears to be changing his mind about where symbolic meaning and 'myth' come from. In his original theory of signification, 'myth and connotation are close cousins'. Barthes believed that as icons photographs are especially prone to a 'mythical' reading. But how could a photograph be mythical when there are supposed to be no connotations which can arise from it? Although myth is close to connotation, it is supposed to be a *new* type of second-order meaning, in which a sign itself (the combination of the physical existence of the sign and the mental concept associated with this physical element) becomes a mere signifier. Therefore connotation and myth are both 'second-order' meanings, growing out of first-order meaning.

The example given by Webster is taken from Barthes, in which he reported seeing a front-cover magazine photograph of a black soldier in the uniform of the French army. In Barthes' example, the connotations of the picture have become fixed and carry a dominant meaning, making the photograph of the soldier a signifier. In other words, the meaning of such an image has become fixed. This meaning is supposedly the concept that French society in general and the French military in particular allowed all to serve the nation without discrimination; a myth of equality. Myth would appear to attempt to narrow down the range of other possible readings.

The problem: denotation and connotation

At this point the problem discussed above needs to be restated. Barthes' theory of signification argued that there is 'no space' for the development of connotations (secondary meanings) in photographs. In addition, Barthes believed that photographs, as icons, are especially prone to a 'mythical' reading. This would suggest that myth grows directly from denotation. It could not, according to this theory, come out of connotation because that is absent in photographs. If myth grows directly from denotation, then connotation as a category becomes less important. If myth is just a certain type of 'fixed' connotation, then it is not a second-order meaning but a 'third-order' meaning, a new type of connotation. We would have to imagine a system which looked either like this:

1 **Denotation**	a **Connotation**	b **Myth**
leading to:	(cut out in the case of photographs)	(as separate second-order systems)
or like this:		

1 **Denotation**	2 **Connotation**	3 **Myth**
leading to:	(as suggested meanings) leading to:	(as fixed meanings)

Despite arguing, at one time, that the photograph is purely denotative, Barthes went on to say that, after all, the photograph *does* carry connotations. It does suggest meanings to people. He admitted that it has been worked on, edited, shaped, and needs to be interpreted or decoded by an audience. He eventually decided that it was denotation, rather than connotation, which led to mythical readings. But then he also stressed the 'paradoxical' nature of the photograph. In other words, the photograph was both close to reality and a highly artificial representation of it; this seems very neat, but in fact leaves the problem intact. The contradiction is left standing.

We are therefore encouraged to understand the photograph as having two opposite properties; it is clear and it is misleading. It is clear in terms of its image, misleading in terms of what it suggests about the world.

DENOTATION AND CONNOTATION AS A RELATIONSHIP

Instead of leaving the problem here, there might be a method which helps us to move forward. Perhaps denotation and connotation should be thought of as a *relationship*, rather than as just a process. In most approaches to semiology, denotation is taught as the first stage, with connotation as the second. We see a sign, we can describe what it represents, then we supply all the associated concepts which this representation suggests.

But the human mind does not work in exactly this way. We do not, for example, see a photograph of a gun and think simply of the object 'gun'. This is because the sign 'gun' is a concept made up of more than just the physical existence of the sign. It is made up of the physical existence of the sign and its associated concept. It is made by its connotations. We think immediately of the object's associations – depending on the particular weapon, we might think of different associated images and concepts.

An image of a silver-mounted shotgun is likely to bring to mind the kind of person who might own it, as well as the uses to which it might be put. An image of a shotgun with sawn-off barrels might lead to other connotations. The point is that denotation and connotation are ways of describing a thought-process which is instantaneous. The reason why a new-born baby is unable to produce connotations is that it is unable to recognise the sign at the 'denotative' level. But an older child

211

is only able to make sense of the meaning of a sign because it knows the connotations that the sign carries. The sign 'gun' is created through its connotative associations; it depends on its present cultural meanings. If guns were used only for starting races, then the meaning of the sign 'gun' would be quite different.

- **Denotation** is a category which appears as the 'natural' meaning, but all meanings are in fact subject to general context (culture) and immediate context (place or position in relationship to other objects). It is difficult to imagine the 'thing itself', precisely because we have a name for it. That naming helps to categorise the real object, but in a way which sets limits to our understanding.
- **Connotation** grows directly out of our instantaneous recognition (or indeed misrecognition) of the object or the representation of the object. We are then likely to use this set of connotations to 'colour' the real object according to our individual (culture-specific) observations. The shades of colour will be different for each human subject.
- **Myth** could be both a series of 'fixed' or 'dominant' meanings arising from the first order (denotation) because other meanings have been 'closed down', or a series of meanings which become 'fixed' through the accumulation and public airing of connotations or discourses.

A diagram of this relationship would therefore appear as follows:

Object (perceived through culture) > Denotation < > Connotation } Myth Connotation < > Denotation } Myth > Object (perceived through myth)

Barthes could have saved everyone a great deal of trouble had he seen right from the start that the photograph is not especially close to the real. Instead of agreeing with the idea that the photograph appears, in the words of Alvarado *et al.* (p. 97–8):

> 'more "realistic" because it seems to have a more direct relation with what it represents than language does; its realism allows us to believe in it almost as the thing itself',

we should see that it is a partial and limited representation of the world. As such it is prone to manipulation and is especially suitable to the construction of myths about that world. This is quite different to saying that photographs tend to create mythical interpretations all by themselves. They need a context (physical as well as cultural) in order to generate social meaning.

Photographs as symbols

We all know that there is some limited (iconic) resemblance between the photograph and its subject. Barthes eventually came to believe that it was exactly the most 'innocent' signs (associated with the denotation of a word or image) that were the most loaded with myth and ideological meaning. He did not, however, abandon the division of signification into denotation and connotation.

An object or sign becomes a symbol when it has picked up (through use and over time) a meaning that allows it to stand for some general concept; a rose or a picture of a rose might be a symbol of a political party as well as of romance. Therefore it would be more than just an icon.

Webster (p. 173) acknowledges the fact that photographs 'can develop quickly into symbols'. By this, he means that photographs tend to suggest a variety of meanings beyond their simple resemblance to the real world. For example, a photograph of Marilyn Monroe, shown to a variety of people who share, broadly, the same culture, may bring out a number of responses in its audience, and is likely to signify a great deal more than just 'young female'. A whole range of meanings connected with sexuality, the Hollywood star system, early death, and so on, will be brought to mind and will seem to be combined in the image. The photograph will not need a caption to produce its connotations, unless it is seen by someone for the first time. Captions, however, cannot generate every nuance of meaning; we need a wider experience of the representations associated with the sign.

Barthes, however, believed that photographic connotation can rarely be separated from a linguistic message. Some authors see language as crucial to visual communication. If we investigate this idea, we ought to be aware of how, exactly, a written text affects our understanding of the visual sign. Clearly, any caption which is attached to an image will tend to make us 'read' the image in a certain way. Barthes thought that the image was 'polysemous'; that is, it could be read in a variety of different ways. Language would therefore be used to limit the possible number of meanings. This is known as 'anchorage'. (Sometimes, a caption will emphasise certain elements of an image or photograph at the expense of others.) Another term used by Barthes to describe the relationship between image and linguistic text is 'relay'. In this case, image and text are in a 'complementary' relationship, working together to produce a narrative, in sequence.

How then are we able to produce meaning from a photograph or sequence of images which have no captions or titles? How is it that some photographs appear to need no caption? Part of the problem lies with the type of caption we are used to seeing. Captions in newspapers do more than simply provide information about a photograph. Whereas many books on photojournalism are careful to describe the exact locations, conditions and even the technical choices which go to make up a finished shot, the newspaper or magazine is mostly interested in using the image to support the ideological or moral point that a story is attempting to make. In other words, the caption is used to *position* or *interpellate* the reader, requiring the readership to fall into line with the preferred interpretation of the image. Of course, we should not regard the written text as the 'natural' part of the equation between image and words. The story that is chosen can be inflected to produce a variety of readings.

It is difficult to produce new meanings from a photograph which has already become symbolic of some idea or force in society. To return to the example mentioned earlier, a photograph of Marilyn Monroe will produce a certain range of meanings; it will do so not because we rely on captions, but because we know something about the individual biography of the star represented by the photograph. Types of photographs will also tend to acquire a number of meanings which will depend on an audience's knowledge of the image under study. Photographs of undernourished Africans will always give rise to connotations which include reference to famine. This may have some negative effects if, for example, the connotations produced work to place the inhabitants of Africa in a subservient or helpless role whenever they are represented, an idea described again in Chapter 6.

PHOTOGRAPHY AND PHOTOJOURNALISM

In *On Photography*, Susan Sontag writes (p. 3) that photography has taught people a new way of seeing the world. She takes the view that there are quite extensive moral implications which arise from this new code:

> 'In teaching us a new visual code, photographs alter and enlarge our notions of what is worth looking at and what we have a right to observe. They are a grammar and, even more importantly, an ethics of seeing.'

Photojournalism has come to inherit many of the moral questions which arise from the debate over the social role of photography. Most of the photographs taken by private individuals do not achieve a very wide circulation. On the other hand, news photographs which are made with the aim of publication must be seen in a different light. They are made as part of a continuous process, in which the news values held by the media institutions and by the journalists who work in these institutions help to determine what images are sought in the first place. News photographs are designed to be accessible to large numbers of people, and are often thought to be instrumental in changing or reinforcing opinion. Sontag (p. 4) believed that:

> 'photographed images ... now provide most of the knowledge people have about the look of the past and the reach of the present.'

If this is the case, then photographs exercise considerable power over how we see the world. When Sontag writes about this power, we should remind ourselves that it is the context of the photograph (where it is seen) that will often determine exactly how powerful it is. If a photograph is seen in a person's family album, then it takes on the domestic and semi-private connotations of personal history. Seen in a mass-circulation newspaper, however, the case is very different. In a newspaper, a photograph carries an impact for two reasons: first, through the very fact that it has been selected to represent or reinforce the essence of a story. Secondly, because it achieves widespread exposure in terms of the numbers of people who see the image.

Miniatures of reality?

Sontag believed that, for whatever purpose it is produced, the photographic image holds a central place in our conception of the real:

> 'What is written about a person or an event is frankly an interpretation, as are handmade visual statements, like paintings and drawings. Photographed images do not seem to be statements about the world so much as pieces of it, miniatures of reality that anyone can make or acquire.'

This view of the photographic image seems to echo Barthes' approach, setting up the same kind of dichotomy, as if to say 'the photograph appears to be close to the real, but in actual fact we are being fooled' – or, again, 'the photograph is both very real and extremely false'. One of the effects of this kind of approach is to create a kind of pessimism about the private uses to which we put photography, as though it is a kind of magic which we practice, while remaining blind to the 'down side' – its dire ideological consequences.

The more dramatic statements made by Sontag, used presumably to draw attention to the thesis of the book, do not work very easily as theory. When she claims (p. 3) that 'to collect photographs is to collect the world', or 'photographs are perhaps the most mysterious of all the objects that make up, and thicken, the environment we recognise as modern', we know we are meant to value such statements as impressive insights, rather than to take them as literal pointers to theory.

There may well be more truth in Sontag's idea that photography is an attempt to *appropriate* the object photographed. That is to say, taking a photograph is a way of possessing a part of whatever is in the frame. The State, too, has found photography a useful way of gaining control over its citizens, in a more practical sense. Sontag cites the case of the oppression which followed the destruction of the Paris Commune, when photographs which had been taken of Communard militants posing beside the wrecked symbols of the French State were used to identify suspects. These individuals were then usually executed.

Even 'well-intentioned' photography is not regarded as innocent by Sontag. The pictures taken by the photographers of the Farm Security Administration during the great Depression in 1930s America stand as an example of her argument that photographs are carefully constructed to reflect the interests of those behind the viewfinder. The FSA photographers strove, according to Sontag (p. 6), to catch the exact appearance which supported 'their own notions about poverty, light, dignity, texture, exploitation and geometry'. The idea of 'constructing' subject-matter and meanings, of making representations which suit a preconceived idea, is one with which we are probably now familiar.

Sontag is right when she says that photographs are as much an interpretation (or representation) of the world as are paintings and drawings. There are few occasions, in her opinion, when photographs are taken in entirely innocent ways, and even these rare examples of the 'self-effacement' of the photographer do not remove (p. 8) 'the aggression implicit in every use of the camera'. Early photography had a different effect because, in Sontag's words (p. 8) there was 'no clear social use … no professionals and no amateurs either'. Modern uses of photography by comparison, appear as (p. 8) 'mainly a social rite, a defence against anxiety, and a tool of power'.

Photojournalism

The move from considering the 'domestic' application of photography to the more 'public' and commercial aspects of its use, leads on to a consideration of the different public forms. Portraiture, for example, may reach a wide audience once the images concerned are published in some form which has a mass outlet.

However, there are clear differences between the audience for photographic books and for newspapers and mass journals. There is a clear difference in the way the image in each case is handled. The portrait may well be printed on good quality paper, displayed in a special context, or published in book form, while the news-photo is supposed to lend itself to widespread reproduction and must act as a visual 'key' to the story. The news-photo will be given, in turn, its own interpretative caption. The matching of the visual element and the written text is achieved through the careful manipulation of size, relative position and the editing of the text.

One of the most thorough explorations of the way that images are 'tailored' to the newspaper as a form is Harold Evans's *Pictures on a Page*. Although a 'mainstream' news editor, Evans often reveals a great deal more about the aesthetic and moral dilemmas which confront photojournalism than some of his more politically astute contemporaries. This is largely because he is able to use such a wide range of pictorial sources; he shows the reader a variety of effects which have moral implications. He demonstrates the range of editorial decisions which have to be imposed on the raw material provided by the photojournalists themselves. His perspective, as an editor, makes an interesting contrast to the role adopted by the photographer and reporter.

Evans's introduction to *Pictures on a Page* provides some remarkable insights into the practices that on occasion have made photojournalism renowned more for its daring than for any regard for the objective truth. He reveals how many photographs which make an impact on the consciousness of the public, photographs which seem to symbolise something about the human condition, have been obtained with less than scrupulous honesty. A prominent example (and one which shows us that the news editor is by no means always the villain of the piece) is the famous Bert Hardy photograph of a young American soldier in the Korean War 'sharing his last drops of water with a dying peasant'. Evans reports Hardy as having said:

> 'I set it up. Everybody was walking past but I had the idea and asked a GI to give the old man some water for the sake of the picture. He said he would if I was quick – and if we used my water ration.'

So, what appeared (by virtue of the caption which 'anchored' it) to be an illustration of human compassion was entirely artificial. Evans goes on to reveal how the news values held by editors would sometimes work against the intentions of photographers working on particular assignments. During the Vietnam War, according to Evans, routine pictures such as the test-firing of a gun would be more likely to achieve publication than photographs of a less spectacular nature which more faithfully recorded the nature of the conflict. (The whole issue of choice, intention and the role of the photojournalist will be explored in an interview with the freelance photographer Mick Garland, later in this chapter.)

Although Evans's examples would seem to reinforce Sontag's point about the general unreliability of the photographic record, Evans is keen to disassociate himself from her approach. He writes:

> 'These opening observations … are not intended to supply a single live round to the

critics who maintain that photojournalism is dead: that, in the words of Susan Sontag, it deludes the mind and deadens the emotions, posing as an accurate "miniature" of reality when it is only a symbol ... to warn of the risks of being deceived by a photograph is not to admit that photography permanently deludes.'

Equally, to argue that photographs stand at some distance from reality is not to deny the possibility that photography may reveal aspects of the social world which would otherwise escape our attention. It is worth noting that it is the school of thought which describes photographs as being very close to reality that also holds them to be especially misleading.

The importance of photojournalism

The importance of photojournalism is described in a variety of ways by different authors. Arthur Rothstein in *Photojournalism* (p. 15) claims that:

'the photographic image speaks directly to the mind and transcends the barriers of language and nationality.'

The idea of the 'universal' ability of the image to speak directly to people across all national and cultural boundaries is common to many studies of photography. Webster (*The New Photography*, p. 203) agrees that the photographic image and photojournalism are at least very widespread since they are 'encountered by each of us virtually every day of our lives ... [and hold] a special place in the way we see the world'.

However, where Rothstein argues that the photojournalist's job is 'to mirror the world' Webster is critical (p. 230) of 'photojournalism's special plea ... that it presents us with *accurate* pictures of the world'. Webster, writing as one who was championing the cause of a radical photography, is quite clear that the photojournalist has a distorted understanding of his/her own role, describing their view of themselves as a kind of self-delusion: 'they will quite affably [say] that their aim is to transmit news in an objective manner.' There is strong criticism of photojournalists in that simple word 'affable' – as though the journalists are too comfortable in their assigned roles.

In agreement with Sontag, Webster is convinced that (p. 231):

'no communication is "natural" because culture always intervenes in the process of encoding and decoding. We necessarily see the world as our culture has taught us.'

Here, the concept of what is natural and what is cultural are seen as quite different, but we might ask if Webster really wants to explore what a 'natural' communication would be. Would it be one which stands outside culture? How then would it qualify as communication at all? As he says, all forms of human communication, whether mediated or not, are part of, and grow out of the culture we inhabit.

We have been concerned, so far, with a moral argument concerning the honesty of the photojournalist and/or editor, and whether or not photography deceives people. These are important issues, but it seems unlikely that we will make very much progress with them until we begin to examine and understand the media institutions which rely on photojournalism, and the news values to which the institutions and journalists subscribe.

Photojournalists are often represented as mavericks, whose basic instinct is to escape from the constraints of the more 'narrow-minded' institutions which employ them. They are often freelance and therefore have attained a reasonably glamorous status in some film and television representations. The central character in the film *Salvador* is represented in these terms, and the fictionalised Tim Page in *Frankie's House* is shown in an equally romantic light.

News values, the institution, and the role of the journalist

When we talk about 'news values' we are referring to the ideas or assumptions which form the ideological background to the work of the journalist and the news editor. These values are not always clear to the casual observer; many of them are absent from the formal discourses of journalism and remain hidden or implicit. It is mostly the practices of journalism that reveal the underlying values which drive individual journalists to collect certain types of material.

News values have been categorised by a number of writers. It is often the case that each new definition of news values will build on the list outlined by earlier writers. In *Using the Media*, Denis McShane sets out five central tenets which journalists are likely to follow in their news-gathering operations. These are conflict, danger to the community, the unusual, scandal, and individualism. Brian Dutton, in *The Media*, produced a list of twelve of the 'most significant' news values. This was based partly on earlier work, such as that carried out by Galtung and Ruge in 1973. The list may be summarised as follows:

1 **Frequency**. This refers to something Dutton calls 'the time span taken by the event'. He cites the example of murders, which happen suddenly and whose meaning is established quickly. More lengthy structural developments in society are outside the 'frequency' of the daily papers and achieve notice only through the release of certain figures on a particular day.

2 **Threshold**. This means the 'size' of an event. There is a threshold below which an event will fail to be considered worthy of attention, and it will not be reported.

3 **Unambiguity**. Although events do not have to be 'simple', the range of possible meanings they are able to generate must remain limited. In this way, the event will be 'accessible' to the public.

4 **Meaningfulness**. Dutton divides this into two categories, following Galtung and Ruge, who called this news value 'Familiarity'. The first category is *cultural proximity*, in which the event agrees with the outlook of a specific culture. The second is *relevance*, where events will be reported and discussed if they seem to have an impact on the 'home' culture. This impact is usually represented in terms of some type of threat.

5 **Consonance** or 'correspondence', where the familiar (that which meets our expectations) is more likely to be thought important than the unfamiliar.

6 **Unexpectedness** or 'surprise', where it is the rarity of an event which leads to its circulation in the public domain. Galtung and Ruge appeared to think that

this category was an important antidote, a kind of balance, to the tendency for news to be predictable, but Dutton notes that the 'newness' of an unexpected event is usually processed through a familiar context. Unexpectedness has to operate through the categories of the meaningful and the consonant.

7 **Continuity**. This is where a story, once it has achieved importance and is 'running', will continue to be covered for some time.

8 **Composition**. Most news outlets will attempt to 'balance' the reporting of events, so that if for example there has been a great deal of bad or gloomy news, some items of a more positive nature will be added. Balance may also be achieved if news happens to come overwhelmingly from one source over a certain period. An example may be a period when most news comes from abroad; 'balance' will be sought by adding some items which reflect the domestic scene.

9 **Reference to elite nations**. Elections, natural disasters, wars and other significant events, are more likely to be reported in the Western press if they occur in the developed world. A disaster which involves loss of life will not automatically qualify as important news – this depends on a kind of sliding scale of importance given to the number of deaths, measured against the country in which they occur. The loss of a few lives in a Western country may achieve recognition, whereas a considerable number of deaths in a Third World country would need to have occurred to achieve similar recognition. This is an example of events having to attain a certain 'threshold'. Of course, it is possible that this value could operate in reverse, in exactly those countries regarded as 'less important' by the Western press.

10 **Reference to elite persons**. The famous and the powerful are often treated as being of greater importance than those who are regarded as 'ordinary', in the sense that their decisions and actions are supposed to affect large numbers of people. In addition, the social activities of such people are given importance because these combine the public's supposed interest in the famous with general interest in special events.

11 **Personalisation**. Events are often seen as the actions of people as individuals. An institution and its functions may be 'personalised' by referring to a prominent individual who is associated with it.

12 **Negativity**. What we sometimes refer to as 'bad news' is often good business for the newspapers and news programmes. The threshold is lower for reporting bad news than for good news; such news is also usually unambiguous, consonant, and occurs in a short space of time.

The role of the journalist

Denis McQuail examines the difference between what are known as the **neutral** and **participant** roles of journalists (*see Mass Communication Theory*, p. 146). The concept of the neutral reporter is closely associated with the idea of the press as a channel of information. The participant role, on the older hand, is where the journalist behaves as a representative of the public.

Past research would seem to suggest that most journalists are likely to cast themselves in the neutral role, since it fits in with dominant ideas about objectivity as a core value in journalism. Surveys of US journalists, however, have found that the role adopted has tended to be one which is critical of government. McQuail believes this to be part of an American journalistic tradition, but he also understands it as a reflection of the political era when the surveys were conducted. Weaver and Wilhoit (1986) confirmed some of the enduring features of journalists' view of their role. There had been some change in the critical perspective brought out in the early 1970s, but there was significant minority support for an **adversarial** role.

TWO ROLES: A LIMITED APPROACH?

The idea of two opposing types of role has come to be seen as rather too simplistic. Weaver and Wilhoit opted instead for a three-part division of roles: **interpreter**, **disseminator**, and **adversary**.

The interpreter would be there to analyse events and raise questions, discuss national policy and explain the actions of the powerful. This is much the same as the idea of the journalist as participant. The disseminator is a role which would involve a view of journalism as a service. A central idea in this case would be the speedy dispatch of accurate information to the public. The role of the adversary would involve taking a consistent and principled stand against the whims of powerful individuals and institutions, in the belief that they might otherwise be able to practice a variety of abuses unchecked.

This is not to say that all journalists fall easily into one or other of these categories. Some clearly see themselves as having a plurality of roles. In the 1986 survey of American journalists, carried out by Weaver and Wilhoit, only some 2 per cent of the respondents described themselves as having only one role. There are, however, differences in the outlook of journalists originating from different countries. Donsbach's 1983 survey (*see Mass Communication Theory*) showed that British journalists were more content to play a purely informative role than their German counterparts.

The role of the photojournalist: a scandal-monger?

It is clear that the photojournalist must work within many of the same constraints as the reporter who relies on a notebook or tape-recorder, or the editor who remains desk-bound throughout the working day. Nevertheless there are significant differences. To explore this area a little further, it would be a good idea to remember that not all journalists who use cameras are 'photojournalists' in the sense that Webster or Evans or Rothstein would use the term. The rise of the 'paparazzi', journalists who work for newspapers which are interested only in a narrow range of news (usually concerning the famous and their public and private excesses), shows how the 'traditional' role of the photojournalist can be neglected in favour of a more limited approach, where news values are even more restrictive. The photographer who sets out to catch revealing pictures of public figures is in the business of innuendo; the photographs themselves hardly need captions. We all understand the intention of the photographer and the newspaper concerned – it is to reveal embarrassing details about the famous. The photographs are essentially similar as a result. Often of the most mundane kind, with little time spent on composition, they are out of focus if taken at an extreme distance, or else the subjects are bathed in flashlight as they emerge from venues like night-clubs. Very little of any interest appears to be happening in such pictures, but then the whole purpose of this type of journalism is to allow readers to draw specific conclusions from sometimes insubstantial evidence. It is a practice based on making money. The photographer who gets a good shot can make a fortune, and the newspapers can maintain sales.

Some sections of the British tabloid press appear, at first sight, to have adopted a position which is critical of royalty and the rich and famous. In reality, such newspapers offer no real critique of the system which produces this class of rich and leisured people. They depend, in fact, on the continued existence of such a group.

WHAT KIND OF PROFESSION?

The existence of the opportunist journalist/photographer can partly be explained through what McQuail calls (*see Mass Communication Theory*, p. 149), 'the weak "institutionalisation" of the profession compared, for instance, to law, medicine or accountancy'. Webster (p. 233) is careful to look behind the scenes to 'the process of news production', where news production is described as a process of 'gatekeeping'. Reporters and editors can 'block certain issues, but ... allow others to filter through to the audience'. According to Webster, 'stories cannot leap from the "reality" of events straight onto the front page. They must be interpreted by human beings'.

It is important to note that editors, photographers and reporters (who deal with the material at source) are all subject to the news values which are held not just by their own papers, but by the press in general. As Webster points out (p. 233), 'the news ... is the account of the event, *not* something intrinsic in the event itself'. There are deadlines and constraints of time, and these too act to structure what the public is likely to read. There are places where photojournalists go because they know those places regularly make 'news' (demonstrations, the police, the courts, the House of Commons). Journalists go to those places they and their institutions have already designated as significant. There are also regional variations in the number of journalists who will turn up at a particular event. Overall, Webster concludes that (p. 235) 'the news is a carefully manufactured activity'.

THROUGH THE EYES OF A CULTURE?

According to Frank Webster, 'it is through the eyes of a culture that photojournalists see the world. They are thus susceptible to the values which are inherent in their culture.' Webster admits that 'culture is not homogeneous', yet he also insists (p. 237) that the BBC is 'thoroughly pro-establishment'. This book has tried to argue that culture, and the ideologies which thrive within it, are never free from contradiction. The establishment itself, particularly in times of stress, is never completely united on all issues. 'Thatcherism' was not the brain-child of the establishment: it was a reaction to events. The class background of leading 'Thatcherites', including Mrs Thatcher herself, was one indicator of how far this grouping originally stood from the centre of power. Where exactly the establishment can be found, let alone where it stands on various issues, is often difficult to work out.

A brief history of photojournalism

Sontag observes (p. 85) that 'nobody ever discovered ugliness through photographs'. Her argument is that photography has had a marked tendency to beautify the world. She goes so far as to argue that to regard oneself as attractive (p. 85) 'is, precisely, to judge that one would look good in a photograph'. Some, however, would dispute this, and may regard the 'essence' of their appearance as something that is not easily captured on film. We use the term 'photogenic' to describe the positive impact that some people are able to make when photographed.

Sontag repeats a well-known point when she argues that there is a tension between two tendencies in photography, the tendency to beautify and the tendency to represent the truth. This tension applies equally to photojournalism. When she quotes (p. 87) from one of Hawthorne's books, in which a photographer talks of how the photograph 'brings out the secret character' of the individual, we need to remember that no such truth would be available were we not used to decoding not simply the codes of photography, but also the codes of human appearance – in particular, the appearance of the human face.

The birth of photojournalism

How exactly did photojournalism first emerge in the press? Some of the early photographers, such as Du Camp, made records of great monuments in the Middle East. However, this was not photojournalism, any more than the comparable work of a landscape painter could be described as social comment. Roger Fenton's photographs of the Crimean War are now historical documents, but the action of war was impossible to capture with the technology of the day, even had Fenton intended to make a critical approach to the subject. The photographs themselves could not be published. In their place, wood engravings were made from the original pictures, and were printed in the *The Illustrated London News*. The practice of making engravings from photographs, and then using the engraved plates for printing, meant a curious kind of image was produced, without the close representation of reality characteristic of the photograph, and yet lacking the liveliness of the freehand drawing. Not until the introduction of the half-tone process did it become possible to reproduce inexpensive prints of the photograph in conjunction with words set in type. The first American photograph of this type appeared in March 1880.

However, it was possible for a photograph to have what we might call a political impact before this date; as Rothstein notes, Abraham Lincoln attributed his election success in 1860 both to a speech he made, and to a photographic portrait produced by Matthew Brady. The image was widely circulated in lithographs and woodcuts. Although these in no sense can be understood as the reproduction of the actual image, they served to counter the other 'image' of Lincoln as a rough and uncouth man from the backwoods. In addition, 'tintypes' from the Brady portrait of Lincoln were circulated as badges – one of the earliest uses of photography for political ends.

Images of war in the early photographic era

The early photographic processes required a kind of travelling darkroom which had to accompany the photographer. Fenton and Brady both used vans to transport their equipment, and Fenton used a tent as a darkroom. As technology became more reliable (although few processes could match the clarity of the earlier daguerreotype), the range of subjects which it was possible to photograph increased considerably.

War has long provided an opportunity for a certain type of journalism, giving rise in the modern era to what some regard as the archetype of the photojournalist – a freelance adventurer. However, as Rothstein points out (*Photojournalism*, p. 15), photojournalism is a practice where 'the photograph is not the final effort; the publication is'. Photojournalism did not exist in the proper sense in the years which saw the advent of the Crimean and American Civil Wars, because the pictures could not be published as part of the representation of events. Since the reproduction of images was impossible, so far as their successful circulation to a mass public was concerned, photographers had to be content with selling individual prints or stereoscopic pictures, or else with mounting exhibitions of their work. These methods operate in a conceptual framework which turns 'news' into commemoration. (The photographers who gained experience during these conflicts were nevertheless able to make other images which would eventually have 'news value'.)

'REALIST' WAR PHOTOGRAPHY

Matthew Brady's role in recording aspects of the American Civil War marked the genesis of 'realist' war photography. He toured the battlefields photographing the dead and the various scenes of devastation. However, he was not above composing his shots in ways which later became standard practice for some photographers. For example, the removal of a sniper's corpse to a visually more effective site is probably the best known early example of the almost universal tendency to set up 'good pictures'. In addition, Brady used groups of employees who were sent into the field with the purpose of capturing shots which would enhance his own reputation. The photographs they made were circulated under Brady's own name, just as some modern photographs will carry the title of a news agency rather than the name of the photographer.

The American Civil War received massive coverage and certainly helped to push forward the practice of war photography and, eventually, photojournalism itself. Some five hundred news reporters from the North, for example, were sent to cover the war. In *The Camera and its Images*, Arthur Goldsmith reveals (p. 86) that photographs of bloodied corpses did not seem to cause revulsion in the public, but rather a kind of morbid curiosity. It is instructive to note that the Northern authorities made no attempt to restrict the circulation of the photographs, nor did they try to doctor the images before their release. It was still the case, as we have seen, that the images did not appear in their own right in any newspapers or journals. If they had done so, the question of censorship may well have arisen.

Technical developments

In the late 1870s the invention of dry, instead of wet emulsions led to a revolution in the practice of photography. The immediate need to develop film-stock no longer applied: plates could be developed at a later stage in the darkroom. The dry plates were also considerably faster than the older wet-plate method and the prospect of exposure times of a fraction of a second came closer. A significant development was the fact that the camera was now able to record movements and actions which the human eye itself was unable to catch.

The improved ability to make faster enlargements of photographs led to an increase in the practice of 'cropping' pictures, which certainly, as Goldsmith writes (p. 95), became a 'powerful aesthetic and remedial tool' but also had powerful political implications. A major improvement was the ease with which cameras could be carried, since hand-held cameras allowed the photographer greater flexibility. There was a craze for portable cameras, and Goldsmith notes that one invention, a camera that looked like a pocket watch, was ordered in large quantities by the Tsarist secret police.

LE JOURNAL ILLUSTRÉ

The first interview to be illustrated by photographs (published in Le Journal Illustré) was conducted by the Nadars, father and son, in 1886. It featured the chemist Michel Chevreul, who had reached his hundredth year. The pictures were 'snapshots', taken with an Eastman camera and roll film. As it became possible to take photographs with faster and faster exposures, the question 'How long is a "moment"?' began to receive attention. Thus the nature of recorded reality came to depend partly on the moment caught. The name of Eadweard Muybridge is associated with the time-stop photographs which recorded human and animal movement in sequence, and confirmed, for example, that, at a certain point in its progress, a galloping horse did lift all four hooves from the ground.

DELAYED BEGINNINGS?

Goldsmith's history of the photographic image deals specifically with the beginnings of photojournalism. The first photograph produced in half-tone appeared (printed on an extremely small scale in a bottom corner) in the New York Daily Graphic in 1880. Goldsmith believes that, along with the first photographic interview, this should have begun the era of photographic journalism. In fact, it was some twenty years before half-tone printing became widely used.

Social crusade or art form?

Photography was used by various social reformers to document the neglected labouring classes of the late nineteenth century. This was one strand of the approach which would make photojournalism a powerful social force. The daguerreotypes of Richard Beard were reproduced as woodcuts in Henry Mayhew's famous *London Labour and the London Poor* of 1864. Dr Barnado made studies of young vagrants and their placing in foundling homes in the 1880s. The immigrant photographer Riis made important studies of the poor of New York in the 1880s. His book, published in 1890, *How the Other Half Lives* helped to bring housing reforms to some of the poorest areas.

The photographer Alfred Stieglitz ran a journal called *Camera Work* (published from 1902 to 1917) which was intended to convey the artistic qualities of the medium. Stieglitz maintained that photography was an art form. By way of contrast, Lewis Hine's 1908 pictures of child labour gave an impetus to protective legislation. Once again, the tension which existed between a practice which emphasised 'beautification' and one which pursued the 'truth' continued to provide a simple frame of reference for many critics. Others, such as the film-maker and writer Su Braden, see a more complex relationship between the photographic image and social issues. In *Committing Photography*, she stresses the need to produce more than images of poverty, since she believes that there must be images also which draw attention to the reasons for it (p. 15):

> 'Lewis Hine, by producing images ... of only one side of the story, appealed only to pity ... what would the effect have been had Hine offered a wider choice of images, had he pictured the exploiters as well as the exploited?'

Getting the best 'shot'

Newspapers had to rely on news-photo services at the end of the nineteenth century. Photographs were most certainly used, but not in a way we would expect. They supported written text, rather than working to illuminate it. Gradually, with the employment of staff photographers, and the use of lighter cameras, newspapers and journals began looking for the 'best' or most expressive picture, rather than any shot which might simply represent an event. Rivalry between newspapers drove photojournalists to make greater efforts to achieve the most dramatic picture possible. Goldsmith describes how photographic images used in newspapers came to be categorised into (p. 153) 'two basic groups – "spot news" and "features"'. The first refers to pictures taken at the scene or aftermath of an event, while the second type relied largely on 'human interest' stories and were often used if there was a dearth of exciting news stories.

The impulse to create sensational stories during the First World War, however, did not include the use of front-line photographs. Wilfred Owen wrote to a friend that he had spent one morning 're-touching a photograph of an officer dying of wounds'. No sense of the reality of the conflict was conveyed in the newspapers, and the most severe restrictions were placed on the use of photography at the front.

Inter-war growth of photojournalism

European photojournalism made great strides during the inter-war years. An early centre was Hungary, in particular Budapest, where names such as Munkacsi, Halasz and Kertesz became famous in the field of news photography. Germany also underwent a period of great creativity after the upheaval of war and a failed leftist revolution. Many publications specifically devoted to the pictorial appeared at the time, both in Berlin and elsewhere, such as *Berliner Illustrierte*, *Die Dame*, *Münchener Illustrierte Presse*, and *Kölnische Illustrierte*.

Other publications, owing allegiance to political parties, also appeared at this time, such as the German Communist Party's *Arbeiter Illustrierte Zeitung*. Some of these publications had a sophisticated sense of what constituted 'news'. Different styles of journalism were made possible by the invention of new, miniature cameras such as the Ermanox (introduced in 1924) and the Leica. The Leica became the most favoured amongst photojournalists after 1925. Faster shutter speeds meant that pictures could be taken indoors without flash. This was another boon to the photojournalist. The Leica was the camera which established the dominance of 35mm film, which had previously faced some practical difficulties in day-to-day use. The Leica also enabled photographers to make a series of rapid exposures, leading to the tendency to portray events sequentially. There was also more opportunity to catch the 'prize-winning' single image.

Photography: sins of omission and sins of commission

Goldsmith describes how the ability to manipulate, crop, and generally 'improve' the still image, rapidly became one of the special weapons of the propagandist. (There is, of course, a difference between tinkering with an image or a set of images, and photographing public events which are from the very start, stage-managed and highly artificial.)

Propagandist use of still images is often associated, rather narrowly, with the era when it reached particularly dizzy heights. In the 1930s, both Soviet Russia and Nazi Germany used photography to great effect, not merely by restricting the freedom to take pictures in certain sensitive areas but also (in the case of the Nazis as a matter of deliberate policy) by setting up propagandist events. Rallies, projects, speeches could all be photographed by party workers. In Soviet Russia, a slightly different approach was the use of 'worker-photographers', who were (*The Camera and Its Images*, Goldsmith, p. 166):

'trained to produce pictures and picture stories imbued with the spirit of "social realism". That is, only didactic, upbeat pictures that showed positive aspects of Soviet life and followed the current party line were permitted.'

Such practices, the selective use and manipulation of photography, also took place in countries regarded as having broadly democratic traditions. In America, for example, there was a 'self-imposed' censorship at work during the Presidency of Franklin Roosevelt, whereby (p. 167):

'no newspapers or magazines ever showed [Roosevelt] in a wheelchair, and only in rare, shocking instances showed the braces on his polio-crippled legs. Many people who grew up during that period were not aware that the President was almost totally crippled from the waist down.'

Whereas the Nazis tended to arrange events which, according to Goldsmith, 'stage-managed and [manipulated] reality on a large scale', there were other, much less laborious methods of deceiving an audience. There is the obvious instance of using misleading captions, so that an event is read in a particular way. Rothstein (*Photojournalism*, p. 21) gives the example of a 'steer's skull', photographed in 1936, which supposedly illustrated a drought in a particular American state. There was widespread outrage when it was discovered that the photograph had in fact been taken in a different place altogether. Again, it is possible to remove some element of an image so that the remainder of it gains (perhaps unjustified) attention. The bewildering number of times Stalin appeared together with Lenin in photographs which purported to date from the early years of the Bolshevik revolution (when Stalin had been a relatively minor figure) may have led some to imagine that Stalin was a carefully chosen (rather than merely a natural) successor to the older dictator.

Another example of duplicitous practice is where images are rephotographed and then recombined in some way, in order to produce an image which could prove damaging to an opponent. Rothstein cites the example (pp. 21–2) of composite photographs used in a US election, of a Communist leader apparently in conversation with a mainstream but left-leaning politician, which contributed directly to that politician's defeat.

A more difficult question arises when the principal elements remain unchanged, but some other aspect of the composition is altered. An outstanding example of this was a famous war photograph made by Dimitri Baltermants. The caption which accompanied the picture was 'Grief', and it illustrated the aftermath of a Nazi atrocity carried out in the Crimea during the Second World War. Distraught women search for the bodies of their menfolk, while corpses lie scattered in all directions. The tragic drama of this scene is reinforced by a sky filled with threatening formations of cloud.

The sky, an important element in creating the general mood of the photograph, was in fact transposed from another negative. This technique was used by early practitioners of photography because it was difficult to capture the contrast between earth and sky.

Photojournalism as myth: the Vietnam War

Of all the conflicts that have been represented in various ways by the mass media, the most obsessive recapitulation seems to have been reserved for the Vietnam War. A host of films re-examining the experience from the viewpoint of the US veteran are available on video. Vietnam has become a *motif*, and where there is no direct reference to the conflict, or where it is simply a background to character or narrative, it still seems to act as a symbol of a generation's betrayal. Under this accumulation of fictive material, the direct experience of those involved seems confined to documentaries (many of which seem to have the same ideological purposes as the narrative film), or else is lost. The images produced by photojournalists have been replaced by images produced by Hollywood.

One of the problems with reporting war is that photographers are placed in a situation where their presence is actually superfluous to the action. They often go to war expecting to make 'great pictures' and to some degree great reputations. Since it is clear that the majority of the developed world's population has no direct experience of the battlefield, and since the visual and emotional expectations of warfare remain so high, all the conditions for a classic 'mediated' experience are in place.

In its retrospective of the photojournalism which flourished during the Vietnam conflict, the photographic magazine *10/8* (*see* Ed Barber, 'Vietnam after the Apocalypse', *10/8*, no. 5/6, spring 1981) described the type of character who hunted for pictures at this time as (p. 34) 'the macho, predatory photojournalist at work'. This may be rather a sweeping generalisation for a group of photographers which included some notable women (*10/8* mentions Leroy and Webb), and may even be misapplied to journalists with a more considered or ambiguous response, such as Don McCullin.

McCullin first encountered armed conflict in Cyprus during the Emergency there and spoke of taking photographs of dead Turkish civilians (*Past Exposures*, BBC, 1989):

> 'I felt a bit lousy about it, but I thought, you know, this is just a still-life job . . . keep your nerve and just shoot pictures . . . in fact there's nothing more unlike still life than just-dead bodies.'

McCullin's dilemma lay in the conflict he felt between his own enjoyment of war and his sense of purpose in recording it:

> 'I'm trying to get the message over to people, that even though I like being in a war . . . because it's a great adventure for me . . . my duty is to be there for a reason, not just to have a bloody good time . . . I've got to make sure that when they look at my pictures on a Sunday morning after breakfast it's going to hit them hard.'

In 1971 Don McCullin produced his first book on the war, entitled *The Destruction Business*. He had covered the war for the *Sunday Times* colour supplement and the book contained some of these images. The criticism the book faces in some quarters is that the images describe the human condition in war without explaining the reasons behind the suffering. This is partly a general argument about the use in photographic journalism of captions and accompanying text, but it is also about the value of composing beautiful or intriguing images when the subject matter itself is so horrific. There are arguments to be made that representations of the Vietnam War needed (and still need to be) set in a political as well as a moral context. Nevertheless, McCullin's pictures remain an effective portrayal of the human condition in extreme circumstances.

The contrast with journalists who do not perceive any anomaly in their situation is adequately served by referring to the career of Tim Page, whose perspective on the conflict did not alter particularly over some twelve years. Interviewed in 1968 (*Past Exposures*), he emphasised the excitement and the 'reality' he encountered in his role as a war photographer. In a review of his work in 1980 at the ICA in London, he still felt that 'all war's glorious – it was fun while it was there'. The *Life* photographer, Larry Burrows (killed in a helicopter crash in 1971), composed pictures which, against the grain of common practice, attempted to help his audience understand the reasons behind the war. He avoided making the sort of picture that was pure horror, since he thought that people would simply turn away from such photographs and learn nothing.

NEWSWORTHY IMAGES?

The retrospective Vietnam study by *10/8* refers to Philip Knightly's remarks about the peculiar nature of the war:

> '... no clear cause, no borders to defend, confusion about war aims, confusion about the enemy.'

The confusion and mayhem have been turned by Hollywood into a selling-point. Images of surreal devastation have become fashionable, but atrocities and massacres were not necessarily considered to be newsworthy at the time the war was actually in progress. Here we return to the question of news values and the roles that journalists choose to adopt. *10/8* quotes Philip Jones-Griffiths as saying:

> 'If I had gone back to Saigon and into one of the agencies and had said, "I've got a story about Americans killing Vietnamese civilians", they would have said, "So what's new?" It was horrible, but certainly not exceptional, and it just wasn't news.'

The infamous My Lai massacre resulted in the US public becoming more aware of the nature of the American involvement in Vietnam; one response from the authorities to the publicity it generated was to question the authenticity of the images. The photographs of the massacre were never, in fact, widely syndicated in America.

The *10/8* article acknowledges the tendency to make 'good pictures' out of something that is fundamentally repulsive. Mark Jury's *The Vietnam Photo Book,* which examines the hippie generation in the war, and David Douglas Duncan's *War Without Heroes* are taken to task for assuming that we already understand what the war was about. *Vietnam Inc.,* on the other hand, produced in 1971 by Philip Jones-Griffiths, is praised for concentrating on the effects the war had on Vietnamese civilians. Jones-Griffiths was told that the book was 'too harrowing' for the US market, but its most distinctive feature is a thoroughly 'contextual' approach. There is a coherent use of text and photographs. As the review by Ed Barber says (p. 36), 'this is no book of icons of horror – it is a well-argued and carefully designed visual and textual statement'.

Photojournalism under constraint

Frank Webster writes about an interesting case which arose during the 1976 funeral of the Irish Republican activist Maire Drumm, who had been shot by paramilitaries. Individual photographers had to seek permission from the Republican Movement to take photographs of the cortege. The images that the papers obtained would be unlikely to stir up much sympathy for the IRA in mainland Britain, whoever had taken them; there was already a negative impression of the IRA, created by the organisation's bombing campaigns on the mainland and by the previous news coverage given to all things Republican. The problem the newspaper editors faced was to give the pictures of the funeral an ideological 'spin' in keeping with their perception of public response.

Ultimately, no matter how biased the 'reading' offered by the tabloids, the fact that audiences respond in different ways in different contexts, as we saw in Chapter 2, will determine to a large extent the impact of any slant put on events by journalists. Are photographs more powerful, more emotive in their effect, than text? Can the image 'overcome' the text to some extent? Different verbal interpretations of the photographs were used by the mass-circulation papers, but to what effect?

Some of the editorial decisions made might seem to have given a faintly ambiguous 'feel' to the story. The *Daily Mirror* used a heavy black border around its picture, which in some situations might signify grief, but in this case seems to have referred more to the seriousness and gravity of the event. The reader was certainly told what to think by the accompanying headline, which read 'Gun Salute for Granny of Hate'. According to Webster, such 'anchorage' was an attempt to defuse the 'IRA codes' carried by the photographs. Pictures of masked members of the IRA firing over the cortege would clearly not be printed without comment. The *Mirror*'s headline would act to 'inflect' the violent connotations of the masked figures, the weapons, the accessories of paramilitary display. However, the usual connotations of 'granny' could still have carried some positive overtones. This is why the word 'hate' is so important, because it pointed up how 'unnatural' this particular grandmother was; a 'granny' is not supposed to stir up 'hate'. By comparison, the *Sun*'s front page, at least in visual terms, appeared more humane (if not actually sympathetic). This is because the paper used photos of a different kind, reflected by the headline: 'Daughters weep at the funeral of Maire Drumm'. The front page again featured a black border, but perhaps in this case indicating the mourning of the daughters.

In the first chapter of *Pictures on a Page* Harold Evans argues that a 'good news photograph' may attract 80 per cent of a newspaper's readership. He opens his book with five photographs, none of which were taken by professional photographers. The quality usually demanded of a news photograph may sometimes be waived in favour of the immediacy of interest which certain types of image may provoke in their audiences (for instance, pictures of the 'Royals' and other well-known figures).

Clearly, some inferior professional work, or the work of amateurs, will be used if there is seen to be a good reason to do so. But what criteria are used to decide on the selection of news photographs? The choice of image is made at what Stuart Hall *(The Manufacture of News)* calls a number of 'levels':

1 The **technical** level, where the technical elements of photography act to shape or restrict what kind of images may be produced (including the range of a lens and the speed of film used) – the photojournalist will understand that the lens has what Rothstein calls a 'different standard of values [to] the human eye'.

2 The **formal** level comes from the ability of the audience to distinguish between objects in the world, and the ability we have to recognise objects despite their two-dimensional representation, from features such as contrast.

3 **Composition** is a level where the relationship between the internal elements of the photograph are set out according to conventions established by artistic and photographic practices. How, for example, different degrees of focus are used, how foreground and background interact – Alvarado *et. al* (p. 101) outline some conventions of pictorial perspective: 'larger objects look small if they are distant from the point of vision; items actually smaller may be represented as apparently larger if closer to the point of observation'.

4 **Expression** describes how the elements within photographs are interpreted according to different cultural codes.

5 **News value** operates as a level of selection, because the choice of people or settings is recognised by an audience as carrying pre-existing meanings; they are already 'encoded' and known from previous material, so the range of possible meanings they might carry becomes restricted.

6 The next level is that of **frame manipulation** where the processes of cropping, retouching and enlarging or reducing can all give certain inflections to meaning.

7 **Page integration** refers to sequential codes and the placing of a photograph within a specific page lay-out.

8 **Anchorage** is the level at which captions, headlines and the main body of accompanying text are used to fix the meaning of the picture.

It is at the fifth level, that of news value, that Hall (*The Manufacture of News*) sees the whole apparatus of news production coming into play; but it seems clear that photojournalists will carry news value with them, and will in many cases be directed before the assignment commences to take a certain kind of picture. The freelance, or the photographer allowed a wider remit, will still carry with them certain news values, though perhaps these will differ in some respects from those mainstream values described earlier in this chapter.

PHOTOMONTAGE

We have discussed, in passing, the fact that it is possible to alter the meaning of photographs by changing the size or the parameters of a frame. Photomontage is another method which has been successful in altering the meaning of images. The term is a combination of two words: photography, the action of light on a chemically-prepared surface, which produces an image; and montage, a technique used by artists to combine different images. Other definitions point out that much photomontage involves a form of collage, the application of fragments of photographs to a surface, rather than the combination of negatives or the rephotographing of images. Sometimes photomontage has been understood as a sort of trick photography, which has a history as long as the science itself. 'Spirit photographs' were sometimes unintentionally obtained when old collodion plates were imperfectly cleaned, so that the previous images appeared faintly when the plates were reused. The cutting out and reassembling of photographs, however, belonged on the whole to the realm of popular diversions – souvenirs, comic postcards, and so on. An early montage of this type was Rejlander's *The Two Ways of Life* (1857), constructed from more than thirty negatives.

It was common practice in the nineteenth century to use combination printing to add figures to a landscape photograph, and to combine different elements from pictures taken at a variety of locations. This was often done in order to achieve an improved representation of the sky. According to Dawn Ades (*Photomontage*, p. 11), this was done because it was:

'almost impossible … to obtain in one exposure both sharp foreground detail and interesting skies.'

In late nineteenth century France, the members of the Photographic Society were banned from exhibiting any sort of composite works. Although eventually there was no need for photomontage as a way of overcoming technical difficulties, it still continued to flourish as a branch of trick photography.

The term 'photomontage', which was not invented until after the First World War, gained currency during the Dada movement. The Dadaists used photographic images as subsidiary elements in painting, but they soon came to employ the technique in its own right. The Dadaists were 'anti-art' in the sense that they were responding to what they believed to be the limitations of conventional representational art. They saw themselves as emerging from a different tradition as, according to Raoul Hausmann (*Photomontage*, p. 12):

'… engineers (hence our preference for workmen's overalls) … we meant to construct, to assemble our works.'

This reference to a collective self-image is echoed by Hannah Hoch, who said (*Photomontage*, p. 13):

'… our whole purpose was to integrate objects from the world of machines and industry in the world of art.'

As in the case of photography itself, there were a variety of claims for the invention of photomontage. George Grosz, the artist and satirist, insisted that it came about in 1916 (*Photomontage*, p. 19):

'Johnny Heartfield and I invented photomontage in my studio at the south end of town at five o'clock one May morning … we had no idea of the immense possibilities, or of the thorny but successful career, that awaited the new invention. On a piece of cardboard we pasted a mish-mash of advertisements for hernia belts, student songbooks and dog food, labels from schnaps and wine bottles, and photographs from picture papers, cut up at will in such a way as to say, in pictures, what would have been banned by the censors had we said it in words.'

Hausmann, speaking at the time of the first exhibition of photomontage, in Berlin in 1931, described it as having 'a propaganda power' which all but the Dadaists lacked 'the courage to exploit'.

John Heartfield and anti-fascist montage

Perhaps the most famous practitioner of photomontage was the satirist and anti-fascist John Heartfield (born Helmut Herzfelde). His work in photomontage emerged from Dadaism at the end of the First World War. Heartfield turned photography to a use which he believed would 'express the truth, tell the simple fact, report the reality'. Here the idea of a close approach to reality through the image, as outlined by Barthes and others, is not what is meant. Instead, a kind of moral truth is approached through the manipulation and recombination of fragments of images. In a sense, photomontage is actually a recognition that the single photograph is wholly inadequate as a representation of social truths.

An early member of the German Communist Party (which eventually followed the disastrous Comintern line on fascism), Heartfield was hounded by the Nazis. He used his skills to oppose fascism and to comment on war. He said that his work 'emerged in the struggle, under persecution, not afterwards'. Even when he found himself exiled to Prague, he was still under threat from the Nazi regime: 'I was hardly a week over the border when I was making montages for the *AIZ* [a Communist publication directed at workers] again.' Heartfield's montages drew attention to his major themes: war, hardship and their relationship to greed and power.

Heartfield's technique was to create an illusion of space and perspective within the frame; he was very concerned to produce rounded images through the use of airbrushing. He most certainly did not want 'the joins' to show, unlike some of his contemporaries who were less interested in technical perfection or who, like Hannah Hoch, deliberately used figures and objects whose proportions are mismatched, together with blank areas of space which add to the impression of energy and chaos. Dada as a whole seemed to represent a system founded on confusion, but in 1925 Grosz and Herzfelde (Heartfield's brother) wrote (*Photomontage*, p. 36):

'. . . we saw then the insane end-products of the prevailing social order, and burst out laughing . . . we did not yet see that a system underlay this insanity.'

Heartfield's work reveals the way this system functioned, through his ability to produce an outstanding clarity of image, combined with some extraordinary juxtapositions within the frame. One of his montages depicts an unemployed worker with a placard around his neck which reads 'any work accepted'; this figure is looking out at the spectator from the right foreground; he has his feet on the long train of a bride's gown. She stands in the left background, raised above the unemployed man. The title is 'The Finest Products of Capitalism'.

With the rise of fascism in Germany, Heartfield used photographs of Nazi leaders to powerful effect, making clear their true characters and actions. In one photomontage, Streicher (one of the earliest members of the Nazi Party) stands against the background of a Stuttgart police photograph depicting a murder victim; blood covers the pavement and runs into the gutter. Streicher appears to be standing, unconcerned yet menacing, in the blood itself. In another montage, Goering carries an axe and wears a blood-spattered apron, while behind him the Reichstag burns. One of Heartfield's most famous works shows Hitler, hand raised backwards in a Nazi salute which becomes an open palm to receive the banknotes pressed into it by a giant figure representing German capitalism. The montage is entitled 'Millions stand behind me', playing on the concept of numerical support; in addition, the picture carries the text, 'The meaning of the Hitler salute: a little man asks for large gifts.' Heartfield saw through the quasi-revolutionary nature of German National Socialism, and its real adherence to its capitalist paymasters. Heartfield's extraordinary political clarity is expressed through the graphic felicity of his images. John Berger offered an explanation for part of the effectiveness of such political photomontage (*Photomontage*, p. 48):

> '... the peculiar advantage of photomontage lies in the fact that everything which has been cut out keeps its familiar photographic appearance. We are still looking first at *things* and only afterwards at symbols.'

The contemporary British practitioner of photomontage, Peter Kennard, is often cited as the inheritor of Heartfield's mantle. He worked for organisations like Greenpeace, the Campaign for Nuclear Disarmament, and the Greater London Council. Kennard's view of montage (*see Independent Media*, May 1987) was that it needed to get a message across in the shortest possible time (p. 6):

> 'I'm certainly thinking all the time of the things I do communicating themselves in three or four seconds flat, which tends to limit some kinds of experimenting with the form.'

Asked by the *Independent Media* interviewer if Heartfield had taken a certain kind of photomontage as far as it would go, Kennard noted that:

> '... whilst I find that people ... do like caricatures of Thatcher, [with] heads on different bodies, I get a bit bored with that way of working, though obviously that's where Heartfield's great strengths lay. I've been working with strong, almost iconic images that can be used almost anywhere in the world or, like in the case of nuclear issues, that people can copy and put on banners ... I think there's an area where montage is still useful, making images of things that often seem remote to people's lives, which may develop things in a different direction from the tradition of Heartfield's work.'

Kennard used to look through magazines to find an idea and then produce the image, but by 1987 he would think of the idea and then go out to find the images, sometimes getting photographers to take the pictures for him. (This last method had been Heartfield's usual practice.) A great deal of Kennard's output was commissioned. Kennard believed that a lot of very hard work was needed to struggle against (p. 6) the 'enormous bombardment of imagery' produced by advertising. Kennard was unhappy with the way that the left in the 1980s could not:

> '... see any value in artists who are actually committed to its programme and its terms. They've all been sold on this idea that the only way to communicate with the world at large is to go through an agency.'

This remark throws an interesting light on the decision of groups like the British Labour Party to mediate every aspect of their political campaigning through the 'professional' filter of the 'communications agency'.

With regard to post-modernist influences on culture, Kennard felt that:

'... there's a kind of rationality about montage that isn't fashionable at all right now. A lot of art seems simply to be saying that all we can really do is simply mirror or decorate the chaos that surrounds us, to play with images without any real criticism of things. I think it's a terribly pessimistic position to hold.'

Interview with a freelance photographer: Mick Garland

Mick There was very bad snow in Somerset at the time; people could hardly move about the streets. I simply ran out to these huge snow-drifts, when an old man wandered by me, trying to climb the snow-drift. It looked such a stark image. He had a long black overcoat on against the whiteness of the snow. I moved in and tried to photograph him as well as I could against the buildings to make a pleasing composition of a stark image in black and white (Figs 4.2–4.4). And from there more or less retained my position ... if you look at the contact sheet without looking at the number sequence, it looks as if I have photographed the man close up and let him recede into the distance – but in actual fact, the *first* shot (Fig 4.4) was the distance shot, then I moved closer to the man. I was able to catch up with him quite easily, as he had problems climbing the snowdrift. That shows how deceptive it is to read a contact sheet – it can be misinterpreted.

Q How do you know how to compose a shot; are there rules?

M It's an instinct, composition – and something you can't teach. You can teach rules of composition but it's a gut feeling inside, as to whether it's a strong image or not.

Q Once students of photography know 'the rules', presumably then they have to go off and break them creatively?

M Absolutely – apply them then break them. It's like looking back into history and then you can look forward. But at the end of the day it's still not going to come off perfectly because I could have shot it so that the man's head appeared *between* the two buildings, instead of getting lost against one building; but when you're struggling against a snowdrift and it's bitterly cold ... but it's been a successful image despite that.

Q Sticking to this idea of successful images, this widely circulated image of the dog lying in the guitar case: where did you take that? (Figs 4.5–4.7.)

M Well, that was a day out wandering in Exeter, purely a shopping trip. I'd started a series of photographs of buskers. But I was particularly interested in the containers that buskers collect their change in. You have to approach the busker, of course, because you can't just get the camera out and start firing away. You'd get comments from the crowd that you're from the tax people! Having taken shots of the busker, I looked to the left of him, and I saw that inside the guitar case was a small Jack Russell lying there asleep. It was very reminiscent of the little dog that you see on the HMV label. I had a small compact camera in my pocket, so I took one shot (which was Fig 4.5). I don't find it such a pleasing composition as the next one, where I was able to move slightly closer and tighten up the composition.

Q Would you consider cropping Fig 4.5?

M Cropping Fig 4.5 could be done very, very successfully, actually. It can work but there's no point in cropping unless you've got to; it's almost an identical shot to the next one, Fig 4.6. It's far better to fill the frame if you possibly can without any cropping, because you don't lose quality that way. By enlarging you lose quality. So I knew it was quite an exciting image, moved in and got the second shot. When you find you've got an exciting image on your hands, you try to take not one or two but perhaps four or five, because it's good to get plenty down. Going for that third shot a coin (remember that the

Figs 4.2, 4.3 and 4.4
(Photographs: Mick Garland)

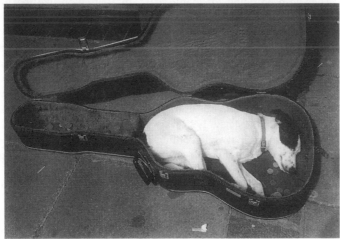

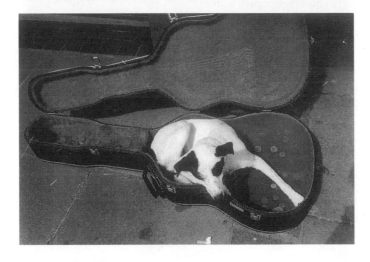

Figs 4.5, 4.6 and 4.7 *(Photographs: Mick Garland)*

guitar case is being used as a container for money), a coin hit the dog and it got up and it spoiled the composition. There's no chance of it going back to sleep ... you've got this peaceful little image and then it changes without you realising it's going to change. You have no control over that.

Q Do you think the way we see things through photography is slightly distorted, exactly because the photographer recognises an exciting image? Do you think there's any down side to that?

M There can actually be a down side to that. I mean a perfect example of that is George Roger the Magnum photographer who entered Belsen and found when he was photographing bodies laid out that he was actually starting – and it's well quoted in books – that he was actually making pleasing compositions of all these masses of dead bodies. He was not rearranging them in any way but he was making interesting angles from dead bodies. When he stopped that night and thought about it ... he felt disgusted with himself. Most photojournalists have a certain integrity and they wish to put a message across to wake people up to what's going on.

Q This demonstration, is it outside South Africa House? (Fig 4.8.)

M It is. They've been going for many years. In a situation like that there are police around and the traffic whizzing by and ... a lot of those people have gone out on a limb with their protest, and the worst thing you can do is introduce a camera and just fire away; many tourists do just that, but what I always do is go and talk to the demonstrators first, explain that I'm actually interested in photography. In this particular case I was very supportive, because I felt a personal support for the type of work they were doing. They are to be commended for actually turning up every day and doing this; when you go back to London, time and time again you see the same faces there.

This particular one in March 1990 was an interesting case because it was a protest against some executions that were coming up in South Africa. It really was quite moving. It's actually wrong, though, to go in cold and start photographing. Around that time they introduced TV cameras right around Trafalgar Square. There's one hanging off the National Gallery, and there's one above the door of South Africa House. When the demonstrators questioned the police, they said it's purely to watch the traffic flow, but as the demonstrators pointed out to me, the traffic doesn't actually flow on the pavement past South Africa House. So the demonstrators know they're being filmed. It was all treated as quite subversive activity.

Q What kind of lens are you using?

M It's a very wide angle lens – a 20mm wide angle lens – which is something I use where perhaps there's a crowd scene and I want to show a lot of what's going on. It does

Fig 4.8
(Photograph: Mick Garland)

give a certain amount of distortion, but what I wanted to show was that there's a lot of posters and text and a collection bucket. I wanted to show the lady on the right-hand side who's quite a regular there, include the banner in the middle and some of Nelson's column and a bit of Trafalgar Square.

It's what we call a scene-setting shot; if you were doing a demonstration you would show an overall shot of as many people marching in the environment as you possibly could and then you'd move in for detailed shots. It gives a picture editor a choice then. An editor could get away with printing that picture without having too much caption or too much text.

Q Where was this sequence taken? (Figs 4.9–4.12.)

M This is actually Berlin, August 1991, eighteen months after the Wall came down. It's quite a strange feeling to walk through the Brandenburg Gate and be in the East, where this picture was taken. This guy with a barrel organ seemed to travel Germany – you see many of them in German cities – and quite spontaneously a young couple, who were tourists, started to dance. They danced tune after tune. There was a really friendly, international, happy sort of atmosphere. Not everyone will recognise the Brandenburg Gate. The clue to knowing which side of the old division you're on, is to look at which way the horses are facing. They're driving cars beneath the Gate now. That was a pedestrian precinct while I was there.

Q This picture has a strong atmosphere to it (Fig 4.13).

Figs 4.9, 4.10, 4.11 and 4.12 *(Photographs: Mick Garland)*

Fig 4.13 *(Photograph: Mick Garland*

M Yes, it's from a sequence I took of the Broomfield, Kingston and Cheddon pilgrimage.

Q Did you realise you had this shot?

M It's part of a whole series of pilgrimages that I did. It's a small pilgrimage which takes place between three churches on the Quantock hills in Somerset. Thirty to forty people turn up with a cross singing hymns. They're all straight Anglicans, C of E. The sequence emphasises the friendliness overall, but this particular image here is rather strange, even sinister. Cartier Bresson spoke of capturing the 'decisive moment'. I feel I've really captured a decisive moment. In the preceding shots, I'd actually climbed on to a hedge to get a look down at what was happening. They were singing, and at the end of that someone had to pick up the cross, and take it away. It happened to be this man, and his face is slightly obscured by the cross; his dog ran up to him and ran away again. The whole thing just came together.

Q Would you say that text or a caption is superfluous to this image, that it might spoil its effect somehow?

M I wouldn't put more in the way of a caption than Kingston, 1988. You can actually detract from a photograph by writing a lot. People may look at it and say what a lucky shot, but there was nothing lucky about getting up early in the morning and climbing that hedge and following that group.

Q At first, this looks like a group of demonstrators (Figs 4.14–4.19)

M In fact, it was a small group of youths in Germany who were acting out a passion play on the streets. They were German evangelists. It just goes to show how images can be read the wrong way. I'm not a religious person, but I am interested in what happens when religion comes out on to the streets.

Q Where was Fig 4.20 taken?

Figs 4.14, 4.15, 4.16, 4.17, 4.18 and 4.19
(Photographs: Mick Garland)

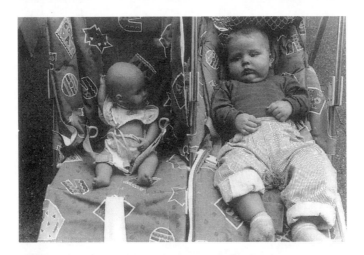

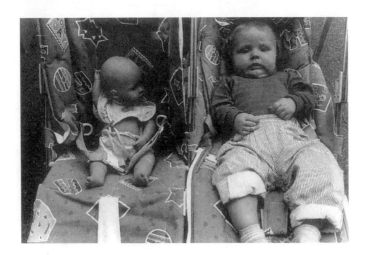

Figs 4.20, 4.21 and 4.22
(Photographs: Mick Garland)

M I took these at the church where Sir John Betjeman is buried. It's opposite Padstowe – the church was uncovered from the sand. The sand bent the spire.

Q The picture of the child in the buggy is interesting – amusing but maybe a bit worrying (Figs 4.21 and 4.22)?

M It was taken in Northern Germany in 1991. Usually, you don't see German children uncovered. It's a question which shot people prefer. I prefer the one where the child is looking at the doll. The reason that the child looked at the camera in the second shot is because it turned round because of the noise of the shutter going off!

Q This next one is a peace demonstration in London, isn't it (Fig 4.23)?

M This was three days before the Gulf War bombing campaign. There was a massive peace demo and I happened to be in London. I went over and photographed the crowds collecting. There were some young Iraqi students, putting their point of view across and making a lot of noise. An old man got into a row about it. The TV crew's arrival made it worse. I think the students played to the camera a bit. I tried to include the camera. You could crop the right hand man, but you have to remember that when you're in the hands of a picture editor, things can be misreported.

Q Do you think, in some respects, that photographers are increasingly losing control over the use of their images, or has this always been a problem?

M To an extent, this has always happened to photographers. Take the example of *Picture Post*. Photographers didn't even retain the copyright of their own negatives. We rely heavily on the integrity of the picture editor. An added problem these days is one of technology. The use of computer terminals instead of the system where photographs were sent by wire often means that the photographer has even less control over the image. With the wire system, a photographer could choose a negative and advise the picture desk as to the potential strength of an image. But now, not only are pictures received through a computer terminal, many picture editors use 'frame-grabbers'. This means that a TV image received by satellite can, with the permission of the TV companies, be taken directly from television news and reproduced on a front page. It also means, if you think about it, that the image is even easier to manipulate. This rush to be first with a picture means that the quality of an image is less important to some papers. Take the case of the Gulf War – the more revealing images, which are made by photographers, are either seen only after the event, or in many cases they stay in files and the public never see them. The end result could be that history is distorted. In my opinion, if a photographer like Don McCullin had been allowed to make pictures in the Gulf, or in the Falklands, then we might have had a more honest overview of events, and the state of public opinion, with regard to those wars, could now be quite different.

Fig 4.23 Cropping a photograph *(Photograph: Mick Garland)*

SUMMARY

An image is usually taken to mean a pictorial representation of something in the real world: a person, scene or object. Images can be produced in a variety of ways using a number of different media. Another meaning of 'image' is those pictures of things that we carry around in our minds.

Susan Sontag put forward the idea that 'the images that have virtually unlimited authority in a modern society are mainly photographic images'.

■ THE PHOTOGRAPH: EARLY DEVELOPMENTS

It is clear that the invention of photography should really have occurred sooner than it did; the two 'halves' of the technology needed to produce photographs had been in existence for some time.

The most important initial question raised in this chapter is how close photography is to reality. Fox-Talbot introduced his 1844 volume of photographs with an assertion about the 'natural' status of photographic images. From the first, photography impressed both practitioners and critics by its apparent closeness to reality. Some believe that photography and film are naturally 'realist' forms.

The point to be considered is the difference between reality and its photographic representation, and the idea that photographs in no way transmit 'the literal reality'.

■ BARTHES AND PHOTOGRAPHY

Barthes believed that there is no need to set up 'a relay' or a code between the reality and the image. He saw no need to construct a link between object and image; he believed object and image to be so close. This is set out as part of the general misunderstanding about the supposed close-ness of photography to the real world.

■ SEMIOLOGY AND THE PHOTOGRAPH

Issue is taken with Saussure's emphasis on the arbitrary nature of the sign; most signs are more likely to have a 'conventional' link with the things they represent. The continued use of the terms 'arbitrary' and 'conventional' together, and even sometimes as interchangeable concepts, may act as a barrier to understanding the sign.

■ THE ICON AND PHOTOGRAPHY

Photographs can be more than icons, and can rapidly become symbols. When Webster says that icons are present 'in a real sense' beyond the 'vagaries of an audience's reading practices', the question arises whether there is supposed to be a 'real' meaning which an audience is unable to reach, and how this real meaning could exist *outside* the 'vagaries' of human perception.

■ DENOTATION AND CONNOTATION

Barthes claims that the photograph is so purely denotative that there is 'no space for the development of a second-order message' – in other words, that there are no connotations. In all this, Barthes appears to be changing his mind about where symbolic meaning and 'myth' come from. In his original theory of signification, 'myth and connotation are close cousins'. Barthes believed that photographs, as icons, are especially prone to a 'mythical' reading; myth is close to connotation, and is supposed to be a new type of second-order meaning, in which a sign itself (the combination of the physical existence of the sign and the mental concept associated with this physical element) becomes a mere signifier. Therefore connotation and myth are both 'second-order' meanings, growing out of first-order meaning. Barthes eventually came to believe that it was exactly the most 'innocent' signs (those which were associated with the denotation of a word or image) that were most loaded with myth and ideological meaning.

The problem of denotation and connotation may be partly resolved if we see the two stages as being in relationship, instead of being simply a process.

■ PHOTOGRAPHY AND PHOTOJOURNALISM

An important issue here is the moral status of some forms of photojournalism. The contrast between public and private photography is mentioned. The power of the widely-circulated news photograph is considerable, as are the moral dilemmas which are part of photojournalism as a practice.

Where Rothstein argues that the photojournalist's job is 'to mirror the world' Webster is critical of 'photojournalism's special plea . . . that it presents us with *accurate* pictures of the world'. Writing as one who was championing the cause of a radical photography, Webster is quite clear that the photojournalist has a distorted understanding of his/her own role, describing their view of themselves as a kind of self-delusion.

An understanding of media institutions and the news values to which these institutions and journalists subscribe is most important. Fictional representations of photojournalists are covered briefly.

As well as examining news values, the role of the journalist is brought into focus. The ideological background to the work of the journalist and the news editor is not always explored as it should be. These values are not always clear to the casual observer, and remain absent from the formal discourses of journalism.

■ The role of the journalist

This is set out using McQuail's reference to two types of role: the **neutral** and the **participant** roles taken by journalists. The first is closely associated with the idea of the press as simply a channel of information. The participant role, on the other hand, is where the journalist acts as a representative of the public.

The idea of two opposing types of role has come to be seen as rather too simplistic, however. Weaver and Wilhoit opted instead for the division of these roles into three parts: **interpreter**, **disseminator**, and **adversary**.

The role of the photojournalist as a possible contributor to scandal was examined. The problem turns on the professional role of the photojournalist, which McQuail thinks is a reflection on 'the weak "institutionalisation" of the profession'.

A brief history of photojournalism is given, including specific reference to photojournalists and to places where the profession flourished. The subject of war in the early photographic era is introduced. The delayed beginnings of photographic journalism testify to the importance of the development of technology; for a long time, photographs could not be printed in newspapers. When at last they began to appear, the practice of printing them with news stories was at first not regarded as particularly interesting. The chapter also examines the practice of photojournalism during the Vietnam War.

■ Photomontage

Photomontage was always regarded as a more political medium than straightforward photography. The career of John Heartfield (born Helmut Hertzfelde) is examined, as a practitioner who turned photography to a use which he believed would 'express the truth, tell the simple fact, report the reality'. This stands against the idea that we gain a close approach to reality through the image. Through the manipulation and recombination of fragments of images, the use of photomontage acknowledges that the single photograph may be wholly inadequate as a representation of social truths.

An interview with the freelance photographer, Mick Garland, concludes the chapter.

STUDENT ACTIVITIES

Analysis: Image analysis and the internal elements of meaning

Students are presented with a series of photographs, in which some of the internal elements within the frame are masked. The exercise 'Reading Pictures' uses this method, presenting three versions of a photograph. The first two show only sections of the picture, the third the full version.

Purpose: to introduce the idea that meaning derives in part from the internal juxtaposition of elements within the frame.

Method: each complete photograph chosen must work as a combination of distinct elements. The three or so versions of the photograph are given to the class in turn. After each version of the photograph a number of questions must be answered on paper concerning what the visible elements are (denotation) and what they appear to mean (connotation). The final picture will reveal the complete internal arrangement of meaning. The class discussion may then turn also on where and when the photograph might have been taken, and where it might have appeared.

Image analysis: the internal arrangement of meaning

Exercise 1: a number of photographs are presented, in which some element of the picture has been cropped. The area which replaces the cropped element is left blank.

Exercise 2: students are given a variety of photocopies of complete photographs.

Purpose: to draw attention to the composition of photographs and how meaning is created by the interaction of certain elements.

Method: it is a good idea to refer in the first instance to Harold Evans's *Pictures on a Page*, which contains some fine examples of how meaning may be altered by the use of photocropping. It is an easy process to use photographs which are not in copyright.

Stage 1: students are asked to sketch in or write down what they think might be missing from the photographs provided in exercise 1. In each case, they must provide a reason for their choice.

Stage 2: in groups, students are requested to crop each of the photographs provided, so that a variety of meanings are obtained in each case. For this, a number of copies of each photograph must be provided. The results should be pasted on to card and each should be provided with a caption.

Image analysis: the external frame of meaning

The class is broken into groups and given a series of photographs from different 'genres' (news pictures, portraiture, advertising images, 'social conscience' photographs, etc.), but without any contextual clues.

Purpose: to begin work on context.

Method: The groups are asked, from the appearance of the photographs alone, to decide in what type of publication or public display they might expect to see the images. Each group in turn reports back to the rest of the class. It is helpful, if possible, to have prepared in advance either large-scale versions of the pictures or overhead projector sheets so that students may speak to the images without needing to remind each other of the photograph under discussion. At the end of the session, the actual context of the photographs should be given or displayed.

Research: Biographies of photographers

Each student is asked to carry out research into a well-known or established photographer, from any era of photography. Subjects may be photojournalists, portrait photographers, 'art' photographers, and so on.

Purpose: to explore the different paths of development taken by photographers and to familiarise the class with the widest possible variety of practitioners by encouraging student presentation through seminar work.

Method: a written piece of 600-800 words should be produced, giving details of the photographer's biography, career and influence on their time. The student should also reveal why they decided to choose the particular subject. At least three copies of the subject's photographs should be included. Students are given an allocation of ten minutes in which to present their biographical study in the next available class.

Production: The self-portrait in words and pictures

Students work in pairs to produce a self-portrait which will reveal, through written text and supporting photographs, aspects of each person's public and private persona (it will be up to each individual to judge how detailed they wish the portrait to be).

Purpose: to continue the exploration of persona and image begun in the previous exercise; to explore representation, and to put students at the centre of the process of meaning-creation.

Method: students are put into pairs and provided with the following outline of the exercise:

> You are required to produce a written self-portrait of no more than 800 words, accompanied by a selection of six photographs of yourself. The photographs should illustrate some aspect of the written work. Your portrait may include different aspects of your personality, history, private and public roles, as well as information on what you would like to be, now or in the future; this exercise could involve elements which are not part of the 'everyday'. You should choose a variety of settings and contexts for the photographs.

Suggested modes of representation for the photographs (which need not all be 'realistic' and may include elements of fantasy) could include: formal portrait, you at work, you in a social setting with friends, you as film icon, you on the cover of a magazine, and so on. Try to use a variety of technical approaches and experiment with colour and black and white film. The use of photocopying (colour or black and white), and the use of experimentation with size and quality of image is perfectly acceptable.

At the end of the exercise, each student presents the self-portrait of the other group member to the whole class. Details of production skills acquired and problems encountered should be given. Discussion could centre on the presentation of self and the question of whether a 'documentary' approach is closer to our self-perception than currents of representation which depend more upon fantasy. (An alternative exercise would be to construct a documentary and a 'fictional' representation as separate and contrasting exercises.)

Production: Negative and positive images

This exercise has been used in many schools and colleges. It requires the provision of a number of point-and-shoot cameras and rolls of colour film. Copies of a college or school prospectus are helpful for this exercise; promotional material for a company or perhaps a holiday destination is also useful, but the images presented must be of places as well as of people and objects.

Purpose: to explore how the same institution can be presented in an entirely different light by the deliberate selection of, on the one hand, positive representations, and on the other, negative representations. Students should see how easy it is to construct a partial and limited representation of the world. The use of supporting written text shows how the image can be manipulated; this is quite different to saying that photographs tend to create myths all by themselves. They need a context (physical as well as cultural) in order to generate social meaning. The exercise can then be set out as a photo-board or as a magazine report, though the latter implies that questions of address to a specific audience will need to be considered.

Method

Stage 1: students are asked to think about the way that institutions present themselves. Promotional material from various sources is circulated. The desire of public and private institutions to put a gloss on their external appearance should be noted. What would class members do if someone they wished to impress was due to call on them? Would they tidy up the appearance of their flat/house/room?

Stage 2: photographs from available material are studied in order to discover how positive representations are made, in terms of the subject chosen, the technical codes deployed and the way that texts are 'anchored' with captions.

Stage 3: the students must produce a series of six to eight images which represent their institution in a good light, and six to eight which represent it in a bad light. Accompanying text should be written to support the images.

Stage 4: when the photographs are available and the supporting text has been produced, students should mount the results for display and discussion.

Audience research and production: Photomontage and advertisements

Students are encouraged to research into the types of imagery found in two-dimensional advertisements. They are also required to make a study of photomontage as a method of representing familiar objects. (See Chapter 3 for information on advertising formats, and this chapter for a description of photomontage.) The aim is to produce a series of advertisements for ideas rather than for products. It is a 'public information' exercise for concepts.

Purpose: to interrogate the commercial mode of representation and to contrast it with a method which has long been associated with political comment and activism. As a result, to produce a set of advertisements which each attempt to address a selected audience with a specific message.

Method

Stage 1: in groups, students choose an audience within easy reach. For example, a class of art and design students or sociology students, or a group with whom students work or spend leisure time.

Stage 2: the chosen audience is provided with a questionnaire asking it to outline its work or leisure activities. In the case of students following a particular subject, they may be asked to list those aspects they most enjoy or most remember, or on which they most need to work.

Stage 3: the media students investigate the topics, concepts or ideas provided by their audience, carrying out some in-depth interviews and undertaking research into secondary sources.

Stage 4: the students sketch out a visual representation of the topic and produce a two-dimensional advertisement using images taken from magazines, photographs they themselves have taken, advertising images and so on. Diagramatic and design elements may be included, as well as limited written text. All images must be reasonably clear as they will be reproduced on a copier.

Examples: a sociology group may wish to look at the concept of the 'amplification of deviance', where the mass media take an issue and turn it into a 'moral panic'; the media students would find a variety of visual images and turn these into a two-dimensional 'advertisement' for the concept. A group of friends may wish to explore the idea of the dance culture, or pub-crawls, or any other uplifting activity. The media students would attempt to represent this in the visual montage form already described.

ESSAY TITLES

1 'The images that have virtually unlimited authority in a modern society are mainly photographic images.'

   Do you agree that the authority of the photographic image is taken more or less on trust, or are there any significant doubts about the reliability of photographs? Refer to both the private and public uses of photography.

2 'Photographs create meaning through the interplay of the following elements: internal content, technical treatment of the image, external context (including captions) and audience expectation of certain photographic genres.'

   Discuss, with reference to the work of any photographer you have studied.

3 To what degree is the war photographer accurately represented in (a) documentary studies (on video or in print) and in (b) popular television and film?

4 Study the six photographs in Figs. 4.24 to 4.29 and comment on the intention of the photographer in each case. Produce a semiological analysis of each photograph.

Figs 4.24, 4.25 and 4.26
(Photographs: Mick Garland)

Figs 4.27, 4.28 and 4.29
(Photographs: Mick Garland)

STARTING PHOTOGRAPHY - 529

Rob Stopford

Aperture and Shutter Speed

Aperture is the relative size of the opening which lets light through to the film plane.

Shutter speed is the duration that the shutter remains open, letting light fall on the film plane.

The two are directly related

For example, if a given shot is correctly exposed with an aperture of F8 @ 1/125 sec, the same shot could be taken using settings of F11 @ 1/60 sec, or F5.6 @ 1/250.

Given the same shot under the same lighting conditions, all these three settings produce exactly the same density of exposure.

F number is the notation for relative aperture, which is the ratio of the focal length to the diameter of the aperture.

Fig 4.30 Example of task set

CHAPTER 5

Cinema: history and theory

EARLY CINEMA

The word 'cinema' comes from the Greek word *kinema*, meaning movement. The origins of cinema can be discovered in various forms of public entertainment, including theatre, small-scale performances given by illusionists, the diorama, magic-lantern slides and experiments in photography. Bill Douglas' film *Comrades* contains a lively account of these early visual traditions of entertainment.

The reason for studying early cinema is not merely because it represents the background to modern achievements, but because it can teach us such a great deal about the development of film technique and narrative. It shows that while the dominant mode of representation (the accepted way of shooting and editing a film – the 'Hollywood' method) may seem 'natural' to us, it is in fact only one current of film technique.

In film, there is a close relationship between what a director wishes to express in artistic terms and the technology at his or her disposal. Meaning is not expressed purely through artistic criteria – technology also helps to shape meaning.

In the nineteenth century, a number of optical instruments were introduced which produced the illusion of movement, achieved through 'persistence of vision', where the brain retains each separate image for a moment, creating the impression of continuous action. Henry Fitton's Thaumatrope (1826), Joseph Plateau's Phenakistoscope (1833), W.G. Horner's Zoetrope (1834) and Emile Renauld's Praxinoscope (1877) used images mounted in revolving drums or other cylindrical devices. The English photographer Eadweard Muybridge was able to demonstrate the mechanics of human and animal movement by using a battery of cameras which each took a single photograph of the subject as it moved across a defined and measured space. In 1878, Muybridge set up a line of 24 cameras, each connected to a trip wire. A galloping horse ran past each camera and produced a set of images which, connected as strips of film, were projected using an instrument called the Zoopraxiscope. Muybridge's work featured in a car advertisement in the autumn of 1992, where it was run as a film sequence.

Other developments included Louis Le Prince's work of 1885, showing horse-drawn traffic passing over a bridge in Leeds. Woodville Latham, an American, invented a projector for large screen projection (1895). This was the same year in which the Lumière brothers began a series of public film shows in the *Salon Indien* in Paris (*see* below). In 1896, the inventors Edison and Dickson developed their Vitascope and exhibited films in a New York music hall. As the century closed, films grew in length and variety and the scale of production increased.

Photography and visual art

The connection between photography and painting, and the cross-fertilisation that still takes place between the two (we can think immediately of Hockney's famous 'Splash' and his more recent experiments with composites of photographs and still video images), forms a background to the history of the development of film-making, and also of cinema as a practice and an institution. Monaco, for example, notes that Monet's 'flip-books' are interesting 'precursors of the movies' (*How to Read a Film*, p. 23). However, there are obviously many different reasons for an artist's interest in the still photographic image, and a host of reasons also why a photographer may wish to study a painting. Many of these reasons concern technical questions of light, perspective and other matters; but a major battleground has been 'realism' in general, a study of which will form a later part of this chapter.

An early example of the split between realist (a category related to but separate from realism) and non-realist film-making may be seen in the difference between the approach of the Lumière brothers (who came to film through experiments in still photography) and that of Melies, who could best be described as a dedicated illusionist with a background in stage magic. The 'opposition' between these two examples can, however, be overplayed.

Lumière

The Lumière brothers produced films which were highly popular, because audiences were unused to seeing the technical form of film, and marvelled at the representation of reality which was brought to them. They could see how faithfully the form reproduced spontaneous human and animal movement, or how familiar objects and places were called up on the screen.

The Lumières' *Leaving the Factory* (1895) records a crowd of female workers walking through the brothers' own factory gate. It would be easy to see this type of early film as having nothing in common with more 'sophisticated', narrative-based experiments. However, the first act in all attempts to communicate is choice of subject (in this case, setting the camera up outside the factory). The next stage is the reproduction of the event for an audience. Most people recount their experiences through the use of 'stories', however straightforward those experiences might be. The filming of a crowd of workers at a certain time in a certain place is not an unstructured event, however simple the presentation may appear to be. The film is structured by choice of subject, choice of viewpoint, choice of where to begin and where to end.

Leaving the Factory illustrates the complexities of the new medium. Problems of perspective, which had been solved in painting, re-appeared exactly because of the new technical possibilities of film. Richard de Cordova (writing in Elsaesser's *Early Cinema: Space, Frame, Narrative*, p. 78) notes how the Lumière film contains footage of three cyclists who also emerge from the gate. Their appearance is sudden, and is masked at first by the emerging crowd of workers. In painting and photography, the masking of an element would have to be partial, because otherwise no one would realise that it was *meant* to appear 'hidden'. If it was not seen, it would not exist. In film, if something is not seen, it may simply mean that it is waiting to be seen.The cyclists also appear distorted as they move off-frame. The addition of the dimension of **time** to that of **space** makes possible a whole new type of imagery.

A very perceptive comment about an early Lumière film was made by Dai Vaughan (*Early Cinema*, pp. 64–5), who related the moment when the 'unpredictable' occurs in *Barque sortant d'un port* (*A boat leaving harbour*). At one point, the men rowing the boat encounter some difficulty and a woman standing on a jetty turns to watch the brief struggle. Vaughan argues that it is this element of unpredictability which is important. Instead of human subjects who performed for the camera, here was a scene where real events in the natural world asserted themselves.

Early audiences were fascinated by the faithful reproduction of pictures of their everyday world – brick dust rising from a wall that has just been demolished onscreen, or steam rising from the funnel of a locomotive. Vaughan believes that the element of unpredictability in the boat sequence brought out the natural wonder felt by audiences at events which could not be planned.

The frame

The frame in television and cinema is understood as the rectangular or 'square' outline which marks out the focus of our attention. Film-makers are generally regarded as working within this space. It is an essential part of the way a shot is composed. We are aware of the artificiality of the frame as a device when we watch television, and the film to which we are devoting our attention has been made for wide-screen projection. Essential parts of the action may be lost, or have to be recaptured by allowing a noticeable break and a shift in what is being shown.

The Lumières, using a fixed camera which was unable to pan across a scene, were faced with the problem of confining significant action within the frame; while at the same time any movement which took place within the limitations of this space would tend to disrupt the 'evenness' of composition. de Cordova (p. 79) describes how the effect of movement was minimised by the technique of maintaining 'a centred space'; in simple terms, the subject was kept, as far as it was possible, within the centre of the frame. de Cordova gives two examples of this. In *Barque sortant d'un port*, the boat moves slowly through perspective into the distance. It is not therefore causing disruption by moving *across* the frame. The other solution employed was to show relatively insignificant actions taking place *against* the centred space. As an example, we might imagine a person or object moving across the frame and causing briefly a disruptive effect – because the frame cannot include it unless it is still, the frame or centre basically remains unaffected. The frame or centred space still defines what is important.

The tendencies of the 'static' camera frame to limit what may be viewed, are seen in *L'Arroseur arose*, where a man on the left of the frame, facing to the left, is shown watering something off-frame. Someone plays a joke by standing on the hose, causing the flow of water to stop. The rest is fairly predictable. The man using the hose looks into the end of it, and the water spurts into his face as the joker takes his foot off the pipe. After the man with the hose has dispensed justice (both characters disappear briefly from the frame during a chase), he returns to his watering in exactly the same off-centred position as before.

In the first place, the space behind the man was there as 'active space', allowing the joker to appear. By the end of the sequence, a modern audience would find the continued representation of the space a puzzle. They would expect the person playing the joke to return, or the camera to dispense with the extra space left behind the central character. We might ask how a modern film-maker would shoot and then edit this narrative.

The Boer War: 'actuality' and propaganda

Britain's first war cameraman, Jack Rosenthal, working at the time of the Boer War, was faced with the same problems as the Lumière brothers in France. The technical constraints again included the inability to pan across a scene, so that all the film taken during the conflict is again concerned with a 'centre' across which action passes, or within which action takes place. Troops march across a ford, artillery is seen in action, a great assembly on a parade ground takes the Boer surrender. These are examples of what we might now call 'actuality' footage – real action. One thing which is striking is that the footage resembles very closely the extremely 'static' war film which was taken during the Falklands War. The Falklands material is static in two senses: first, camera movement is limited, despite much greater technical flexibility than was possible at the end of the nineteenth century. Secondly, the locations where the camera operator was allowed to set up appear to have been restricted. The Falklands material shows artillery firing, troops on the march, and the British flag being raised at the conclusion of a successful campaign, just like the Boer War footage.

AN EARLY EXAMPLE OF CINEMATIC PROPAGANDA

During the Boer War, many short films were circulated as genuine war footage. One film is an attempt to represent the opponents of the British as evil and monstrous, in some ways prefiguring British propaganda during the early stages of the First World War. A tent marked with a large (presumably red) cross, clearly signifying 'dressing station', is attacked by a group of 'Boers'. Filmed on Hampstead Heath, it demonstrates the difficulties which beset film-makers trying to show this kind of 'outrage'. It is difficult to make out precise detail (no close-ups are used), the action is often 'off-centre', and the scene, at least to a modern eye, looks extremely artificial and melodramatic.

At the time, none of this need have mattered, since propaganda in some forms is clearly meant to be 'over-stated' and narrative lines are meant to be clearly drawn. Propaganda often serves to 'act out' perceptions an audience already has. The little scene may therefore have been effective, even if it seemed obviously to have been a reconstruction rather than an actual event.

What is interesting from our point of view is that we, as a 'sophisticated' audience, can see propaganda at work in this example because its techniques are so 'unsophisticated'. Yet we might accept an even cruder set of tricks if they were dressed up in a more convincing technical form. This was certainly the problem when a crop of late 'cold war' films like *Top Gun* appeared in the 1980s. The message was mediated by highly convincing photographic techniques – and through the stars who appeared in the films.

Early cinema: growing from the popular

Some theorists have seen the development of early films, particularly those made before 1907, as being dependent in the main on theatrical traditions. The fact that the action which takes place before the camera is set within the limits of a frame and is often uninterrupted by an edit or cut, seems to suggest that what we are seeing is a theatre set and a theatrical performance, contained within the traditional proscenium arch.

The tendency to regard early films as 'primitive' can lead us to overlook some of the techniques which capable practitioners like Melies employed. Tom Gunning (*Early Cinema*, p. 99) describes how one of Melies' cinematic tricks (the 'disappearance' of an object or character) consisted of more than simply stopping the camera, rearranging the scene, and then starting the action again. The film showing the beginning and end of the interrupted action had to be spliced together. Early film-makers had what Gunning calls a 'unified viewpoint of the action' which they used even when they employed splices to achieve trick shots. This is a form of 'continuity' framing, which is very different from what is often referred to as the 'classical' system (represented to some degree by Hollywood), which uses continuity *editing* to represent the events of the narrative as proceeding in an ordered sequence. Gunning takes early cinema to be concerned primarily with display, with what he calls 'showmanship'. In the case of the illusions produced by Melies, this display is not in fact the relatively 'passive' presentation of events, it is a trick designed to make the viewer believe that there is also a 'unity of time' which goes on alongside the unity of framing. Instead of a limited, unimaginative 'theatrical' presentation, the unity of framing is used to conceal what Gunning calls 'the actual cinematic process at work' (p. 100). To many theorists, early film-making is a 'cinema of attractions', as opposed to later practice when cinema became concerned for the most part with story-telling.

Narrative and early cinema

A narrative is a chain of events in cause-effect relationship occurring in time. We should realise straight away that the plot of the story being told is only part of the narrative; the cinematic devices used in its telling are also part of the narrative (these devices include linguistic and sound effects, as well as visual devices). Narrative is often centred on conflict. The conflict faced could be described as person against nature, person against person, or person against self. There seems inevitably to be conflict in the narrative form. Resolutions, when they happen, tend to favour the hero/heroine/central character. Some of these conventions of narrative will emerge in later discussion of theorists like Vladimir Propp.

'Genres' of editing and narrative codes

As we have seen, when the cinema began in around 1895, the codes we are used to applying to film did not exist in their present form. How was the transition made from the 'cinema of attractions' to something we would regard as 'modern'?

The beginnings of an answer might be found in an examination of the development of early films themselves. Gunning suggests four distinct 'cine genres' in the early period, which he takes to be the period 1895–1910. A 'cine genre' can be understood as 'a complex of compositional, stylistic, and narrative devices' (Piotrovskij, *Early Cinema*, p. 88). In this case, the definition of such devices refers to the way that shots are used in time and space.

We must bear in mind the tendency of genres to overlap, in terms of the years during which they flourished. (If we exclude for a moment the first and fourth genres, we can see that the problem faced by the film-maker is how to minimise the disruption caused by cuts between action.) Gunning discusses the following cine genres:

1 The **single shot** narrative, which emerged in fictional pieces in 1895 and which includes any film 'in which some narrative action is developed within a single shot' (the camera remains in one set-up). This genre lasted from 1895 to 1905.
2 The genre of **non-continuity** refers to those films which show a contrast between two elements of the narrative, and which use a device such as a blurring of the picture or a dissolve to show this contrast between the two. For example, some early films show characters who are seen doing things, which are then revealed to be dreams because the next scene (linked by the dissolve or blurring) shows them waking. This type of practice, as a *main* device in story-telling, ends by 1904.
3 The genre of **continuity** narrative is associated with the 'chase film', where definite movement is required. Characters tend to leave the frame at the end of one shot. The next shot is signalled by their reappearance in the frame. This takes the audience over the disruption caused by a cut in the film. This form was important from about 1904 to 1907.
4 The genre of **discontinuity** marks the reintroduction of the cut as a disruption. Instead of needing to 'disguise' a cut, the cut is made between different actions. This is known as 'parallel' editing and was used to show rescues or other dra-

matic situations where the film-maker needed to demonstrate that two events, happening in different locations, were taking place at the same time. These events usually converged (came together) at the end of the sequence. This form began in about 1907 and then ran in parallel to a system of representation which began to develop the idea of using scenes. Concentrating on scenes meant that a single setting was used and the cuts were made *within* that setting; the earlier system of discontinuity used cutting to make a contrast *between* settings. It is possible to see here the beginnings of a dependence on 'linear' time – events happening which progress in an ordered way, and in which all the elements obey the same rate of progression. As we shall see below, some theorists (including Charles Musser), believe that 1907 marks the beginning of the now dominant 'classical' mode of representation.

Each of these four separate genres was dominant, or appeared at a certain stage, but they were not completely replaced by the next genre on the list. The classification is useful because it shows how early film moved from the single shot, through simple editing used to link two sequences, to clear cuts between shots marked by character movement, and finally to the ability to represent separate events which happen simultaneously. Gradually, a number of **codes** (a system into which signs are organised) were being presented to the public. Once these codes became recognised and accepted, then the 'language' of film was beginning to be established and **conventions** (established practices within film or other forms) could be used as a kind of 'shorthand' to get a message or an idea across to the public.

THE MOVE TO THE 'CLASSICAL' SYSTEM

Charles Musser ('The Nickelodeon Era Begins', *Early Cinema*, p. 256), argues that the cinema should be seen as a system which exists as a relationship between production and representation. The production side of the equation has three elements: the actual production of films for public display, exhibition, and reception (the audience's consumption of the product).

As the narrative element of films became more complex, a problem arose with the audience's reception or consumption of the product. The codes provided by the film-makers and circulated so that they became recognised conventions were perhaps outstripped by the development of narrative. Musser repeats a story about a film which showed a young couple walking across a field. The audience appeared mystified when the two people stopped, bowed their heads for a few seconds and then carried on walking – as well they might, because the vital explanatory element was a sound. At another public showing of the film, a sound effect (the tolling of a bell) was included. The couple's action was then understood as a rather touching example of piety. Sound effects could not, however, explain all the new complexities appearing in film. Film-makers discovered that many of their productions, adapted from books or stage plays, were simply not being understood. There was also a difficulty in using more simple narratives that relied on audience foreknowledge, since the plots were so over-used that audiences had become bored with them.

In some theatres, lectures were given to explain the background to the action. At other times, actors stood behind the screen and spoke the vocal parts. Or again, phonographs were used to produce synchronised sound. The easiest and cheapest method, however, was the use of inter-titles to explain the action and these soon became the standard method for a description of events on the screen.

Representations of time

It was the way in which the passage of time was shown which marked the move towards what became known as the 'classical' mode of representation in the cinema. A much stricter use of linear time was introduced around 1907 and rapid cutting between actions and objects gradually became standard practice. Action was 'set free' from the single shot, which had once acted to structure the entire narrative. Action now moved 'across' shots, rather than being structured by them.

Once we have an overview of how film may be divided into historical periods, we may look at the narrative devices which make up the 'classical' system. The idea of a dominant way of portraying events in the cinema (a dominant mode of representation) should then be easy to appreciate.

Labelling the eras of film

In *How to Read a Film*, James Monaco gives a breakdown of film history, which may be summarised thus;

1 A prehistory, including all the technical developments which led up to the distinct practice of film.
2 1895–1912: the evolution of the cinema from what he calls a 'side-show gimmick' to a developed 'economic' art, with the feature-length film appearing at the end of the period.
3 1913–27: the silent period.
4 1928–32: a state of transition, about which Monaco remains vague.
5 1932–46: the classic Hollywood era.
6 1947–59: the period in which film responded to the challenges of television.
7 1960–80: characterised by a concern with social and political issues and a series of 'new wave' experiments from various directors.

The drawback with such a list lies in the fact that the different periods seem to be distinguished from one another by a variety of criteria. Sometimes it is the technical development of a period which marks it out; at other times it is a response to a new mass media form, or perhaps an era is marked off because it displays some particular artistic quality. There is still disagreement about how the different eras should be divided. Monaco, for example, finishes with those films he believes to be broadly progressive, but the whole range of material from the later 1980s and the early 1990s suggest a number of directions, not all particularly forward-looking.

Dominant modes

There are obvious reasons why action in the early cinema was regarded as more important than characterisation. The very early films were short – by later standards we might regard them as ludicrously short – so there was little scope for complex character development. Single takes, from 1895 to about 1905, were very much the order of the day, showing a great deal of action in one long shot. Close-ups were in use quite extensively by 1912, sometimes to pick up significant detail, but often appearing to be used quite arbitrarily. In some cases, vital narrative information was lost because directors continued to favour the tableau, where a number of characters and a lot of movement appear within the frame.

By 1919, the most significant narrative conventions had been established. If we realise that narrative is not just the story but the way the story is told, we can begin to understand that narrative organises our perception of 'screen time'. Obviously, if a film is two hours long, we don't expect to see an exact presentation of two hours in the lives of the characters. (Andy Warhol's film *Empire* runs counter to these expectations. Made in 1964, it is an eight-hour shot of the Empire State building, from morning until night.)

Compositional codes

There are three sets of visual compositional codes which have to be taken into account. First is the plane of the image. Second is the geography of the space photographed. Third is the plane of depth perception, perpendicular to (at right angles to) both the frame plane and the geographical plane. (Lighting techniques will be discussed later.)

The categories of narrative device which depend on these visual codes include types of shot and methods of structuring shots.

TYPES OF SHOT

In still photography, it is useful to realise that shots may be most simply described according to their distance from the subject, and the angle from which they observe the subject. Film, by contrast, moves backward from and forward to the subject; but when a film is planned, storyboards are often used to sketch out individual shots. When this happens, the use of a combined distance and angle notation provides the director with the information needed to set up the shot. There are fine variations between each of these descriptions, but they are adequate for our purposes.

- **Distance** The most basic description of distance-to-object is **long shot**, **medium shot** and **close up**.
- **Angle** The basic description of angle in relation to object is **high angle**, **straight angle** and **low angle**.

If we were to summarise the categories of distance, they could be annotated as **LS, MS** and **CU**. For angle, we could use **HA, SA**, and **LA.** Any shot may be described as a combination of a certain distance and a certain angle. There are nine possible combinations (shown in Figures 5.1–5.9), as follows:

Fig 5.1 Long shot, high angle

Fig 5.2 Medium shot, high angle

Fig 5.3 Close-up, high angle

Fig 5.4 Long shot, straight angle

Fig 5.5 Medium shot, straight angle

Fig 5.6 Close-up, straight angle

Fig 5.7 Long shot, low angle

Fig 5.8 Medium shot, low angle

Fig 5.9 Close-up, low angle

LS/HA, MS/HA, CU/HA
LS/SA, MS/SA, CU/SA
LS/LA, MS/LA, CU/LA

The effects of using these types of shot will vary according to the intention of the director and the type of film. For example, a close-up/low angle shot of a house may be regarded as sinister in the context of a horror film, whose conventions lead an audience to expect something unpleasant. The same shot of the house in the context of a romantic comedy may have a different effect; it may be a way of introducing the audience to an idyllic retreat used by the central characters.

However, there are shots which are used in all types of film to signal the onset of certain events or to draw the attention of an audience to some significant detail. The first type, angle and distance shots, may be thought of as having a meaning dependent on context; they are **contextual.** The second type carry a more universal meaning, from film to flim. They are **intertextual.** Close-ups form a type of shot which is both contextual and intertextual.

SHOTS WITH A 'UNIVERSAL' MEANING: INTERTEXTUAL

- **Establishing shots** are used to show where a scene is about to take place – a building or location may appear briefly at the begining of a scene, without having to show, as film-makers had to do in the early stages of the industry, the characters themselves on site.
- **Insert shots** are used to show important detail – for example, an object which some characters are about to fight over, a mark on an object which gives a clue to an event, and so on. The use of an insert does not imply that the characters are able to see what the audience can see in the insert.
- **Close-ups** are used in order to help point up significant detail and to reveal important psychological moments through facial expressions.
- **Over-the shoulder shots** demonstrate conversation between two individuals. Part of the back of the head and shoulder of the person being addressed is seen, as well as the frontal view of the speaker's face.
- **Point-of-view shots** show a person or an object from the viewpoint of a single (usually important) character.
- **Reaction shots** follow a significant action or speech made by one character; they show the reaction of another character.
- **Shot-reverse-shot** is the practice of showing two individuals in conversation, filmed over the left shoulder and then over the right shoulder (*see* Figures 5.10–5.11).

EDITING

Besides the use of recognised or conventional shots like those above, there are also establised ways of editing film which help to structure narrative, shape screen time, and thus create meaning. Barry Salt (*see* Film Form 1900–1906 in *Early Cinema*) argues that certain technical shots in the early cinema do not have stable, fixed meanings, but must be understood in relative terms; for example, Melies' dissolves do not signify dream states or time lapses, but may simply indicate a

Fig 5.10 Shot-reverse-shot, over right shoulder

Fig 5.11 Shot-reverse-shot, over left shoulder: reverse of Fig 5.10

change of location. In the modern cinema, however, dominant meanings for certain editing techniques have definitely evolved.

- The use of **real time**, where the time taken by the recorded action on the film is equal to the time that the performance took. (It quickly became accepted in the early cinema that 'redundant' information could be cut out by stopping the camera and starting it again at the next significant point of action. The next step was to arrange the 'best' positions for the camera so that the audience could have a certain view of the action.)
- **Montage**, the technique of cutting from one shot to another in order to create meaning. There is a modern technique known as a *justified cut*, where for example, a shot of a woman drinking out of a glass can lead quite naturally to a close-up of the glass. If an audience sees an 'unjustified' cut in a mainstream film, it will be regarded as a mistake. The Russian director Eisenstein used montage deliberately in order to make different shots 'collide', thus unsettling and perhaps provoking thought in his audiences.
- **Cross-cutting**, the practice of using contrasting shots achieved by parallel editing, to establish an idea of simultaneous action in different places.

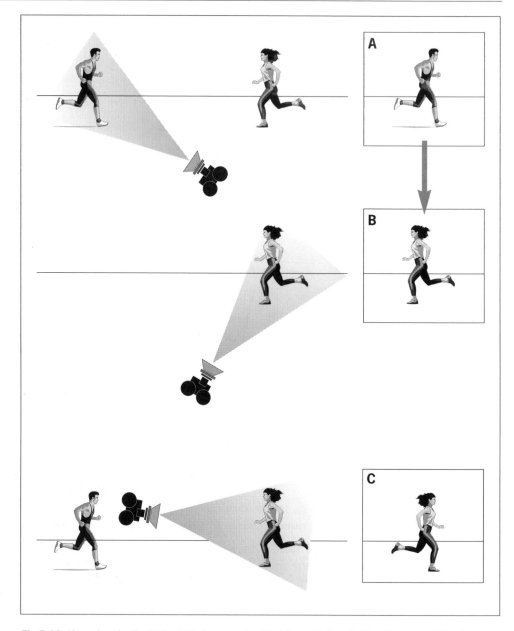

Fig 5.12 'Crossing the line': the 180 degree rule. Shot B can follow A. Shot C cannot follow A because the camera has broken the 180 degree rule

- **Fading in and out** is a technique used for representing the passage of time and preparing an audience for some change in the action. When a dissolve takes place, it is where a fade-out is superimposed over a fade-in.
- **Flashbacks** are a form of editing and are used to signify a past event, which is inserted into the 'present' of screen time. Flashbacks are often linked to the experiences of a specific character in order to explain their present motivations. When we return to the screen present, the scene is more or less identical to that

which came before the flashback, with the character who has had the flashback shown emerging from the experience.
• **Crossing the line** is a rule established in mainstream film-making which prevents a camera moving across a line of 180 degress. Breaking this rule gives the impression that the actors have changed position, whereas in fact the camera has made an 'unjustified' move from one place to another (*see* Figure 5.12 on page 266).

LIGHTING AND 'TEXTURE'

Lighting can of course be an important code. In many films, lighting is exactly what the frame is designed to show, and some directors may even choose certain objects or settings specifically to allow a certain type of lighting to be effective.

'Film Noir' is often used an example of a system of lighting which is in keeping with the general mood of the genre; underlit rooms and dark shadows were used to emphasise the gloomy view of human nature which ran through these films. Originally, however, the reason that the 'noir' sets were underlit was because their budgets did not always allow the full panoply of lights used in 'A' pictures to be employed. The immense cost of producing modern 'noirs' (or films with a 'dark' overtone, like the *Batman* films) makes an interesting contrast to the original reasons for the practice.

'Texture' means the appearance of the film, its physical quality as an element of meaning. Monaco gives the example of grainy film, which usually means that the frame has been enlarged; it can be used as a code for documentary narration.

Codes and meanings

From our study of semiology in Chapter 2, we have learned that images can be 'read' by an audience. If an image is clear enough and in a reasonably familiar context, then the viewer will be able to make sense of it – it will carry meaning for that individual and for other members of the same culture. The cinema is bound to produce, as some of its most familiar codes, the codes of everyday existence. These include human communication (verbal and non-verbal) as well as human actions which are not specifically communicative (eating and sleeping for example). Then there are codes which the cinema shares with other forms of artistic production: codes of composition, including framing, lighting and tinting/colouring. Finally, there are codes that are peculiar to the cinema, the most obvious of which is montage.

SEMIOLOGY AND FILM

If we agree that images can be 'read', then we should investigate the process through which this happens. Some theorists argue that images carry two meanings: the first as an optical pattern, the second that of a mental experience. Clearly, the optical pattern leads to the mental experience.

Monaco makes a distinction between language, where the power of the system lies in the great difference between the signifier and the signified, and film where, he believes, the power of the system lies in the fact that the signifier and the signified are almost exactly the same.

Shot choice: paradigm and syntagm

Paradigm and syntagm are often described as two different ways of reading a menu, both of which need to be done in order to understand what is on offer. A paradigm could be understood as an example of a starter: lentil soup as opposed to mushroom soup. A syntagm could be seen as the way the menu is written out, with different classes of food following on from one another; starter followed by main course, and so on. A paradigm is an example of a class of objects. A syntagm is an element which follows another in a recognised sequence.

After a film maker has decided *what* to shoot, the two questions which must follow are how to shoot it and how to *present* or edit what has been shot. Deciding how to shoot an object (for example) represents a paradigmatic choice. If we were to take the example of a tree, it is clear that this is one type of tree chosen from other available types. The director of a film might decide to take a shot which shows it in a soft light from medium close-up, using a straight angle. The meanings we gain from the shot grow from its relationship to the other possible shots which could have been taken at the same point, made up of the range of choices of distance, lighting and angle.

Deciding how to present what has been shot represents a syntagmatic choice. This means, in the case of the shot of the tree, deciding which shots will come before or after it, and also how the movement from one shot to another will be made. If the shot which follows our original paradigmatic choice is of a tree-cutter, then this seems to suggest a particular type of narrative choice. If the shot which follows the original shows someone hiding in the branches, another type of narrative is on offer.

These two different kinds of connotation have their equivalents in literature. In *How to Read a Film* (p. 132) Monaco argues that a word alone on a page has no particular connotation, only denotation. By this he means that it has in fact many *potential* connotations and that we are never sure of an author's intention until we observe what other choices are made, what other words are placed on either side of the first word. We then find ourselves presented with a syntagmatic connotation. Whatever choices a director *might* make, there are obviously choices that have *not* been made. Meaning is structured by what has not been shown as well as by what has been revealed. Choice means that there must be a series of rejections – silences in the text.

WAYS OF UNDERSTANDING FILM NARRATIVE

One of the most important points to note is that narrative is a way of organising material. It happens to have become the dominant form in cinema, but then it is also very widely used in other disciplines – history is an example where narrative is used extensively. Narrative should not be associated simply with 'fiction'. Edward Branigan (*Narrative Comprehension and Film*, p. 3) describes narrative not simply as a chain of events, but as an 'activity that organises data into a special pattern which represents and explains experience'.

Some commentators have observed that narrative is a development whose component parts tend to modify each other as they go along. Others are now concerned mostly with how individual subjects make sense of actual examples of narrative.

Film as fairy-tale

Vladimir Propp, a Russian critic active in the 1920s, published his *Morphology of the Folk-Tale* in 1928. This was at a time when Soviet cinema was still producing some exceptionally interesting texts. Propp, however, was concerned with the written narrative. He noticed that folk-tales were very similar to one another in many respects. They seemed to be about the same basic situations and struggles. They appeared also to have the same 'stock' characters in each case.

Propp identified no less than thirty-two basic categories of action, which he called 'functions'. He also identified a set of basic 'spheres of action' or character roles. Characters are not used in the folk-tale to promote discussions about their individual psychology. They have, according to Propp, a narrative function in the text. Characters are there to help provide a structure for the text.

For our purposes, we could identify some eight basic characters who inhabit the world of the Russian fairy-tale, each of whom performs a certain function:

- the **hero**, who is the character who seeks something;
- the **villain**, who opposes or blocks the hero's quest;
- the **donor**, who provides an object which has some magic property;
- the **dispatcher**, who sends the hero on his way by providing a message;
- the **false hero**, who disrupts the hero's hope of reward by pressing false claims
- the **helper**, who aids the hero;
- the **princess**, who acts as reward for the hero and as object of the villain's scheming;
- her **father**, who acts to reward the hero for his efforts.

ACTIONS AS FUNCTIONS

The actions or events described by Propp are as follows;

Preparation
A community, kingdom, family; an ordered state of being:
- A member of the family/community leaves home.
- A warning is given to the community or its leaders/a rule is imposed on the hero.
- The warning is discounted/the rule is broken.
- The villain attempts to discover something about the victim.
- The villain discovers the required information.
- The villain tries to deceive the victim to gain an advantage.
- The victim is deceived by the villain and unwittingly helps him/her.

Complication
A state of disorder:
- The villain harms a member of the family/community.

- One of the family / community desires something.
- The hero is sent out to find what is desired.
- The hero plans action against the villain.

Transference
- The hero leaves home.
- The hero is either tested or attacked; he meets the challenge and receives a magical agent or a helper.
- The hero reacts to the donor.
- The hero arrives at or is transferred to the place where he will fulfil his quest.

Struggle
- There is a struggle in a specific setting between hero and villain.
- The hero is branded.
- The villain is overcome.
- The state of disorder is settled.

Return
- The hero returns.
- The hero is pursued.
- The hero escapes or is rescued from the pursuit.
- The hero arrives at home or at some other place and is not recognised.
- A false hero presses a claim.
- A task is set for the hero.
- The task is accomplished.

Recognition
- The hero is recognised.
- The false hero or villain is unmasked.
- The false hero or villain is punished.
- The hero attains the princess and the wealth and power of the state.

As we have seen, the point about the functions described by Propp is that they are not just seen as events, actions, or characters, but rather as elements of narrative which can occur at different places in the tale. We should realise that exactly the same action can have a completely different meaning, depending on where it is found in the narrative. In 'Film Narrative' (*The Cinema Book*, p. 234) Sheila Johnstone gives an example of this point;

> '. . . the same event, "the prince builds a castle", could represent in one tale the *violation* of an interdiction [instruction] which forbade this, in the second the *solution* of a difficult task and in a third the preparation of a *wedding*.'

Johnstone also notes that two completely different events, involving different characters, can carry the same meaning. She demonstrates this by showing how a Tsar's gift of a ring to a hero can carry the same meaning as a princess giving another hero a horse. In both cases, we witness the function called 'the provision of a magical agent'.

Some critics have argued that the film as narrative is based on the fairy-tale or folktale, sharing their limited number of characters and plots. Of course, there are clear differences between the male-orientated categories listed above (reflecting the patriarchal fantasies of the tales) and those films which deliberately set out to challenge the gender-roles of its characters; but Propp's system may still be applied, because *function* rather than *gender* lies at the heart of the analysis. (It is interesting to note how some films have used women in roles written for men – the part of Ripley in *Alien*, which caused some debate about gender and role, would be a prime example.)

CRITICISMS OF PROPP

A number of writers found that Propp's analysis could be applied to film with a surprising degree of accuracy, although the method is supposed to work *from* the material in hand, in order to reach a set of conclusions. What should really be done, therefore, is to set up a new project to investigate the functions found in modern films.

Others felt that the system could be applied most easily to the simple texts – present in the bulk of the formulaic, popular cinema which dominates the market-place. More complex art would not fit the system. The application of Propp's system to film has also been attacked by those who believe that it takes no account of pleasure and the tendency to identify with characters. Some films, however, seem to 'fit' the system well. Oliver Stone, the director responsible for two narratives centred on the Vietnam War, has produced films which are powerful by virtue of their subject matter, but are not very complex in terms of their narrative. *Platoon* for example, conforms in some respects quite closely to Propp's analysis, in which the role of hero is divided between the newcomer Taylor and the experienced Sergeant Elias. The false hero and villain is Barnes, but the villainy can be made manifest in any number of ways. The NVC/NVA (North Vietnamese) remain outlines, shadows, figures crouching in the dark, reduced almost to psychological traits against which the central character must fight.

A major fault in the system appears to lie in Propp's casting of the thirty-one functions in chronological order. Theorists like Wright believe that a strict order of events/characters is restrictive, and that thinking of 'clusters' of functions is more helpful. The theory remains useful, however, because it avoids an approach which treats characters as though they are real individuals, demonstrating instead how important character is to the structuring of narrative.

The logical schemes of Propp and Todorov (mentioned above and below) have been challenged by a newer wave of interest in how readers interpret texts. The grand designs of structuralism are very useful as a starting point, although perhaps a little inflexible when dealing with actual 'reading situations'.

Equilibrium and disequilibrium: Todorov

Tzvetan Todorov wrote about the structure of the 'fantastic', advancing the theory that a narrative is a fictional environment which begins with a state of equilibrium (all is as it should be) which then suffers some disruption (disequilibrium), before a new equilibrium is produced at the end of the story. There are in fact five transformations through which an event can pass:

1 a state of equilibrium – all is in order;
2 a disruption of the ordered state by an event;
3 a recognition that a disruption has taken place;
4 an attempt to repair the damage of the disruption;
5 a return to some kind of equilibrium.

This structure can be applied to fictional and even non-fictional forms. The problem is that it remains very general and cannot reveal the close detail of a narrative.

Readers and narratives

Branigan (*Narrative Comprehension and Film*, p. 14) notes that subjects tend to remember a story in terms of what he calls 'categories of information', rather than in (p. 15), 'the way the story is actually presented or its surface features'. But what are these 'categories of information' ? Branigan proposes the following narrative schema (an outline of how any narrative will work):

1 introduction of setting and characters;
2 explanation of a state of affairs;
3 initiating event;
4 emotional response or statement of a goal by the protagonist;
5 complicating actions;
6 outcome;
7 reactions to the outcome.

These elements, rather than details of shot and angle, are what people tend to remember, according to Branigan.

Discourse in narrative forms

As soon as we remove the storyteller from the audience's immediate physical presence, we have to deal with the new factors that grow out of the distance between the two. The relationship between the author of a book and the people who read it is at a greater remove than the relationship in a face-to-face communication. Although the individuals concerned (author and readers) cannot see each other, they probably have ideas about each other's personality. The author may use a certain style of address to talk to the readers, while the readers for their part are bound to have some conception of the author, through the content and form of the book.

Narratives 'position' readers

The way we are spoken to, the way we are led through a story, having certain things revealed, certain things withheld, helps to place us as the subjects of the narrative. But the relationship is more complex than this suggests. Who is doing the 'positioning'? It seems that someone in the text is speaking to us.

If we take the example of a literary narrative (a novel), there is a 'narrator' within the text, through whom the author speaks. Sometimes this narrator is given a name and a persona, sometimes the narrator is supposed to be none other than the author. But many would argue that it is impossible in a work of fiction for the narrator to be the same as the real author. This perspective suggests that, as soon as a writer begins to address an audience, he or she does so through a 'persona', an assumed identity. The identity the author has assumed to write even this non-fiction book is of someone rational and knowledgeable; suited, in other words, to what the author assumes the audience expects. At times, it is not just that the audience demands a certain type of approach; the author will have an expectation of his/her audience's needs.

Many authors appear to play with narrative personae in order to give themselves a variety and flexibility in the address they make to the reader. Emily Brontë's only novel, *Wuthering Heights*, begins by detailing the adventures of a man called Lockwood who has moved North to take up the occupancy of a house, Thrushcross Grange. He speaks to us as narrator, as 'author' of the narrative which follows. The personal experiences he relates to us, however, are not particularly interesting, except in the personal inadequacies which they reveal. After an unfortunate experience during an enforced overnight stay at the house of his nearest neighbour, he becomes ill and has to be helped to recovery by his housekeeper, Mrs Dean. During this period, Mrs Dean begins to tell Lockwood (and through Lockwood, the reader), the history of the family dramas she has witnessed. Mrs. Dean becomes the narrator. Later, other characters' stories are told through Mrs Dean. Yet they speak in their own voices. We sometimes forget that there is any mediation between their stories and our reception of them. Letters and diary entries form part of the text, and again people speak in their own voices, narrating events as it were, direct to the reader. Where is Emily Brontë in all this? Which voice is hers? Or should we expect that voice to reveal itself in the choice of themes, functions, characters and above all in the 'way of telling' which she employs?

In film, the narrator-position is sometimes used to deceive the viewer. The storyteller, the narrator, is in a powerful position with respect to the reader and this may be used to help to complicate our view of what is happening as the narrative unfolds. In one of the 'Hammer' horror films, *Dracula*, someone begins to read from a journal. We assume that this narrator and the author of the journal are one and the same. But in fact the author of the journal is dead, and the journal is being read by someone else. When we are misled in this way, it can affect our whole perception of the events which take place within a film.

A system of 'participants'

In an essay on narrative in *Channels of Discourse* (p. 55), Sarah Ruth Kozloff reproduces a system of the relationships which go on between the participants when a text is read. This system may remind us of the simple communication diagram in Chapter 1. According to this theory, no less than six participants take part in the relationships set up by the text. A diagrammatic representation would appear as in Fig. 5.13.

If we take the example of *Wuthering Heights*, we could describe the *real author* as

Emily Brontë. The *implied author* would be the conception of Emily Brontë that each reader acquires from reading the text. The *narrator* is, variously, Lockwood, Nelly Dean, Cathy, and so on. The *narratee* appears whenever the text addresses a 'you', or speaks to the reader directly as a person. The *implied reader* is the subject-position that the text offers the reader, whether or not it is taken up. In the case of this particular novel, the reader is regarded by the writer as being unfamiliar with the habits of existence and styles of life found in the community described, and is addressed accordingly. But exactly which point of view the reader is supposed to agree with is more difficult to describe. Heathcliff's fierce romanticism is 'mediated' by the manipulative interventions of Nelly Dean. It is possible to agree with either of two competing discourses. The *real reader* is the actual individual subject who engages in the physical task of reading the book.

APPLICATION OF A SYSTEM OF 'PARTICIPANTS' TO FILM

It is more difficult to get a firm sense of the actual or implied author in film, partly because films are collaborative efforts. But we can still use the term 'authorship' to look at those individuals, collectives, and institutions which work together to initiate a film project. In the sense that the institution of 'cinema' is one which is based very much on what the big production companies believe audiences are prepared to watch, the audience or readership is part of the whole equation from the very start.

The role of narrator in a film is sometimes more complicated than might be the case in many novels. This is because the narrator is not always the same as the central character. There may be a voice-over describing the action, but even in this case the narrative itself might reveal that the voice-over is misleading or mistaken. Nor is it quite correct to identify, as some theorists do (*see Channels of Discourse*, p. 57), the camera as the narrator, since the use of sound may sometimes work to contradict the image that has been presented on the screen. What we are being told through the soundtrack must therefore also be taken into account. Terms like 'grand image-maker' as a title for the narrator are worse than useless for this reason. *Diegesis* is the term used to describe all the 'denotative' material which goes to make up a film, including fictional space and time, codes and conventions, sound and narration. Narration is the act, the process of revealing the narrative. If diegesis is the sum total of the feature film, then the *collective actors* which reveal the diegesis (narration) must stand for the narrator.

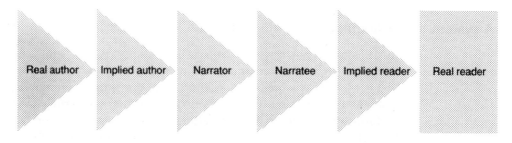

Fig 5.13 Diagram showing relationships of six participants when a text is being read

Real author   Implied author   Narrator   Narratee   Implied reader   Real reader

Kozloff (p. 58) notes that 'consciously or not [the institution] ... invites ... audiences to make the communicative act concrete'. She notes how often television networks run shows that include live studio audiences as narratees. But who would be identified as the narratee in a film, where no audience is present at the point of production (i.e. when the film is being made)? I would suggest that the narratee is part of the film's mode of address; it is the person or persons for whom the sum total of the action is played out. The narratee may be 'inside' the film if the film's narration addresses someone or something specific.

The *implied reader* here is the authorship's *conception* of the representative viewer. When audience research is carried out, there are groups which the film institution will regard as 'target markets' for their products, and to some extent there are likely to be things in the film which are designed to appeal to all these groups. The film's address is made to an implied viewer who will agree with the ideological intent of the film. For example, the openly sexist use of female models in a film like *Used Cars* is shown within an ideological framework which allows it as part of the spirit of fun and 'small-town capitalist rebellion' which the film offers. The implied reader is imagined falling into step with the dominant viewpoint of the film.

The *real reader* is the actual audience member, taken at random, who watches the film.

The organisation of time and space in narrative

It is clear that there must be a difference between the time it takes for an event to occur (an actual time-event, measurable by an accepted method), and the time it takes to represent that event once it is completed. Our brief investigation of the early cinema shows how the use of 'real time' could not be maintained once complex narratives were attempted. The first method of editing was to stop the camera and start once the information regarded as 'redundant' had passed by. The next was to show simultaneous events occurring through the use of cross-cutting. Then came the 'compression' of time by making the scenes themselves stand for different time-periods, so that events which would take place in the real world over a long period could be summarised.

FIVE CATEGORIES OF TIME IN THE CINEMA: TECHNICAL APPROACHES

An understanding of cinematic time can be helped using a system described by Genette and adapted by Chatman. A comparison is made between 'discourse time' and 'story time'. Discourse time is the time it takes to narrate an event. Discourse here is not used with its proper ideological meaning, but rather a much looser definition. It involves a choice, including selecting and shaping the original material. Story time refers to the description of a complete story with the inclusion of all its elements. Kozloff (p. 64) makes a list of five possible 'matches' between discourse and story time:

1 **Summary**. In this case, discourse time is shorter than story time. The film uses techniques like rapidly changing seasons, montage to show life-events, and calendars changing to represent the passage of time. It is a kind of compression, or short hand.

2 **Ellipsis**. This is a system we are all used to; it involves cutting out all intervening time between two shots. If someone is shown getting out of bed, followed by a shot which shows them eating breakfast, followed in turn by a shot which shows the person travelling to work on a train, we don't find this odd. It has become a natural way of representing an event. Discourse time is regarded as non-existent during an ellipsis.

3 **Scene**. In this, story time and discourse time are equal. The camera is allowed to present the events of a story in full. No cuts as such are made; the camera is free to move, provided it does not disturb the use of 'real time'. Important dialogue scenes are shot in this way.

4 **Stretch**. Here, discourse time is longer than story time. The use of slow-motion is the most useful example. The real time of events (the story time in this system) is lengthened for some dramatic purpose.

5 **Pause**. Here, story time is non-existent. Sometimes, at the end of a film, a freeze-frame is used and narrative information flows past in the form of words, or a voice-over is heard drawing conclusions about the story.

These categories were clearly developed for dealing with the image-based components of a narrative. In a later chapter the part played by sound will be investigated more fully. In the meantime, we should realise that the visual is only one channel of information in film. Christian Metz identifies five channels of information:

1 the visual image;
2 print and other graphics;
3 speech;
4 music;
5 noise/SFX (sound effects).

It seems significant, considering the neglect in many quarters of the study of sound, that the majority of the channels are auditory. The visual image and sound effects work most closely together, and are continuous. The other elements are not always in evidence, even in densely-written works such as films based on the plays of Shakespeare. Some films make a deliberate attempt to unify the image with sound; an example could be the French film *Delicatessen*, where the effect of reinforcing images with sound is used in order to achieve a comic effect.

The pervasive nature of sound is its main strength. Sound tends to make time in film 'feel' more concrete and natural. According to the theorist Reisz, sound is either **synchronous** or **asynchronous**. Synchronous sound comes from within the frame and the editor must work to synchronise it with the image. Asynchronous sound comes from outside the frame. Another set of useful terms describes the way sound works with, or against an image. **Contrapuntal** sound is opposed to or in counterpoint with the image; **parallel** sound is connected with the image, which it reinforces.

The idea that the soundtrack works either with or against the image produces what some believe to be the basic 'dialectic' in aesthetic terms. The Hollywood style was thought to be strongly parallel, and the programmatic music of the thirties particularly so, since it seemed to underline and heavily reinforce even the simplest scenes. Some modern films use contrapuntal sound because it makes the audience wary of what the image appears to be telling them. It acts as a commentary on the image, or as an important element of contrast. In a way, audiences often trust sound above the image. It is often used to warn of impending danger, when the image might otherwise appear completely innocent.

GENRE

Most people who have come across the term 'genre' take it to mean 'type'. This is a good place to begin. Films are, at first sight anyway, easily sorted into types: musicals, westerns, horror movies, comedies, and so on.

Take the example of a western. We can list all the features which make up this genre. There are men in stetsons, women in long skirts. Horses are used as transport. There are saloons, boarding-houses, jails, banks. The roads are dusty and things which look like huge bits of fluff blow through the streets when it is windy. There are gunfights, arrests, jailbreaks, love affairs, bank robberies – all the ingredients which go to make up the action of a western. From this we may be confident that setting, characters (who usually have a clear appearance and a limited number of personality traits for easy identification), the symbols in the frame (guns, for example), the type of conflict shown, and the way that the conflicts are resolved, all contribute to genre.

But the problem has always been to find the point at which one genre ends and another begins. Suppose we allow the cowboys to wear bowler hats instead of stetsons? This may only mean that the action is set further east. Suppose that everything remains as it should be, except that the characters in the film are shown riding camels instead of horses? This definitely begins to confuse the viewer. Are we watching the same genre? Why should one change alter all our expectations of the western film?

We find ourselves up against a similar problem to the one we came across before, when an attempt was made to identify specific genres of discourse. How are we able to say 'this is a western, this is science fiction'? As Andrew Tudor wrote (*see Theories of Film*, quoted in 'History of genre criticism', *The Cinema Book*, p. 59):

> 'To take a genre such as the "western"... and list its principal characteristics... is to ... isolate the body of films which are "westerns". But they can only be isolated on the basis of the "principal characteristics" which can only be discovered from the films themselves after they have been isolated.'

There is no point in following this circular process (unless we are prepared to give up the search for an accurate definition of genre!).

We might agree with the idea that 'the cinema' is not simply the collection of institutions which physically produce and circulate films, but that it also includes the wider *social* institution, which must include audiences as well. In *Genre*, Stephen Neale solved the problem of how best to understand genre when he drew attention (p. 19) to the notion that genres are 'systems' of 'expectations and conventions' that circulate between 'industry, text and subject'. The idea of an audience's foreknowledge (knowledge of genre in advance, based on experience of other texts) will obviously lead to a certain set of expectations. It is these expectations which are then used to catch the attention of an audience whenever a film is being publicised.

Genre, narrative, discourse

Using the scheme set out by Todorov, Neale describes how certain types of narrative are bound to crop up in, and are likely to match, specific genres. Taking the second 'event' in Todorov's system, disequilibrium (the disruption of the original ordered state), he writes (p. 21) that 'in the western, the gangster film and the detective film, disruption is always figured literally – as physical violence'.

In each of these cases, the tension between the ordered state and the disruption of that ordered state (equilibrium and disequilibrium) is represented by a struggle over the meaning of the law; its effectiveness or ineffectiveness. Therefore, discourses about the meaning of the law will feature prominently in the western, gangster and detective genres. Neale argues that, although violence may feature in, for instance, a musical like *West Side Story*, it is not what he calls a d*efining characteristic* of the genre 'musical'.

Genre: examples of audience foreknowledge and expectation

One way of investigating this approach to genre would be to ask if genre is an internal or external characteristic of a film text. We have listed some of the internal evidence of genre: setting, characters, symbols, the type of conflict and the nature of the resolutions offered in the text. Other evidence will include type of music, style of titles, etc. But what do we mean by external evidence? How can we prove or disprove the theory which says that genres are 'systems of expectations'?

The answer to this question lies in finding an audience and discovering what filmic 'clues' will fire up their expectations; what images and sounds lead them to believe they will see certain things on the screen. The best method is to show a short part of the opening of a film and to freeze the frame after a few seconds. The examples here are taken from a study carried out with a group of first-year A level students.

To start with a fairly easily-recognised example of genre, an extract from Oliver Stone's film *Platoon* was shown, ending as soon as the rear of the military transport plane revealed a group of soldiers waiting to disembark. Immediately, the concept of a war film was established. The central disequilibrium would of course be the fighting that the audience expected to take place, but the exact nature of the film's discourse, its address to the 'narratee' and the 'intended viewer' would remain obscure until the film got further under way. Similarly, the exact delineation of character, or the use of character as a structural function in the narrative, would remain obscure until more evidence came into view. What is significant here is how some members of the audience 'read' the opening clues of image and sound as simply stating 'war film'; but of course, the name of the war is the important focus we need in order to make certain judgments about what precisely to expect. If this is a Second World War film, then the suffering undergone by the characters may be signalled clearly as 'self-sacrifice' in the interests of the 'defence of democracy', the 'liberation of fascist-occupied Europe', and so on (although it is by no means certain that this is the only possible type of 'message' of films set during this period).

When an audience is allowed to discover that this is an example of what most of them already suspected (the Vietnam War film), then another set of expectations begins to make itself felt. This may amount to a perception of the characters' situation as being one of 'sacrifice in an uncertain cause', or the 'oppression of a people by an ignorant invader'. Once the audience witness the interaction between the new recruits and the veterans, certain 'confirmatory' codes come into play. In other words, some of the audience's expectations are confirmed by the contrast between the appearance of the recruits and that of the veterans; and also particularly by one veteran's linguistic appropriation of the term which signifies both the country and the situation the recruits have entered into. The moment when a soldier tells the new draft that 'you're gonna love the Nam – for f***in' ever' shows how 'the Nam' is the soldier's redefinition of the full proper noun, Vietnam. It is meant to signal an understanding of a situation which the recruits will soon experience for themselves.

The opening of Spielberg's *Gremlins* uses a number of codes which can mislead an audience. The form of direct address used by the first character and the dark and mysterious setting suggested the police or detective drama to some members of the audience. The first character to speak does so to the narratee through a voice-over, declaring that 'it all started here in Chinatown. I was hitting the shops, trying to move some merchandise.' This parodies the style of address found in many mainstream police adventures, at the same time as it contains a clear reference to the actual occupation of the character. This character appears to stand at the centre of the narrative, but this is misleading. He soon becomes a secondary element of the film, only resuming this narration at the very end. In fact, during much of the drama, he appears to be in complete ignorance of the situation which arises in his home town. Some may interpret this as 'bad' or inconsistent filmmaking.

The Orient is suggested by the setting, music and the dress codes of some of the extras who appear, though we soon learn that this is in fact an ethnic enclave in one of the big American cities. The sequence in the basement shop which follows includes a racial stereotype which was probably current in pre-war cinema. The old Chinese grandfather seems to signify the mystery of the Orient. (This tendency to draw inspiration from old sources is a feature of Spielberg's film-making, a point which some in the audience appeared to understand.) The scene in the old man's store begins by following the already established representation of the Far East, but then becomes rapidly farcical as the inventor attempts to sell the grossly inefficient 'bathroom buddy' to the venerable and unusually silent gentleman. With the introduction of this unsuccessful invention, a new genre appears to be signalled; the comic farce. Spielberg's large repertoire of effects sometimes leads to a confusing jumble of generic codes, pointing in some cases to an exercise in narration, rather than encouraging the creation of a coherent narrative.

The task in the case of *To Kill a Mockingbird* was for the audience to work out, before any interaction between characters took place, what kind of film they were about to see. There were various responses from students. These responses may be partly shaped by their reaction to a text which was produced in black and white and which did not suggest, therefore, an experience that would be relevant to them.

One view was that this was was an historical drama. A film about childhood was another common response, but many were less certain about the exact signification of the music on the sound-track, which was orchestrated with a kind of romantic sweep. (In the author's opinion, the film would have considerably less emotional impact without this introduction.)

The music also included a child-like piano score, which one student felt was sinister because of the modern use of such music as a sound-effect which often accompanies films where the apparent innocence of character or circumstance is later undermined. In other words, through repeated use in a certain context, this type of child-like music has become associated with the horror genre.

When a further extract was shown, more audience members felt that they had found their bearings. The story is located in the past. 'A day was 24 hours long, but it seemed longer,' says the mature female narrator (as yet unseen). The languid tone of this statement, together with the refined tones of the female Southern accent, may remind some of the other texts they have seen, which begin with a description of the deep South as hot, humid and perhaps the setting for high passions.

It is not just the plot of a film which creates the narrative, but also those technical codes which 'deliver' the plot. For example, the long sweep of the camera which takes place at the beginning, first following a man delivering papers, then changing to follow the movement of a horse-drawn buggy, helps to reinforce the mood of the opening sequence. There is a slow dissolve between two shots which also helps to express the introductory discourse of this film.

We are seeing this film through a sort of double historical lens. From our position in the present, we observe a fiction which was produced in the 1960s with all the attendant acting and directing styles, and discourses about racism then current; both these positions go towards interpreting life in a Southern state in the 1930s.

FILM FROM BOOK

To Kill a Mockingbird was used widely in British schools for many years. It is a classic liberal text both as a book and as a film, in the sense that it deals with racial injustice but proposes solutions which keep carefully within the bounds of recognised morality and the law. Gradually, however, its liberal discourses (which focused mostly on white society) came to be deemed unfashionable, and it was replaced by texts which addressed the same concerns more directly.

The central characters are a widowed lawyer, Atticus Finch, and his two children, a girl called Scout and her older brother, Jem. Scout, Jem and their friend Dill create their own fantastic stories about a never-seen neighbour and recluse, Boo Radley, who becomes, in their minds, a fascinating and dangerous figure. Atticus is assigned to defend a black farm-worker, Tom Robinson, who has been accused of beating and raping a young white woman called Mayella Ewell. The persecuted and clearly innocent farm-worker fails to receive justice from the court which tries him; we hear later that he is shot dead while making what seems to be a deliberately suicidal escape attempt.

A more radical and violent response to the problem of racism shadows the text. This emerges during an early scene in which Atticus attempts to use persuasion to stop a group of men lynching the accused man. The appearance of Atticus's children prevents the lynching, since the men are shamed by Scout's innocent chatter. However, the local newspaper editor had all along been watching events with a shotgun from an upper storey window. The lynch-mob and Atticus are unaware of his presence.

In a dramatic conclusion to the text, Boo Radley (who has acted all along as the children's 'guardian angel', without their knowledge), prevents Bob Ewell killing Jem. Ewell is fatally injured by his own knife, but Boo Radley is not brought to book for the death because of his simple state of mind. Justice is served outside the law, but by an agent who is allowed this leeway because of his 'special' position. Racism is represented as being most virulent in the poorest and most ignorant section of Maycomb society. The idea that there is a more enlightened class is marked out by the attitudes of Atticus and his professional acquaintances.

NARRATIVE CHOICES

The film displays the words 'based upon the novel by Harper Lee' among its opening credits. This means that the film uses the novel as a basis for its story. Of course, the film and the book are very similar in many ways. Many of the same things happen and the sentiment of the film is close to that of the book.

However, the exact order of events in the book is not followed. Some things are missed out, some events are moved around, and some characters are removed. The idea has been to create a 'tighter' story-line. The film obviously has less time to tell the story, but this is not the only reason that big changes have been made. The medium of film has to be used differently – a simple look from Atticus, for example, can be known and understood in a second on the screen. The meaning of the same look or expression has to be described in words by the writer. But narrative choices are also choices about effect.

The first thing to note is that the story is told in the first person (by the little girl, Scout) and that the narrator looks back at events which took place in the past. We are told various thing about these past events, and as we read the book we stand in an actual, as well as a fictive present. In other words, we stand in our own present, and experience the 'present' of the narrator, but where and when exactly that is, is not made clear – we hear the voice of an adult speaking to us, while the figure in the frame is that of a child.

Below are eight major structuring events from the opening chapter of the book. A contrast may then be made with the events which the film chooses to reproduce, together with the places in the book from which the film's narrative was taken. The page numbers are approximate.

page 1 Jem had his arm broken when he was nearly 13 years old.

page 2 The children look back at the injury and discuss the root cause of it.

page 3 Scout thought it possible that the root cause of the injury went right back in the history of Alabama.

page 4 Scout tells the narratee about Simon Finch, their ancestor.

page 5 We are told that it was customary for the Finch men to stay on the original Finch homestead.

page 6 Reference is made to the American Civil War and then Scout's father, Atticus.

page 7 We learn that Atticus's first two clients were hanged.

page 8 Scout reveals that Atticus used his earnings as a lawyer to finance his brother's education.

This concludes the first chapter of the book. As a narrative, certain of its elements are designed to emphasise the length and legitimacy of the Finchs' Southern heritage. The Civil War is part of their heritage, but no residue of bitterness attaches to its memory. It is marked as history.

The Finchs' position as a historically placed family acts as a context for Atticus's position; he is someone who is established and respected. The financial assistance he provided for his brother establishes his goodness and strength. The execution of his first two clients is directly attributed to their own stubbornness, rather than incompetence on the part of Atticus. However, a certain light-hearted and irreverent tone is used here, which seems to reappear in the book at intervals, and which sounds a note of reassurance and even complacency.

SELECTION

The film begins with a specific 'historical' setting. These examples are not broken down into individual shots, but are for the most part composite scenes.

1 Narrative event: a payment. Extract from voice-over:
'Maycomb was a tired old town when I knew it ... somehow it was hotter then ... Ladies bathed before noon ... and by nightfall were like soft teacakes with frostings of sweat and sweet talcum ... that summer I was six years old ...'

Walter Cunningham appears at the Finchs' house with a bag of hickory nuts, as part of his payment for the legal work Atticus has been doing for him. Scout runs to fetch her father, which Cunningham does not want – because he is ashamed of having to pay in such a way. Cunningham leaves and Atticus advises Scout that next time she had better not call him to the door. The general question of the poverty of all in the locality is introduced, further reinforcing other codes such as dress which announce this as the 1930s.

The introduction formed by the voice-over is taken from Chapter 1, page 11 of the book. But the drama of the payment and Cunningham's embarrassment are narrative devices, rather than the simple social statement they might appear to be. The delivery of the payment is not made in the way the film suggests, since we learn from Chapter 2, page 26 that the goods are simply found by Scout and Jem. No meeting with Cunningham takes place. The simple delivery of the payment matches the narrative intentions of the book, where other mysterious gifts are left (by Boo Radley). This scene serves to show, this time in an immediate and not a historical context, that Atticus is both respected and considerate, which helps to legitimise his role, just as the story of his old Southern background did in the book.

2 Narrative events: a clash between generations and a new friend. Jem is shown in a tree, refusing to come down until Atticus agrees to play football for the Methodists (Chapter 10, page 95 first mentions Atticus' reluctance to play football). Atticus leaves. A neighbour, Miss Maudie, is seen in her front yard. Dill Harris is introduced into the story (Chapter 1, page 12 in the book).

3 Narrative event: fear of a social 'outsider'. The children watch Mr Radley senior walk down the street.
Sound: Jem says 'There goes the meanest man who ever drew a breath of life'.
   (Chapter 1, page 18 has the Finchs' cook Calpurnia say, 'There goes the meanest man ever God blew breath into.') This starts the Boo Radley story in both film and book. The effect of the adult judgment is therefore lost in the film. The film appears at this point more concerned to establish the central importance of the children's view of their environment. The tale of the Radleys is recounted by Miss Stephanie Crawford (Chapter 1, page 17 in the book). At this point in the film's narrative, there appears to be a rush to establish story-lines and characters for the viewer, and this works to bring about an effect of 'crowding' and some confusion. The 'tired old town' suddenly appears to be packed with incident, and we lose the rather nostalgic feel of the original voice-over. In its place, the imaginative world of the children begins to assert itself.

4 Narrative event: running battles with an enemy. The children run to meet Atticus as he returns from work and pass Mrs Dubose on her front porch. She shouts at Scout in particular and then Atticus rounds the corner and is polite and kind to the old lady; he says she looks 'like a picture' (this element is taken from Chapter 11, page 106).

The way the film hops about in order to plunder the written text, so that a new narrative scheme is constructed, may be seen from this outline.

THEORIES OF SPECTATORSHIP:
VISUAL PLEASURE AND NARRATIVE CINEMA

One of the questions most asked about the effects of the cinema on its audience is what kind of pleasure it provides. There was a time in the 1970s when it looked as though an 'alternative' model of film could grow to challenge mainstream cinema. Laura Mulvey wrote a widely-discussed article about pleasure, mainstream cinema, and the possibility of a new kind of film which challenged the dominant system. This was 'Visual Pleasure and Narrative Cinema', which appeared in *Screen* in 1975 and was subsequently re-printed in *Popular Television and Film* (OUP, 1981). One of her central aims, which remains important, was to attack the way that the dominant system in film presents only certain types of pleasure. She thought that the narrative fiction film created images of women which were used for the gratification of men.

Mulvey argued that cinema had changed from the 'monolithic' system which flourished between the 1930s and 1950s, and that it had become easier to make small-scale productions. (This was before the late 1980s film industry crisis in Britain.) She contrasted the two modes of production as capitalist (big studio production) and artisanal (small-scale radical film). Of course, the way in which the artisanal sector (sometimes now referred to as 'independent cinema') raises finance is still based on capitalist notions of profitability, whatever is done ultimately with that profit. Mulvey did not examine this.

Mulvey believed that the 'magic' of Hollywood style arose largely from its skilled 'manipulation of visual pleasure'. Mainstream film (the classic realist text, as it is sometimes known) took the pleasures of watching erotic images and turned them into a reflection of the dominant system. Or, as Mulvey put it, the erotic was encoded into the 'language of the dominant patriarchal order'. This may sound difficult, but in fact simply means that Mulvey saw the most powerful institutions in society, including the cinema, as being run for the benefit of men; the dominant order, made up of powerful men (film directors, producers, financiers, etc.) takes something which all human beings appear to enjoy (erotic images) and turns them into one kind of 'pleasure' – heterosexual male pleasure. Mulvey draws on Lacanian psychology and feminist theory in order to support this view.

Pleasure in looking

Mulvey noted that the cinema offers a pleasure she described as 'scopophilia'. This isn't something you can catch exactly – it could be characterised as a voyeurism, subjecting other people to a controlling and curious gaze. The cinema, she argues, produces a fantasy in which the audience observes from a darkened auditorium. Individual members of the audience are isolated from each other by the conditions of viewing. The illusion is created of being able to look in on a private world. A sort of repressed desire in the spectator is then focused on the performer on the screen.

There may be some truth in all of the above, but other factors which should be taken into account include the varying nature of the material on the screen, the different compositions of the audience, and finally the different psychological states of individuals. Mulvey's theory is useful where it is used to describe a certain type of situation, rather than an established set of effects which always take place.

LACAN AND THE MALE GAZE

Mulvey referred to the French psychoanalyst Lacan, who used the idea that the human child's first recognition of itself in a mirror was crucial to the formation of the ego. He believed that this recognition predated language for the child. One of the conclusions Mulvey reached from this study of Lacan is that the cinema experience is close to the mirror experience. The mirror image seen by the infant is supposed to be fascinating, because the infant supposes that the image of itself is more complete than its real body – more 'perfect', if you like. The cinema experience is described as being just as fascinating. People tend to forget their immediate concerns if a film interests them (Mulvey called this 'temporary loss of ego'). However, in another way, the cinema reinforces the ego, because the stars on the screen tend to be 'ego ideals' that people can identify with.

Mulvey summarised her theory, conceptualising two distinct pleasures – the one where we sit in the dark cinema and 'peek' in at someone else's world, and the one where we identify with what is on the screen – applying psychological ideas to both types. She argued that 'scopophilic' spectatorship suggests a *separation* from what we see on the screen, because we, as subjects, are supposed to gain pleasure from the use of another person's image. The other type, narcissism, or the mirror experience, implies that we tend to gain pleasure from identifying with the image on the screen – quite different to wishing to control what we see. The first type is supposed to be a function of the sexual instincts, the second of ego libido.

Woman as image, man as bearer of the 'look'

This theory turns on the idea that, because we live in a sexist society, pleasure in looking (in an erotic way) has been split into two. The idea is quite easy to remember in terms of **active/male** and **passive/female**. It is, according to Mulvey's theory, the *male* look which determines what we see on the screen much of the time (there would be institutional reasons for this, since the film industry would be largely male dominated). In other words, the interests, obsessions, fantasies and so on which we see on the screen will be those of the dominant males who more or less 'run' the whole society.

An interesting idea which emerges at this point concerns questions about narrative. Since mainstream film uses women as erotic objects, the effect can be to slow down the story, because time is spent within the film on erotic contemplation. If the movement of the narrative is slowed down in order to give the male heterosexual spectator time to stare at the women on display, then we seem to have a clash between two 'dominant' practices. In some cases, the camera dwells so long on some physical aspect of a woman that the image becomes almost abstract, and is referred to as an icon (in semiology the term symbol, rather than icon, would be used). An example may be a close-up of a star's face, dwelt on for longer than the usual length of shot. Such an image may be further abstracted from the narrative by its use as a film poster designed to attract the audience's attention.

Buddy films: avoiding women?

Some narrative films have dispensed with the 'problem' of women as central elements of imagery, concentrating instead on a central male relationship (for example, as in *Butch Cassidy and the Sundance Kid*). Commonly called 'buddy movies', such films tend to make use of a male-centred eroticism. Some supposedly 'macho' war films contain such eroticism, but objections only seem to be raised when homoeroticism is made explicit (an example would be *Sebastiane* by Derek Jarman).

Ruling ideology?

Mulvey advanced the idea of a 'ruling ideology' which leads the male onlooker to identify with the male protagonist, or hero, in the film. Two things may be misleading here, however. To 'rule' at all, as argued earlier, an ideology needs to contain elements of 'subordinate' systems of belief (unless the social system it exists within depends on outright repression, when less effort may be put into taking account of opinion generally). If it contains elements of a subordinate system, then there will be moments in film when feminist, working-class, and ethnically-centred demands may gain expression (this is not to argue that such demands will always be progressive). It may also be the case that the more unpleasant aspects of the 'male gaze' are present in certain members of the audience – and that, instead of taking their lead from the mainstream cinema, such individuals go to other outlets in order to gain their pleasure or to reinforce their view of women.

It can be argued that to be male is not automatically to identify with a male protagonist. Some males will, for example, decide that the male hero of a film is not a model of the right sort of behaviour. This is easily seen when we look at films from the 1970s, some of which made claims for male powers which now seem outrageous – the James Bond films are an excellent example. As the James Bond series wore on, Bond changed from the confident chauvinist of *You Only Live Twice* to a less assured modern persona (aided also by a change of actor in the title role).

Mulvey argued that the male hero in the film acts as 'the bearer of the look'. This means that he possesses the controlling power of the male gaze and that the film 'sees' everything in the narrative through his eyes. The male spectator is therefore put in a privileged position, seeing the female characters through the gaze of the hero, sharing as it were in the power of the hero. This is certainly the case with a great many films, but some films seem to work deliberately to show the male protagonist as flawed. Does this mean that films which show a more 'realistic' picture of men are always outside the mainstream? Or does this mean that the mainstream provides a much wider variety of male types than Mulvey will allow?

In *The Last Detail*, Jack Nicholson plays a character whose control over events is limited, whose triumphs are small, whose attempts to impress women are a failure, whose life is frustrating. Is the 'anti-hero' less, or more easy to identify with than the perfect hero? There are many different types of 'anti-hero'. *Rambo* could be seen as a right-wing version of an anti-hero, whereas films like *Easy Rider* come more perhaps from the romantic leftism of liberal America.

Mulvey believed that films like *To Have and Have Not* (which opens with a clearly 'sexualised' female at the centre of male attention) work in such a way that the woman becomes the possession of the hero and therefore has her eroticism subjected to him; the spectator can share in this 'ownership' of the female through his identification with the hero.

Critics of Mulvey

Among the authors who disagree with some of Mulvey's points are Lapsley and Westlake (*see Screen*, vol. 33, no. 1). They argue that male and female spectators do not identify with characters simply in terms of their respective genders; instead, they will tend to identify with figures in particular 'fantasy scenarios'.

For instance, spectators identifying with Robocop have no wish to be robots but they approve of his methods of dealing with troublesome villains. Lapsley and Westlake made a study of the film *Pretty Woman*. They note that when Vivien, played by Julia Roberts, passes through the hotel lobby and attracts admiring glances, she is at once the object of the voyeuristic gaze and a point of identification for spectators of both sexes. In other words, both of Mulvey's categories come together at once. In this particular fantasy scenario she is looked at from the position she would *like* to be looked at from. If this is correct, we may agree that 'identification in the Cinema is multiple and dispersed, with both sexes identifying across sex boundaries' (Lapsley and Westlake, *Screen*). If there is a question mark over this argument, it might be connected with the idea that Vivien is, after all, a female character who is ultimately positioned by a male director working within a largely male institution.

Text or spectator?

Lapsley and Westlake ask why in *Pretty Woman* the central characters do not meet, fall in love and simply stay in a perfect state of harmony throughout the film? This seems to be connected with Todorov's idea, mentioned above, that films work between a state of equilibrium and disequilibrium. As we have seen, the Structuralist approach proposes that the text itself determines 'the way in which it is read', and therefore that the text positions the spectator. These authors note that ethnographic criticism puts more emphasis on the role of the spectator, pointing to the evidence of varied responses among spectators to the same text. They believe that a better approach would be to explain the relation between the text and the subject as a dialectic. This means that the spectator might 'produce' the text, changing it through his or her associations, memories, and so on. On the other hand, they say, the spectator is positioned by the text, because 'the shared meaning and the affective states' which come from an understanding of that message are determined by its narrative and other structures. The subject 'is both transforming and transformed'. By the very process of constituting the text, the spectator is in turn constituted by it and comes to care about the characters and their situation.

More questions on the 'look'

E. Ann Kaplan, in *Women and Film* (p. 11), describes the 'dominant' cinema as being composed of films which, taken individually are 'a feature-length narrative sound film made and distributed by the Hollywood studio system'. The 'classic' period of this Hollywood system, she believes, was 1930–1960.

Kaplan notices, from her position as a theorist in the 1980s, that film has undergone some important changes since Mulvey's description of the 'male gaze'. She argues that a whole crop of films place a man at the centre of a 'female gaze'. In some cases, she thinks that female characters exercise extensive control over the male ones. The problem, however, is that the 'controlling' women in these films also seem (p. 29) to lose their 'traditionally feminine characteristics' once they are in a position of dominance.

In an essay in *Women in Film Noir* (edited by E. Ann Kaplan), Janey Place argues that myth not only expresses dominant ideologies, it is also responsive to what she calls (p. 36) 'the *repressed* needs of a culture'. This is similar to the notion of 'dominant' discourses needing to take account of subordinate ones, in order to create meanings which will have an impact on subordinate groups. Although Place can see perfectly clearly that film noir is a genre of male fantasy, within which women are still defined by their sexuality, she is convinced that film noir represents a period of film where women are (p. 35) 'active, not static symbols ' and 'derive power, not weakness, from their sexuality'. Place's work reminds us that the needs of a culture change, and also that perhaps the 1980s may not be our only model for a 'female gaze'. We do not therefore simply have to hope for a 'progressive' development; there may be useful lessons for film-making in some periods of past practice.

It should not be imagined that all feminist film theorists agree with the Lacanian arguments about the sexuality of women. Some think that women have been kept in a 'childlike' position by the dominant currents of psychoanalytical film theory, and that new agendas need to be set. Julia Kristeva has in fact argued that it is impossible to know precisely what the 'feminine' might be, because all the ways we have of imagining the feminine have been constructed by men. There is much dissatisfaction also with the tendency to study the 'dominant' cinema instead of looking at what was really one of Mulvey's most important ideas: that critics should look at a cinema which *challenges* established film practice. At the same time, it is generally accepted that film has always, and should continue to provide female viewers with pleasure.

REALISM

There are various ways of understanding what realism means. Ian Watt (in 1957) argued that realism depends on the belief in a reality 'out there' that can be accurately experienced by human beings through their senses. Already we can see that the 'real' and 'realism' are two quite different things. The most obvious thing to say in the first place is that 'realism' is based on the 'real'. It is also a way of representing the real.

Because of the confusions about what realism actually is, we need to state the obvious straight away. Realism can mean 'realistic' (where a painting or a novel is said to be very much like the real situation depicted), but cinematic realism is a practice, an established convention. There is not even much agreement as to what a 'realistic' film is like.

Photography (upon which film is based) started its life as a 'realistic' medium. A photograph *looked* like the subject matter it represented. What seems more obvious to us is the great number of deficiencies photography had in its earliest manifestation. Some photographic methods, such as those which used paper negatives, produced a very grainy image. The images were in black and white; and, like modern photographs, they were two-dimensional and could not reproduce the sounds or smells of the environment in which they were made.

Considering these drawbacks, it seems odd that some still regard the reproduction of the image as central to notions of realism. For example, the theorist Kracauer produced five arguments in favour of the idea that film was naturally a 'realist' form. He believed that:

1 photography naturally inclined towards the straightforward recording of reality;
2 film involves photography as one of its elements;
3 photography is the decisive and most important aspect of film, the element which gives film its distinctive form;
4 film therefore shares with photography the inclination towards capturing 'unaltered reality';
5 realism is part of the nature of film and the major artistic value in the cinema.

Since everything Kracauer wrote here, apart from the second point, is dependent on the first proposition, and since that is wrong, it follows that most of what he says is hopelessly flawed. Photography can be entirely misleading in its representations. Even its technical abilities, as mentioned above, may be regarded as lacking in those elements which might bring it even close to the real world.

There are, in fact, some people who argue that the attempt to get close to the real world by carefully imitating aspects of its appearance is a lost cause and may in fact produce a sterile art-form which, in intellectual and emotional terms, keeps us at an even greater distance from actual experience. Artists who worked in the Cubist tradition argued that their representation of objects and people (showing for example different angles of faces, all on the flat surface of a single canvas) was more realistic than conventional graphic methods. Presumably they thought it closer to actual experience.

From what we learned earlier, we should be able to sort out some of the problems presented by questions of realism and representation by returning to semiology. Rather than call a photographic image of a person more 'real' than a description of the same person in words, we should say that the photograph is *iconic* – that is to say it *resembles* the thing in the real world that it represents. The 'portrait in words', on the other hand, is symbolic – if we saw the words from a distance, crowded together on a page, we would not say that they resembled the person being described. The written description, however, might give us a greater sense of the individual. So we should not substitute 'realistic' for iconic, since iconic is really a better description of the nature of a photograph.

An important complicating factor in film is the fact that it is usually presented as a narrative. We are not only looking at an image and judging how true or faithful it is as a representation, we are dealing with a realism which can only be appreciated if it takes the narrative form. When we see a film, we are likely to consider it highly 'unrealistic' if it does not obey the rules of story-telling. We have some doubts when a narrative is told in a different way. Some of Dennis Potter's work for television is a good example of an 'anti-realist' approach.

Realism and realist projects

John Corner, writing in the film magazine *Screen*, argued that the concept of realism was becoming more trouble than it is worth. His most important insight lay in the idea that theories of realism seem to be concerned with two things: in the first place, there is a trend which is interested in examining 'the pleasures of realist forms'. Secondly, there is an interest in the 'documentary potential' of realism, because these forms are thought to be suitable for examining society.

As a result, there seem to be two distinct realist projects happening at present (Corner applies this to television, but his work is useful in clearing the realist undergrowth which obscures our understanding of film). The first project is concerned with making films which are *like* the real (so-called 'naturalistic' film). The second is concerned with making films *about* the real.

Realism of form and realism of content

One way of making more sense of realism is to split it into two distinct parts: realism of **form** and realism of **content**.

For example, if form is taken to be an arrangement of parts, the structure of a text, then there are clearly films whose form is realist. The situation is slightly complicated by the fact that there are 'big' forms and 'little' forms; 'form' can mean the broad external structure of more than one text (i.e. 'film form'), as well as the internal ordering of content in a single text or a set of similar texts. The films which we could call 'realist in form' might arrange their representations in a way which feels broadly similar to our surface experience of life. Time might be represented sequentially. The documentary is thought of as *being* a realist form, but many films are thought of as *having* a realist form or structure.

John Fiske, writing in *Television Culture* (p. 24), notes that realism is often understood as a narrative arrangement (a form), and that this is especially useful for films or programmes that contain a large element of fantasy, because these fantastic actions and abilities 'conform to the laws of cause and effect, they are related logically to other elements of the narrative, and work according to ... a recognisable system'. Writing about television news, John Corner (*Screen*), notes that:

> 'viewers may clearly regard the News as real because of its form but if they do so they
> block questions about the nature of its construction.'

If content is taken to mean the collected elements which are contained within the form of the realist text, or which are organised by the internal structures of form, then a realist content must be the subject matter itself, rather than the order in which it is presented. Here, too, there are differences of opinion in defining what a realist content might be, but we might start from Raymond Williams' definition of realism in drama. He identified three main characteristics of such a realism:

1 it has a contemporary setting;
2 it represents human action and human beings;
3 it shows the lives and activities of ordinary individuals.

The emphasis on individual lives and experiences is very important in notions of realism in art and stems from a belief that representing this 'ordinary' experience is a way of understanding the concrete manifestation of moral, political and social questions, which would otherwise remain abstract.

If we remember the idea put forward by Stephen Neale, that genre or type is understood partly as an expectation held by an audience, then this could also apply to film form. John Corner draws an interesting distinction between the expectations brought by an audience to a form such as the news, and those they bring to a form such as drama. He suggests that audiences in each case bring different 'questions' to the individual texts. In the case of news, they may ask, 'Is this truthful?' In the case of drama, or the realist narrative film, they are more likely to ask, 'Is this plausible?'

Debates about realism: the classic realist text

Colin MacCabe, a one-time structuralist, began his investigation of 'realism' and the cinema by arguing that the dominant idea of realism comes from the nineteenth-century novel. He then made an attempt to define the structure of the novel. MacCabe's theory is that there is a **hierarchy of discourses** in the classic realist text/novel/film. In other words, there is an approval (expressed by the author, or by the text, and sometimes quite subtle) of one type of discourse in preference to another.

We must already be familiar with the idea of discourses – identifiable sets of beliefs/values/attitudes, expressed (in film) in a combination of language, image and sound. For example, a film about a robbery might display different discourses within the narrative. One discourse may be about poverty (perhaps the robbers are from a desperate class). Another may be about law and order (the robbers may harm the innocent). A third discourse may concentrate on the notion of love (policeman falls for injured bystander).

The main question is therefore: which discourse becomes dominant? In other words, which discourse does the film itself seem to favour? Does the film in fact make a choice at all?

The film MacCabe uses as his example of a classic realist text is *Klute*, which was made by Pakula and starred Jane Fonda and Donald Sutherland. This film was widely noted for its 'realism' upon its release, especially in the portrayal of the prostitute, Bree. The whole film is interspersed with scenes showing Bree (played by Fonda) talking to her psychiatrist, providing a commentary which is often in contradiction to the narrative flow. Bree is in fact unaware of many of the details of the narrative, whereas the detective who protects her (Klute, played by Sutherland) is in possession of more knowledge, power and insight. His role as a policeman and his gender ensure a privileged 'position', comparable to the position of the viewer. The film is also notable for the opportunities it provides for the exercise of the 'male gaze', and for the way in which the spectator is manipulated and positioned.

Realism and the novel

MacCabe uses an example from the great nineteenth-century novel, *Middlemarch*, by George Eliot. The author intends to show that two characters, Brooke and Dagley, are mistaken in their beliefs and are ignorant of reality. Eliot reproduces a conversation between the two. The author is in a privileged position, and uses the clear shortcomings of the characters she has herself created to make judgments about people and society in general.

The implication is, as MacCabe notes, that the narrative prose achieves its position of dominance because it is 'in the position of knowledge'. The narrative prose therefore claims to have 'direct access to a final reality'. The process MacCabe notes is fairly obvious. In her novel *Shirley*, Charlotte Brontë clearly disapproves of the working-class Luddites who attack the mill-owners. She reinforces her view of what the reader's attitude should be to them by making their main spokesman dishonest and repulsive. This is, if anything, an even cruder approach than that employed by Eliot; it is one which has found widespread favour in mainstream films.

To sum up the main point of this criticism of nineteenth-century narrative fiction, it appears that the author gives us a certain knowledge (often not possessed by the characters) which we can use as a yardstick against which to measure the discourses of the characters, whom we can then find inadequate. MacCabe believes that there are two important conclusions to his study:

1 The classic realist text cannot deal with the real as contradictory (in other words, it always tries to force a certain view of the world on its own material – no opposing positions are allowed to succeed).
2 The classic realist text ensures that the subject (the human subject) is placed in a relation of dominant specularity (i.e. the viewer is forced to see all questions raised by the narrative – morality, politics and so on – through the 'dominant' point of view expressed in the film).

Returning to questions on discourse

The questions we asked before were:

- Which discourse becomes dominant?
- Which discourse does the film itself seem to favour?
- Does the film in fact make a choice at all?

In the institution of the cinema, films often deal with similar subjects, while allowing different discourses to triumph. Vietnam War films are a good example of this. *The Green Berets* represents a discourse which emerges from a ruling-class ideology. The war is treated as a re-run of the Second World War, positioning the Americans as champions of morality, protecting a smaller ally. *Born on the Fourth of July* shows, and supports, the emergence of a soft-left humanism amongst Vietnam veterans – and by implication in the wider society. *Hamburger Hill* seems to approve of the weary right-wing positions adopted by the troops it represents and allows their expression of hostility to liberal politicians. *Platoon* sides with the counter-culture developed by the more liberal soldiers, while being openly critical of the group which sides with the vicious Sergeant Barnes. What all of these films share is a pre-occupation with the emotional and political impact of the war on American soldiers.

Criticisms of MacCabe

It is one thing to identify realism as being concerned primarily with narrative, quite another to claim that realist film texts are drawn from the form of the nineteenth-century novel. There are many other narrative sources which have provided realist film with models upon which to base itself: the theatre, the music-hall, popular folk-tales and legends, and so on. These forms should not necessarily be regarded as more progressive than the realist text. Terry Lovell, in *Pictures of Reality*, takes issue with the idea that some 'non-realist forms' (anarchic comedy and melodrama, for example), are as radical as some who have followed MacCabe like to make out.

In addition, MacCabe has since recognised that a single dominant meaning in a text, which constructs a single subject-position, cannot take account of variations in audience response. The notion of a 'preferred' reading has been circulated as a substitute, and takes us back to the criticisms made in Chapter 3, of the division of subject-positions into artificial 'bands' of audience response.

By way of explaining how the 'dominant' reading theory has major flaws even before we realise that an audience is free to reject or modify it, we could argue that, if there are contradictions in its own structure, it is by no means guaranteed that a film will be able to gain approval for the discourses of which it itself most approves.

It is often the case that a certain discourse is represented by a particular person, or group of persons. A useful example might be the version of the Robin Hood legend, *Robin Hood, Prince of Thieves*, starring Kevin Costner. Clearly, the people of whom we are meant to approve are on Robin's side: they reproduce a discourse based on friendship, faithfulness, trust, weakness turned to strength, ennobling love, etc. The opposing discourse, represented by the Sheriff (played by Alan Rickman) and his supporters, is nevertheless meant to appeal to us. Ultimately, there are important reasons in the narrative structure of the film for there to be a strong opposing contrast marked as evil.

The interests represented by the Sheriff are clearly marked by the film (and by legend) as the losing side. The film suggests that the discourses of good will overcome those of evil. But in this text, Robin himself is perhaps not a strong enough or interesting enough character to make dominant the discourses he represents in terms of the overall impression an audience receives. Janey Place noted a similar tendency in some examples of film noir; in this latter case, the 'narrative closure', in which the 'deviant' female is destroyed, is less powerful than the more enduring image of the 'alternative' mode of life the noir heroine represents. MacCabe's original scenario seems overly pessimistic and restrictive.

A way forward?

John Fiske provides an account (in *Television Culture*) of alternative ways of imagining how filmic (and televisual) discourses work in terms of the arguments and agendas they present to the viewer or subject. He mentions the fact that Barthes thought that narratives were (p. 89) an 'interweaving of voices that cannot finally be structured into any controlling hierarchy'. This is to throw away the best part of MacCabe's theory, which does at least recognise that some kind of 'will to power' is going on in many realist narratives. 'Discourse' is not a neutral term if it is taken to mean a way of suggesting certain subject-positions to members of an audience. If the will to power fails to achieve its objective (if, for example, a discourse is no longer relevant) then this does not take away the 'guilt' of its original intention.

A more productive notion, though one which is still limited and which does not go into the variations and contradictions which must surely appear in all texts, was advanced by Bakhtin. Fiske discusses how Bakhtin distinguished between 'heteroglot' and 'monoglot' texts. The 'heteroglot' text is one which is composed of many voices, where there is an inevitable struggle over meaning, as different groups attempt to put forward their own discursive variants. The 'monoglot' text attempts to control the various differences in ideas and arguments, advancing a single 'world-view' which it hopes will find acceptance. The first idea is probably more useful, since any good propagandist knows that the best form of persuasion is that which speaks in the accents of, and about the concerns of, the group to be persuaded. The ruling powers in cultural production cannot simply take account of their own ideological and cultural interests; if they want to stay in business, they must be able to adapt their messages to consumer taste. Voloshinov spoke of the way that language could be 'multiaccentual', though it appears that he made the mistake of imagining that the ruling powers always attempted to speak in a unifying, 'uniaccentual' voice. It is perhaps easier to 'divide and rule' if the ideological issue is pursued within a 'multiaccentual' approach.

FILM AND SOCIETY

Early Soviet cinema

Following the 1917 revolution, the Bolshevik leadership was quick to grasp the potential of using film as a propagandist device. It seemed the best and most immediate method of reaching an audience, which in many cases would be illiterate or only semi-literate.

The excitement generated by the new order gave a great boost to all those artists and writers who had found the outlook of the old regime restrictive. For a time, it seemed as though the beliefs and interests of the new authorities and those of the radical artist ran side by side.

However, the gradual transfer of power from the newly-created soviets to the Bolshevik state led to the beginnings of a split between the new authorities and many of the 'cultural workers' who had once seen Bolshevism as a liberating force.

Under Lenin, the repression of rival socialist and anarchist groups clearly signalled how rigid the Bolshevik view of socialism was to become. Although Soviet society ceased very quickly to be revolutionary, the idea of a socialist purpose, however distorted, continued to animate its artists and theorists for some time.

EISENSTEIN

Eisenstein's name continues to be the best-known of the Soviet directors who worked in early Russian cinema, partly because he was both a theorist and a film maker. Since Eisenstein was concerned to make an impact on audiences for explicit political ends, he developed theories about how best to manipulate their responses. The immediate problem in any such project would be how exactly to 'reach' people through the use (in the main) of images.

EISENSTEIN AND THEORY

Eisenstein was interested in the social and psychological conditions which he believed prevailed both in the society and more particularly in the cinema. It was a curious mix of what Andrew Tudor calls (*Theories of Film*, p. 20) 'fairly straight Soviet socialism and a Pavlovian behaviourism'. Since he was interested in communicating with an audience, his major preoccupation was with the language of film. In a similar way to semiologists working at much the same time, this interest in language often extended to attempts to find the basic units which contributed to meaning; according to Eisenstein, the equivalent of the sentence in language.

If it seems that the traditions of thought Eisenstein worked within were never really adequate to the task of understanding the behaviour of the human subject, it is even more obvious that the political 'foreshortening' of Marxism which took place under Stalin led to a constant pressure on Eisenstein to conform to an aesthetic which he did not find to his taste. The idea, held by the authorities, that audiences would respond to mundane reproductions of Soviet life under the heading of 'socialist realism' cramped Eisenstein's cinematic style.

MONTAGE AND THEORY

Eisenstein believed that film could be used to agitate his audiences and to inspire them with socialist ideals. He began to put his beliefs into practice through the use of a theory centred on montage, which remained the base of his whole conception of film. Montage as an idea grew from the dialectic which many Marxist thinkers still take to be one of the key concepts in socialist thought. Dialectics is the study of how meaning is created through the interaction of contradictory opposites. This is sometimes referred to as thesis, antithesis and synthesis. A proposition is made, its opposite is posed, and a new meaning is created as a result, the synthesis.

In the context of this theory, the simplest form of montage is nothing more than the development of narrative through shots which are related to one another. A *justified* cut is one which uses the first shot to prepare the viewer for a subsequent shot. For example, a medium shot of a person drawing a pistol can quite justifiably be followed by a close-up of the gun, of the person's face, or by a medium shot taken from a new angle. An *unjustified* cut would show a completely different scene, unrelated to the original. Of course, the question of what is or is not 'justi-fied' is really a matter of convention – established and accepted practice.

While some directors used montage simply as a way of building a narrative, Eisenstein attempted to use it to create meaning by making apparently uncon-nected shots 'collide'. The deliberate contrast between two shots was, he felt, both more creative and more in tune with the spirit of the dialectic. His belief in this method derived partly from the Kuleshov experiments, carried out in order to investigate audience response to images on the screen. These experiments had involved showing the expressionless face of a man intercut in turn with a series of other shots. The face would be followed by a shot of a bowl of soup, then by a coffin, and so on. The experiment discovered that the audience viewing these sequences thought that the face was showing whatever emotion appeared to be suggested by the shot following it; in the cases mentioned here, hunger and sad-ness respectively.

In his later years, Eisenstein moved away from his original position, putting less stress on the idea of the shots having to 'clash' to produce meaning. By 1938, he believed that montage could be defined as (Tudor, p. 32):

> 'two film pieces of any kind, placed together … [which] inevitably combine into a new concept, a new quality, arising out of that juxtaposition.'

FIVE TYPES OF MONTAGE

Andrew Tudor describes five types of montage in Eisenstein's system:

- **Metric** montage is the most straightforward method, based on the length of the film-strip. Each sequence on the strip is proportionate to the next sequence.
- **Rhythmic** montage involves considering the pattern of movement within a shot, which may set up a rhythm within it.
- **Tonal** montage is based on emotional effects brought about by light qualities and visual patterns in a shot.
- **Overtonal** montage is an elusive concept, based on the totality of all the elements of a shot. It appears that it is a process made up of all three of the previ-ous elements.
- **Intellectual** montage is where a direct point is made by the film-maker through the use of contrasting shots, so that one sequence is shown in a certain light by another. The audience is manipulated into 'reading' the sequences in a particular way.

Of these categories, it may be argued that *overtonal* montage should have been set by Eisenstein at the head of the whole list, since it appears to encompass at least three other elements. *Intellectual* montage appears to be the closest to propaganda. The reason for the emphasis placed on image-based theories in the early Soviet cin-ema is obviously derived from the fact that these films were silent. Notwithstanding the importance of investigating the image, modern theory still appears to be dominated by debates over visual impacts and effects, almost as a left-over from the days of the silent film.

Eisenstein went on to develop a theory of what he called *vertical montage*, the most obvious example of which would be the relationship between sound and image. Not only did Eisenstein's creative vision seek to break free from the restrictive ideologies of the Soviet state, it did not seem to fit his own system of laws and structures. Part of the reason for this was the clash between Eisenstein's socialism and the rather simplistic notions he had about being able to achieve complex emotional and political effects through film. He seemed convinced that there is some kind of 'one-for-one' relationship between cause and effect. The film would represent some situation or event which an audience, influenced by the power of montage, would respond to in an emotional manner; there would ultimately be some kind of socialist 'outcome' to this response. Such beliefs would appear to have been founded on assumptions, remain largely untested and seem not to have been based on research.

THE INFLUENCE OF SOVIET FILM

Some of the techniques which were pioneered in the early Soviet cinema have become part of the repertoire of film-makers. Andrew Tudor notes in *Film Theory* (p. 59):

> 'It is now a commonplace to assume that accelerated cutting raises the level of emotional tension in an audience.'

The idea of 'tempo' in montage is that the rate of cutting will have certain effects on an audience. But it is the assumption that audiences will behave in a predictable way, regardless of the immediate context, that we may now regard as mistaken. Such 'cause and effect' theories may be concerned less with liberating audiences than with 'mobilising the masses' in some social cause. The idea of accelerated cutting, for example, may in fact have no emotional effect upon an audience which is used to the rapid editing of the popular music video.

The French 'new wave'

The French 'new wave' (or *nouvelle vague*, a term first used by Giroud, the editor of *L' Express)* of the late-1950s to mid-1960s arose partly as a result of an economic downturn in the French cinema industry. Vadim's film *And God created Woman* of 1956 was made cheaply, and yet proved extremely profitable. It seemed logical for the industry to encourage low-budget films. It was in this way that an oppositional practice of sorts emerged on a national scale in France.

The films of Jean-Luc Godard are notable for the way in which they attempted to establish a different kind of filmic practice. Some believe that challenging dominant modes of film-making involves a change in the *way* that content/subject matter is presented. This means attending to the codes and conventions of meaning-creation in film, even more perhaps than to questions of content.

Although the French new wave marked a break with dominant modes of representation, some of the subject-matter, particularly in Godard's film, was of course highly familiar to audiences. Images were recycled from Hollywood films and put to new uses. Godard would deliberately mix different film conventions in order to force his audience into reassessing their relationship to what they saw. Instead of allowing members of an audience to be drawn into the narrative, various devices would be used to remind them they were witnessing a deliberate fiction. The action would be divided into sections or acts, in line with the Brechtian idea of providing opportunities for an audience to step back to a critical distance from the drama. Another method adopted by Godard was to allow the characters/actors to be interviewed on film, again making it difficult for the viewer to become engrossed in the familar pleasures of identification.

New wave has been associated with the '*Cahiers du cinéma*' group made up of influential film critics (including Chabrol, Godard, Truffaut, Rohmer and Rivette), first-time directors and a number of established film-makers. The films of Agnes Varda helped to set a style which other directors followed. Susan Hayward (*see Key Concepts in Cinema Studies*) suggests that new wave cinema falls into two historical periods: 1958–62 and 1966–8, the latter being more overtly political than the former. *Nouvelle vague* films include Varda's *La Pointe courte* (1954), Vadim's *Et Dieu crea la femme* (1956), Truffaut's *Les 400 Coups* (1959), Godard's *A bout de souffle* (1959), and Godard's *La Chinoise* (1967).

NEW WAVE AND TECHNICAL CODES

In terms of technical procedure, new wave films were characterised by what could be described as unjustified or 'jump' cuts, a lack of attention to eye-line matches, long shots which were allowed to continue without cuts, and the use of hand-held cameras. Locations were usually real ones, with available light used to shoot the action. Sound was often 'natural'; that is, recorded directly on to the soundtrack at the time of shooting, rather than being dubbed on afterwards in a studio.

The film industry, however, remains stuck with a dominant practice, which means that the highly codified nature of narrative construction favoured by Hollywood remains in force. The 'anti-realist' and 'anti-narrative' currents which have existed in film seem most likely to be seen only in those forms which are used for experimental purposes, such as animation.

Early Indian cinema

The first film programme to be screened in India was advertised on 7 July 1897 in *The Times of India* as 'The Marvel of the Century – The Wonder of the World'. The Lumière Brothers had brought the Cinematograph to a land ruled by the British; thus the announcement of the event was made in English throughout. The programme included 'Leaving the Factory' and 'Arrival of a Train', as well as three other items. Entry was fixed at one rupee, and the entire programme was repeated at 6, 7, 9 and 10 pm. It ran until 15 August.

The following year, from 4 January, more imported films were shown. An entrepreneur called Stewart used his Vitugraph to show what would now be called 'documentary' films such as *The Jubilee Procession*, together with some others which were clearly fictional: *Death of Nelson* is an example. Gradually, films with some reference to the sub-continent itself were introduced. For instance, in 1898, a Professor Anderson (and his assistant, 'Mademoiselle Blanche'), produced *A Train Arriving at Bombay Station*, *Poona Races '98* and *A Panorama of Indian Scenes and*

Processions. In the final months of 1899, an Indian film-maker appeared on the scene: H.S. Bhatvadekar showed two short films, one of a wrestling-match (set up for the cameras) and one of a man training a monkey.

On the first day of the new century, 1 January 1900, the Tivoli theatre used Edison's Projecting Kinetoscope to show twenty-five films, all of which had been imported from Europe. Another Indian, F.B. Thanawalla, produced films like *Taboot Procession* (a Muslim ceremony) and *Splendid Views of Bombay*, using a Grand Kinetoscope. Hiralal Sen, working in Calcutta in 1901, produced extracts from no less than seven popular Bengali plays. Four years later, J.F. Madan moved into regular production, introducing a system which foreshadowed the hugely successful Indian film industry. It was not until the years immediately preceding the First War, that fully-fledged dramatic productions began to be conceived. The first was R.G. Torney and N.G. Chitre's *Pundalik*, based upon the life of a saint. It was released on 18 May 1912, and was shown as a double-bill with a feature called *A Dead Man's Child*. *Pundalik* received extensive publicity and was extremely successful, though advertisements which claimed 'almost half the Bombay Hindu population has seen it' may be treated with caution.

One of the most important pioneers of the early Indian film industry was D. J. Phalke, who acquired a Williamson camera and the necessary supporting equipment in 1912. Lacking the funds to finance a major project, he made a short film using time-lapse photography. Using this short piece (the growth of a pea) as a kind of self-advertisement, he received financial backing from a dealer in photographic goods and produced as his next work a story from the *Mahabharata*, the tale of King Harischandra.

Phalke found that he was unable to obtain female actors for his first long feature, *Rajah Harischandra*. He had approached prostitutes with the request that they might consider appearing in the film, but no woman in any walk of life was prepared to risk the public disapproval which acting in film would entail. (The first actresses to work in the Indian cinema faced severe disapprobation from families and acquaintances.) Phalke solved his immediate problem by finding instead a young man to play the heroine Taramati. The film itself was released in 1913, to great acclaim; but the film industry at this stage was divided between those outlets showing western films, and the small beginnings of a genuinely indigenous cinema. Phalke showed those legends which his contemporaries knew through an oral tradition, a tradition given a physical presence in festivals, painting and sculpture.

Viewing the early films of Phalke, a number of practices make themselves apparent. In the first place, the actors appear often to look towards the camera, presumably for direction from Phalke. In addition, the inability to pan across a scene means that the action is played out entirely in front of the camera. The actors are prone also to a great deal of what seems, to a modern eye, the same 'unnecessary' movement apparent in western cinema of that time. It is sometimes difficult to be sure precisely which character is supposed to be the focus of attention. The other practice, one which makes Phalke stand out as a great innovator, is the use of trick photography to represent the remarkable and often supernatural events of the Indian legends. Phalke's cinema was especially close to his own culture, and grew out of a fund of images and discourses with which his audience was extensively familiar. These 'organic' links with his own culture were probably considerably stronger than the connection between the Russian avant-garde and the new 'working class' culture of the early Soviet Union. On some occasions, when Phalke's films presented gods from the Indian legends, members of the audience would prostrate themselves before the images on the screen. It is interesting to note that the technical and laboratory work, down to the loading of cameras, was left to Kaki Phalke, the director's wife. It may remind us of the essential role played by the women who were married to the first photographers, and how they still often remain 'hidden from history'.

On a promotional visit to London in 1914, where his work was greeted with great critical acclaim, Phalke was asked to make films in Britain. He did not take up this offer, choosing to return to India. During the First War, when interest in the cinema declined somewhat, Phalke and his associates had to struggle to keep their projects afloat. In 1917, however, he produced *Lanka Dahan*, another success. Phalke then helped to create the Hindustan Cinema Film Company, which produced two successful first films, *Krishna Janma* (*Birth of Shri Krishna*) and *Kalia Mardan* (*Childhood of Shri Krishna*) in 1918 and 1919 respectively.

Rivals to Phalke began to emerge: J.F. Madan (mentioned above) made Bengal's first silent feature film. Nataraj Mudaliar's *Keechaka Vadham*, made in Madras, appeared in 1919. As Firoze Rangoonwalla writes in *A Pictorial History of Indian Cinema* (p. 14) 'from 1917, there followed a period of 15 years when silent films held sway and some 1,280 were made in different genres'.

The development of the 'talkies'

In India, films using sound did not initially supplant silent movies, chiefly because the technology had not been developed on the sub-continent. Some two hundred films were made in the first year of sound. The earliest Indian performance containing sound was actually achieved using synchronisation of separate aural and visual sources.

The first Indian 'talkie' was *Alam Ara* of 1931, but sound brought problems which had not previously existed in the industry. There are sixteen distinct languages in India and therefore there was no longer a potential audience of several hundred million people for any one film. Even this does not reveal the full complexity of the problem; there were different versions of some languages, which were used in different contexts. The solution to this problem came partly through the use of a particularly potent genre of film, the 'music-drama' form. This genre, because it allowed for a profusion of song and dance, guaranteed that an audience would understand what the film had to communicate. Another solution was an extraordinary challenge to any film maker: the reshooting or even the complete remaking of a film in a number of languages. Chandulal Shah remade his famous *Gun Sundari* no fewer than three times, and in each case it was a commercial success.

Alam Ara (Light of the World) had achieved its popularity through the use of a simple mixture between Sanskrit-based Hindi and Persian-based Urdu, and the presentation of seven songs which became popular in India.

THE CULTURAL FUNCTION OF INDIAN CINEMA

The Indian cinema had a strongly 'integrative' effect on Indian culture as a whole. It continues to have such an effect, and remains a central institution, similar in some respects to that of Hollywood in the 1930s. The early industry had little in the way of serious financial backing, with the result that it was more or less an 'improvised' industry. Western influence did eventually creep into the industry in the 1920s, and some films were made which owed much to American cinema in particular. Universal Studios succeeded in penetrating the Indian market and by the mid-1920s was offering Indian film theatres a total of fifty-two features, fifty-two comedies, and fifty-two newsreels a year (*Indian Cinema*, p. 41). The Indian film industry began to make new progress at the same time as the movement for independence from Britain began to grow in strength.

Myth and religious tradition was used extensively as subject-matter. The strong cultural resonance of such material helped to ensure its popularity across the country. Rangoonwalla (*A Pictorial History of Indian Cinema*, p. 16) believes 'faith in divine deities as miracle workers plus a craving for magic solutions to the various problems of life lie behind the weakness for the mythological epic and its sister genre, the devotional'. It was not just film-makers in the silent era who concentrated on such traditions; the interest in this material continues to the present. In Rangoonwalla's opinion, 'the most popular myths have been those from the epics Ramayana and Mahabharata and the countless tales connected with Lord Krishna from his childhood onwards'. He is clearly opposed to what he sees as the melodramatic qualities of much production emerging from the religious tradition, calling the majority of films 'pseudo-devout', repetitious and mechanical, and expressing concern about the sexualised appearance of 'goddesses and other revered females'. Other themes treated include tales from folklore, love stories, and adventures featuring outlaws and bandits. Non-myth genres, Rangoonwalla believes (p. 24) 'have functioned as mythological byproducts', existing in 'a supernatural miracle world and promoting old-world beliefs and superstitions'. Other genres included historical films, biographical pictures (or 'biopics'), romances, and 'social' films, dealing with a range of public issues. A trend for dealing with modern subject-matter was pioneered by Dhiren Ganguli, who made a series of satirical films in the silent era, including *England Returned* in 1921 and two short features, *Lady Teacher* and *Marriage Tonic*. The advantage of using English titles was that they catered to the 'elite' audience used to watching English and American imports. One of the most influential films of the 1930s was *Devdas*, a social drama of 1935 which showed the destruction of a love affair by class differences. Directed by P.C. Barau, two versions were made, one for Bangali audiences and another for Hindi filmgoers. Socially progressive statements, like those found in *Devdas*, became popular, but also gave rise to what Rangoonwalla calls (p. 38) 'currents of gloom' and 'frustration as a credo'. Throughout the twentieth century, films focusing on social problems were extremely popular. One theme which recurs, is that of Muslim and Hindu unity, used often because of the violent confrontations which took place between the two communities after the country's partition.

One enduring feature has been the use of music, to the extent that many films approach the status of musicals, even where the intended genre is quite different.

Some movies broke from this tradition, though others retained music but kept it in the background. In a number of cases, however, narrative would be used to lead up to a major song. The 1970s saw a more humane approach to a number of important issues, including prostitution and the conditions faced by lowly workers like dancing girls and singers. Literacy, domestic drudgery and independence from the British all provided material for films. One theme which failed to ignite a new genre was found in *Amar Jyoti* (*Immortal Flame*) produced in 1936 by V. Shantaram. It featured a species of female revolt, in the person of a woman pirate who punishes and enslaves men and incites other women to do the same. A year later, the same director made the powerful *Duniya Na Mane* (given the English title *The Unexpected*). The actress Shanta Apte played a young woman who refuses to accept an old man as her husband. In the 1950s, the Indian Prime Minister, Pandit Nehru, made a call for children's films to be made, which brought about a deluge of such dramas. Overseas influences on the style of films can be seen in films like Bimal Roy's 1953 *Do Bigha Zamin* (*Two Acres of Land*), which was close in spirit and execution to Italian neo-realism. Other 'leftist' films of the period, like Raj Kapoor's 1956 *Jagte Raho*, found a ready market in what was then the Soviet Union, and followed the success of Kapoor's *Awara* in the same country in 1951.

Censorship of films was not unknown: during the Emergency of the 1970s, a film called *Aandhi* (*Storm*) attacked the then Prime Minister, Indira Gandhi and was withdrawn from circulation, while another controversial production (*Kissa Kursi Ka*, or *The saga of the chair*) was seized and burnt in the same period. In the normal course of events, censorship in India is enforced by the Central Board of Film Censors (set up in 1952), based in Bombay, with regional offices in Madras and Calcutta.

Rangoonwalla (p. 100) considers that, in the years before independence, 'censorship was mainly political'. References to the struggle for independence and Indian national leaders were usually excised, though there were considerable differences in the degree of censorship exercised in different provinces. Owing to the differences between regions, the size of the country, and the inconsistency of regulation, film-makers have resorted to a number of ploys to present various unsuitable events (like sexual encounters, for example), as initiated by accident, while ritual dances are used to spell out the theme the director wishes to represent. The output of the Indian film industry is phenomenal: between 1931 and 1978, 13,560 films were made. The current output is some 500 to 600 films a year. One of the most important film directors was undoubtedly Satyajit Ray, who first emerged in 1955 with a film called *Pather Panchali* (*Saga of the Road*). Ray had the ability to make films belonging to a range of genres. In 1960, he produced *Devi* (*The Goddess*), a critical study of religious dogmatism. Films by Ray include *Postmaster, Monihara, Mahanagar, Seemabaddha*, among many others.

Commercial problems in contemporary Hollywood

During the 1980s and early 1990s, Hollywood seemed to rely heavily on a succession of action-adventure films. Profit returns at the end of the 1980s reached a peak with *Batman* in 1989. As has often been the case before, Hollywood tended to go overboard for whatever had most recently been popular and successful. Ever more elaborate special effects, for example, were thought to be one way to ensure a good return on an investment. Strictly speaking, the film industry is now a multi-national enterprise that simply speaks with an American accent and uses American locations. Four of the seven major studios are now owned by companies which are not native to the US.

If we talk about the 'Hollywood studio system', a fairly heavy emphasis could be put on the word 'system'. During the golden age of films in Hollywood, from the 1930s to the 1960s, the system was an integrated operation. The studios controlled the whole cycle of production (they owned the facilities) and distribution (they owned the cinemas). Writers, producers and directors in this 'golden age' were employed full-time as part of the whole operation. The decline began when the studios were forced, as part of an anti-monopoly drive by government, to sell off the cinemas they owned.

Studios are now run as divisions of even bigger businesses. Jobs depend on the studios always making a bigger profit than the previous year. Out of an average of between fifteen and twenty films made by each studio every year, most of the profits will come from perhaps two of those films. Which of the films will make a substantial profit is of course not known in advance.

Spending huge sums of money is no guarantee that a film will be successful. In fact, whole sections of the film industry can be destroyed by over-spending. *Heaven's Gate*, made by Michael Cimino and released in 1980, was a financial disaster, and the more recent *Revolution* destroyed the Goldcrest company which produced it.

There are definite constraints on the types of film which are made, since the average age of consumers lies between seventeen and twenty-five years old. It is worth noting that the 1960s was a particularly difficult period for Hollywood. The studio system of the classical era came to an end. Television was a major rival, at the very time when the French new wave was turning out films which did not depend on vast amounts of capital investment.

The industry was revived by the *Rocky* films and by Lucas's *Star Wars* saga. Hollywood began to look for a formula based on previous successes. However, an increasingly sterile cycle of narratives can only sustain profitability for so long, before a new formula is needed. That, in its turn, will have a tendency to become over-used.

HISTORIES: BRITISH FILM

American penetration of the British market began as early as 1915, when the Essanay company required its British exhibitors to take the Essanay output in its entirety, together with the Chaplin films which formed the real centre of the attraction for audiences. Block-booking meant that British theatres were unable to afford space for the relatively small output of its own industry's films. An attempt was made in 1917 to require such outlets to show a specific quota of British films, but the proposition failed and the British distributors were at the mercy of the stronger American industry.

Between 1945 and 1960 the British film industry was known largely for a series of light comedies, a number of war films and for the more dramatic work of directors such as David Lean, who made *Brief Encounter* in 1945. A series of films which examined the life of the English working class began with Jack Clayton's *Room at the Top* in 1959. In the 1960s, when the industry was doing well, the production of the Hammer Horror cycle and the 'Carry On' series helped to attain a peak figure of 126 films released in a single year. The decline in vigour, at least, is shown by the fact that this number had fallen to thirty-eight films in 1989, and twenty-five by 1990.

In the early 1980s British films were again successful and the industry appeared set to continue to grow in strength. *Chariots of Fire*, produced by David Puttnam, took four Oscars. The following year there was another highly successful Goldcrest production, *Gandhi*. This film won eight Oscars. Films such as these brought in more money, but also a host of illusions about competing with Hollywood. This was possibly the worst mistake that some influential producers and directors could have made. The British industry has been unable to sustain losses on unsuccessful films, whereas Hollywood has both enough capital, and sufficient power of distribution, to thrive on one or two commercial successes out of a total of some twenty projects.

In some respects it might be argued that modern audiences expect more from a film than the generations who went before. But these expectations would appear to relate to certain elements only, such as special effects. A common argument is that the virtues of 'sound plot' and credible characterisation have been neglected in order to reflect the latest technological advances. To many, however, the most urgent problem is not one of artistic credibility and integrity, but of structure and finance. Investment in the industry had fallen from an estimated £270 million in 1986 to under £50 million in 1990. David Puttnam noted what he described as an 'extraordinary paradox', in that audience figures are climbing and the construction of multiplexes will help sustain a growing demand for films, at a time when production is dropping. Clearly, the large American distributors will reap the rewards of this growth in audience numbers.

Of course, part of the problem lies not just in how much money is being spent, but where exactly it is likely to go. If the result of financial constraint is sometimes better film-making, and the result of generous funding is another *Revolution*, then some may argue that the industry performs badly just when it is awash with money. In reality, however, the problem is made worse by the danger that the whole structure of the industry may fall into decay; the major studio at Pinewood, which was once used to produce the Bond films, now has the appearance of a disused aircraft hangar. Camera operators and producers may move overseas, production and editing facilities may be broken up into smaller parts and hived off. Any sort of recovery might therefore be faced with a reduced capacity to sustain it. A return to more manageable projects which reflect British culture, represented by films like *Trainspotting* and *The Full Monty*, has inspired more positive hopes for the future of British films.

A NON-COMMERCIAL MODEL?

Some directors work on a different basis altogether, avoiding the traditional model based on commercial success. By taking a different route they must also accept smaller public access to their films. Derek Jarman, for example, deliberately kept his projects cheap and manageable so that he could concentrate on the message he wanted to convey. His budget for *Imagining October* (1984) was only £3,800. At the time the average production cost for a British film was £4,000,000. In *Art Monthly*, Michael O'Pray declared, 'Jarman's films are the work of a painter in their refusal to tidy up the edges, or to cover the canvas.'

In *Take 10 Contemporary British Film Directors* (eds Hacker and Price, p. 211), Peter Greenaway, who found his influences in films like Bergman's *The Seventh Seal*, said that:

'no film maker should be castigated for not conforming to the dominant mode. There is no one way to make a film. The cinema community makes itself look very conventional – their model for cinema seems narrow.'

FINANCE AND GOVERNMENT

The British film industry relies on various sources for its funding, one of which is an organisation called 'British Screen' which was aided by the government with a grant of £1,500,000 a year to stimulate film production. With the uncertainty of the renewal of this grant, other shareholders such as Rank became scared by the risk and took their money out of film production. Government policies have proved to be another hurdle for the industry. In 1985 the Eady Levy, which had given producers a share of cinema takings to make new films, was abolished. In 1986 capital allowances for investing in British films were abolished.

As long as a competitive model is applied to a 'national 'industry, then the mirage of a purely British cinema will continue to misdirect resources. Some projects, such as the British Film Institute's support for productions like *Young Soul Rebels* (despite that film's major weaknesses as a political statement and as an artistic achievement), point to an alternative model of practice, while revealing currents of British life which might never otherwise have reached the screen. The story of the production of *Memphis Belle* seems to illustrate a failure of nerve which is directly linked to the problem of achieving adequate funding for 'national' projects. A Warner Brothers production made in 1990 and produced by David Puttnam it had originally been intended as a study of RAF Lancaster bomber crews in the Second World War. Financial backing could not be found for a British story. The result was a film which deals with an American bomber crew. Perhaps the project was all along limited in 'ideological' terms.

Entertainment: no boundaries between film and theme parks?

The US industry has already recognised a vast potential European market for reproductions and reflections of the filmic experience. It will probably not be long before films are actually made with the theme park in mind, instead of being recreated in three dimensions once an audience has already experienced the adventure on film.

The use of a kind of 'wrap-around' virtual or computer reality would certainly have intrigued Eisenstein, since the emotions called up by simulation rides like 'Back to the Future' at Euro-Disney are at least more easily measurable than the 'pathos' he proposed as the ultimate aim of advanced film-making. The immediate limitations of this kind of entertainment are exactly those felt by audiences who have sat through the more mundane parts of a Spielberg adventure – the emotions of the audience are only engaged at the most basic and superficial level. Action will continue to be the key to these theme park recreations of filmic experience.

Universal have opened a theme park in America and would like to site a second one near Paris or London as part of their studio complex which could become a base for a huge European film business. The French government has offered Universal millions of pounds in grants. The reluctance of the British government, by comparison, to fund the industry to any significant degree, has left the way open for private investment; one of the most significant examples of this being the decision of British Satellite Broadcasting (now BSkyB) to invest in film production. In addition, the drama department of the BBC is to invest up to £3 million in six theatrical feature films a year. Channel 4 and some of the ITV companies are also to invest in film.

These diverse sources of finance underline an important aspect of British film production; it is dependent on money from the television and video sectors, showing that film may not often be made primarily for cinema release, but for the television, cable and home video markets. What does this mean for film as a distinct element of European culture? In recent years Hollywood has been able to thrive on video sales, which had previously seemed to threaten its profitability.

Looking for the formula

Once audiences had seemed to tire of action-adventure films, a genre which produced some good box-office returns was romantic comedy. *Pretty Woman*, *Green Card* and *Ghost* all formed part of this wave of sentiment. They were followed by the release of *Love Potion No. 9*, *The Marrying Man*, *Frankie and Johnny*, *The Favor*, *LA Story*, and many others. Why, however, should romantic films be popular during an economic depression? Elizabeth Kendall, in a book called *The Runaway Bride*, describes the reasons as follows (quoted in 'Farewell Romeo, Hello Romeo', Mike Bygrave in *The Guardian*, 6 June 1991):

> 'Depression romantic comedies responded to their audiences' loss of faith [in the social and economic system] by making a virtue of personality traits usually thought of as feminine ... [audiences] wanted to watch the woman, who was supposed to be weak, become strong, and the man, who was traditionally strong, become vulnerable.'

Bygrave makes the interesting observation that the male and female protagonists sometimes meet in a setting where the class differences which sometimes exist between them may be more easily overcome, thus revealing their 'true selves'. He also repeats *Time* magazine's comment on *Ghost*, one modern version of the romantic comedy: 'Hollywood's … definition of a perfect couple is a man and a woman, one of whom is dead.'

Radical voices

A number of mainstream films in the early 1990s used women characters to portray what some have called the 'female usurper' (Joan Smith, *The Guardian*, 9 July 1991), an ambitious woman who enters a male preserve. The audience is perhaps supposed to feel that the disasters which occur are entirely deserved. If we follow the theory that a dominant mode of representation will not register an awareness of trends in society, but will wish to engage with them in order to provide fresh material for representations (just as advertising does in order to restock its own displays), then it comes as less of a surprise that 'versions' of feminism should be produced by mainstream male directors.

Ridley Scott's *Thelma and Louise* was described by many critics as a 'feminist road movie'. (Scott's own *Blade Runner* was certainly not noted for its pro-feminist stance – in fact, its representation of the female 'replicants' caused not simply unease but also protest amongst feminist critics.) At the core of the film is the attempted rape of Thelma in a car park. Louise shoots dead the man involved, after he has released his intended victim. Rough justice is meted out to unpleasant men throughout the film, but the nature of their actions leads Thelma and Louise to appear as largely similar to other heroes of movies which seem to thrive simply on mayhem and the motivations of revenge. Meanwhile, feminist directors have spent many years producing films which have failed to reach the mass audience. *Thelma and Louise* made money, with the result that the mainstream film industry has had to take this genre seriously.

Criticisms which remain, however, have concerned the fact that the female heroes of many films such as *Alien* and *Terminator 2* remain trapped in the action-adventure genre. Do feminist concerns stand a chance of a full representation in a genre which some believe sets severe limitations to future developments? It depends partly upon the gender of the director. It seems almost laughable that a 'feminist' agenda should need to be mediated not simply through the concerns of Hollywood, but also through the vision of a male director, when there are plenty of women making films which explore such concerns more directly. Kathryn Bigelow's *Blue Steel* is an example of a film which takes an unremarkable idea and uses it to investigate 'male anger' in a convincing psychological framework.

It is the question of who has power over production and distribution, however, which may deny the circulation of alternative images, representations and ideas to the wider audiences. The female lead in the Costner *Robin Hood*, Mary Elizabeth Mastrantonio, noted that (*see* Cynthia Rose, 'What happens after *Thelma and Louise* in *The Guardian*), 'Even the most successful director rarely has the final say.'

An independent practice?

E. Ann Kaplan, discussing future strategies for independent feminist film in her *Women and Film* argued that (p. 195):

'we have been so concerned with figuring out the "correct" theoretical position ... that we forgot to pay attention, first, to the way subjects "receive" [read] films; and second, to the contexts of production and reception.'

Kaplan faces the problem of the under-representation and marginalisation of feminist independent film-making by referring to the vital need to examine problems of production, exhibition and reception. She clearly identifies (p. 196) the contradictions which have 'dominated alternate practices of all kinds.' These are:

1 The fact that alternative film-makers have had to rely for funding on the very system they oppose.
2 'Anti-illusionist' (and presumably anti-narrative) films have used 'cinematic strategies' that are difficult for audiences to understand.
3 American alternative film-makers, in particular, have not had the opportunity properly to exhibit their films once they have been made.
4 The film-makers who have been most intent on changing people's 'ways of seeing' have found that the only audiences they are able to reach are those which are already committed to their values.

Kaplan believes that alternative film practice is (p. 197) 'never independent of the society in which it is embedded'. The solution is therefore to make new *institutions* which are independent of the mainstream. In terms of film theory, Kaplan emphasises the central position of pleasure, since for many feminist film practitioners and theorists, it is (p. 205) 'here that patriarchal repression has been most negative'.

Doing the right thing?

Representations of the experience of black Americans seem to have caused more disquiet when those providing the images have themselves been black, than when white directors have used black actors in roles which have sometimes been little more than supporting cameos. The shameful racism of D.W. Griffith's silent *Birth of a Nation* is perhaps unusual, but there are many films whose portrayal of the 'African American' is just as ridiculous. One of the most difficult genres in this respect is the Southern drama or adventure. Representations of black people as loyal simpletons abound in films like *Gone with the Wind* and more particularly in that maudlin vehicle for Shirley Temple, *The Littlest Rebel*. History is in some respects rewritten in such narratives. Progress of a sort was made under the liberal banner of *To Kill a Mockingbird*, but only in the sense that the film stands on the side of justice for whoever is disadvantaged. There is little movement here in the way that black people are represented, and few psychological insights into their position. Alan Parker's *Mississippi Burning*, more than two decades after *Mockingbird*, was notable for its return to muted representations of black characters. In both films, the black experience is mediated through white 'authority figures'.

In moving to a contemporary black experience in an urban setting, Spike Lee's films present black characters who are allowed to speak for themselves and who are far from idealised. This is particularly the case in *Do the Right Thing*, where the inhabitants of a close-knit neighbourhood become increasingly polarised during a heat wave. Irritation caused by an exclusively Italian-American 'hall of fame' in a local pizzeria blows up into a climactic scene in which the pizza house is set on fire. At one point, the extraordinary display of verbal clashes is represented by a series of ritualistic outbursts in which members of each ethnic group vent their spleen on the negative characteristics of some other race. Lee's direction allows an almost alarming closeness to each character, and yet through various technical devices allows us to maintain a critical distance from the passionate irrationality they display. The suspicions of the black section of the populace seem confirmed by the end of the film, and yet there is a sense also that their prophecy was self-fulfilled. Lee's *Jungle Fever* also depends for much of its impact on representation of a kind of endemic racism, as a black lawyer's affair with a white woman becomes the object of a series of virulently negative reactions from all ethnic communities. Lee's films remain examples of a positive cinematic project. They not only avoid some of the restrictive practices of realism, thus opening up some kind of critical distance between the narrative and their audience, they also raise controversial questions with a serious intention. This must be one of the vital differences between directors who use issues of public concern as gimmicks, and directors who are closely involved with issues of which they have direct experience. Despite its flaws, Lee's *Malcolm X* is also notable for its powerful representation of the black American community.

SUMMARY

■ EARLY CINEMA

This chapter begins by examining early cinema, which is so instructive about the development of film technique and narrative. While the 'dominant' mode of representation may look 'natural' to us, it is in fact only one current of film technique.

Eadweard Muybridge pioneered the study of human and animal movement, using a battery of cameras which each took a single photograph of the subject as it moved across a defined and measured space. Two of the earliest film-makers proper were the Lumière brothers. Their audiences were unused to seeing the technical form of film, and could marvel at how the representation of reality was brought to them. It would be easy to see very early film as having nothing in common with more 'sophisticated', narrative-based experiments, but the first act in all attempts to communicate is choice of subject (in the case of the Lumières, setting up the camera outside their factory). The next stage is the reproduction of the event for an audience.

The frame in television and cinema is understood as the rectangular or 'square' outline which marks out the focus of our attention. Film-makers are generally regarded as working within this space.

■ The use of film during the Boer War: 'actuality' and propaganda

The technical constraints of early film-making resulted in a rather limited representation of the war, but again comparison with a modern example is instructive. Footage from the Boer War resembles very closely the extremely 'static' film of the Falklands War.

Early film in general, however, drew on a variety of popular sources of entertainment. Much early film owed its form to the tradition of magic-lantern slides and dioramas which flourished in the nineteenth century.

■ NARRATIVE AND EARLY CINEMA: 'GENRES' OF EDITING AND NARRATIVE CODES

When the cinema began in around 1895, the codes with which we are familiar did not exist in their present form. A transition was made from the 'cinema of attractions' to something we would regard as 'modern'. Some critics suggest that there are four distinct 'cine-genres' in the early period, 1895–1910. The genres are thought to be the **single shot** narrative, the genre of **non-continuity**, the genre of **continuity**, and the genre of **discontinuity**. Some theorists believe that 1907 marks the beginning of the now dominant 'classical' mode of representation. 1919 is regarded as the year by which the most significant narrative conventions had been established.

The cinema should be seen as a system which exists as a relationship between 'production and representation'. The production side of the equation has three elements: the actual production of films for public display, exhibition, and reception (the audience's consumption of the product).

The chapter goes on to consider 'screen time' and how it differs from real time.

■ TYPES OF SHOT

Types of shot are described in order to give a straightfforward idea of how shots are set up using angle and distance. Film also moves backward from and forward to the subject. The descriptions of angle and distance are set out. Distance is specified as long shot, medium shot and close-up. Angle is understood as high angle, straight angle and low angle.

The categories of distance may be annotated as **LS, MS** and **CU**; angle may be described as **HA, SA,** and **LA**. Any shot may be described as a combination of a certain distance and a certain angle. The nine possible combinations are given as:

LS/HA, LS/SA, LS/LA
MS/HA, MS/SA, MS/LA
CU/HA, CU/SA, CU/LA

Shots appear as establishing shots, insert shots, close-ups, over-the-shoulder shots, point-of-view shots, and reaction shots.

■ Editing

This is also carried out according to established practices. Terms include montage, cross-cutting, fading in and out, and flashbacks.

■ Shot choice: paradigm and syntagm

A paradigm is an example of a class of objects, while a syntagm is an element which follows another element in a recognised sequence. After a film-maker has decided *what* to shoot, the two questions which must follow are *how* to shoot it and how to *present* or edit what has been shot. Deciding how to shoot an object (for example) is known as choosing from the **paradigmatic** range. If we were to take the example of a tree, it is clear that the one type of tree had been chosen from other available types. But this is not quite what is meant in the case of film, because this would ignore the technical codes which may be used. The director of a film might decide to take a shot which showed the tree in a soft light from medium close-up, using a straight angle. The meanings we gained from the shot would depend on its relationship to the other possible shots which could have been taken, from different distances, under different lighting conditions, using different angles. Deciding how to present what has been shot is known as choosing from the **syntagmatic** range. In the case of the shot of the tree, this means deciding which shots will come before or after it, and also how the movement from one shot to another will be made. If the shot which followed our original paradigmatic choice was of a tree-cutter, then this would seem to suggest a particular type of narrative choice.

■ WAYS OF UNDERSTANDING FILM NARRATIVE

Narrative is a way of organising material. It happens to have become the dominant form in cinema, but it is also very widely used in other disciplines. Edward Branigan describes narrative not simply as a chain of events, but as an 'activity that organises data into a special pattern which represents and explains experience'.

Vladimir Propp is introduced as a very important example of a theorist of narrative who noticed that folk-tales contained many similar themes dealing with the same basic situations and struggles. They appeared also to have the same 'stock' characters in each case.

Some critics have argued that the film as narrative is based on the fairy-tale or folk-tale, sharing their limited number of characters and plots.

■ Readers and narratives

Branigan notes that subjects tend to remember a story in terms of what he calls 'categories of information' and that a narrative schema would encompass the following:

1 introduction of setting and characters;
2 explanation of a state of affairs;
3 initiating event;
4 emotional response or statement of a goal by the protagonist;
5 complicating actions;
6 outcome;
7 reactions to the outcome;

These, rather than details of shot and angle, are what people tend to remember, according to this approach.

■ Discourse in narrative forms

Narratives 'position' readers. It is possible to describe a system of 'participants': according to this theory, no less than six participants take part in the relationships set up by the text;

Real → **Implied** → **Narrator** → **Narrattee** → **Implied** → **Real**
author   **author**   **reader**   **reader**

■ FIVE CATEGORIES OF TIME IN THE CINEMA: TECHNICAL APPROACHES

An understanding of cinematic time can be helped using a system described by Genette and adapted by Chatman. A comparison is made between 'discourse time' and 'story time'. Discourse time is the time it takes to narrate an event. There is a list of five possible 'matches' between discourse and story time: summary; ellipsis; scene; stretch; and pause.

Christian Metz identifies five channels of information in film: the visual image, print and other graphics, speech, music, and noise and sound effects.

Sound tends to make the time in film 'feel' more concrete and natural. According to the theorist Reisz, sound is either **synchronous** or **asynchronous**. Synchronous sound comes from within the frame and the editor must work to synchronise it with the image. Asynchronous sound comes from outside the frame. Another set of useful terms describes the way sound works with or against an image. **Contrapuntal** sound is opposed to or in counterpoint with the image. **Parallel** sound is connected with the image, and reinforces it. The idea that the soundtrack works either with or against the image produces what some believe is the basic 'dialectic' in aesthetic terms.

'Genre' is another important concept covered in this study of film. It is usually taken to mean 'type'. At first sight, anyway, films are easily sorted into types: musicals, westerns, horror movies, comedies, and so on. From genre we may be confident that setting, characters, symbols in the frame, the type of conflict shown, and the way that the conflicts are resolved, will be recognised. However, if we agree with the idea that 'the cinema' is not simply the collection of institutions which physically produce and circulate films, but that it also includes the wider *social* institution, which must be made up of audiences as well, then we should accept Stephen Neale's notion that genres are 'systems' of 'expectations and conventions' that circulate between 'industry, text and subject.' The idea of an audience's foreknowledge (knowledge of genre in advance, based on experience of other texts) will obviously lead to a certain set of expectations. It is these expectations which are then used to catch the attention of an audience, whenever a film is being publicised.

Examples of audience foreknowledge and expectation are given in this chapter, as well as an analysis of how part of *To Kill a Mockingbird* was translated from book to film.

■ THEORIES OF FILM: SPECTATORSHIP AND REALISM

The theories advanced by Laura Mulvey are examined, as well as her critics, such as Janey Place.

Realism is explored as a way of representing the real. Kracauer's five arguments in favour of the idea that film is naturally a 'realist' form are critically examined. Attempting to understand the difference between realism of form and realism of content is posed as a way of avoiding some of the pitfalls of a description which some have described as being more trouble than it is worth.

Colin MacCabe's notion of the classic realist text is subjected to scrutiny. His belief in a hierarchy of discourses in the classic realist text/novel/film is noted, as well as Bakhtin's concept of 'heteroglot' and 'monoglot' texts.

Film and society   The analysis of film and society explores early Soviet cinema, the French 'new wave', early Indian cinema, commercial problems in contemporary Hollywood, ideas about the decline of the British film industry, and non-commercial models of cinema.

The relationship between film and public entertainments like theme parks is noted. The chapter ends with an exploration of the difference between those directors who have used certain themes because they appear fashionable, and feminist and black film-makers, some of whom have used film to present a range of sub-cultural experiences.

STUDENT ACTIVITIES

NARRATIVE AND FILM ANALYSIS, RESEARCH, PRODUCTION, ESSAY TITLES

Analysis: Analysis of representation and typage in the cinema

Under the general heading 'casting', a set of photographs showing a range of physical types, ages and genders, is presented to the class.

Purpose: to investigate how physical appearance is linked to a certain specificity of role; to link this to the industry's practices and the audience's expectations; to prepare students for an investigation of character as function.

Method: the photographs (these should not be well-known individuals) are distributed with instructions to consider what type of cinematic role they would expect each individual to assume. A set of cards describing a variety of roles (taken from Propp's analysis) is given to the class. How do students match the sets? This works on the idea of audience expectation. Upon tabulation of the results (i.e. how many students put a certain type in a certain role), discussion should turn on the reasons for the selection. Does audience expectation form an agreement with the practices of the industry which no one wishes to disturb? 'Casting' is central in the construction of meaning. The career of 'leading men' like Robert Redford would be a useful study. Leading roles often monopolise the wide range of social competencies which people in general possess.

Work to follow this type of exercise would be the study of famous cinema 'remakes' and the differences in type (style and changing social customs could also be considered) used to represent the central characters. Also, an investigation of the 'multiple' heroes/heroines of some films would make an interesting contrast. Students can be shown the way that characters are introduced in mainstream Hollywood narratives, and asked to predict what will be the fate of each character. The clues are there in the physical appearance and the role assigned to characters as well as in the length of time they appear on screen.

Analysis: The construction of masculinity: *The Big Sleep*

Students would study the film career of Humphrey Bogart, a star actor who began by taking on supporting roles which cast him as a criminal, then as a detective (in line with the industry's change from pre-war gangster to post-war detective genres), and who was eventually redeployed as a romantic lead. The class then studies the first fifteen or so minutes of the 1946 film *The Big Sleep*.

Purpose: previous work on the story-line is not the object of study (neither Raymond Chandler, the author of the original book, nor Howard Hawks, the director, appeared to understand the plot), but rather the way in which Bogart's 'masculinity' is constructed through a number of devices.

Method: students are presented with a guide for writing an analysis as follows:

The construction of masculinity: *The Big Sleep*, 1946.
Director: Howard Hawks. Stars: Humphrey Bogart, Lauren Bacall.

In this assessment, you will be given some information from the film as a guide, and a list of questions and suggestions for a piece of textual analysis which you will write yourself. The central question will turn on how masculinity and the male star persona is presented or constructed in the early sequences of the film. Other subjects for analysis will include the representation of women. Take note of setting, characterisation, *mise-en-scène* and ideology as revealed in role and action and dialogue. Study the opening scenes at the Sternwood residence and the early part of the enquiry Marlowe undertakes. His encounters with women will form a central part of your analysis.

The opening shots are as follows:

A   Silhouettes of Bogart/Bacall. Two lighted cigarettes lying together. Music and titles.
1   'Stenwood' plaque outside the house and a hand pressing the bell.
2   Door opening, and beginning of dialogue: 'My name's Marlowe.
    General Sternwood wanted to see me.' (Deep note of music.)
3   Carmen Sternwood in shot.
4   Marlowe gives an appreciative look.
5   Carmen: 'Morning. [Pause] You're not very tall, are you?'
6   Marlowe, looking down at himself: 'I try to be.'
    Carmen: 'Not bad-looking, though you probably know it.'
    Marlowe: 'Thank you.'
7   Carmen: 'What's your name?'
8   Marlowe: 'Riley, dog-house Riley.'
9   Carmen: 'Funny kind of name.'
10 Marlowe reacts.
11 Carmen 'faints'.
12 Marlowe catches her.

Please note the following elements of non-verbal communication: looks, gestures, stance and actions. What do these elements tell us about the different ways in which men and women are represented? What is the verbal 'play' (echoed soon in Marlowe's conversation with Vivien) meant to indicate?

In the scene in the conservatory, played between Marlowe and General Sternwood, give examples from the dialogue which would seem to reinforce a 'shared masculinity'. What is the point of the biographical details Marlowe gives, such as his having been fired from the District Attorney's office? What is the purpose of the conversation about Sean Regan? Sternwood describes Regan as 'my son, almost', and congratulates Marlowe on having survived his encounters with Regan: 'Few men swap more than one shot with Sean Regan. He commanded a brigade in the Irish Republican Army ...'

How does Sternwood characterise his daughters? Where is their 'corrupt blood' supposed to come from? In the scenes which follow, how is Marlowe represented in the encounters he has with women?

Analysis: Audience foreknowledge and expectation; genre

A series of very brief extracts from the opening sequences of a number of films is shown.
Purpose: to find out why certain images and sounds lead students to expect that they will see certain events and representations on the screen.
Method: to show a short part of the opening of a film and to freeze the frame after a few seconds, then ask questions about what will happen. It is best to avoid the film's title, or to use films which have a pre-title sequence. Films used should form a contrast with one another, not merely in terms of genre, but also in the way in which they have been made. For example, the opening of *Solaris* proceeds at what many students regard as an extremely slow pace. The aesthetics of Tarkovsky's cinema are misunderstood and the sequence where Kris stands amongst the fauna in the country-side is taken to be a prelude to some unpleasant discovery, while the close-up of water running through reeds has caused students to speculate about the possibility of a dead body rising to the surface. This is because we are used to certain codes and conventions. We interpret images and sounds according to the values we have already acquired.

Research: Cinema: audience and institution

Students may be asked to research a number of areas of film. The most profitable exercises may be the relationship between audience and institution. It is sometimes difficult to keep these areas of enquiry apart.

Purpose: to allow students to develop skills in research; to illustrate the interdependence of institution and audience, and to explore the relations of power between the two.

Example of problematic: (taken from a research project by Saira Bradford, Somerset College, 1992).

'Cinema attendance appears to have been an important part of life during the Second World War. How can we account for the marked popularity of the Cinema during this period?'

There are a number of elements which need to be considered. The study would be made up of qualitative interviews, statistical information on cinema attendance, narrative outlines of the films shown during the period; and theory on the attractions and effects associated with the mass media.

Examples of sources of information: (note – the project became a study of female attendance).

Primary data collected from in-depth interviews carried out amongst a number of people who had attended the cinema during the period under study, including questions about personal circumstances and experiences of the war. A list of the films the subjects remembered would have to be compiled.

Secondary data of a qualitative nature to include diaries, reminiscences and fictional works from the period (for example, *Lime Street at Two* by Helen Forrester).

Secondary data from studies of society, including *Leisure and Society, 1830–1950* and television programmes such as *A Century of Childhood* (Channel 4) and *Out of the Doll's House* (BBC).

Enquiry could include books like *Media Sociology* by David Barrat, since it looks into effects and suggests reasons for an audience's use of the mass media.

Books on the cinema would need to include volumes such as Pam Cook's *Cinema Book*, but more specific information, considering the move in the project towards a study of women and leisure, would be required. An excellent article in this respect would be *Gender and Sexuality in Second World War Films*, by Christine Gledhill and Gillian Swanson.

A complete list of all cinema exhibitions made in the area where the audience attended showings of films would need to be compiled. (Newspaper files from a local library or the records of a newspaper itself should provide such data.)

Structures of response in report-writing: The following format was used to write up the project's findings;

- Problematic
- Introduction to scope of research
- Examination of established theory
- Main research findings
- Conclusion: relationship of findings to theory
- Evaluation of the research process
- Appendices
- Bibliography

(Extracts from this research project are given on pages 316–317.)

Production: Narrative and editing conventions

Students are required to produce a short, straightforward narrative involving no more than three characters. For this purpose, a more advanced storyboard will need to be provided (see Storyboard Fig 5.16 at the end of this section).

Purpose: to concentrate on the technical and aesthetic conventions which together produce a distinctive approach to film.

Method: in groups of three, students will produce a storyboard featuring a simple narrative. They will then be shown a number of film extracts which represent different styles or traditions of editing, including montage from Eisenstein (*October* would be a good example), the practice of the French 'new wave' (Godard's films provide a good introduction), and Hollywood narrative 'realism'. They will then be asked to produce a total of three more storyboards, each featuring a different approach to editing and narrative. The storyline must remain the same, but the shots used to tell the story must obey a different set of conventions. It is perfectly possible, if the story and setting has been kept simple, to record the three narratives on video tape, shooting in strict sequence for the sake of ease of editing. (*See* Figures 5.14, 5.15 and 5.16 for examples of storyboards.)

Production: Marketing a film

Students are asked to choose a genre of film and then to produce a set of posters designed to stimulate audience expectation.

Purpose: to investigate the conventions of publicity and marketing in film; to encourage design work.

Method: students are asked to list (a) all the types of pre-publicity (interviews, merchandise, advertising, etc.) which are used to draw the public's attention to a film, and (b) to make a study of any recent publicity surrounding a film which has recently been released. They are then required to produce material for a mainstream narrative film; in this case a poster which must include some strong iconic link with the film itself and a phrase, slogan or even extract from the film's dialogue, designed to attract the attention of a specific audience.

EXTRACT FROM STUDENT RESEARCH PROJECT (by Saira Bradford)

This fact, that British films were valued by their British audience, was backed up by my primary research from the interview with the elderly ladies. One of the women I interviewed said she preferred the British films and actors to American ones. 'I tended to go to the serious ones like Gielgud or Olivier and I went to foreign ones if I could. I didn't really like American actors, I preferred British or French, I think, on the whole.' She said she liked George Bernard Shaw and actors or actresses like David Niven, Alex Guiness, Wendy Hiller and Celia Johnson. In fact Celia Johnson was her favourite actress. The majority of the women I interviewed started to go to the cinema when they were about eight or nine but the older women didn't start going until they were in their teens, at about thirteen or fourteen. So most of them started to go to the cinema between 1920 and 1930, but not on a regular basis. Most of the women would go with at least one other individual or a group of friends. However, a small number would often go alone. According to one of the women there was no question of her attending a film showing on her own because it was too dangerous in the black-out. 'I remember walking along the pavement in the black-out and falling over a great big iron bar, a terrible fall! I've got the scar on my leg still.'

A lot of the women were married with children by the mid-forties so it would be a great treat for them to go to the cinema and if their husbands were not away at war they would often babysit.

'I went on my own after I was married because my husband would look after the baby, that was why it was such a treat. He would say, "Would you like to go to the pictures tonight?" and I was out the door as quick as I could go.'

* * *

One of the other interviewees describes how she would go up to London to see films. 'I went for the experience. I went to a particular film with a friend who'd also like to go with me.'

'Picture houses were compulsorily closed at the outbreak of war and were not allowed to reopen until factory managers had made strong representations to the Government about the effect on morale of this pathetically negative attitude. The trade pointed out that the chief form of recreation of possibly thirteen million people could not be written off in a moment, and that incidentally, closed cinemas lost the Exchequer £200,000 a week in taxation.' (*Where we came in* by Charles Oakley.)

Therefore it was a combination of audience influence, i.e. the need to keep morale up in factory workers, and financial pressure in the government's loss of taxation, that determined the cinemas were reopened.

'The movies, perhaps even more than any other form of entertainment, *sustained* people through the war. Cinemas were full from noon onwards, and audiences rarely left their seats for the shelters during air-raids.' (*The Forties in Vogue* by Carolyn Hall.)

This extract more than anything shows how appealing the cinema was to its audiences. They would risk being bombed in the cinema instead of going to the safety of a shelter, for the sake of watching the end of a film. Maybe they were just being complacent or were just bored with constantly rushing out to sit in a cold, dark, cramped, frightened atmosphere needlessly, when they could be in a nice warm, spacious, amiable atmosphere watching an exciting film. 'People got tired of leaving during air-raids and seeing only half the film, and generally stayed put throughout the performance.'

Although American films seemed to be the most popular form of escapist movies, the British film industry also took advantage of this rise in cinema attendance and made a number of well-made, sympathetic films which seemed to appeal all the more to the British audience.

ESSAY TITLES

1 'Propp's analysis may be applied to film with a surprising degree of accuracy, provided the method based on it is applied to the more straightforward narratives; it is impossible to analyse more complicated narratives using Propp's ideas.'

Discuss, with reference to at least three different films you have studied.

2 'Mainstream film is unable to represent women as anything other than the objects of the male gaze.'

Comment on this view, with reference to feminist approaches to film. Use examples of films from more than one period of this century.

3 To what extent is the independent film and video sector truly independent?

Answer with reference to the economic conditions under which this sector operates, and the extent to which it maintains an alternative political and artistic agenda.

4 Describe the ways in which the contemporary Indian cinema industry provides a parallel to the Hollywood system of the 1930s.

Refer to the structures and practices of both industries, and also to the content of at least two films from each period (you may find it useful to include reference to the star system, narrative practices, characterisation, genre and the relationship with the audience).

Story Board

Production 'ALIEN BREEDING 2'_____ Story Board No. _35_

	Picture	Description	Audio & effects
Shot 346 Cam 1		CLOSE-UP ON WOMAN'S FACE_____ TIME: _LENGTH OF_ DIALOGUE_____	"WHAT'S THE MATTER?" EERIE_MUSIC_CONT...
Shot 347 Cam 2		EXTREME CLOSE-UP ON MAN'S FACE (LIPS) TIME: LENGTH OF DIALOGUE_____	"YOU'VE BECOME TOO__ SCARY".
Shot 348 Cam 3		OVER-SHOULDER SHOT_____ TIME: LENGTH_OF DIALOGUE"	"I DON'T UNDERSTAND)".
Shot 349 Cam 2		EXTREME CLOSE-UP ON EYES_____ TIME: LENGTH OF DIALOGUE_____	"I THINK YOU'RE WORKING FOR PROFESSOR DREAD) IN__ HELPING ---"
Shot 350 Cam 1		CLOSE-UP ON WOMAN'S FACE TO SHOW____ SHOCKED REACTION SHOT. TIME: MAX 3 SECONDS_____	"..TO BREED THE ALIENS."
Shot 351 Cam 4		MAN SWIVELS AROUND FROM LOOKING AT WOMAN___ TO _WALK___ OFF-SHOT, PASSING CLOSE TO____ CAMERA FOUR.	"I'M GOING. I NEED TO REPORT BACK ABOUT THE PODS IN_ THE BASEMENT_."
Shot 352 Cam 3		{Match on action shot. Man walks out of the door. Woman goes to window.	"JOHN, WAIT! YOU'VE GOT IT _WRONG!"
Shot 353 Cam 5		{TIME 352: LENGTH to walk to door TIME 353: LENGTH OF walk to CAR. ← N/A.	
Shot 354 Cam 3		AFTER DIALOGUE, WOMAN BLURS TO _SHOW CAR_ DRIVING OFF, THROUGH _WINDOW_____ ARTWORK: IAN MERCHANT_ STORY: DAVID KEMP___	"PROFESSOR DREAD. HE'S LEAVING IN HIS CAR".

Fig 5.14 A completed storyboard

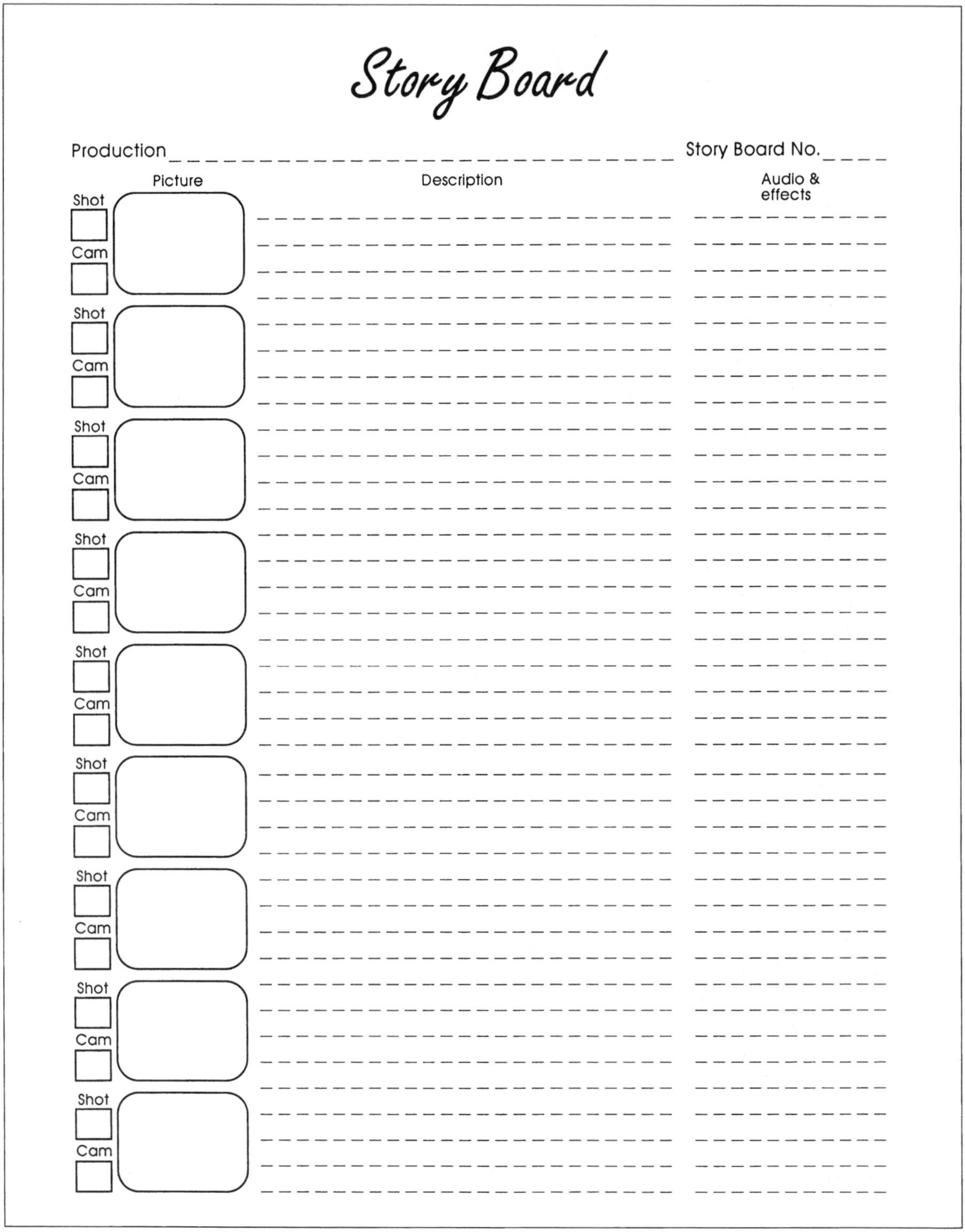
Story Board

Production __________ Story Board No. ____

Picture	Description	Audio & effects
Shot / Cam		
Shot / Cam		
Shot / Cam		
Shot / Cam		
Shot / Cam		
Shot / Cam		
Shot / Cam		
Shot / Cam		
Shot / Cam		

Fig 5.15 A film-video storyboard

Story Board

Production _ _ _ _ _ _ _ _ _ _ _ _ _ _ _ _ _ _ _   Story Board No. _ _ _ _ _ _ _ _ _ _.

	Picture	Floor plan	Description	Audio & effects
Shot ☐ Cam ☐				
Shot ☐ Cam ☐				
Shot ☐ Cam ☐				
Shot ☐ Cam ☐				
Shot ☐ Cam ☐				
Shot ☐ Cam ☐				
Shot ☐ Cam ☐				
Shot ☐ Cam ☐				
Shot ☐ Cam ☐				

Fig 5.16 A television studio storyboard

CHAPTER 6

Popular forms: television, radio and technology

THE SOCIAL IMPACT OF TELEVISION

In *Television, Technology and Cultural Form*, Raymond Williams begins by examining the simple statement (p. 9) that 'television has altered our world'. The idea that the advent of television marked a change in the social order has become part of the received wisdom of our time. The coming of television is ranked among other events of great significance, largely because of its widespread proliferation as a technology, and the assumption that such a popular form would be bound to have significant social effects. It is not unusual to hear the claim that television programmes exercise direct effects on human behaviour; the question of effects on audience will be raised later in this chapter.

Despite its gradual evolution into a 'dominant' form, many commentators still regard television as an inferior visual medium by comparison with the older technology of the cinema. The impact television has had on film, however, has been considerable. Barry Norman, writing about the tenth anniversary of *Film on Four* (*Radio Times*, 31 October 1992) observed that:

> '... though TV has welcomed [the film industry] into bed, it's television that owns the bed and it's television which chooses the side it wants to sleep on.'

The new relationship between television and film has resulted in the production of 'hybrid' forms; films made specifically for TV which take account of the characteristics of television as a medium. Some films do not achieve success at the box-office but make a considerable impact on video. Television has certainly affected other mass media forms, as well as the culture those forms reproduce.

Technology and the uses of technology

Williams was concerned to establish-specific – rather than general – meanings about television and its impact on society and culture. One of the earliest distinctions he made was between a technology and the *uses* of a technology; or as he put it, between *content* and *form*. He posed the following question: is technology a cause or an effect? In examining this question, he noted that 'technological determinism' (a belief in the idea that technology is directly involved in *making* modern society and the people in it) and 'symptomatic technology' (which sees technology as marginal to society, but beneficial when discovered and put to use), both view technology as an isolated and 'self-acting' force.

Williams preferred to think of technology (p. 14) 'as being looked for and developed with certain purposes and practices already in mind'. In other words, technology arises from the drive to make ideas and concepts work in practice. It is not so much stumbled upon as actively looked for.

Television as 'objective' and 'enterprise'

Williams insisted that television did not come about as the result of a *single* event. It depended on (p. 14):

'a complex of inventions and developments in electricity, telegraphy, photography … motion pictures, and radio.'

Williams believed that television can be understood as developing as a specific *objective* roughly between the years of 1875 and 1890. It then developed as a technological *enterprise* from around 1920 through to the first public television systems of the 1930s.

A 'complex' of inventions

Williams detailed the historical background to the invention of television in order to show that there was a close relationship between technology and human need. He called this the 'social history of television as a technology', identifying a much earlier beginning to the 'history of television' than is usually the case. Williams began his study of television with the discovery of electricity. He characterised it as an exploration which began as the study of 'a strange natural phenomenon'. The invention of Volta's battery, combined with Faraday's demonstration of electromagnetic induction, resulted within a short time in the production of generators; as a consequence electricity began to lose its status as a natural wonder. The further development of electrical power was closely related to the needs of industry (industry in turn then going on to push demand to new heights).

Mechanical forms of telegraphy were commonplace in the eighteenth century. Electrical telegraphy was first suggested in 1753. According to Williams, the spread of the railways led to the more extensive development of this form of communication. By the 1870s, a general system of electrical telegraphy had been established, the same decade in which the telephone was developed as a system. The idea of transmitting pictures by electrical methods over great distances was first proposed in 1842 and given a practical demonstration in 1862. (The development of photography and the beginning of the 'motion picture' industry were described in Chapters 4 and 5.)

Television as an idea was closely linked to developments in photography and studies of motion. The eventual production of multi-shot cameras, and the establishment of the first cinematic picture-shows in the 1890s, combined with inventions such as photoelectric cells and the cathode-ray tube, meant that the required elements for a television system were in place by the 1930s. The outbreak of the Second World War interrupted the full development of a public television system, which had been established in Britain (on a limited scale) by 1936.

Public service television: models of regulation

Throughout the history of British broadcasting, formal enquiries have been set up to review the output and conduct of those bodies engaged in mass communication. The earliest inter-war Committees (Sykes, Crawford, Selsdon and Ullswater) confirmed the status of the BBC as a **public service broadcaster**. Those which followed (Hankey, Beveridge, Pilkington, Annan, and Peacock) studied the development of broadcasting as a public institution, and grappled with the difficulties presented by commercial models of television and radio. In most cases, the membership of the committees was drawn from the ranks of the political and cultural establishment of the day. Final reports are thus often characterised by an enlightened but cautious form of paternalism. The use of peers, knights and viscounts to provide leadership for the various commissions, appears highly unrepresentative, but the choice of such figures was intended to demonstrate how the groups they led were composed of 'the great and good' and, by implication, that they were above narrow party politics. The list provided here gives an overview of the various committees which examined broadcasting in Britain, and also gives information about the government Acts which followed the publication of some reports.

The **1923 Sykes** Committee (chaired by Sir Frederick Sykes), was appointed by the Postmaster General (a government Minister). Its enquiries were carried out at a time when the broadcasting service was controlled by six large private companies. These were the largest manufacturers of broadcasting equipment, each of which had the power to appoint one BBC director (providing six out of a total of nine). The committee noted that radio broadcasting was 'of great national importance as a medium for the performance of a valuable public service'. It also argued that 'control of such a potential power over public opinion and the life of the nation ought to remain with the State', and that 'so important a national service ought not to be allowed to become an unrestricted commercial monopoly'. The BBC was at this stage the British Broadcasting *Company*.

Crawford, set up in **1925** (it took its name from its chairperson, the Earl of Crawford and Belcarres), created the BBC's Charter, which enshrined the three principles which guided the early development of British broadcasting. These were the institution of a monopoly, the use of a licence fee to support programme-making, and the creation of an independent corporation to oversee the whole system. The Crawford Committee authorised the BBC to broadcast for a period of ten years from 1 January 1927. Thus the British Broadcasting *Corporation* came into being.

The **Selsdon** Committee (led by Lord Selsdon) was appointed in **1935** to consider the development of television and then to advise the Postmaster General on the relative merits of different systems. The aim was to establish a clear idea of 'the conditions under which any public television should be provided'. The Selsdon report suggested that the BBC should be given the task of planning the service, and that the cost of television broadcasting should be taken from the radio licence fee.

Ullswater was the **1936** Committee (chaired by Viscount Ullswater), given the task of making recommendations on the future of the BBC as it approached the end of its first term of ten years (its Charter ran initially from 1 January 1927 until 31 December 1936). The report praised the impartiality of the Corporation, but expressed some reservations about its Sunday programming. It recognised the public responsibility of broadcasting and pointed out that 'the influence of broadcasting upon the mind and speech of the nation' meant that there was an 'urgent necessity in the national interest that the broadcasting service should at all times be conducted in the best possible manner and to the best possible advantage of the people'. The ban on advertising remained, though sponsorship of television programmes was to be allowed – this was a right only rarely exercised by the BBC. The number of Governors was increased from five to seven. One other issue which the Committee considered was the structure of the Corporation: a measure of internal and regional decentralisation was recommended. In a 'reservation' written by Clement Attlee (a future Labour Prime Minister), attention was drawn to the need to allow other opinions, besides those of government, the right to be heard.

Hankey was a wartime Committee (chaired by Lord Hankey) formed in **1943** in order to prepare plans for the development of television after the end of the Second World War. The report produced by Hankey and his colleagues characterised television as a medium of actuality; it declared that television performed its 'greatest service' when it televised 'actual events', giving the viewer 'a front-row seat at almost every possible kind of exciting or memorable spectacle'.

The **Beveridge** Committee (led, once again, by a Lord) submitted its report in **1950**. It had carried out a wide-ranging and thorough enquiry into post-war British broadcasting. Lord Beveridge wanted to ensure that the BBC remained outside the direct control of government. Thus, he was not in favour of closer Parliamentary supervision. The Beveridge committee identified the dangers which lay in a monopoly of broadcasting, but did not suggest a market alternative. Commercial development seemed to threaten a decline in quality, because competition was thought to lead to lower standards. Sponsorship, in the opinion of the majority of the Committee, was a bad idea because it would place control 'in the hands of people whose interest is not broadcasting but the selling of some other goods or services or the propagation of particular ideas'. Advertising would 'sooner or later endanger the traditions of public service, high standards and impartiality which have been built up over twenty-five years'. The report also recommended that programme content should be monitored by the BBC's Governors, that there should be public representation, five-year reviews, and some devolution of the BBC's functions. A commercial television service was established by the Television Act of **1954**, together with a new regulatory body, the Independent Television Authority. The conditions under which the new Authority was to work, reveal the Conservative government's anxiety over any possible diminution of public standards: the ITA was to ensure that 'nothing is included in the programmes which offends against good taste or decency or is likely to encourage ... crime or lead to disorder or to be offensive to public feelings'. Advertisers were another source of disquiet. Rules were made to ensure that they would not begin to control programme content. The ITA's governing body was to be similar in structure to that of the BBC.

The **Pilkington** Committee, set up in 1960 (and led by the glass manufacturer Sir Harry Pilkington), examined the cultural effect of commercial television. Its report, made in **1962**, argued that ITV 'operates to lower standards of enjoyment and understanding', showing a 'comprehensive carelessness about moral standards generally'. The Committee attacked the Independent Television Authority for not sufficiently recognising 'the influence of television on values and moral standards'. It came as no surprise, therefore, when the BBC (described as 'a successful realisation of broadcasting as defined in the Charter') was awarded the second channel in 1964. Thus, BBC 2 came into being. A notable member of the Committee was Richard Hoggart, the author of *The Uses of Literacy* (an early contribution to cultural studies). He is believed to have been instrumental in framing the report. In **1964** the Conservative government introduced a Television Act which increased the powers of the ITA, but forced it to introduce a code which governed the portrayal of violence and reinforced overall standards.

The **Annan** Commission report on the future of British broadcasting appeared in **1977**. Lord Annan was given charge of the committee by a Labour government in 1974. It produced a report which laid out four principles which should characterise British broadcasting. These were 'accountability through Parliament to a public which is given more chance to make its voice heard'; 'diversity of services'; 'flexibility of structure'; and 'editorial independence'. The Annan committee was dissatisfied with the duopoly of the BBC and the ITA which, it noted, seemed like 'a highly restricted club'. A more diverse approach was suggested, one which took account of minority interests. It argued that 'we do not need more of the same. There are enough programmes for the majority. What is needed now is programmes for the different minorities which add up to make the majority'. The Act of **1980** which followed the Annan report endorsed this view, stating that Channel 4 (established in 1982) should contain 'a suitable proportion of matter calculated to appeal to tastes and interests not generally catered for by ITV'; the new channel acted as a commissioning agent for independent producers. The Committee was also in favour of Breakfast Television, a Broadcasting Complaints Commission, an Open Broadcasting Authority for the new commercial channel, and a Public Enquiry Board.

The **Peacock** Report on public service broadcasting appeared in **1986**. Its major concern was to explore the possibility of alternative sources of income for the BBC. The committee (chaired by Professor Alan Peacock) argued that broadcasting should 'move towards a sophisticated market system based on consumer sovereignty', a system which 'recognises that viewers and listeners are the best ultimate judges of their own interest'. The committee advocated a free-market approach, based on 'consumer choice rather than the continuation of the licence fee'. It used, in addition, the notion of 'consumer welfare', which could be achieved through the provision of a 'considerable range of broadcast programmes' especially ones which dealt with matters of 'serious national concern' and which helped to expand consumers' 'range of taste and preference'. The members of the Committee appeared to think that established broadcasting principles could be supported through the market, rather than simply by relying on public service traditions. The Conservative government's White Paper, which appeared in 1988, proposed the expansion of Direct Satellite Broadcasting, a fifth terrestrial channel, and three new national radio networks. The Broadcasting Act of **1990**, based on the White Paper, replaced the Independent Television Authority with the Independent Television Commission, a less powerful organisation. Its first duty was to organise the franchise bids to run the commercial television network (this process is described on page 335).

Public service and commercialisation

Raymond Williams characterised the British ruling class as 'unusually compact', which helped it produce and control 'an effective paternalist definition of both service and responsibility' (*Television Technology and Cultural Form*, p. 33).

This observation requires a little more discussion. We could point out the dominant class's ability to achieve three things: to set an agenda for its own conduct; to use this moral/behavioural 'code' as a guide for those individuals entrusted with power; and to make other classes/groups aware of these beliefs and standards of behaviour.

This may be reminiscent of Gramsci's concept of hegemony (where a ruling group or class has managed to persuade other groups to accept its own cultural and moral values). When using this concept, it is worth remembering that there are various forms of 'acceptance', from genuine and enthusiastic conviction, to passive concurrence.

The real issue here, however, is to explain why the British ruling class in this period was particularly attached to notions of service and responsibility. Of course, this is not to suggest that all powerful factions always agreed with this approach, but public service remained a dominant current in the political and cultural sphere. One of the reasons for the strength of the public service tradition has already been suggested: power works best, in any period of history, where it has a 'moral' basis. That is to say, the business of government runs most smoothly when the deeds of the powerful appear fair and rational. This happens when their actions appear to conform to publicly recognised values. Direct, coercive power can, of course, always be used in an emergency. Another reason for the existence of the public service ideal, is that the notion of service was already well established in other spheres. Parliamentary and municipal politics, colonial administration, and aristocratic and military rank all involved the use of power, but power exercised within the rhetoric of responsibility. Paternalism, characterised by its 'benign' regulation of the lives, habits, or conduct of those for whom it believes itself responsible, was an established feature of a class society which, although essentially capitalist, had significant reservations about the worth of domination and 'commerce' as guiding *principles*. In other words, the pursuit of power alone could not provide a wide enough range of reasons to justify the exercise of authority. The accumulation of wealth through trade and manufacture may well have been a central part of economic reality, and the use of coercion a feature of everyday life, but neither provided an entirely respectable public discourse in a society which, for example, still expressed itself within a Christian framework. In the reproduction of culture, particularly one which attempts to speak with moral resonance (expressing 'national' sentiments), straightforward 'capitalist' discourses simply do not provide the degree of moral authority required.

Public service broadcasters were seen as 'trustees of the public interest' (in the words of Stuart Hood in *On Television*, p. 53). From the early years of the BBC, the concept of public service was formed in direct opposition to the notion of profit-making and commercialism. In 1931, Lord Reith (the first Director General of the Corporation), declared that he had attempted to 'found a tradition of public service rather than public exploitation'. A year later, he said that 'the serving of public interest and the serving of financial interest are not normally fully compatible'.

The idea of public service is not, from what we have seen so far, simply a convenient disguise behind which another agenda is pursued. Despite its shortcomings, it is a real alternative to the rule of the marketplace. It is not, however, a democratic model of media organisation. When Reith wrote about 'public interest', we may remember that the history of the British ruling class is littered with blunders and misdemeanours which have been actually been suppressed 'in the public interest'. Reith's position should not be taken to indicate a politically progressive outlook; his authoritarianism is revealed in his own diaries (for example, Hood mentions the Director General's approval of Hitler's purge of the Nazi party in the early 1930s).

Reith's position is a variant of corporate paternalism, a creed wide enough to appeal to all the mainstream political parties of the time, containing elements of which each could approve: national unity, public education, technological progress, and so on. Hood maintains that the parties were (p. 54) 'attracted by the idea of public bodies' which seemed to offer the prospect of reconciling different groups. In his essay on public service broadcasting (*see* Raboy, *Public Broadcasting for the 21st Century*, p. 26), Paddy Scannell maintains that the mission of the BBC in these early years 'was, essentially, a task of democratic representation on the terrain of culture rather than politics' and goes on to argue that 'the task was to create a common culture that speaks to the whole society'. Stuart Hood is convinced that the goal of a common culture at this early stage was very far from being attained. On p. 60 of *On Television*, he writes that 'pre-war television was aimed at a small and affluent audience in London and the Home Counties'. The programmes received were 'dominated by the concept of the West End show ... the kind of entertainment which was the middle-class audience's idea of a night out'. Hood's criticism goes further – he argues that many of the BBC's listeners were 'turned away by middle-class accents, middle-class interests and middle-class taste and standards'. He also notes that, in the pre-war period, '66 per cent of the radio audience tuned in at weekends to foreign commercial stations'.

Perhaps Scannell's notion of 'democratic representation' is a little premature, especially considering his belief that, after the 1918 Representation of the People Act, 'the state was now representative of the whole population'. In fact, in Britain it took until 1928 for women to attain the same voting rights as men.

The development of public service broadcasting

Paddy Scannell divides the development of public service broadcasting into three phases: **national service, competition**, and **cultural pluralism**. The first period, from 1927–54, saw the establishment of the BBC and its mission to 'educate, inform and entertain'. The principle which guided the broadcasters in this period, expressed in a BBC report of 1933, was that 'the general needs of the community [come] before the sectional'. Denis McQuail, in *Media Performance* p. 55, argues that the BBC at this time behaved 'as if it was above politics – an instrument of public enlightenment'. Broadcasting was a form of mass communication, carried out on a national scale. With the creation of a single 'Home Service' in 1939, the BBC established a unitary voice. Although the development of television was interrupted by the Second World War, radio broadcasting became a significant resource. McQuail (op. cit.) recognises that 'the standing of the BBC was at its peak in the immediate post-war years after it had been seen to play its part in the national war effort and to have enhanced its own reputation and that of Britain'.

In the post-war era, the Corporation divided its radio network into the Home Service, the Light Programme, and the Third Programme; television broadcasting was resumed in 1946. Finding what Scannell calls the 'right tone of voice' was a difficult task – one which became imperative with the advent of the commercial sector.

According to Scannell, the era of **competition** began in 1954, when the Conservative government passed the Television Act, and ended in 1977. The 1954 Act introduced the first commercial channel, which was regulated by the Independent Television Authority and allowed an initial term of ten years. Although commercial, 'independent' television was set up within the public service tradition, and its progress was closely monitored by the state. In effect, a duopoly had been created, where previously there had been a monopoly. The area contested by the two channels was popular programming, a field which ITV was well placed to dominate. As Scannell notes, within two years, the BBC's audience share was falling below 30 per cent. However, when Hugh Carleton Greene was made director general, he began to create innovative and irreverent programmes which (Scannell p. 28) made fun of 'authority, religion, and traditional values in general'.

As a balance between the BBC and ITV began to be achieved, the latter was criticised by the Pilkington Committee of 1962 (see above, p. 325). ITV, in the words of the Committee, 'operates to lower standards of enjoyment and understanding' and demonstrated 'carelessness about moral standards'. By the end of the 1960s, the BBC was also under pressure, its leadership less self-assured in a political landscape which had become considerably more radical. In 1968, the BBC produced a document which lamented this situation, containing this mournful judgement: 'a country divided and disturbed inevitably has the BBC on the rack'. The unitary voice seemed to have faltered.

The Annan report (see above) reflected increasing dissatisfaction with the duopoly of the BBC and the IBA, and turned its attention to the different audience groups whose potential, it felt, was being ignored. The era of commercial and **cultural pluralism**, identified by Scannell as lasting from 1977 to 1995, had begun. Annan looked back on the strategies of public service broadcasters in the 1960s, and found them wanting. A proportion of the audience at the time perceived broadcasters, in the report's words, to be 'not challenging enough' and thought they 'were cowed by Government and vested interests to produce programmes that bolstered up the *status quo* and concealed how a better society could evolve'. The solution was, in the Committee's view, the introduction of greater pluralism (a system which recognised the existence and legitimacy of multiple viewpoints). In addition to minority opinions, other forms of social and cultural diversity were to be sought out and represented. Although the Conservative government introduced the spirit of pluralism when it set up Channel Four (see below), it did not follow the report's bold proposal to set up a truly independent regulating body, an Open Broadcasting Authority. Channel Four thus fell under the overall direction of the IBA (see below). Ultimately, however, the marketplace would decide whether innovations like Channel Four were to survive. In their analysis of the market forces which were encouraged to thrive in broadcasting, Corner, Harvey and Lury (*see Behind the Screens*, 1994) note that 'such a perspective was in line with dominant tendencies in the broader political culture of Britain at the time ... Mrs. Thatcher and her government were concerned to promote both a "reconstructed" British economy and a "reconstructed" national value system'. This helps to explain the role of bodies like the Independent Television Commission which, in the words of Coleman and Rollet (*see Television in Europe*, 1997) 'does not review programmes but rather acts as a monitoring body within the framework of its own Code, acting on the assumption that licensees themselves will decide on the suitability of programmes'.

In examining the evolution of broadcasting from the early phase of national unity, to the later commercial pluralism of the 1980s and 1990s, care should be taken not to over-simplify each model of public service. What I have called the 'unitary voice' of the BBC was not always successful; its heyday was probably during the Second World War, when it used the medium of radio to broadcast across occupied Europe. (It is significant that the medium of radio still provides the corporation with an important international voice: 125 million people listen to the English language programmes of the BBC World Service). The concept of national unity can be quite radical, especially at times when a nation is forced to defend a moral principle against threats such as fascism. In other circumstances, where national unity has to be manufactured for narrow political gains, it can have largely negative effects. Equally, the notion of cultural pluralism is vastly beneficial to a society which has a great diversity of interests and opinion. The only drawback appears when significant public issues are given less attention because the airwaves are sacrificed to trivia – in such a case, cultural fragmentation rather than diversity may be the end result.

When, in November 1992, the Conservative government published a Green paper called 'The Future of the BBC', it supported the idea that the BBC remain a public service broadcaster and that the licence fee should continue to be its main source of funding. In 1994, a government White Paper renewed the Corporation's Charter. The Broadcasting Standards Council and the Broadcasting Complaints Commission were merged to form a new council which would monitor standards.

An interesting contrast with the British experience was that of the United States, where an attempt to centralise broadcasting failed because the industrial manufacturers asserted their independence. As a result, broadcasting in America was 'regulated' by the market itself. The forerunner of the Federal Communications Commission attempted to keep the competitive market intact, against the tendency towards monopolisation in the industry. After 1944, the FRC (as it was then called) tried to define the public interest in new ways, and sought to introduce concepts of fairness, social usefulness and public morality. The control which this commission exercised was over individual stations, rather than over the networks which controlled those stations.

Forms of television: technology before content

One of Willams's most useful observations is that the technology (the capability to produce moving pictures for domestic consumption) preceded the content of television. One of the results of this is what he called (p. 29) 'the familiar parasitism on existing events: a coronation, a major sporting event'. In other words, television was forced to search for pre-existing material. This might remind us of the early film-makers, who at first took their subject-matter directly from life. However, by the middle of the 1950s, new kinds of content were being produced specifically *for* the medium.

Television would appear to be a combination of earlier forms of public communication, and examples of innovation which grew from the medium itself. Williams provides a list of television forms (p. 44):

- **News** was at first entirely dependent upon the news agencies, but the use of special correspondents developed during the Second World War. This led to the television news broadcasters having a system in the immediate post-war era which possessed its own news-gathering facilities.
- **Argument and discussion** is the term used by Williams to describe the way that public debate had been 'broadened' by broadcasting in general, but particularly by television.
- **Education** is an example of a case where a public practice (which had previously taken place in schools and colleges) was taken over by the television medium. Williams saw this aspect of television's role as extremely positive, provided that television did not attempt to take on all the functions of education; he saw it as best used to support the education system.
- **Drama** was an interesting case, since television appeared to lend itself to the direct transmission of the dominant forms of theatrical representation, at the

very time when major radio experiments were taking place in the use of speech and sound to create new dimensions of meaning and new experiences for listeners.

- **Films** came to provide television with a vast and ready-made source of material. (Eventually, companies would make films specifically for television broadcast and some bodies, such as Channel 4, now commission films which otherwise would not have been produced). Williams noted how some films are sold as a 'package' and that this can constitute a form of 'dumping' of material.
- **Variety** is described as a form of spectacle originating from the music-hall and traced back to a class-based division between mainstream and alternative forms, with the mainstream conceived of as legitimate theatre.
- **Sport** is regarded as a wide-ranging practice which television, to some degree, helped to stimulate. However, sport was always of a spectacular nature and in that sense is suited to representation through television. The ability to draw attention to detail through the use of close-ups is one of the advantages of television, and a bonus for sport.
- **Advertising**, which obviously pre-dated television, underwent a change as the result of industrialisation; the possible scale of production and distribution was vastly increased, to the extent that in the US, radio and television were organised around advertising features, as well as being funded by them.
- **Pastimes**, according to this view, include parlour games and other activities which television has 'updated' and cast in the form of game shows.

Williams argued that television had pioneered a number of new forms. These include the drama-documentary, 'education by seeing', discussion, features, sequences and even, according to Williams, television itself, by which he means 'some of its intrinsic visual experiences', which are unique to television and which allow us to see things in new and unexpected ways.

Television as institution

What is the meaning of the term 'institution'? It is all too easy to attempt to explain the term by giving an *example* of a familiar media institution, like the BBC, rather than a *definition*. In *A Dictionary of Communication and Media Studies* (p. 87), Watson and Hill define institution quite differently, as '[a] term generally applied to patterns of behaviour which are established, approved and usually of some permanence'.

Here we have an idea which might help us to break the habit of imagining institutions simply as large buildings in Central London. 'Patterns of behaviour' suggests that there is a human dimension to all institutions. In *Mass Communication Theory*, McQuail writes that various media have become institutionalised, which means that (p. 37) 'they have acquired a stable form, structure and set of functions and related public expectations'.

The key to both definitions is to be found in words like 'patterns' and 'structure', 'established' and 'stable'. In other words, institutions are bodies which have a settled structure and a set way of functioning. Alvarado, Gutch and Wollen (*Learning the Media*, p. 48) use the definition employed by Williams:

'Institution is one of several examples of a noun of action or process which became, at a certain stage, a general and abstract noun describing something apparently objective and systematic; in fact, in the modern sense, an *institution*.'

These authors create no surprises when they insist (p. 49) that:

'... no text without production and without audience is possible, and to teach about institutions is to teach about the relations ... between those three.'

Here, the idea of institution as a *relationship* is stressed – a relationship between production, text and audience. But the authors are moving into different territory when they propose that there have traditionally been two understandings of 'institution', the first, conventional term being used to describe 'patterns of ownership and control' in various public or private industries, while the second is a term which examines how a text, or a set of texts, can be 'contextualised' in the following ways (p. 50):

1 how it generates, or partially composes an ideological currency;
2 how it comes to construct an audience;
3 how it operates its own terms of address, its own reference.

Why this sudden turn to the text as the central aspect of institution? It may be because the text is the aspect of institution which creates the relationship between producers and audience. It is certainly the element which most of us are most likely to experience. Reading this book, for instance, you are engaged in an experience which has been shaped by institutional factors. It isn't exactly a private communication between two people; although the author writes at times as though it is a personal interaction, he is aware of the public and institutional context of the message he wishes to offer. The trouble is that an emphasis on text can lead us to believe that this is the only level at which we can really understand institution. In fact, texts can be produced which bear almost no resemblance to the true values of the systems which produce them.

Alvarado and his co-authors offer a more useful model when they argue that educationalists should (p. 49), 'engage with three determinations'. These are described as:

1 the relationship between the artifact and the institutions through which it is produced, circulated and consumed;
2 the relations between media institutions and private and public capital – teaching about television as an industry involving a number of institutions;
3 the relations between media institutions and the State – teaching about television as an institution, a duopoly of the BBC and the IBA, regulated and increasingly controlled by central government.

These authors recognise that the idea of a broader category of Institution will tend perhaps to make their concept too vague and unwieldy for the purposes of analysis. But the real problem appears to lie in the tension between a view of institution as a monolith and hierarchy (which limits an understanding of its relationship to audience and how audience may become part of institution), and a view of institution as a set of relationships (which obscures a clear understanding of the political nature of the capitalist media industry). A partial solution may be to separate the *core* of institution from its wider functions, by considering first all those operations which are internally regulated and self-sufficient (such as internal hierarchies).

Channel Four: new directions?

As long ago as the late 1960s, television engineers had calculated that there was room for another channel on the 625-line standard that BBC 2 television had pioneered. The political debate over who should be awarded the new channel turned on the notion of a 'balance' between the existing institutions and between the types of channel already in existence. The debate continued throughout the 1970s, but it seemed all along that the BBC would be very unlikely to gain control of the new channel, since it already possessed two. Equally, the existing ITV companies did not seem the best guarantors of what was sought – a completely fresh approach.

One option was that the new channel should be commercial but should be controlled by separate operators, and should be in competition with the existing ITV channel. As a result, two channels would compete for the advertising supplied to the independent television network. This immediately provoked concern over rather imprecisely defined 'standards'. Another option, which now appears quite remarkable, was that the channel should be devoted entirely to education.

Campaigns to widen the sources from which television found its material were initiated. In 1977 the Annan Committee on Broadcasting had proposed that an Open Broadcasting Authority be created, but two years later the 1979 election produced a Conservative victory and a new solution. This recommended that the channel should be within the independent television system. It should have, however, a new direction and should select programmes which would encourage new and independent talent. The Independent Broadcasting Authority established an autonomous subsidiary to run the new channel, called the Channel 4 Television Company. This was to be financed by means of a subscription collected from the independent television companies, whose existing income was thought enough, initially, to run two independent channels.

The original annual subscription to the new channel from the other companies was 17 per cent of the total advertising revenue generated by ITV. Channel 4 was set up to be a purchaser and commissioner of other people's work, and therefore sought material not simply from Britain, but from international sources. The fact that the channel existed encouraged the creation of several hundred new companies in the first year of its operation. Some independents gained commissions from the BBC and ITV networks on the strength of their work for Channel 4, which therefore became something of a showcase.

When deregulation came into force in 1991, Channel 4 had to earn all its own advertising revenue; this it did with some success, securing 95 per cent of its revenue from this source. Having achieved an enviable financial position, the company came under threat from the Conservative government of the day, which suggested that it should be privatised. Valerie Swales (*see* 'Television in the United Kingdom' in Coleman and Rollet, *Television in Europe*, p. 32) notes that Channel 4 had moved away from its original remit, and considers that its decision to build up its audience share has had an impact on programming: 'between 1992 and 1993 entertainment rose from 25.5 per cent to 31.0 per cent, quizzes from 2.8 per cent to 3.5 per cent ... feature films decreased from 17.1 per cent to 16.4 per cent, news output dropped from 7.7 per cent of output to 3.8 per cent whilst documentaries and current affairs fell from 10.4 per cent to 9.8 per cent.' Its financial success enabled it, in Swales' words, to win 'partially its case to keep more of its profits', which should result in an increase in original, as opposed to imported programming.

Deregulation

Deregulation has been defined as 'the dissolution of rules and regulations which restrict but also protect the status of public services' (*see* Stuart Price, *The Complete A–Z Media and Communication Handbook*, 1997). Watson and Hill, in *A Dictionary of Communication and Media Studies*, point out that another term in current use is 'privatisation', which 'emphasises the practical nature of the shift, from public to commercial control'.

While it is certainly the case that the public sector in broadcasting has suffered from significant commercial inroads, deregulation is not just the introduction of competition (which public service broadcasters have encountered since the introduction of cable and satellite). Deregulation is also the process of allowing private enterprise greater freedom to manoeuvre, while providing the public with fewer safeguards over quality of service. This had been recognised by the Peacock Committee of 1986, and was also a major concern of the Home Office Committee on Broadcasting, which noted in 1988 that 'British television is seen to be amongst the best, if not the best in the world', and argued that 'the principles of public service broadcasting must be an integral part of the new broadcasting environment'. Minority interests had to be served, while there must be 'safeguards against concentration of ownership'. Market-led broadcasting would not, the 1988 Committee believed, maintain diversity of programming.

This was not quite at the heart of the Conservative government's agenda. It envisaged a system where 'the viewer' was to be placed at the centre of policy, which actually meant that a certain notion of a typical viewer replaced the more complex idea of audience shared by many who actually worked in television. The provision of more channels was another Conservative idea, in the belief that this would offer 'more choice'. Again, this suited the zealous support shown by Tories for free market economics, a faith which co-existed so comically with their government's increasing authoritarianism, applied as soon as the real effects of free market chaos had been felt.

The Broadcasting Act of 1990 replaced the 1980 Cable and Broadcasting Act and established (or re-vamped) five institutions to replace the rather more independent bodies which had previously managed the commercial stations and the 'complaints' industry. The ITC was allowed 'a lighter touch' than the Independent Broadcasting Authority. The other new (or newly overhauled) institutions were the Radio Authority, Wales Channel 4 (S4C), the Broadcasting Complaints commission and the Broadcasting Standards Council.

The ITC was set up to oversee the licensing and regulation of commercial television, including ITV, Channel 4, satellite and cable services. In each ITV region the Commission awards a fixed term licence to a company responsible for providing commercial television output for that area. The present licence period runs from 1993 until 2002. At that time, the ITC will be allowed to redraw regional boundaries or alter licence requirements. It has no direct responsibility for the content of commercial television. It was, however responsible for overseeing the extraordinary steeplechase that followed the new bids for media ownership (which were invited from 16 October 1991). A 'quality threshold' was introduced which consisted of three key requirements; to provide regional programmes, to broadcast high quality news programmes at peak viewing times, and to provide a wide diversity of programmes to cater for 'a variety of tastes and interests.' Once the quality threshold had been assured in each case, the private companies competing for the franchises which were available (each of the fifteen constituent ITV companies, plus Breakfast television) had to submit sealed bids to the ITC. The ITC would then award the contract to the company making the highest offer (though there was a provision that the ITC might make an award to a low-bidder under 'exceptional circumstances', which were not defined).

The dangers were immediately obvious. Making a bid that was too high would mean that less money would be available for programme-making, while too low a bid would ensure defeat. Or again, if we take the case of those companies trying to fight off a challenge, they could easily enter into the bidding with a vengeance, only to find later that the other interests had withdrawn; the franchise would then return to its 'rightful' owner, and the company executives would feel as though they had bought their own old boots at an auction. The whole process did not quite reflect the free market philosophy which supposedly inspired the whole exercise. (If there were any individuals who thought they would like to club together and buy a TV station, they would certainly need to cram their hands down the back of the sofa and take the empty pop bottles back to the shop in order to gather up their loose change: there was a non-returnable deposit of anything between seven and a half thousand and eighty thousand pounds.)

The debates which emerged in response to the White Paper on the subject (which had appeared in 1988) turned on issues of 'quality' and fears about the increasing monopolisation of broadcasting. In terms of content, the White Paper proposed that a staple diet of at least three news programmes per day must be provided. One and a half hours per week would be given over to religious programmes and at least ten hours a week of children's programmes would be produced. There were to be no provisions for the broadcasting of documentaries during peak-time viewing.

Under the new Act, as it became, the Secretary of State managed to increase his already impressive powers, reserving the right, in 'exceptional circumstances' (again, not defined in the original Bill), to overturn a decision made by the ITC. In addition, this minister may also be able to exercise the power to make appointments to the broadcasting institutions.

THE MARKET-PLACE AND THE UNEMPLOYED

The 'big five' independent television companies found that the 1990 Act abolished their right to provide programmes to the ITV network; 25 per cent of programme production was to be carried out by independent producers. Some television companies began a 'rationalisation' of what now appeared to be an over-capacity at their studios, where many directly-employed staff were released from their obligations. Companies were then at liberty to employ some of those made redundant, on short-term contracts. The industry began to adapt itself to the new 'privatised' environment, while many skilled workers remained unemployed.

It would perhaps be a little unfair to say that some of the new franchise holders had spent more time on logo design than on coming up with original ideas for programmes. (A proposal for a show which surprises a celebrity with his or her life-history and an admiring group of loyal friends does seem to carry some echoes of past light-entertainment triumphs.)

A TABLE OF 'RESULTS'

Four television companies lost their licences and were replaced by new groups: these were Carlton, Meridian, Westcountry and the breakfast TV station GMTV (Sunrise TV). The new arrangements came into force in January 1993. (Compilation of results by Claire Till).

LWT
Founded in: 1967
After 1980 Cable and Broadcasting Act:
retained franchise (not challenged)
Position after 1990 Broadcasting Act:
defeated one rival
Other 1990 contenders:
London Independent Broadcasting
(Polygram, Working Title Holdings,
Mentorn Films, Palace Pictures)

Thames Television
Founded in: 1967
After 1980 Cable and Broadcasting Act:
retained franchise (one challenger)
Position after 1990 Broadcasting Act:
lost to Carlton Communications
Other 1990 contenders:
CPV-TV
(Charterhouse Merchant Bank, Virgin,
Paladine Productions)

Granada Television
Founded in: 1955
After 1980 Cable and Broadcasting Act:
retained franchise (one challenger)
Position after 1990 Broadcasting Act:
defeated one challenger
Other 1990 contender:
North West Television

Anglia Television
Founded in: 1958
After 1980 Cable and Broadcasting Act:
retained franchise (one challenger)
Position after 1990 Broadcasting Act:
defeated two challengers
Other 1990 contenders:
CPV-TV and Three East Entertainment

TVS
Founded in: 1980
After 1980 Cable and Broadcasting Act:
gained franchise from Southern TV

HTV West and HTV Wales
Founded in: 1967
After 1980 Cable and Broadcasting Act:
retained franchise (one challenger)

Position after 1990 Broadcasting Act:
lost franchise to Meridian TV
Other 1990 contender:
CPV-TV

Central Television
Founded in: 1967
After 1980 Cable and Broadcasting Act:
retained franchise (two challengers)
Position after 1990 Broadcasting Act:
retained franchise
Other 1990 contenders:
none

Yorkshire Television
Founded in: 1963
After 1980 Cable and Broadcasting Act:
retained franchise (one challenger)
Position after 1990 Broadcasting Act:
defeated two other challengers
Other 1990 contenders:
White Rose Television (Chrysalis) and
Viking Television

Grampian Television
Founded in: 1960
After 1980 Cable and Broadcasting Act:
retained franchise unopposed
Position after 1990 Broadcasting Act:
defeated two challengers
Other 1990 contenders:
Channel 3 Caledonia and
North of Scotland Television

Ulster Television
Founded in: 1958
After 1980 Cable and Broadcasting Act:
retained franchise unopposed
Position after 1990 Broadcasting Act:
defeated two challengers
Other 1990 contenders:
Television Northern Ireland and
Lagan Television

Position after 1990 Broadcasting Act:
defeated two challengers
Other 1990 contenders:
Merlin Television and Channel 3 Wales
(backed by RTE)

Tyne-Tees Television
Founded in: 1958
After 1980 Cable and Broadcasting Act:
retained franchise (two challengers)
Position after 1990 Broadcasting Act:
retained franchise
Other 1990 contenders:
none

TSW
Founded in: 1980
After 1980 Cable and Broadcasting Act:
won franchise (two other bidders)
Position after 1990 Broadcasting Act:
lost franchise to West Country TV
Other 1990 contender:
Telewest

Border Television
Founded in: 1960
After 1980 Cable and Broadcasting Act:
retained franchise unopposed
Position after 1990 Broadcasting Act:
retained franchise
Other 1990 contenders:
none

Scottish Television
Founded in: 1956
After 1980 Cable and Broadcasting Act:
retained franchise (two challengers)
Position after 1990 Broadcasting Act:
retained franchise
Other 1990 contenders:
none

337

Channel Television	TV-am
Founded in: 1959	Founded in: 1980
After 1980 Cable and Broadcasting Act: retained franchise unopposed	After 1980 Cable and Broadcasting Act: only bidder
Position after 1990 Broadcasting Act: defeated one challenger	Position after 1990 Broadcasting Act: lost franchise to Sunrise Television
Other 1990 contender: Channel 13 Television	Other 1990 contender: Daybreak Television

The 1995 Broadcasting Bill

In May 1995, Conservative minister Stephen Dorrell declared that the ownership of media in Britain would be 'liberalised', attacking what he called the 'complex, myriad' rules facing media companies. On 15 December 1995, the Broadcasting Bill was published. It featured a number of important points, which appear below:

- the rule which allowed television companies to operate more than two broadcasting licences was replaced by a limit of a 15 per cent share of the television audience;
- any newspaper group with less than a 20 per cent market share of national circulation would be allowed to own up to 15 per cent of the total television market, defined by audience share; any newspaper group with more than 20 per cent of national circulation would be barred from owning ITV licences;
- ownership of cable and satellite by terrestrial television stations, was permitted provided no individual group had no more than 15 per cent of audience share; the same principle operated in the case of those satellite or cable groups which might express an interest in terrestrial television;
- newspaper groups and radio stations holding a market share below the 20 per cent threshold would be able to apply to the Radio Authority to control radio stations; where local newspapers had more than 30 per cent circulation in an area, only one national licence could be awarded;
- the limit on the number of radio licences which could be held was raised, from twenty to thirty-five; restrictions on television companies owning radio stations would be ended;
- up to thirty-six digital television channels were proposed, with special provision for the BBC to operate its own digital 'multiplex';
- the Broadcasting Complaints Commission and the Broadcasting Standards Council were to merge from 1 April 1997;
- from 1998, Channel Four's funding formula would be revised.

The Conservative government, which crashed from power in the General Election of 1997, was unable to see all these proposals through to their conclusion. However, the call to limit the influence of Rupert Murdoch's News International had been heeded, in the sense that the 20 per cent ruling on newspaper circulation prevented the expansion of its interests in terrestrial television.

Many other consequences of the Bill remain to be seen. It appears, however, that the BBC will have the largest geographical cover (through the possession of its own multiplex) for digital television, while Channels 3, 4 and the Welsh S4C will share the second multiplex. Channel 5 will be offered half of the third multiplex. With regard to digital television, Valerie Swales (*see* her contribution to Coleman and Rollet's *Television in Europe*, p. 26) draws attention to 'doubts about the consumer's willingness to bear the cost of new set-top decoders estimated at between £300 and £500'.

Judging the Bill as a whole, Stuart Price (*see Communication Studies*, p. 353), insists that the changes 'must be seen within the framework of a capitalist or market-driven philosophy, in which 'diversity' is supposedly assured through allowing established organisations to create an interlocking structure based on political power and commercial strength'. He uses McQuail's 'Democratic-participant' theory as a challenge to other models of media organisation, in which 'the needs, interests and aspirations of the active "receiver" in a political society' are placed before the drive for profits (*see Mass Communication Theory*, p. 122). Amongst those with a stake in broadcasting, however, the Bill (particularly considering its origins in a Tory administration), was seen as a reasonably liberal document.

Satellite, cable and new technology

New developments in technology do change viewing habits, but these changes have not always been as obvious as the advent of satellite television. The sight of satellite dish receivers on houses acts as a constant reminder that broadcasting has undergone something of a revolution.

By early 1997, the Independent Television Commission had listed over eighty cable and satellite programme channels which could be eligible for a licence (one third of this number were, however, non-operational). In addition to domestic channels, some 130 overseas satellite services were also on the ITC's books. Among the better known channels are Sky One, Sky Movies, Sky Sports, Sky News, Sky Movies Gold, UK Gold, Adult Channel, Movie Channel, MTV Europe, Cable Jukebox, Live TV, Disney and Nickleodeon. How did non-terrestrial television manage to expand so rapidly?

In July 1981, the Conservative government appointed the Information Technology Advisory Panel to examine the commercial potential of cable and other 'new' technologies. In March 1982, despite its own admission that it had carried out no detailed market research, the ITAP recommended a rapid expansion of privately-owned cable networks. It estimated the cost of wiring up British households at £2.5 billion. The Hunt Committee, appointed in the same month in order to 'secure the benefits for the United Kingdom which cable technology can offer', produced its report within a breathtaking six months. Hunt put little emphasis on regulation, favoured the creation of a number of cable channels, and envisaged the major source of income as commercial advertising. Pay-per-view television was regarded as a threat to important sporting events, while cable services directed only at affluent suburban areas, were barred. The Cable and

Broadcasting Act was introduced in 1984, and proposed the creation of a cable network for the United Kingdom overseen by a Cable Authority. Few rules were made for the actual laying of cable systems, such was the rush to establish profitable networks.

Despite the fact that cable and satellite programmes are regulated by the ITC, individual companies are not required to meet quality thresholds, nor have any rules been laid down about the range of material which should be produced. Essentially, in the words of Valerie Swales (*see* 'Television in the United Kingdom' in Coleman and Rollet's *Television in Europe*) 'regulation is confined to the prevention of abuse in the form of unacceptable programming and advertising'. The ITC's codes only apply to services transmitted from Britain, while material from other sources is simply monitored. Satellite and cable regulation also envisages a different relationship between viewer and broadcaster (if broadcasting is the right term for the activity). In the belief that the viewer has selected cable or satellite as a conscious choice, the 'watershed' is split into two periods. The first is set at 8 pm, roughly equivalent to the terrestrial threshold of 9 pm. Programmes aimed at an adult audience are transmitted after 10 pm.

The Sky's limits

An enthusiastic and lenient government was central to the growth of cable and satellite. The other factor was the existence of rapacious commercial organisations prepared to take advantage of new opportunities. Sky, one of the best-known media players in the satellite market, began by acquiring a small station and investing heavily in its development.

The first European satellite programme was broadcast in 1982 from a small studio in London. 'Satellite TV Ltd.' used material which it thought suitable to a range of countries, concentrating upon items which would make a visual impact. In 1983, the company received interested visitors from Australia; it was not long before Rupert Murdoch took over the operation and re-named it 'Sky Channel'. Three years later Murdoch secured broadcasting space on the *Astra* European satellite, run by the *Société Européene des Satellites* (SES) on a twenty-two year franchise from the Luxembourg government.

Meanwhile, also in 1986, the Independent Broadcasting Authority solicited bids for the British satellite contract. The winning bid came from a group called British Satellite Broadcasting which, under a European Community Directive, was told that it had to invest in a high quality transmission system called MAC. The belief was that only high-powered satellites using the MAC system, could provide acceptable standards for sound and picture quality. Sky, however, invested in the rival PAL system, which BSB had been prevented from using because of its supposed inferiority. Once the Astra satellite was launched in November 1988, time counted against BSB; Murdoch was ready to transmit programmes in early 1989. Although the majority of viewers relied upon cable transmission because of a shortage of satellite dishes, the picture quality generated by the PAL system was perfectly adequate. Sky had stolen a march on BSB which, forced to invest in the MAC system, had suffered a serious disadvantage.

BSB, supposedly the owner of a satellite monopoly, found that Sky was immune from prosecution because it was based in Europe. Sky also had a powerful ally: the Conservative government. News International, the British subsidiary of Murdoch's newspaper empire, was a firm supporter of the Tory party which, in turn, had agreed with Murdoch's inflexible opposition to the printworkers during the Wapping dispute of 1986. Just six months after BSB finally managed to get on air, a merger was announced; neither group could sustain the financial trauma of the contest. The new company was called BSkyB and, in the light of subsequent developments, it must be seen as a triumph for Murdoch's interests. By 1995, BSkyB had established itself in four million homes in Britain. Two years later, it had secured over six million subscribers.

Competition, profit and 'parasitism'

The satellite channels have become part of the landscape of broadcasting, even managing to penetrate the terrestrial channels through the increasingly familiar 'Sky News' logo, which appears in the corner of reports borrowed by the traditional news programmes.

In the first year of Sky's operation, Murdoch had budgeted for an expenditure of £170 million, but although the actual sum was probably considerably higher, Sky continues to grow. In managing BSB, Murdoch's strategy was based on the employment of experienced personnel from Australian television. Sam Chisholm, for example (Sky's chief executive until his departure in late 1997), spent fifteen years as managing director of Australia's commercial Channel 9 station. Responsible for the takeover of BSB, Chisholm presided over the expansion of Sky's interests, exemplified in 1993 by the deal made with the Premier League for the right to televise soccer fixtures. In addition, he secured the growth of Sky's network, to 6.2 million subscribers, and supervised the company's flotation on the stock exchange. BSkyB's profits for 1996 reached £257 million. Chisholm, who had negotiated a 0.5 per cent share of annual profits, drew a total salary in 1997 of approximately £4.5 million.

In May of the same year, BSkyB and British Telecom (together with two junior partners, the Midland Bank and the Matsushita company), agreed to sign a deal to create a new organisation called British Interactive Broadcasting (BIB). BIB planned to operate a number of new services, including fast access to the Internet, and home shopping facilities. The consortium also hoped to gain subsidies which would halve the cost of digital set-top boxes; these decoders are required for the reception of multi-channel television. The first order made by BIB was for one million such devices.

In an interview with the *Guardian*'s Maggie Brown (*see* 'Reaching for the Sky', 12 May 1997), Chisholm insisted that 'no one anywhere has managed to pull together this sort of combination and to get the box subsidised ... we are going to lead the world in this UK operation'. It is worth noting that the nature of BSkyB's undertaking is revealed in the term 'UK operation' – it is not a 'British' development so much as a corporate venture with a base in one particular nation-state. Despite this, some writers find it difficult to treat the Sky 'revolution' with a sense of detachment. Brown, in the article cited above, felt 'it is impossible to be neutral about BSkyB's dramatic impact on British TV in the last eight years'. According to Brown, BSkyB has 'single-handedly kick-started the mass subscription market, now worth more than £1 billion a year', as well as dominating that market (taking some 90 per cent of the revenue) and leaving other broadcasters (such as Granada and the BBC), floundering in its wake. Indeed, Chisolm's boast was that BSkyB had become 'a media and information company in the broadest sense'. The goal of many companies in the digital age is still, according to some commentators, too limited. As Anthony Feldman in *An Introduction to Digital Media* argues (p. 13) 'organisations call themselves – and understand themselves to be – television companies, record companies, book, magazine or newspaper publishers ... in every case, they identify themselves explicitly by the physical form in which they have always delivered their products'. The strength of BSkyB has been its ability to imagine a more integrated media environment, closer to Feldman's definition of a business which is 'an exploiter of content wherever content can viably be exploited'.

The words used by Feldman are very revealing: a media firm should be 'an exploiter of content'. Notice that Feldman does not seem to expect it to *produce* content. The shortcomings of Sky's approach becomes clear; it is an exploiter, concentrating on sport, news, and British film, with little commitment to original programming. Like many satellite and cable enterprises, therefore, it demonstrates what we encountered at the beginning of this chapter, the 'parasitism on existing events' which Raymond Williams identified as a feature of early television. It remains a feature of all those media forms which have as their prime function the creation of profits rather than the extension of public horizons.

Chisholm, nevertheless, appeared convinced that 'Sky has made terrestrial television better ... because we have introduced competition and forced them to sharpen up'. The opposing argument is that the consequence of increased competition has been a scramble to satisfy the 'lowest common denominator' (for a full discussion of commercialisation in the case of television and other news forms, see pp. 347 and 439; refer also to 'European fears', below).

Trouble at the mill

As disquiet over the extent of the Murdoch empire continued to appear in public debate, a series of problems began to shake confidence in BSkyB itself. The relatively sudden departure of senior management from the Sky hierarchy began with the announcement on 17 June 1997, that Sam Chisholm was to leave by the end of the year due to ill health. His deputy, David Chance (originally tipped to succeed as managing director), was also to leave. On 20 June the *Financial Times* announced that the independent sector's regulator, the ITC, would ask BSkyB to drop its 33 per cent equity stake in British Digital Broadcasting (see 'Digital dreams' below).

Despite these problems, the threat to the organisation was not as severe as had been forecast; on 24 June the Independent Television Commission awarded the digital licence to BDB, insisting that Sky remained a core supplier of premium channels to the entire consortium, an arrangement attacked by the director general of Oftel, Don Cruickshank, who pointed out that BSkyB's provision of sports coverage raised 'substantial competition concerns in the pay-TV network'.

The ascent of Murdoch's daughter Elisabeth, in the Sky hierarchy, posed another problem for the company. On 22 June, the *Sunday Telegraph* noted that the advancement of Murdoch's daughter had angered investors, and suggested that tension between Chisholm and Murdoch had grown as it became clear that Elisabeth was being groomed to take over the company. Faced with other difficulties, including the inability, by 27 June, to reach final agreement with the Premier League (which had already begun to consider setting up its own TV service once its deal with BSkyB expired), Sky found that £3.5bn had been wiped off its share price. In other words, by 30 June one third of its former worth had disappeared. Murdoch's response was to insist that Sky's market value had always been seriously inflated.

Digital dreams

Digital technology uses a series of binary digits (0 and 1 in a variety of combinations) to represent data. Any media form (video images, photographs, printed text, etc.) can be digitalised. Digitalisation converts information into 'formal relationships in abstract structures' (Timothy Binkley, in *Future Visions*, 1993) stripping away the physical property of the source. By contrast, analogue reproduction transcribes the physical arrangement of the original source, into a similar configuration in another form. Price (1997) gives this example (p. 15): 'representational painting depends on the transcription of the scene/figure chosen, into a similar arrangement on the canvas'. He notes that 'photography is an example of direct analogue production, while video is indirect, requiring the translation of light patterns into electrical signals and then their transformation back into recognisable images'. Tony Feldman lists the key features of digital information. Digital data is:

- manipulable;
- networkable;
- dense;
- compressible;
- impartial.

When Feldman describes digital information as **manipulable**, he means that it is flexible enough to be re-shaped and presented in a new order. This, he believes, 'means something quite extraordinary: users of the media can shape their own experience of it' (p. 4). He cites the example of the 'Primis' publishing service, created by McGraw-Hill in the United States. It allows teachers to select a variety of material from a wide range of existing McGraw-Hill publications, the idea being that a new textbook can be composed of whatever choices individuals have made.

When digital media is described as **networkable**, this means that users have (*see* Feldman, *An Introduction to Digital Media*, p. 6) 'simultaneous access to networked information'. The same content may be reproduced many times, without 'the difficulties and costs implied by shifting physical products through a supply chain'. This alters the traditional model of media distribution, but whether this will really mean the creation of what Feldman calls 'a new form of electronic community' remains to be seen.

The concept of **density** refers to the compactness of the digital format, and the way in which information can be stored in a relatively small space. **Compressibility** is that quality of digital information which allows it to be reduced in size, so that it can be transferred along narrow electronic bandwidths. Feldman considers this to be (p. 7) 'the single most important ingredient in making it possible to handle video in digital environments' because digital files may be compressed and then decompressed when they need to be used. Feldman explains: 'instead of fiddling with the pipes [whatever conduits are being used to convey information] to find more capacity, we can for more or less the first time fiddle instead with the information we propose to send through the pipes ... by compressing digital information we can effectively make thin pipes fat and fat pipes fatter' ... that is the miracle of compression and it has transformed our ability to handle large bodies of information over transmission systems ...'

Impartiality refers to the 'indifference' of computer systems, to the actual meaning, source and ownership of bytes of information. This is an odd observation to make, since technology is usually thought to be 'neutral', at least in the sense that it cannot make judgments about the value or status of the material it stores or transmits. Feldman goes on to say that (p. 8) 'digital data can represent any form of underlying information'. Perhaps a better term would be **adaptability**.

The competitive edge

Predictions about the value of the new media and the 'digital economy' often point to the extended degree of 'choice' offered by new systems to consumers. Feldman is certainly interested in what he calls the 'commercialisable opportunity' digital television (for example) offers for television companies. If (p. 9) 'going digital' can offer benefits that 'users will pay more to receive' (in Feldman's terms 'greater choice of programming, more freedom to choose what they want to watch ... higher quality reception'), then it will be worth pursuing. Other forms taken by the new media may include electronic books, magazines and newspapers, but Feldman is quite sure that these 'cannot just be books, magazines and newspapers in electronic form'. The process of digitalisation requires some form of transformation into 'a new medium with substantial unique, added values ... the unique characteristics of digital information have to be put to work to deliver new benefits to customers – benefits they will recognise as benefits and be prepared to pay for ...'

Feldman speaks almost exclusively of the customer or consumer, revealing his perspective on the development of digital media – as a commercial proposition. He notes that 'a satellite broadcaster probably spends currently £4 million to £5 million a year to lease time on an analogue transponder of a satellite' (transponders are the devices which receive an incoming signal from an Earth station and retransmit it to viewers). With the use of compressed digitalised data, the capacity of transponders can be substantially increased. Feldman argues that (p. 10) 'instead of each transponder handling a single analogue television channel, they will soon be routinely capable of handling up to about 30 ... the practical reality will probably be that most transponders will handle about 18 channels'. Feldman's celebration of satellites which could begin to offer 324 channels instead of a mere 18 has one flaw: will viewers across Europe really appreciate a choice of 'thousands of individual channels by the turn of the century'? Will the large number of channels mean an extensive number of companies, or will only a few major multi-nationals offer what could be a cornucopia of mediocrity? Feldman thinks that 'a substantial lowering of leasing prices' will offer a new economic model for satellite broadcasting 'which could open the industry to many non-traditional broad-casters'. The extent of his conception of broadcast democracy is revealed when he writes: 'satellite transmission could soon become an increasingly effective way of delivering a whole new range of core content ranging from in-store information systems for retailers to data feeds for corporate networks'. This limited, commer-cial model of 'non-traditional broadcasters' is very far removed from the more utopian visions which envisage use of the 'new media' as one means of strength-ening public democracy.

The origins and development of cable

Cable television is at least thirty years old, yet it is still regarded as a 'new tech-nology'. At least in the sense that it is not yet widespread in Britain, cable probably still remains a novelty to most people. In the optimistic days of cable's first appear-ance in the US, there was some speculation about the social uses and what was seen as the 'progressive' nature of the technology. A truly 'democratic-participant' and community-based service would, according to some, end the isolation of in-dividuals, and would lead to harmony between groups which had previously existed in mutual antagonism. This little Utopia never came about – not just because of economic recession, but also because no mass media form of itself is able to swing a community towards good-neighbourliness, let alone towards forms of communal socialism. The expansion of cable in the US, in fact, provided a chance for the big firms to monopolise the system, so that by 1980 the three biggest distributors of cable programmes (HBO, Showtime and The Movie Channel) had control of almost the whole distribution business.

The cable strategy in Britain was from the start to establish a good film channel, but competition has been fierce. Premiere, a cable channel, was driven out of busi-ness by the prices demanded for post-video releases. The surviving cable firms have at least the advantage over satellite that they can be two-way and interactive, but there is little point in imagining this holds the potential for democratic devel-opments which have already failed to materialise in the USA.

It is generally accepted that the potential for the expansion of cable will be in the field of popular entertainment. In the US, 80–85 per cent of the material shown on cable TV consists of feature films. A number of other developments are in evid-ence. Besides shows devoted to public spectacle, studio-bound shows centred on the general public, and the expansion of formulaic adventure series, the amateur video show has been made possible owing to the proliferation of cam-corders. People submit 'amateur' videos but then appear to be increasingly interested in learning directly from television and film, in terms of composition, and even editing (usually in the camera). The rise of cable, VCRs and home video might well be a kind of choice which is not based on a wide variety of different types of programming, but on a choice of 'flexible viewing', where the viewer takes increasing control of the timing of viewing, but views perhaps a narrower range of material.

Some theorists argue that television began in the US not simply as a domestic medium, but as a medium aimed specifically at women. David Morley, involved in running a project on the household uses of information technology, argues that, considering television's multiple uses (video, video games, computer link-ups), it makes little sense to study television in isolation. Instead, it should be seen in the context of the 'technological culture' of the household. Morley, who had previously published research on television and the way it was for the most part incorporated into a masculine domain of leisure, notes how the VCR in particular has taken on the status of a 'male' toy. The same would appear to be true of video games, whose emphasis is on 'masculine' actions: adventure, combat, survival and quest. In conclusion, Morley warns against neglecting to investigate what he sees as a split in our culture between a public/masculine sphere and a private/feminine sphere.

European fears over loss of identity

In the USA there are some 49 million subscribers to cable; the American experience provided a model for the introduction of cable in Britain. In fact, US cable operators have made investments in Britain as part of a series of general incursions into Europe.

It is perhaps precisely because we share a common language with the Americans that we are unable to appreciate fully the arguments current in Europe about 'cultural imperialism'. For Europe, there is a fear that national cultural identities will be eroded by the influx of US material, not simply from cable and satellite ownership, but also because European networks buy and show US-made material on their own networks. At one time, the collapse of European space and satellite programmes, and the slow demise of the Soviet 'Intersputnik', seemed to have left the field wide open for increasing American influence. The French government has talked of 'English language imperialism', while the Italian authorities have cited 'cultural colonisation' as a threat. In 1984, the French government decided that no more than 30 per cent of total programme time should be given over to foreign material. In Holland, there is a policy which aimed to attain a target of 20 per cent national cultural material by 1989. Denmark and Finland import some 43 and 37 per cent respectively of their television from foreign sources. However, the rekindling of interest in European satellites in the mid-1980s has resulted in some forms of national control over a market which appeared to have become increasingly 'sewn up' by the American corporations.

Another development has been the tendency for programmes to be undertaken as co-productions, designed from the outset for a global market. Therefore some American programming has already attempted to take account (for purely commercial reasons) of different cultural values held elsewhere in the world. It is in any case extremely difficult to separate 'negative' effects which may be due to television from the wider cultural influences which arise from other contacts, especially where nations share a border or a language, but not a culture.

Some commentators, however, have set out to oppose what they see as a negative cultural influence. Nicholas Fraser, for instance, in an article called 'A New Moronism' (the *Guardian*, 1997), argues that the domination of global television by companies based in the United States, has produced 'a world media culture … consisting predominantly of reach-me-down Americana'. He cites 'Lite TV, a California news bulletin destined for the reality-averse or merely Prozac-stuffed'. His belief is that American TV forms have been first exported and then 'copied throughout the world'. There is some evidence as he says, that the conglomerates 'are not in the business of doing good deeds, or preserving what remains of our public, national cultures'.

In a speech given to an international conference on the future of public service broadcasting (held in London in 1994), Albert Scharf, President of the European Broadcasting Union, listed a number of anxieties which troubled those committed to PSB in Europe (*see* Groombridge and Hay, *The Price of Choice*):

• Could national or European legislation create defences against the increasing power of 'a few media moguls'?
• What is the impact of cross-media ownership of print and electronic media by groups such as Bertelsmann and News Corporation?
• How can national regulations on taste and decency be applied when so many programmes can be introduced from unregulated sources?

The problem does not always lie, however, in threats from outside the European market. Scharf revealed how, in another public forum, he was involved in a discussion with the chief executive of a successful German commercial channel. The executive was asked about the place of culture in his programming, to which he replied 'What do you mean, culture? Culture in television means nobody looks at it. This we cannot afford.'

The State as saviour?

Some writers look to the State to protect society from the commercial values of the new broadcasters. John Ellis, in an article on broadcasting ('Broadcasting and the State: Britain and the experience of Channel 4', *Screen*, no. 27, 1986, p. 7), insists that 'the State has to ensure that social values countervail those of the market'.

The evidence so far is that the State has instead been used by the executive arm of government to oversee the widening of market influence, rather than to maintain the 'social values' Ellis believes are important. He also goes on to note that culture seems everywhere to be under threat:

'Even in the United States, those equivalents of magazines … specialist cable channels … have had an extremely difficult time: though MTV … and weather forecasts have proved financially viable, the attempts at a 'Culture Channel' have all collapsed, and even some feature film entertainment outlets have had to merge.'

The point here may be that 'culture' and some types of film are simply not best served by television as a form. We should not automatically assume that it is the ignorance of the public which is to blame. It also seems curious when Ellis calls for the State to:

'conduct its broadcasting policy according to publicly debated principles rather than a disorganised retreat in the face of (false) calls for a free market.'

By what mechanism would the State, if it so wished, be able to turn itself into the defender of the public and of principle? At exactly the same time, Ellis recognised that it was the 'Thatcherite State' that was attacking some of the values many people held dear. The State is hardly likely, unfortunately, to come to the rescue of the BBC.

Knocking the BBC?

The BBC, of course, was originally a private company set up by a conglomerate of radio manufacturers. It was nationalised by a Conservative government and made into a state broadcasting monopoly. Two principles lay at the centre of this monopoly. First, that the BBC should be a single corporation with a monopoly of radio (and subsequently of TV) broadcasting. Secondly, that it should have formal independence from the government in its own internal affairs, yet the government should appoint a Board of Governors. The dangers of this system must be apparent to all.

Independent television provided the real Trojan horse. Its creation was seen by some as the first move towards the eventual replacement of the BBC ethos. There were certainly many private companies which, from the start of the independent network, wanted to see advertising on all channels.

Although one of the basic principles of the commercial system established in the mid-1950s was to have a regulatory body which would award contracts to regional contractors, rather than a single national body, the third channel has operated in effect as a national station. The TV companies were allowed to form what amounted to a network, with each company providing a proportion of the programmes to be shown by all at peak times of viewing; some of the independent companies made only minor contributions to the overall production of programmes.

RADIO AND PUBLIC COMMUNICATION

The status of radio within Media Studies

Within media and cultural theory, the study of radio has suffered from neglect. Pete Wilby and Andy Conroy, writing in *The Radio Handbook* (p. 15), believe that 'its cultural significance is only beginning to receive wider recognition in academic circles'. Wilby and Conroy believe that one of the reasons for this, lies in the fact that media students have 'studied film and television in terms of their textual qualities, their means of relating to audience experience and their cultural significance', while students' encounters with radio have concentrated on practice, and the study of 'how programmes are made'.

This view may also be discovered in the work of Peter Lewis and Jerry Booth, whose book, *The Invisible Medium*, begins by examining the position of radio in the wider context of broadcasting. Their Introduction (p. xiii) states that '... radio is hardly noticed in academic literature and as a practice is mostly taught in a vocational context as a preparation for journalism'. Lewis and Booth are convinced that, as a result 'radio practice and policy lacks a language for critical reflection and analysis'.

The absence of such a critical language is in one sense rather curious: after all, the dominant analytical current, Saussurean semiology, emerged from the study of linguistics, and might be thought an ideal instrument for the study of a form whose signs are often composed of linguistic 'units'. However, the adaptation of semiology to serve the purposes of visual analysis, directed towards the interpretation of television and film, has perhaps obscured other lines of development. Such problems have, in the words of Lewis and Booth (p. 16) culminated in a situation where 'radio education has taken on a somewhat functional role'.

The nature of radio as a medium

Wilby and Conroy present radio (*see The Radio Handbook*, p. 1) as 'an intimate medium'. This view of contemporary radio provides a significant contrast to its great days as a *public* medium when, during the Second World War in particular, it became an important instrument in the ideological armoury of the British State. The fact that it was an unrivalled source of information helped bolster its status, while the often collective manner in which radio was 'consumed' indicates its role in the maintenance of a 'national' consciousness. Groups of people would gather together, in private and in public, to listen to the broadcasts made by the BBC.

Now, Wilby and Conroy feel, 'people rarely sit round the kitchen table in groups to listen to the radio'. Instead of a collective experience, radio as a form 'addresses each listener as an individual' (*The Radio Handbook*, p. 1). Lewis and Booth make a similar point, describing radio as 'a mass medium, and yet, in the Western world, now received personally' (Introduction to *The Invisible Medium*, p. xii). The mode of reception encompasses a variety of 'personal, variant, or subversive readings ...'

The act of listening to radio does not require extensive re-adjustments to domestic arrangements. Wilby and Conroy (p. 1) note that it 'does not demand the virtually exclusive level of audience attention that the press and television require for effective communication', though their belief that radio 'offers the greatest potential for building up a one-to-one relationship with each member of its audience' confuses, perhaps, the imitation of personal address with real interaction. They insist, however, (p. 26) that 'common to most of the forms that radio programmes can take ... is the simple characteristic of one person talking to another' which allows a programme's 'instantaneous and personal communicative impact'. They are probably nearer the mark when they describe the ability of commercial programmes to reproduce (p. 28) 'the discourse of companionship'. Lewis and Booth draw attention to the idea that individual activities carried out during the process of listening 'colour the meaning of what's heard' (p. xii).

Radical radio in Italy: the background

The potential of radio to offer what Wilby and Conroy (p. 27) call 'a more spontaneous, less planned experience', has meant that certain stations have on occasion been able to offer a creative alternative to the structured output of most broadcasts. This was certainly the case in the mid-1970s in some of Italy's major cities. Escaping the kind of monopoly which had once in Britain 'justified control by a few professionals' (*The Invisible Medium*, p. xiii), *radios libres* (free radio) provided a new model of European practice. In Italy, a number of stations were closely allied to the revolutionary left. An appreciation of this era requires a brief overview of the circumstances under which 'free radio' emerged.

The power of the PCI (the Italian Communist Party) was challenged by a host of groups which opposed the 'historic compromise' made between the increasingly moribund Communists and the right-wing Christian Democrats. The Radical Party, various Trotskyist organisations, Maoists, feminist groups, anarchists and the libertarian group '*Lotta Continua*' ('Continuing Struggle') all contributed to a movement which took radical action against the forces of the Italian state.

The period from the 'Hot Autumn' of 1969 until 1976, saw the growth of a number of political controversies. In the words of Pete Anderson (*see* p. vi of the Introduction to *Dear Comrades: Readers' letters to Lotta Continua*) 'the far left in Italy won many fundamental victories and were taken very seriously by the ruling class'. At first it appeared as though the gains of the left would continue; Anderson explains 'as long as they thought that revolution was around the corner, most militants were prepared to postpone their desire for personal liberation'. However, when it became clear that fundamental change was not an immediate possibility, attention switched to more personal issues. Feminists in particular made new demands using the slogan 'the personal is political' but found their perspective opposed by the largely industrial politics which still dominated the left.

Another major problem lay in the escalation of violence which characterised life in Italian cities. Demonstrators were shot dead by police, fascist groups (secretly encouraged by state organisations) planted bombs attacks in public places, and some elements of the far-left decided on a strategy of 'armed struggle'. The Red Brigades and the NAP (Armed Proletarian Nuclei) were involved in shoot-outs and assassinations (though the kidnapping and murder of Aldo Moro, blamed on the Red Brigades, was actually organised by a secret right-wing group). Quite apart from the physical dangers of left-wing activism, the issue of violence caused widespread disagreement amongst socialists. Some supported the NAP and the Red Brigades, seeing in them the continuation of armed resistance to fascism organised by partisans during the Second World War. Others saw such groups as elitist, and dangerous to the very cause they claimed to advance. It was in this context, of militancy, violence and political confusion, that the radical radio stations flourished.

Radical radio in Italy: democratic forums

All forms of community radio are, to an extent 'an open or implied criticism of mainstream radio', as Lewis and Booth put it, (p. 9) *The Invisible Medium*. The intention of '*Radio Bologna per l'Accesso Pubblico*', which began illegal transmissions in November 1974, was rather more wide-ranging. The station hoped to hasten 'the reform of the information system' and demonstrate 'the possibility of decentralisation and free access at a very moderate cost'. This experiment was run by a co-operative of workers, students and communications experts. Lewis and Booth note that 'the station's reach, with a 20 km radius, was local, but its effect was national and sensational'. Scores, then hundreds of stations followed the Bologna example. The authorities tried to end such broadcasts, but control was quickly lost.

In 1976, state regulation was further eroded when Italy's Constitutional court decided that the monopoly held by the national radio station (RAI), was unconstitutional if applied to local enterprises. Two years later, in June 1978, a survey revealed that there were 2,275 radio stations in the country. Most of these were commercial, extensions (in Lewis and Booth's words, p. 141) of the 'music, electronics and publishing industries'. The authors of *The Invisible Medium* believe that 'most such broadcasting simply reproduced the traditional relationships between broadcasters and listeners'.

In some cases, however, social experiments were made by the new broadcasters. '*Radio Citta*', for example, was run as a co-operative, its operational decisions being taken by an assembly which met once a fortnight. News and information formed important parts of the schedule, which also allocated space for reports from trade unions, the women's movement, prisoners' groups, and so on. Sundays were set aside as a day for free access to the station.

One of the most famous of the Italian stations was '*Radio Alice*', situated in Bologna. This station was notable in that it 'denied reality' and rejected the idea of schedules. Set up by revolutionary leftists belonging to the group '*Potere Operaio*', and by 'autonomists' who owed allegiance to no particular party, 'Radio Alice' declared that it wished to 'break the logic of the mirror', arguing that information should be used not merely to 'display' reality, but to effect some transformation in the order of things. Lewis and Booth refer to Umberto Eco's response to the phenomenon (Eco is a cultural theorist and the author of *The Name of the Rose*, among other novels). He wrote that:

> '*Radio Alice* is made up of literary citations, classical music, political songs, non-structured dialogues, free-wheeling language, and direct reporting of such varied events as strikes, squatting, demonstrations and fetes.'

During this period, it became noticeable that surreal forms of language use, initiated by the station, had spread to its listeners. In various other ways, the left-wing groups involved in radio broadcasting, broke with the conventions of mainstream practice. Stations used telephone reports made by their own listeners.

In 1977, during confrontations between students and police, *Radio Alice* was charged with inciting riots. During the police raid which ended its broadcasts, the station remained on air until the moment when armed officers entered the studio. A Roman station, '*Citta Futura*', avoided a similar fate by calling upon its listeners to turn out in force to protect it. The presence of crowds, including some politicians, prevented police action from taking place.

Another station, *'Radio Popolare'*, was described by a media analyst called Cavalli-Sforza (*see The Invisible Medium*, p. 146); 'each person who telephones has something to say ... they don't telephone simply to give their personal opinion, but ... make their call a political intervention and in this way add something to the debate'. Networks of volunteer correspondents made the audience for these broadcasts (p. 147) 'an active partner in information production'.

Dreams of community

Lewis and Booth go on to note that 'the remarkable degree to which some stations broke down the traditional barriers between sender and receiver' was 'a symptom and a product of a historical phase of unusual intensity, even for Italian culture and politics'. In other words, they see this type of close interaction between audience and broadcast media as the product of specific historical circumstances, and do not imagine that it can always be reproduced. Their caution is expressed in the comment 'We do not believe that radio can create communities where none exist' (p. 187). The idea that communities can really be brought into being by a type of broadcasting should, they note, 'be treated with suspicion'.

The pressure to experiment with new radio forms comes, they believe, from two sources (p. 188); 'those seeking to set up commercial stations and those who wish to use radio for community development'.

Radio and the language of freedom

Felix Guattari, writing on the subject of 'Popular Free Radio' (*see* Strauss and Mandl, *Radiotext(e)*, p. 85), believes that there are two possible ways in which communication could develop. One is 'toward hyper-concentrated systems controlled by the apparatus of state, of monopolies, of big political machines with the aim of shaping opinion'. The other, in Guattari's opinion, is 'toward miniaturised systems that create the possibility of a collective appropriation of the media'.

Guattari proposed this division between types of communication in response to his experience of Italian radio, then at the height of its radicalism. There is no denying the polarisation which affected public communication at this time, but the problem is that anything which falls between these categories may be ignored. Guattari presses forward with his theme, however, noting on the one hand 'always more centralisation, conformism, oppression' and on the other 'the perspective of a new space of freedom, self-management ... and the fulfilment of the singularities of desire'.

In his view, 'a breakthrough in the second direction' was achieved through 'a relatively old technology like radio', in the form of the Free Radio phenomenon in France and Italy. Perhaps the reason for the success of stations like *'Radio Alice'* lay in their ability to mobilise a pre-existing community around wider issues. Guattari, writing about the Alice phenomenon, identifies its position as 'one element at the heart of an entire range of communication means, from daily, informal meetings in the Piazza Maggiore to the newspaper – via billboards, mural paintings, posters, leaflets, meetings, community activities, celebrations, etc.'

The use of radio in the fight for social justice cannot ignore the language in which that struggle is conducted. In *Radiotext(e)* (p. 87), Guattari speaks of 'direct speech, living speech, full of confidence, but also hesitation, contradiction, indeed even nonsense'. He believes this to be 'the vehicle of desire's considerable burdens'. It is this form of discourse, free-ranging and thus able to express fundamental human needs, which Guattari sets against 'the language of official media' which is 'traceable to the police languages of the managerial milieu and the university'. We encounter here a strict division between good and bad practice, reflecting a real divergence between language genres, but allowing it seems for no cross-infection between one type of discourse and another. 'Bureaucrats of every stamp', Guattari feels, try to reduce the potency of living speech.

Political structures and radio broadcasting

If 'free radio' cannot be created by an effort of will, then we should perhaps look at the political structures which make such a phenomenon difficult to achieve. In the United States, Lewis and Booth believe that the emergence of 'giant corporations', the 'development of mass production techniques' and 'the growth of advertising' (together with 'an ideology that honoured profit'), produced a stridently commercial form of radio.

In Britain, the de-regulation of radio broadcasting in the late 1980s, did not recognise the considerable difference between commercial stations and those broadcasters with a genuine interest in a particular community. The 1987 Green Paper stated that the BBC must 'judge the size and commitment to local radio alongside the other claims on its resources'. Bob Franklin, writing in *Newszak and News Media*, translates this quite bluntly as meaning that 'BBC local radio was a shoestring operation to be funded from existing licence revenues'. The BBC, faced with competition from Independent Local Radio, reproduced the tried, trusted and cheap format of playing music, making dedications, and encouraging phone-ins. The type of listener interaction thus obtained, based on either controlled contributions to public debate, or more often on straightforward response to questions during phone-in competitions, is far removed from the use of listeners as informal correspondents.

The 'independent' sector itself was no more creative or democratic than the BBC. As Kevin Williams writes in *Get Me a Murder a Day!*(p. 247) 'most of Britain's local stations are owned by a small number of larger companies ... commercial considerations make such companies play safe in terms of the content of their stations ... throughout Britain there is a remarkable similarity as to what can be heard over the airwaves'. In Williams' opinion, the larger regional stations have developed 'at the expense of the local community stations'.

Lewis and Booth believe that (p. 9) 'the push for free, alternative or community radio ... has been overtaken by commercial radio operating under the same label ... similarly opposed to a state monopoly/duopoly but for different reasons'. Their argument in favour of 'a redefined public service' and the founding of a new radio station which can act as 'a radio publishing house', invites the state to support the more democratic or community-based projects which have achieved expression through forms such as pirate radio. Instead of this enlightened but limited proposal, the direction chosen by John Birt, Director General of the BBC, has caused some consternation amongst the supporters of radio broadcasting. Franklin (*Newszak and News Media*, p. 137) writes that 'critics immediately denounced the plan for downgrading domestic services, threatening the World Service, presaging widespread job cuts ... and triggering an explosion of bureaucracy'. Restructuring at the BBC seemed to guarantee the downgrading of radio as a distinct and autonomous arm of British broadcasting.

Interview with a lecturer in media and radio: Eryl Price-Davies

Q Do you consider that radio has been neglected, and why do you think it hasn't received the attention it might deserve?

Eryl Clearly radio is neglected as a medium in Higher Education. You've only got to look through prospectuses, and lists of courses in the UCAS handbook and so on, and you will be very lucky to come across the word radio at all. Lots of film studies courses, lots of media studies courses ... if you look more closely at media studies curriculum in most institutions, radio doesn't warrant a mention. So we have this huge medium that has a vast and diverse history, that is truly global and international, that encompasses community, public service broadcasting and free market models, that millions of people still listen to every day, yet there is massive critical neglect; there is no critical discourse, no language, no grammar in which to discuss radio in the way that there is for film or the novel, or women's magazines, or subcultures, and so on.

Q Do you think it's possible to adapt the frames of reference used for the novel, or the image, or is there a whole new project which is required to create a language in which radio can be discussed?

E I think a mixture of both strategies is required. What a lot of us have been trying to do for many years now, is to rework some basic structuralist methodology, and apply this to radio texts. What this has revealed is a number of interesting weaknesses, weaknesses which I've also found when you use semiology to try to analyse anything which moves, whether it's performance art, dance, theatre, or even film. Semiology seems to work best when it's dealing with fixed objects which aren't based in time.

Q Is part of the problem the fact that semiology has emerged largely from the Saussurean tradition, and that other currents of thought have had less impact? Could the system associated with C.S. Peirce, which is more concerned with action and meaning, be applied to radio?

E It would seem like a useful avenue to explore. There are, however, some other existing theories which can be adapted to the study of radio, such as the work of David Morley on television audiences, and methods of textual analysis drawn from film studies. But at the same time we're still left with the tyranny of the image and the very fact that we use visual metaphors all the time in trying to analyse this non-visual form. There is a clear difference between the visual form and radio. Film, for example, is infinitely reviewable; it exists as an object which is designed, particularly in the video era, to be seen and re-seen. The greatest strength that radio has, it is the most ephemeral of all media.

Q Some people would baulk at that; they'd say, if it's not there any longer, what's the point?

E Well absolutely, there is an absent centre in radio studies, which is the text itself. There is an exalted end of radio theory, which looks at mostly speech-based radio where scripts do exist and there's a clear literary tradition of broadcast talks which can then be studied using the tools of literary analysis. Other high status forms include the kind of radio phonic works like Dylan Thomas' *Under Milk Wood*. The vast majority of radio in the current era is music radio, and this music radio is characterised by its ephemerality. It doesn't mean that we can't make sense of it, just that we're struggling to find a critical language with which to discuss it.

Q Surely most of the stuff you hear in terms of music has been designed to be reheard, so why's that ephemeral?

E If people just wanted to listen to music, they'd listen to music on CDs. And there are in fact some music-only stations; Melody is one, Capital Gold in London is another. But for the vast majority of listeners, the reason for listening to one station as opposed to another is not the music, it's the presenters. So there is something there about the chat that goes on. Presenters are a key element. It's a personality-driven industry.

Q Don't you think that there's a lot of meaningless blather produced by many presenters, a kind of babble which is designed to get you through to the next record?

E Well the blather could have a number of different functions. It's non-threatening and not very demanding; radio is a background medium – you tend to listen to the radio when you're engaged in some other activity. There's a difference between listening and hearing. You hear the radio a great deal, but you only listen intermittently.

Q What do you think of the phone-in system on commercial radio; would you call that a move towards democracy or is it a sop to the listening public?

E I think it's purely economically driven for the most part, it's one of the cheapest forms of radio, you don't have to pay any money to the Performing Rights Society, for example. You just need a presenter and some phone lines, and people pay the station by phoning in. That's why the phone-in dominates talk radio. When it happens on television, it shows how dull television is as a medium for those kind of things. Watching people sitting on a sofa listening to someone's voice is dull.

Q In terms of introducing radio-based work into colleges, schools and universities, what should be done? Is there a way of basing radio work on theory, or should radio be introduced chiefly through practical methods?

E The single biggest opportunity available for educators is the Radio Authority's granting of Restricted Service Licences, which run for twenty-eight days. The first ones were granted in about 1994. It provides the chance to give students real experience of live broadcasting. Across the country, there are something like thirty, thirty-five student radio stations.

Q Do you think there is a kind of democratic potential in these Restricted Service Licences?

E There can be, but some RSLs are purely commercially driven. There are companies that run them as businesses, and will set up a twenty-eight day RSL in different parts of the country and they can work more or less round the year. They have an advertising team in each part of the country. There's one called Show FM which goes round agricultural shows. At the other end of the scale, there's groups like Bradford Community Broadcasting which run an RSL to involve local kids, to get them on air. They're funded by the local council and local arts groups – they carry no on-air advertising. The RSL is, I think, a tremendous tool for educators.

Sound and meaning

Andrew Crisell, in *Understanding Radio*, makes the distinction between words and sound. As signs, words count as symbols; it is their symbolic status which Crisell believes is the basis of radio's imaginative appeal. Of course, words are also used in those media traditionally regarded as visual, but it is a fact that words are spoken and therefore given the inflection of a human speaker's personality, which Crisell sees as having a particular impact on the listener.

Language: more emotional than cognitive?

Some theorists expand on the idea that the human voice carries a particular emotional quality, returning to the nature of language itself. There are arguments to be made for investigating more than simply the logical structures of language. Expressing dissatisfaction with the rather mechanical nature of Saussure's system of 'signifier' and 'signified', some teachers of language insist that the *sound* of an utterance is equal in importance to its structural qualities. Meaning is conveyed by both elements. The next stage is to argue, as Rivers Barry does in a recent paper *Sound and Meaning*, that:

> 'Language has an impact that is more emotional than cognitive in many instances ... the sounds themselves are certainly the building blocks of the mechanical system that all languages follow but their purpose is not necessarily one of separating and labelling ... sound is the emotional signposting, as much as it is the expression of ideas, of the "psychological reality" or significance of an utterance.'

Barry notes that a limited understanding of language is not necessarily an impediment to meaning. For example, he argues that 'don't' as an utterance is understood by children in the earliest part of their language development:

> 'They are not, at least usually, aware that it is a contraction of "do not" but they are aware that it is a negative and a command or warning, especially if it is given tonal significance.'

Sound and narrative

Sounds, as opposed to tone of voice, are by contrast 'natural', in that they are a form of signification which exists in the world. Crisell takes sounds to be indexical, rather than primarily symbolic. In the real world, individuals tend to pick out sounds if they are motivated to listen for something in particular, or if, for example, they unexpectedly hear their own name in the midst of other noise.

Radio and film technicians, however, must be able to reproduce the specific noise a producer requires and, more significantly, must be able to make certain sounds a priority. Erving Goffman, writing about radio drama, notes the difference between the individual subject's experience of a party (where individual speech would have to compete with a level of background noise), and the conventions which are used in order to *represent* the same event on the radio. There is a high degree of artificiality in the solutions which could be used. The alternatives would be to hold the background noise under the level of the foreground conversation, or to allow the occasional low sound to signify what would in reality be a stream of background noise.

A number of students working on an advanced production (at Somerset College) addressed the problem of how a 'semiology of sound' can be investigated using an audience of fellow students. Taking the idea of context as an important determining factor in the creation of meaning, they presented a number of sounds in turn to their selected audience, and required them to write down the connotations associated with each sound. Laughter on its own, for example, generated the response that happiness was signified. The same laughter, overlaid with sinister music (which acted as the contextualising factor), produced an idea of threat and suggested the horror genre. By contrast, used with a light-hearted piece, the laughter appeared innocent. This type of exercise may be a prelude to thinking again about the use of sound in film.

We saw, for example, how sound is either synchronous or asynchronous. The first comes from within the frame and the editor must work to synchronise it with the image. The other comes from outside the frame. Sound works either with or against an image. Contrapuntal sound is opposed to or in counterpoint with the image, whereas parallel sound is connected with the image, and reinforces it.

Barry distinguishes between the use of sound in film and in radio drama;

'The fact that music prompts certain feelings in given contexts means that musical "keys" are logical conventions of TV and film, where a narrative or context is not exclusively linguistic … it is unusual for music to be used as a form of emotional punctuation in radio … it is a medium of voice and of language, so the use of music would tend to inhibit rather than encourage the uptake of the narrative.'

APPROACHES TO THE STUDY OF TELEVISION

There are a number of approaches to the study of television, most of which have emerged from film theory. Some of the main strands of enquiry are summarised here. If we examine any specific approach to television, it is obvious that we will be studying the subject from just one angle, and that each approach will be unable to cover all the possible perspectives. Is there one perspective which covers more ground than the others? Or are the different approaches simply a reflection of the complexities of television texts themselves?

Feminist criticism of television

It is to some of the theories of Jacques Lacan that many feminist theorists have turned. It is not difficult to see why. Lacan's work examines the 'displacement' of the female, whereas in Freud the female seems to appear as an 'incomplete' version of the male. The work of Julia Kristeva (amongst others) is based on Lacan's theories of the way the female subject is constructed in a 'patriarchal language order'. This order is known as the 'symbolic', and it is one in which a woman is normally relegated to the position of 'absence' or 'lack'.

One of Lacan's most famous and controversial ideas, as we have seen, was that there was a 'mirror phase' which first marks the infant's awareness that its original sense of oneness with the mother is illusory. Lacan imagined the mother holding the child in front of a mirror in which both appeared. The child was supposed to catch sight of the reflection of itself and its mother, and to see the mother as an object *distinct* from itself. In addition, it would also make it recognise the mirror image of itself as an ideal image. The human subject is therefore, in Lacan's view, a split subject. In the first place, there is a mother and a non-mother. In the second place, there is this side of the mirror and there is the other side of the mirror.

The child is supposed unconsciously to incorporate the image of the mother as *another* image – and it begins to symbolise its own look as the Other. This sets in motion the desire for the mother. This desire in turn is displaced into a desire for what she desires. The recognition of the mother as the Other is, according to Lacan, a universal experience and one that is essential for the human-to-be to become human. The use of Lacan's theory has been extensive. As we have already seen in Chapter 1, the 'mirror' phase is incapable of proof; nor did Lacan attempt to carry out any clinical investigations in order to support his theories.

Feminism often appears, like many social theories, to carry a range of meanings. E. Ann Kaplan (*Channels of Discourse*) writes of 'feminisms', referring to the different strands of feminist thought and practice. She distinguishes between what she calls *political* approaches and *philosophical* approaches. Since any political conception of feminism is linked closely to the broad philosophical position held by theorists, it is worth describing the difference between these categories first.

Kaplan defines the **philosophical** approach to feminism as composed of two types: 'essentialist' and 'anti-essentialist'. Essentialist feminism starts from the idea that:

> 'there is a particular group called "women" that can be separated from another group, "men" – in terms of an essence that precedes culture and is ultimately biological in origin.'

Female values would, in this view, make up a contrast to the competitive and individualistic 'male' values that govern society. Female values would be seen to have an essential 'humaneness'. The other, anti-essentialist view, does not look for an essential 'femininity' which is supposed to be hidden or obscured by a male-dominated culture. An anti-essentialist approach would instead attempt to understand the processes through which the 'female' is constructed in patriarchal culture.

Kaplan divides the **political** categories of feminism into four types: 'bourgeois feminism', by which she means the concern of women to obtain equal rights and freedoms within a capitalist system; 'Marxist feminism', which links the specific oppression of women within the larger structure of capitalism; 'radical feminism', which is the designation of women as different from men and which pursues the goal of separate female communities to forward women's specific needs and desires; and finally, 'post-structuralist' feminism, where the idea is to analyse the language order (p. 216) 'through which we learn to be *what our culture* calls women'.

In the first case, **bourgeois** feminism contains what Julia Kristeva has called domestic or liberal strands, in which women (particularly in the nineteenth century) were likely to see (*Channels of Discourse*, p. 219):

> 'the patriarchically constructed "feminine" . . . as "natural", and . . . celebrated the qualities assigned to women as morally better than the male values of competition and aggressive individualism.'

This type of feminism made demands for equality of opportunity in the workplace and for access to institutional power. It is this strand which some critics believe has led to a great deal of quantitative analysis of mainstream television, in an attempt to analyse the range of roles that are assigned to women. Kaplan gives as an example of this approach a study of female roles in television made by Diana Meehan, in which she makes an exhaustive study of television roles and actions as they pertain to women. Meehan found that:

> 'the composite impression of the good-bad images was a forceful endorsement of a secondary position for women, a place in the world as selfless, devoted adjuncts to men.'
>
> (p. 221)

Kaplan regards Meehan's conclusions as rather inadequate, however, because Meehan simply ends with a clarion-call for new representations of women:

> 'it's time to tell the stories of female heroes – heading families, heading corporations, conquering fears, and coping with change.'
>
> (p. 221)

The next type described by Kaplan, is an **orthodox Marxism**, used by some feminist critics who regard television as a capitalist institution and examine both how women are *portrayed* by the institution, and how female viewers are *positioned* as consumers. As a result of this use of women by capitalism, a variety of images of women may appear on the screen, according to the needs of the capitalist economy. Lillian Robinson made a study using this perspective, one which used content analysis and investigated the real work roles of women in the American economy. Robinson found that much of the television representation of women's jobs entailed the trivialisation of their role in the workplace or, alternatively, showed the woman with professional status coming to grief, as though the 'career woman' has to be punished for her success. As Kaplan notes (p. 225):

> '[Robinson's] objective is to expose the workings of the patriarchal Symbolic rather than arguing for women's access to it.'

The next type, **radical feminism**, has somewhat different aims and uses a different analytical standpoint. Here the feminine is celebrated and a struggle for autonomy, or even separation from men and male-dominated institutions, is undertaken. Kaplan cites the work of Carol Aschur in the United States, which attacks television in that country for circulating two myths: that virtually everyone is middle class in America, and that the family is the sole location of (p. 226) 'love, understanding, compassion, respect, and sexuality'. The advent of series like *Roseanne* have marked a break with the almost exclusive concentration on the middle class, but it is certainly true that even this programme continued to filter all problems and ideas through the institution of the family. To radical feminist critics, the family is the place where the patriarchal order is reproduced and maintained. Soap opera, to their mind, is incapable of representing accurately the negative side of male roles in the family.

Post-structuralist feminism is based on the attempt to achieve:

> 'transcendence of the categories of sexual difference ... or at least recognition of their cultural construction.' (p. 227)

The aim in this type of feminist approach would be to examine and analyse the symbolic systems through which we communicate, in order to find out how men and women learn to 'be' men and women in this culture. The use of Laura Mulvey's work on the 'male gaze' and scopophilia in the cinema is useful to an extent, but only when applied in the main to what have become known as 'male' genres, or what might be best described as 'mainstream' narrative film. It seems obvious that the (heterosexual male) *television* viewer does not quite experience the necessary conditions for 'scopophilia' which are available in the cinema, even if such an opportunity for voyeurism is available. (There are plenty of men who find watching representations of sex on the television or cinema screen just plain embarrassing.)

Some feminist critics have moved away from the limitations of Mulvey's system towards an approach which allows them to explore the way that television functions: as a technology, as a carrier of a variety of texts, and as a form which is 'received' in a variety of ways and in a variety of locations. Kaplan refers to Tania Modleski's interest in soap opera as a genre which breaks down the distance which is maintained between spectator and text, since this genre works on a relationship of 'nearness' (just like that between mother and daughter) and has a structure which allows for interruption. Some authors go on to note the relationship between the fictive soap opera texts and television advertisements, which both deal with the sphere of the domestic, yet represent them in quite different ways. Television commercials tend to represent the family unit as less subject to problems and difficulties (and where it is, these problems tend to be 'resolved' by the product being advertised).

Charlotte Brunsdon drew the important distinction between the cinema's creation of narrative suspense, and the television soap opera's manipulation of ideas about personal life. One of the problems Brunsdon finds in teaching 'women's genres' (*see* 'Pedagogies of the Feminine', *Screen*, vol. 32, no. 4) is the resistance put up by different groups of students (for sometimes quite different reasons) to the material which makes up the accepted canon of 'women's texts'.

Anti-racist critiques of television

Anti-racist critiques of television start from a view which emphasises both the inadequate scale of the representation of black people, and the stereotyped nature of many of those representations which do exist. Angela Barry's essay on 'Black

Mythologies: Representation of Black People on Television', in *The Black and White Media Book* (Trentham Books, 1988) registers her initial surprise when, as a teenager newly arrived from Bermuda, she first experienced the content of *Till Death Us Do Part*, which featured the supposedly satirical outbursts of Alf Garnett. It was not that she was unused either to meeting racism or seeing racist stereotypes, but rather that she had not encountered these in the context of (p. 83), 'British social realism'. Other forms of racism were evident in the contemporaneous speeches of Enoch Powell, which became a rallying cry for right-wing forces, including some overtly fascist groups. Barry's experience of television in Bermuda had been quite different; it had at this time been broadcasting what Barry calls 'American icons', the images of US Civil Rights marchers, forming a definite contrast with the material broadcast on British television.

Objection to the representation of diatribes *against* certain ethnic groups is not the only element which concerns anti-racist critiques of television. Another is obviously the way that Afro-Caribbean and Asian people are themselves represented on television. Television's view of ethnicity is built upon older understandings of the differences between Western culture and what have been called Third World societies. Alvarado, Gutch and Wollen describe this pre-existing 'mind-set' as emanating from the cultural and economic relationships established between (p. 204) 'the mercantile Europeans of the sixteenth century' and the lands and peoples they were to exploit. In an echo of Lacan's phrase, these authors argue that:

'those who inspired [the Europeans'] wonder were marked as "other", which served a useful purpose when later the search for resources and markets became so rapacious that the "other" had to be subjugated, robbed, controlled.'

According to this idea, it is the *difference* between the two ethnicities which mattered to the Europeans. An inability to understand the cultural formations of these 'native' peoples led to various customs and artifacts being taken out of context and, importantly for an insight into some of television's practices, the people from this 'new world' were regarded as 'exotic'. The 'other', the exotic, continue to circulate as important elements in the meanings television constructs when it addresses the question of racial difference.

Most authors acknowledge the progress that has been made in the way that television approaches ethnicity, but such progress has been extremely problematic. Whereas certain types of programme now seem unthinkable, and comedians like Bernard Manning and Jim Davidson are more readily seen as 'controversial', those writers who have investigated the question see new difficulties arising at the very moment when the programme-makers seemed to have made an effort to introduce more positive images.

It would seem that images of black people are allowed to appear 'positive' provided they pose no threat to the status quo. Angela Barry notes (p. 86) that it was part of the change from the 'ideology of Empire' to ideas about 'Commonwealth' which allowed the patronising but 'benevolent' television and newsreel depictions of black Commonwealth citizens arriving in England in the early 1950s. The general 'invisibility' of black people, so far as television was concerned (apart from the strange case of *The Black and White Minstrel Show*), lasted until 1958, when what are still known as the 'Notting Hill Riots' took place. (How exactly attacks on black people, carried out by hooligans and racists, came to be known as 'race riots' is difficult to understand.) According to Barry, this marked the beginning of a change in the attitude of the authorities.

The 1962 Commonwealth Immigration Bill began to restrict the right of Commonwealth citizens to enter Britain. Barry goes on to argue, however, that the institution of television did not reflect this new negativity; instead, it made a number of representations which might have appeared positive, had the black artists involved not been restricted to certain roles, in particular ones which were centred on dance, music, and light entertainment. It is not the importance of music and dance to black cultures which Barry challenges, but rather the fact that such images were so predominant in British television at this time. She describes three images of black people which circulated during this period; the trouble-maker (an image not used by television), the entertainer, and the victim of famine and misfortune.

This last category is described by Alvarado *et al.* (p. 218), as 'the Pitied'. During 1985 representations of famine were particularly widespread in television and the mass media. These authors attribute a new form of negativity to the fact that the representations of starving Africans de-contextualise and de-historicise their plight by concentrating on images rather than on analysis:

> 'Nearly all the images of black people – in particular mothers and children – represent them as victims and sufferers.' (p. 218)

The mid-1980s also featured what Salman Rushdie called 'the Raj revival'. Rushdie noted the trend for making programmes, films and 'mini-series' set during the time of the British Raj in India. At the same time, very few Indian actors were allowed to represent major characters in the various projects which flourished at this time. Rushdie's opinion of some of the television versions of Indian life was hardly complimentary. He described *The Far Pavilions* (in *The Black and White Media Book*) as a part of a long trend for manufacturing (p. 131) 'a false Orient of cruel-lipped princes and dusky slim-hipped maidens'. His response to the mini-series is also based unashamedly on artistic and literary criteria:

> 'the great processing machines of TV soap opera have taken the somewhat more fibrous garbage of the M.M. Kaye book and pureed it into easy-swallow, no-chewing-necessary drivel. Thus, the two central characters, both supposedly raised as Indians, have been lobotomised to the point of being incapable of pronouncing their own names.' (p. 130)

In the last analysis, Rushdie returns to what he sees as the cause of the proliferation of Raj-fictions. This is the nostalgic wish to return to an era when Britain was a colonial power, so that the poverty and lack of direction which characterised much of the Thatcherite era could momentarily be forgotten. Rushdie makes the argument, that:

> 'works of art, even works of entertainment, do not come into being in a social and political vacuum ... the way that they operate in a society cannot be separated from politics, from history. For every text, a context ... the rise of Raj revisionism ... is the artistic counterpart to the rise of conservative ideologies in Britain.' (p. 133)

Narrative approaches to television

Narrative, as we have seen in the chapter on film, concerns itself with the structural aspects of both plot and plot-device (including character as an aspect of structure). Propp and Todorov have stood out as exemplars in this field, but narrative theory deals also with ideas about the interaction between plot and subplot. Narrative is an intrinsic part of how we represent actions and events in our lives. Edward Branigan, writing about film (*Narrative Comprehension and Film*, p. 3) describes narrative as an 'activity that organises data into a special pattern which represents and explains experience'.

Narrative in film and narrative in television are, however, different in many respects. Some theorists argue that television has so much predictability and so little of the normal 'cinematic' ingredients of suspense, that it fails to fulfil one of the main goals of narrative – to keep the reader guessing. This is partly to do with a number of constraints placed on many fictional forms. In the first place, time is a major constraint. A crime in *The Bill* must be solved by the end of half an hour, or the connection between the various subplots must at least be made clear, leaving the way open for future resolution. Each episode of *Eastenders* and *Brookside* must end on a dramatic note, the traditional soap opera cliff-hanger.

Another constraint is that of character; for the sake of clarity and ease of identification, people must behave according to type. If Grant in *Eastenders* gets it into his head to pay off a debt by burning down the Queen Vic and collecting the insurance, we feel pretty sure he will attempt to do just that. It seems that television's fictional forms compensate for the high levels of predictability they display by creating a number of story-lines and character types – which in turn probably diffuse the dramatic impact of the programme. Film, by contrast, requires a single sitting but a high rate of commitment throughout, and an audience probably expects an emotionally satisfying conclusion.

Jane Feuer (in Fiske, *Television Culture*, p. 144), argues that the 'dominant' forms of television's narrative practice are the series and the serial. Although some regard television programmes as 'predictable', Feuer believes that these dominant forms are much more open to different interpretations than the complete, 'closed' narratives of the novel and film. This seems to be true in the sense that the multiple plots of the series and serial in many cases never reach a point of 'closure', partly because they depend on having plots which can develop in a number of directions. This is connected with the fact that often a team of writers is responsible for developing the story-line. It seems possible, however, that film too is often reluctant to make a complete narrative closure, to leave open the option of making a profitable sequel at some later date. (There are sad cases where a film is well and truly over, but the plot is revived anyway because of the scent of money.) Television 'sitcoms', in particular, are cases where (Fiske, p. 145) 'the comedy may be resolved each week, but the situation never is.'

Narrative theory should not be thought of as confined to fictional forms, since the news, for example, can be described as a narrative, with definite structures at work; the serious tone of many opening reports and the gradual move towards the day's sporting highlights, with perhaps an amusing story thrown in as a conclusion. Sarah Ruth Kozloff, writing about narrative theory (*see Channels of Discourse*,

p. 67), describes 'short-stories, novels, and films' as 'freestanding', in the sense that the narratives are allowed to develop without too many 'outside constraints' . Television narratives are different, however, because they are embedded within the 'metadiscourse' of the station's schedule or overall programming. The word 'discourse' is one with which we are familiar: 'Meta', from the Greek, means 'after' or 'with' and the term as a whole refers to the overall effect of the many addresses, narratives, and structures which are found in television.

Reader-orientated criticism

Reader-oriented criticism is a term used by Robert C. Allen in *Channels of Discourse*. It is an idea which tends to oppose the structuralist perspective upon which much narrative theory rests. The critic Wolfgang Iser was an opponent of the idea that meaning is located solely in the text, objecting to the notion that it was the professional critic who provided explanations to an ignorant public. An important alternative to the idea that the text has a fixed, accessible meaning would be that texts are made to mean things through the process of reading.

Phenomenology is the term given to the relationship between the perceiving individual and the world of things, people and actions that might be perceived. According to this theory, all thought and perception involve mutually dependent subjects and objects. Reality amounts to individually experienced phenomena. Mass media and other texts are brought to life in the imagination of the individual reader. According to Roman Ingarden (*Channels of Discourse*, p. 77), the literary text starts as an intentional act on the part of the author. However, once the work has been written and published, it exists separately from these originating intentions. Ingarden uses the example of music, where the text has a material status as written notes on paper that have resulted from the composer's activity. At this point, the text is still only a list of possibilities (although it could be argued that these possibilities are strictly circumscribed). Ingarden believed that the performer had to 'concretise' the text through performance and that the same was true for the literary text. The literary text was characterised as a 'schema', a skeletal structure of *meaning possibilities* awaiting concretisation by the reader's own activity. Each reading would therefore be a 'performance' of meaning. The text is 'waiting' for the intending (human) subject. Although it may appear that (p. 78) 'the text leaves much up to the individual to decide', these decisions may in fact be no more than the details of the narrative, leaving intact the wider structures, which provide all readers with a set of definite parameters. In other words, the individual is able to 'recast' the text only within certain limits.

It must be made clear that there are differences between literary narratives and the televisual text. In the case of television, the initial expectations the reader has of the text form a constantly changing fictional world, but one (*Channels of Discourse*, p. 79) 'that appears to us as whole and complete at any given moment during the reading act.'

According to the theories of Wolfgang Iser, paintings are available to us as audience 'all at once', whereas the only time we experience a novel or a film as a whole is when we have finished reading it. There are some possible faults in this approach, however. To characterise a painting as immediately available is to ignore the fact that the eye cannot cover all the ground of a picture at once, and is usually attracted only by certain areas at a time. Equally, many of the codes of painting might not be easily accessible to the viewer; certain references may not be understood. To sum up the objections which may be made, we might consider that it takes time to come to an understanding of a painting.

The reader of a narrative takes on what Iser (p. 79) calls a 'wandering viewpoint' – a constantly changing position within the text itself. Iser's theory of the 'wandering viewpoint' emphasises its **diachronic** nature, that is to say the way it occurs over time. We have to pass between what we *anticipate* and what we *remember* of the text. Iser calls this an alteration between **portension** (what we expect or anticipate) and **retention** (what we have remembered from the text).

Allen goes on to apply Ingarden and Iser's theories to soap opera. Soap opera seems to him to be a typical example of a form which (p. 83) 'does not give us a position after "The End" from which to look back on the entire text'. Therefore, as viewers we 'cannot help but be inside the narrative flow of the soap opera text'.

Ideological analysis

Ideological analysis is the term given to a current of thought which looks at the political and social meanings offered by the mass media, both on the surface (explicit) and below the surface (implicit). In line with our understanding of the term, we could say that an analysis of discourse is a natural route for understanding ideological concerns in their material context; actually looking at what texts appear to 'say'.

There are clear differences between the British and American contexts. Mimi White, in 'Ideological Analysis and Television' (*Channels of Discourse*, p. 134) notes that:

'In the context of American television, advertising is normal ... the integral presence of commercials is taken as a given, regulating the rhythm of programmes and viewing. The viewer, familiar with the regularity of commercials as an integral feature of textual flow, is addressed as a potential customer.'

The purpose of ideological criticism, according to White, is to show how cultural artifacts 'produce particular knowledges and positions for viewers'. One strength of this approach is that it relates what we see on our television screens to the wider structures of society. A text is not something which entirely escapes from the time and place of its production – we are aware of this when we view a fictional text from ten or more years ago. For instance, we may notice that there are considerable differences between the fashions of dress displayed in the text and the fashions we are used to seeing in the present. But we may also notice that the themes which are explored in the programme, or more likely the characters' *attitudes* to these themes, are different to the attitudes displayed in contemporary dramas. We could say that all texts, whether produced under the influence of a certain ideology or not, have a 'shelf life'. As White argues:

'Because of this social and historical specificity, artifacts express and promote values, beliefs, and ideas that are pertinent to the contexts in which they are produced, distributed and received.'

(p. 136)

Orthodox Marxist theory, which divides society into a *base* and a *superstructure*, has not proved quite flexible enough to explain how discourse in mass media texts produces meaning. According to this theory, the crucial organising factor of human society is its economic base. The main class division is between the owners of the means of production and the workers within the mode of production (*see* Chapter 2 for theories of society).

From this fairly primitive perspective, texts carry a 'dominant' ideology within themselves, because they were created within a capitalist system. This point of view would tend to imply (p. 137) that 'a transformation of television's ideology would require a shift in the mode of production'.

By a change in the mode of production, some Marxists would imagine a total reorganisation of the present ownership and control of the economy, and all its related social structures, in favour of some kind of system based on the interests of the working class. But, as we saw in our study of advertising, some changes in the discourses of television can occur when less dramatic changes happen in the economy and in society in general. Although it is true that a partial reorganisation in the structures of British broadcasting has taken place through the process of de-regulation, this has simply confirmed the movement towards a commercial model of television.

Most commentators are not convinced by the argument that the working class are basically 'kept quiet' and docile by the mass media (although it is difficult to be active about things that one does not even know about – for example, we might cite certain events which occurred during the Gulf War). We have explored the shortcomings of ideas about 'false consciousness' in a previous chapter, but it may be that certain groups in British society have acquired a rather limited set of cultural perspectives.

There are clearly preferred readings in a text, but (as we saw in the chapter on film) television programmes tend also to carry alternative readings in their very structure. This is because the male hero, for example, must be clearly set against an opposing force which reviles his values. Are any valid criticisms of the hero made during his 'legitimated' quest against the villain? Can programmes be read 'against the grain'?

White believes that the ideological position of some programmes may become contradictory. The example she uses is the American series, *Cagney and Lacey*. This programme appeared to be made from a 'liberal' feminist viewpoint. However, White notes that the conventions of framing and *mise-en-scène* (what is actually seen in the frame, the content) may work against the dominant (liberal) discourse of the programme. In the episode discussed by White, Cagney is threatened by a suspect in a murder to which she was a witness. White describes the action as follows:

'this episode included repeated shots of Cagney isolated in her apartment, almost cowering, trapped by the camera and the suspect as he watched her through the rooftop skylight. In this instance, her ability to perform as a cop (aggressive, strong, confident) was displaced by conventions for representing women as subject to the menacing threat of a narrative character and the look of the camera.'   (p. 154)

This idea is quite a familiar one from our study of film. White believes that, although the programme offers two strong and competent women, this is undermined in visual and narrative terms by the codes and conventions which the makers of the series have used. Jane Feuer argues (*see* Fiske, *Television Culture*, p. 144) that traditional narrative theories are better at describing 'masculine' narratives (such as the adventure or police drama) than 'feminine' narratives, such as soap opera. It may also be that the programme-makers themselves are used to codes and conventions which allow the male perspective a privileged position.

Cagney and Lacey (*Channels of Discourse*, p. 155) may, according to Mimi White, 'orchestrate a variety of perspectives, without clearly insisting that only one position is acceptable'. White's political position is an interesting one, since she believes that the 'system' contains and neutralises any possible challenges exactly through its power to express them:

> 'This system allows the programme to raise questions about the police system, or to suggest that it has problems, but it never poses a thoroughgoing challenge to the system itself. Instead, dramatised problems are seen as weaknesses or aberrations in a fundamentally good (natural and necessary) system, within which the characters of Cagney and Lacey represent an ideal.'   (p. 156)

This idea is very close to the concept of 'recuperation' which was explored in Chapter 2. White sees (p. 157) the 'unusual degree of strength and independence' of the narrative roles of these female characters, as a threat which has to be contained by the use of 'conventional visual strategies ... along with domestic plots that emphasise the more traditional roles of wife, mother, and daughter'. If we are to understand television as a 'meta-discourse', and not simply as a collection of ideas scattered among different programmes, then we could learn from White's remark that the commercial breaks which come between different segments of the programme (showing quite traditional female roles), serve to 'contextualise' the more challenging aspects of the programme through a 'dominant' view of the place of women.

White's work represents an important updating of the Marxist perspective on ideology, one which is flexible enough to recognise that there is no single valid interpretation of a text (this is presumably learned from reader-oriented approaches) and which also avoids the more mechanical systems used by Morley to describe the possible range of interpretations he found in the *Nationwide* study (the divisions described as oppositional, negotiated and dominant). White concludes:

> 'thus, over time, within and across individual episodes, *Cagney and Lacey* produces a range of ideological effects and meanings. The contradictions and multiplicity of views help explain its appeal to a broad potential audience because one can recognise progressive, liberal, and traditional values working at once through the fabric of the show.'
>   (p. 158)

DEBATES ABOUT TELEVISION: FORM AND CONTENT

Feminist critics who have stressed the greater accessibility of some forms of television, have advanced arguments which emphasise the approach television makes to the 'personal' and the 'domestic'. Television is often cited as an example of realism. John Fiske, writing in *Television Culture*, notes (as we saw in the chapter on film) that realism is often understood as a narrative arrangement (a form). Content, on the other hand, is taken to mean the collected elements which are contained *within* the form of the text; content must be the subject-matter itself, rather than the order is which it is presented.

The emphasis on individual lives and experiences is, as we have seen under the heading of feminist criticism, very important in notions of realism. The idea of representing ordinary lives comes from a belief that moral, political and social questions can be examined in a way which makes more immediate contact with an audience.

Text and audience

Stephen Neale's idea that genre or type is understood partly in terms of an expectation held by an audience, clearly applies to television as well as film. It is worth reminding ourselves of John Corner's distinction between the expectations brought by an audience to a form such as the news, and those they bring to dramatic fiction. Corner's suggestion was that audiences may ask, 'is this truthful?' in the case of new programmes, and 'is this plausible?' in the case of film and narrative television forms.

The relationship between text and audience is an important element in the creation of realism in television. John Fiske explains the codes of television precisely in terms of this relationship:

'Codes are links between producers, texts, and audiences, and are agents of intertextuality through which texts interrelate in a network of meanings that constitute our cultural world.' (p. 4)

He also argues that a text is:

'the site of struggles for meaning that reproduce the conflicts of interests between the producers and consumers of the cultural commodity.' (p. 14)

The struggle over meaning is able to take place because, according to Fiske:

'an essential characteristic of television is its polysemy, or multiplicity of meanings. A programme provides a potential of meanings which may be realised, or made into actually experienced meanings, by socially situated viewers in the process of reading.' (p. 15)

Any study of television must take into account the formal qualities of television programmes, as well as the intertextual relations of television programmes with one another. The other element must be the investigation of audience and the study of the way in which texts are read.

Reality and the code

Fiske believes that 'reality is already encoded' and gives the example of people's appearance. His idea was to divide the codes of television into three (though it would have been better had they been categorised into four sections). In the first case, an event to be televised is already encoded by social codes; this is described as level one, or the level of **reality**, and includes such things as appearance, dress, environment, speech, expression, sound and so on. These elements are further encoded by technical codes, producing the second level, which consists of the mediating effects of camera, lighting, editing, music, and reproduction of sound. Fiske calls this level **representation**. Representational codes (of narrative, conflict, character, action, dialogue, setting, and so on) produce another level, or according to Fiske do so when **ideology** organises these things into (p. 5) 'coherence and social acceptability' by individualism, patriarchy, race, class, materialism, and capitalism.

Fiske argues that what passes for reality in any culture is:

'the product of that culture's codes, so "reality" is always already coded, it is never "raw". If this piece of encoded reality is televised, the technical codes and representational conventions of the medium are brought to bear on it so as to make it a) transmittable technologically and b) an appropriate cultural text for its audiences.' (p. 5)

Following this line, he suggests that different sorts of trees have different connotative associations and decides that:

'a tree reflected in a lake, for example, is fully encoded even before it is photographed and turned into the setting for a romantic narrative.' (p. 6)

But it seems, according to his previous argument, that such a scene is really encoded at the level of reality. The individual human responses which then interpret that reality, could produce a variety of meanings. These meanings could be entirely different to the representation produced by the photograph.

Realism and television drama

John Corner, whose work was introduced in Chapter 5, felt that the notion of realism had become little more than a collection of begged questions. Realism seemed to be either a 'straight imaging of the real' such as news and documentary (which tends to block questions about the nature of their construction as texts), or an 'imaginatively convincing' piece of artifice such as the drama series, plays, films and so on. The real itself is at some distance from both of these practices. Realism appeared to mean some kind of conformity to what are called 'generic norms' in such a way that the 'illusion' of realism is produced. Corner thinks that realism is (*Media Culture and Society*, vol. 13, no. 2, April 1991, p. 99):

'an acknowledged effect whose separation from (and discernible difference from) "reality" forms part of its appreciation.'

In other words, we would not be able to spot the difference between realism and the real itself, if the practice of realism were not in fact just another way of representing reality.

According to Corner, the 'realism' of news, current affairs television and documentary are connected with 'veracity of reference' (underpinned in its turn by 'veracities of image and speech'). In drama, on the other hand, the criteria usually applied by audiences are faithfulness to the truth, and credibility. The *Days of Hope* debate (*see* below), in Corner's view, made a link between television representation and social and political realities. Corner talked of realism of form (conventions of staging, directing, acting, shooting and editing) and realism of theme (characterisation, circumstance, and action).

It is Corner's belief that realism of form has been the dominant strand in the formation of television theory, owing to the influence of film theory on studies of television. In Britain, the use of documentary conventions in social or historical drama gave rise to theories of 'progressive realism'.

Days of Hope

Day of Hope was a television series transmitted in 1975, which became an issue debated throughout the 1980s. It was used as a focus for study in various centres of higher education and seemed to fulfil Barthes' adage that 'what is noted becomes notable'. In terms of content, the series is easy to describe. It consisted of four filmed plays based around the experience of an English working-class family over ten years from 1916 to 1926. In other words, the narrative began during the First World War and ended in the year of the General Strike. There were three principal characters in this drama: Ben and Sarah (a brother and sister) and Sarah's husband Philip.

Philip begins as a conscientious objector on the run from the police. Ben, by contrast, joins the Army and is first sent to Ireland and then to Durham. The function of the armed forces in Durham is to put down a miners' strike which is in progress. However, Ben becomes radicalised, and by the fourth episode has become a communist, helping his sister to organise working-class action during the General Strike.

The producer was Tony Garnett, the director Ken Loach, and the writer Jim Allen. *Days of Hope* remains important because of its commitment to a certain kind of realism and to a political view of television. There was a clear political message in the consciousness of the people who produced it. In September 1975, Garnett, interviewed in the *Radio Times* (*see Popular Television and Film*, BFI, 1981, p. 302), said:

'Our motive for going into the past is not to escape the present; we go into the past to draw lessons from it. History is contemporary.'

Ken Loach, who had originally wanted to make the series as a film, stressed that:

'we wanted to show that England is founded on a violent past which involves the forceful suppression of dissent ... We want anybody who feels themselves to be suffering from crises today, people who are caught by price rises, inflation and wage restraint, to watch the films and realise that all this happened before. And we hope they will learn some lessons from the opportunities that were lost in 1926 and the defeats inflicted on the working class that time. We haven't given any solutions, though the judgment we make is clear.'

The writer, Jim Allen, went so far as to say that:

'The General Strike offered the opportunity for the creation of a workers' state in Britain. This opportunity was lost by the sell-out of the TUC, the Labour Party and the Communist Party. The message is: don't let it happen again.'

The programme provoked a great response; letters to all sorts of newspapers began to appear. Although many accusations were made about the political bias shown in the series, some complaints were based simply on the grounds of historical accuracy. Again, the fact that actors worked without much more than improvised scripts (in an attempt to achieve a 'naturalism' which might be able to escape the artificial constraints of a great deal of screen acting), led to other debates, equally heated. One reviewer (*Popular Television and Film*, p. 303) made the comment that the naturalist approach to the subject:

'militates against form, for instance. It tends to preclude a writer rounding off a scene as neatly, making a point as concisely, constructing his drama with as much craft, as he would if he were writing a conventional play.'

Some felt that the parts where the action was based on real speeches were more effective than those scenes which emerged from what the critic Keith Tribe calls the conventions of family romance. *Screen*, the film and television journal, began a debate on the issues which surrounded *Days of Hope*. Screen was concerned with the idea that the use of realism set up limitations to what could be achieved politically. One of its contributors, Colin McArthur, wrote (*see Popular Television and Film*, p. 306):

'Its authors' refusal to countenance auto-reflexive devices, i.e. devices which directly create an awareness of the process of production, guaranteed that much critical response would take the irrelevant lines it did ... it is reasonable to expect an allegedly radical film to tell us something about the problems of making films for a large broadcasting institution within a dominant artistic discourse as well as about the "reality" it signifies.'

In other words, this writer believed that there should be 'built-in' devices designed to break the viewer's usual habit of suspending his or her disbelief. The technical and artistic methods used in constructing the programme should be made obvious, to remind the viewer that he/she is watching a fictional construct. These devices might include the deliberate inclusion of film equipment, which usually remains unseen. It might involve a character talking direct to camera, or the use of anomalies (such as the rather self-conscious references to modern US imperialism in Alex Cox's *Walker*).

The reason for this belief in the need to 'alienate' the audience is easy to see. Some writers at this time, following Brecht, believed that the audience was otherwise too easily sucked into the traditional narrative structures of mainstream film and television. There was nothing left for audiences to do but enjoy the ride, as it were. If there was going to be a useful reaction, in political terms, to a piece of fiction, then the audience would have to feel that the central dilemma of the narrative remained unresolved at the end of the action.

McArthur looked at the *Days of Hope* controversy by referring to Colin MacCabe's article concerning Brecht's theses on the theatre. (The account given above of Brecht's ideas about the purposes of drama is a rather loose one.) McArthur goes on to describe MacCabe's theory of the 'classic realist text'. This would be the idea that more than one discourse or ideological standpoint is present in a text, but that one only (the one favoured by the author) would remain in a position of dominance.

The notion that a number of discourses comprise the text and that these discourses are placed in a hierarchy, with the dominant point of view at the top, does seem plausible, except that many texts in practice seem to allow a greater internal equality between discourses than this suggests. (Sometimes it may seem as if an author does not quite have control over his/her material and that discourses are not particularly favoured one over another). The idea that the dominant viewpoint or discourse is never revealed but is presented as obvious or natural, seems to underestimate the ability of an audience to recognise artifice.

McArthur in fact doubted the applicability of MacCabe's theory of the classical realist text to *Days of Hope*. In particular, MacCabe's idea that the classic realist text 'cannot deal with the real as contradictory', struck McArthur as far removed from the truth. In his opinion, *Days of Hope* dealt very well with the contradictions of actual existence. McArthur cites the scene where a northern colliery owner lectures Ben and three arrested Durham miners on the British tradition of peaceful and gradual constitutional reform, while we see in the background troops brought in to suppress the strike, practising bayonet drill (*see Popular Television and Film*, p. 308). *Days of Hope* would appear to avoid certain Hollywood practices (such as the use of stars and narrative climax) but in almost every other respect is produced as a classic text. McArthur argued that the series was at least a 'progressive realist text', and he went on to accuse *Screen* of tending towards the 'utopian'.

MacCabe's response to McArthur (*see Popular Television and Film*, p. 310) was to highlight the way that *Days of Hope* compared subordinate discourses with the 'narrative' or dominant discourse and then used the dominant discourse to force the reader into an 'imaginary unity of position'. The text was therefore 'repressing its own operations'.

The example given by McArthur (the bayonet drill set out as a contrast to the colliery owner who praises the moderate nature of the British State) is one which MacCabe finds unconvincing:

> '[McArthur] cites the sequence in which the mine-owner speaks about the peaceful and constitutional British tradition while in the background the troops brought in to quell the miners indulge in bayonet practice. What McArthur here confuses is the narrative's ability to state a contradiction which it has already resolved, and the narrative's ability to produce a contradiction which remains unresolved and is thus left for the reader to resolve and act out.'
> (p. 312)

MacCabe is obviously keen to emphasise that the narrative has simply set up its own very dubious 'proof' in order to make the point that the British State is in fact highly repressive. This is quite a convincing argument, but he also imagines the audience as an active body of individuals who are closely involved in matters political, even as spectators. However, there is no necessary link in present circumstances between a political play and its audience. In other words, the audience may feel no need to rush off and act out the unresolved contradictions; the loose ends of social action may continue to hang loose. The Brechtian thesis may operate to some degree in certain types of society and more importantly at certain times, but not in other times and places where public protest is regarded perhaps as eccentric, or as undesirable.

There is nothing wrong with distinguishing between fictional forms which resolve all their internal conflicts (or force a resolution to them) and those which allow the reader to do some work. But to imagine that an audience will be always forced to act out the contradictions as some kind of political imperative might be regarded as something of a fantasy.

MacCabe believed that it was the dominance of the novel form which led to the confusion of realism with 'the particular forms of the nineteenth century realist novel'. This reliance on the idea that the novel was still the predominant form, is the weakest part of MacCabe's argument, but he made some interesting remarks when he noted that *Days of Hope* was really trying to offer the working class a set of 'memories' close to their own history, while at the same time the actual history appeared to be fading from their consciousness. He was therefore confident of his ground when he identified a classic realist trick, that which occurs when the *image* used is supposed to reassure the audience that they are watching something 'true':

> 'The reality of the character is guaranteed by the shot, and the reality of the shot is guaranteed by the character.'   (p. 315)

MacCabe noticed that some characters did not have the 'guarantee' of the visual to underline their truthfulness:

> 'Philip's politics are presented without any visual evidence to explain their origin or form . . . as such, and opposed to Ben's, they are simply "unrealistic".'

MacCabe's most telling attack on the limitations of *Days of Hope* comes when he recalls what Marx had to say about the value of the past as an inspiration for present struggles:

> 'just when [the revolutionaries] seem engaged in revolutionising themselves and things, in creating something that has never yet existed . . . they anxiously conjure up the spirits of the past to their service and borrow from them names, battle-cries and costumes . . . The social revolution cannot draw its poetry from the past but only from the future.'
> (p. 316)

MacCabe's argument is that a proper investigation of political and social themes would need to start from an examination of the present, but this would be impossible in the context of *Days of Hope*, because to do so would undermine the importance given to the visual (the 'faithful' representation of the past in terms of setting, dress codes and behaviours). The 'truth' of the series depended heavily on the visual and a break with it would have destroyed the whole thesis of the series. As John Caughie wrote (*Popular Television and Film*, p. 324), the careful reconstruction of the past, down to the smallest detail, would result in '[a] history . . . recognised as Truth by the viewer not by virtue of the "facts" being correct, but because the image looks right'.

But the ability of the Loach/Garnett/Allen attempt to use working-class history in a political way was possible partly by virtue of the tradition of the 'innovative' drama-form, where certain plays were allowed to extend television's general range of discourse, and where, most importantly, alternative ways of imagining the world are *shown* to an audience. This idea extends to other dramas besides *Days of Hope.* According to Caughie:

> 'The effect of *Cathy Come Home* was derived precisely from the *showing* of evidence which was already available as statistics for discussion.' (p. 329)

GUARDIANS OR PUBLIC SERVANTS?

The controversy which surrounded the showing of *Days of Hope* had somehow to be rationalised and contained by the BBC. Caughie believed that broadcasting had developed a vocabulary for dealing with a confusion of roles; one role being that of guardian of morals, and the other being that of public servant. Since explicit censorship has always been a problem for a broadcasting system which (p. 329) 'claims public responsibility', some kind of discourse has to be used in order to justify restrictions on what is allowed to be seen.

On the one hand, censorship of a documentary would be likely to be justified by reference to concepts such as 'national security', 'civic responsibility', 'objectivity', and so on. In Caughie's opinion, this might possibly (p. 139) 'throw a shadow' over notions of 'independence' and 'the public's right to know'. The censorship of drama, on the other hand, would tend to rely on a 'much less secure language' which would include terms such as 'taste' and 'public sensibility'.

To Caughie, the discourse of television is not static, but is subject to continual change. He suggested that 'the single play or play series has a crucial functional role in that revision and extension'. The single play or series is advanced here as the standard bearer of freedoms which need to be won for television as a whole. It is of course the 'seriousness' of drama which allows its themes to be perceived as serious, and which therefore makes people think it worthy of attention. John Caughie's outstanding point is:

> 'that the political importance of television drama is tied up with the place which drama occupies in the movements of relationships within the institutions, and cannot be thought of simply in terms of its form or its content'. (p. 330)

This is worth thinking about, because we might otherwise imagine that it will *always* be the case that a certain form will cause controversy and argument, and that somehow there is a way of avoiding trouble by adopting alternative forms. There is, however, some evidence to suggest that certain forms will be less prone to trouble. For example, we might cite a play like *The Black and Blue Lamp*, which worked to criticise contemporary policing methods through reference to (and contrast with) the image of the police set up by the original film, *The Blue Lamp*. Dirk Bogarde featured in the earlier film as the youthful villain who shatters the whole of Britain's post-war consensus by shooting George Dixon (resurrected as *Dixon of*

Dock Green in the long-running television series). The *Black and Blue Lamp*, however, used a surreal comic form very similar to plays like *Accidental Death of an Anarchist* by Dario Fo, and escaped the kind of outcry provoked by *Days of Hope*.

CURRENTS OF DISCOURSE

The Listener (vol. 94, no. 2427) published a transcript of a debate which took place on the BBC *Tonight* programme, hosted by Sue Lawley. What is interesting from the vantage point of studies of discourse, is the way that the interviewer immediately picks up the dominant current of discourse – the view that *Days of Hope* was openly propagandist (*see Drama-Documentary: BFI Dossier 19*, BFI, 1984, p. 21):

> 'Sue Lawley: "Days of Hope has met with a storm of abuse – not just for its alleged Communist propaganda. The BBC itself has been criticised for allowing it to be broadcast ... ".'

The audience is addressed as though it is part of a consensus which sees the whole debate from a certain perspective. Lawley set the tone with a list of questions supposed to outline the main concerns:

> '"How factually accurate is Jim Allen's script? is it a documentary or a drama? Should the BBC have broadcast what some have called open political propaganda?"'

The 'some' here is unspecific, while the unspoken 'others' who might have thought the programme harmless, or justifiably leftist, or simply of no interest, are excluded from this agenda and have to make their replies framed by the dominant discourse. Allen was obliged to answer the question according to the agenda set by the programme and, more immediately, the interviewer:

> 'Lawley: "Jim Allen, how accurate a picture of the period were you attempting to portray?"
> Jim Allen: "As accurate as possible. We did our homework. Especially, we used books like Citrine's. We leaned very heavily on Citrine. And, of course, Tom Jones' diaries of what went on between him and Baldwin ... But, let me say this, our business is to write fiction. We don't make documentaries ... I don't think we can be made accountable in the same way that *Panorama* is."
> William Deedes: "What I think is almost dishonest is the way in which the BBC have presented it. If I look at the *Radio Times*, it is put: *Days of Hope*, a series of four films from the Great War to the General Strike. What am I meant to conclude from that? Fiction or fact, documentary or drama?"'

While official defence of the series might stress the right of a dramatist or artist to investigate and represent controversial issues, one of the objections of the political right was clearly based on the 'confusion of forms', as though a straightforward exercise in leftist propaganda would have been less objectionable, had it appeared within a form which signalled to its audience a different set of expectations.

The political message of *Days of Hope* seemed to sound out through this controversy loud and clear, although the confidence its originators expressed in the possibility of creating a 'workers' state' in 1926 seems out of keeping with the historical evidence. How far had the working class been prepared to go in 1926?

Had there been coherent plans for the creation of working-class structures of power? Were the same opportunities (whatever opportunities those were) really available in the mid-1970s?

The *Monocled Mutineer*

Alan Bleasdale's 1986 series *The Monocled Mutineer* triggered off what was almost a small-scale rerun of the *Days of Hope* controversy. In the first place, the historical period represented was comparable. Secondly, it dealt with a similar theme: rebellion against civil and military authority. However, many aspects of the series formed a strong contrast to the naturalistic atmosphere and ragged improvisation used in *Days of Hope*. The dialogue was polished, inventive and barbed. The BBC was again praised for its ability to stage a convincing costume drama. The experience of watching the carefully crafted *Mutineer* would produce for many viewers a more convincing dramatic experience than *Days of Hope*, partly because the later series obeyed mainstream codes and conventions. It lay more clearly in the accepted current of television drama; both dialogue and setting created a compelling fictional world, reminiscent of the cinema.

Fig 6.1 Paul McGann as the Monocled Mutineer
(© BBC Photograph Library)

Extract from the script by Alan Bleasdale for *The Monocled Mutineer*

48/2 INT/EXT. THE GAS HUT
LATER THAT DAY

[*A darkened wooden hut of some size. Full of sand, and various gases at various times –
chlorine would produce a green/yellow haze. Two pairs of curtains contain the gas inside the
hut.*

We see the HARD MAN *being released from the gas hut. He staggers out, coughing.*

*We see outside. Most of the men have gone through, and have been allowed to sit and
recover.*

Only the GEORDIE *is left for the experience of a lifetime.*

The men who have got through sit on a small ridge, watching the GEORDIE.

Several of them are mumbling and debating together.

TOPLIS *is one of them.*

As the GEORDIE *is next, the* HARD MAN *returns and goes towards the gas hut,
stepping in front of a Canary*]

GAS CANARY: Next.

HARD MAN: He's not going.

GAS CANARY: Who says so?

HARD MAN: I do.

GAS CANARY: Who are you?

    [*Shouts*]

 Sar'nt!

HARD MAN: The bloke who's just told you he isn't going. He's not fit.

GAS CANARY: Oh I see, a doctor in disguise.

    [*The* LANCASHIRE LAD *stands up. As he does so,* WALL EYE *approaches and takes
in the scene, taking off his cap. Three other Canaries join him*]

LANCASHIRE LAD: None of us want him to go. He's ill, any fool can see that.

WALL EYE: . . . Anyone else share those views?

    [*Slowly the lot of them stand up, and face out silently.* TOPLIS *is the last to stand*]

    Well then, let's see if I can't change your minds for you.

A DISTORTION OF THE TRUTH?

The Etaples mutiny of 1917 took place in a British Army training camp to which, in
rather negative terms, Wilfred Owen had once referred. There are a few scattered
histories of this period, but the best known book on the subject (written by two
authors called Allison and Fairley) appeared in 1979. The television version was
closely modelled on the book, and carried the same title. The upset and debate
which greeted the series again seemed to offer a dispute which led to a natural
division between left and right. However, there were some significant dissentients.
The libertarian socialist journal *Solidarity* argued (*see* Ken Weller, 'Cherished Myths
of Radical Action', *Solidarity*, Issue 14, summer 1987, p. 4):

'there is a tendency among some leftwingers to see socialism as a sort of conspiracy in
which socialists should keep silent and defend "our side" in any dispute.'

Solidarity felt that the *Mutineer* programmes 'profoundly distorted the events of the Etaples mutiny', and that the series in fact reflected the idea that all working-class rebellions needed 'expert leaders' in order to achieve anything. Once again, according to the *Solidarity* reviewer, the working class was being 'written out' of history, and their autonomous role downplayed, while the programme-makers concentrated on (p. 5), 'the "essential" role of an elite.'

The historical accuracy of the *Mutineer* came under attack, partly because the publicity for the series emphasised exactly this aspect of the production. The *Radio Times* of 30 August to 5 September 1986 promoted the series through an article entitled 'Class War on the Western Front' (*see* Fig. 6.2). The first paragraph contained a sentence which declared (p. 73):

> 'It's adapted from a true story about a British army mutiny led by a dashing rogue, Private Percy Toplis, on the eve of the Battle of Passchendaele in 1917.'

The article went on to repeat the stories associated with Toplis as though they were entirely factual and uncontroversial.

The series' researcher, Julian Putowski, was drawn into the public debate because he felt that the BBC's stance on the issue of historical accuracy had forced him publicly to distance himself from some of the incidents (reproduced in the main from Allison and Fairley's book) which he regarded as (*Solidarity*, p. 7) 'either questionable or untrue'.

A twentieth-century myth?

One writer began his study of what he called 'The twentieth-century myth of facts' by asking, 'Why has a "documentary" inflection to a "dramatic" work become evident in the second half of the twentieth century?' He paid particular attention to the television drama *Tumbledown*, which portrayed the experiences of a Guards captain who was severely wounded in the battle for the Tumbledown mountain during the Falklands war. He argued:

> 'what was really at issue was the way the war as public event was to be re-presented. The existence of controversy indicated the lack of easy consensus about what the Falklands War stood for'.
> (p. 9)

Tumbledown was transmitted in 1988, two years after *The Monocled Mutineer*. This author believed that the arguments over the Falklands war were displaced by another debate which concentrated on the treatment of what he called the 'Wounded Hero.' The author repeats Raymond Williams' dictum that to believe in a *real* achievable objectivity is to create 'a fiction about reality itself'.

The 'factual' text: television coverage of the miners' strike

The most notable feature of the coverage of the 1984–5 miners' strike, according to Len Masterman (who wrote an essay entitled 'The Battle of Orgreave' while the dispute was still in progress), was the way that picket line violence was highlighted (*see Television Mythologies*, p. 99). Television news appeared to adopt a

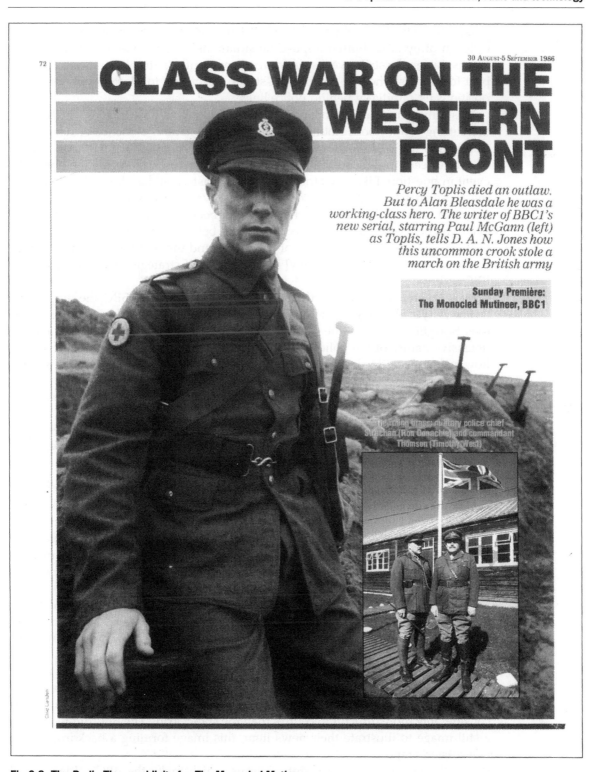

Fig 6.2 The *Radio Times* publicity for *The Monocled Mutineer*
(Courtesy of Radio Times; Photographs by Clive Landon)

perspective which concentrated on 'problems facing the police in trying to keep order in difficult and often impossible situations'. Masterman also believed that events during the strike were seen from an apparently 'natural' perspective of support for miners who did not join the strike. According to Masterman, 'television positions us, familiarly, behind police lines'.

Masterman emphasised the importance of looking at those images which 'lie on the cutting room floor', noting that, 'by its very nature, evidence of television's absences is difficult for viewers to establish'. Investigation of this theory would therefore seem to depend on the fullest possible access to information about the event in question. Like any other researcher, Masterman had limited evidence, in the sense that he had to rely on what was available through the mass media (together with any material which might have been produced by the NUM). In the event, he believed that it was a contradiction between the coverage given by the ITN news of the Orgreave picket of June 1984, and the comparable BBC coverage of the same event, which, '[threw] into sharp relief strategic omissions' from the BBC account.

Masterman perceived three themes being developed by the BBC: the supposedly military-style planning of the operation by miners' leader Arthur Scargill, doubt over Scargill's claim that he was hit on the head during a police charge, and the defensive nature of the police role during the picket. The BBC version of events, however, appeared to be undermined by the ITN coverage, which emphasised the violent action of heavily-armed riot police.

Masterman described the ITN report of events on the picket-line as follows:

'the film showed the police lines opening up, the horses galloping into a group of pickets, who were simply standing around, and the riot police following up wielding their truncheons.'

Making a comparison of the two film extracts, Masterman established that the BBC film ran to the point at which a policeman was about to begin beating a picket with his truncheon, but there the film had been cut. The cut away from this point was to show the violent *response* of miners to the attack made on one of their number. The point Masterman makes is that the upshot of such a selection was to make it appear (p. 103) that 'these de-contextualised images can only signify *unprovoked* violence by pickets'.

The manipulation of the image, however, is only part of the story, so far as Masterman is concerned. We may also identify here some general principles of journalistic practice in television. It is not the image alone which 'dominates' the point of view of an audience. Clearly, Masterman felt the BBC had chosen a set of images which reflected badly upon the striking mineworkers, whereas a more objective report would have shown the police bearing responsibility for the escalation of violence. The problem the Corporation faced was that the moving image is considerably more difficult to control than the static 'icon'. The BBC did in fact use a still image to illustrate their news item, this image forming a backdrop to the newscaster's report.

It is the use of certain descriptive terms which make the BBC's 'ideological' approach plain: 'hand-to-hand' fighting, a term used in the news report, is so broad a reference that it fails to explain where the violence began. 'Horrific' attacks on policemen is, by contrast, a clear allocation of blame, and taken together with 'hand-to-hand' conflict, works to demonise the mineworkers. Masterman shows also how the distortion of the event had implications for the media coverage which immediately followed the BBC early evening news.

Setting the agenda

Television is clearly able to frame an event in such a way that it sets an agenda which can then help to determine how the public perceives a debate. In this case, so many vital facts seemed to have been neglected or distorted by the BBC that an entirely misleading picture of the 'Battle of Orgreave' was the result. But a single television text alone cannot force the public into believing anything. Meaning must *circulate* if there is to be any chance of an effect on an audience. *Sixty Minutes*, which followed the early news, was based on the viewpoint already established. Nick Ross's opening question to Jack Taylor (leader of the South Yorkshire miners) clearly signalled the fact that the agenda had become 'semi-official' (p. 103): 'Mr Taylor, how on earth do you explain what happened at Orgreave today?' This question functions in precisely the same way as Sue Lawley's opening remarks to Jim Allen, in the case of *Days of Hope*. Both examples use a dominant agenda which has already been established elsewhere in the mass media.

The difference here was the fact that the ITN footage had provided the material for an alternative discourse, so that cracks began eventually to appear in the BBC's account of the Orgreave conflict. As Masterman notes, the *Nine o'Clock News* was forced to make a number of significant changes to the commentary it had previously employed, this time emphasising how the police themselves had used a considerable amount of violence. In particular, the key phrase 'it was a marvel/ miracle no one was killed' was completely altered in its significance. In the early evening news, it had referred, by direct implication, to the threat to police lives:

> 'the attacks on individual policemen were horrific. The police commanders said it was a marvel no one was killed.'

By the later edition of the news, the phrase could apply equally to either pickets or police:

> 'the attacks on individual policemen were horrific but the riot squads gave no quarter, using their batons liberally. "It was a miracle no one was killed," said one police commander.'

As we have seen, this commentary (by John Thorne) had to alter in the light of another text which acted to contradict his original report; therefore other meanings had challenged the one which had at first seemed dominant. The BBC report failed to convince because it had too narrow a factual base and too limited a discourse to sound as though 'both sides' of the case had been adequately represented. There is a common dictum which insists that there are 'two sides to every argument', and in this case the BBC did not seem to have presented two sides. (The notion that in many cases there are *not* two equally guilty parties, but instead a clear division between right and wrong, was borne out when, some years later, mineworkers arrested at the Orgreave picket had their convictions overturned.)

Masterman notes that the still image from the early evening news, showing a miner lashing out at a policeman, had been dropped by nine o'clock. However, one of the most significant points that his article makes is that the 'deeper structures' of the BBC's approach remained intact. His conclusion is that (p. 108) 'the control of information … is the very cornerstone of political power'. We might also add that the ability to shape a convincing discourse for public consumption is vital to maintaining that power. If the discourse is unconvincing, then it follows that power will not be maintained to the same degree.

Does limited information produce 'limited audiences'?

Although Masterman has successfully demonstrated that the BBC coverage was misleading, he does not investigate audience response to it. He is justified in wanting to have a fuller picture of an event like Orgreave, since an informed opinion can only be built on access to a wide range of sources. The ability of a news programme to limit or distort information does not always mean that it will achieve a position of power or influence over the public (partly because other sources may discredit it, but partly owing to the experiences and beliefs brought to a text by an audience).

While it is true that the BBC failed to produce a discourse which could survive the test of public knowledge of *other* ways of understanding the event, there is no record of public response to the bulletin. In the supermarket of ideas and images, John Thorne's original report was of course very quickly past its 'sell-by' date, but our conception of the relationship between authority and institution on the one hand, and audience on the other, needs to be informed by research into how audiences are influenced by what they read, see, and hear in the mass media.

Audience response to media messages

The *Social Studies Review* of May 1991 carried an article ('Seeing is Believing?') by Greg Philo, who carried out research into people's memories of the miners' strike of 1984–85. Philo accepted the idea (p. 174) that 'TV news is our main source of information for national and international events', but went on to ask 'what do *we* bring to our understanding of television?' The research carried out by Philo and the Glasgow University Media Group puts the case that what we understand and believe about the television message is 'influenced by our own personal history, political culture and class experience'.

Philo gave groups of people from different parts of the country news photographs from the miners' strike, and then asked them to imagine they were journalists who had to write their own news items. These people were also questioned about their memories of the strike and about specific issues such as, for example, whether the picketing that took place was mostly peaceful or mostly violent.

One of the results was the close resemblance of the stories written to the original items which had appeared on BBC and ITN. A group from Shenfield in Essex wrote: 'as the drift back to work in the mines began to gather momentum, violence erupted'. A group from Glasgow wrote: 'on a day that saw an increased drift back to work ... further violence was taking place'. Some pieces written by the research groups were extremely close to the original news items, in terms of the words and phrases used – 'drift back' was a particular example which (according to Michael Crick) had been coined by the Coal Board itself. This process should not, however, surprise the media theorist. People will use words and phrases which are part of a current linguistic 'fashion', but will also recall other 'labels' from the past which are triggered off by images or associations. As Philo points out, being able to recall images and language does not mean that we will automatically *believe* what those in authority suggest to us.

Television and the individual subject

Philo continues his argument by noting that:

> 'The extent to which [the research subjects] believed in the television version of the world depended on several factors, particularly on whether they had access to alternative accounts.'
>
> (p. 174)

We already have some idea of how alternative accounts can operate as a very important factor in the individual's creation of meaning. Some would compare television news with other sources of information, such as the 'quality' and local press or 'alternative' current affairs programmes and radio. Some 16 per cent of Philo's sample made such comparisons between television news and these other sources. About 14 per cent of the sample were critical of television news for a tendency to over-emphasise violence on the picket line to the exclusion of other events. This sample explained that this was the reason that they had rejected the explanation given by the television news. However, where such beliefs existed they did not always lead to rejection of what was seen on the news.

Philo mentions also how personal experience can work to give perspective to television news reports. He says that 'no one who had actually been to a picket line thought that picketing was mostly violent'. However, attending a picket line might imply a degree of commitment to the miners' cause in the first place (and it would look rather curious if a person had attempted to stand with the police on their lines). Some people involved in the study clearly believed that the camera operators had filmed violent bits on purpose, since their experience of the picket line was considerably muted by comparison.

Philo discusses the complicated 'sets of filters' that some individuals have acquired as a result of their background, and proposes that these act to produce quite complex readings of images. One example would be the policeman's daughter who sympathised with both miners and police, because of her experience of how police would very often break or bend rules and procedures in order to achieve a desired result.

Another significant finding was that, when asked about their key memories of the strike, there were sharp differences between various groups. Women from the working-class districts of Glasgow and London (p. 176) 'remembered queues for food and the loss of jobs during the dispute', whereas among a group of women from the middle-class area of Bromley in Kent, no respondent gave this as their memory. The effect of 'experience on memory' was also reflected upon in the survey where one woman from Essex, although occupying a class position which might suggest antipathy or indifference to the miners' case, remembered the hardship she had experienced as a child in South Wales and this produced an alternative reading.

Over half the sample believed that picketing was mostly violent. Philo's response was to read out eyewitness accounts of the picket-line experiences of strikers and police officers, by way of contrast to the dominant idea of violent concentration. However, Philo also found that 'at least some of the information which is used when these audiences think about the world is itself provided by television and the press'. He concludes by arguing that it:

'can be very difficult to criticise a dominant media account if there is little access to alternative sources of information. In these circumstances we should not underestimate the power of the media.' (p. 177)

Cognition

Perhaps at this stage we should perhaps ask again to what exactly Philo attributes different responses amongst his sample. It comes down in the end to background, class location and experience, a complicated 'set of filters' as Philo puts it. We have seen already that researchers such as Birgitta Hoijer questioned David Morley's work on the grounds that it did not reveal exactly how groups decode television messages and that this had led some scholars to propose the idea that there is a 'missing link' between the construction of the mass media material and its reception by an audience. We saw this link described as the 'cognitive level'. Hoijer refers (in *Media Culture and Society*) to the fact that mass communication research had, by the 1920s and 1930s, already discovered that:

'individual characteristics and social background ... influenced the way in which the audience gave meaning to messages.' (p. 583)

Hoijer argues that cognition ('knowing', or preception) includes emotional and intuitive elements, as well as the purely logical reasoning processs. Therefore, in the study of audience reception, Hoijer uses a model of cognition which includes emotional elements (some theorists believe that emotions arise as a result of certain kinds of cognitions). Of course, cognitive processes encompass a number of different levels, from the simple identification of objects to what may be described as 'higher' intellectual dimensions.

Thinking in a frame?

The everyday processes of making decisions and solving problems make up what we could describe quite simply as 'thinking'. Glass and Holyoak (*see Cognition*) describe thinking as involving:

'the active transformation of existing knowledge to create new knowledge that can be used to achieve a goal.'   (p. 333)

They go on to emphasise that goals may be relatively simple, or highly complex, drawing a distinction between *reasoning*, which is described as drawing new inferences from knowledge and beliefs which are already held, *decision-making*, which involves evaluating options or making choices between them, and *problem solving*, where attempts are made to achieve a wide variety of 'types of goals'.

Glass and Holyoak divide logic into two types, deduction and induction. Deduction is (p. 335) 'a judgment that something *must* be true if other things are true'. The example they give is the statement 'the earth circles a star', which is based on two other ideas, that the earth does in fact circle the sun and secondly that the sun is a star. Induction, on the other hand, is a process whereby a judgment is made that something 'is *probably* true on the basis of experience'. A case of the latter type of logical deduction would be the conclusion that day follows night because it has done so in the past.

Cognition and research

If we apply the categories of reasoning, decision-making and problem-solving to Philo's research, we could argue that all these processes were used by the research groups involved in the study he carried out, but that there were definite limitations to what he was able to discover. He was able to establish, in effect, that people were able to *reproduce* the discourses of certain mass media texts. Part of the problem lies also in the very fact that this was an exercise, a game perhaps, in which the usual consequences of having to make a decision are absent.

In a sense, the whole experience of watching television news is removed from the need to make significant choices, or indeed to do anything. Of course, we may still continue with the processes of reasoning, which may eventually lead to action of some type, but it is the removal of any sense of personal involvement in events (partly because the *form* of television news sets us at a distance from those events), which may seem to result in a tendency to produce *generic* material. In other words, as Philo's research appears to demonstrate, we do not necessarily reveal our beliefs in an exercise where we may instead be able to rely upon the familiar modes of address learned from television.

We may find that terms like the 'drift back to work' are 'parroted' not simply out of political ignorance, but because there is a tendency to use established terms as a handy frame of reference. It happens to be the case here that the term carries an ideological loading because it appears to have been invented by the Coal Board as part of a propaganda drive against the mineworkers. Thus a certain meaning is recirculated by virtue of the very usefulness of the term and the lack of a powerful alternative to challenge it; thus the term 'drift back to work' becomes an accepted discourse, a piece of shorthand for more complex meanings. In turn, it limits the meanings that would otherwise be available.

Socio-cognitive approaches

When Hall describes ideology (*see Media Culture and Society*), he is referring to:

'the mental frameworks – the languages, the concepts, categories, imagery of thought, and the systems of representation – which different classes and social groups deploy in order to make sense of, define, figure out and render intelligible the way society works.'

(p. 585)

This bears a relationship to 'ethnomethodological' approaches which set out to study the methods used by people to make sense of the world. However, ethnomethodology also proposes that there is in fact no such thing as a social order, but instead a kind of fiction of order established by people in order to allow them to describe their own actions and functions in a meaningful way. Most approaches to cognition and meaning take social order as a given fact. Hoijer talks of a 'social world' rather than a 'social order'.

Hoijer argues that people:

'carry within them, concealed in their cognitive structures, all the experiences and collected world knowledge they have developed through interaction with the surrounding world.'

(p. 586)

Therefore, according to this author, consciousness is inseperably connected with the social world. In addition, 'almost all' human experiences may be divided into three types: universal experiences, cultural experiences and private experiences.

Although we may accept the idea that experience can be divided into different categories, we rarely make an active effort to distinguish between these types while we are engaged in the process of living. Also, all efforts to categorise human thought or action are bound to create areas which overlap. Despite these draw-backs, such categories may still be useful, since they might clarify the background to the statements and decisions made by the individual subjects of research. Another advantage may be that the ability to consider 'universal' experiences may help in breaking out of the limitations imposed by the kind of research which expects certain socio-economic groups to behave in specified ways.

Three types of experience

All the experiences described by Hoijer are, it should again be emphasised, connected to the social world:

- **Universal** experiences are shared by all, and include life and all its elements and features, like childhood, ageing, health and the universal experiences we have of nature.
- **Cultural** experiences include all those areas which are the products of a specific society, culture or subculture, so that socialisation will take place differently in different societies.
- **Private** experiences are those which are supposed to be unique to individuals since, even within the same family, individual members of that unit will not have exactly the same experiences.

Generally speaking, it is the interaction between the 'micro' level of individual understanding (constructed by the individual's experience of the world), and the 'macro' level of the society and its structures, which produces what we may call the 'socio-cognitive' process through which meaning is created. The cognitive structures found in the human mind are (p. 587) 'neither solely a mental creation nor a mechanical reflection of the environment'.

Research into audience cognition

Hoijer and the Swedish Broadcasting Corporation used a science programme about HIV and Aids as the centre-piece of their study. A broad range of social and educational backgrounds was sought among prospective respondents to be used in the research. Interviews were carried out individually, the idea being to discover how the viewers each structured their experience of the programme.

The response to the programme was divided into the three categories (universal, cultural and personal) described above. The results of the research appeared to support the concept of meaning as something created as a network of relations between text, audience, social reality, and other texts already seen or due to be seen. The multiple meanings seen in media texts (their polysemy) should therefore be balanced against an investigation of the multiple ways in which reception is made by audiences.

MEDIA EFFECTS

The effects tradition concentrates on the supposed effects that particular forms or contents of the media have on their audience. In the case of television, one current of interest has been the general social effects of viewing. Another strand of research undertaken into television's influence has concentrated on the more specific and dramatic outcomes that are supposed to result from audience exposure to the mediated message. Ideas about the way that violent behaviour might be attributable to television, for example, have been the stimulus for a number of funded studies.

Effects: competing definitions

Shaun Moores (*Interpreting Audiences*) reserves the term effects for a straightforward causal relationship. O'Sullivan's entry for the term in his *Key Concepts* dictionary notes that it is 'commonly used to refer to the supposed direct consequences and impact of media messages', before moving on to mention that a range of human attributes (behaviours, beliefs, values and ideas) may be subject to media influence. Watson and Hill opt for a broader definition from the start, saying that effects are 'any change induced directly or indirectly by the recording, reporting, or filming of events' (*Dictionary of Communication and Media Studies*). Price, in *The A–Z Media and Communication Handbook*) also favours a broad interpretation, using the term to indicate 'the various types of impact made on audiences by media content' before drawing attention to the 'media forms and / or media content [which] have a measurable impact (direct or indirect) on the behaviour, attitudes or actions of audiences'. The differences between these definitions will become important when the limitations of the 'violence' debate are considered below.

Investigative analysis of media effects

A number of methods are used by researchers to investigate media effects. Traditionally, two types of audience research have stood out. The first is the laboratory approach, in which closed experiments in an artificial environment are carried out in order to ascertain how subjects may respond to a television stimulus. The second is the field study, where researchers go into the social environment and test audience opinion against available data, or against the attitudes or performance of a control group. Another method, which does not involve direct contact with an audience, is content analysis, in which quantitative data is collected and the nature of that material is assessed. Care needs to be taken not to use this method alone, since it is not useful merely to make assumptions about how an audience might react to a certain kind of content.

Descriptions of effects

There are various effects which have been identified over the years. This list of supposedly observable effects is brought together from a wide variety of different ideas and expectations about what kind of 'behaviours' are likely to emerge in human beings as a result of exposure to communication from mass media sources.

- **Socialisation** is the idea that the media, as well as other social forces which act upon the subject, help to 'initiate' an individual into the social framework. The media are imagined as helping to present a range of norms and behaviours which the society regards as 'normal'.
- **Social control** is the term given to the way that the media are supposed to reproduce the given social order, by circulating arguments for the continued maintenance of things as they are; this would include at present arguments in favour of lawful behaviour and a 'moderate' political outlook. (The hierarchical nature of most media organisations seems to force out much open dissent. The result is a kind of knowing professional cynicism.)
- **Agenda setting** is a more indirect process, based on the idea that the mass media have the power to decide which events or issues (or indeed which *aspects* of an event or issue) are most deserving of attention. It is not an effect, as such, because the agenda may be rejected out of hand, even if no alternative agendas are on offer. It is one of the means by which socialisation and social control is effected.
- **Moral panics** are effects which are supposed to emerge when the media consistently represents a subgroup or subculture as dangerous or deviant, to such an extent that 'folk-devils' are created, and sections of the community begin to

attribute all kinds of mishaps to the supposed malevolence of the group under scrutiny.

- **Attitude change**, where the public or sections of it are imagined to be vulnerable to persuasive messages, so that changes in attitude towards a range of issues may be effected. This is often associated with political campaigns.
- **Behavioural change** is meant to occur as a direct result of 'traumatic' exposure to a media input which is exciting or distressing, or as a result of a successful alteration in the way that people think about an issue (*see* attitude change above), thus preparing them to act on their new perceptions.

Theories of effects: effects on individual behaviour (Comstock's model)

As we have seen above, some models of television effects began with the idea that aggressive, anti-social or deviant behaviours may be attributable to the influence of media texts (particularly texts whose purpose is to entertain). Comstock's psychological model proposes that the main input which may affect behaviour is the 'TV act'. This is the portrayal of a specific action. The following list of elements from Comstock's model is taken from McQuail and Windahl (*Communication Models*, Longman, 1981, p. 47):

- **TV act** is any form of human behaviour shown on television.
- **TV arousal** is the extent to which a person is motivated to perform an act as a result of the TV act.
- **TV perceived consequences** are described as the sum of all positive (minus all negative) values which are learned from television and which go with a given act.
- **TV perceived reality** is the degree to which a person perceives the TV act to be true to life.
- **TV alternatives** are other social behaviours shown on television.
- **'P' TV act** is the probability of carrying out the TV act.
- **Opportunity** is the real-life chance of putting the TV act into practice.
- **Display behaviour** is the observable performance of social behaviour shown on television.

Thus, the act or behaviour seen on television will have an impact on the individual viewer, depending on the degree of positive value attached to the act and on the degree to which it is shown to be close to real life. Comstock believed that the further removed a television act was from reality, the less likely it was to have relevance to the viewer. McQuail and Windahl provide two examples of TV acts which lead to different effects. In the first case, they imagine (p. 48) 'a realistic police story in which the police hero deals brutally with a drug dealer'. The physical beating the dealer receives is shown centrally and realistically. The context given by the narrative shows approval of the act; therefore a positive value has been given to the act. Such an example is fairly likely to provide a model for aggressive behaviour. The second example is of a cartoon in which a witch poisons a princess. It does not provide a model for aggressive behaviour, because the act is given an unrealistic context and is carried out by an unattractive protagonist. The probability of imitation is non-existent.

Such models of audience response are mechanical and founded on a pessimistic view of human nature as highly impressionable and irrational. Its abstractions are useful only where a simple and observable process may be recorded, but its use as a model of response is limited, since it was constructed as part of an approach to behaviour which is now regarded as both outdated and, in its basic premise and aims, reactionary.

Direct and 'hypodermic' effects

Perhaps one of the earliest models of effects was that concerned with establishing the idea that the mass media could have a **direct** and quite spectacular impact on the public who received mass communication messages. The attempted manipulation of audience response through mass communication by dictatorships in Western and Eastern Europe may have led to this perspective.

Audience manipulation during a period of dictatorship depends ultimately upon the threat of violent coercion, and cannot be considered in isolation from the communicative forms it has chosen and applied. The 'direct' effects theory may be defined as a stimulus-response theory of mass communicative effects, which includes the famous concept of **hypodermic** effects, whereby media content is supposedly 'injected' into the consciousness of an audience. The reaction which might then take place is seen as being largely predictable. This idea depends not just on a view of the media as a unified and single-minded (almost omnipotent) force, but on the people who receive the messages being part of a 'mass society' which can easily be reached.

Hypodermic models of effects continue to enjoy a kind of posthumous support from 'moral campaigners', who see television as having effects on certain audiences that are regarded as being vulnerable. In this model, little account is taken of the variety of 'filtering' mechanisms which may act to block or alter the message being received. These mechanisms would reflect the social groups to which the individual may belong and also include the attitudes, values and beliefs of the individual audience member (*see* page 393 for further discussion).

Inoculation theory

Another view of effects was that continued exposure to specific television messages (such as representations of violence) would lead to an audience becoming desensitised. This theory is close to the argument that over-exposure to television leads ultimately to a kind of permanently stupified populace. A group called the 'couch potatoes' in America took advantage of this idea to gull interviewers into reporting their new 'cult' which involved 'multiple viewing' of programmes and endless 'TV meals' taken with plenty of alcohol. The joke was apparently lost on some journalists. If the joke is lost, then so too are its implicit criticisms of the 'anti-TV' lobby.

Psychodynamic effects

Modifications to the simple 'cause and effect' thesis included DeFleur's 1970 **psychodynamic** model, in which the persuasive effect of the message is seen as depending on the psychology of the individual. We may recall the definition of persuasion offered by O'Keefe (*see* Chapter 2):

> 'a successful intentional effort at influencing another's mental state through communication in a circumstance in which the persuadee has some measure of freedom.'

This would imply a need to affect the attitudes, values and beliefs of an individual; these three attributes of human personality were described in Chapter 2, adapted from O'Keefe and Myers and Myers. In summary, an **attitude** is a person's general evaluation of an object, where object stands for a person or people, an event, an incident, a commodity, an institution. Since attitudes are supposed to be learned, new attitudes may appear as new learning occurs. Attitudes are supposed to be relatively enduring, and are not the same as temporary states such as moods. **Values** are ideas about the relative worth of things and the nature of good and bad. Values often 'cluster together' to form systems of belief. Values 'grow out of a complex interaction between basic needs and the specificity of a given environment' (Myers and Myers, p. 93). **Beliefs** generally express a perceived link between two aspects of a person's world. Beliefs operate as thoughts or statements about the relative truth or falsehood of a thing. Some beliefs are central to a person, while others are less important.

Some of the supporting research which appeared on behalf of the 'psychodynamic' model was devoted to the idea that particular types of individual were susceptible to persuasion. Other investigations concentrated on the attitude of the receiver towards the source, before any new message was sent. Although all 'stimulus-response' models appear to be rather crude, they serve to highlight the way that the concentrated power of the media can be used at least to send messages which may, by their sheer volume, push other alternatives to one side.

Two-step flow theory

Lazarsfeld, Berelson and Gaudet made a study of the 1940 US presidential election campaign, initially based on the idea that a 'stimulus-response' theory was adequate to the task of exploring the mechanisms of influence. The earlier theory proved completely inadequate. The researchers therefore moved to a new perspective, one which emphasised the concept of 'opinion leaders' who passed on ideas received from radio and newspaper sources to the less 'active' members of the society. In 1955, a re-evaluation of the model was published by Katz and Lazarsfeld.

This model moved towards a conception of audiences as members of social groups, rather than isolated individuals. Mass media sources would therefore be in competition with other influences on the individual, an idea already indicated above. It would be a mistake to imagine that specific individuals are always the 'opinion leaders' on every single issue, and that distinct numbers of people unfailingly assume the role of impressionable drudges. Nor were opinion leaders, according to Katz and Lazarfeld's 1956 study, necessarily those who had most wealth and power in society.

Models of diffusion

Models of diffusion are useful because they emphasise the role of personal interaction in the spread of news. We may recall from Chapter 4 the discussion of news values which institutions espouse. The first type of news diffusion 'event' is one in which a low threshold of importance is given by the mass media to an occurrence which is in fact of very great importance to a limited number of individuals. A small-scale, local accident reported in a national television report might prompt a significant response among the people directly concerned. The response might occur despite the small size of the relevant group who might have seen the original report. They might pass on the information in turn to other members of the interested group. As McQuail and Windahl note (p. 56);

> 'a rather high proportion will have heard [about the relevant event] through a personal intermediary.'

The second type of event is the sort which is not usually passed on from person to person because it is assumed to be known by the majority of people; such an event would be regarded as of general public importance.

The third type of event is one of extreme urgency and a particular dramatic quality, such as the assassination of a major public figure, where news of the event is spread very quickly between people. The eventual proportion of people hearing of this event through others (rather than through the mass media) will be higher than in either of the two previous examples.

Problems with research into effects: television violence

It would perhaps be a little unfair, although perfectly understandable, to laugh at a survey of television violence which cost a million dollars to carry out, yet which had failed properly to define its own terms before it began. The US Surgeon General's report of 1972 which investigated 'Television and Social Behaviour' was made up of no less than twenty-three separate projects. The projects were not co-ordinated and no distinction was made between types of violent behaviour. This illustrates perfectly the problems which are created when assumptions are taken as proven effects. The money would clearly have been put to better use had it, for example, been deployed to alleviate poverty, from which certain kinds of social violence might have a tendency to grow.

William Benson's research in the early 1970s was intended to discover possible connections between the delinquency of boys involved in violence and petty crime, and their viewing habits. Unfortunately, the study was flawed from the start. It relied on asking the boys to remember features from a quite extended sample of one hundred programmes; the boys were then asked to report any violent behaviour that they had been involved in during the previous six months. Belson also used a rather broad definition of violence. There is, of course, great scope for disagreement as to what constitutes a violent act, depending largely on the nature and context of the act itself. Belson was not interested in taking the context into account and ended up with a measure of 'serious violence' which ranged from vandalism to serious assault. It seemed from his research that those most keen on viewing television violence were those who admitted to committing the smallest number of violent acts. Some theorists believe that the violent behaviour recorded by Belson could only be understood in the context of a male working class 'street culture'. The media would therefore have some kind of effect, but through the filtering mechanism of this particular culture.

Gerbner, using a content-analysis model, carried out research into television violence and found that the characters in television drama encountered more violence than the typical viewer. Why then is violence so often represented? A theory which may help to explain this phenomenon is that, as 'television fiction' is naturally a dramatic form, violence becomes a kind of motif for conflict in general. According to Gerbner, one unexpected effect of exposure to television violence was that 'heavy' viewers of television, far from becoming violent themselves, were more likely to over-estimate the levels of crime in society and even to become more afraid of walking the streets late at night.

Content analysis is still extremely useful when it comes to supporting campaigns against stereotyping, since some studies suggest that violence on television serves to make scapegoats out of certain (often physical) types of people, and to strengthen demands for more powerful, and perhaps less accountable police and judicial systems. A myth we seem to hold, that the legal system can never produce any form of lasting justice, seems to give rise less to demands for legal reform than to a fantasy in which a lone hero (usually it is a man) 'oversteps' or bends the rules and dispenses justice on his own terms.

Real *vs.* screen violence

Before the limitations of the 'violence' debate are considered, it would be useful to acknowledge an important and obvious distinction between actual violence against real individuals, and the violence we encounter through media outlets. In the first place, 'screen violence' (whatever its source or origin) is mediated and therefore, to some extent at least, altered in meaning and quality. This applies to both fictional and non-fictional forms. If we were to make a further distinction, it would be reasonable to describe fictional violence as a dramatisation of human behaviour, while footage of real violence (war reports, or other material which shows actual harm to individuals) would retain its status as a form of recorded evidence. Films and television programmes (television being the main subject of this chapter) which adopt a realist approach to the depiction of violence, are often singled out for particular criticism.

MEDIA REPRESENTATIONS OF VIOLENCE: LIMITED DEBATES

Those campaigners who advance the idea that media representations of violence have direct, observable effects, have been vigorously opposed by media researchers in Britain. The academics, faced as they have been by a simplistic but popular line of argument, have been forced into expending a great deal of energy on what is, in fact, only one part of a larger issue.

Barker and Petley, for example, in their 1997 book *Ill Effects*, write of their own work, 'this is not a standard academic book ... it is a polemic drawing on a body of academic research'. A polemic is a controversial argument which is usually framed as an attack on another point of view. Such controversy, generated by opposition between two positions, is nothing new. In 1967, thirty years before the appearance of *Ill Effects*, Mary Whitehouse (chair of the National Viewers' and Listeners' Association), blamed the 'heat of the moment' for her failure to recognise the positive aspects of work done by the BBC (in 1964 she had made a headlong attack on the Corporation). As a consequence of the polarisation between 'moralists' and researchers, aspects of the wider debate have been neglected.

Public discourse and public morality

Two issues, in particular, seem to have been ignored by many media academics. The first is the idea that their opponents, despite the 'primitive' form of their pronouncements, are actually engaged in an important task – raising arguments about public morality and individual freedom. There is no doubt that the way in which these concerns have been expressed, seem at times quite bizarre (Whitehouse, in *Cleaning up TV*, accused the BBC of promoting 'promiscuity, infidelity and drinking'), but this does not alter the fact that the core of the debate contains a very real argument about public conduct. As Justin Lewis wrote in *Are You Receiving Me?* (p. 157):

> '... underlying the "effects" approach were perfectly legitimate questions about the influence of television on the way we think and behave ...'

David Buckingham, in a contribution to the *Ill Effects* volume on media and violence, also recognises that the debate 'invokes deep-seated moral and political convictions' and that it may actually provide an outlet for other anxieties, including worries about the nature of contemporary culture and 'the shortcomings of capitalism' (p. 45). The point which must be answered is the one which comes as no shock to the new wave of discourse theorists: are public discourses and public conduct in any way influenced by public forms of communication? Before this is explored further, we should recall the second aspect of the argument which has suffered from neglect. This is the nature of the term 'effects'.

Effects and influences

At the beginning of this section, I noted the different ways in which 'effects' could be defined. If we consider only direct effects, where cinematic or televisual representation gives rise to real instances of violence, then of course we will discover only limited evidence. This would include those individuals who, already predisposed to anti-social behaviour, have their tendencies confirmed or triggered by exposure to similar acts on television or in the cinema. This is, of course, enough to prove the argument that media violence has some negative effects, but is certainly not sufficient to support the idea that the bulk of audiences will respond in the same way.

Although some researchers, like David Gauntlett in *Moving Experiences*, declare (p. 1) that 'the work of effects researchers is done', the tradition cannot as he hopes 'be laid to rest', partly because there is an unacknowledged link between 'effects' research, and those other forms of enquiry which he believes lie outside the whole paradigm. Gauntlett makes a distinction between effects and another less clear-cut category, that of 'influence', which might work on the 'thoughts and perceptions' of viewers. He presents 'influence' as an alternative, something which may alter 'attitudes to life, and relationships, and ... expectations about the world'.

If we were to accept the idea that 'influence' is confined to 'viewers' thoughts' while 'effects' belongs to the realm of behaviour, we have created a new problem; an idealist separation of one type of consequence (emotional, cognitive) from another (material, behavioural) without recognising that the first is often a pre-condition of the second. In other words, the performance of an action (visible effect) depends on an attitude which orientates an individual towards reality in a particular way. Attitude (growing perhaps from some form of influence) is necessary for action; Gauntlett's point of view threatens to remove thought from 'action' in order to create an artificial distinction between ideas and behaviour. The real purpose seems to be to preserve his argument about the shortcomings of 'direct effects'.

Disturbed behaviour

It is interesting to note that some other, 'non-academic' commentators, hold a reasonably complex view of media effects. One example may be found in the comments of an American police sergeant called Jerry Townshend, who was featured in a documentary which studied the violence debate (broadcast in the mid-1990s and called, confusingly, *Natural Born Killers?*). His comment on the case of a teenager accused of carrying out murders after seeing Oliver Stone's *NBK*, does not contain assertions about the existence of a direct, 'knee-jerk' reaction, but instead speculates about the role of a particular text within the context of disturbed behaviour:

> 'I just think, personally, that he thought his problems were so bad, that he had to find a way out, and I think the movie helped him connect, to find this way out.'

The man at the centre of the disquiet which surrounded this particular movie was its director, Oliver Stone. In the same documentary cited above, he produced the following argument:

> 'Most people are equipped to see movies. I cannot of course talk for lunatics, people who accept movies at face value, and believe exactly what they see on the screen and go out and do something.'

This is quite an interesting tactic; if those who seem to be influenced by screen violence can be characterised as lunatics (or victims of drugs like marijuana, another of the examples used by Stone in this interview), then it is possible to avoid what some people suspect – the idea that film may have a general social impact, by virtue of its position as a public form of communication (thus contributing to exactly those attitudes which researchers like Gauntlett try to separate from the world of real consequences). In remarks which immediately followed this statement (see the documentary *Natural Born Killers?*), Stone took a rather different line:

> 'Film is a powerful medium, film is a drug, film is a potential hallucinogen, it goes in your eye, it goes in your brain, it stimulates, and it's a dangerous thing, it can be a very subversive thing.'

Here, the director is no longer talking about a deviant minority; he seems to be arguing that film has a general social effect. (Incidentally, he ended up making this point because he took up his *theme* of brainwashing and dope-smoking, instead of pursuing his earlier line of *argument*).

Tired arguments: the 'moral panic' thesis

At this point, my suggestion that there has been academic resistance to the moral aspect of the violence debate, deserves fuller exposition. Reluctance to acknowledge the underlying issue of public morality is sometimes expressed through the very common argument that public concern is actually just another variant of 'moral panic'. Guy Cumberbatch, speaking in the documentary *Natural Born Killers?*, insisted that the whole debate should be seen in the context of 'the anxieties that have always existed about popular culture'. Gauntlett also pursues this theme, when he notes that 'the moral panics' about 'penny dreadfuls' in the nineteenth century, 'raise only a wry smile today'. Martin Barker and Julian Petley seem equally convinced of the strength of this parallel when they write (*Ill Effects*, p. 8); 'for more than 150 years, moral campaigners have been making wild claims about the effects of media which they don't like'.

There is certainly some truth in this perspective, but the comparison between nineteenth-century objections to novels, plays, and other material, and criticism of a more advanced form of industrial culture (television programmes and films), can be overplayed. The suggestion that all concern about screen violence and morality is merely a prelude to calls for censorship, or that it comes solely from right-wing ideologues, stifles debate on the public issues which media studies should address.

The moral question arises whenever we consider the industrial production of culture, and the representation of values which audiences may encounter in no other context. The danger lies not so much in imitation, as in the restricted range of actions and limited forms of public discourse that surround some representations of violence. Screen violence can be used to initiate arguments about power and justice; the opening sequence of the Italian film *La Scorta* is a good example, while the representation of police violence in series like *Homicide: Life on the Street*, serves as a reminder of the relationship between authority and coercion.

However, particularly as it appears in many Hollywood productions, screen violence can appear in a number of degraded forms: as a ready-made narrative device, as a model of amoral conduct which is 'justified' by the circumstances of the protagonist, or even as part of fashion and public style. In this sense, some forms of screen violence may reduce the range and quality of public discourse.

However, calls for greater censorship (always exercised by centralised bodies) do not address those issues which lie behind the violence debate: power, accountability, and democratic participation in media.

Selective perception and 'uses and gratifications'

Ideas about 'selective perception', where the audience is imagined as being able to look after itself, depend on the idea that there are certain social and psychological defences which will act to protect people from the worst effects of television messages. This idea was founded on the belief that, where opinions were expressed which were in accordance with strongly held beliefs, these ideas would be accepted, but where this was not the case, they were likely to be rejected. This came to be developed into a 'uses and gratifications' theory, in which the different needs of individuals were satisfied by the mass media in different ways; furthermore, individuals were actively engaged, according to this notion, in selecting and refining what they wanted from the mass media. Television, in this scenario, would become the servant rather than the master of the general public. Lewis (*see Are You Receiving Me?*) believes, however, that the 'uses and gratifications' approach, in 'asserting the viewer's power to select and interpret', abandoned not only the 'effects' methodology, but also 'the questions ... that methodology failed to answer'.

Audience and discourses of taste

Pertti Alasuutari ('The Moral Hierarchy of Television Programmes', *Media Culture and Society*, vol. 14, no. 4, October 1992) carried out research into the *way* that audiences explained their reasons for watching certain programmes. His analysis was based on 'unstructured thematic interviews' with ninety families and ninety-nine adult interviewees from Tampere in Southern Finland. He restricted his report of this research to the parents' responses. He found a 'moral hierarchy' in programmes; in other words, certain programmes were regarded by his respondents as being 'better' or more worthy than others.

People watching soap operas, for example, tended to (p. 562) 'defend, justify or excuse themselves for their programme choices'. People do in general seem to be aware of a kind of 'attitude' towards culture which they must take into account as they speak about what they watch. In other words, people know that there are different levels of 'worth' attached to different genres of television, and they are anxious to show that they are aware of what they perceive as a 'pecking order' of television programmes.

Alasuutari describes how:

'the most highly valued types of TV programme in the Finnish moral hierarchy are represented by news and documentaries, while at the bottom of the hierarchy we have American soap operas. Male viewers in particular seemed to need to justify their interest in soaps.'
(p. 563)

He went on to discover that there were four basic types of discourse or ways of speaking which people used as a frame within which to talk about the programmes they watched:

1 a laconic statement that one (p. 564) 'likes or watches' a certain programme;
2 that one dislikes or never watches a certain programme;
3 a reflective discourse where the person comments on the fact that he/she watches a programme; these comments may be about why the person concerned watches the programme, or again they might be about his/her frame of mind when watching the programme, or may offer an analysis of the programme itself and its attractions; comments could be the reverse of this where the same ideas are expressed to describe or reflect upon the fact that the subject does not watch a certain programme;
4 that one used to watch a programme but has 'given up'.

Most of the references in the interviews consisted of remarks about two types of television programmes, current affairs and documentaries on the one hand, and soap operas on the other. It seems that these two categories play a major part in the 'characterisation' of the audience's tastes. Of course, the two categories were not talked about in precisely the same way. Alasuutari argues that:

> 'criticism of soap operas may serve as a reverse strategy of communicating one's values, whereas documentaries are mentioned frequently because of their highly valued position.'   (pp. 564–5)

It was from these findings that Alasuutari constructed a 'moral hierarchy' of television programmes. For him, the vital importance lay in the statements which can be categorised as either 'watches' or 'explains-why-does-not-watch'. Such comments are:

> 'indicative of a high valuation of the programme type in the sense that either the interviewee does not consider it necessary in any way to explain the fact that he or she watches the programme, or that he or she feels it is necessary to have some excuse for not watching it.'

In this research, for example, no one explains why they are interested in current affairs programmes and no one feels the need to explain why they do not watch certain fictional serials. This is clearly significant; no justification is required because no guilt or social unease is associated with either not watching fiction or with watching current affairs.

Alasuutari went on to divide the proportions of men and women choosing certain types of programme, and then divided the audience between those with high education and those who had not gone on to further or higher education.

The highly educated reported watching detective serials and situation comedies, while the particular interest of those with a lower level of education was reserved for sports programmes and action serials. From the data collected, this author discovered that one of the women's top favourites came lowest in the moral hierarchy of television programmes. However, the highly educated as a group favoured detective serials, which only came third from last in the hierarchy.

It would at first appear that the better-educated were engaged in watching programmes which had a low status, but the research went on to discover that in fact detective serials were a particular favourite of highly educated *women*. It was therefore still the case that the dominant type of programme in the hierarchy was the sort valued by highly educated men.

Television: low involvement?

Barwise and Ehrenberg (*see Television and its Audience*) describe television as a 'low-involvement' medium:

> 'People mainly use television to relax with and be entertained ... There may be two or three programmes where we are rather concerned about what is happening on the screen ... but we watch the news mainly because we do not like to be out of touch rather than because we necessarily care all that much about the stories themselves.'

They describe watching television as 'a passive activity in two senses'. In the first place, it involves little physical, emotional, intellectual or financial effort or investment. It may require, in some cases, an intellectual effort and there is little doubt that it has some marked emotional *effects*. The second reason given by these authors for seeing it as a passive activity is that most of the time television is watched as 'a "filler" when we have nothing better or more important to do'. A sense of proportion is certainly needed in all studies of television; for example, Barwise and Ehrenberg note that:

> 'although some 40 million Americans ... are all tuned to the same highly popular prime-time programme, another 60 million or so have chosen to watch one of the less popular programmes, while the other half of the population, 100 million or more, are not watching television at all.'
>
> (p. 124)

These authors note all the variables which affect the viewing habits of the public. These include the range and quality of the programmes available at the time, the mood of the viewer and their need for variety, the amount of time available and viewing habits. Switching channels is common and has increased as a result of remote-control. The 'low-involvement' model suggested by these writers is drawn from observation of the rational choices that people make about why and how they watch television.

For example, people may choose to watch something relaxing, but at other times they will choose a demanding text, as long as it is rewarding in some way; to see something as both enjoyable and challenging is perfectly possible – the two categories should not be mutually exclusive. The context in which viewing takes place is an important consideration in television research.

However, the claim that (p. 125) 'The majority of most people's television time occurs in the context of family viewing' has to be treated with some caution, once we realise that there may be a number of sets in one home and that family members may even be watching the same programme in separate places. Television is not really much of an 'event' unless there is some specific programme or film which people consciously plan to watch.

As we have seen, a great many theories of television have approached the subject with the idea that it has had dire effects on society. The power of television has perhaps been over-estimated; too much loose talk and too many poor definitions have served to popularise the idea that people are unable to resist its power. Of course, television does have a number of attractive aspects which ensure that it always gains attention, but this attention is, according to this theory, of a limited and specific kind.

Although television may well demand only a low level of involvement, it is nonetheless true that, as a form, it is:

> 'to some extent compelling, irrespective of the programme. If we are in a room with a television set on, our eyes are almost continually drawn to the screen.'   (p. 126)

One of the key statements that Barwise and Ehrenberg make in their 'rationalist' and rather distant assessment of television is that:

> 'the degree of attention required for television viewing is at a comfortable level: less than for reading or speaking, and far less than for writing, but enough to distract us.'

SUMMARY

■ SOCIAL IMPACT OF TELEVISION

Raymond Williams proposed the idea that the advent of television marked a change in the social order and had had a major impact on the world as a whole. The coming of television is ranked among other events of great significance, largely because of its widespread proliferation as a technology.

■ TECHNOLOGY AND THE USES OF TECHNOLOGY

Williams was concerned to establish specific rather than general meanings about television and its impact on society and culture. One of the earliest distinctions he made was between a technology and the *uses* of a technology, or, as he put it, between **content** and **form**.

■ Television as 'objective' and 'enterprise'

Television can be understood as developing as a specific objective roughly between the years of 1875–90. It then developed as a technological enterprise from around 1920 through to the first public television systems of the 1930s.

■ Public Service television models of regulation

Those formal enquiries set up to review the output of **public service broadcasting** are listed as follows: the **1923 Sykes** Committee, the **Crawford** Committee set up in **1925**, the **Selsdon** Committee of **1935**, the **Ullswater** Committee (**1936**), the **Hankey** Committee formed in **1943**, the **Beveridge** Committee which submitted its report in **1950**. This was followed by the **Pilkington** Committee, set up in **1960**, the **Annan** Commission which reported in **1977**, and the **Peacock** Committee which submitted its findings in **1986**.

■ The development of public service broadcasting

Three phases of public service broadcasting, identified by Scanell, are introduced: **national service, competition**, and **cultural pluralism**. The first period ran from 1927 to 1954. The second began in 1954 and ended in 1977. The third ran from 1977 until 1995.

■ FORMS OF TELEVISION: TECHNOLOGY BEFORE CONTENT

The technology preceded the content of television. One of the results of this is a kind of 'parasitism' on existing events; in other words, television was forced to search for pre-existing material.

Television was regulated in quite different ways in different countries; in Britain there was 'an effective paternalist definition of both service and responsibility', but in the United States the attempt to centralise broadcasting failed because the industrial manufacturers asserted their independence.

Television would appear to be a combination of earlier forms of public communication, and examples of innovation which grew from the medium itself. A list of television forms would include news, argument and discussion, education, drama, films, variety, sport, advertising, and pastimes. Williams argued that television had pioneered a number of new forms including the drama-documetary, 'education by seeing', discussion, features, sequences and even, according to Williams, television itself, by which he means 'some of its intrinsic visual experiences' which are unique to television and which allow us to see things in new and unexpected ways.

■ TELEVISION AS INSTITUTION

Institution is investigated as a term 'generally applied to patterns of behaviour which are established, approved and usually of some permanence'.

Institutions are bodies which have a settled structure and set ways of functioning. Hence the idea of institution as a relationship is stressed as being one between production, text and audience. The danger is that the particular distinctiveness of institution as a powerful agent in social reproduction may be lost if too much emphasis is placed upon its status as a relationship.

Channel Four was born after the 1979 election, when it was recommended that the channel should have a new direction and should select programmes which would encourage new and independent talent. The Independent Broadcasting Authority established a new, autonomous subsidiary to run the new channel.

■ DEREGULATION

Deregulation has been defined as 'the dissolution of rules and regulations which restrict but also protect the status of public services' (*see* Stuart Price, *The A–Z Media and Communication Handbook*, 1997). Watson and Hill, in *A Dictionary of Communication and Media Studies*, point out that another term in current use is 'privatisation', which 'emphasises the practical nature of the shift, from public to commercial control'.

Deregulation is not just the introduction of competition but also the process of allowing private enterprise greater freedom to manoeuvre, while providing the public with fewer safeguards over quality of service.

Deregulahon is examined as a process made formal by the Broadcasting Bill of 1990. The debates which were aired in response to the White Paper on the subject turned on issues of 'quality' and fears about the increasing monopolisation of broadcasting. One and a half hours per week would be given over to religious programmes and at least ten hours a week of children's programmes would be produced. There were no provisions for the maintenance of documentaries during 'peak-time' viewing.

■ The market-place and the unemployed

The 'big five' independent television companies found that the 1990 Bill abolished their right to provide programmes to the ITV network; 25 per cent of programme production was to be carried out by independent producers. Considerable redundancies in regional workforces were made by various television companies.

A table of 'results' is provided setting out the outcome of the 1990 franchise bids. Details of the 1995 Broadcasting Bill are provided.

■ SATELLITE AND NEW TECHNOLOGY

This is studied in relation to the way that new developments in technology change viewing habits. The launch of the powerful Astra satellite in the late 1980s has allowed viewers to receive programmes direct. The earlier technology meant that satellite broadcasts were relayed by cable companies to subscribers who had cable installed. By early 1997, the Independent Television Commission had listed over eighty cable and satellite programme channels which could be eligible for a licence. The reasons for the growth of non-terrestrial television are examined, with particular reference to Murdoch's Sky network.

■ Competition, profit and 'parasitism'

A detailed study of management strategies in BSkyB is given, with reference to the mass subscription market and rival broadcasters such as Granada and the BBC. The position of BSkyB as an integrated media business is discussed. Financial and managerial problems in the Murdoch empire are also examined.

■ Digital dreams

The increasing use of digital technology is acknowledged. Digital technology uses a series of binary digits (0 and 1 in a variety of combinations) to represent data. Any media form (video images, photographs, printed text, etc.) can be digitalised. Digitalisation converts information into 'formal relationships in abstract structures' (Timothy Binkley, in *Future Visions*, 1993) stripping away the physical property of the source. Tony Feldman lists the key features of digital information. Digital data is:

- manipulable;
- networkable;
- dense;
- compressible;
- impartial.

■ THE ORIGINS AND DEVELOPMENT OF CABLE

Cable television is at least thirty years old, yet it is still regarded as a 'new technology'. In the optimistic days of cable's first appearance in the US, there was some speculation about the social uses and 'progressive' nature of the form. A truly 'democratic-participant' and community-based service would, according to this view, end the isolation of individuals, and would lead to harmony between groups which had previously existed in mutual antagonism. This vision did not materialise.

The cable strategy in Britain was from the start to establish a good film channel, but competition has been fierce. The surviving cable firms have at least the advantage over satellite that they can be two-way and interactive. The potential for the expansion of cable will probably be in the field of popular entertainment.

Some theorists look to the domestic adaptation of technology as the saving grace in the expansion of televisual communication, while others hope that the State will act to ameliorate the worst effects of televison expansion.

■ EUROPEAN FEARS OVER LOSS OF IDENTITY

Such fears turn on the penetration of the European market by American television networks and production companies. US cable operators have made investments in Britain as part of a series of general incursions into Europe. Another development has been the tendency for programmes to be undertaken as co-productions, designed from the outset for a global market. Therefore, a European country which fears the imposition of US cultural values may find that they receive American programming which has already attempted to take account (though for commercial reasons) of different values which may be held elsewhere in the world.

■ KNOCKING THE BBC?

The BBC was originally a private company set up by a conglomerate of radio manufacturers. It was nationalised by a Conservative government and made into a state broadcasting monopoly. Two principles lay at the centre of this monopoly. First, that the BBC should be a single corporation with a monopoly of radio (and subsequently of TV) broadcasting. Secondly, that it should have formal independence from the government in its own internal affairs, yet the government should appoint a Board of Governors.

Although one of the basic principles of the commercial system established in the mid-1950s was to have a regulatory body which would award contracts to regional contractors rather than a single national body, the third channel has operated in effect as a national station.

■ RADIO AND PUBLIC COMMUNICATION

Within media and cultural theory, the study of radio has suffered from neglect. Pete Wilby and Andy Conroy, writing in *The Radio Handbook* (p. 15), believe that 'its cultural significance is only beginning to receive wider recognition in academic circles'. Peter Lewis and Jerry Booth, in *The Invisible Medium* argue that '... radio is hardly noticed in academic literature and as a practice is mostly taught in a vocational context as a preparation for journalism'.

The absence of such a critical language is in one sense rather curious since the dominant analytical current, Saussurean semiology, emerged from the study of linguistics, and might be thought an ideal instrument for the study of a form whose signs are often composed of linguistic 'units'. The nature of radio as a medium is also discussed with reference to its public nature and the largely private mode in which it is consumed.

■ Radical radio in Italy

In Italy, a number of stations were closely allied to the revolutionary left. The period from the 'Hot Autumn' of 1969 until 1976, saw the growth of the far left in Italy. With the birth of 'Radio Bologna per l'Accesso Pubblico' new forms of democratic public communication became possible. Hundreds of stations followed the Bologna example. The authorities tried to end such broadcasts, but control was quickly lost. In June 1978, a survey revealed that there were 2,275 radio stations in the country. Most were commercial but some helped to advance radical social experiments. The case of 'Radio Alice', situated in Bologna, is explored.

403

■ Dreams of community

Most commentators see the Italian model as a rare case and do not believe that communities can be created by radio broadcasts, however forward-looking. The pressure to experiment with new radio forms appears to come from two sources: commercial bodies and community activism. The relationship between political structures and radio broadcasting is examined. An interview with a lecturer in media and radio is reproduced in this section.

■ SOUND AND MEANING

Andrew Crisell makes the distinction between words and sound. As signs, words count as symbols; it is their symbolic status which Crisell believes is the basis of radio's imaginative appeal. Of course, words are also used in those media traditionally regarded as visual, but it is the fact that words are spoken and therefore given the inflection of a human speaker's personality which Crisell sees as making a particular impact on a listener.

■ Language and sound

Some theorists expand on the idea that the human voice carries a particular emotional quality by returning to the nature of language itself. There are arguments to be made for investigating more than simply the logical structures of language. Expressing dissatisfaction with the rather mechanical nature of Saussure's system of 'signifier' and 'signified', some teachers of language insist that the *sound* of an utterance is equal in importance to its structural qualities.

Sounds, as opposed to tone of voice, are by contrast 'natural,' in that they are a form of signification which exists in the world. In the real world, individuals tend to pick out sounds if they are motivated to listen for something in particular. Radio and film technicians, however, must be able to reproduce the specific noise a producer requires and, more significantly, must be able to allow listeners to interpret the relative importance of different sounds.

■ APPROACHES TO THE STUDY OF TELEVISION

These include feminist approaches, anti-racist critiques, narrative approaches, reader-orientated criticism, and ideological and discourse analyses.

■ Debates about television: form and content

Some critics have advanced arguments which have stressed the approach television makes to the 'personal' and the 'domestic'. Television is often cited as an example of realism. Realism is often understood as a narrative arrangement (a form). Content, on the other hand, is taken to mean the collected elements which are contained within the form of the text; content must be the subject-matter itself, rather than the order in which it is presented.

■ Text and audience

Stephen Neale's idea that genre or type is understood partly as an expectation held by an audience applies also to television.

The relationship between text and audience is an important element in the creation of realism in television. Any study of television must take into account the formal qualities of television programmes, as well as the intertextual relations of television programmes with one another.

■ Realism and television drama

John Corner felt that the notion of realism had become little more than a collection of begged questions. Realism seemed to be either a 'straight imaging of the real', such as news and documentary, or an 'imaginatively convincing' piece of artifice, such as drama series, plays, films and so on. Corner sees realism as 'an acknowledged effect whose separation from "reality" forms part of its appreciation'. In other words, we would not be able to spot the difference between realism and the real itself if the practice of realism were not in fact just another way of representing reality.

■ *DAYS OF HOPE*

Days of Hope, a television series transmitted in 1975, became an issue which was debated throughout the 1980s. It was used as a focus for study in various centres of higher education and seemed to fulfil Barthes' adage that 'what is noted becomes notable'. The producer was Tony Garnett, the director Ken Loach, and the writer Jim Allen. *Days of Hope* remains important because of its commitment to a certain kind of realism and to a political view of television.

A great response was created by the programme and letters to all kinds of newspapers began to appear. Although many accusations were made about the political bias shown in the series, some complaints were based simply on the grounds of historical accuracy.

Colin McArthur looked at the *Days of Hope* controversy by referring to Colin MacCabe's article concerning Brecht's theses on the theatre. McArthur doubts the applicability of MacCabe's theory of the classical realist text to *Days of Hope*. MacCabe's response to McArthur was to highlight the way that *Days of Hope* compared subordinate discourses with the 'narrative' or dominant discourse and then used the dominant discourse to force the reader into an 'imaginary unity of position'.

MacCabe made some interesting remarks when he noted that *Days of Hope* was really trying to offer the working class a set of 'memories' close to their own history, while at the same time the actual history appeared to be fading from their consciousness. He was therefore confident of his ground when he identified a classic realist trick as that which occurs when the image used is supposed to reassure the audience that they are watching something 'true'; 'the reality of the character is guaranteed by the shot, and the reality of the shot is guaranteed by the character.'

■ Guardians or public servants?

The controversy which surrounded the showing of *Days of Hope* had somehow to be rationalised and contained by the BBC. Broadcasting had developed a vocabulary to deal with a confusion of roles; one role being that of guardian of morals, the other that of public servant.

■ *THE MONOCLED MUTINEER*

Alan Bleasdale's 1986 series *The Monocled Mutineer* seemed almost to provoke a small-scale rerun of the *Days of Hope* controversy. The historical accuracy of the *Mutineer* came under attack, partly because the publicity for the series emphasised exactly this aspect of the production.

■ THE 'FACTUAL' TEXT: TELEVISION COVERAGE OF THE MINERS' STRIKE

Len Masterman's study of television news reports of the Orgreave picket found that they adopted a perspective which concentrated on problems facing the police in trying to keep order in difficult and often impossible situations. Masterman also believed that events during the strike were seen from an apparently 'natural' perspective of support for miners who did not join the strike. The BBC version of events, however, appeared to be undermined by the ITN coverage, which drew attention to the violent action of heavily-armed riot police.

Making a comparison of the two film extracts, Masterman discovered that the BBC film ran to the point at which a policeman was about to begin beating a picket with his truncheon, but there the film had been cut. The cut away from this point was to show the violent response of miners to the attack made on one of their number.

■ Audience response to media messages

Greg Philo carried out research into people's memories of the miners' strike of 1984–5. Philo accepted the idea that 'TV news is our main source of information for national and international events', but went on to ask, 'what do we bring to our understanding of television?' The research Philo and the Glasgow University Media Group carried out puts the case that what we understand and believe about the television message is 'influenced by our own personal history, political culture and class experience'.

Philo gave groups of people from different parts of the country news photographs from the miners' strike, and then asked them to imagine they were journalists who had to write their own news items. One of the results was the close resemblance of the stories written to the original items which had appeared on BBC and ITN.

Philo attributed different responses among his sample to background, class location and experience, a complicated 'set of filters' as Philo puts it. Researchers like Birgitta Hoijer, however, suggested a 'missing link' between the construction of the mass media material and its reception by an audience. This link may be described as the 'cognitive level'.

There may well have been definite limitations to what Philo was able to discover. In a sense, the whole experience of watching television news is removed from the need to make significant choices; we do not necessarily reveal our beliefs in an exercise where we may instead be able to rely upon the familiar modes of address learned from television.

Hoijer argues that people 'carry within them, concealed in their cognitive structures, all the experiences and collected world knowledge they have developed through interaction with the surrounding world.' Therefore, according to this theory, consciousness is inseparably connected with the social world. In addition, 'almost all' human experiences may be divided into three types: **universal** experiences, **cultural** experiences and **private** experiences.

■ RESEARCH INTO AUDIENCE COGNITION

The response to a selected programme on Aids was divided into the three categories described above. The results of the research appeared to support the concept of meaning as something created as a network of relations between text, audience, social reality, and other texts already seen or due to be seen. The multiple meanings seen in media texts (their polysemy) should therefore be balanced against an investigation of the multiple ways in which reception is carried out by audiences.

■ MEDIA EFFECTS

The effects tradition concentrates on the supposed effects that particular forms or contents of the media have on their audience. In the case of television, one current of interest has been the general social effects of viewing.

■ Effects: competing definitions

Shaun Moores (*Interpreting Audiences*) reserves the term effects for a straightforward causal relationship. O'Sullivan's entry for the term in his *Key Concepts* dictionary notes that it is 'commonly used to refer to the supposed direct consequences and impact of media messages'. Watson and Hill opt for a broader definition, saying that effects are 'any change induced directly or indirectly by the recording, reporting, or filming of events' (*Dictionary of Communication and Media Studies*). Price, in *The A–Z Media and Communication Handbook*, also favours a broad interpretation, using the term to indicate 'the various types of impact made on audiences by media content' before drawing attention to the 'media forms and/or media content [which] have a measurable impact (direct or indirect) on the behaviour, attitudes or actions of audiences'.

■ Investigative analysis

A number of methods are used by researchers to investigate media effects. Traditionally, two types of audience research have stood out: the laboratory approach, in which closed experiments in an artificial environment are carried out in order to ascertain how subjects may respond to a television stimulus, and the field study, where researchers go into the social environment and test audience opinion against available data, or against the attitudes or performance of a control group.

■ DESCRIPTIONS OF EFFECTS

A variety of effects have been identified over the years. This list of supposedly observable effects is brought together from a wide variety of different ideas and expectations about what kind of 'behaviours' are likely to emerge in human beings as a result of exposure to communication from mass media sources. They may be listed as: socialisation, social control, agenda setting, moral panics, attitude change, and behavioural change.

■ Theories of effects

Some models of television effects began with the idea that aggressive, anti-social or deviant behaviours may be attributable to the influence of media texts. Comstock's psychological model proposes that the main input which may affect behaviour is the 'TV act'. This is the portrayal of a specific action. The following list outlines the areas Comstock considered: TV act, TV arousal, TV perceived consequences, TV perceived reality, TV alternatives, 'P' TV act, opportunity and display behaviour.

Such models of audience response are mechanical and founded on a pessimistic view of human nature as highly impressionable and irrational.

■ Direct and 'hypodermic' effects

Perhaps one of the earliest models of effects was the idea that the mass media could have a direct and quite spectacular impact on the public which received mass communication messages.

■ Inoculation theory

Another view of effects was that continued exposure to specific television messages (such as representations of violence) would lead to an audience becoming desensitised.

■ Psychodynamic effects

Modifications to this simple 'cause and effect' thesis included DeFleur's 1970 psychodynamic model, in which the persuasive effect of the message is seen as depending on the internal psychological structure of the individual.

■ Two-step flow theory

Lazarsfeld, Berelson and Gaudet made a study of the 1940 US presidential election campaign initially based on the idea that a 'stimulus-response' theory was adequate to the task of exploring the mechanisms of influence. The earlier theory proved completely inadequate. The researchers therefore moved to a new perspective, one which emphasised the concept of 'opinion leaders', who passed on ideas received from radio and newspaper sources to the less 'active' members of society. By 1955, a re-evaluation of the model was published by Katz and Lazarsfeld.

■ Models of difflusion

Models of diffusion are useful, because they emphasise the role of personal interaction in the spread of news.

■ Problems with research into effects: television violence

Many studies of representations of violence failed to set out proper definitions at the start of the study. Problems with the concept of 'effects' are also described in this chapter.

■ Real vs. screen violence

An important distinction between actual violence against real individuals, and the violence encountered through media outlets, is provided.

■ Media representations of violence: limited debates

The media violence debate in Britain has become polarised, setting academics and public campaigners at opposite ends of the debate. Academics have been forced into expending energy on what is only one part of a larger issue. As a consequence of the polarisation between 'moralists' and researchers, aspects of the wider debate have been neglected. The issue of public discourse and public morality is outlined, in the belief that, behind the controversy, important arguments about public morality are being made. David Buckingham recognises that the debate 'invokes deep-seated moral and political convictions' and that it may actually provide an outlet for other anxieties, including worries about the nature of contemporary culture and 'the shortcomings of capitalism'. An important question is posed: are public discourses and public conduct in any way influenced by public forms of communication? Certain arguments, particularly the 'moral panic' thesis, seem to have become part of the reluctance to acknowledge the underlying issue of public morality. The moral question arises whenever we consider the industrial production of culture, and the representation of values which audiences may encounter in no other context. Behind the violence debate lie issues concerning power, accountability, and democratic participation in media.

■ AUDIENCE AND DISCOURSES OF TASTE

The research carried out by Alasuutari into the way that audiences explained their reasons for watching certain programmes was examined. He found a 'moral hierarchy' in programmes; in other words, certain programmes were regarded by his respondents as 'better' or more worthy than others.

Alasuutari went on to analyse the proportions of men and women choosing certain types of programme, and then divided the audience between those with higher education and those who had not been to university. From the data collected, Alasuutari discovered that one of women's top favourites came lowest in the moral hierarchy of television programmes.

■ TELEVISION: LOW INVOLVEMENT?

Barwise and Ehrenberg describe television as a low-involvement medium. They describe watching television as 'a passive activity in two senses'. In the first place, it involves little physical, emotional, intellectual or financial effort or investment. In the second place, most of the time television is watched as a 'filler' when there is nothing better or more important to do. These authors note all the variables which affect the viewing habits of the public. These include the range and quality of the programmes available at the time, the mood of the viewer and the need for variety, the amount of time available, and viewing habits. Switching channels is a practice which is widespread, and one which has increased as a result of remote-control. The 'low-involvement' model suggested by these writers is drawn from observation of the rational choices that people make about why and how they watch television.

STUDENT ACTIVITIES

TELEVISION AND RADIO: ANALYSIS, RESEARCH, PRODUCTION, ESSAY TITLES

Analysis: Content and functional analysis of popular soap operas/sit-coms

A content analysis of the gender, age, class, ethnicity, etc. of characters in popular soaps and sit coms must be linked with an analysis of their roles and functions within the narrative structure of the programme, together with the typical settings within which certain types of action or event take place.

Purpose: to gain a detailed insight into the representations on offer in popular television series, and to explore the typical events which are used to maintain audience engagement with the programmes.

Method: a system of tabulation of results is set up as in Figures 6.3 and 6.4.

■ Analysis and exercise in sound and image: Analysis of national news bulletins/party political broadcasts

Equipment required for this exercise: microphone plus lead with correct plug for video recorder audio output; television set; editing suite or second video recorder. A VHS tape of news footage, and blank tapes for copying. Students are required to rewrite news commentary or voice-over in order to produce an alternative version of the discourses favoured by television news.

Purpose: to investigate the relationship between image and discourse by dubbing new commentary on to existing images; to demonstrate in practice that images are polysemic; to explore the central role of sound in the creation of meaning; to examine questions of 'bias' in the news and in party broadcasts (see Chapter 7 for a discussion of bias and notions of impartiality).

Method: a number of copies of the same news or PEB sequence will have to be produced. The most useful footage is the kind of material which includes exterior or stock footage, rostrum work, graphics, and so on. The students are shown the selected piece with the sound turned down. They are divided into groups and asked to write a commentary for the material they have seen, which should be run through a number of times. Each shot should in the first instance be timed with a stop-watch.

An alternative approach is to ask the groups to assume the role of different interest groups with different perspectives, or to work from the perspective of different news stations, perhaps from a

Name of series:		Episode:	
Scene No.	Character	Attributes	Role/Function

Fig 6.3 'Soap' grid 1

Name of series:			Episode:
Scene No.	Setting	Characters appearing	Actions performed

Fig 6.4 'Soap' grid 2

different national perspective. Each group then proceeds to record its commentary over a tape containing the images, using the 'audio dub' facility on the video recorder. Each group's work is then reviewed, and discussion is invited on the different commentaries.

■ Research: Television, gender, children and violence

Students may be asked to carry out research into a number of areas of television. The most useful exercises may be the relationship between television and audience. (See the work in Chapter 6 on effects.)

Purpose: to allow students to develop skills in research; to investigate effects; to encourage contact between students and younger pupils in the education system.

Example of problematic: (taken from a research project by Jacqui Gale, Somerset College, 1992).

'What is the effect on children of violence and the representation of gender roles in cartoons? To what extent do children reproduce these influences in their social behaviour?'

A number of elements need to be considered. The study would be made up of: research in schools, consisting of both qualitative interviews of children and adults, quantitative surveys, and some degree of observation; content analysis of cartoons, together with brief narrative outlines; a critical examination of previous studies (many of them flawed, whether undertaken in the field or in laboratory conditions); and theory on the attractions and effects associated with the mass media. At first it appears that the project title has set two tasks related to media effects, one on gender and one on violence, though the general thrust is the susceptibility of children to media influences (see Chapter 7 for Masterman's theories on cartoons, as well as comments on the approach taken by a number of researchers). This kind of project has defeated many people in the past, but if it is kept to a manageable scale, it could result in some useful insights.

Sources of information: Secondary data such as the work of the 'moral campaigners' associated with the National Listeners and Viewers Association, books like *Amusing Ourselves to Death*, the analytical work carried out on children and video nasties by Martin Barker, *The Box in the Corner* by Gwen Dunn and *Children and Television* by Hodge and Tripp. Issues of the *Media Education* journal often carry reports on work with children. Psychological studies, including the famous 'Bobo' doll experiments, should be investigated. The study of children and television by David Buckingham of the University of London Institute of Education would be essential reading.

Primary data collected from in-depth interviews with schoolchildren was produced to support the project, which was illustrated with a number of cartoon drawings and flicker books made by children. The project successfully drew out responses which showed interesting differences between boys and girls on the subject of violence, thus justifying the use of gender as an important perspective.

Structures of response in report-writing: the following format was used to write up the project's findings;

- Problematic
- Introduction to scope of research
- Examination of established theory
- Main research findings
- Conclusion: relationship of findings to theory
- Evaluation of the research process
- Appendices
- Bibliography

(See Fig 6.5 for general questionnaire given to children; their drawings appear in Fig 6.6.)

QUESTIONNAIRE TWO: What is watched, preferred.
Concepts of reality/fiction.
Effects.

1. Name Natalie Storey

2. Age 7

3. What is your favourite T.V. programme? Pikkxie & Dixey

4. Do you watch cartoons?   Sometimes   ☐
   Not very often   ☐
   All the time   ☑
   Never   ☐   Tick ONE box

5. Have you ever seen a cartoon film <u>like</u> Snow White, The Little Mermaid, Fantasia, Babar the Elephant?

   Yes   ☑
   No   ☐   Tick ONE box.

6. Do you like cartoons?

   Yes   ☑
   No   ☐

   If 'yes', do you like them because they are...
   Funny   ☑
   Realistic   ☐
   Better than other programmes   ☐
   Short   ☐   Tick ONE box.

7. Do you have a favourite cartoon?

   Yes   ☑
   No   ☐   Tick ONE box.

   If 'yes', what is it ......Pxie & dixie............

8. Are there any cartoons your parents don't like you watching?

   Yes   ☐
   No   ☑
   Don't know   Tick one box.

   If there are, what are they? ....

9. Have you ever pretended you were a particular cartoon character?
   <u>Like</u> Raphael, Cheetarah, Lion-o, He-man.

   Yes   ☐
   No   ☑   Tick ONE box.

This question is continued on the other side of the page.

Fig 6.5 Television research project: example of general questionnaire given to children

If 'yes' how many times?

Sometimes ☑

A lot ☐

All of the time ☐   Tick ONE box.

10. Have you ever acted out a cartoon with your friends?

Yes ☐

NO ☑   Tick ONE box.

If so which one ....

11. Have you ever bought/been given a toy who is a character from a cartoon/cartoon film.

Yes ☑

No ☐   Tick ONE box.

12. Do you ever use guns/swords/sticks when you are playing at school - even if they are just pretend?

Yes ☐

No ☑   Tick ONE box.

13. What makes a cartoon different to other T.V. programmes? 💬

the pictures on a film look real.

....

14. Have you ever been scared by a cartoon/cartoon film?

Yes ☐

Nc ☑   Tick ONE box.

Natalie

Fig 6.5 *(continued)*

Tom. cant Find
Jerry .

Tom looks bay
his side and he
runs afder. Jerry

and catches
him and edts
him up.

Tom and Jerry

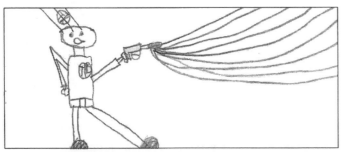

Virgil from Thunderbirds

From series of pictures showing man being attacked with hammer

Fig 6.6 Examples of drawings by children on the theme of violence on television

Production: Radio broadcast

Equipment required: tape recorders, microphones, tape and pre-recorded music.

Purpose: to investigate student perceptions of different audiences; to encourage collaborative groupwork; to investigate performance under pressure and to investigate the constraints under which broadcasters work.

Method

Stage 1: students are presented with a list of elements which must be included in a radio broadcast of no more than four to six minutes: DJ/announcer links or introductions, a news bulletin, two short musical extracts, and a selection of readers' letters or phone-responses on a specified subject. The news and the subject-matter of the phone-in/readers' letters should be identical in each case and held centrally until given to each group by the teacher.

Each group is assigned a different institutional position and a different target audience, as follows: a chart-music show on a mainstream commercial station catering for an inner-city audience; a show concerned with all aspects of the dance culture, running from a pirate station; a BBC radio station featuring a long-established 'magazine' show aimed at women.

Stage 2: students write the show, choosing how to frame the readers' letters/phone-in, and where to place this in relation to the identical news bulletin and the musical extracts.

Stage 3: a piece of late news is given out just before transmission. This should be of an important sensational nature and will be used to see if the group is able to respond under pressure and work to fit the new piece into the broadcast. (Some groups actually ignore the last 'newsflash'.) Note: this exercise may be used as a 'television' broadcast devoted to news, using a number of items which are released piecemeal from a central 'agency' and causing the progressive alteration of the schedule throughout the exercise until the transmission deadline. The same room organisation is used as shown in the Chapter 2 student activity.

Production: Creating a soap opera from character, setting, and narrative elements

Students are required to produce a synopsis, script extract and accompanying storyboard for a new soap opera/sit-com produced by one of the new commercial television licence-holders, with a bias towards new representations of groups revealed by content analysis to have been either under-represented or to have been assigned secondary or supporting roles.

Purpose: to investigate the possibility of reproducing a number of successful elements which together will make a viable prime-time soap or sit-com; to combine the visual and aural techniques learned to date with an extension of script work produced for studies of advertising; to explore some of the institutional constraints faced by individual researchers and writers in television.

Method: it is best to require each group of students to act first as the research department, and to base their proposals and suggestions on the content and audience analysis carried out in the previous exercise.

Stage 1: each group must produce a list of elements upon which the soap/sit-com will be based. The following headings must be used for script and storyboard work:

1 six leading characters, with details of age, occupation, gender, ethnicity;
2 a setting for the series which will allow a base for the characters, but which will be in some way innovatory, in line with the new channel's attempt to differentiate itself from its main rivals;
3 a basic plot-outline for the first episode.

Stage 2: each group will presumably imagine that it will be using its own proposals. Not so! The proposals would then be collected and recirculated between groups, so that no group will receive its own proposals. Each group will then assume a new role, as the team of writers who have to do their best with the research they are given (the hand they have been dealt, as it were).

This is when the synopsis, script extract and accompanying storyboard must start to be produced. It is possible that short extracts may also be filmed using video cameras; the work may additionally be turned into a photo-storyboard, or publicity material for the series.

ESSAY TITLES

1 'Instead of being forced to accept greater deregulation and dependence on a commercial model, television as an institution should be based in the community and workplace.'

What in your opinion would be the differences between programmes made within a 'democratic-participant' model of television, and those reaching our screens from any of the newer commercial franchises?

2 'Television is chewing-gum for the eyes.' Discuss.

3 Have cable and satellite increased or decreased consumer choice in television?

Illustrate your answer with examples of programme content on cable, satellite and the established public channels.

4 'Radio serves no useful purpose in a society dominated by the image.'

Discuss the validity of this statement, and the assumptions upon which it is founded.

CHAPTER 7

Popular forms: printed media, news and the music industry

THE EARLY HISTORY OF THE PRESS

It is usually assumed that mass communication cannot begin to take place unless there is some kind of technology which is able to mediate between authors and authority on the one hand, and a significantly numerous audience on the other. Most of those who examine the history of the mass media ascribe the birth of mass communication to either the expansion of newspapers in the nineteenth century, or the invention of printing using metal type in the fifteenth century. Some theorists consider the question of the size and role of audience, pointing out that the literate (those who could receive the communication in the first place) would have formed only a small proportion of the total population in either of these cases. James Curran, for example (*The Media: Contexts of Study*) argues that:

> 'church liturgy . . . in pre-industrial society probably reached a larger and more heterogeneous audience than any mass communication before the rise of the cinema in the twentieth century . . . it was mediated to the overwhelming majority of the population in Christendom who attended Church on Sunday.'

The development of the English press: 1620 to the Civil War

Although the English press seems to have originated during the seventeenth century, with the first newsbooks, or *corantos*, appearing in London during the early 1620s, the publication of literature, entertainment and various currents of opinion was already well established. For example, the first true pamphlet (a printed argument in its own right, one which had not first been written as a sermon) was published in 1529. Written by one Simon Fish, it was called 'A

Supplication for the Beggars' and argued against both the Roman Catholic church and the existence of the monasteries. There was perhaps no danger in expressing such ideas at the time, since Henry Vlll was to pursue a course of action which ended with the break from Rome in 1532. Under Henry's daughter, Elizabeth I, both Catholic and Puritan sects were suppressed. Elizabeth's regime hunted for the underground presses which, from time to time, printed religious polemic. One Puritan press was found in Manchester in 1589, for example, and closed down.

For those whose motivation was commercial rather than political or religious, it was much more profitable to publish stories or entertainments (often about notorious villainies, or the criminal underworld) than it was to produce, for example, books of verse. Thomas Harman's pamphlet on the criminal fraternity in London, which appeared in 1566, became a sort of best-seller. Robert Greene, a poet remembered for describing Shakespeare as 'an upstart crow beautified with our [the established poets'] feathers', turned to writing about London's rogues, their robberies and confidence tricks.

The press and the Civil War

The earliest newsbooks carried foreign news, in the main, because of the extent of censorship exercised over events at home. It was the English Civil War of the 1640s which gave a new impetus to the development of the press. Information was eagerly sought and reproduced by the various political factions. *A Perfect Diurnall of some passages in Parliament*, published in 1645 when the war had been in progress for three years (Giles and Hodgson, *Creative Newspaper Design*) reveals the sense of urgency which early news reports could generate during this era of violent civil conflict, even when those reports appeared only on a weekly basis:

> 'a Letter was read in the Commons House from a Gentleman of worth and quality in Sir Thomas Fairfax Army setting forth the great necessities of the Souldiers of that Army for Cloathes for this winter season and the House thereupon entering into debate, ordered that 6000 suits of Apparell should be speedily provided and sent to them, which we hope will bee accordingly dispatched without Intermission as the occasion requires and calls out for.'
>
> (p. 39)

Radical political sects

New forms of radical politics emerged from the religious and political turmoil resulting from the war. The expansion of print meant that the Bible was much more widely available; the population, in particular its Puritan element, was therefore able to receive religious teaching unmediated by Church or State. The idea of divine authority bypassing the monarchy and being established directly in the lived experience of ordinary people was indeed a revolutionary development.

Some religious sects went further; they began by questioning the established practices of the Church, and ended by casting doubt on the 'literal truths' supposed to be contained in the Bible. While the leaders of both sides were usually men of property and influence, many of the Parliamentarian rank-and-file began to argue for democratic reforms. Print (Curran, p. 37) 'helped to provide a new social identity that legitimated opposition to the crown'.

Political movements such as the Levellers proposed measures (widening of the franchise and the establishment of yearly parliaments) which went far beyond what the victorious Cromwellian leadership was prepared to contemplate. Records of the Putney debates of 1647 (held in an attempt to defuse the conflict between the leaders of the New Model Army and the 'Agitators' who represented rank and file soldiery) reveal the mood which existed in the more radical wing of the Parliamentarian camp. Colonel Rainsborough, as one of those who spoke in the radical cause, asked (see Brailsford, *The Levellers and the English Revolution*, p. 277):

'what the soldier hath fought for all this while? He hath fought to enslave himself, to give power to men of riches, men of estates.'

Another asked if the whole purpose of the war had not been to settle 'whose slaves the poor shall be'.

Censorship and supervision

In London, at least a dozen weekly newsbooks were in circulation. They bore little resemblance to present-day newspapers: they carried no headlines, but instead provided a list of notes or 'footlines' at the base of the page, detailing the contents of each edition. The first newspaper to carry headlines, albeit grouped together under its title, was *Mercurius Brittanicus*, which appeared in the spring of 1649.

Censorship of these early newspapers was strict, as part of the attempt by government to suppress democratic demands. In 1648, the censor (at the time a man called Gilbert Mabbott) refused to license a newspaper because it carried a French phrase which referred approvingly to the notion of holding parliaments of short duration. Cromwell eventually created a state monopoly of news under the supervision of government censors. No printing was allowed to take place in cities other than London, Cambridge, Oxford and York. By the early 1650s, there were eight long-running weeklies on sale in the capital. The Royalists, who had sustained a number of underground publications during the Protectorship, simply inherited this system at the time of the Restoration in 1660. The press was then supervised by a series of licensers.

Developments after the Civil War

In 1679 Parliament allowed the Printing Act of 1662 to lapse – this had previously kept the press under tight parliamentary control. A whole host of new publications appeared as a result. The Act, however, was reintroduced in 1685, but was allowed to fall into disuse just ten years later. The early history of the press is a history of the struggle to establish the right to free speech (and commercial success) against the tendency of the State to restrict both what could be said, and the number of publications which could appear. Only in the modern era has the State been able to rely upon the relative quiescence and loyalty of a large section of the newspaper industry.

During the second half of the seventeenth century the form of the newspaper changed, from the pamphlet to the single-leaf layout. By the early years of the eighteenth century, no fewer than twenty papers were being published and circulated in London – some weekly, some appearing at longer intervals, and one daily. In 1712, however, the first of the Stamp Acts was introduced. This comprised a tax on the papers themselves and on the advertisements they carried. Sales fell as a result, and some papers went out of business. A curious anomaly of the Act was that it charged more tax on single-sheet newspapers, so as a result it encouraged the growth of longer newspapers, which were taxed at a lower rate – such newspapers could simply register as pamphlets. There was a second Stamp Act in 1725, which forced the proprietors of newspapers to charge an increased price and in addition to reduce the size and quality of their publications. There were however a whole host of unstamped and therefore unofficial newspapers making a regular appearance. Harris (*see Newspaper history from the 17th century to the present day*, in Boyce, Curran and Wingate) quotes from an author of the late 1730s who most certainly did not approve of the unofficial press (p. 85):

> 'others print news in papers of a miscellaneous kind, containing scraps of Poetry, History, Trials of Highwaymen, pickpockets and many other subjects, that tend to debauch the morals of the community, for which they insist by *law* that no duty is payable.'

There were thought at the time to be at least thirty such unstamped papers in London. The passing of a new Act in 1743 meant that the hawkers who sold unstamped papers were driven off the streets. Not only did the Stamp Acts hold back the growth of the press, they (p. 86):

> 'tended to aggravate the competition between different forms of publication, and between papers of the same type struggling for a foothold in overlapping geographical and social areas.'

The cost of some papers meant that their readership was restricted to those classes which could afford the cover price. Therefore these types of paper had what we may regard as a fairly limited range of content, reflecting the commercial and social aspirations of a particular class. According to Curran (p. 42), the expansion of the press and journalism contributed to 'the growth of a bourgeois political culture'. The first issue of the *Newcastle Chronicle,* which appeared in 1764, had its news organised into sections, while the actual content included (Giles and Hodgson, p. 41):

> 'cattle plague, the death of Viscount Townshend, the arrival of a wheat cargo, beef prices in Germany, regimental movements, murders in America, the shortage of grain in Naples and various royal functions.'

There is nothing on the first page which is of a specifically local, or even a more generally northern bias, despite the paper's masthead and its expressed intention of service to the northern counties.

During this era, the circulation of an established newspaper rarely exceeded 5000 copies, though that would have been regarded as fairly high. By the end of the eighteenth century, few cheap newspapers were available, since the established papers and their vested interests were largely able to eliminate competition. The improvement of roads and the expansion of the General Post Office assisted the growth of the established papers, and London newspapers came to achieve a national status.

The pursuit of profit

Throughout the eighteenth century, the London coffee houses provided newspapers for their customers, while other such establishments existed in the bigger provincial towns, such as Winchester, Bath, and Birmingham. At some points in the century, it was estimated that a single copy of a London newspaper could have as many as twenty individual readers. The papers were supported through a system of shareholding. Profit was not simply made on sales, but on advertising. *The London Daily Post* brought in an after-tax profit in 1746 of £753. 10s. Once papers became reasonably profitable, booksellers were interested in stocking them. There were of course negative aspects to the increasingly integrated system which produced a successful press. Harris notes that the author of the *National Journal* of 1746 complained that:

> 'there seems to be a combination among the proprieters of all the daily papers but one, not to suffer any Newspapers to be set up, in which they have no concern; and as most of the pamphlet shops ...are by necessity or choice become such slaves to them, as to deny selling any paper which has not had the good fortune to be licensed by these demagogues; it has prevented the first two or three numbers of this paper, from coming to the hands of many gentlemen.'

Under prime minister Walpole, some newspapers were bought and turned into instruments of government propaganda, written by government employees and given an extremely wide circulation. By 1741, a paper called the *Daily Gazetteer* was being sent around the country at government expense, to the tune of some 11,000 copies a week. Walpole spent over £50,000 on government propaganda over a period of ten years in office – a huge amount for the time. Some journalists were bought off and became in essence the paid lackeys of the rich and powerful. However, the career of John Wilkes, the son of a prosperous distiller, helped to shatter the complacency of the press, and threatened the ease with which governmental power could be exercised to silence its critics. Imprisoned for writing an article attacking the government, Wilkes began an intense campaign of propaganda against this injustice. He used his newspaper the *North Briton,* as well as printed songs, posters and broadsheets to carry out this attack. Despite his re-election to the House of Commons, Wilkes' repeated exclusion from Parliament became an issue of national importance. Mass action on the streets of London, and demonstrations throughout the country, helped to destroy the use of 'general warrants' to gag the press. The ban on the reporting of Parliament was abandoned in 1771.

New challenges to the status quo

The development of new printing technology served the growing commercial enterprise which the British press had become by the beginning of the nineteenth century. From the late years of the previous century, there had been an increase in the number of journals and newspapers available. There had been daily news-papers, together with some evening papers, in London, and a number of weeklies which had appeared in the provinces. From 1780 onwards, evening papers appeared each day and Sunday newspapers were also produced. Various radical journals and newspapers appeared in the years after the Battle of Waterloo, but this growth of alternative voices died back again around 1819, only to be revived in the 1830s with the advent of Chartism. The influence of radical perspectives was never quite lost in the early years of the nineteenth century. The first issue of *The Sunday Times* for instance, which appeared in 1822, contained material which the same journal's modern readership might find surprising (Giles and Hodgson p. 45):

> 'we feel an awful presentiment that damps our spirits, and almost induces us to lay down our pen in despair. If we glance our eye to the state of foreign politics, we are appalled by the sickening view of unnatural alliance with a combination of despots . . . [Turning to] the internal state of our country, an endless and unvarying succession of almost general distress presents itself to our view.'

Another weekly, *The Poor Man's Guardian,* made a more strident avowal of inde-pendence and commitment to radical change. Facing prosecution in July 1831, one edition opened with a direct address to its readership (*see* Curran, p. 49) which reflects a more fundamental critique of the whole structure of society as it was then constituted:

> 'our tyrants have summoned us to Bow-street, to act over again the farce of the "Law", before "their worships" Birnie and Halls. Our course is adopted, nor shall we waste any more of our valuable time in striving to evade the power of tyranny . . . we depend upon your support, and fearless and confident as the unarmed David, will we grapple with our giant foe!'

It is easy to lose sight of these currents of media history which, ignored once in one text, are soon regarded as mere footnotes to those events which retain an estab-lished place in our consciousness.

The inability of government to control the radical press and radical democratic movements in the early to mid-1840s (there was a general strike in 1842) had reper-cussions throughout the rest of the nineteenth century. Two of the most successful papers in the mid-1850s, just prior to the abolition of Stamp Duty in 1855, were *The Times,* appearing daily in London, and the weekly *Northern Star,* a provincial jour-nal with a wide national readership. Part of the reason for the latter's popularity was its status as the leading Chartist newspaper.

Revenue, politics and editorial control

The editor of *The Times,* Thomas Barnes, built up the world's first network of news correspondents. Although there were fewer direct attempts by government to control the press, there were other factors which acted as a brake upon the freedom of a paper to take its own course in social or political matters. Increased sales and profits did bring a degree of financial independence, but as Ivan Asquith observes (*see* Boyce, Curran and Wingate, p. 113):

'the dependence of a proprietor on his advertising income could make it difficult for him to oppose the political or commercial interests of his advertising customers.'

Asquith reports the proprietor of the *West Sussex Advertiser* in 1854 as bemoaning the fact that he depended 'absolutely more upon . . . advertising connection for profit than the sale'. Proprietors were '*compelled* to be respectable – even if [they] should wish otherwise'. We may see this as part of a process which Curran calls 'restabilisation'. The papers which arose from the period following the liberalisation of the press seemed to have a different view of society and their role within it. Curran writes (*The Media: Contexts of Study,* p. 51):

'a view of society as a system of class exploitation gave way to a new definition of reality in which different sections of the community were portrayed as being interdependent, with shared interests in common. The portrayal of labour as the source of wealth was replaced by the portrayal of "profits" as the mainspring of the economy.'

The discourses which grew from this view of society were hardly likely to disturb the increasing power of the bourgeois class. Curran refers (p. 52) to the 'incorporation . . . of the working-class movement into bourgeois political parties'. The rise in publishing costs saw the press being increasingly monopolised by those interests which had access to substantial amounts of capital. The future pattern of ownership and control of the mass circulation papers was being laid out in the latter half of the nineteenth century. It may seem surprising to note that, according to Alan Lee (*see* Boyce, Curran and Wingate, p. 119):

'in 1886, 60.6% of the columnage of *The Daily Telegraph*, 49% of that of the *The Times* and 40.5 % of *The Scotsman* was devoted to advertisements.'

The newspaper industry as a whole was driven (mainly by rising costs and the very substantial amounts of capital required to start and sustain a publishing venture) to move away from a diversity of small-scale operations towards a more integrated model of practice.

Entertainment or information?

The expansion of mass markets in the later part of the nineteenth century brought with it an increase in the number of newspapers prepared to include features designed purely as entertainment; these accompanied the usual fare of straightforward news reports. The debate over material which is not cast in a serious form, or which reproduces content associated with leisure and light-hearted pursuits, has long been the focus of criticism and suspicion. The whole 'effects' tradition, examined in Chapter 6, arose partly from concern over the form as well as the content of mass media texts.

The role of the 'alternative' press: the 1980s

The early 1980s saw a number of issues forced into the open by the revival of public interest in governmental secrecy. This accompanied the existence of the Campaign for Nuclear Disarmament in the early 1980s, and led to the existence of a variety of radical magazines with an agenda which involved more than the call for an end to the arms race. The conduct as well as the whole purpose of government and government departments was called into question.

This was a time when investigative journalism seemed to make new revelations every week. There are many examples of such journalistic enquiries, but the following will provide a small sample. The *New Statesman*, as a long-standing magazine of the left, ran a variety of articles by Duncan Campbell, which in one case revealed how the Ministry of Defence had dubbed the beginning of their 1981 propaganda war against CND the 'spring offensive'. The *Leveller*, a magazine of the libertarian left named after the seventeenth-century political movement, linked the 'Council for Social Democracy' (the forerunner of the SDP) with the right-wing 'Committee for a Free World', which the *Leveller* in turn claimed had links to the American Central Intelligence Agency. The government's ill-conceived Civil Defence exercise of 1982, 'Hard Rock', was publicised and ridiculed by magazines like *Sanity*.

A number of regional papers and magazines flourished at this time. They seemed to have decided, as John Hartley notes (*Understanding News*, p. 135), to turn away from 'the mass', and to have abandoned ideas about obtaining a large readership, seeking instead 'to build counter-hegemonic consciousness in specific areas of cultural and political activity'. The result of the proliferation of alternative papers meant that such publications were 'addressing different but "interlocking" constituencies of readers'.

Some regional papers or magazines were particularly successful in doing exactly this. In the late 1970s, *Alarm*, an A4 publication avowedly anarchist in orientation, stole a march on the 'respectable' press of Swansea by making accusations about corruption, which ended in the jailing of a number of local councillors. *Alarm* relied on a mixture of a strong core of student and local working-class support, and developed an impressive network of casual informants. *Leeds' Other Paper*, *Rochdale's Alternative Paper* and the *Islington Gutter* Press were examples of papers which were particularly successful in establishing a base in their communities. The *Exeter Flying Post*, first established in the nineteenth century, was revived in the twentieth as an outlet for information which the mainstream press neglected. A number of nationally-based magazines and papers also used similar methods in their investigative journalism, and stories which were neglected by other parts of the mainstream press were circulated in the *Observer, Private Eye*, the *Guardian* and others, including on occasion in the music press (*Melody Maker* and *NME*). When the London-based *Time Out* changed some of its working policies and sacked a number of journalists, the magazine *City Limits* was founded as a rival outlet for listings and news. A proportion of the *Time Out* readership duly defected to the new magazine.

It was to a great extent the mass membership of organisations such as CND and the Anti-Nazi League, and movements like Women's Liberation, together with gay and lesbian groups, which provided the readership for a variety of radical magazines. A number of community, co-operative and socialist presses operated on the basis of 'servicing' the needs of radical and community groups. However, with the decline in numbers of committed activists and the collapse of a wider periphery of supporters (certainly the case with CND), together with the availability of commercial technologies such as photocopying, many small presses (which used for the most part offset-litho machines) ceased functioning or turned to commercial printing.

In 1982, John Hartley was still able to declare (p. 136) that:

'the radical press is alive and well, but invisible among the consumer commodities in the High Street.'

At present, it is more the case that some publications are just about able to survive, while a very few which have better funding, and which appear to have adopted the familiar style and design of the tabloid press (*Socialist Worker* would be an obvious example), have still some kind of limited public profile. The short-lived attempt in 1987 to produce a 'left-wing' version of the populist *Sun* (a newspaper called *News on Sunday*) foundered on problems connected with distribution and the low proportion of the cover price offered to newsagents. Behind this failure lay a host of other problems connected with the balance between leftist content and traditionalist form.

Issues in the modern press: effects on voters

In 1991, a group of academics at Glasgow University, led by William Miller, published a book called *How Voters Change*. This research challenged what had long been an accepted notion in the sphere of mass media studies; that the openly partisan press in Britain tends in the main only to *reinforce* pre-existing beliefs among its readership, rather than bringing about change in public opinion. An article by Ivor Crewe in the *Media Guardian* ('Revenge of the mind benders', 19 November 1990), which reported the Glasgow research, outlined those older currents of thought which had been used to support the idea that the press has very little impact on the opinion of the electorate. They were:

- that television is gradually replacing the popular press as the medium regarded as most 'reliable' in terms of providing unbiased information during election campaigns;
- that readers of tabloid newspapers tend to have a low involvement in things political, and so ignore whatever political content their paper might contain;
- that readers choose newspapers which reflect their own political positions;
- that voters who read papers which run against the grain of their own political opinions, are either too sophisticated to be caught out, or else too ignorant to be influenced; and in the final case,

- that 'partisan conversion' was on so small a scale as to be unworthy of serious consideration.

As an example of this earlier research, we might look briefly at Lazarsfeld, Berelson and Gaudet's 1948 study of newspaper readers, *The People's Choice*, which concluded that readers were selective in their perception, and that they chose messages which reinforced their own opinions. Klapper, in a 1960 study, suggested that the mass media usually reinforced rather than altered opinions. Butler and Stokes (1969), who argued that the press may influence uncommitted voters through a kind of 'magnetic' attraction to the political party that the newspaper supports, suggested that newspapers could also act to 'demagnetise' readers if they attacked a certain party.

All these theories have been called into question by Miller's research of 1987–90, which demonstrates that the Conservative Party (then led by Margaret Thatcher), managed to make an impressive recovery between April 1986 and March 1987. The party moved from being 1 per cent behind Labour, to being no less than 16 per cent ahead. The Conservative recovery was strongest, however, among certain sectors of the electorate: the revitalisation of the party's fortunes did not occur equally across all groups. Amongst *Guardian* readers for example, it was very low. There was a modest recovery in the popularity of the Conservative Party amongst readers of *The Daily Telegraph* and the *Daily Express*, at 9 and 10 points respectively. Crewe notes that:

> 'The really big swing occured among readers of the Tory tabloids – 30 points among *Star* readers and an even more massive 36 points among *Sun* readers.'

The ability to manufacture news, to set agendas, to create headlines, seems in some instances to have offset the more 'balanced' approach of the television news.

BALANCE, NEUTRALITY AND IMPARTIALITY

Before we consider the question of 'bias' in the press, it may be worth considering the ways in which television and radio are generally regarded as more reliable sources of information.

The Annan report of 1977 was the largest and most important government sponsored enquiry into broadcasting, and dealt specifically with the notion of impartiality. The idea of impartiality was contrasted with that of balance, on the one hand, and neutrality on the other. Balance operates in television and radio news by concentrating on how much of what has been said by each interested party is actually reported in a news bulletin. This is often measured in a strictly mathematical sense, so that each participant can tell to what degree they have been accorded equal time. Neutrality, the idea that a broadcasting institution should observe from the sidelines, treating all material with the same seriousness or indifference, was rejected as a model for broadcasting by the Annan report. 'Due impartiality' was the concept favoured by the Annan team. Three elements went to make up this concept; the need to establish a range of opinions, the need to take account of the relative weight of opinion, and the need to recognise that the range and weight of opinion is subject to regular change.

On the face of it, this sounds like a reasonable approach which might, if the broadcasters continue to take it seriously, produce a fair hearing for all concerned. But this view of impartiality was founded on the understanding that the broadcasting institutions remembered that they operate (Hartley p. 51) 'within a system of parliamentary democracy', as though such a system was already perfect and therefore stood outside all controversy and was not subject to critical enquiry. As Tony Bennett once wrote, this is 'tolerance ... exercised only within the sphere of the tolerable'. In conclusion, it may be the case that television and radio news reporting may appear more 'rational' and impartial, but is sometimes unable to take the bolder gambles which are second nature to some newspapers. The issue of Royal 'accountability' for example, was forced into the public sphere not by measured enquiries into the state of the constitution, but by the sensational disclosures of the tabloid press. In the whole saga of Royal taxation, divorces and separations, the medium of broadcasting followed the initiatives made by the press – but at a discreet distance.

Language and ideology

It would also be misleading to imagine that the difference between the press and broadcasting is that broadcasting is somehow free from any form of ideology. Any institutional use of language as a mode of communication, whether in print or as a reproduction of the human voice, will carry some meanings which are ideological. Fowler argues that:

> 'news is a representation of the world in language; because language is a semiotic code, it imposes a structure of values, social and economic in origin, on whatever is represented; and so inevitably news, like every discourse, constructively patterns that of which it speaks.'
>
> (p. 4)

This patterning is ideological in the first instance because all language has been produced in societies, and in all societies there is always a 'will to power' being exercised; but the use of language is not always consciously ideological. John Hartley (in *Understanding News*), demonstrates how linguistic choices may also be ideological choices.

Take, for example, a photograph of combat in the Vietnam war featuring American troops in action. These captions could be used to create widely differing meanings:

a Heroes under fire
b A taste of their own terror
c The horrors of war

People may sometimes, as suggested earlier, appear to reproduce a particular ideological stance because only certain types of discourse are available. The example Hartley gives is the phrase 'terrorists liberated' which, although grammatically correct, would be unlikely to be used in a conversation or news report because the two words carry quite different values. Together, they are confusing. It would be more 'natural', argues Hartley, for someone to use the term 'terrorists' with words like 'captured', 'overran' or 'occupied', which give the same idea that some target has fallen by force of arms, but without the positive connotations of 'liberation' being attached. The ideological choices made by news broadcasters have become 'time-honoured'. The language they use may be less irritating and certainly less extreme that that used by sections of the tabloid press, but it reflects a concern to maintain an impartiality which depends upon an adherence to a linguistic and political status quo.

'Bias' or discourse: two approaches to communication in the press

It seems that the particular talent of the Conservative press is to persuade specific groups of voters to rally to the causes of the Right at times of crisis or pressure; election campaigns are an example of such crises. If we accept the idea that news-papers are able, in certain circumstances, to alter attitudes, and are even able to affect short-term behaviour as a consequence, then the possession of such power has immense implications for the democratic process. It is obvious that the deci-sions made during elections will affect the lives of people for a number of years following polling-day. A relentless, large-scale newspaper campaign in favour of any party, and especially a campaign which is partially co-ordinated by a govern-ment, is one symptom of a serious imbalance in power.

We have already studied the relationship between public relations, advertising and politics. During elections, many front pages in the press are, in terms of their direct mode of persuasive address, little more than advertising, and might usefully carry the words 'advertisement feature' in the margin. Advertising, as we have seen, does not need to describe the product in factual terms. It can still function effectively in the short-term, even where the product is useless or harmful. Of course, the extreme heights of pro-Conservative rhetoric are only reached during an intensive propaganda campaign. It is not usually necessary to produce such material when a government is not under pressure, and may even be counter-productive if the discourses used do not seem to match the actual experience of those reading the headlines.

Some newspaper editors maintain that being partisan is a relatively harmless tendency in newspapers. Sir Nick Lloyd, editor of the *Daily Express*, said in a 1991 interview (*see* Nina Arnott, *Political Bias in the Press*, Communication studies project):

> 'Obviously newspapers do pick and choose stories to use, rather like rooting for a foot-ball team.'

Of course, the consequences of the two types of choice would be quite different, although some may wonder how exactly the economy would fare under the elect-ed stewardship of, for example, Millwall Football Club.

Overall, the question of bias in the press is one which has long featured as a central issue in the study of mass communication. The term 'bias', as applied to sections of the media, refers to the idea that they appear to favour one viewpoint over another, or that they have a tendency to support a certain political party, social group or institution at the expense of other sections of society. 'Bias' may be created through an open prejudice in favour of something, or by deliberately neglecting to provide all the information necessary for a more complete view of events.

'Bias' in the press: a useful concept?

It is clear that the press in Britain is overwhelmingly Conservative in political orientation. To some degree, therefore, 'bias' is a useful concept. It lets us know that a large part of one mass communicative form is likely to be deployed in support of one political creed, come what may.

However, attacks on political bias in general face a major problem. What do such critiques hope to achieve, apart from a general acceptance of the idea that some papers are 'unfair' in their treatment of certain issues? Is it worthwhile campaigning for the adoption of some kind of 'neutral' political stance in the national press? (If, of course, it were really possible to find a perfectly neutral position from which to judge events.)

One solution to the problem of 'bias' may be to argue for a strictly 'factual' approach to reporting. But this ignores the role and function of the newspaper as a form. Many newspapers are not primarily in the 'information' business; facts are often regarded as less important than 'stories'. In a way, we could argue that *all* newspapers regard facts as subsidiary to the 'narratives' that they produce. Roger Fowler (*Language in the News*, p. 1) argues that:

> 'the "content" of newspapers is not facts about the world, but in a very general sense "ideas".'

If we accept that newspapers are really in the business of circulating ideas (or perhaps discourses in narrative form), rather than facts, we may be able to suggest a different approach to the question of political bias. Fowler makes it clear that his intention was not (p. 8):

> 'simply to expose "bias", certainly not to maintain that newspapers are especially "biased".'

In one sense, ditching the usual obsession with 'bias' allows us to see that discourse, an address with a 'will to power' behind it, is able to operate in all forms of communication. In other words, an approach which concentrates on discourse allows us to examine all the ways in which meaning is created, and lets us escape from the problem of having to contrast 'bias' with some notion of 'balance'. As Fowler puts it:

> '[nearly] all meanings are socially constructed . . . all discourse is a social product and a social practice.'

Instead of trying to expose the 'evils' of a partisan press, therefore, a more general investigation of meaning-creation and meaning-circulation would have to be carried out.

The disadvantage is that some studies of discourse neglect the question of political and social power. Ideas about 'bias' at least point to the fact that sections of the press operate in the interests of the powerful. Fowler is careful to emphasise the *social* nature of news production, but goes on to argue that 'newspapers are not especially biased'. But the point we have already established is that, taken as a whole, newspapers can be exactly this. Not only are they often owned by one particular interest or individual, the *form* of newspapers (particularly the use of headlines, photographs and captions) lends itself to a propagandist approach. During a political fight, newspapers are often used as blunt instruments.

We should not forget that newspapers make no attempt to attract the kind of general audience which, for example, the early evening television news must secure. This means that newspapers are at liberty to pursue a sometimes quite out-spoken political line, once they have identified an audience which is prepared to endorse or tolerate that line. Individual newspapers cater for carefully chosen target groups (although there will be times when they wish to widen their audience). Free from the constraints of having to speak a universal dialect, as it were, they may appeal to their chosen audience in narrower terms. If the appeal is made through a popular discourse which emphasises what used to be called 'the lowest common denominator' (or 'enjoyment and light-heartedness' if you prefer), it may be possible to carry a variety of political messages on the back of a generally cheerful 'down to earth' attitude to the world.

One of the side-effects of approaching all discourses in the same way is that we may lose the more critical edge which is offered by characterising *certain parts* of the national press as 'biased'. We need to accept the idea that 'language is a semiotic code' and that the newspaper articles based on it are therefore involved in the social construction of meaning; but we must distinguish between the linguist's use of 'discourse' as 'all speech' and the media theorist's use of 'discourse' as 'ideological address'. 'All speech' is bound to reflect (rather than merely reimpose) the social structure from which it springs. 'Ideological address', on the other hand, has an extra element. It refers to that type of speech which is based on a system or systems of belief, and which is loaded with a systematic and coherent intention (the address).

The 1987 election campaign

The fact that newspapers have a relatively small readership may lead some to argue that their partisan approach is bound to be limited in effect. Sir Nick Lloyd (*see* Arnott) made the point that:

> 'You can only get over to your own readers. The Express has four and a half million. That's only a small percentage of the electorate and if people buy newspapers that reinforce their political view then you won't change much.'

One response to this, quite apart from the fact that the 'reinforcement' argument has been shown to be flawed, is that there is more than just one Conservative newspaper (there were no fewer than eleven in 1987), and that the accumulated power of so many publications of one political hue may be considerable. Again, the editor of the *Daily Express* opposes this view, and emphasises the relative harmlessness of political allegiance:

> 'Newspapers have a character and part of that character is a political view: maybe as a result of the ownership of that newspaper or maybe as a result of the journalists working on it.'

POLITICAL CONTACT BETWEEN PRESS AND POLITICIANS

The close relationship between many newspaper editors and the leaders of the Conservative Party was attested to by Rodney Tyler, who worked for a number of national newspapers before writing a study of the 1987 election called *Campaign!* (p. 125):

> 'Many, many times, in both 1979 and 1983, potential disasters were averted … by frank exchanges over an evening drink in the editors' offices of Fleet Street.'

In an emergency, advice could be proffered more easily over the telephone. The advice would very often be from editor to politician, rather than vice versa. Such support was important, since Mrs Thatcher's position in the 1987 general election was not as strong as it had been in 1983. Thatcherism operated through what Fowler (p. 6) calls the 'paradoxical ideology of conflict and consensus', and the Conservative press was instrumental in mobilising this ideology. By a 'paradoxical ideology' Fowler means that:

> 'the Conservative government under Mrs. Thatcher … theorised social and international relationships in terms of conflict … but while the practice was to segregate and marginalize threatening and undesirable elements, the official discourse of government and media spoke of national unity of interest and common purpose: consensus.'

CREATING AN AGENDA

It was up to the Conservative press to provide the discourses which might best help to 'marginalize' those elements which stood in the way of victory at the polls. One of the main targets for the campaign was the Labour leader, Neil Kinnock, since he posed more of a threat in terms of image and capability than had Michael Foot, the previous leader. The attacks on Kinnock and the party he led tried to place them as far as possible outside the 'consensus' the Tory press hoped to create.

The *Sun* ran an article with the headline, 'If you want union bully boys back, vote for Kinnock', while the *Daily Mail* repeated Thatcher's warning that 'The Tyrants are Waiting'. Both of these are recognisable as the type of address which tries to place the Labour Party beyond the limits of what is politically acceptable. They are appeals to the fear which is supposed to be created by political extremism. On 9 June, the *Daily Express* announced that 'Labour is more extreme today than it has ever been' and that the election was being fought by 'the largest collection of left-wing nasties west of the Berlin Wall'. In a variation of the theme which dealt with political extremism, this paper argued that Kinnock would be the 'prisoner' of these malevolent forces. On election day some attention was given to the positive virtues of the government, though even this editorial gave more space to the threat posed by Labour.

BOADICEA CASTS HER VOTE

Other attempts to denigrate the 'new model' Labour Party were more humorous. In an attempt to bolster the patriotic credentials of Mrs Thatcher, the *Sun* carried interviews which had been conducted via 'a medium and psychic investigator', the reason being to discover the voting intentions of a variety of notable figures from history. Stalin was, apparently, determined in his support of Kinnock, while Henry VIII and Nelson were both firmly in the Conservative camp. Boadicea, also speaking from beyond the grave, declared, 'When I hear the words of Kinnock and his treacherous ilk I feel ashamed for England.' It appears that this Queen managed to feel ashamed for the nation, although it had not existed as such in her own lifetime.

HISTORIC ROLES AND PERSONAL ATTACKS

The *Daily Mirror,* in support of the Labour Party, carried a front-page article which might in fact have proved a little uncomfortable for the Labour leadership, concerned as it was to avoid presenting the Conservative press with any evidence of past socialist instincts. Dated 10 June 1987, it insisted that:

'The Conservative Party exists to preserve privileges. That is what it was created for. That is its historic role. The Labour Party was created to fight privilege, the degradation of poverty, the humiliation of unemployment, the misery of slums. That is its historic duty.'

Arnott, in the conclusion to her study of bias in the press, writes that:

'Sectors of the "quality" press grudgingly admitted that the Labour campaign was much better organised and presented more professionally than that of the Conservatives. Perhaps this is part of the reason why the Conservative press concentrated more on ridiculing the Labour Party than on promoting the policies of the Conservatives.'

The precedent set by the attacks on the private lives and public characters of Labour politicians, such as Benn, Kinnock, Mandelson and a host of others, later proved an uncomfortable experience for Conservatives such as Mellor and Lamont. Benyon (*Social Studies Review,* November 1987) revealed there had been rumours that a team of journalists had gone so far as to question Neil Kinnock's neighbours in attempts to discover anything that might be construed as scandalous. Kinnock described the press as 'more irresponsible, more prone to slander, more filthy than we have had in this country before'. The use of personal attacks seems to have become almost a dominant feature of newspaper practice. Sir Nick Lloyd believes that public figures must be prepared for such coverage:

'If a politician is going to stand on a pedestal and make speeches about how we run our lives, then how they run theirs is relevant ... if you stand for public office you have to be aware that people will be interested in parts of your private life that you'd prefer them not to be interested in.'

Although all the editors of the national newspapers observe a code of conduct agreeing not to investigate private lives unless it is in the public's interest to know, the difficulty remains that editors have quite widely divergent ideas about where exactly the public interest lies.

Profit from the popular: the *Sun*

The *Sun* remains an outstanding success, a publishing phenomenon whose profits allowed its proprietor, Rupert Murdoch, to finance his Sky satellite project. Even when it seemed that millions of pounds each month was being lost in the repayment of loans, profits from the newspaper helped to sustain the satellite venture. The *Sun* remains the most lucrative newspaper run by Murdoch in any of the three continents in which he operates. In the financial year 1985–6, for example, the subsidiary which publishes the *Sun* and *News of the World* accounted for over a quarter of all the profits made by all the worldwide subsidiaries of News Corporation, the parent company. Together, the two newspapers produced a profit of £34 million.

Murdoch's vision of a mass media empire is one in which each sector helps to support the others. It is a vision of integration. Murdoch's take-over of the Twentieth Century Fox film and television facilities was intended both to help construct a large US television network, and to provide the Sky project with film-stock, of which there are some 2,500 features available to be shown. Profits from the *Sun* were used to help acquire American newspapers, including the *New York Post*, purchased in 1976. There appears to be a fortune in the 'information' industry, with £800 million worth of newspaper revenue and £560 million from magazines, TV and films flowing into News Corporation in 1985–6. However, News Corporation needs to continue to make substantial profits in order to repay debts and make interest payments incurred as a result of its acquisitions (*see* Wollen, 'Institution' in *The Media Studies Book*, Routledge, 1991).

News International in Britain

News International, the British end of News Corporation, consisted in the early 1990s of the following interests: in terms of newspapers and journals owned, we may list the *Sun, Today, News of the World, The Times, The Sunday Times, The Times Educational Supplement, The Times Higher Education Supplement, The Times Literary Supplement, TV Guide, New Woman,* and a 50 per cent holding in *Sky Magazine.* In addition, the group owns Sky Television, the Harper Collins book publishing interests, and has a 20 per cent stake in *The Financial Times.*

The *Sun* and its discourses

If we take the linguist's conception of discourse first, we may sometimes find an approach which emphasises 'speech genres'. The *Sun* works on the basis of addressing or 'interpellating' its readers in a way which allows them to imagine that there is a *common-sense* approach to society's problems. Stuart Hall described how the language used by a newspaper will attempt to reflect the usual modes of address employed by its readership (Hartley, p. 96):

> 'the language employed will thus be the newspaper's own version of the language of the public to whom it is principally addressed.'

We should know by now that language grows from, and acts in turn upon the society it is used within. If a newspaper works by speaking in the mode employed by its readers, then it must be able to mobilise a variety of language genres. Hall describes this as:

> '[the newspaper's] version of the rhetoric, imagery and underlying common stock of knowledge which it assumes its audience shares.'

A newspaper may indeed begin by imagining a mode of address which will be successful in targeting a specific group, but once that address is established, the readership may come to assume it themselves, at least during the time they are in reception of the address. Of course, it is the whole idea of what constitutes the accepted view of 'common sense' that needs some explanation. John Hartley makes an important point when he asks how it is that basing journalism and broadcasting in 'the everyday' and the 'real concerns' of the people ends up by:

> 'land[ing] the media straight back into the laps of those who are the current beneficiaries of the way power and rewards are unequally distributed?'   (p. 96)

Here there are two views which might be worth contrasting. The first answer to Hartley's question might be that the dominant classes in society themselves produce the 'common sense', which is then passed down to all other groups below. The second may be that the whole of society is engaged in producing versions of 'common sense', from which the press and the broadcasting institutions make *selections*. Many people's opinions appear contradictory, in the sense that passionate feelings about one issue may be directly undermined by their stance on something else of an essentially similar nature. John Westergaard (*see* Hartley) talks of how the 'diverse and ambiguous reality of popular outlooks on the world' is sacrificed by the tendency of newspapers to select only those discourses which they feel conform to their ideas of the way the world should be represented. One point worth remembering is that really successful newspapers, like the *Sun*, sometimes end up by reproducing an ambiguous stance themselves, not usually within single articles, but when a reading is made of a single issue's overall content.

THE *SUN*: A 'WORLD-VIEW'?

To castigate the *Sun* for depending on the lowest common denominator (in this case, scandal and sex) is to lose sight of how it achieved its unique market position. There are other publications which manage to be even more basic, but which do not quite possess the ability of Murdoch's leading journal to frame every story in terms of what some have called a 'naughty' but cheerful sexuality. Moving further downmarket from the *Sun*, we encounter a species of pornography which is not only distinctly tacky but which also seems to cater for a certain kind of viciousness. the *Sun* could be said to have inherited something of the sexual liberation and anti-authoritarianism of the late 1960s and early 1970s, and to have been a factor in the increasing liberalisation of society's attitudes to sex. This process has, however, gone only so far, and many authors argue that the sexual liberation of the 1960s and 1970s benefited men considerably more than it did women.

In addition, the paper's broad-mindedness does not apply when the activities in question carry any suggestion that they are not strictly heterosexual. The paper will print stories about gay and lesbian relationships, but only in order to denigrate and undermine the subjects of such articles. On the face of it, this is one of those issues which calls into question what some have called the 'anti-authoritarianism' of the *Sun*. How can it be 'liberated' about sex if it both exploits teenage models and employs double standards on the simple basis of sexual preference? In matters of 'straight' sexuality it might seem to be carefree and fun-loving, but its apparent liking for a more authoritarian society, and its calls for harsher discipline and the punishment of what it sees as social deviance, mark it out as part of the Thatcherite inheritance. The *Sun's* antipathy to homosexual relationships is not of course unique. As Derek Jameson said (in *Out of the Gutter*, Campaign for Press and Broadcasting Freedom, 1987, p. 15):

> 'Fleet Street takes the view that homosexuality is abnormal, unnatural, a bit evil ... they're not going to say that gays are normal, natural people.'

The *Sun* has a certain populist approach which manages to combine a kind of spiteful enjoyment of stories involving gay relationships with the exercise of moral outrage. The CPBF's 1985/86 survey of press treatment of homosexuality found that certain stories (such as one which featured a 'love triangle' of three women) were used day after day, with much of the material simply being repeated time after time. Such stories reveal how some papers like the *Sun* are in fact highly formulaic; the same set of criteria are always used in judging the participants, and the language deployed appears to reflect a pre-existing ideological frame. The use of the same approach, the same 'house-style', leads the journalist to produce the same kind of story, no matter what the details of the individual case. Overall, the paper's open hostility to alternative forms of sexual behaviour must surely form part of its marketing strategy. A positive or even tolerant response to stories featuring gay and lesbian issues would appear to be perceived as a threat to one of the *Sun's* main selling-points: its 'fun-loving' commitment to the commercial exploitation of the female body for the benefit of the heterosexual male reader.

RACISM AND THE *SUN*

Many commentators believe that black people are 'invisible' except when a news report can cast them as a 'problem'. The notion of equality or impartiality of treatment is something that fails to convince many black writers. Kofi Hadjor writes (*see Searle*, p. 7);

> 'For committed black journalists there is no such thing as an objective impartial viewpoint. We should start from the assumption that the establishment press propagates establishment views ... [we] should seek out and expose every example of injustice against our people.'

Where the *Sun* can combine a number of its pet dislikes it will certainly do so. A visit by Neil Kinnock to a number of front-line African states during the 1987 election campaign was recast as 'Kinnock's in Jungleland at vote time'. All foreign states and their subjects have become the targets of the *Sun's* racism, although particular venom seems reserved for black people. Searle (p. 20) believes that the *Sun's* racism has been refined over the years:

> 'It [racism] is the sharpened form of national jingoism which was brought into populist fullness during the war in the Malvinas [Falklands], and has developed almost to the level . . . of self-parody.'

Once a newspaper is expected to engage in a certain kind of abuse, this becomes part of its stock-in-trade. The famous 1984 headline, 'Hop off you Frogs', or the equally ridiculous 'Up Yours Delors', emblazoned with a life-sized picture of a two-fingered salute, are both memorable examples of this approach. But the paper's 'self-parody' can obscure an important feature of its overall success, which is based on a spurious kind of reader 'participation'. At noon on the day of the anti-Delors attack, loyal *Sun* readers were supposed to take a few minutes off work to stick their fingers up in the direction of France. Kelvin MacKenzie, the paper's editor, once associated the mass-produced picture entitled 'The Crying Boy' with a curse, because it had survived a fire in which a fatality occurred. He appealed to his readers to send in their own copies of the picture, so that the curse could be exorcised. Some thousands of reproductions of the picture duly arrived at the paper's offices.

ADDRESSING THE READERSHIP

While some of the more unusual publicity stunts of the *Sun* have undoubtedly been quite harmless, certain of its campaigns have carried none of this unintentional humour. Some of its campaigns have targeted those individuals and groups who have attempted to criticise its racism and sexism. The Labour MP Clare Short, who has campaigned since 1986 to introduce legislation which would result in the banning of 'page three' displays, was attacked at some length in the paper. The *Sun* instituted a 'Stop Crazy Clare' campaign, complete with badges and stickers issued to the readership. Chris Searle's two-year monitoring of the paper revealed that only half a dozen stories in all that time could be regarded as positive treatments of the subject of race. One of the most consistent campaigns run by the paper has been to reinforce far-right propaganda on the subject of repatriation. In terms of address, the *Sun* would appear to encourage a reaction to a variety of groups based on an appeal to the most uncharitable and mean-spirited of human instincts. Many of its articles appear to encourage responses in its readership based on mockery and resentment founded on a deep-seated anxiety about national identity.

The Wapping dispute

In January 1986, some 6000 members of SOGAT '82, the NGA and the AUEW went on strike after months of negotiation with their employers, News International and Times Group Newspapers. The management had proposed the introduction of

Fig 7.1 Wapping strike leaflet

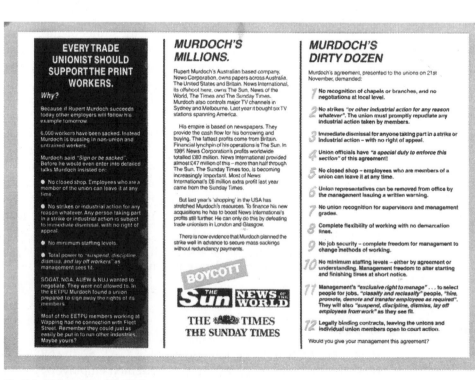

Fig 7.1 *(Other side of leaflet)*

new working conditions, as part of a legally-binding five-year contract to include flexible working, the end of the union closed-shop policy, the introduction of new technology, and a no-strike agreement. The ability of trade unionists to interfere with some of the *Sun*'s more extreme propaganda stunts had been one factor in the decision to discipline the workforce through the move to a new plant in Wapping. For example the refusal on 15 May 1984 of all production chapels at the *Sun* to handle a front-page photograph of Arthur Scargill waving at a Mansfield rally, on the grounds that the caption ('Mine Fuhrer') suggested he was giving a Nazi salute, resulted in the paper being printed without caption or photograph.

As soon as the strike was announced, dismissal notices were issued to all those taking part in industrial action. The workforce was replaced with members of the EETPU (the electrician's union). Outside the new Wapping plant, demonstrations were organised on Wednesday and Saturday evenings, sometimes with relatively low attendance (in the hundreds), but quite often attended by considerably more. One of the largest demonstrations took place on 24 January 1987, the anniversary of the beginning of the dispute. Some 20,000 people attended the event, with the first marchers moving off at five o'clock that evening. Clashes between police and demonstrators resulted in a police operation which was organised as a series of baton charges made by officers on foot, combined with the use of mounted officers. Thirty-nine police officers and thirty-four demonstrators received hospital treatment (over two hundred demonstrators were injured). Some five years later, a number of police were found guilty of having used excessive violence in their attacks on demonstrators. The unions failed to get their members reinstated. During the dispute, a variety of alternative journals and newsletters flourished, of which the best known were the *Wapping Post* and the radical news-sheet Picket, which gave details of the movement of TNT strike-breaking lorries and of the marches and sometimes irregular actions carried out by pickets.

NEWS AND POPULAR JOURNALISM

The new 'moronism'?

Media commentators have become increasingly agitated by the idea that serious news journalism (in print and television) is under threat by what *Guardian* reporter Nicholas Fraser has called 'the new moronism' (see his article of 2 June 1997). In his attack on the 'vacuity of contemporary media', Fraser refers to a common theme in the campaign against falling journalistic standards – the example set by news organisations in the United States. He mentions in particular 'Lite TV, a California news bulletin designed for the reality-averse or merely Prozac-stuffed'. Fraser believes that 'there is a world media culture now and it consists predominantly of reach-me-down Americana'. Meanwhile, programme-makers and editors in the United States have offered an explanation for the seeming frivolity of their practices. In the words of Van Gordon Sauter, President of CBS News from 1982–3, the aim was simply to make 'stories simpler, more accessible', and to provide 'stories that people could understand'. Changes of this kind are often justified by referring to the 'needs' of audience. The process of change is not confined to America, however; nor is a rather patronising attitude towards audience. In 1997, an internal BBC study revealed that world issues were, in the words of Andrew Culf of the *Guardian* 'a no-go area for large sections of its audience'. A leaked programme review document revealed concern among BBC's management that the extent of many viewers' interest in 'foreign affairs' is confined to holidays abroad. Serious or 'heavy' issues like world economics, famines and wars, appeared to make little impression unless the presentation could be made particularly 'frothy'. A certain group of celebrities were thought suited to the task of presenting news to younger viewers, including the following: Chris Evans, Gaby Roslin, Ulrike Jonsson, Vic Reeves and Bob Mortimer. The 130-page review had gone further than this, however, dividing the BBC audience into six categories:

- **Saga travellers** (6.6 million): mainly divorced or widowed women, interested in foreign culture, and avid viewers of the Antiques Roadshow, Heartbeat and Countdown;
- **Club 18–35ers** (6.8 million): mostly males who watch satellite television and 'do not want to understand foreigners';
- **Stay at homes** (3.5 million): a retired, xenophobic group with an interest in soap operas and shows hosted by Michael Barrymore;
- **Keen travellers** (9.5 million): young parents who are fairly adventurous, unconcerned about language barriers, and used to taking holidays abroad;
- **2.4 children** (10 million): this group is composed of families who go on sightseeing holidays to the Mediterranean, watch Wildlife on One and Heartbeat;
- **Discerning and serious** (8.7 million): educated and 'up-market', the individuals who make up this group read the *Guardian* or *The Times*, and are interested in foreign affairs.

This piece of 'research' seems to recall the practice of segmentation, studied earlier in this book. The BBC report notes that 'the groups at the bottom [of the social scale] are looking for entertainment, not information. Any educational message to this group cannot be explicit'. As before, the idea that sections of the audience are incapable of coping with serious coverage of world events, provides news organisations with a ready excuse.

There are two aspects to the problem of 'dumbing down', as it was sometimes known during this period. The first is a question of content. Are the critics of the 'new' journalism worried about the kind of items that now achieve circulation in news bulletins and newspapers? Or do they object to the fact that news formats have become more informal? The answer is that both seem to cause offence; content and presentation together have created the response noted above.

Content and format in news

The 'trivialisation' of news is also noticed by Bob Franklin, who begins his analysis with two examples, from an ITN news report and from a story carried by the *News of the World*. The first piece he cites uses the funeral of James Bulger (whose murder was popularly linked with the negative influence of videos like *Child's Play*). In its report, ITN opened with the following introduction: 'Hello. The teddy bears he loved so much sat side by side in church today. The day of the funeral of James Bulger.' Franklin considers the item to be an 'insensitive conjoining of the sentimental and the sensational, the prurient and the populist', bearing 'all the hallmarks of tabloid journalism' (*Newszak and News Media*, p. 3). The second example of bad taste is taken from an article which advertised itself as a 'world exclusive' concerning the alleged relationship between the Conservative MP Jerry Hayes and his House of Commons researcher, Paul Stone. The *News of the World* carried the headline 'Tory MP 2-Timed Wife With Under-Age Gay Lover'.

Both of Franklin's examples are certainly rather tawdry, and may well reflect changed attitudes to news among both journalists and the public. However, there is another aspect of this fondness for sensation which Franklin may not have considered, and which is revealed in a third example where 'little regard is shown for the privacy of the individuals concerned'.

This is the *Daily Mirror's* serialisation of interviews with Sarah Ferguson, which represent in Franklin's opinion 'a particularly unpleasant and ugly downturn in tabloid coverage of the royals' (p. 4). The *Mirror's* material included a picture of a goat and invited readers to choose between Fergie and the animal. This wretched and sexist comparison does, however, exemplify the death of deference, in the tabloids and amongst the British population. The tabloid press followed a populist agenda where royalty was concerned, but it was an agenda which grew from a source which was in some respects political, though expressed as disillusionment with many of the characters who populated the royal soap opera. This form of disenchantment was reflected in newspaper attacks such as the one above – personalised, limited, offensive – yet a potent confirmation of public feeling. This leads directly to two questions which could be explored in any discussion of changing news priorities:

- Does poor taste and an informal mode of presentation always convey trivial content?
- Does seriousness of purpose and formal presentation always promise a useful insight into important issues?

Form, content and structure: visibility and invisibility of media

Our experience of the media is somewhat contradictory: we encounter media which are at one and the same time **visible** and **invisible**. *Visible* in the sense that we can quite easily observe and grow to understand media **content**, such as television commercials, films, and in this case newspaper articles and television news bulletins; and *invisible* in the sense that what lies 'behind the scenes', the **structures** of the media (the hierarchies, the financial framework, the practices, ownership and control), remain largely *hidden* from our view.

Media structures are not usually democratic – that is to say, the internal relationships between workers and the executive class (certainly within the largest corporate bodies) are just as hierarchical as those within other industries. In addition, the relationship between the media and their 'clients' or audience is founded on an absolute inequality of power. When called upon to address its audiences, however, the media must 'speak' in a form which the bulk of the population understands, based on a description of content which a variety of groups are able to recognise as relevant.

Although there is much criticism of the media's tendency to appeal to the 'lowest common denominator' (those morally reprehensible interests which all or most individuals are supposed to find entertaining), the 'lowest' denominator can still carry, under certain circumstances, a political agenda. When Franklin claims that (p. 4) 'the pressures on news media to win viewers and readers in an increasingly competitive market have generated revised editorial ambitions', and Nicholas Fraser argues that television journalism 'is now best understood as an extension of showbusiness', we may lose sight of the fact that successful journalism has always contained a strong element of spectacle; it is a narrative form pressed into commercial service.

The news we receive is the result of what could be called an *industrial* as well as an *intellectual* process. In other words, 'news' is a product or commodity, something for sale in a marketplace. It has thus always been 'entertainment', though it is fair to say as Franklin indicates that (p. 4) 'news media have increasingly become part of the entertainment industry'.

It is **the status of news as a commodity**, rather than the degree of its 'seriousness', which determines its position within the entertainment market. The problem neglected by Franklin and others, is the difficulty of drawing a firm dividing line between real news and trivia. Franklin complains that 'the world of sport or the royal family are judged more 'newsworthy' than the reporting of significant issues and events of international consequence'. Are the royal family, then, not 'of international consequence'? The way in which royal issues are discussed ('would you prefer Fergie or a goat?') may well at times seem trivial, but such material emerges from, and contributes to a public debate about the real value of the whole institution (even where such a debate ultimately confirms that the institution itself has some function).

'It's a safe pill, and it ain't doing you no harm. I don't see the problem'

The use of celebrity, sensationalism and entertainment are never devoid of political significance. As an example, consider this statement; 'It's a safe pill, and it ain't doing you no harm. I don't see the problem' made in 1996 by a singer named Brian Harvey, who belonged to a group called East 17. Hours after declaring that Ecstasy was harmless, the unfortunate Harvey had to issue a new statement, rather different to the first: 'All I'd like to say now is: Never take Ecstasy. It can kill you.' Leaving aside the issue of which of these statements sounds most authentic, one more statement either way on the subject of drugs is hardly 'new information' about events. Why then does it 'make the headlines'?

Imagine for a minute that the first remark took place during a private conversation; it might have caused some argument, perhaps, if the other people present had disagreed, but it would not have provoked the same controversy. Three factors make this news:

- the **status** of the individual concerned – this idea is sometimes associated with the 'news value' called *personalisation*;
- the **content** of the original statement – it has *relevance* and *simplicity*;
- and the **context** within which the remark was made.

Celebrity confers status; if a person is already in the public eye, anything they do has the potential to become significant. Content is the apparent *meaning* of the material (in this case, a declaration that ecstasy *is* or *is not* a harmful drug). Context, on the other hand, is made up of the following elements: the **situation** and the **discursive environment** within which the event takes place. The situation or 'immediate' context was the radio interview in which the remarks were made, while the discursive environment was the continuing public debate about the dangers of drug abuse. Harvey got into trouble because his statement fell outside the boundaries of acceptable public discourse (at the time, the issue of Ecstasy was linked to the idea of teenage deaths). Once he had 'broken the ice', however, less nervous public figures pursued the same agenda and received more serious treatment. A short while later, Noel Gallagher made similar remarks and received qualified support from the *Daily Mirror* which reported his opinion under the headline 'E's got a point'! (On a practical note, Gallagher's position, unlike Harvey's, was not undermined by his fellow artistes).

News as 'factual' information?

Although the proper definition of news is 'new information about events' (so, for example, one friend might say to another 'what's new?') the real meaning of the term in our society is rather different. News has come to mean information which has been **collected, shaped** (or given form) and then passed on or **reported** by professional, profit-making organisations.

The extent to which perceptions of news and the role of the media have changed, is revealed in the contrast between the work of Franklin, who sets 'entertainment' against the more desirable 'news and information', and the perspective found in John Fiske's *Television Culture*, 1989. In this book Fiske attacked what was then an established idea: the notion that news is somehow factual or 'objective'. Speaking of television, he wrote that (p. 281) 'the basic definition of news as factual information ... gives us only half the story'. In other words, Fiske objected not to *sensation dressed up as news*, but the idea of news as 'fact' (quite appropriate to a study of television news in the 1970s). Fiske goes on to speak of 'norms', a set of values which 'embody the ideology of the dominant classes'. This point of view casts the news organisation in a certain role - as the servant of the dominant forces in society. News is therefore, according to this scenario, a reflection or embodiment of dominant interests and values.

Fiske selects an example to make this point, using media treatment of industrial disputes to explore the ways in which workers are represented in television news. He notes (p. 285) that 'their [trade unionists'] actions are always represented as "demands" whereas employers are said to "offer".' This convention, Fiske thinks, is read by trade unionists as 'further evidence of the power of the dominant classes to naturalise their [the dominant class'] social interests into 'ordinary' common sense' (this was before Fiske's celebration of audience, described in Chapter 1).

So, according to this theory, news bulletins use the word 'demands' to describe the actions of workers because this makes the rule of the powerful seem 'natural'. But might the use of the word 'demands' actually *reveal* rather than *conceal* true power relations? Of course the workers have to *demand* a pay increase from their bosses! The bosses hold the purse strings and are therefore able to *offer* what they see fit. The use of these words may reveal the dominance of one group's interests, but they are also an accurate representation of unequal power relations; the alteration of such terms (in an attempt perhaps to create a more liberal discourse), may serve only to soften the reality of industrial relations.

News and the discursive turn in media

The 'dominant ideology' thesis remains a powerful force in media and cultural theory. This model of the communication process seemed to suggest that the media was engaged in some form of conspiracy, serving the interests of those in power. The idea, as we have seen above, was that messages which actually served the interests of dominant groups were made to appear 'natural' rather than sectional, part of the wider 'common sense' of a society.

Leaving aside the suspicion that those in authority might not always be as united as we sometimes imagine, it is quite possible that the media have their own agendas. Certainly, media treatment of industrial conflict has often been straightforwardly anti-working class, but there are other issues which have caused long disputes between news organisations and state agencies (Alastair Milne's BBC under the Thatcher government is a case in point).

In recent years, some writers have pointed out the limitations of academic analysis of the kind we have encountered above. Peter A. Bruck (*see* 'Discursive Movements and Social Movements: the Active Negotiation of Constraints' in *Democratic Communications in the Information Age*, edited by Wasko and Mosco) is one of these commentators.

He argues (p. 138) that 'critical work separates phenomena in the world into what they appear to be and what they 'really' are, and it relates them to what possibly should be'. This is precisely the method adopted in the early work of writers like John Fiske and John Hartley (*see* Hartley, *Understanding News*). The media do not, however, just make up events or reflect the opinions of the powerful. Bruck believes that most 'critical media theories' are inadequate, because they fail 'to account for the often contradictory operation of the news media'. Looking beyond the arguments about trivia *vs.* seriousness (p. 140), Bruck turns his attention instead to the bureaucratic organisation of news work, which 'ties journalistic practice ... to the operational modes and agendas of the management apparatuses of the state and the economy'. Although certain sections of the media tend, at first sight, to have 'a proclivity for the sensational', and therefore 'the unbureaucratic', Bruck believes that on closer examination, the news media prove to be 'an integral part of present-day social administration and control'.

Bruck departs from the perspective as represented by the early Fiske, in his belief that identifying the news media as part of the dominant system, is only 'a starting point of analysis'. The dominant system, in Bruck's view, does not 'reproduce itself in an uncontradictory or conflict-free fashion'. He also insists that the news media (the press, television and radio) do not do operate in a uniform way. Finding that most critical research of news assumes that the media 'do their job in a consistent manner', that the media reproduce 'the dominant ideology largely without slip or hitch', and that most studies concentrated on the theory of 'ideological closure', Bruck searched for alternative approaches. He advanced the idea that (p. 141) 'the news media do their work in differing ways at different times depending … on topic, political circumstance, and … the alternative social and discursive pressures exerted at a given time'. In other words, the media are subject to the general social and discursive context in which they operate, and must consider a range of material and opinion. Bruck makes the following important statement (p. 142): 'the media do speak in their own particular ways about the world … the discursive material they work with, however, is not their own'. Despite the fact that the media have their own methods of interpretation, their own codes and conventions, they 'build their accounts of what happens in the world' on material taken from 'eye-witnesses, police officers, experts, lobbyists, politicians, or business leaders'.

The 'survivor' and the 'traitor'

The idea that the media are involved in a re-presentation of 'discursive material which is not their own', can be applied to the analysis of news. Following the death of Diana, Princess of Wales, one edition of the *Daily Mirror* ran two stories which dealt with individuals associated with her; first, they carried a report on the return to Britain of Diana's bodyguard, Trevor Rees-Jones. The front page carries the caption 'survivor'. This is of course no more than a statement of fact; the man survived a car crash which killed his companions.

Inside the newspaper, an *interpretation* of the event is offered. The headline used above a photograph of the bodyguard reads 'Walk of Courage'. This is not a neutral description of Rees-Jones' arrival, but a positive appraisal drawing on discourses of human tenacity and courage. The article goes on to read: 'This was raw courage on parade yesterday … despite his terrible face and neck injuries, he managed to walk unaided.'

It might have been possible for the paper to take a different line, and to accuse Rees-Jones of neglecting to do his job properly, of failing to protect Diana and her boyfriend; but, for various reasons, including the reluctance to attack someone who has suffered, that course of action was not chosen. A second study of 'categorisation' at work can be found by turning to another article in the same edition. A forthright attack is made on the royal author Andrew Morton, for making money out of the new edition of his book on Diana. In this second article, quite different attitudes are displayed. The notion that Morton might be justified in printing a book which includes more detail of his subject's strongly held views, is rejected in favour of a perspective which describes him as a 'traitor'.

Apart from the tendency shown by the press to create saints and sinners, the reason for this difference in treatment of the two men lies not simply in their actions, but in the interpretation of their actions *already made* by those individuals and groups which constitute the newspaper's sources. At the hospital where Rees-Jones was recovering, a doctor had already described him as 'a very brave man'; and, in the case of Andrew Morton, television news presenters, Bob Geldof, and members of the public had already attacked the author. In both cases, the *Mirror* took a lead from 'pre-existing' views and opinions.

The provisional nature of news

Ultimately, however, all news is always **provisional**. The status of any report is temporary and subject to change in the light of new information. We see this process at work most clearly when the unexpected happens and news organisations have to fight to interpret events. At such a point, there is a struggle to categorise the occurrence and establish meaning. In such cases, news reporting is essentially an attempt to establish order from chaos, coherence from the flow of events.

Modest demands: public reaction to the death of Princess Diana

The accident which befell Diana, Princess of Wales, is an example of the 'unexpected' (though BBC news had been prepared for an almost identical scenario). The event was extraordinary enough for the main political parties to cancel official political activity. The *Guardian* of 2 September 1997 reported that 'Politics goes on hold until after service' (a reference to the funeral which was to take place on the following Saturday). The main parties' response to the event was, however, political in the broader sense. William Hague, for example, praised the charitable work of the Princess, without mentioning the landmine campaign which had caused such discomfort to his party. Tony Blair's description of Diana as the 'People's Princess' was a political manoeuvre which helped to shape public response (though his attempt to achieve the same effect for the 'post-Diana' monarchy did not succeed).

The agreement to observe a political truce was, nonetheless, part of what I would call the 'suspension of the everyday' which manifested itself particularly strongly on the occasion of the funeral. This is not to say that the funeral itself did not contain unusual and quite significant departures from more traditional events. The BBC's 6pm news of 1 September 1997, for example, acknowledged departures from tradition when, discussing the processions organised for Churchill in 1965 and Mountbatten in 1979, the newsreader said that '... it was felt that similar military emphasis would not be in harmony with her wishes or character, and it's a decision that is supported by the charities she helped'.

However, the agreement to suspend open political controversy made attempts at a more explicit political interpretation of the event itself more difficult to achieve. As a result, during the struggle to establish the meaning of the fatal crash and the controversies which followed it, certain types of response failed to make much headway. Those newspapers, the *Independent* in particular, which suggested the growth of active republican sentiment, did not achieve much credence. The reasons for this failure may be summarised here.

In the first place, even if substantial republican sentiment had really existed, it would have been difficult to translate into action. Established forms of political action (marches, protests, etc.) were not suited to the event or the period of 'national mourning' which followed. The forms of public demonstration which actually occurred (queuing for hours outside the Royal palaces, laying flowers, etc.) reflected the modest intentions of the participants and were more appropriate to the form of behaviour which mourning requires. There is no doubt that there was a real sense of anger directed at the royal family (which emerged during phone-ins to GMTV, for example), but the reason for this annoyance must be understood.

The rather more vocal demands made as the week progressed, grew not from militancy but from the 'inadequacy' of official royal response. Public agitation, mediated by news organisations, centred on demands for an increase in the number of condolence books, for the display of the royal standard above Buckingham Palace, for direct statements from members of the royal family, and for a longer route for the funeral itself. Many people justified their outbursts by referring to the needs of the 'two boys' – Diana's bereaved sons.

The amplification of public response

News organisations, therefore, found public reactions which could be *amplified*; the laying of flowers, inscriptions in books of remembrance, and the demands for a royal standard to be flown over Buckingham Palace, all provided evidence of attempts to create public **symbols** of Diana's passing (and thus some consensus over the meaning of her life).

In the course of events, simple oppositions were created, between modernity and tradition, spontaneity and protocol, emotion and restraint. For example, on 3 September 1997, under the heading 'The People's Princess', the *Sun* set out a simple contrast between a Britain which 'unashamedly pours out its grief for Diana' while 'the Royal Family remains aloof'. It mentioned the absence of a 'flag at half-mast over Buckingham Palace', the lack of any 'expression of sorrow from the Queen' and the fact that 'not one word has come from a royal lip', and 'not one tear has been shed in public from a royal eye'.

These are demands for public signs of feeling, not for the overthrow of an institution. Little wonder then, that when the royals met some of these demands, the tabloid papers turned from flights of fantasy (see the *Mail*'s 'Charles Weeps Bitter Tears of Guilt') respectful pleas (the *Mirror*'s 'Your People are Suffering, Ma'am'), and subdued attacks, to a celebration of the signs themselves.

The scope of public response was thus circumscribed by a number of factors: its own informal organisation, the restricted agenda it found itself setting out, the interpretations of this agenda made by the media, the means of expression available, and finally the spontaneous forms of behaviour enacted during the 'suspension' of normality.

This spontaneous behaviour did not go so far as the 'booing' of Prince Charles,

Fig 7.2 The amplification of public response: 'Your people are suffering. Speak to us Ma'am'
(Courtesy of the Mirror)

Daily Mail

GOOD HEALTH
PAGES 34-39

TUESDAY, SEPTEMBER 2, 1997   35p

Death crash driver was criminally drunk	Could Diana yet destroy the monarchy?	James Hewitt: I loved her so very much
SEE PAGE 7	SEE PAGE 12	SEE PAGE 6

CHARLES WEEPS BITTER TEARS OF GUILT

By RICHARD KAY

EARLY yesterday Prince Charles went walking on the heather moors around Balmoral Castle.

It was 6.30am, an hour earlier than he usually rises, and he was alone.

It was grey and cloudy but he walked like a man reliving images of his life that were clear.

For the second successive night he had had little sleep. He had stayed up into the early hours drinking stiff gin-based martinis and making telephone call after call to friends, most of whom had

long gone to bed. By now the tears that had coursed down his ever-suntanned cheeks had gone.

In the 24 hours since he first learned that his former wife Diana had been killed, he had wept a lot, especially when he went to the Pitie Salpetriere hospital in eastern Paris to collect her body.

It was at the hospital, when he saw the broken remains of the

elegant women who bore his children and was his wife for 15 years, that he cracked.

He had been consoling Diana's sisters Lady Sarah McCorquodale and Lady Jane Fellowes on the plane that brought them over, but now, as they stood and wept, so did he.

As he emerged into a corridor outside the hospital mortuary,

Turn to Page 4, Col. 1

Charles: Walked alone on the Balmoral moors

INSIDE: Weather 2, Femail 18-19, Dempster 31, Good Health 34-39, Letters 40-41, TV, Radio 42-44, Coffee Break 46-48, City 53-55, Sport 56-64

Fig 7.3 News as speculation: 'Charles weeps bitter tears of guilt'
(Courtesy of Mail Newspapers)

which some newspapers thought might occur during the funeral procession, but did include applause for the pronouncements of Charles Spencer during the service in Westminster Abbey. In such a case, 'unusual' forms of public demonstration were tolerated as part of an 'extraordinary' occasion. Although active public participation in this process (attendance at the funeral, and so forth) was confined to a minority, television coverage provided another mode of involvement which although passive, was 'shared' and thus social. The attack made by Earl Spencer on media conduct and royal protocol became a talking-point as a result of its mediation by television news.

In this period, news did not act as the mouthpiece of the ruling class; however, certain consequences of media intervention were noticeable. The disagreements of two factions of a privileged, 'non-executive' ruling class (both of which relate to 'ordinary' people as objects of charity) were made public. In addition, a grieving 'public' was definitely 'created', partly through the media's ability to broadcast and thus sanction its behaviours (even where aspects of public response could not be predicted), and partly through the exclusion of dissenting opinion (the media were drawn to the public spectacle they had helped to aggrandise and did not, with some notable exceptions, seek out those who found the whole event distasteful).

The origins of news agendas

Mainstream media theory seems to argue that news organisations set public agendas. Watson and Hill, for instance (see *A Dictionary of Media and Communication Studies*), claim that the media (p. 3) 'set the order of importance of current issues' while O'Sullivan in 'Key Concepts' (p. 8) argues that the media 'wittingly or unwittingly structure public debate and awareness'. Gill and Adams (*ABC of Communication Studies*, p. 6) talk of 'the ways in which the media decide which information and which issues are most important for the public'. If true, this would mean that the terms of public debate could be set in newsrooms and newspaper offices. It is, perhaps, an over-estimation of the media's power.

Dearing and Rogers, in their book on the subject (*Agenda-Setting*), take a different view, calling the process 'an on-going competition among issue proponents to gain the attention of media professionals, the public, and policy elites'. This means that the media is just one part of the contest to form points of view, and that much of the time media professionals can actually be the *target* of attempts to persuade or influence.

During the Diana 'incident', the role of the news organisation was to reproduce 'discursive material' which originated in the wider social environment, not simply to invent ideas or to repeat what the dominant classes wished to circulate. Michael Schudson, writing on 'The sociology of news production'(see *Social Meanings of News*) recalls Richard Hoggart's idea that the most important filter through which news is constructed is 'the cultural air we breathe, the whole ideological atmosphere of our society'. This 'cultural air' is 'one that in part ruling groups and institutions create, but it is one in whose context their own establishment takes place'.

This 'ideological atmosphere', in Hoggart's words, 'tells us that some things can be said and others had best not been said'. What may and may not be said can be

THE EXPRESS

ON TUESDAY

SEPTEMBER 2, 1997   35p

Diana's driver had drunk the equivalent of two bottles of wine

He was a hotel security officer not a chauffeur

The car's speedometer was jammed at 121 mph

DRIVEN TO HER DEATH

SHE TOUCHED OUR LIVES ● ORDINARY PEOPLE REMEMBER DIANA ● PAGE 28

Fig 7.4 Changing news agendas a) 'Driven to her death.' Chauffeur identified as culprit
(Courtesy of Express Newspapers)

THE ✠ EXPRESS

SEPTEMBER 3, 1997 • ON WEDNESDAY • 35p

NO MERCY

●Police reveal sick antics of paparazzi as Diana lay dying

●Six photographers face death charge

PURSUING PAPARAZZI went to incredible lengths to capture Diana's dying moments on film.

Two of the photographers who surrounded her crashed car allegedly fought with police.

It was revealed that one officer was prevented from helping the victims as they lay trapped in the wrecked Mercedes in a Paris underpass.

Last night six photographers and a courier arrested at the scene were facing manslaughter charges.

The chaos moments after the crash was disclosed in an official police report. A policeman said the paparazzi were "aggressive and pushy". Taking photos through one of the car's open doors, they stopped him from going to the occupants' aid. One photographer told him: "You make me sick. Let me do my job."

Another officer quoted in the report said: "I could not help the injured and hold back the photographers at the same time."

A photographer objected to being removed from the scene, complaining: "You only have to go to Bosnia and you would see that I'm only doing my job."

The seven arrested men are being investigated for manslaughter and failing to assist people in danger.

If charged and convicted, they could face jail sentences of up to 15 years for manslaughter and five years for the other offence. The men were freed by

FROM JACK GEE AND SHEKHAR BHATIA
IN PARIS

Paris judge Herve Stephan as police and court officials continued their investigations.

Two photographers, Romuald Rat of the Gamma agency and Christian Martinez of the Angeli agency, were released on £10,000 bail and forbidden to work as journalists pending the case. Police accused Rat of obstructing the work of the first officers on the scene.

His lawyer, Philippe Benamou,

WAS DIANA'S CAR SAFE? Page 3

insisted he took Diana's pulse while taking pictures of the wreckage. Freed without bail were Nikola Arsov of the Sipa agency, Jacques Langevin of Sygma, Stephane Darmon of Gamma, Serge Arnal of Stills and freelance Laslo Veres.

The men had been held in custody since their arrest at the underpass by the River Seine. The toughness of the court decisions came as a surprise

PAGE 2 COLUMN 2

DIANA: A photographer said he felt her pulse as he took pictures

TOUCHED BY THE QUEEN OF HEARTS ● ORDINARY PEOPLE REMEMBER DIANA ● PAGE 28

Fig 7.5 Changing news agendas b) 'No mercy.' 'Paparazzi' identified as culprits
(Courtesy of Express Newspapers)

gauged from the discourses that appeared and failed to appear during the aftermath of Diana's death. The meaning of the event (including the emotive public response to it) could be described in a number of limited and inter-related ways: as the demise of hope for royalty as an institution, for example, as a national tragedy, as confirmation of the 'feminisation' of the public sphere, and so on. Discourses which cast Diana in the role of tireless (and tiresome) media manipulator, like the *Sunday Mirror* journalist whose column advised the Princess to stop making public statements and buy a 'Gucci zip' for her mouth (a suggestion which appeared in print on the day she was killed), could not be sustained.

POPULAR FORMS: WOMEN'S MAGAZINES

Although the first women's magazine proper was probably *The Ladies' Mercury* of 1693, it was *The Lady's Magazine* of 1770 to 1847, which Janice Winship (*Inside Women's Magazines*) believes introduced the form imitated by so many of the publications which followed. *The English Woman's Magazine* of the early 1850s marked the beginnings of a diversified market, being aimed at the middle-class woman who had some responsibility, albeit indirect, for running her own household.

Discourse and address

The first personal and 'friendly' address, which Winship sees as typical of modern women's magazines, was to be found in journals like *My Weekly* (1910) and *Woman's Weekly* (1911). A 'personal-inclusive' address does not, however, imply that such magazines reflected all the currents of thought and opinion of their readership. As we have seen when considering the types of address made by newspapers like the *Sun*, the audience is imagined in only a limited number of ways. A *Woman's Own* article of 15 October 1932, entitled 'Looks do count after marriage', gives an insight into the way that an 'interpersonal' mode of communication is used between writer (in this case Mary Carlyle) and audience;

> 'don't let yourself "go" – especially in the mornings. Wear a pretty, crisp overall, and leave him with a good impression for the day! . . . you have to rise early, prepare your lord and master's breakfast, and see him off the premises before 8.30 am.'

Woman, a magazine with colour pages, appeared in 1937. The Second World War resulted in an expanded role for women, one that was reflected in the kind of magazines which appeared then and in the post-war years.

The discourses mobilised in wartime and in the post-war period reflect the ability of the advertiser to echo and then to re-order those messages coming from authority via the mass media. During the early part of the war these discourses gave recognition to the way that women could work in occupations previously imagined as being suitable only for men; the problem as the war came to an end was how to mobilise the women to make a return to the home. Advertisements in magazines had also to reflect the austerity of the post-war era. An advertisement for Horlicks from 1948 reads:

> 'Of course the Government is right to urge "more and more production" to earn the dollars we need. But what is a man to do if he begins the day already tired and feels like a piece of chewed string by the end of it? Not to mention his harassed wife, standing in queues and coping with rations.'

The answer was a drink of Horlicks at bedtime, dressed up with homely advice about where to position the bed and the importance of keeping the feet warm and the head cool.

Winship explains the contradictory positions that post-war women's magazines could find themselves pulled between; on the one hand, the ideals of femininity and on the other:

> 'the foregrounding of the nation's needs over those of the Individual and the family that licensed . . . a limited questioning of traditional femininity.'   (p. 31)

The impact of a kind of muted feminism had led to some articles which had resisted some of the demands made by government, but such a stance did not last very long. With the introduction of the National Health Service in 1948, and other policies which were of benefit to women, there was something of an improvement in many lives.

Modern women?

Winship believes most strongly that feminism *in combination with* socialism is not tolerated in commercial magazines, though some forms of feminism are tolerated on their own. She writes also about the way that modes of address work to draw their readers into the ideological world of the journal:

> 'by ideology . . . I refer to commonsense knowledges to be found in newspapers and magazines . . . which shape how people think and feel and act in their daily lives . . . from a political position "outside" them it is possible to see ideologies as partial and selective . . . seen from the "inside", ideologies appear to be right and appropriate for deciding how to conduct one's life.'   (p. 21)

Here, Winship identifies an idea we have explored in previous chapters, that different types of address can be accepted under certain circumstances (albeit on a temporary basis), and furthermore that one can respond in both a critical, 'academic' way, and in a more uncritical mode. Questions of 'belonging' are central to this notion. To take an example from interpersonal and group communication, we may imagine a situation where, although we have a set of quite strong beliefs, we feel unable to articulate them in the midst of a group of people who have opposing views. When we see an address in print, we might be inclined to accept the terms of the address simply in order to be able to make sense of what it is telling us. Just as a film will signal its genre and the 'subject position' we are invited to assume, so a piece of writing will carry a 'register' appropriate to its address. It is not impossible for a vehement critic of the *Sun* to accept its mode of address for a certain period. Simply reading the narrative form taken by most news stories is to enter into the 'fictive' world offered to us.

However, there are clearly occasions when certain groups are deliberately excluded from a discourse. Again, if a discourse is not framed in a generally credible way, then it may be refused. Some types of address tend to suffer under the weight of the years and the reader's awareness of a changed context which casts a new light on the original. For example, a photograph of the Queen, Prince Philip and their two children (which appeared in a 1953 edition of *Woman*, accompanied by a caption which emphasises the 'priceless value of a happy home') may now seem to carry an ironic overtone.

A clear example of exclusion from the address supposedly offered to 'all' readers is the failure to represent the different ethnic groups which constitute a readership. This is not just a matter of what is written, but of who is represented in visual terms. Winship, writing about *Woman's Own*, believes that:

> 'A liberal intent also informs the magazine's moves towards addressing and including Britain's black women. It gestures towards including them, but on white women's terms. On the whole its unashamed address is to white women. Many issues have no black women anywhere and a black model has yet to grace the cover.' (p. 94)

Interviewing the magazine's editor in August 1982, Winship discovered the rationale behind such a tentative approach to the inclusion of black women:

> 'I'm fair to our readers, because I don't believe that the bulk of them are anti-black … but they would be unnerved by a black face and you do it two weeks running and they will start to think, "Oh what's happening, my way of life" … it's the one thing that shakes any race to the roots. "Is everything I've known and become familiar with going to be shaken up and changed overnight?" ' (p. 95)

Although this situation improved as the 1980s progressed, Winship is quite correct to note that the inclusion of only the occasional black face in the magazine is distinctly ambiguous. It includes the single representative of the black readership but 'renders blackness an irrelevant factor in the issues being discussed'.

Spare Rib and *Cosmopolitan*: opposite poles?

Cosmopolitan, which appears in some seventeen different countries, was founded in 1972, the same year as *Spare Rib*. The former has an image founded on an individualistic pursuit of social freedoms, strongly centred on ideas about independence in the workplace and laced with open discussions of 'straight' sexuality. *Spare Rib* was the best-known magazine of a more overtly political feminism, which during its history had embraced a number of different feminist currents. (Both magazines provided a forum for the exploration of issues which concern women. Both were caught within the contradictions which face women as a whole in this society.) *Spare Rib* had encountered difficulties in maintaining a clear 'market position', especially as different groups of readers have, over the years, raised issues which the magazine itself has been slow to assimilate. Winship describes this as being due to Spare Rib's attempt:

> 'to meet incompatible demands from "inside" and "outside" the women's movement . . . the main attack on Spare Rib is that it falls between two stools.' (p. 123)

The influence of *Spare Rib*, however, extended much further than the 20,000 print-run which it had in the mid-1980s.

The criticism of *Cosmopolitan*, on the other hand, is that it often fails to carry far enough its critique of the social iniquities faced by women; that it is only able to articulate its version of feminism through the very things which continue to soften the impact of women's demands – an obsession with the ways of men and the elusive dream of independence through the 'good career'. There certainly seem to be a large number of fatuous and sloppy articles written by men in this magazine, something that *Spare Rib* has avoided, since it would appear ridiculous for a woman's magazine not to concentrate, as a matter of principle, on the experiences of women. Winship considers that it is the *imagery* of *Cosmopolitan* (the appearance of both advertisements and text) which is particularly at odds with the demands for equality that it sometimes makes. *Cosmopolitan* did, however, begin by making a logical extension of the 'sexual liberation' which had previously applied almost exclusively to men. An article which appeared in the magazine in 1972 insisted that:

> 'The ability and right of women as well as men to enjoy sexual satisfaction is as import-ant and relevant a subject today as any other physical ability or civil right.'

There is almost no argument to be made with such a statement, but it is still of immediate relevance to students of the mass media to ask how this right is *represented*, quite apart from how it is exercised. Letters from readers sometimes raise this very issue. One, published in 1983, attacked *Cosmopolitan*'s use of imagery, which seemed to sit uneasily with its avowed aims (Winship, p. 121):

> '*Cosmopolitan* publishes articles which aim to raise female consciousness, decrying male chauvinism, yet the pictures seem to contradict these views. I was prompted to write by the picture taken at the Porchester Baths . . . who was the picture aimed at? Surely not women. The picture of four tousled girls lounging around looking provocative . . . could not have been more pornographic.'

The main point, however, is not to argue that *Cosmopolitan* is either entirely progressive, or entirely reactionary, but to recognise its contradictory position. It is, for many commentators, at best a muted version of feminism, but as we saw in our study of advertisements it is often the 'diluted' version of a theory or idea which achieves widest circulation. It is impossible to erase all traces of the political origins and implications of an address, even where that address is almost entirely mediated through discourses which concentrate on sexuality. The problem would then arise when those discourses are tailored, as we must admit they are in *Cosmopolitan* as much as in the *Sun*, to only one kind of sexual orientation.

MAGAZINE DESIGN

The magazine as a form could be described as a collection of articles in either a sequential or non-sequential order (since an article does not always have any relationship with what goes before or after; nor do many readers scan journals starting from the beginning). The magazine has been described (Sue Watling, 'Magazine Design', Somerset College, 1992) as a 'laboratory for design innovation'. Part of the reason for this is the fact that magazines are ephemeral. They do not therefore 'date' in the same way as book design, and are able to adapt to changing circumstances. They are 'a synthesis of images and words'.

Origins of the magazine

The birth of the magazine was made possible in the nineteenth century by both the increase in literacy and the development of more sophisticated means of production. By the 1830s cheap weekly magazines were often printed in runs of 100,000 or more. The 1840s saw the appearance of illustrated news weeklies such as the *Illustrated London News*, which was founded in 1842. The 1870s saw an innovation which became central to the development of magazine design, the use of colour lithography, which could also reproduce the paintings and other graphic work of famous artists for a wider public than had hitherto been possible. In the 1880s, the development of the half-tone screen process allowed the reproduction of photographic material together with printed text.

Modernism and magazines

We may recall the extensive use of photomontage made by Dadaist publications, and the central role of practitioners like John Heartfield. The German Communist Party's AIZ (*Arbeiter Illustrierte Zeitung*) produced a fresh approach to design, finding new and innovatory ways of expressing a socialist politics. The Russian Constructivists attempted to create 'a new typographical language ... a fresh approach to the materials of printing [Maholy-Nagy]'. A host of new magazines appeared, including *Das Neue Russland* (the *New Russia* (Germany)) *Blok* (a Polish magazine) and *Red* (published in Czechoslovakia). Many of these European developments were interrupted by the rise of fascism and the onset of the Second World War, so that the next wave of developments took place in the United States, where *Life* magazine had been founded in 1936. The 'golden age' of magazine design took place in America between 1945 and 1968, with the rise of *Vanity Fair, Harpers Bazaar* (which featured the design work of Alexey Brodovitch), *McCall's* and *Mademoiselle* (designed by Bradbury Thompson). The mid-to-late 1960s ushered in a revival in European design led by innovators like Harry Peccinotti and Willy Fleckhaus, who worked on *Nova* and *Twen* respectively. In Britain, one of the most important developments was the *Sunday Times Magazine*, which had Michael Rand as art director and which featured the designs of David King. This was the magazine, as we already know, which featured the photographs of Don McCullin.

Recession and revival

The 1970s were perceived as a bad time for magazines, with what Sue Watling calls 'a loss of nerve by publishing houses'. The 1980s appeared to have a different approach to production altogether, relying on much the same kind of 'home-grown' approach as the new wave of musical experimentation known as punk rock. Independent magazines, although possessing only small budgets, used new technologies which gave the designers themselves a high degree of control over their work. Britain was the centre of such developments, marking a move away from reliance on the advertising agencies, the big publishing houses and design studios.

i=D was founded in September 1980, under the art direction of Terry Jones. The design of the magazine was central to the editorial policies pursued in the magazine. Also launched in 1980 was *The Face*, edited by Nick Logan, who was joined some eighteen months later by the highly influential designer Neville Brody. Brody's designs were not limited to the images which in many magazines simply accompanied the text; the written text itself was subjected to a rigorous approach to design. In terms of its overall style, *The Face* became hugely influential, spawning a host of imitators. Brody insisted that:

> 'I wanted other people to challenge *The Face*, not to copy it ... I was pointing out the means to a way of thinking and a way of working, not the solution.'

Brody was also involved in the design of magazines like *City Limits* and *Arena*, and worked on soft-left publications which flirted with post-modernism, such as *New Socialist*. At its best, the new design represented in *The Face* and *i*=D, and by practitioners such as Brody and Phil Bicker, achieved (Watling) 'an interesting synthesis of politics, fashion, text, image and design'.

Incorporation of the radicals?

Once an innovation is noticed, and once the magazines which pioneer it become financially viable, then the big publishing houses are sure to fasten on to the new avenues of profitability suggested by such success. *Italian Vogue*, under its art director Fabien Baron, became noted for its bold and effective use of image. Large single letters were used as design motifs in themselves. In America, *Interview* appeared under the art direction of Tibor Kalman, while *Beach Culture*, also a US publication, was designed by David Carson, noted for his 'post-modernist' layering (and random distribution) of text. Debates about form and content are central to all questions of magazine design, while political integrity is still something that motivates some designers in the onset of new depths of economic recession. Brody declared:

> 'The establishment adjusts to any change and eventually engulfs it. You can't touch the foundation of the establishment. It changes its clothes as fast as you can cut them up. If you are radical, it's only a matter of time before you are automatically accepted – that is provided you don't go bankrupt.'

POPULAR FORMS: COMICS

The comic began as a form in 1796, when the *Comic Magazine* carried a series of Hogarth prints in its pages, though the appearance and purpose of the publication was of course quite different to its modern counterparts. William Randolph Hearst, the American press magnate, was able to produce comic supplements to his newspapers. This was made possible by advances in colour printing. The modern comic book, as a form in its own right, established itself rapidly in the United States in the 1930s, beginning with *Famous Funnies*, drawn by an artist named Gaines. The usual cover price at this time was ten US cents; rare items are now worth thousands of pounds. Crime and detective strips were well established in the mid-1930s. After the Second World War it became more common for the US comic book to be aimed directly at adults.

As the industry began to grow, the characters appearing in the strips became the major selling point. Will Eisner, a well-known comic-book artist, declared (quoted in *Comic Book Confidential*, Channel 4, 1987), 'in the beginning ... the identity of the artist involved became submerged'. Some of these artists set out to develop their own characters and styles, free from the constraints of working within a framework over which they had little direct control.

The rise of the 'super-being'

The transformation of men and women into super-beings featured prominently in many comic books. The hugely-built Captain America, the scourge of the Third Reich in many comic book adventures, was produced after 'a frail young man' was injected with a 'seething liquid':

> 'the first of a core of super-agents whose mental and physical ability will make them a terror to spies and saboteurs.'

Stan Lee was the originator of a range of US superheroes, including Spiderman and the Incredible Hulk. Spiderman was the transformed state of Peter Parker, who was bitten by an irradiated spider. This character, in his daily life, had to face a number of personal difficulties and problems which marked him out as a more 'realistic' type of super-hero. The Second World War saw a variety of titles, often with patriotic themes to the fore: *Our Flag*, *Victory*, and *Major Victory* are some examples. Stories such as 'The Spirit' ran as strips in newspapers as part of a strategy to offset the growing readership of comic books, which threatened to reduce the newspapers' market-share.

Post-war developments: anxieties over effects

After the war, the interest in comics remained strong and the range of titles again began to increase. Strips illustrated certain post-war anxieties which were perhaps not expressed elsewhere. For example, fear of atomic war entered the consciousness of many people. The rise of the horror comic, featuring a variety of unpleasant representations of physical decay, was regarded as encouraging moral aberration in adults and equally unhealthy developments in the young. A widespread propaganda campaign against this type of comic was instituted by a number of self-appointed guardians of morality. The effects such comics were supposed to have were regarded as both direct and dramatic in nature. Television and film played a part in identifying this new 'menace', and in mobilising sections of the public against it (archive film from *Comic Book Confidential*, Channel 4):

> 'what a wonderful thing this would be if they [young boys] were reading something worthwhile … but … they're reading stories devoted to adultery, to sexual perversion, to horror, to the most despicable of crimes … one of the wonderfully appealing things about children is that they haven't yet come to the age where reality and unreality are divorced. The emotional impact of something they read in a comic book may be much the same as a real life situation they witness.'

This particular excerpt went on to argue that 'immediate and noticeable effect[s]' were apparent in the children; the director of this film made his young actors display a range of threatening and unbalanced behaviours as a result of an illicit session of comic-study, including sticking a penknife into a tree and banging rocks together. One boy is shown approaching another with a rock in one hand and a mad gleam in his eyes. The case of an eleven-year-old who shot a woman dead was cited as a direct consequence of reading unsuitable comics. Lack of proper evidence has never stopped any of the assumptions which have been made about the way that mass media messages influence audiences. Comic books were burned in public, and the move towards censorship was hastened. In 1954 a Senate sub-committee on juvenile delinquency took evidence from a variety of witnesses, expert and not-so-expert alike. William M. Gaines, whose father had produced *Famous Funnies* in the 1930s, appeared in front of the committee. He described the 'harmless thrill' children experienced when reading horror comics. The point here is that neither side produced much in the way of research to support their positions; the argument was resolved because one side was able to use the power of the local and national state, combined with short-term mobilisations of 'public opinion'.

When the Comics Magazine Association was formed, it moved immediately to outlaw the words 'horror', 'terror' and 'weird', through which many comics had been able to signal their contents to the reading public. Comics began to appear with a stamp of approval which read 'Approved by the Comics Code', one of the forerunners of the 'Parental Approval' stickers which now appear on many records in the US. Judge Charles F. Murphy was able to report that, in less than one year, his office, set up to censor comics, had 'eliminated' more than 'five thousand six-hundred drawings', replacing them with panels which conformed to the new code. Some of the titles which appeared in the place of the old ones were perhaps a little tame. *Cowboy Love, Nature Boy* and *The Adventures of Jerry Lewis* are clearly aimed at a different market from that served by *Tales from the Crypt*. Meanwhile, some magazines escaped persecution by adopting humour as a defence. *Mad* magazine even lampooned the McCarthy hearings.

Underground illustrators

In the 1960s, a number of comic-book artists evaded the constraints of the new mainstream by participating in underground publications centred in San Francisco. Robert Crumb, creator of Mr Natural and Fritz the Cat, declared that 'the straight medium was so atrophied ... you were pretty much locked-out'. The freedom that artists like Crumb sought included, in the initial stages, 'racist images and any sexual images that came to mind'. Alternative heroes from this era included 'Trashman', noted for stunts like spraying the dinner-parties of the rich with indiscriminate machine-gun fire. Forms of rebellion ranged from the moral degeneracy of Gilbert Shelton's 'Fabulous Furry Freak Brothers' to Dan O'Neill's subversion of Mickey Mouse, in which the venerated Disney creation engages in various forms of sexual activity with his partner Minnie. O'Neill's intention was to 'wreck the airwaves, disrupt the body politic'. With his co-workers he set out to challenge the institutions which seemed to limit the creative range he sought (*Comic Confidential*):

> 'it was impossible for one person to stem the conservative tide, so five of us thought we would.'

Some artists are more overtly political and do more than attack a culture's icons. Sue Coe's representations of state oppression in South Africa have the power of a Heartfield photomontage, and resemble the satirical drawings of George Grosz. On the other hand, there are magazines which push against the boundaries of accepted form, like *Raw*, which looks as though it has been designed along similar lines to *The Face* and *City Limits*.

British developments

Viz sells a million copies to its 'adult' audience every time it produces an issue. *The Pathetic Sharks Bumper Special* is a venture from the same 'stable', but this time aimed specifically at children. Chris Donald, the editor of *Viz* said, in a *Guardian* interview with Martin Wylie (12 July 1991):

> 'I think you have to go down to eight or nine-year olds to find naivety and innocence these days. There's a deterioration of values throughout society. People like me, scraping a living without full regard to the consequences, are part of that.'

The reference here to what we would refer to as media effects is clearly designed to acknowledge such criticisms, while at the same time being facetious. Since the vast majority of *Viz* readers are male, he was asked if this factor will be reflected in the readership of the *Sharks* comic:

> 'I expect it'll be mainly boys. It's in the nature of kids isn't it? Boys read comics ... [girls] play with dolls and kitchens and all that. Anyway, girls mature a lot younger, don't they?'

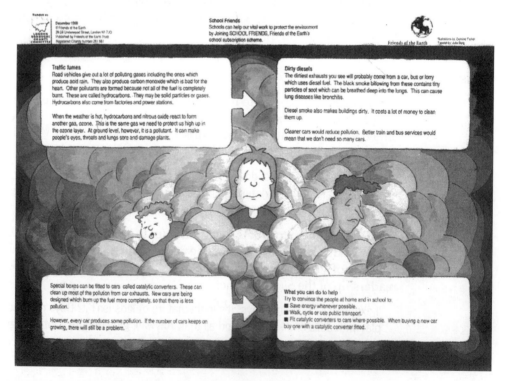

Fig 7.6 Adaptation of the comic form – an appeal to children

Comics: a male preserve?

There have been numerous attacks on the comic industry as the preserve of an especially retrogressive male culture. The products of this industry are regarded by many as a fantasy world for men and boys who waste their time looking at lurid cartoon strips. One development which comes from this conviction may be seen in the increasing involvement of women in graphic art. The photomontagist Cath Tate and the comic publisher Carol Bennett combined their energies to produce a magazine, entitled *Fanny*, written from a feminist perspective. The first edition was called 'Ceasefire' and concentrated on the Gulf War. Bennett thinks that:

> 'boys stay with comics far longer than girls. They start with the *Beano* and then go on to *2000 AD* ... Girls have *June and Schoolfriend* and then they go on to magazines like *Just Seventeen*, which is all about make-up tips and how to keep your boyfriend. That becomes more important to girls than graphic art, so they cease to read comics at 13 to 14.'

The idea that girl's magazines are 'all about make-up tips and how to keep your boyfriend' was investigated, as we shall see, by Martin Barker. Feminist challenges to the male hero are sometimes described as being led by the militant and futuristic Tank Girl, taken from a comic for adults called *Deadline*. Tank Girl is in fact drawn by two men, and was taken up with great enthusiasm by Wrangler Jeans, who were clearly alive to the potential power of using a cult figure to sell their product to certain groups of young women. The question is always whether or not such material loses its broadly political impact when it is turned into an advertising campaign. Brody's remarks on the deadening hand of the establishment seem appropriate here.

Film as comic strip?

Some writers believe that the comic strips have had a significant influence on film as well as on advertising and other mass media. J. G. Ballard, writing in the *Guardian* in 1991 used this idea to throw new light on a certain genre of film:

> 'The Star Wars series, Sylvester Stallone's entire career, and recent movies like *Die Hard* and *Total Recall* are little more than imitation comic strips ... the bizarre success of Arnold Schwarzenegger makes complete sense if one accepts that his grotesque physique and hesitant approach to speech and thought exactly mimic the ... comic-book super-hero.'

We should remember that it may be a mistake to imagine the comic-book hero (where it is not a heroine instead) as always being quite so brutish and inarticulate as this description suggests. The enigmatic 'Spirit' has his monologues, 'Spiderman' struggles in the web of his own angst, while the 'Silver Surfer', the first philosopher and environmentalist amongst super-beings, is so thoughtful that it is almost painful. The content of comics should not be thought to be entirely vacuous because they are wrongly thought to rely solely on visual imagery.

The power of the visual?

It would appear that the majority of forms which attract criticism on the basis of their supposed *effects* (see previous chapter) are those whose predominant mode of communication is thought to be 'visual'. When dealing with the dissemination of propaganda, however, our conception of television as a visual medium is sometimes undermined; in the midst of a propaganda offensive, television becomes a sort of 'colour radio'. Clearly, when the purpose of using an image is purely 'emblematic' (when it is intended merely to support or reinforce a dominant discourse), the image is not allowed the range of meanings it might otherwise produce. But it is not always the case that an image has a particularly wide range of meanings to start with. A photograph of a jet bomber can be given negative or positive inflections, but it can only be properly understood as a symbol of destruction.

Approaches to the comic form: Martin Barker

In his book *Comics* (Manchester University Press, 1989), Martin Barker is anxious not to accept the usual approaches used by critics of the comic form, since he thinks these may (p. 92) 'stop us looking positively at the ways kids use their comics'.

The current of criticism which insists that comics lead to a general lowering of standards, or else to forms of direct imitation (where children are supposed to carry out undesirable acts they have seen represented), are labelled by Barker 'the traditional end' of the various attacks on the comic form. Barker cites the case of the critic Clare Dellino, who claimed that (p. 93):

> 'These so-called "comics" are a major influence on the attitudes and behaviour of children today.'

Barker is not convinced that comics hide some 'negative' message behind an 'innocent' appearance. Other critics singled out for disapproval under the 'traditional' heading include George Gale, who noted that:

> 'week after week children are invited to laugh at people who are fat, deformed, handicapped or ugly, especially when pain is being inflicted.'

This seems to be a reasonably fair criticism, but it is not one that Barker chooses to investigate. He attacks instead what he calls Gale's worries about the 'deformation of language', though what Gale actually says is that the undesirable content of comics 'is accompanied throughout by crude, ugly language'.

CONTENT ANALYSIS: NEGATIVE ROLES?

As we have seen, comics once came in for a great deal of criticism from the political right in America, but they have also been investigated by theorists who have used content analysis to depict a more specific failure: a failure to offer accurate pictures of reality to young readers. The fashion for content analysis has been taken up in particular by feminist theorists. The work of Judith O'Connell may serve as an example. She discovered an 'overpowering imbalance' between the number of male and female characters represented in the *Beano*, which she believed was (in Barker) 'hardly a fair representation of society'.

Barker's view of O'Connell's findings is that she is simply making assumptions, if she believes that comics *ought* to be reflections of society. This is a point worth discussing. If only 15 per cent of the *Beano*'s characters are female, then it could be argued that girls are being offered fewer opportunities to identify with the characters and indeed with the comic as a whole, though it would depend partly on the roles that girls were shown adopting in the pages of the comic. If the female 15 per cent were in a leading position (shown in major roles), then the size of the percentage would perhaps matter less.

The question we should address is, are there any really serious social implications in the smaller percentage of female characters to be found in the *Beano*? Barker appears to think not, insisting that it is an argument that will not bear extension. He uses a parallel example to attack O'Connell's position:

> 'Is the proportion of pets correct? I won't even dare to ask whether the ratio of humans to non-human species is right . . . stick with pets. Dogs feature hugely, hopelessly out of proportion with the number of gerbils and hamsters actually owned. Does that also constitute a distortion? Hardly, because such an "imbalance" has no relevance.'

Of course, we might argue that the fact that the misrepresentation of the proportion of pets is largely irrelevant, and has no social implications whatsoever, which is exactly why Barker has used this rather mischievous example to ridicule the method adopted by O'Connell. He believes that her findings have no bearing on the actual meanings offered by the comics:

> 'How do we know that the gender-imbalance is "relevant" to the comics? O'Connell, I'm afraid, mainly takes this for granted, with just one argument to support her case – that the imbalance of characters is mirrored in the imbalance of readers . . . The implication is made clear; girls lack models for identifying with the *Beano* and are presumably therefore denied its pleasures.'

What this distrust of comics like the *Beano* rests on, according to Barker, is the notion that their readers relate to the stories as boys and girls. In his opinion, they are more likely to relate to such material as *children*. He takes issue with the whole idea that there is a process called 'identification', in which children see a character in a mass media text and identify with that character, taking on to some extent the values that are offered in the text. The clear implication would be that children are identifying with wholly 'negative' values in many cases. There are, of course, so many variables in this process, and so many other possible influences on children, that it does seem impossible to measure exactly how, and to what extent, identification might work to 'place' the individual child in a system of values or beliefs. We may remember from Chapter 5 that Mulvey's ideas about identification in the cinema came in for criticism from authors who believed that audiences are more likely to identify with actions or situations. If we use the idea of interpellation, we might find that the different varieties of address offered to children are not always accepted, or if they are, then it may be that this is only a temporary adoption of the 'role' the text suggests.

SEXISM IN *JACKIE*?

The view of *Jackie* as a magazine which will negatively affect the self-confidence of young women and inculcate them with sexist attitudes is again one which Barker resists. He advances three arguments which point to the flaws in the methodology of the critics:

> 'first, their [the critics'] methods of understanding how an "ideology of femininity" might be embodied in such magazines are grossly unsatisfactory. Second, there are politics implicit in their accounts, tightly related to those inadequate methods. And third, all the accounts I have looked at just cannot account for the enormous changes that *Jackie* has undergone.'
> (p. 134)

Barker read samples of one month of *Jackie* since its start in 1964. He believes that the methods used by previous researchers to produce meaning from the stories have been too insensitive. He notes that many stories carry events which are what he calls 'unmotivated'– in other words, the incidents in them (p. 137) 'were not causally or purposefully connected with each other'.

So what is the method being pursued in these narratives? What are the narratives supposed to do for, or to, their readers? Barker says that the point of some of these stories is that they often involve (p. 138) 'a transformation of the emotions'. In other words, we could say that events occur not in order to make a moral point about something, but because they allow what Barker later calls 'emotional self-realisation' to take place in their female protagonists:

> 'To identify the ideological elements in such stories, we must start from how sequences of incidents, otherwise disconnected, relate to kinds of emotional self-realisation in their women characters.'

Barker believes that other critics have treated the stories as parables when in fact they are not like that:

> 'most of the time, leading characters retain their individuality and are not simply lessons for readers.'
> (p. 138)

We should not think from this that Barker is unable to see that some of the stories are actually quite retrogressive; describing one tale he calls it 'a thoroughly reactionary story', not because of its content as such, but because of the way in which it reaches its conclusion.

It does appear to be the case that the critics of texts like *Jackie* take it for granted that somehow all the various parts 'accumulate and form a pattern to make up a single kind of influence'. Barker accuses the critics of arguing that there have been no really important developments in the messages offered by Jackie over the last thirty years. He argues that there is:

> 'a total absence of history in all the the varieties of feminist work on teenage romances'.

What exactly would be the nature of the message which some critics perceive in *Jackie*? Barker believes that most critics imagine the female reader as being forced to see herself in a limited role, centred on trying to appear attractive in order to capture a mate. Angela McRobbie, in *Feminism for Girls* writes that:

'It must be clear by now that the one concept which holds *Jackie* together, which gives it coherence, is romance.'
(p. 118)

It is certainly true that the interest expressed in love in girls' comics seems to be very strong, but is it also the case that nothing else is regarded as important? If love is being used, again, as a means of expressing the 'self-realisation' of characters, are there other states of being or personal achievements which should also stand out as desirable for female characters? Why use just one metaphor for personal growth? If we refer back for a moment to Chapter 2 and its work on advertising, we may recall that Maslow's hierarchy was a model which put 'self-realisation' at the very apex of the pyramid of human development, but there was no specification as to the exact nature of this state, and certainly no differentiation between genders. In other words, there is nothing to say that young women should achieve 'self-realisation' through romance alone. It is worth noting that much of what we would call 'serious literature', whether for men or women, places love at the centre of human experience.

APPROACHES TO ANALYSING GIRLS' COMICS: MASS CULTURE AS A NEGATIVE INFLUENCE

Barker goes on to look at the different analytical approaches to girls' comics. First, he examines ideas which begin by treating comics as part of mass culture. Connie Alderson is one author he identifies with this view. She sees comics of this type as (p. 140) 'amoral', 'anti-intellectual', and 'emotionally immature'. Young women are supposed to enjoy reading the magazines because of something called 'strong reader-identification'. Escapism is frowned upon and attacked, because Alderson wants women to be good mothers and home-makers as well as being public figures.

Barker sees this as elitist, and identifies the approach as part of a trend which emphasises that, in the world of female endeavour, 'doing' is better than 'dreaming'. Because Alderson sees the stories themselves as quite boring, a question arises as to why the young women continue to read them. They do so according to this 'pre-feminist' author because they hope that the next story might (p. 142) 'prove more interesting'. All of this amounts in Barker's view to the use of criteria which work on the basis of what the stories *ought* to do.

On the other hand, critics should surely be free to suggest alternative activities besides the consumption of fictional narratives, which they honestly believe might enhance the development of young adults. This is presumably why Angela McRobbie (*Feminism for Girls*) argues that:

'instead of having hobbies, instead of going fishing, learning to play the guitar, or even learning to swim or play tennis, the girl is encouraged to load all her eggs in the basket of romance and hope it pays off.'
(p. 118)

McRobbie is concerned not simply with how young women will spend their leisure, but how the choices they make will effect their whole futures. *Feminism for Girls* as a text is designed to investigate both the political and the material chances that girls are presented with, and those which they may create for themselves.

IMAGES OF WOMEN: STEREOTYPES

The next school of thought to fall under Barker's scrutiny begins from the idea that the mass media bear a responsibility for maintaining social inequality. The mass media produce a series of ideal 'images' of women, which according to Sue Sharpe (p. 144) 'force comparison on their recipients'. Sharpe sees gender roles divided into the active and the passive, summarised as follows:

'The active and passive dimensions of traditional male and female roles can be seen clearly in the way that a man's major activities are outward-directed and a woman's inner-directed.'

Barker argues that *Jackie* may well play a part in reproducing stereotypes, but it is not the source of them. Sharpe seems to make a similar case when she says that:

'this literature probably only acts as a reinforcement to the limited views and interests that have already developed, but it is important in what it omits from its content. Like much of the mass media it endorses the status quo by leaving out suggestions for the possibility or desirability of change.' (p. 146)

Barker's response to this is to say that 'anything not openly acknowledging those things of which Sharpe is convinced, is ... hiding them'. The same current of thought runs through Barker's work here; that most methods of analysis appear to start from an assumption, which then tries to fit the material to a ready-made conclusion. This is also Barker's approach when he looks at semiological critiques of girls' comics. Yet the idea of omission, the idea that the mass media do not present a wide enough range of possible roles for some groups, needs to be taken seriously.

SEMIOLOGICAL ANALYSIS OF *JACKIE*

First published in 1979, Angela McRobbie's approach to *Jackie* was one which saw the 'feminine career' being mapped out in such a way that there would be no room for any alternatives; central to her analysis was the idea that readers were being denied other choices by the magazine's concentration on the theme of romance. McRobbie believed, as we have seen, that there were a number of positive activities which were neglected. *Jackie* is popular, according to McRobbie, because:

'it offers its exclusive attention to an already powerless group, to a group which receives little public attention and which is already, from an early age, systematically denied any real sense of identity, creativity, or control.' (p. 128)

This last point should always generate broad agreement, but this is not to say that girls are of necessity more vulnerable to media influence. In fact, McRobbie is careful to argue that there is a whole range of factors in the lives of girls which limit the range of alternatives with which they are presented. *Jackie* alone would be incapable of producing such effects; its power is seen in the context of (p. 116) 'a whole range of institutions'.

MORE PROBLEMS WITH SEMIOLOGY

Barker addresses himself to questions of the *operation* of semiology. He notes that semiology has a tendency to push us in the direction of imagining (*Comics*, p. 152) 'the surface features of a cultural object like *Jackie*' having to be understood 'as expressions of an underlying pattern or structure'. The problem as Barker sees it, is that semiology thinks of meanings as created in systems – but then it is exactly the case that systems are not apparent on the surface of a culture. It is this important contradiction which leads Barker to ask *which* surface elements we should focus on, in order to get beyond the surface to the deeper meanings.

As an example of this problem, he cites the practice of *Jackie* in the 1960s and 1970s, when it was dependent for its artwork on poorly-paid Spanish artists who were sent the story-lines and who then had to provide the pictures. This system resulted in drawings reminiscent of English fashion models from the 1960s, images which seemed to many to be rather out of date. Did such drawings reflect the simple fact that *Jackie* was involved in a straightforward economic arrangement, acting perhaps as a barrier to what the magazine was attempting to say, or did they reveal (p. 153) 'the comic's fundamental ideology'?

Barker insists that, if we are to follow the lines of semiological analysis (looking beyond surface features for an underlying pattern), then we must treat *all* surface features as meaningful. This must include all content, but since it seems unlikely that taking all content together would produce any sensible results, the critic is forced to use his or her own judgment. If this in turn is done, then the critic is likely to end up with data which simply confirm the judgments brought to the text in the first place.

It is worth reminding ourselves that if, as Barker believes, semiology 'commands' the investigator to look for a unified system underneath the surface features, there will be a tendency, once the system is found, for the researcher to obliterate any evidence which does not fit the system, or else to treat what doesn't fit as simply irrelevant.

Barker refers to McRobbie's claim (p. 155) that the female readers of *Jackie* are presented with 'an ideological bloc of mammoth proportions'. It is also the case that McRobbie accused *Jackie* of having created a 'false totality' in which class and ethnic differences among girls are passed over so that the girls appear as essentially similar, with a similar range of interests. She imagined the readers as being (p. 156) trapped in 'a claustrophobic world of jealousy and competitiveness'. Barker disagrees, analysing McRobbie's claim that on the surface (as it were), the girls are doing things in groups, but underneath are in fact simply isolated and alone. Barker argues that, far from being a 'unified' text, *Jackie* is a collection of parts which act in contradictory ways.

Such an approach would fit more closely with the idea put forward in this book, that the mass media text may contain a variety of discourses which act sometimes in opposition to one another. The very act of address, if it is to be effective, must be able to refer to a variety of elements within the lived experience of the audience. We have seen some of the shortcomings of both a semiological and a content-analysis approach, just as Leiss, Klein and Jhally discovered a similar range of failures in their study of advertising. At the same time, we should be extremely wary of imagining, because the effects tradition has proved so dismally wrong-headed in the past, that mass media texts will never produce negative and potentially damaging representations. One of the major factors to consider would be the context – the times and places – in which representations are seen; the other would be the way they are mobilised within that context.

Television cartoons

At this point, it may be useful to refer to Len Masterman's approach to television cartoons, because of its relevance to the debate which surrounds comics, and more particularly because of the way in which children are supposed to respond to the comic form.

In *Teaching about Television* (p. 68), Masterman describes cartoons as (p. 68) 'the simplest of all of television's dramatic forms'. It seems to be for this reason that he proposes their use in the classroom. From his work on cartoons, Masterman is able to isolate a number of characteristics and points, raised by the pupils used in the study. These might apply to cartoons in general. He begins the list with considerations of narrative, and goes on to other elements.

- **Narrative structure** According to the pupils with whom Masterman worked, the narrative structure of cartoons is easy to discern. There will be what Masterman calls an *exposition*, in which a situation or a theme is outlined, a *development* which ends in a climax (or a series of climaxes), and a *resolution*, in which conflicts are settled and problems solved.
- **Narrative devices** These are 'a number of variations on a theme', or else there is a specific problem which is set out. The *motifs* which make up the narrative devices are chases, swift changes in fortune, reversals of situations, and finally what is described as retribution, which is physical, violent and impermanent in its effects.
- **Morality** In common with many other narrative forms, cartoons 'tend to present us with situations in which there is a moral conflict'. The two sides to this conflict are presented as being clearly opposed in many respects, including often the physical attributes and appearance of the characters involved.
- **Anthropomorphism** In cartoons, animals and other beings and/or objects, understand language and talk and behave like human beings.
- **The cartoon image** Masterman uses the pupils' observations to note how the individual frames in cartoons are 'quite lacking in the detail of photographs'. There is what he calls a kind of visual shorthand at work in the cartoon form, which means that generally only one meaning is offered for each particular event at one time. In order to obtain clarity in the delivery of meaning, actions, emotions and physical features are exaggerated. There is extensive use of stereotyping.
- **Humour** The humour found in cartoons takes a variety of forms. Masterman points up the use of *analogy*, in which a sound or an image is used in an unusual way to suggest something else. (One example he gives is the way that characters who are running along sound like cars as they screech to a halt.)
- **Political implications** Masterman reports that his young respondents noted that

The Flintstones (one of the cartoons studied) did not portray stone-age life in a 'realistic' way (whatever that might be), but as an extension of American suburban life. He believes this is because in American cartoons and comics:

'different cultures, historical periods and ways of life are not presented as being of some importance and interest in themselves but as either essentially the *same* as American society, or as so strange and odd as to be funny.' (p. 72)

• **Simplicity** Masterman sees the cartoon form as presenting us with:

'a simple, instantly recognisable and uncomplicated world, in which all situations and characters can be instantly comprehended; they provide a refuge from a real world which is fraught with ambiguity and complexity.'

One or two of these points seem to reveal a rather over-simplified approach to ideology. It is worth noting that Masterman's concepts of *retribution* (as part of 'narrative devices') and his ideas about *morality* might be contrasted with Barker's 'emotional transformation', in which incidents and events function not as 'lessons' but as transformations of the human state.

When Masterman deals with *political implications*, and argues that American cartoons and comics tend to treat 'different cultures, historical periods and ways of life' as of little importance and interest in themselves, being presented as 'either essentially the *same* as American society, or as so strange and odd as to be funny', it may be that he has simply misunderstood the type of humour used in *The Flintstones*, which seems to be both about 'stone age' *and* 'modern' values. Jokes about a record player which uses a bird's beak as the needle, or about cars powered by bare feet which poke through their floors, seem at first sight to be making fun of a pre-technological society, but the values held by the characters (particularly those held by Fred) are recognisable as belonging to a 'modern' period. It is the contrast between the primitive technology and the aspirations and 'lifestyle' of the characters which seems to produce the humour. The joke cuts both ways, and can be read as making fun of American society, particularly when the series is seen in a different cultural context. Seen in a British context, where there has also been a considerable lapse of time between the making of the cartoon and its reception by a contemporary audience, we may imagine that some of the values portrayed appear distinctly old-fashioned. Which looks more quaint, the 'stone age' setting, or the relationship between Fred and Wilma? We should be aware, however, that the mass reintroduction of cartoons and adventure programmes originally made in the 1960s, may in itself have something to say about the retreat from more forward-looking attitudes, as well as the more restricted economic outlook faced by many broadcasting institutions.

Masterman's view that the cartoon form presents us with 'a simple, instantly recognisable and uncomplicated world' which provides children with 'a refuge from a real world which is fraught with ambiguity and complexity' may be rather misleading. If we take the question of 'simplicity' first, then we can see that cartoons may well work to a formula, and clearly contain a number of limited situations and characters. They would, in addition, seem very likely to provide a simplified narrative 'closure'; but they will often manage to raise a number of issues in the course of the narrative. We should by now be used to the idea that viewers and readers may be most impressed by certain elements of narrative which might well 'conflict' with the narrative closure. This is to make a point about ideology, but it is also a question about the way in which people perceive and understand meanings. We may remind ourselves that we need to investigate perception and cognition. Edward Branigan, in *Narrative, Comprehension and Film*, notes that:

> 'what perceivers remember from a narrative, as well as what they forget, is not random, but dictated by the specific method used in searching for global properties.' (p. 13)

In other words, all people, including children, will tend to remember broad categories of ideas or functions, because human beings appear to search for 'categories' of information. The simplicity of cartoons could be seen as an aid to this process.

The other point Masterman makes is that cartoons offer a 'retreat' from reality. In many ways, however, the cartoon 'world' is not particularly comfortable, and may present a number of difficult issues. Although many cartoons are entirely serious in their intentions, it is through humour that some of these difficult matters are exorcised. We could see cartoons as being 'rehearsals' of problems and solutions; children may find cartoons instructive for this reason. Referring back to the comic form (p. 395), there are examples of cartoon strips which show a high awareness of social and political issues. 'The Toad War' story in *Bucky O'Hare* (Fig. 7.7) illustrates this point.

Masterman's categories provide a useful overview of the cartoon form, but they have limitations. One of these is the way that the **moral** category is not connected to the **political** category. In addition, the political category is used in an inflexible way to attack the presumed 'bias' of the cartoon under study, without allowing either for the different 'readings' made by viewers or for the fact that any discourse chosen is bound to express contradictions in its very structure. (It is partly these contradictions which allow different readings to be made.) Using the category **discourse** to encompass the concerns of both these categories, and pursuing research which helps to reveal perceptual and cognitive processes, might be a step forward to a more structured and less subjective approach to the political or ideological content of cartoons and comics.

POPULAR CULTURE: MUSIC AND THE MUSIC INDUSTRY

In any study of music and the music industry, the issues which surround popular culture seem to apply with a particular force. These issues include censorship and free expression, profitability, the recuperation of radical forms, national and international culture, questions of originality, and enquiries into the relationship between institution and audience. Dick Hebdidge (*Hiding in the Light*) places the relationship between US music and the British media in the immediate post-war period within the context of the economies of the two countries:

Fig 7.7a Bucky O'Hare – a children's comic which also employs a political discourse
(taken from 'The Toad Wars', Courtesy of DC Comics, © Continuity Graphics 1992)

Fig 7.7b

Fig 7.7c

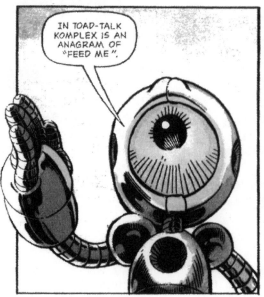

Fig 7.7d

'In magazine articles and newspaper reports, Britain's austerity was frequently contrasted against the booming American economy and the strong dollar.'   (p. 54)

After the Second World War, the majority of the British people were still suffering the kind of deprivation which had been accepted as necessary during the conflict itself. Rationing was still in force. The winter of 1946–7 was particularly bleak, with fuel in short supply. In 1948, the first records to be produced in vinyl appeared on the market.

The antithesis of good taste

Hebdidge notes that, according to the BBC and the 'literary and cultural establishments', American imports (records and films) were regarded to be in rather dubious taste. In fact, throughout the 1940s and 1950s, the BBC laid down detailed guidelines as to how much US material could be presented, with rock and roll music being deliberately resisted by the BBC radio networks. In 1956, for example, not a single rock and roll song featured in the annual review of popular songs. *Melody Maker* resisted readers' requests to run a 'top ten' until the same date. During the 1950s *Melody Maker* declared:

'Viewed as a social phenomenon, the current craze for Rock-and-Roll material is one of the most terrifying things to have happened to popular music ... The Rock-and-Roll technique, instrumentally and vocally, is the antithesis of all that jazz has been striving for over the years – in other words, good taste and musical integrity.'

When Hebdidge describes (p. 56) the attempts made to 'tame' this dangerous import by 'elaborate monitoring and framing procedures', he makes an interesting reference to what we would call the incorporation of a supposed threat. The early TV music shows, for example, were all hosted by already established professional presenters. They acted almost as responsible 'chaperones' to the youthful audience which followed the new music, mediating between product and consumer. *Oh Boy!* on the commercial channel had by contrast rather more deviant overtones.

The 1960s saw an explosion in popular music in America, and a proliferation of new studios set up to capitalise on the scores of talented groups which appeared. Cynthia Wild, for example, who formed a production and song-writing team with her husband Barry Man, searched for the kind of sound that would be acceptable 'to white kids', new to the black music which had suddenly become fashionable. Many studios operated almost like factories, with a very high turnover of songs, little preparation and almost immediate access to the recording studio. It was partly the sheer volume of material emanating from the US which led to the growth in 1960s Britain of pirate radio stations. These existed to provide listeners with a more immediate experience of popular music; ultimately, they forced the hand of the BBC. Faced with such competition and unable to close pirate stations like 'Radio Caroline' (which operated from a ship in the North Sea, moored outside British jurisdiction) the BBC introduced Radio 1, the first legal, all-pop station. With the advent of 'The Beatles', British musical credibility was high in the US. In one year, 'The Beatles' hed the first five top places in the US charts.

Industry and audience

Popular music cannot be separated from the way it is produced and the variety of ways in which it is consumed. From its origins in the 1950s, the popular music industry had to address a youth audience which had in previous years been told what was good for it by an older generation. Popular music seemed to speak directly to the young, and very often to speak up for its interests as well. This is in one sense curious, because in the case of the big music corporations, there are a great many mediating processes which take place between the original conception of a song and the consumption of the end product. In *Rebel Rock*, John Street describes the:

> 'record executives, lawyers, accountants, producers, engineers, publicists, sales personnel, radio programmers, disc jockeys, music journalists and a host of others who come between a song's composition and its first hearing.' (p. 6)

There is no indication here of the relative influence of each of these roles, but it does emphasise how the larger sections of the music industry try to leave nothing to chance when it comes to the production of music. We may also realise that many recording artists are themselves part of a marketing strategy, and some are doing no more than mouthing ideas brought into being by their corporate mentors. One point which is often made is that a record, CD or tape is not 'a piece of pure art' but, as Street puts it:

> 'the result of countless choices and compromises, using criteria that mix the aesthetic, the political and the economic.'

Whether or not we argue that art is never 'pure' and has always been the result of the kind of compromises detailed above, we should recognise that popular music is never 'meaningless'. It may well be mass-produced, but some genuine contact seems to be established between artist and audience which goes beyond what Street calls its 'exchange value'. We should perhaps understand the growth of 'independent' labels partly as an attempt to exercise more control over a highly commercial process. In whatever way music is actually produced, it will always remain part of the lifestyles and subcultures of millions of people.

Types of music companies

There are usually said to be three different types of company which operate within the music business. The **majors** are large, multinational organisations which manufacture and distribute their own product, combining a number of functions. They sign up artists, operate their own recording studios, run their own production technologies, and have extensive marketing, promotional and distributive networks. Amongst the largest of these giant corporations, sometimes called the 'big six', are Sony, Philips/Polygram, Time Warner, Thorn-EMI, Bertelsmann/BMG, and Matsushita/MCA. The **independents** were originally those smaller companies such as Virgin (since taken over by EMI), Island and A&M (both taken over by Philips/Polygram), which established a share in the market by making production or distribution deals with the major labels, or through establishing links with independent studios or production facilities. The third type, the **new independents**, emerged originally in response to the rise of a large number of the bands during the 'new wave' and punk era of the mid to late 1970s. These companies offered deals to bands which were not yet established, often being in a position to capitalise on the arrival of cheaper and more efficient technologies. The new independents included companies like Illegal, Stiff, and Rough Trade. The short-lived EMI record deal with the Sex Pistols (terminated after the band members were provoked into using bad language during a television interview) demonstrates how the majors found it difficult to balance their interest in new sources of profit with their worries about bands that might eventually represent a threat to their respectability.

Profit and loss

Live music plays a central role in maintaining the profits of the music and record industry. According to the Arts Council, in 1984–5, nearly five million people attended pop or rock concerts in the five hundred or so venues which cater for such events. Box office receipts of £36.8 million (Euromonitor Consumer Market Surveys) were taken at pop concerts in 1985. In the same year, when Bruce Springsteen toured Britain he was seen by almost 500,000 people, who paid out in total £6 million. A sell-out crowd at Wembley Arena could bring in over £90,000 in box office receipts. Overall, in terms of both consumer and industrial spending, the music market is worth well over £2,000 million.

The decline of the single

Although in 1985 Band Aid sold 750,000 singles in one week, this was exceptional. Overall, singles sales have continued to fall. On average, a single which goes to number one will achieve sales of some 60,000 a week, although the figure needed to achieve prime position in the charts may in fact be much lower. New Kids on the Block's number-one record, *Hanging Tough*, sold a mere 28,000 in January 1990.

In order to maintain sales the price of a single is kept artificially low, with suggestions that, at the beginning of the 1990s, record companies lost 20p for every single sold. Why then do labels continue to release singles? In the end, singles help both to launch and sell the albums which follow. Vinyl LP sales themselves, however underwent a decline between 1975 (91.6 million) and 1990 (24.7 million).

The rise of the CD

The cassette player and the music cassette proved a highly successful format, with some 2.6 billion tapes sold around the world every year, but it was the compact disc, first brought out in 1982, which first secured and then increased the music industry's profit margins. In 1990 the CD market was worth £273.4 million in Britain. Millions of pounds were spent by consumers on the replacement of vinyl albums with CDs. New versions of the disc include the Digital Compact Cassette and Sony's 'Mini Disc' system. All such innovations are a risk, since the manufacturers must be able to persuade the public to give up older systems. Equally, once an innovation appears, the rest of the market has to watch its success or failure very carefully. No one wants to get involved in a commercial failure, but equally, few are anxious to miss a genuine money-making opportunity.

The music industry is not prepared to make any false moves in time of recession. Focus groups, examined in Chapter 3, are used to conduct research on general taste as well as on more specific issues like public perception of the images of individual artists. The BBC 2 programme *Reportage* discovered that all aspects of the product are investigated, including the sleeve design and even the order of the tracks; single-sex groups are used to investigate the sex appeal of an artist. Since compilation albums account for a very high proportion of album sales, the industry spends a lot of time on this aspect of its marketing strategy. Good old-fashioned 'hype' is no longer quite enough to maintain sales, and certainly not whole stations. The experience of Jazz FM is a good example, since it failed to maintain itself as a specialist outlet for jazz, and other music genres had to be introduced. Classical music has benefited from careful marketing, which puts more emphasis on attracting an audience through the use of new packaging designs and alluring titles; the composer's name can sometimes fail to achieve even equal prominence.

A British music industry in slow decline?

In America in 1985 (from spring to summer), there were eight consecutive hits by British artists, with 30 per cent of the 'hot one hundred' being produced by British acts. By 1992, only 13 per cent of the American market was being taken by British bands (*Reportage*, BBC 2). Sales of British records in 1992 were half what they had been six years earlier.

Various reasons are advanced for this decline. In the first place, Americans seemed in the early 1990s to take their lead from home-grown music, with radio networks and the all-important MTV showing little interest in British bands. MTV, of course, has to be concerned with the image of the musicians it presents. While rave and dance music have secured a strong internal market in the UK, this type of music has not taken hold in America. Videos for rave and dance do not seem to provide the type of images required by the US television networks.

As Dave Kendall, presenter of 120 *Minutes* on MTV said (*Reportage*): 'An image is more easily presented with a face but Techno and Rave music ... is faceless.'

While dance music remains unpopular in the US, British acts have also suffered a drop in popularity in the third largest record market in the world, which is Germany. British sales there fell by half between 1985 and 1992. In Sweden the popularity of British music, judging by sales, halved between 1987 and 1992. Inside Britain, the story of decline was similar. In 1984 70 per cent of the top acts in the UK charts were British, but by 1991 the figure had dropped to 45 per cent.

The net result of this recession in the industry was inevitable; firms began to retrench and risks were no longer taken. In 1992 Chrysalis were signing one band a year, and in general trying to keep costs down. The number of new bands signed by the major labels had fallen dramatically. Since as many as twenty new bands who begin contracts with major labels fail to achieve success (and often disappear from sight), the majors look for acts that may be successful abroad, even if this means producing music written to a formula. Clearly, while the British market can sustain only 6 per cent of world music sales, as opposed to America's 40 per cent share of the global market, the UK market is not big enough to justify spending large amounts on an artist who is popular in Britain but of no interest to other markets.

Takeovers in the music business

The tendency, present throughout the later 1980s, for the big record names to make takeover bids for the larger independents, developed more strongly as time passed. The larger independents, companies which had once stood for a more innovatory approach to music (and which were in many ways closer to the artists they signed), were ripe for takeovers by huge conglomerates. In a way, the independents could only ever grow to a certain size before they had to begin operating like their bigger rivals. Having grown large, they would at some point lose the advantages which their original compact size had given them. RCA was one of the first to be incorporated, in this tendency to create monopolies. At the time of the take-over of the Virgin music business by Thorn EMI, in March 1992, the European Commission was expressing concern at Thorn EMI's domination of the Greek and Portuguese record markets. Thorn EMI paid £560 million for Virgin, which had previously estimated the value of its business at some £200 million higher than this figure. However, the value of Virgin's physical assets (the buildings and their contents) was thought by some commentators (*Independent*, 12 March 1992) to be only some £10 million. The money paid would really have been for Virgin's share of the music market and the earning potential of artists who were part of the Virgin stable, including The Rolling Stones, XTC, Bryan Ferry, Phil Collins and Simple Minds. Although Virgin would remain largely independent, some musicians expressed mixed feelings about the take-over. Andy Partridge of 'XTC' responded to the change of employer by saying (*Independent*):

> 'maybe I do mind being on a label organised by people who make missile guidance systems, but what can you say? Virgin had been growing a little more faceless, a little less personal through the years. But now I feel a bit like Jonah, in the belly of this vast beast.'

The independents rise again

One response to this increasing concentration of power has been the beginning of new cycles of independent activity. The whole institutional process can be imagined as one in which companies grow until the logic of this type of capitalist enterprise forces amalgamation or take-over. At the base, new companies arise because they are closer to the newest acts. New ventures are then 'tested' and draw the attention of the majors if they prove profitable. Most dance records, for example, are made on computers. Sonz of a Loop Da Loop Era's record *Far Out* went to the charts at number 36, selling 25,000 copies (*Reportage*). Using relatively cheap equipment, such groups can make a record in a day. Some of the individuals concerned do not see themselves as musicians at all, but rather as technicians. With costs in the early 1990s relatively low (£1.40 each to press a CD and £1.20 each to press a 12-inch record) a band could, with good promotion and judicious use of 'white labels' (promotional copies sent to DJs), create a reasonable demand for their music. The independent sector may be rather misleadingly named, but it still survives. In fact, some in the industry believe that, as soon as bands go mainstream, many of their fans begin to lose enthusiasm and look elsewhere for inspiration.

An end to independent charts?

The attempt by the major companies to replace the 'independent charts' with a new 'alternative chart', which took place in March 1992, was clearly meant to reduce the influence of the independent companies. Instead of producing a chart which was compiled by CIM/Gallup from independent labels with independent distribution, the majors proposed that the new chart should include music they themselves had released, provided that the records concerned were of an 'independent style'. Martin Mills, who runs the Beggar's Banquet label, was one of the many who opposed the move (the *Guardian*, 12 March 1992):

> 'If you start getting records by major labels on an independent chart, firstly it's going to harm the independents, and secondly it's going to devalue the chart.'

Radio plays: a corrupt system?

Over the years, since its inception in 1967, Radio 1 has held the power to make or break new records. If Radio 1 favours a release and it achieves airplay, then there is a better chance of the record in question entering the charts. As one EMI executive said (Street, *Rebel Rock*, p. 113):

> 'Radio is incredibly important. It probably does more to influence public taste than anything else . . . I'm sure there's a direct correlation between airplays and sales.'

This is not to say that those who purchase music tapes, CDs and records, do not have other sources of information, but it is the certainty of a large-scale and very public reinforcement of popular hits which ensures that (p. 116) 'what the listeners receive is a highly selective populism'.

Since airplay depends on what radio producers select, and considering that the producers are influenced by the charts, the key to obtaining airplay comes back again to the manipulation of public awareness of the releases. There are a number of perfectly legal ways of boosting a record into the charts. One method is to circulate free copies, usually of singles, to record shops. These may then be placed as bargains and sold for relatively small amounts. The numbers thus disposed of will help to boost sales, as an addition to 'legitimate' sales. The net increase would assist the record in its rise through the charts.

The music industry in Britain and in other countries has certainly been involved in direct corruption, including a form of bribery called payola (or 'pay for play') where record companies pay DJs to allocate their records extensive airplay. It caused a major scandal in the US industry, where a clutch of disc jockeys were found to be corrupt. Payola was outlawed, though other more subtle methods still flourish, ranging from the inevitable private functions which launch new releases, to the offer of holidays and other inducements to producers and DJs.

Advertising on the airwaves

A recent content analysis of a number of programmes' 'links' (the addresses made by DJs between records) found that much of what was said could be described as advertising, for bands, records and public performances. (*See Nothing local about it: London's local radio*, Comedia/LRW, 1983.) In one case, the address of the DJ was concerned with release dates and gigs, which:

> '[were] already covered in a much better fashion in the local press … all in all the programme added up to little more than a vehicle for the promotion of records that because of their chart position were already receiving plenty of airtime.'

However, such a practice on a specialist programme may not be particularly sinister, since the DJ may take it for granted that the audience is sufficiently dedicated to the genre to tolerate a high level of commercial information.

The second programme analysed by the Local Radio Workshop was the Robbie Vincent show, which at one time was broadcast between 11.30 a.m. and 2 p.m. on Saturdays:

> 'On this occasion, the show had two guests, the first of whom was treated like a co-presenter, given duties and asked to rate records played. Less than two minutes was spent discussing her music and career. The second guest was questioned about his career and had his music played. During the interview the presenter mentioned the trade paper *Billboard* and with good reason too, as twenty-two out of the thirty-three records played were in the Billboard charts … five were Billboard selections. It appears the show was simply an advertising tool.'

Although research is able to show quite easily that Radio 1 was being used as an advertising tool, with the remarks of disc jockeys a mixture of commercial references and value judgments, we should not imagine that one institution alone is guilty in this way. Pop magazines and children's television programmes are obviously suffused with references to pop stars and bands, and in some senses this could be seen as a mutually-beneficial relationship for the institutional partners involved.

Pop videos are a major selling ploy in recorded music. They give a distinct visual style to the bands and individual artists featured. Queen are often regarded as the pioneers of this form, with the video for *Bohemian Rhapsody*. Some commentators attributed the success of artists such as Adam Ant to the power of the pop video. Although retail sales of pop videos in 1985 were estimated to be worth in the region of £11 million, some companies appear to have taken significant risks in spending vast sums on the form. In 1991, for example, Michael Jackson's record company spent no less than £3 million on one ten-minute pop video.

Increasingly, some television programmes have come to rely quite heavily on the video, which works to standardise the image of a band and which helps to secure its market position. The vogue for making promotional videos seems split between practices which seek to record spectacular live concerts, those which concentrate on dance and the human form as an added attraction to the music, and those which produce complete narrative or fictive experiences for their audience.

Hip-hop and rap

When Normski (the presenter of BBC 2's *Dance Energy*), appeared in a 1992 edition of *Rapido* dedicated to the exploration of hip-hop culture, he began his presentation in New York:

> 'Here in the South Bronx Project is where it all started. DJs would plug their sound systems into the street lamps and jam away in the streets and parks. In those early days it was a black and Hispanic thing and it was by all accounts wicked.'

The film-stock used on the programme featured the Bronx in 1974, and the interviews emphasised the way that the community was drawn to events which were free, open-air celebrations, starting in the summer at two in the afternoon, and growing in size until thousands of individuals would be present in the streets. The electricity was obtained, as Normski admitted, from the public grid via street lamps. This was a public culture brought out at minimal cost, in one of the poorest neighbourhoods of New York. In the winter, community centres and high schools were used as the venues.

The music and dance phenomenon now known as hip-hop soon became an extensive and influential movement. The vocal aspect of the broader culture was called rap, and many of its more recent practitioners look back to artists such as Isaac Hayes and Millie Jackson, as well as to forms of rap associated with poetry, represented by movements like 'The Last Poets'. There are a variety of rap 'forms'. Jamaican 'toasting' and funk were among those included, as well as forms of public speech used by black religious leaders. It would be possible to identify all such variants as belonging to a specifically African cultural heritage, but only if distinctions are made between the component parts of the music: the beat comes from hard funk, whereas the style of speech or song emanates from reggae, and specifically from what is sometimes called 'DJ reggae'.

The exact timing of the origins of rap are a matter of debate, reflecting the various influences to which it has been subject. The singer James Brown argues that he started rap music years before its vogue in the 1980s and early 1990s. Others point to the West Indies and oral traditions, where information was spread by rhyming verses. Valal Nuridon, of 'The Last Poets' claimed: 'it's also part of the oral storytelling tradition'.

EARLY DAYS

DJ Kool Herc, a Jamaican-born West Indian, is credited with the introduction in the late 1960s and early 1970s of rhythmic speech set over the instrumental part of a record. Finding that people at house-parties were unenthusiastic about dancing to reggae, he would introduce a variety of phrases designed to prompt greater involvement from his audience. He began buying records but was chiefly interested in the instrumental parts of each track which could form a background to his own phrases. He ended up buying many copies of individual records for use on two record decks, so that he could reuse certain instrumental pieces. He was followed by musicians like Grandmaster Flash. Soon, there were many different crews, or groups of musicians. The practice of using turntables to mix tracks to produce scratch rhythms became widespread. The use of turntables allowed many different musicians from a variety of traditions to be heard together in a new synthesis of sound. Television commercial themes began to be mixed; the practice had few boundaries. The term 'scratch' has various origins, but according to performer Jazzy Jay, this was based on the fact that someone in the crowd had misunderstood the use of turntables:

> 'I remember the first time a guy came and said "Yo, It's marvellous the way you scratch the records." I said "I'm not scratching them, you see me scratching them?" But after a while I guess that sort of set in as what we did. They called it scratching . . . the transformer style, the style where they slow the record down actually break it down, into beats . . . evolved from what we were doing . . .'

Red Alert was a DJ and producer who worked with Jazzy Jay; together they would 'dig around for all the old records and just listen to certain great beats – didn't matter what type of record it was'.

Rap remained an underground scene until the shop release of *Rappers Delight* by the Sugarhill Gang. No one knew who they were or where they had come from. Sylvia Robinson was instrumental in putting the Sugarhill Gang together:

> 'I was at a disco in New York and I saw these guys just talking on the microphone . . . and everybody was just going into a frenzy . . . I said to myself: if I put a concept like that on record it would be a smash . . . I called them the Sugarhill Gang.'

Sylvia Robinson later released the influential *The Message*, by Grandmaster Flash and the Furious Five. The content was overtly political. *Planet Rock* by Afrika Bambaataa and the Sonic Soul Force also appeared at about this time. This was more of an electronic sound, using synthesisers. Bambaataa felt that there was no real black punk or rock group producing music. Rap gained exposure in mid-town Manhattan and was eagerly taken up as a commercial proposition by the influential 'Soho set', who exploited this new talent by bringing rap artists, graffiti artists and break dancers to new and more affluent audiences. Upmarket New York clubs like the 'Roxy' and 'Palladium' used the new music. Gallery openings also featured the work of some graffiti artists who saw more profitability in using canvas than in pursuing (at some danger and risk to themselves) trains on the subway. Artists like Fab 5 Freddy and Jean-Michel Basquiat exhibited in galleries in the East Village area of Manhattan. The galleries, feeling that there had been no movements since pop art, and always looking for something new to sell to the public, took up graffiti work with enthusiasm. Another home-grown art form was being exploited commercially, in much the same way as its musical counterpart.

GANGSTER RAP?

Public Enemy, once described as the most successful rap act in the world, was always closely associated with the politics of 'The Nation of Islam' and its leader, Louis Farrakhan. This militant sect has been publicised by the activities of Public Enemy. Indeed, according to Harry Allen, a journalist on the *Voice*, a New York magazine for the black community, it has done more than this (*Guardian*, 9 January 1992): 'Public Enemy' and their music give the 'Nation' credibility, an air of acceptability.' Dotun Adebayo, another journalist on the *Voice*, argues that:

> 'Rap bands and heavy metal bands certainly have the same message about power or gaining power, whether the message is depicted with Satanistic metaphors or with gangster violence as in rap.'

The relationship between Islam and music performed specifically for entertainment has not usually been close. Traditionally, the Muslim world has kept music and religion separate. The call to prayer and the use of chants in the reading of the Koran are not considered to be music as such. There is a clear division between those black Muslims in America who are closely involved in the music world and some Muslims in other countries who remain unconvinced of the place of music in religion.

Comments made by one member of Public Enemy about the Jewish community caused his departure from the group. Other anti-semitic remarks which have allegedly emerged from another member of Public Enemy led their manager, Mike Adler, to say (*Reportage*):

> 'It's a dumb fight to pick. The Jews are not his enemy ... I wish he'd chosen more powerful enemies –systems which really do oppress the black people.'

It is perhaps unfortunate that the public debate has at times become locked into a discussion of censorship rather than how to oppose racism. At the close of the *Reportage* study, for example, viewers were asked simply to cast a telephone vote for or against stricter controls of music.

In a sense, music is already strictly controlled. It might be as well to remember that almost all of America's more than 5000 radio stations are owned by large corporations such as CBS and NBC.

Censorship: banned in the USA

The first amendment in the United States guarantees freedom of speech. However, a sixteen-year-old in a US record store will not be sold Prince's album *Graffiti Bridge*, released in 1990. Notices in US record shops warn: 'Due to explicit lyrics you must be 18 years old and show proper ID to purchase LPs, cassettes and CDs with Parent Advisory Warnings.'

At one point in 1990, 9 per cent of the top two hundred albums in America carried warning stickers on their covers. Groups which have been awarded warning stickers include rap groups NWA, Public Enemy and Ice Cube, and thrash bands such as Extreme and Danzig. How had this situation come about? In the first place, there had long been censorship of popular forms in the United States. In

1939 there was a manual dedicated specifically to outlining taboo subjects in popular songs. References to drinking and 'necking' were as undesirable as any mention of 'labor' – by which was meant any favourable references to the working class.

In the early 1980s Prince's *1999* album included a line which had not been listed on the lyric sheet. A parent called Rick Alley complained to the American PTA (Parents' and Teachers' Association) which began a campaign of letter writing to all the major record labels. The PTA proposed a rating system for records based upon the content of the lyrics. This campaign proved unsuccessful until the PTA president, Ann Kahn, enlisted the help of the 'Washington Wives', a group of wealthy women whose husbands were at the centre of power. Tipper Gore, wife of then Democratic Senator (now Vice-President) Al Gore, founded the Parents' Music Resource Centre in 1985. At a press conference held by the PMRC in the same year, one member recited the lyrics of songs produced by Sheena Easton and Prince, referring to them as lewd and profane. The organisation (which had always advocated the voluntary labelling of record sleeves by the record companies themselves) suggested the introduction of a certificate scheme with labels for violence (a capital 'V') and lewdness and profanity (a capital 'X').

This campaign may remind us of the Comics Magazine Association and its struggle against specific types of 'unacceptable' content; just as comics once had to appear with the 'Approved by the Comics Code' stamp of approval, music covers were now to be labelled. The pressure for legislation, rather than simply a voluntary code, began to grow. The State Representative for Missouri proposed a law that would make the labelling of certain music publications mandatory and some twenty American states joined together to propose legislation for a new standard sticker. The legislation was introduced in the spring of 1990, but then most states withdrew their bills and it was left to Louisiana to pass the first labelling law in July 1990. Although this was later vetoed, the US music industry appeared to be labelling itself on a voluntary basis. Warnings on albums soon turned into extensive lists of possible offences: 'may contain explicit lyrics descriptive of one or more of the following: Nudity, Satanism, Suicide, Sodomy, Incest, Bestiality, Sadomasochism, Adultery, Murder, Morbid Violence, Deviant Sexual Conduct ...' and so on.

The rather surprising inclusion of 'nudity' amongst this alarming list may lend weight to the argument that a sense of proportion was being lost, or else that a proper definition of the actual offences had not been set out in the first place, rather like the way that some researchers into media effects failed to define their terms before starting their enquiry.

Heavy metal in the dock

Cardinal John O'Connor announced from the pulpit of the New York Cathedral in 1990 that 'Heavy metal has led to a rise in satanism in the city.' Publications from religious groups accused rock music of corrupting youth. One such pamphlet carried the propagandist title *Stairway to hell: the well-planned destruction of teens*.

In Nevada in 1990, Judas Priest and CBS records faced the accusation that their album *Stained Class* contained 'subliminal messages' – concealed messages which could only be 'read' subconsciously, or which appeared when the record was played backwards. Two teenagers had committed suicide (one had died at the time and the second some three years later), supposedly as a response to subliminal messages in the album's lyrics. Judas Priest were acquitted, although the judge did find that subliminal messages were present on the album, whether intended or not. On the last day of the trial the group's singer, Rob Halford, appeared in court with a cassette machine and played tracks both forwards and backwards. Non-sensical messages then appeared, but they clearly had no connection to any evil suggestion or influence.

The BBC begs to disapprove

There have been a number of occasions when the BBC has banned records which were thought morally dubious or politically sensitive. Famous examples include the song *Je t'aime* by Birkin and Gainsbourg, *Wet Dream* by Max Romeo, and *Relax* by Frankie Goes to Hollywood, all for reasons of the sexual impropriety they seemed to suggest. Political censorship was clearly exercised when *God Save the Queen*, by the Sex Pistols, was banned during the sovereign's silver jubilee. This was guaranteed to make the Sex Pistols notorious. (Copies of this particular record were passed around in schools and colleges, thus investing the single with a par-ticular potency.) Other examples of political censorship include a very peculiar list of 'unsuitable' records circulated during the Gulf War.

Censorship has always been, of course, a rather uncertain weapon in matters concerning popular culture, failing as it clearly does to pick up all the sexual or political, or even cultural references contained in songs, and pouncing on some innocuous material. Direct censorship is usually a response to a release which has already established itself in the public consciousness. John Street argues that a more sinister form of censorship is that which is partially exercised through the charts and the shops, and through radio and TV's (p. 116) 'ability to act as gate-keeper for public taste'.

Provocation on and off-stage

In some cases, however, there is material in circulation which is intended to be offensive, and which it would be hard to misunderstand. Although most instances of racism and homophobia are usually found in remarks made by artists off-stage (sexism appearing to be an integral part of some musical forms), there have been examples, in both Britain and the US, of provocative nonsense spoken in public during live performances, and of lyrics and images which carry discriminatory messages. The band Guns 'n' Roses suffered a blanket ban of their *Appetite for Destruction* album cover in the USA, because it featured a picture of a woman who appeared to have been raped by a robot. Some retailers in Britain withdrew the album.

The best method of combating material which is openly anti-social (often exactly that material which is aimed at those who are least able to fight back) is difficult to determine, since it may depend on the nature of each case. Some acts, such as Guns 'n' Roses, have produced homophobic material in their lyrics of an explicit nature; this from a band whose debut album sold over 10 million copies. The response of the left has usually been to agitate in public against such abuses, whereas the right has more commonly spoken in terms of censorship and government action.

One of the most effective responses to offensive material would be that which comes from within the industry itself, whether in America or Britain. The emergence of female-led bands, such as Hole, The Nymphs, and Daisy Chainsaw, which use rock to address all those issues which affect women, acts as an important contrast to the wilder assertions made by bands founded on male posturing. Many of these bands are reminiscent of the strong female orientation of some punk acts in the 1970s.

Rebellion or public relations?

All bands are interested in promotion of one sort or another, and deliberately outrageous behaviour seems to be a regular recourse for many performers. Does this constitute a type of resistance to commercialism, or is such public behaviour designed more to capture a market position, with so many acts having trouble establishing a clear identity? Stories of anti-social behaviour which leads to the banning of some acts from public venues would appear to be part of the image that certain groups wish to project.

Collective consumption: dance, gender and club culture

Popular journalism is fond of identifying cults among young people, particularly where the devotees in question engage in 'deviant' activity. In Britain, the dance phenomenon gained a degree of notoriety, beginning in the late 1980s with reports of 'acid house' raves. In the summer of 1988, the *Sun* carried a story about the use of recreational drugs at raves, under the headline '10,000 DRUG CRAZED YOUTHS', while in 1989 another of the paper's front-page scoops was introduced with the words 'SPACED OUT!'. It featured a group of dancers 'at a secret party attended by more than 11,000'. Even in these two reports, the common theme of uncontrolled youth (gathered in large numbers), are clearly reproduced.

The young adherents of dance were outraged at the tabloids' representation of their culture, but possibly more unsettled when the same newspapers began to run positive reports on their activities. *Touch* magazine of December 1991 interpreted this change in attitude to mean that the *Sun* 'knows absolutely f*** all about what's happening on the Rave scene' just as they 'knew f*** all in 1988 and 1989' (in Thornton, *Club Cultures*, p. 135). As Thornton notes (p. 6) 'approving reports in mass media like tabloids or television ... are the subcultural kiss of death'. Positive coverage led to 'a quick abandonment of the key insignia of the culture'.

Although the *Sun* had decided that drug abuse no longer constituted a part of the club scene, and was running stories which praised the physical benefits of the dance forms associated with rave, interviews with adherents of this new 'cult' showed that drug use remained a central part of the culture. It did not, however, appear to create the vacuity or blankness first suggested in the news-papers.

Ravers seemed to 're-configure' their relationship both to 'mainstream' society and to each other. Ideas about freedom, 'connectedness' between individuals, and the worth of collective behaviour, were 'lived' during – and sometimes beyond – the dance event itself. Ecstasy was often an essential component of the state of mind which gave rise to the positive atmosphere which dancers described.

In an essay called 'Women and the early British rave scene' (*see* McRobbie, *Back to Reality*) Maria Pini describes her interviews with female dance enthusiasts. Among the opinions expressed, is that of a woman called Miriam, who described the scene as feeling 'like it was almost a cult ... a different society ... you were yourself – you had your own identity – but you were also part of the whole group'. The sense of trust and freedom produced in the early manifestation of rave, is revealed in the remarks of Ann, who noted that 'unlike discos and many pubs – people may look at you as being there to pick someone up ... but I wouldn't hesi-tate to go raving on my own ... it's fine for a woman to go to a rave, pop anything they want to, skin-up a huge joint and no one bats an eyelid'.

Academics have long expressed a keen interest in youth culture, particularly as it so often seems to provide alternative lifestyles to the 'mainstream'. In Pini's view, such research has, however, concentrated on groups of young males, dealing with 'questions of "deviance" and "resistance"', and neglecting the question of women's activities and experiences. Pini points out that (p. 152) , for well over a decade, 'feminists involved in researching youth culture have sought to contest the familiar association of "youth" with "masculinity"'. Furthermore, Pini believes that (p. 153) 'the actual location of women' within the rave culture, seems to have been neglected.

While men appeared to be involved in music production, the organisation of events, and the distribution of drugs, women took little part in these 'profit-making' activities. It is not merely the existence of difference that disturbs Pini, but the way that this difference is theorised or understood. Thus the more visible and by extension the more 'meaningful' experience of male participants often becomes the object of study. Despite the exclusion of females at one level of participation, Pini believes there is much to be learned from studying the activities in which they do engage. In general, women have been denied what Rumsey and Little in 1989 called 'unsupervised adventures' and which Pini believes the dance culture pro-vides. Her research method was to elicit 'stories' from female participants in order to gauge what kinds of identities they constructed through the experience of rave.

For those directly involved in the early rave scene, the activity in which they engaged was (p. 156) 'surrounded by an air of thrill, illegality and mystery'. This atmosphere was partly created by police attempts to prevent meetings taking place, which in turn required coded directions to be sent out to party-goers from pirate radio stations. Devotees, therefore, often had to cover extreme distances to reach events which might ultimately prove to have been cancelled. Writing about the post-rave rise of Jungle, Martin James recalls that parties were held (*see State of Bass*, p. 6) 'in direct opposition to the overpriced and designer-centred legal clubs ... warehouse events appealed to individual spontaneity ... venues could be anything from an old abattoir to a disused car park, anywhere which had a power supply and relatively easy access'. The aim was to get the site established and the party underway before the arrival of the police. As time went on, however, the police used a computer database to track organisers and thus the ravers themselves; eventually, using the power of laws which raised the penalty for unlicensed parties from £2,000 to £20,000 and six months' imprisonment, police forces were emboldened into taking direct repressive action.

In the early days, before illegal raves were suppressed, successful conflict with the authorities was only the build-up to a sense of excitement heightened by computerised music, and the feeling that (Pini, p. 161) 'the raver [loses] her sense of "self" and becomes part of something "bigger"'. Many of the interviews carried out by Pini reveal the opinion of respondents that, during the early period of rave, in the late eighties, social, ethnic and gender divisions did not matter. One woman, Catherine, noted 'it's a very strange sensation really – an ideal state is where you're not centred on yourself ... you're part of the whole crowd of people – like your identity is a much broader one'. Another interviewee called Jane found that 'you're part of something, and that feeling of being inside something that's bigger than yourself is really lovely'.

The drugs, music and feelings of unity were strongly related in many cases to a 'New Age' philosophy in which the interrelation of mind/body/spirit was emphasised and (p. 163) 'any prioritisation of mind over body, or rational thought over pleasure, [was] seen as imbalance'.

Culture and commodities: incorporation or rebellion?

In *Popular Culture and Social Relations* (edited by Bennett, Mercer and Woollacott), Richard Middleton's work on the 'pleasures of musical repetition' examines the aspect of musical culture that had, during the rave era, been elevated into a symbol of deviant practice. Music with a 'repetitive beat' had become the target of legal restriction. Yet Middleton, writing in 1986 before the dance phenomenon had properly begun, notes that (p. 159) 'the most widely applicable aspect of popular music syntaxes ... is that of repetition'. He goes on to look at common complaints about popular music and repetition, based on the idea that it gives rise to monotony, sameness and predictability and that these in turn lead to outright slavishness in audience response.

From a commercial point of view, 'the significance of the role played by such techniques [repetitive syntax] in the operations of the music industry' lies in their (p. 160) 'efficacy in helping to define and hold markets, to channel types of consumption, to preform response and to make listening easy'. (Middleton cites the work of Jameson, who argues that repetition is 'simply a fundamental characteristic of *all* cultural production under contemporary capitalism'). Yet, at the same time, the reduction of repetition to a requirement of music's 'political economy' or an 'ideological effect' would be to miss what Middleton calls 'the pleasures produced by musical syntaxes themselves'. Henri Lefebvre argues that 'musicality communicates corporeality ... it renders the body into social practice ... music binds bodies together (socialises them)'.

Negative attitudes to music and dance, by comparison, have linked large-scale participation to the notion of a mass (and thus cheapened or impoverished) culture. This theme has reappeared from the days of the Frankfurt School to what Sarah Thornton calls Baudrillard's 'dismissal of the discotheque as the lowest form of contemporary entertainment' (*see Club Cultures*, p. 1). In Thornton's words, dance music 'has been considered to be standardised, mindless and banal, while dancers have been regarded as narcotized, conformist, and easily manipulated'.

Incorporation of the fittest?

In many accounts of the rise of popular musical forms and the cultures which accompany them, there is a sense of initial enthusiasm and then, ultimately, some form of decline or decay. Dick Hebdige, in *Subculture: the Meaning of Style* writes that (p. 96) 'youth subcultural styles may begin by issuing symbolic challenges, but they must inevitably end by establishing new sets of conventions; by creating new commodities, new industries and rejuvenating old ones'. Anne Beezer's analysis of this position is given in her essay in *Reading into Cultural Studies* (edited with Martin Barker). She believes that (p. 110) 'the "semantic disorder" of subcultural style is defined against the symbolic order issuing from the "anonymous ideology" pervading mainstream society'. Perceiving that 'the moment' of subcultural innovation is identified by writers and then 'contrasted with its later ideological incorporation', Beezer points out that critics see subcultural subversion 'as a momentary break in a social and symbolic order characterised by consensus and conformity'.

Beezer is closer in sympathy to writers like Simon Frith, who views Hebdige's approach as 'too romanticised and overly pessimistic'. She believes that 'a view of subcultures as a movement from subversion to incorporation is a romantic story with a tragic ending'. Frith, she is interested to find, sees important distinctions within subcultures 'between those who are committed to subcultural identity and those who have a transient relationship to it', a view similar to that held by Thornton, who studied the 'hierarchies' which existed within subcultures themselves. Other established notions are also revised in Beezer's work: using Frith's *Art and Pop* as an example, she repeats its insight into the links between 'art school education and involvement in pop and rock music', marking a departure from the construction of music-based sub-culture as class rebellion. Frith, for example, was convinced that 'punk rock was the ultimate art school music movement'.

While Hebdige celebrated punk as politically meaningful, Beezer thinks that 'the signs of punk style resist the act of semiotic translation, presenting only a blankness and absence of meaning to the theorist'. This appears to be confirmed by the judgement of the sometime rock journalist Julie Burchill, who writes about the punk explosion in her 1998 autobiography *I Knew I Was Right* and insists that 'punk was about a break with convention ... what we all shared was Attitude ... liberal-baiting and hippie-baiting ... celebrating the ephemeral, the possibilities and products of the new industries, the importance of style and taste, and the new freedom offered by cultural confusion'. Despite the feeling that some movements are more 'disordered' than oppositionist in a political sense, an alliance of activists in the late seventies did at least secure the support of many punk bands for Rock Against Racism, thus mobilising a vital element in the growing resistance to far-right politics.

SUMMARY

This chapter proposes that mass communication cannot begin to take place until there is some kind of technology to mediate between authors and authority on the one hand, and a significantly numerous audience on the other.

■ THE DEVELOPMENT OF THE ENGLISH PRESS

The institutional factors at work in the growth of the press are introduced through issues of censorship and independence. During the English Civil War of the 1640s, political and social conflict gave a new impetus to the exchange of information.

New forms of radical politics emerged from the religious and political turmoil which the war produced. The very fact that the Bible was much more widely available to people is attributable to the expansion of print; the wider availability helped people to make their own decisions about religion and their place in the social order. Censorship of these early newspapers was strict, as part of the general attempt by government to suppress democratic demands.

In 1679 Parliament allowed the Printing Act of 1662 to lapse, which had previously kept the press under tight parliamentary control. A number of new publications appeared as a result, although the Act was reintroduced in 1685. The first of the Stamp Acts, which comprised a tax on the papers themselves and on the advertisements they carried, was introduced in 1712. Sales fell as a result and some papers went out of business. Taking advantage of flaws in the Act, however, newspapers registered as pamphlets and avoided tax.

Readership of newspapers was restricted to those classes which could afford the cover price. Many types of paper had what we may regard as a fairly limited range of content, reflecting the commercial and social aspirations of a particular class. Once papers became reasonably profitable, however, booksellers became interested is stocking them.

Under prime minister Walpole, some newspapers were bought and turned into the instruments of government propaganda, written by government employees and given an extremely wide circulation.

■ New challenges to the status quo

The use of new technologies served the growing commercial enterprise which the British press had become by the beginning of the nineteenth century. The type of press available to the populace had expanded. Daily, evening and weekly newspapers appeared in London and the provinces. Various radical journals and newspapers appeared in the years after the Battle of Waterloo, but this growth of alternative voices died back again around 1819. The political newspaper was to be revived in the 1830s, however, with the advent of Chartism.

The inability of governments to control the radical press and radical democratic movements in the early to mid-1840s had important repercussions. Two of the most successful papers in the mid-1850s were *The Times*, and the weekly *Northern Star*, a provincial journal with a wide national readership. Part of the reason for the latter's popularity was its status as the leading Chartist newspaper.

■ Revenue, politics and editorial control

Although direct attempts by government to control the press began to decline, other factors acted as a brake upon the political freedom of newspapers, including the dependence of proprietors on advertising revenue.

■ Entertainment

The expansion of mass markets in the later part of the nineteenth century brought with it an increase in the number of newspapers prepared to include features designed purely as entertainment. Material which is not cast in a serious form, or which reproduces content associated with leisure and light-hearted pursuits, has always been the focus of criticism and suspicion.

■ The role of the 'alternative' press in the 1980s

This is given as an example of the revival of a radical current in the press.

■ New studies of effects on voters

New studies seem to suggest that older notions of press influence on audiences are flawed. This work is centred on William Miller's research of 1987–90, which investigated the impressive recovery that the Conservative Party managed to make between April 1986 and March 1987.

■ BALANCE, NEUTRALITY AND IMPARTIALITY

These are outlined as concepts, and the differences between each are explored. The Annan Report of 1977 used the idea that impartiality was the most important guide for broadcasters.

■ LANGUAGE AND IDEOLOGY

Fowler's idea that news is a representation of the world in language and that language imposes a structure of values on whatever is represented is used to lead into a discussion of 'bias' and discourse as approaches to communication in the press.

The ability of the Conservative press to persuade specific groups of voters to rally to their cause at times of crisis is noted, with reference to election campaigns.

The whole notion of 'bias' in the press is examined as a concept, and its worth discussed. To some degree, 'bias' is a useful concept. It lets us know that a large part of one mass communicative form is likely to be deployed in support of one political creed, come what may. However, attacks against *political* bias face a problem. Is it worth while campaigning for the adoption of some kind of 'neutral' political stance in the national press? Many newspapers are not primarily in the 'information' business, and facts are often regarded as less important than 'stories'. If we accept that newspapers are really in the business of circulating ideas (or perhaps discourses in narrative form), rather than facts, we may be able to suggest a different approach to the question of political bias. Discourse, an address with a 'will to power' behind it, is able to operate in all forms of communication. An approach which concentrates on discourse allows us to examine all the ways in which meaning is created, and lets us escape from the problem of having to contrast 'bias' with some notion of 'balance'. We must be careful not to neglect the question of political and social power since ideas about 'bias' at least point to the fact that sections of the press operate in the interests of the powerful.

Newspapers make no attempt to attract the kind of general audience which, for example, the early evening television news must secure. This means that newspapers are at liberty to pursue a sometimes quite outspoken political line, once they have identified an audience which is prepared to accept or tolerate that line.

■ THE 1987 ELECTION CAMPAIGN

This analysis outlines the close relationship which exists between many editors and the leaders of the Conservative Party. The pro-Conservative press appear to create an agenda which is able to aid the Conservative Party during elections.

■ THE *SUN*

The *Sun* in particular is used as an example of how profits are made from the reproduction of openly populist material. Its success is analysed, together with the strong integration of Rupert Murdoch's media empire, News International.

The *Sun* and its discourses are also subjected to analysis, and ideas about how the language used by a newspaper will attempt to reflect the usual modes of address employed by its readership are linked to ideas about the *Sun's* 'world-view', particularly its treatment of scandal and sex; the tension between the paper's anti-authoritarianism is contrasted with its open antipathy to homosexuality and its intolerant attitude on many other issues.

The Wapping dispute is described as the result of the sacking of some 6000 *Sun* employees.

■ NEWS AND POPULAR JOURNALISM

Media commentators argue that serious news journalism is under threat because of falling standards and a fondness for sensationalism. News organisations in Britain and America justify a more informal approach to news by arguing that this is what audiences prefer. There are two aspects to the problem of 'dumbing down' in news: content and form. Both have caused disquiet amongst commentators. The perspective offered in this section argues that condemnation of sensationalism does not recognise the political element of, for example, muck-raking attacks on the royal family. Public disenchantment is sometimes reflected in such material. Two questions are asked:

- Does poor taste and an informal mode of presentation always convey trivial content?
- Does seriousness of purpose and formal presentation always promise a useful insight into important issues?

The argument is made that media are both **visible** and **invisible**. Visible in terms of **content,** and invisible regarding the **structures** of the media. Although some argue that news has become an extension of showbusiness, successful journalism has always contained a strong element of spectacle. News is described as an *industrial* and an *intellectual* process. It is **the status of news as a commodity**, rather than its degree of 'seriousness', which determines its position within the entertainment market.

A remark made by a singer, which denied the harmfulness of Estasy, is studied and its value as news is explained by:

- the **status** of the individual concerned – this idea is sometimes associated with the 'news value' called *personalisation*;
- the **content** of the original statement – it has *relevance* and *simplicity*;
- and the **context** within which the remark was made.

Context is made up of the **situation** and the **discursive environment** within which the event takes place.

The section on news goes on to note that it has come to mean information which has been collected, **shaped** and then passed on or **reported** by professional, profit-making organisations. The difference between current demands for more factual information is contrasted with the traditional academic preoccupation with the status of news as a process of 'naturalisation' of the dominant ideologies.

The 'dominant ideology' thesis is contrasted with the 'discursive turn' in media and cultural theory. Peter Bruck believes that the dominant system does not 'reproduce itself in an uncontradictory fashion'. He also notes that the news media do not operate in a uniform way. The media are subject to the general social and discursive context in which they operate; 'the discursive material they work with . . . is not their own'.

Two news stories from the *Daily Mirror* are studied, to demonstrate how news organisations pick up the viewpoints of their sources. All news is always **provisional**. The status of any report is temporary and subject to change in the light of new information. The death of Diana, Princess of Wales, is used as an example of a major news incident. One of the conclusions from the study is that news organisations find public reactions which can be **amplified**. Public actions after the death are described as attempts to create **symbols** of Diana's passing. The scope of public response was thus limited by a number of factors: its own informal organisation, the restricted agenda it found itself setting out, the interpretations of this agenda made by the media, the means of expression available, and finally the spontaneous forms of behaviour enacted during the **'suspension' of normality.**

The origins of news agendas are described, using Dearing and Rogers' idea that agenda-setting is 'competition among issue proponents to gain the attention of media professionals, the public, and policy elites'.

■ POPULAR FORMS: WOMEN'S MAGAZINES

The history of magazines aimed at women is studied, beginning in 1693. Questions of class, discourse and address are all examined. Janice Winship's study of magazines reveals the contradictory positions that post-war women's magazines could find themselves tempted to occupy: on the one hand, to support the ideals of femininity, and on the other to pursue ideas about women's rights in society.

Winship believes most strongly that a combination of socialism and feminism is not tolerated in commercial magazines, though some forms of feminism are tolerated on their own. She writes also about the way that modes of address work to draw their readers into the ideological world of the woman's journal. The notion that different types of address can be accepted under certain circumstances is one with which we are familiar. The tentative movement towards the inclusion of black women in mainstream magazines is noted.

Spare Rib and *Cosmopolitan* are described in terms of their political positions and their attempts to capture a specific market.

■ MAGAZINE DESIGN

This is presented as a 'laboratory for design innovation'. The origins of the magazine in the nineteenth century, the increase in literacy and the development of the means of production during the Industrial Revolution, made the birth of the magazine possible so that by the 1830s cheap weekly magazines often printed in runs of 100 000 or more.

The revival of innovatory magazines in the 1980s appeared to follow a different model of production altogether, relying on much the same 'home grown' approach as the new wave of musical experimentation known as punk rock. Independent magazines, although able to rely on only small budgets, used new technologies to give the designers themselves a high degree of control over their work. Britain was the centre of such developments, marking a move away from reliance on the advertising agencies, the big publishing houses and design studios.

Notions of incorporation of radical ideas are introduced, since it appears that once an innovation becomes noticed and the magazines which pioneer it become financially viable, then the big publishing houses will see the new forms as a source of profit.

■ POPULAR FORMS: COMICS

This begins by dealing with the rise of the comic in modern times, with particular reference to the establishment in 1930s America, of popular comic-book forms. Issues of censorship and freedom of speech are centrally concerned with this popular form, and the debate about taste in comics prefigures the later controversy which arose over best-selling music albums in the US.

A summary is given of the way that a number of artists in 1960s America evaded the 'mainstream' by producing work which deliberately explored offensive narratives and images. The suspicion that comics are mainly used as a form of entertainment for men stems from studies of the subject-matter of most adult comics. It would appear that the majority of forms which attract criticism on the basis of their supposed effects are those whose predominant mode of communication is thought to be visual.

■ Approaches to the comic form

This is a study of the comic form and the critique of many content analyses and semiological decodings made by Martin Barker. He is not convinced by the argument that comics fail to offer accurate pictures of reality to young readers, because he does not believe that readers relate to comics as gendered individuals so much as children. He takes issue with the whole idea that there is a process called 'identification', in which children see a character in a mass media text and identify with that character, taking on to some extent the values that are offered in the text. Barker says that the point of some of the stories in comics like *Jackie* is that they often involve 'a transformation of the emotions'. In other words, we could say that events occur not in order to make a moral point about something, but because they allow what Barker later calls 'emotional self-realisation'. Angela McRobbie, on the other hand, argues that magazines like *Jackie* offer attention to a powerless group, and that in so doing offer it a negative set of values.

In a study of semiology Barker asks which surface elements the researcher should take seriously, in order to get beyond the surface to the deeper meanings.

Len Masterman's approach to television cartoons as 'the simplest of all of television's dramatic forms' begins a critical exploration of his ideas on the television cartoon form.

■ POPULAR CULTURE: MUSIC AND THE MUSIC INDUSTRY

The issues which surround popular culture seem to make themselves felt with a particular force in terms of music. These issues include censorship and free expression, profitability, the recuperation of radical forms, national and international culture, questions of originality, and enquiries into the relationship between institution and audience. Popular music cannot be separated from the way it is produced and the variety of ways in which it is consumed. From its origins in the 1950s, the popular music industry had to address a youth audience which had in previous years been told what was good for it by an older generation. Popular music seemed to speak directly to the young, and very often to speak up for its interests as well.

■ Types of music companies

There are usually said to be three different types of company which operate within the music business: the majors, the independents, and the new independents.

Profit and loss is a central issue in any study of music. The decline of the single is contrasted with the rise of the CD and the highly successful format which came immediately before it, the tape. The relative decline of the British music industry is attributed to the type of music and associated displays preferred by the American and European markets.

Take-overs in the music business are certainly part of this contraction in popularity and profitability. The tendency, present throughout the later 1980s, for the big names to make take-over bids for the larger independents, became stronger as time passed. The larger independents, companies which had once stood for a more innovatory approach to music (and which were in many ways closer to the artists they signed), were ripe for being taken over by huge conglomerates.

At the base of the system, new companies arose because they are closer to the newest acts. New ventures are then 'tested', drawing the attention of the majors if they prove profitable. Most dance records are made on computers.

The attempt by the major companies to replace the 'independent charts' is noted as another tendency towards the centralisation of power in the music industry. The relationship between radio plays and sales, and the way that other advertising is carried out on the airwaves as an ostensible part of the normal discourses of disc jockeys, are features of modern radio practice.

A study of hip-hop and rap emphasises the orientation of this type of music to the community, while the rise of a kind of 'gangster rap' may be seen as one of the elements which led to increased censorship in the USA. 'Parent Advisory Warnings' seem to mark a return to the censorious outlook which greeted comics in the 1950s.

■ Collective consumption: dance, gender and club culture

The role of popular journalism in identifying music 'cults' among young people is discussed in the context of rave in the late 1980s. Issues of drug use as a central part of dance culture is investigated with reference to ravers' 're-configuration' of their relationship both to 'mainstream' society and to each other. Ideas about freedom, 'connectedness' between individuals, and the worth of collective behaviour is explored with regard to the use of Ecstasy.

In an essay called 'Women and the early British rave scene' Maria Pini describes her interviews with female dance enthusiasts. The sense of trust and freedom produced in the early manifestation of rave, is revealed in the remarks of those interviewed by Pini.

Academics have long expressed a keen interest in youth culture, particularly as it so often seems to provide alternative lifestyles to the 'mainstream'. In Pini's view, such research has however concentrated on groups of young males, dealing with 'questions of "deviance" and "resistance"', and neglecting the question of women's activities and experiences.

For those directly involved in the early rave scene, the activity in which they engaged was surrounded by an air of excitement and mystery, partly created by police attempts to prevent meetings taking place. Early parties were run in opposition to the 'overpriced' legal clubs.

Negative attitudes to music and dance have been much in evidence, linking large-scale participation to the notion of a mass (and thus cheapened or impoverished) culture. Anne Beezer's analysis of the idea that youth subcultures provide 'a momentary break in a social and symbolic order characterised by consensus and conformity' is studied with reference to punk rock.

STUDENT ACTIVITIES

THE PRESS: ANALYSIS, RESEARCH, PRODUCTION, ESSAY TITLES

Analysis: Analysis of discourse in the press: headline creation, writing articles, writing leaders

The class is divided into between two and four groups, with each group consisting of an editor, sub-editors, picture editor and a leader writer. An event is selected on which each of two tabloids of opposite political persuasions has produced in-depth coverage. These newspapers are presented to the class.

Purpose: to investigate discourse, bias, use of language and anchorage in the press, and the poly-semous nature of the press photograph.

Method: the group or groups presented with the tabloids are asked to read through the article chosen and to write a new article, leader comment and headline/anchorage for the accompanying pictures, taking the opposite political viewpoint to the one championed by the paper they are study-ing (the photographs may be cut away from the rest of the text). After each group member has drawn up suggestions for approval by a full editorial meeting, a new page is to be produced using the original photographs, a new set of articles and new headlines/captions. The editor will make the final decision on content. The groups will be brought together and each group will compare its new front page with the text presented to its opposite number. All similarities and differences of treat-ment are to be noted.

Research: Research into press content

A complete day's press output is presented to the class and students are asked to carry out a content analysis of all elements of the papers.

Purpose: to investigate content and audience targeting.

Method: it is easiest to present the class with a set of headings under which all content must appear; the danger otherwise would be that there will be different headings used by each group; the size of each page is gauged and the physical percentage of all types of article or feature or adver-tisement is recorded.

Analysis and production: Analysis of representation in comics

Students are presented with a series of enlarged pictures of a variety of comic-book characters of various types and genders. Each group receives a set of characters from a different type of comic.

Purpose: to investigate the use of physical type without reference to narrative; to investigate gender representation; to investigate character as function in line with Propp's analysis of the folk-tale.

Method: the characters presented are divorced from their context. Students are asked to create a simple narrative based on each of the characters. Many of these characters will already be known, so it may be advisable, if resources allow, to create a new series of physical representations.

Analysis, research and production: Character function in comics

Based upon content analysis of comics, the class is required in groups to draft and produce a comic-book aimed at an actual audience of, for example, children younger than themselves.

Purpose: to conduct research into the tastes of a specific audience; to produce representations and narratives which challenge the accepted representations of mainstream comic forms, if a set of clearly identifiable representations are in fact discovered.

Method: quantitative surveys of a group of children's consumption of various comics is carried out (based on replies from an equal number of boys and girls), followed by a smaller-scale qualitative analysis into preferred characters and narratives. Data is collected and students are required to produce a number of characters who might be instrumental in mobilising a set of narratives which challenge accepted representations along gender-lines. Comics are to be created by each group taking a particular character or narrative; final assembly into a comic is to be followed by the same process of quantitative and qualitative research into the responses of the original groups of children. These should then be the starting-point for a series of enquiries into the notion of 'negative' and 'positive' images in mainstream narratives.

Research and production: college magazine

Students are encouraged to carry out research into the possible need for a magazine representing aspects of their institution. The market can be internal, or may involve an attempt to attract prospective students to the institution by presenting some alternative representations of educational experience from the students' viewpoint. Although this type of exercise is sometimes over-used, it can be very successful if the purpose of such a publication is thought through, and provided the audience research is carried out carefully to ascertain target groups and projected form and content.

Purpose: to introduce students to notions of audience research, marketing, audience expectation and the interplay between mainstream and alternative form, and mainstream and alternative content.

Method

Stage 1: a content analysis of one month's issues of the following or similar titles:

Cosmopolitan
Everywoman
The Observer Colour Supplement
Hello
GQ
The Face
Woman's Own

Mainstream and alternative form is identified, as is mainstream and alternative content. The interplay between form and content in each magazine is expressly investigated. 'House-styles' of design are noted and a design grid is produced for the front cover of each publication, paying attention to typeface, use of space, use of typical design features.

Stage 2: an analysis of the college audience's preferred magazine reading, with a tally system to record the most popular publication which circulates in each designated group.

Stage 3: an analysis of both content and form in the case of each of the most popular publications.

Stage 4: since the frame of questions designed to discover 'what an audience wants to see' in a college magazine invariably produces a list of features which will limit content to a set of variations on material best read out in an assembly or posted in the corridors, the production team should be led by the kind of material read outside the particular educational establishment. To what degree will it be possible to produce a magazine which attempts less to produce a set of outdated sports results than to create a number of features of more enduring interest?

Stage 5: what mode of organisation will be followed? A hierarchical model with designated roles and an editor at the helm? Or a co-operative model with an agreed agenda and a flexible conception of role? What mode of production and distribution will be used? Will the magazine be sold in order to break even or to make a profit?

Production: Image creation for a band

An informal study of a number of bands is carried out, in terms of image, appearance and common themes which appear in lyrical content.

Purpose: to investigate how bands are presented to their audiences.

Method: using the results of an informal study of bands, students are asked to produce a set of materials to advertise a band which is a purely fictional creation. Students then go on to write a series of press releases detailing the band's activities on and off the performance circuit, complete with interviews and musical reviews.

Production: Music video from news images

Equipment required: video recorder with 'audio dub' facility and monitor, pius three or more cassette players.

Purpose: to investigate the relationship between popular music and public images; to decontextualise 'factual' news images; to test the potential of an approach which may be used to alter meaning.

Method: audio music tapes are used to select music for use with prerecorded video tapes taken from news broadcasts, documentaries and other similar genres. (Pre-existing images have been adapted, sometimes in a radical context, at other times by advertisers, to produce what used to be known as 'scratch' video.) Students will need to be presented with copies of a number of sequences, each of some three to four minutes in length.

Stage 1: students are divided into groups and given a selection of audio tapes featuring a variety of musical styles. Each group is required to view all the video tapes and then work to match images to music.

Stage 2: a piece of music is recorded over the images, using the 'audio dub' facility. By beginning the dubbing at different points, a range of possibilities is opened up. Final productions are used for class discussion.

Analysis: Captions in the press – altering meaning through different captions

Look at the photograph in Fig. 7.8 over the page. Three alternative captions have been given. What range of meanings does each caption create?

Fig 7.8 Three alternative captions
a **A mother's love**
b **How much longer will the world ignore them?**
c **How much longer will the West ignore them?**
(Photograph taken in Somalia by Chris Steele-Perkins)

ESSAY TITLES

1 'The history of the British press has been the history of a struggle between censorship and radical calls for freedom of speech.'
Discuss.

2 'The term "bias" should not be used to describe the partisan tendencies of the Press. All news should be analysed as discourse.'
Discuss.

3 Produce an analysis of three of the following magazines, with reference to form, content, and target readership:

19	TV Times
Woman's Weekly	New Statesman & Society
The Spectator	Cosmopolitan
The Tatler	Country Life

What contrasting modes of address are used in each of the three cases you have chosen?

4 Analyse the current state of the British music industry and contrast it with an example of the practices of one other national music industry. How, in your opinion, should any music industry be organised to ensure the widest representation of musical taste?

Bibliography

Ades, D. *Photomontage* (Thames and Hudson, 1986).

Alasuutari, P. *Researching Culture* (Sage, 1995).

Allen, R.G. (ed.) *Channels of Discourse* (Methuen, 1987).

Alvarado, M., Gutch, R. & Wollen, T. *Learning the Media* (Macmillan, 1987).

Anderson, P., Partridge, H., & Kunzle, K. (ed) *Dear Comrades: Readers' letters to Lotta Continua* (Pluto Press, 1980).

Ang, I. *Desperately Seeking the Audience* (Routledge, 1991).

Argyle, M. *The Psychology of Interpersonal Behaviour* (Penguin, 1972).

Barker, M. *Comics* (Manchester University Press, 1989).

Barker, M. and Beezer, A. (eds) *Reading into Cultural Studies* (Routledge, 1992).

Barker, M. and Petley, J. (eds) *Ill Effects* (Routledge, 1997).

Barrett, M. *The Politics of Truth* (Polity, 1991).

Barnouw, E. & Krishnaswamy, S. *Indian Film* (OUP, 1980).

Barwise, P. & Ehrenburg, A. *Television and Its Audience* (Sage, 1988).

Bedwell, R. 'Class Distinctions', *Media Week* May 1990.

Bennett, Mercer & Woollacott (eds) *Popular Culture and Social Relations* (OUP, 1986).

Bennett, T. *The Media: Contexts of Study* (OUP, 1977).

Berkowitz, D. *Social Meanings of News* (Sage, 1997).

Billig, M. *Ideology and Opinions* (Sage, 1991).

Boyce, Curran & Wingate *Newspaper History from the Seventeenth Century to the Present Day* (Acton Society, 1978).

Braden, S. *Committing Photography* (Pluto Press, 1983).

Brailsford, H.N. *The Levellers and the English Revolution* (Spokesman Books, 1976).

Branigan, E. *Narrative Comprehension and Film* (Routledge, 1992).

Brickman, E. 'Is Anarchy boosting corporate profits?' *Solidarity* journal, no. 12, 1986.

Brunt, R. & Jordin, M. *1984 International Television Studies Conference*, Sheffield Polytechnic.

Brunt, R & Jordin, M. (eds) *Constituting the Television Audience: Problem of Method in Television and Its Audience* (BFI Books, 1988).

Burton G. *More than Meets the Eye* (Edward Arnold, 1991).

Cassirer, E. *The Philosophy of Symbolic Forms* (Yale University Press, 1966).

Coates, D. (ed) 'Traditions of Thought', in *Society & Social Science* (1990).

Coates, J. *Women, Men and Language* (Longman, 1986).

Cobley, P. *The Communication Theory Reader* (Routledge, 1996).

Coleman, J. A. & Rollet, B. *Television in Europe* (Intellect, 1997).

Cook, P. *The Cinema Book* (BFI, 1985).

Coulthard, M. *An Introduction to Discourse Analysis* (Longman, 1985).

Crisell, A. *Understanding Radio* (Methuen, 1986).

Crowley, T. *The Politics of Discourse* (Macmillan, 1989).

Curran J. (ed) 'Mass communication as a social force in history', in *The Media: Contexts of Study* (Open University, 1977).

Dance, F. & Larsen, C. *Functions of Human Communication: a theoretical approach* (Holt, Rinehart & Winston, 1976).

Dearing J.W. & Rogers, E.M. *Agenda-Setting* (Sage, 1996).

Dickerson, P. 'The Discursive Construction of Viewer Identity' (in *European Journal of Communication*, Vol. 11 (1), 1996).

Dimbleby, R. & Burton, G. *More than Words* (Routledge, 1985).

Dimbleby, R. & Burton, G. *Between Ourselves* (Edward Arnold, 1988).

Dutton, B. *The Media* (Longman, 1986).

Dyer, G. *Advertising as Communication* (Routledge, 1989).

Edwards, M. & Usher, S. *Greek Orators 1* (Aris & Philips, 1980).

Elsaesser, T. *Early Cinema: Space Frame Narrative* (British Film Institute, 1990).

Evans, H. *Pictures on a Page* (Heinemann, 1978).

Feldman, A. *An Introduction to Digital Media* (Routledge, 1997).

Fiske, J. *Introduction to Communication Studies* (Methuen, 1982).

Fiske, J. *Understanding Popular Culture* (Unwin Hyman, 1989).

Fiske, J. *Television Culture* (Methuen, 1989).

Fiske, J. & Hartley, J. *Reading Television* (Routledge, 1987).

Fiumara, G.C. *The Symbolic Function* (Blackwell, 1992).

Fowler, R. *Language in the News* (Routledge, 1991).

Franklin, B. *Newszak and News Media* (Arnold, 1997).

Gauntlett, D. *Moving Experiences* (John Libbey, 1995).

Giles, V. & Hodgson, F. W. *Creative Newspaper Design* (Heinemann, 1990).

Gill, D. & Adams, B. *ABC of Communication Studies* (Thomas Nelson, 1992).

Glass , A.L. & Holyoak, K.J. *Cognition* (McGraw Hill, 1986).

Goffman, E. *Gender Advertisements* (Macmillan, 1976).

Goldsmith, A. *The Camera and Its Images* (Ridge Press / Newsweek Books, 1979).

Greenberg, S. & Smith, G. *Rejoice!* (CPBF, 1983).

Groombridge, B. & Hay, J. (ed) *The Price of Choice* (John Libbey, 1995).

Gurevitch, M. & Roberts, B. *Issues in the Study of Mass Communication and Society* (OUP, 1977).

Hacker, J. & Price, D. *Take 10 Contemporary British Film Directors* (Clarendon Press, 1991).

Hall, S. *The Manufacture of News* (Owen & Young, 1981).

Halloran, J.D. (ed) *The Effects of Television*

Harris, R. *Gotcha! The Media, the Government and the Falklands Crisis* (Faber & Faber, 1983).

Hart, A. *Understanding the Media* (Routledge, 1991).

Hartley, J. *Understanding News* (Methuen, 1982).

Hayward, P. & Wollen, T. *Future Visions: new technologies of the screen* (BFI, 1993).

Hayward, S. *Key Concepts in Cinema Studies* (Routledge, 1996).

Hebdidge, D. *Hiding in the Light* (Routledge, 1988).

Hebdige, D. *Subculture: the Meaning of Style* (Methuen, 1979).

Hodge & Kress *Social Semiotics* (Polity Press, 1988).

Hoijer, B. 'Socio-cognitive structures and television reception', *Media Culture and Society*, vol. 14, 1992.

Hood, S. *Behind the Screens: The Structure of British TV in the 90s* (Lawrence & Wishart, 1994).

Hood, S. *On Television* (Pluto Press, 1983).

Hymes, D. *Directions in Sociolinguistics* (Holt, Rinehart & Winston, 1972).

James, M. *State of Bass* (Boxtree, 1997).

Jensen, K.B. *The Social Semiotics of Mass Communication* (Sage, 1995).

Jowett, G.S. & O'Donnell, V. *Propaganda and Persuasion* (Sage, 1986).

Kaplan, E. *Women and Film* (Methuen, 1983).

Kaplan, E. *Women in Film Noir* (BFI, 1980).

Labov *Language in the Inner City* (University of Pennsylvania Press, 1972).

Larrain, J. *The Concept of Ideology* (Hutchinson, 1979).

Leiss, W., Kline, S. & Jhally, S. *Advertising as Social Communication* (Routledge, 1990).

Lewis, P. & Booth, J. *The Invisible Medium* (Macmillan, 1989).

Local Radio Workshop *Nothing Local About It* (Comedia / LRW, 1983).

Lovell, T. *Pictures of Reality* (BFI, 1983).

McLennan, G. (ed) 'Politics and Power' in *The Power of Ideology* (OUP, 1991).

McQuail, D. *Communication* (Longman, 1975).

McQuail, D. *Mass Communication Theory* (Sage, 1987).

McQuail, D. *Media Performance* (Sage, 1992).

McQuail, D. & Windahl, S. *Communication Models* (Longman, 1981).

McRobbie, A. (ed) *Back to Reality* (MUP, 1997).

McRobbie, A. & MacCabe, T. *Feminism for Girls* (RKP, 1981).

McShane, D. *Using the Media* (Pluto Press, 1979).

Maslow, A. *Motivation and Personality* (Harper & Row, 1970).

Masterman, L. *Teaching about Television* (Macmillan, 1980).

Masterman, L. *Television Mythologies* (Comedia, 1984).

Matelart, A. *Advertising International* (Routledge, 1991).

Monaco, J. *How to Read a Film* (OUP, 1981).

Moores, S. *Interpreting Audiences* (Sage, 1993).

Moores, S. *Satellite Television and Everyday Life* (John Libbey, 1996).

Morley, D. *The Nationwide Audience* (BFI, 1980).

Myers and Myers *The Dynamics of Human Communication* (McGraw Hill, 1985).

Neale, S. *Genre* (BFI, 1980).

O'Keefe, D. *Persuasion: Theory and Research* (1990).

O'Sullivan, T., Hartley, J., Montgomery, M. & Saunders, D. *Key Concepts in Communication and Cultural Studies* (2nd ed, Routledge, 1994).

Price, S. *Communication Studies* (Addison Wesley Longman, 1996).

Price, S. *The A–Z Media and Communication Handbook* (Hodder and Stoughton, 1997).

Raboy, M. *Public Broadcasting for the 21st Century* (John Libbey, 1995).

Rangoonwalla, F. *A Pictorial History of Indian Cinema* (Hamlyn, 1979).

Rosen, H. *Language and Class* (Falling Wall Press, 1972).

Rothstein, A. *Photojournalism* (Amphoto, 1974).

Sarup, M. *Introductory Guide to Post-Structuralism and Postmodernism* (Harvester Wheatsheaf, 1988).

Saussure *Course on General Linguistics* (Owen, 1916).

Searle, C. *Your Daily Dose: Racism and 'The Sun'* (CPBF, 1989).

Sontag, S. *On Photography* (Penguin Books, 1978).

Steinberg, C.S. &·Belsky, I. *Infancy, Childhood and Adolescence: Development in Context* (McGraw Hill, 1991).

Strauss, M. & Mandl, D. (eds) *Radiotext(e)* (Semiotext(e), 1993).

Street, J. *Rebel Rock* (Blackwell, 1986).

Tetzlaff, D. 'Divide and Conquer' in *Media Culture and Society* (Sage, 1991).

Therborn, G. *Ideology of Power and the Power of Ideology* (Verso, 1980).

Thornton, S. *Club Cultures* (Polity, 1995).

Tudor, A. *Theories of Film* (Secker & Warburg/BFI, 1974).

Watson, J. & Hill, A. *A Dictionary of Communication and Media Studies* (Edward Arnold, 1989).

Webster, C. *The New Photography* (John Calder, 1980).

Webster, C. 'New Social Movements', *Here and Now*, no. 5.

Wernick, A. *Promotional Culture* (Sage, 1991).

Whitehouse, M. *Cleaning up TV* (Blandford, 1967).

Wilby, P. & Conroy, A. *The Radio Handbook* (Routledge, 1994).

Williams, K. *Get Me a Murder a Day!* (Arnold, 1997).

Williams, R. *Television, Technology and Cultural Form* (Fontana, 1977).

Williams, R. *Keywords* (Fontana, 1983).

Winship, J. *Inside Women's Magazines* (Pandora/RKP, 1987).

Wittgenstein, L.J.J. *Tractatus Logico-Philosophicus* (International Library of Philosophy & Scientific Method, 1921).

Zizek, S. *Mapping Ideology* (Verso, 1994).

Index